THE
FEMINIST ENCYCLOPEDIA
OF SPANISH LITERATURE

THE FEMINIST ENCYCLOPEDIA OF SPANISH LITERATURE

A–M

Edited by
Janet Pérez and Maureen Ihrie

GREENWOOD PRESS
Westport, Connecticut • London

Library of Congress Cataloging-in-Publication Data

The feminist encyclopedia of Spanish literature / edited by Janet Pérez and Maureen Ihrie.
  p. cm.
  Includes bibliographical references and index.
  ISBN 0–313–29346–5 (alk. paper: set)—ISBN 0–313–32444–1 (alk. paper: A-M)—ISBN 0–313–32445–X (alk. paper: N-Z)
  1. Spanish literature—Women authors—Encyclopedias. 2. Spanish literature—Encyclopedias. 3. Women authors, Spanish—Biography—Encyclopedias. 4. Feminism and literature—Encyclopedias. 5. Women in literature—Encyclopedias. I. Pérez, Janet. II. Ihrie, Maureen.
  PQ6055.F46 2002
  860.9'9287—dc21   2002019922

British Library Cataloguing in Publication Data is available.

Copyright © 2002 by Janet Pérez and Maureen Ihrie

All rights reserved. No portion of this book may be reproduced, by any process or technique, without the express written consent of the publisher.

Library of Congress Catalog Card Number: 2002019922
ISBN: 0–313–29346–5 (set)
ISBN: 0–313–32444–1 (A-M)
ISBN: 0–313–32445–X (N-Z)

First published in 2002

Greenwood Press, 88 Post Road West, Westport, CT 06881
An imprint of Greenwood Publishing Group, Inc.
www.greenwood.com

Printed in the United States of America

The paper used in this book complies with the Permanent Paper Standard issued by the National Information Standards Organization (Z39.48–1984).

10 9 8 7 6 5 4 3 2 1

Every reasonable effort has been made to trace the owners of copyright materials in this book, but in some instances this has proven impossible. The author and publisher will be glad to receive information leading to more complete acknowledgments in subsequent printings of the book, and in the meantime extend their apologies for any omissions.

Contents

Preface	vii
The Encyclopedia	1
Appendix	697
Selected Bibliography	705
Index	711
Contributors	735

Preface

Like *The Feminist Encyclopedia of German Literature* (Greenwood, 1997), *The Feminist Encyclopedia of Italian Literature* (Greenwood, 1997), and *The Feminist Encyclopedia of French Literature* (Greenwood, 1999), this reference approaches a particular national literature from a women's studies perspective, with entries arranged alphabetically and written by expert contributors. Spanish literature, even when limited to that of the Peninsula, and to literature in Castilian (excluding other Peninsular languages), is nonetheless a far larger subject than can be covered in a single volume. Thus this encyclopedia does not pretend to be exhaustive. Further limitation results from our focus on selected aspects of that literary corpus, as suggested by the adjective *feminist*, which likewise requires some clarification. This encyclopedia is feminist insofar as the criteria of inclusion are narrowed to those aspects most likely to interest readers seeking information in areas including women's studies, gender studies, gynocritics, and feminist criticism: Spanish women writers and their works; Spanish women important as historical and cultural figures; important Spanish feminists and defenders of women's rights; the treatment of women by significant male writers in Spain; overviews of Spanish women's history and of Spanish women's production in certain genres; assessment of women's condition in significant moments of the last several centuries in Spain; and finally, certain terms peculiar to feminine gender in Spain. As an initial consequence, many important male writers do not appear or may be represented by a single work that stands out because of its female protagonist (or conversely, its negative treatment of women). A secondary consequence, therefore, is that some major literary works (including titles in the "masterpiece" category) do not appear, either because they have few significant female characters or because they are essentially neutral in their portrayals of women, neither especially misogynist nor noteworthy for the creation of autonomous women characters or espousal of women's rights.

The editors lament the necessity of excluding the many excellent and important women writers past and present in other languages of Spain, especially in Catalan and Galician. We have included survey articles on the present state of women's literature in those languages and also in Basque (*euskera, vascuence*) in the hope of giving some notion of the richness of current production by women in the vernacular languages and providing readers with guidance on sources of additional relevant information; we have opted not to try to represent the less-used vernacular languages, due to their limited histories and the absence of recognized canons and experts. The inclusion of individual entries on the many significant women writers in Catalan, Galician, and Basque would have necessitated at least a three-volume format, which was not an option. Similarly excluded are other women writers in the Spanish language (in Latin America, on which the publishers contemplate a separate volume). The target area of the present work thus covers works by and about women written in Spanish and limited to Spain.

Within this area, readers may still notice the presence of lacunae, as a number of authors and titles listed in the original prospectus for the project could not be included for several reasons: the lack of qualified experts interested in providing entries on certain topics, the relative inaccessibility of certain materials, the "defection" of would-be contributors who made the commitment to write on various subjects but failed to produce. This scenario will seem familiar to those who have prior experience in editing reference works; it qualifies as an occupational hazard of the genre and merits mention here largely because neither of the coeditors set out to figure among the most assiduous collaborators, but both found themselves forced to fill in resulting gaps where possible. Eventually, it became necessary to delete the remaining desiderata and conclude the project because those materials received early in the course of compilation (some seven years before) risked becoming dated. For this reason also, some early entries may not show death dates for recently deceased subjects (and even when not very recent, these are extremely difficult to secure at times). The varying lengths and degrees of thoroughness of different entries may reflect individual resources available to collaborators and do not necessarily reflect editorial judgments of a subject's importance. Similarly, individual bibliographies are not exhaustive, and what is listed often reflects collaborators' assessments of importance; one constant, however, has been accessibility, for which reason we have privileged books and works in English in the bibliographies.

Anything that dares to call itself encyclopedic is necessarily a perennial work in progress. The explosion of Spain's population of women writers in the second half of the twentieth century and the corresponding increase in research on them and on women's issues in Spain continue unabated, with numerous important new works appearing each year. Spain today has far more artistically important, highly visible, and successful women writers than at any time in its history. Some who have achieved significance at the beginning of the third millennium were only emerging when this project began (and thus did not figure in the original prospectus). As a result, many women who began publishing in the 1980s and 1990s do not appear but would be candidates for inclusion in a future edition. If this work serves its readers well, perhaps it can be expanded at a future date.

A further word concerning the "feminist" orientation: feminist criticism as a discipline is in some respects still emerging from primeval chaos, divided into various national and ideological camps and not taken too seriously in Spain where a majority of women writers—including some of the most important exponents of feminist issues and writers on women's topics—reject the feminist label for varied and complex cultural and political reasons. Many women included here would dispute their inclusion; hence we record the caveat that feminism, political, literary, or otherwise, is not an essential criterion (as evinced by the presence of entries on notorious misogynists and a series of both male and occasionally female writers in the patriarchal tradition who qualify as indifferent or negative in the area of women's rights and condition). Our intention is to present the cultural background against which Spanish women writers have produced their works, the climate in which they were formed, and in many cases, against which they react in their writings, not simply to select those relatively few Spanish women writers who would accept the feminist label.

Similarly, collaborators have not been restricted to "feminist critics" but draw upon many Hispanists both male and female from a variety of methodological and theoretical backgrounds who share an interest in women's writing, gender studies, women's history, and specific writers or works. There is no single or dominant critical methodology represented, as indeed would be well-nigh impossible in any work of collective authorship with hundreds of entries and scores of contributors. The mixture results in a tone much closer to the objective discourse generally associated with reference works than the occasionally trenchant language of the stereotype (or caricature) of feminist criticism, but such moderation of discourse is not the result of editorial intervention; we have generally made only minimal corrections (of obvious errors, misspellings, problems with English style, and the like). Individual contributors' judgments and opinions have been respected, as well as their discourse, where possible.

General Format of Entries and a Word on the Index and the Appendix

Entry titles may be related to biographical names (or, in a very few cases, well-recognized pseudonyms), literary titles or characters, genres, general and specific topics, and specific terms. Authors and titles have been cross-referenced to facilitate locating entries. As much as possible, dates (biographical, composition, publication, time frame) and/or specific focus are also included in titles to clarify the scope of the entry. Because of the time elapsed since original submission of some entries, significant recent events (death of an author, recent major awards, or latest publications) may not appear. Punctuation is consistent with the following examples: Benavente, Jacinto (1866–1954): His Portrayal of Women in *La noche del sábado* and *La malquerida*; *Don Quijote de la Mancha* (Part I, 1605; Part II, 1615): Its Representation of Women.

Within the main text of each entry, the first time a published title authored by the entry subject is mentioned, it is followed by a literal translation to English (unless the title is the name of a character), placed in parentheses. The English translation is generally preceded by the publication date of the original unless the date has already been mentioned. If a published English translation of a work has been found, that title is given, underlined, and followed by its publication date. Only readily available published translations to English are given. Titles of journals, newspapers, and so forth, in an entry are not generally translated unless they are pertinent to the subject. The entry of a work with a published translation appears as follows: *El color de agosto* (1988; *The Color of August*, 1994). A work where a published translation has not been included is listed according to the following example: *La niña lunática y otros cuentos* (1996; The Lunatic Girl and Other Stories). Quotes and other terms in Spanish are also generally translated to English.

Most entries conclude with a two-part bibliography. Part one lists work by the author and part two provides work about the author, work, or entry topic, providing some secondary bibliography. Each part is generally arranged alphabetically, although a few of the longest survey entries may be subdivided further. An attempt has been made to include recent sources, but neither section is exhaustive, and the criteria followed were left in large part to the discretion of individual authors. The intent is to provide a starting point for readers who wish to explore further.

English alphabetical order has been followed; thus *ch*, *ll*, and *ñ* are not treated as separate letters but are interfiled. Just as in English, where *an*, *a*, and *the* are ignored when alphabetizing titles, when arranging Spanish-language titles *el*, *la*, *los*, *las*, *un*, *una*, *unos*, and *unas* have been disregarded when alphabetizing bibliographies. Entry titles begin after any definite or indefinite article. Thus, *El corbacho* is listed as *Corbacho, El* (1438), and the "el" is disregarded when alphabetizing the bibliography.

Queens and canonized saints are indexed under their first names, but surnames (or surnames of pseudonyms) are used for all other biographical figures, including noncanonized religious figures.

Cross-referencing has been indicated with asterisks (*). If a person, topic, title, or term that appears as a main entry elsewhere in the *Encyclopedia* is mentioned in an article, the first mention of the item carries an asterisk that is placed immediately before the part of the name or title under which it is entered. If there are other complementary subjects or titles not indicated through asterisks, they will be listed at the end of the main text of an entry. In a very few cases, plural forms of an entry have been asterisked, although the entry appears in its singular form. Eponymous titles and characters are treated as equal, as are the Spanish terms *honor/honra* and the English equivalent *honor*.

Entry authorship is indicated at the conclusion of each article, following the bibliography.

In addition to a comprehensive general index, an Appendix with a rough chronological listing of entries by century has been provided, arranged according to birthdates, beginnings of movements, and so on. The volume closes with a selected, general bibliography of major studies.

The coeditors offer sincere thanks to all those who helped make this project possible, including those whose names appear in the list of Contributors and those agencies that provided support in the respective academic institutions, especially the Graduate School of Texas Tech University, for assistance to Janet Pérez with early stages of the project, and Kansas State University, which provided a one-semester sabbatical leave for Maureen Ihrie, furthering progress on formatting, indexing, and editorial preparation of the final manuscript. To both, our gratitude.

Abad, Mercedes (1961–)

A writer and journalist born in Barcelona, Mercedes Abad's main work consists of short stories that deal with the problems between men and women in love relationships. Two principal traits of her fiction are the pathological protagonists who exhibit eccentric or obsessive behavior and the unexpected endings that bring about an ironic or derisive twist to a story's interpretation.

One of Abad's most important contributions has been her entry into the field of erotic literature, which, for women writers in Spain, represents a great departure from tradition. In 1986 she was the second woman writer to win the prize awarded by "La Sonrisa Vertical" in its eighth edition, with her book of short stories *Ligeros libertinajes sabáticos* (Frivolous Weekend Libertines). Thanks to this prestigious erotic literature prize awarded yearly by Tusquets publishing house, she became widely known with her first published work.

Abad breaks with her predecessor Spanish women writers in several respects. Biographical exploration of women protagonists' lives is not a predominant feature of her stories; she relates the lives of numerous different characters, men and women, in the first or third person. She does not create an intimate space in which to analyze in depth the personality of one protagonist through time, and she does not use memorialist techniques. In her stories, action prevails over psychological study: Things happen rapidly, tension increases incrementally, and suspense is resolved in a stroke with amazing and usually catastrophic results. Her swift, dynamic, and very often comic prose contributes to this sense of agility. Moreover, the erotic elements in her fiction are very explicit, and she mixes them with a strong element of cruelty; eroticism is not, therefore, sublimated.

In the 10 short stories of *Ligeros libertinajes sabáticos*, Abad creates nonconventional characters and endows their otherwise monotonous lives with disparate elements. Pánfila de Castis, protagonist of "Una mujer sorprendente" (A Surprising Woman), seduces men with sumptuous banquets and chooses her lovers for the capacity they have to surprise. Some of the short stories are ironic, some humorous, some tragic, and many leave the reader with an ambivalent feeling of tragicomedy. Dolores de la Borbolla, protagonist of "Malos tiempos para el absurdo o Las delicias de Onán" (Bad Times for Absurdity, or The Delights of Onanism), dies while masturbating with a bottle of champagne when the cork explodes inside her vagina. Pascualino Fígaro La Pera in "Pascualino y los globos" (Pascualino and Balloons) narrates his sexual experience with a corpulent woman (an obsession he has decided to indulge after 57 years of a successful but meaningless life) while he allows himself to be asphyxiated by her genitals, taking pleasure while nearing death. The man of "Crucifixión del círculo" (Crucifixion of the Circle) waits obsessively in his apartment for his *puta arrabalera* (slum prostitute) in a frenzied anguish and does not open the door when she arrives. In the end, when he lets her in, he chokes her to death.

Abad's stories embody a strong element of the absurd both in the situations described and in the highly clichéd language used by some of her bourgeois protagonists. In "Ligeros libertinajes sabáticos," the story that gives title to the book, Mr. and Mrs. Johnson organize a party every Saturday for their friends. Abad creates a very conventional atmosphere at the beginning of the story, narrating in simple terms and following a logical rhetoric. However, in this seemingly ordinary atmosphere extraordinary things are happening. One guest, Mr. Robertson, plays pool using his penis as the stick, while his wife eats her dessert from Mrs. Smith's vagina. An important component of cruelty is also present in numerous stories as Abad mixes love with death and explores the forms and consequences of morbid, sadistic, masochistic, and violent patterns of behavior. "Juego de niños" (Children's Games) studies the dynamics between a violent protagonist, who likes to watch the suffering he has inflicted on other people, and Bruno, who derives pleasure from the humiliation and pain he suffers.

In her second book of short stories, *Felicidades conyugales* (1989; Conjugal Happiness), the author analyzes the problems with couples in relationship, especially in marriages. The title, therefore, becomes ironic because Abad shows negative aspects of married life such as noncommunication, nonunderstanding, infidelity, treachery, indifference in love, murderous and suicidal instincts, the loss of illusion, and hypocrisy.

Sólo dime dónde lo hacemos (1991; Just Tell Me Where We Can Do It) is a collection of essays and short stories that advocates for an openness in erotic space. Abad's idea is that any place is a good place to make love if people use their imaginations. This capacity of the mind aroused by desire is what adds sensual and inciting qualities to the atmosphere, and therefore it can transform any site into a fine place for sex.

In the short story "Profanaré tu pecho, Yokanaán" (I Shall Desecrate Your Breast, Yokanaán), included in the collection *Verte desnudo* (1992; Seeing You Naked) for which nine women writers each invented a story concerning one part of the male body, Abad chose men's breasts.

Soplando al viento (1995; Blowing in the Wind) is a collection of 13 stories in which cruel and absurd elements predominate. The topic of Cain and Abel is explored in "El pájaro" (The Bird) where a six-year-old boy watches his brother drown with complete indifference. In "El placer de escuchar" (The Pleasure of Listening) a couple offers their son as dinner to their guests in order to have a private laugh at the latter's expense and to rid themselves of the nuisance their drug-using son had become to them.

Abad's mixture of the extraordinary with the habitual blurs the barriers between the possible and the impossible and at the same time displays frightening aspects of human nature. The view of humanity portrayed in her books is extremely bleak as she focuses on the cruelty, hypocrisy, envy, maliciousness, and frivolity of life and people. Many of her characters isolate themselves to the point of becoming autistic, disconnecting from reality and acting in selfish and violent ways. Abad reiterates throughout her stories the need to break with conventional behavior, arbitrary modes of life, and limiting moral precepts in order to combat the monotony of existence. However, she also warns us of the dangers inherent in such an attitude when taken to extremes. Isolated and selfish individuals tend to seek self-satisfaction as their only priority and do not take into account the feelings of others. *See also* Eroticism in Contemporary Spanish Women Writers' Narrative; Short Fiction by Women Writers: 1975–1998, Post-Franco

Work by

Felicidades conyugales. Barcelona: Tusquets, Colección Andanzas, 1989.
"La joie de vivre." *Los pecados capitales.* Barcelona: Grijalbo, El Espejo de Tinta, 1990.
Ligeros libertinajes sabáticos. Barcelona: Tusquets, 1986.
"Ligeros libertinajes sabáticos" and "Pascualino y los globos." *Relatos eróticos.* Madrid: Castalia, Instituto de la Mujer, 1990.
"Profanaré tu pecho, Yokanaán." *Verte desnudo.* Madrid: Temas de Hoy, Biblioteca Erótica, 1992.
Sólo dime dónde lo hacemos. Madrid: Temas de Hoy, Biblioteca Erótica, 1991.
Soplando al viento. Barcelona: Tusquets, Colección Andanzas, 1995.

Work about

Jiménez Morales, María Isabel. *Pertinaz sequía: Mercedes Abad.* Málaga: Universidad de Málaga, Dirección General de Cultura, 1994.
Mandrell, James. "Mercedes Abad and La Sonrisa Vertical: Erotica and Pornography in Post-Franco Spain." *Letras Peninsulares* 6.2–3 (1993–1994): 277–299.

Eva Legido-Quigley

Abarca de Bolea, Ana Francisca (1623?–?)

Entering the Cistercian convent in Casbas at age three, Ana Francisca Abarca de Bolea spent nearly her entire life within the confines of the cloister. She was born to noble parents, don Martín Abarca de Bolea y Castro and doña Ana de Mur, in 1623 or 1624. Her father was an educated man and a literary figure of sufficient renown to be mentioned favorably by Lope de *Vega in his *Laurel de Apolo,* Silva II. The reason why the daughter of such an illustrious family was put into a convent so young is unknown. Abarca de Bolea took her final vows at an early age and served as abbess of the convent from 1672 to 1678.

In the convent Abarca de Bolea enjoyed access to sacred and cultured books. She learned Latin, studied music, and wrote numerous verses, one novel, and four hagiographic books, the first being *Vida de catorce santas del Císter* (1655; Lives of Fourteen Cistercian Saints). This work was followed by accounts of the lives of St. Susana, published in 1671, and of St. Felix Catalicio. The *Vigilia y octavario de San Juan Baptista* (1679; Vigil and Week of the Celebration of John the Baptist) is a compendium of poems, songs, and narratives loosely connected as the celebrations of a fictional group of courtiers along the banks of the Guara during the days before St. John's feast day. Abarca de Bolea's last known work was an unpublished history of appearances and miracles of our Lady of Glory, venerated in the convent at Casbas.

Among Abarca de Bolea's poems figure several to members of the royal household and high nobility, underscoring her familial connections to the highest levels of Spanish society. She wrote an unusual number of poems about female saints, an interest reflected in her prose work as well. A number of poems comment on domestic details of convent life: "A un estuche" (To a Box) complains about another nun's constant borrowing of her things; "A unos velos" (To Some Veils) is a request for a new veil.

A number of Abarca de Bolea's poems have been lost, including one cited and praised by Baltasar Gracián in his *Agudeza y arte de ingenio* (1648). The loss of this and other poems may have occurred in a fire that consumed the convent. The date of the fire and that of Abarca de Bolea's death are unknown. *See also* Autobiographical Self-Representation of Women in the Early Modern Period; Nuns Who Wrote in Sixteenth- and Seventeenth-Century Spain

Work by

Castro y Calvo, José María. *Prosas y versos de Doña Ana F. Abarca de Bolea.* Zaragoza: Artes Gráficas, E. Berdejo Casañal, 1938.
Olivares, Julián, and Elizabeth S. Boyce. *Tras el es-*

pejo la musa escribe: *Lírica femenina de los Siglos de Oro*. Madrid: Siglo XXI de España Editores, 1993. 391–433.

Serrano y Sanz, Manuel. *Apuntes para una bibliografía de escritoras españolas*. Madrid: Rivadeneyra, 1903–1905. I: 1–9. II: 631.

Work about

Alvar, Manuel. *Estudios sobre el "Octavario" de Doña Ana Abarca de Bolea*. Zaragoza: Archivo de Filología Aragonesa, 1945.

Elizabeth S. Boyce and Julián Olivares

Abencerraje y la hermosa Jarifa, El (1561–1565)

This elegant Renaissance sentimental novel (also a precursor of the *morisca* [Moorish] novel) appeared with slight variations in five different works between 1561 and 1565. Drawing from classical mythology, novels of chivalry, epic, the Bible, frontier poetry, and the *courtly love tradition, it presents an eloquent celebration of the self-perfectibility of man in a place and time where differences of religion (Christian versus Islam), ethnicity (Spanish versus Arab), and nation (Christian Spain versus Arab Granada) are overcome through the exercise of spiritual and moral attributes. Although both protagonists are fifteenth-century historical figures, the harmonious *convivencia* (peaceful coexistence) that characterizes the narrative is quite at odds with the strong intolerance, dissension, and persecution of *moriscos* (indigenous Islamics) that were occurring in Spain when the story was written.

The two protagonists, Christian military hero Rodrigo Narváez and Abindarráez, last surviving male of the distinguished and powerful Abencerraje clan (exterminated in 1482 as a result of political intrigues), each possess outstanding attributes of nobility and character. They meet in an adversarial situation where each demonstrates singular prowess in combat—Abindarráez single-handedly defeats five Christian soldiers before Narváez arrives on the scene (rested) and succeeds in subduing him. Once his captive, Narváez observes that his prisoner's reaction to this defeat seems disproportionate to his loss and begins a conversation. The extraordinary exemplarity of character that the two protagonists share becomes mutually apparent, further guiding the conversation. Abencerraje reveals his tragic past, then explains how he was on his way to meet his beloved Jarifa, to take her as his wife, but that fortune again has thwarted the Abencerraje clan. Narváez vows to demonstrate to his captive that he can prevail over fortune, initiating what becomes a series of demonstrations of virtue on the part of each, by allowing Abencerraje to go free if he will give his word to return within three days. Many themes are played out in the work—love of various types, fortune, chivalric values such as justice, loyalty, integrity, generosity, and friendship—but the unifying force of action is personal virtue and its ability to elevate and purify conduct, placing it beyond the reach of "fortune."

Women's roles in the story are much smaller and largely defined by courtly love conventions. The perfection of Jarifa's beauty surpasses that of Salmacis and Venus and is complemented by her honesty, sincerity, discretion, and sense of honor. Abindarráez suffers terribly when separated from his beloved, visiting places she used to frequent as a penitent visits the stations of the cross before Easter. Her absence provokes passionate jealousy, which robs him of his reason. Jarifa is presented as a supremely worthy object of male adoration. She certainly inspired Abindarráez's bravery in combat, and her position as captor of Abindarráez's soul is more significant than Narváez's role as Abindarráez's physical jailer.

Nonetheless, when considering the pursuit of virtue, the key competition between the two protagonists that moves the plot forward, woman's negative role is underscored three times in the story. The first instance occurs when Abindarráez is liberated by Narváez and journeys on to meet Jarifa. After a joyful reunion in which, after exchanging secret vows of marriage, the two consummate the relationship, Abindarráez prepares to return to his jailer, to fulfill the promise given. Jarifa observes that it would be equally reasonable to simply send Narváez a generous ransom in exchange, since that will be precisely what Narváez would be planning to do with him. Abindarráez responds that her love for him is clearly clouding her judgment, for it would be "tan gran yerro" (a great mistake) to fail to keep his word. She accedes to his will, volunteering then to accompany Abindarráez in his return and share her beloved's imprisonment. To Jarifa's credit, her willingness to suffer with him does demonstrate a capacity for selflessness on her part.

The second instance where a woman's influence serves to tempt male virtue involves Narváez. As Jarifa and Abindarráez travel to Narváez's terrain, they meet a fellow traveler who states that he also is going to see Narváez and describes him as the most virtuous gentleman he has ever seen. When Jarifa asks for an example, the traveler recounts how Narváez had become enamored of a certain noblewoman and accordingly had served her as would a courtly lover. At first the noblewoman disdained the interest shown, but after hearing from her own husband what an outstanding, worthy individual Narváez was, she decided to invite him over when her husband was away. Narváez came, and as the lady was about to give herself to him, she commented that her husband was responsible for her interest, since his profession of admiration and love for Narváez had inspired her own feelings. Narváez immediately withdrew, exclaiming that he could never betray the *honor the husband had accorded to him by profaning that man's honor. This altruistic denial of self-gratification for the sake of another man's honor is understood by Abindarráez; Jarifa, however, responds that she would prefer a less virtuous man who would be more moved by female beauty than by another man's honor, thereby providing the third moment in which a woman's influence on male virtue is depicted as negative. In the final analysis, then, in this idealistic, highly Neoplatonic vision of human conduct, the woman's role is largely confined to that of physical beauty, she personifies the temptation to carnal sin, and she does not exercise a positive role in furthering virtue of the soul. *See also Caballerías, novelas de*: Their Treatment of Women

Work

El Abencerraje: Novela y romancero. Ed. F. López Estrada. Madrid: Cátedra, 1987.
Antonio de Villegas. El Abencerraje. Ed. F. López Estrada and trans., and intro. J.E. Keller. Chapel Hill: U of North Carolina P, 1964. Spanish and English.

Work about

Bass, Laura. "Homosocial Bonds and Desire in the *Abencerraje*." *Revista Canadiense de Estudios Hispánicos* 24.3 (Spring 2000): 453–471.
Burshatin, Israel. "Power, Discourse and Metaphor in the *Abencerraje*." *MLN* 99.2 (1984): 195–213.
Carrasco Urgoiti, M.S. *The Moorish Novel*: El Abencerraje *and* Pérez de Hita. TWAS 375. Boston: Twayne, 1976.
Gaylord, Mary. "Spain's Renaissance Conquests and the Retroping of Identity." *Journal of Hispanic Philology* 16.2 (1992): 125–136.
Krauel, Ricardo. "El esquema heroico de la historia de Abindarráez." *Romance Notes* 37.1 (1996): 39–47.

Maureen Ihrie

Acuña y Villanueva de la Iglesia, Rosario de (1851–1923)

Born in Madrid to a noble family, Acuña produced works—plays, essays, and short stories—highly critical of the aristocratic society to which she belonged. Like many other nineteenth-century women, she concealed her true name under a masculine pseudonym (Remigio Andrés Delafón). She married at age 25 but soon thereafter separated from her husband. Acuña initiated her literary career writing poetry: *La vuelta de una golondrina* (1875; Return of a Swallow) and *Ecos del alma* (1876; Echoes of the Soul). In 1876, her play *Rienzi el Tribuno* (Tribune Rienzi) had its premiere. Written in verse, this two-act tragedy with epilogue depicts the strife between nobles and the masses during fourteenth-century Rome and deals with the eternal values of courage, *honor, and freedom. El Padre Juan (1891; Father John), a three-act drama in prose, reveals Acuña's thoughts about contemporary society. Set in Asturias, this extremely anticlerical play illustrates the conflict between orthodox conservatism and scientific progress by presenting two pairs of oppositions: the believer versus the rationalist, and the city juxtaposed to the countryside. Her others plays are *Amor a la Patria* (1878; Love of Country), a one-act tragic drama in verse; *Tribunales de venganza* (1880; Tribunals of Revenge), a tragic drama in two acts and epilogue; and *La voz de la patria* (1893; Voice of the Fatherland), a verse drama in one act. In 1882 Acuña began to publish in the feminist magazine *El correo de la moda* (The Fashion Mail), disseminating her ideas about rural life and her ecological concerns. These themes appear also in her essays *Influencia de la vida del campo* (1882; Influence of Country Life) and *El lujo en los pueblos rurales* (1882; Luxury in Rural Villages), which present the Horatian ideals of "court contempt and village praise."

Starting in 1885, Acuña wrote for *Las dominicales del Libre Pensamiento* (Sunday Supplements of the Free Thinker). In 1886 she became a member of the Constante Alona Masonic lodge, with the name of Hipatía. Acuña was the first woman speaker in the Madrid Ateneo in 1884. In 1911 a letter she wrote decrying male Spanish university students' behavior in an incident involving two North American female students was published in the Parisian paper *El Internacional* and then Barcelona's *El Progreso*. Her criticism provoked a national scandal and temporary closure of Spanish universities. Fearing imprisonment, she sought exile in Portugal for four years. *See also* Drama by Spanish Women Writers: 1860–1900

Work by

Cosas mías. Tortosa: Monclús, 1917.
Ecos del alma. Poesías. Madrid: A. Gómez Fuentenebro, 1876.
El Padre Juan. Prologue by José Bolado. Gijón: Ateneo Casino Obrero, 1985.
Rienzi el Tribuno. El Padre Juan. Ed., intro., and notes María del Carmen Simón Palmer. Madrid: Castalia, 1990.
La siesta. Colección de artículos. Madrid: G. Estrada, 1882.
Tiempo perdido. (Cuentos y bocetos). Madrid: M. Minuesa de los Ríos, 1881.
La voz de la patria. Madrid: R. Velasco, 1893.

Work about

¿Quién fue Rosario de Acuña?. Madrid: Artes gráficas municipales, 1933.
Simón Palmer, María del Carmen. *Escritoras españolas del siglo XIX. Manual bio-bibliográfico*. Madrid: Castalia, 1991.

Carmen de Urioste

Agreda, María Jesús de (1602–1665)

This prolific, visionary nun maintained a 22-year correspondence with King Philip IV, offering advice to him on affairs of state, and was during that time, as Kendrick comments, the most eminent, generally admired woman in Spain. Born to a wealthy, extremely pious family, in 1615 her mother received and carried out an order from God requiring her to evict her husband and two sons and convert the house to a nunnery. María Jesús de Agreda and her mother professed as nuns in the Franciscan order, and María rose to become the convent abbess in 1628. From 1620 to 1623 Agreda practiced extreme self-mortification and experienced frequent visions and illness. During this period she is reported to have begun to levitate, and from about 1620 to 1631, she experienced visions of being transported to the New World to assist in converting the Jumano Indians. Communication of these experiences to her confessor provoked inquiries by the Inquisition, first in the 1630s and again in 1650, and also made her known to the king.

Correspondence between the king and Agreda began in 1643 and continued until her death. Over 600 letters have survived, documenting her unofficial role as his consultant and sounding board in selected practical matters of government and social policy. She saw a need to reform certain customs and dress in society and communicated her disapproval of the idea of royal favorites. Because of her special relationship with God, the king depended on Agreda's prayers for him as his own personal spiritual advocate before the Almighty. A mutual affection emerges in letters of the later years.

Aside from this voluminous correspondence, Kendrick lists some 14 titles, plus sundry minor pieces. Of these, Agreda's most important writing is the *Mística Ciudad de Dios* (composed between 1637 and 1645; *City of God*, 1949), originally titled "Historia y vida de la Virgen" (History and Life of the Virgin), which recounts detailed information about the Holy Family revealed personally to Agreda by the Virgin Mary in her visions. One of Agreda's confessors ordered her to burn it, and she obeyed, but as Philip had requested a copy, his priest deemed it divinely inspired, and the work was saved. Agreda later rewrote it for the king, completing the revision in 1661. Among other things, the text offers a passionate defense of the doctrine of Immaculate Conception, a national cause of the day. Published five years after her death, it enjoyed 89 complete editions and 68 partial ones and provoked furious debate, pro and con, throughout Europe. It was alternately placed on and removed from several papal Indexes over the years.

Efforts to canonize Agreda began at her death and repeated, failed attempts continued into the nineteenth century, as the question of whether her writing represents heresy or divine revelation has yet to be determined. Her remarkable life and writings attest to the turbulent spiritual climate of seventeenth-century Spain. *See also* Autobiographical Self-Representation of Women in the Early Modern Period; Marianism; Nuns Who Wrote in Sixteenth- and Seventeenth-Century Spain

Work by

City of God. Trans. F. Marison (pseud. of Rev. G.J. Blatter). 3rd ed. Santa Fe, NM: Catholic Information Service, 1949.
Correspondencia con Felipe IV: Religión y razón de estado. Intro. Consolación Baranda. Madrid: Castalia, 1991.
Mística ciudad de Dios. Ed. Ozcoidi. 5 vols. Barcelona: Gili, 1911–1914.

Work about

Colahan, Clark. "Mary of Agreda, the Virgin Mary, and Mystical Knowing." *Studia Mystica* 11.3 (1988): 53–65.
———. *The Visions of Sor María de Agreda: Writing, Knowledge and Power*. Tucson: U of Arizona P, 1994.
Kendrick, T.D. *Mary of Agreda*. London: Routledge and Kegan Paul, 1967.

Maureen Ihrie

Aguirre, Francisca (1930–)

The poetry of Francisca Aguirre gives invaluable testimony to her generation from a very personal perspective, that of a woman avidly watching a cultural world that nevertheless remains alien to her. Her creative work is linked to this witness role and is often biographical and profoundly marked by the fact that she is married to poet Félix Grande (1937–). She combines delicate introspective musings about the meaning of culture as collective experience with a deeply rooted, personal, intimate analysis of her own life. Aguirre's poetry, then, is simultaneously social and private, hopeful and desolate, intellectual and domestic.

Aguirre's feminine perspective is distant from a feminist approach; in fact, she responds in a traditional way to cultural values as embodied by androcentrism, of which she is both an expert and an enthusiast. On the other hand, in all her works there is a constant female presence and a constant male absence—father first, husband later—which repeatedly suggests autobiographical undertones. But in the final instance, the androcentric or traditional view truly takes second place and almost vanishes as she stresses, consciously or otherwise, her own female entity to ensure a firm sense of her personal reality. For her, art is paramount, mostly literary and within that poetic, but also musical and philosophical; at the same time her work offers a high social content as she expresses concern for fellow poets, a trait shared by writers of her generation. As witness, Aguirre's poetry refers to Spanish postwar poets and also to Latin American intellectuals of the 1960s, 1970s, and 1980s.

Since her work tends to revolve persistently around her own life, it is possible to equate certain creative cycles with her own life cycles: the stages of childhood and adolescence, the young woman, and the mature woman. The first two are marked by the death and absence of the father; the final by the presence/absence of the lover and the works of writers she knows through her reading or through friendships. Nearly all of the latter are men, with Rosa *Chacel (1898–1994) probably the one exception, not counting a few feminist writers to whom she refers with irony. On the other hand, these same life stages are strongly marked by the real presence of nonintellectual, enormously vital women: her grandmothers, aunts, mother, and sisters during her childhood and adolescence; artist-friends' wives and above all herself in the adult years.

To date she has published: *Itaca* (1972; Ithaca); *La otra música* (1977; The Other Music); *Los trescientos escalones* (1977; Three Hundred Stairs); *Ensayo general* (1996; General Essay), which combines verse and poetic prose; *Espejito, espejito* (1995; Mirror, Mirror), which has a strong autobiographic component; and *Que planche Rosa Luxemburgo* (1995; Let Rosa Luxemburgo Iron), an obliquely autobiographic narrative. She remains active and has several unpublished pieces.

While *La otra música* gives her measure as an excellent poet, deeply fascinated by the aesthetic fact, exploring feelings and emotions, the ethical, and the philosophical, her first book, *Itaca*, and her latest, *Ensayo general*, are probably her most ambitious, valuable creations. Both are written in the classic vein, with Homer and Euripides in the background, as they explore time, destiny, and love. *Itaca* stresses fidelity, and the central character follows a Penelope pattern, a woman in the role of waiting wife. The absent Ulysses upholds her tormented hope. The sea around her (poetry, words) is both a way out and the walls of the prison, friend and jailer. But hope and the return of the husband are still possible. In *Ensayo general* all hope has been abandoned, and there will be no return. A most cruel, unfaithful lover stands laughing at the heart of this tormented soul, the wife who knows her destiny is to love without being loved, who feels passionate, stubborn longing for a lover who in turn runs hopelessly after other women. Aguirre chooses as this work's background a tragedy, the Trojans. The introduction, written in poetic prose, brings in the Greek elements, Time/Chronos, adverse Destiny/Cassandra, uncertain and absurd roles/the Actor, with ephemeral reality, and the Trojan herself, lamenting her blind destiny. The heart of the book, the plot, is comprised of 32 remarkable sonnets that deal with love, with a traitor, executioner/ lover. Nevertheless, like a tragic mythological character, the only life-giving thread she possesses is this murdering, one-way love that culminates in the supreme forgiveness that uncertainly turns the loving body into food and shelter for the stranded lover. The epilogue consists of a different contemporary domestic lament that connects this work to the rest of her compositions and shows the eventual rebellion and lucidity that, in spite of all cultural constructions, might lie behind the erudition whose main role is to keep the pieces working together. The pieces and their heroic resonance break up in the last brief lines, dissolving to a mute but peaceful beast. The waiting, the unending supporting role, the woman, the absent man, the domestic prison are all that remain in the final instance. The way out can be perceived in other books, mostly in her narrative work.

The title *Los trescientos escalones* refers to one of her father's paintings; these poems dwell on Aguirre's past, as an orphan child, as daughter of Lorenzo Aguirre, a great painter and source of happiness for his young family. After escaping Franco's purges but failing to secure exile in any Latin American country from Le Havre (France), he returned to Spain in 1940, only to be put in jail and shot by a firing squad in 1942, when Aguirre was 12 years old. She would never recover from this wound. From the moment of the father's death, she and the women in her family would live "like fish in a waterless tank." The consequence of this tragedy became twofold constants for her: longing for the father's presence first and for the lover later, and longing for knowledge and culture as interpreter and key to life. Culture is represented by a man, while she is always a woman, keeper of the fire and house.

Espejito, espejito combines narrative and poetry. In a very original format, poems are written from the present of the poet as an homage to the Spanish poetic tradition. The *romance* (ballad) predominates, but there are a variety of lyrical structures and the shadows of great poets so well loved by Aguirre: Francisco de *Quevedo (1580–1645), Manuel and Antonio Machado (twentieth century), Federico *García Lorca (1898–1936), Miguel Hernández (1910–1942), José Hierro (1922–   ), Luis Rosales (1910–   ). The narrative part is memory, first the child, the early years in Madrid, the war and the wanderings, following the Republican government, Valencia, Barcelona, then the flight to Paris and Le Havre, the failure and return, the tragedy. Child and poet are hand in hand as Aguirre jumps from an inspired present to her childhood experiences, never forgotten, never even totally in the past. In contrast to the fear that, as her grandmother puts it, is stronger than hunger, there stands a longing for the beautiful, the artistic, the learning in a house where the only furnishings are her father's paintings and where there is no food. But in the house there is the strong presence of a mother offering unfailing support, a grandmother always providing unimaginable food through ingenuity and effort, a singing aunt and three little sisters who support each other as they attend cruel, right-wing schools—these women are towering fortresses. They are for real, they belong to no cultural world, their presence is solid. Then come adulthood and the discovery by herself of the tantalizing world of real culture, the Ateneo, young poets and other writers, companionship and love.

Que planche Rosa Luxemburgo is a different type of work. There is a link here to the epilogue of *Ensayo general* and to *Espejito, espejito*, but the candid autobiographical voice of those works is now a more oblique third person. The book is a duel between androcentric culture, which Aguirre admires, to which she belongs and by which she has been nourished, and the wife, the woman, the peripheral spectator and respectful participant. The duel is manifested in a love-hate relationship to books and poetry as surrogates of life, and to a husband-poet, the master of culture, who disappears. This housewife—who irons, cooks, mops, washes, waters, and cleans up after others in endless, frequently frantic solitude—realizes her life of routine and resents it. Thus the poets and writings frequently quoted by her undergo revision in this text. Books are the way out as she equates them to Aladdin's lamp, an escape from solitude, as book, room, and woman keep each other company. She needs the quiet, clean room in order to feel some peace. But books can possess a hostile side, particularly to the housekeeper who must clean them again and again. Antagonism between culture and life, housewife and culture, is endless in the book. At the end there is a compromise. Feminism doesn't really help; Lidia *Falcón's Marxist approaches are rejected. Aguirre will not turn into a revolutionary, but, following the lead of *Baroja's novels, she puts on her coat and goes out into the streets.

As counterpoint to *Ensayo general*, where she accepts her role as a victim, *Que planche Rosa Luxemburgo* gives way to a clear rebellion. There is a measure of rejection of men's culture; she might not be, after all, emulator of the poetry by her husband and his friends. There is a real interior fight, prolonged moments of truth and loneliness, always walking past the sacred books of sacred poets and sacred minds; always reading and dusting these books, until she no longer feels the urge, the need, to read, but rather to live, until she begins to correct her beloved poets, Machado, Neruda, Rosales; until she begins to realize that *no* reading equals or surpasses living, and she is not living. Hers is the overwhelming loneliness of that woman described by Hélène Cixous, always waiting at the castle door, always waiting for a law that will never enfranchise her.

Work by

Ensayo general. El Ferrol: Esquío, 1996.
Espejito, espejito. San Sebastián de los Reyes: Universidad Popular, 1995.
Itaca. Madrid: Cultura Hispánica, 1972.
La otra música. Madrid: Cultura Hispánica ICI, 1977.
Que planche Rosa Luxemburgo. Toledo: Caja de Castilla La Mancha, 1995.
Los trescientos escalones. San Sebastián: Caja de Ahorros de Guipúzcoa, 1977.

Work about

Miró, Emilio. "Francisca Aguirre y Ana María Navales." *Insula* 35. 404–405 (July–August 1980): 12–13.
Wilcox, John. "A Reconsideration of Two Spanish Women Poets: Angela Figuera Aymerich and Francisca Aguirre." *Studies in Twentieth Century Literature* 16.1 (1992): 65–92.

María Elena Bravo

Alarcón, Pedro Antonio de (1833–1891): Women in His Works

Although most of Alarcón's novels and short stories treat romantic themes, they are rich and varied in terms of characters and descriptions. An important literary figure of the second half of nineteenth-century Spain, Pedro Antonio de Alarcón was born in Guadix, a province of Granada, on March 10, 1833. From an early age he showed interest in politics and journalism. He started writing when only 15 and had composed his first novel by the time he was 17. Although romantic and *costumbrista* (depiction of regional customs and manners) tendencies are present throughout his literary works, later writings tend to be more didactic in nature and are clearly set within the context of the realist novel. "El clavo" (The Nail) from the collection of 11 short selections known as *Cuentos amatorios* (1881; Love Stories) is one of Alarcón's most popular stories. At first, the plot appears to center around three different female characters, but as the narrative unfolds, the reader discovers that all three are the same woman, Gabriela. Gabriela had met the narrator's friend, Zarco, and fallen in love with him. Upon finding out that she is expecting Zarco's child, her only hope for happiness is to return home, murder her husband, and free herself from an unhappy, unfulfilling marriage. Zarco, who is completely unaware of Gabriela's marriage, thinks he has been deserted by her and returns to his hometown, disillusioned with all women in general. A twist to the story is added when Zarco, along with the narrator, stumbles upon a man's skull with a nail driven through it. After investigating the murder, Zarco discovers that the crime was committed by the wife and vows to bring her to justice. When he discovers that the murderess is Gabriela, Zarco attempts to save her from a death sentence. Ironically, as he arrives with the pardon, Gabriela dies, never having found happiness in her life. The story is from beginning to end a tale of passionate love where characters, both male and female, constantly reinforce the melodramatic tone of the narration.

Another story from the same collection is "La comendadora" (The Nun). Here the subject matter deviates from the romantic theme and presents a more in-depth analysis of characters and the forces that motivate their behaviors. It tells the story of a domineering countess and her daughter, Isabel, whom she had forced to join the convent of the order of Comendadoras of Santiago. In the convent, Isabel grows up completely isolated from any type of love or happiness. Her beauty, beyond comparison, soon becomes a source of comfort since those who see her compare her with female figures of the Bible. Isabel finds refuge in these comparisons and, in order to be more like the women she resembles, dedicates her life to mysticism and self-destructive behaviors so extreme that she has to be sent home to recuperate. At home, she finds herself caring for Carlos, her orphaned nephew. This young, unbalanced child manipulates both Isabel and her mother. Upon overhearing a conversation about his aunt's beautiful body the child demands to see her naked. The grandmother's initial denial of this request quickly provokes an out-of-control tantrum. The grandmother, afraid for the health of the child, then commands her daughter to comply. That same day Isabel returns to the convent where she is to spend the rest of her days. Isabel's compliance with her mother's humiliating order shows her weakness and lack of strength. Although dominant, the mother is also a weak victim of society. She chooses to give her entire wealth to the male son and sacrifices her daughter's hopes for happiness in order to conform to societal expectations of the time. Some of the most interesting aspects of the story rely on psychological development in the characters, especially the two women who must conform to extreme measures in order to cover up the decadence and misery of their lives.

El sombrero de tres picos (1874; The Three-Cornered Hat), Alarcón's only critically acclaimed work, tells the story of Lucas, a miller, and his beautiful wife, Frasquita, who has caught the eye of the *corregidor* (local magistrate). Throughout the novel the virtue and devotion that Frasquita shows her husband prove to be immune to the wishful seducer's advances. Although a minor character, the *corregidor*'s wife is also exalted by Frasquita's beauty and dignity when faced with her husband's possibility of adultery. Rather than becoming hysterical, both women prove to be more clever than the *corregidor* and together take control of the situation without compromising their dignity. The only lecher turns out to be the *corregidor* who becomes a comical character and easy target for ridicule.

With *El escándalo* (1875; The Scandal), *El niño de la bola* (1880; The Child with the Globe), and *La pródiga* (1882; The Prodigal Woman), Alarcón changes his style and becomes more interested in ideological novels that convey moralistic themes and develop psychological analyses of characters. *La pródiga*, which is more erotic than any of his previous works, tells the story of Julia, a beautiful but older woman who falls in love with a young idealist, Guillermo. At the beginning of the novel, Julia's reputation is questioned, but as the narrative unfolds, it is revealed that she has been the victim of a series of ill-fated affairs. As Julia herself admits, men have become her enemies. For this reason, she turns into a very determined woman who acts on her own instincts and defies the conventions of the time. She falls in love with Guillermo and is willing to make any sacrifice to preserve that love. Vowing that their relationship will never become a burden, when Julia senses Guillermo's increasing unhappiness, she opts to commit suicide. Since Guillermo is unable to abandon her, she sacrifices her own life in order to free him to lead his own.

In general, the women that appear in Alarcón's works are characterized primarily by their exceptional beauty. However, most are also strong women, determined to maintain their dignity even if their actions do not reflect behaviors that society would generally expect from them.

Work by

Death and the Doctor: Three Nineteenth-Century Spanish Tales. Trans. Robert M. Fedorchek. Intro. Lou Charnon-Deutsch. Lewisburg, PA: Bucknell UP, 1997.
"The Nail," and Other Stories. Trans. Robert M. Fedorchek. Intro. Cyrus C. DeCoster. Lewisburg, PA: Bucknell UP; London and Cranbury, NJ: Associated U Presses, 1997.
Novelas completas. Madrid: Aguilar, 1974.
Obras completas. Madrid: Fax, 1968.
El sombrero de tres picos. Ed. A. Navarro González. Madrid: Nacional, 1975.

Work about

Combs, Colleen Jacqueline. "The Representation of Women in the Short Stories of Pedro Antonio de Alarcón." Diss. U of Illinois, 1996.
Crider, Eneida. "The Pious Woman in Three Works of Nineteenth Century Spain: La comendadora, Juanita la Larga, Marta y María." Diss. Florida State U, 1996.
DeCoster, Cyrus. *Pedro Antonio de Alarcón*. Boston: Twayne, 1979.
En torno a Pedro Antonio de Alarcón. Ed. Fernando García Larra. Granada: Biblioteca de ensayo, 1993.
Ocano, Armando. *Alarcón*. Madrid: Epesa, 1970.
Pardo Canalis, Enrique. *Pedro Antonio de Alarcón*. Madrid: Compañía Bibliográfica española, 1965.

Delmarie Martínez

Alas, Leopoldo

See *Regenta, La* (1885): Female Enemies in the Novel; *Regenta, La* (1885): Protagonist Ana Ozores

Alba

A traditional song, usually with a female protagonist, the *alba* (dawn) describes from her point of view the union and/or separation of lovers at dawn. Examples survive from the *jarchas* (Mozarabic refrains to a type of eleventh-century Arabic poetry) of the early Middle Ages, songbooks of the Renaissance, the cultural poetry of the Golden Age, and even oral Sephardic traditions in Morocco. Some are only a few graphic lines, such as the **jarcha* "Ven, oh hechicero, / un alba que tiene tan hermoso fulgor / cuando viene pide amor" (Come, oh sorcerer, a dawn of such beautiful splendor, comes asking for love), while others portray an entire narrative sequence, as do many of the *romances* (ballads). The female is invariably a passionate lover who eagerly awaits her beloved, rejoices in his presence, and laments his departure. The language is usually simple and direct, using atmospheric imagery associated with the dawning of the day. See also Cantiga de amigo; Hispano-Arabic Poetry by Women

Work

Empaytaz, Dionisia. *Antología de albas, alboradas y poemas afines en la península ibérica hasta 1625*. Madrid: Playor, 1976.

David H. Darst

Alberca Lorente, Luisa (1920–   )

Born in Ciudad Real, Luisa Alberca Lorente was a volunteer in the Spanish Civil War and gained experience writing for and working in radio broadcasting. Over a span of decades, she has produced an astonishing array of radio and television scripts, novels, plays, short stories, and a highly regarded children's book, *Los mensajeros del diablo* (1958; The Devil's Messengers) and has received both the Nadal Prize and the Concha Espina Prize.

Alberca's published works are primarily novels in the sentimental romance genre, often coauthored with Guillermo Sautier Casaseca. Most are popular melodramatic romps, where boy meets girl, boy and girl face incredible opposition, but true love triumphs over all. Betrayal, mistaken identity, and family backgrounds worthy of the most tangled soap opera abound. The characters are widely traveled and often foreign; most of the action of *Extraño poder* (1969; Strange Power) takes place in the United States. Yet underneath the wildly unlikely plots, there is a subtle but firm respect for the morals of Alberca's mostly Catholic audience.

Some of Alberca's works take a more serious turn, focusing on universal problems such as survival, domestic abuse, and the question of a woman's role in a rapidly changing world. Such complex themes also figure strongly in much of her radio work; *Lo que no muere* (1953; That Which Doesn't Die) is a collection of 10 novelized radio serials that focus on variations of good against evil. The combination of escapist plots and support for her readers makes Alberca one of the most popular writers of her time.

Work by

La dama verde. With Guillermo Sautier Casaseca. Madrid: Cid, 1958.
Extraño poder. Madrid: Cid, 1969.
Lo que no muere. Madrid: Cid, 1953.
Los mensajeros del diablo. Madrid: R.E.M., 1958.
Patricia Rilton. Madrid: Saez, 1950.
La última dicha. Madrid: Cid, 1954.

Shannon W. Sudderth

Alberta, Baronesa
See Ballesteros, Mercedes (1913–)

Albornoz, Aurora de (1926–1990)

Poet and critic, born in Luarca, Spain, Aurora de Albornoz moved to Puerto Rico with her parents in 1940, at the end of the Spanish Civil War. She studied at the University in Río Piedras, later attended La Sorbonne in Paris, and received a doctorate from the University of Salamanca in Spain. After teaching a number of years in Puerto Rico, she returned to Spain in 1967 and lived there until her death.

Solitude and aloneness dominate *Brazo de niebla* (1955; Arm of Fog), her first poetry collection, with images of fog, color, and nothingness underscoring the desire for self-expression through poetry and self-doubt about attaining that yearning. In *Prosas de París* (1959; Paris Prose), influenced by Proust, Albornoz searches for time past. That search continues in *Poemas para alcanzar un segundo* (1961; Poems to Catch a Second), where childhood memories of the Civil War lead to feelings of the passage of life toward death, as experienced while in Paris. Questions of identity and insecurity as a poet are posed, as well as the conflict between feelings, memory, and expression in an autoanalysis of her poetry. This volume dedicates some poems to real and fictitious women who are important to the poet (a sister Sonia, Emma Bovary, Ana Karenina, Ophelia). *Por la primavera blanca* (1962; Through the White Springtime), in poetic prose, explores feelings brought by the memory of an event by a person, or by the contemplation of an object. *En busca de esos niños en hilera* (1967; Seeking Children in a Row) the passing of time recurs in the form of a progression from childhood memories as a suppression of bad times, through children's fears caused by adult cruelty and misunderstandings, to, finally, death of childhood with a longing to capture moments of youth from a lost time. *Palabras reunidas* (1966–1977; Collected Words), although not totally devoid of personal content, collects poems with universal subjects. The posthumous collection *Cronilíricas* (1991) is a collage of 20 texts of various contents. There are necrologies (Blas de Otero, Celso Emilio Ferreiro, Salvador Allende, Alejo Carpentier, José Bergamín, Ignacio Prat, León Felipe, Concha *Méndez, Enrique Tierno Galván); journey experiences (Galicia, Florence, Granada, Moguer, Paestum); comments on films by Visconti and Rossellini; memories of Juan Ramón *Jiménez in Puerto Rico; poetic landscape in Claudio Rodríguez; musings ambling through Madrid with José Olivio Jiménez; and thoughts on the Spanish transition after the death of Franco. The compositions are permeated by the author's moral character as well as her defense of freedom in a very poetic, artistic voice.

Besides authoring 10 collections of poetry and poetic prose, Albornoz was the editor of

Puerto (Puerto Rico) and a regular contributor to prestigious journals such as *Insula, Revista de Occidente, La Torre, Sur, Triunfo,* and *El Urogallo.* She wrote critical studies on Juan Ramón Jiménez, José Hierro, León Felipe, and Rivera Chevremont, most of them later collected in *Hacia la realidad creada* (1979; Toward Created Reality). Her work on Antonio Machado merits special attention for its quality and her dedication to it. It includes her essay *La presencia de Miguel de* Unamuno en Antonio Machado* (1968; Miguel de Unamuno's Presence in Antonio Machado), critical studies in her edition of *Poesías de guerra de Antonio Machado* (1961; War Poems of Antonio Machado), her compilation of documents jointly prepared with Manuel Machado of *La prehistoria de Antonio Machado* (1961; Antonio Machado's Prehistory), her critical edition of Machado's *Obras, poesía y prosa* (1964; Works, Poetry and Prose) as well as Machado's *Antología de su prosa* (1970–1971; Prose Anthology). To these must be added her posthumous publication of *Canciones de Guiomar* (1990; Guiomar's Songs).

Raised in a liberal family with a rich cultural heritage, Albornoz benefited from access to a solid academic education that allowed her to be an independent woman whose professionalism as a poet, literary critic, teacher, and editor were widely respected by her peers, male and female. Feelings of aloneness, solitude, a search for time past, recurrent memories of childhood and the war, some doubts and insecurity as to her worthiness as a poet, all of which are found in Albornoz's poetry, perhaps could be construed as feminine attributes. However, there are no traces of strategic subterfuge nor feminist militancy in her discourse. Although her poetry is still conspicuously absent from anthologies, she was part of the community of respected poets and scholars, and her elegant, poetic voice did not hide her liberal allegiances.

Work by

Brazo de niebla. Puerto Rico: Coayuco, 1955.
Canciones de Guiomar. Madrid: Torremozas, 1990.
Cronilíricas. Madrid: Pastor, 1991.
En busca de esos niños en hilera. Santander: Isla de Ratones, 1967.
Hacia la realidad creada. Barcelona: Península, 1979.
Palabras reunidas; 1966–1977. Madrid: Ayuso, 1983.
Poemas para alcanzar un segundo. Madrid: Rialp, 1961.
Por la primavera blanca. Madrid: Insula, 1962.

Work about

Abellán, José Luís. "Los exiliados del absolutismo. (Homenaje a Aurora de Albornoz)." *Triunfo en su época*. Ed. Alicia Alted and Paul Aubert. Madrid: Casa de Velázquez, 1995. n.p.
Homenaje a Aurora de Albornoz. Special issue of *La Torre* 6.21 (January–March 1992).
Miró, Emilio. "Arte y vida en la poesía de Aurora de Albornoz." *Insula* 423 (June 1985): 6.

Pilar Sáenz

Alcahueta

See Celestina, La. Comedia o Tragicomedia de Calisto y Melibea; Tercera

Alcalde, Carmen (1936–)

Born in Gerona the year marking the outbreak of the Spanish Civil War, Carmen Alcalde was the youngest of four children. She was raised by her grandmother and father, a Franco partisan who was an imposing, apparently unloving man. Although deeply affected by this patriarchal upbringing and her Catholic schooling, she grew up rebellious, keen on finding answers to questions that would lead her away from the commonplace path her family would have had her follow. As an adolescent, she believed she had found a solution in the Sección Femenina, the Falange women's organization. Yet her hopes went unanswered. After similar attempts to find her way, as she became increasingly aware of the condition of women in Spain, she had to endure ignorance, deceit, and hostility.

The only woman in her family to reject the traditional roles assigned to females, she pursued university studies in philosophy and journalism in Barcelona, an undertaking that resulted in loneliness and poverty since her family was not disposed to pay for the education of a prodigal daughter. These hardships, however, only reinforced her developing character, fostering expansiveness, generosity, and responsibility for her own situation as well as concern for all the oppressed and unfortunate.

Alcalde published some books of poetry in the 1960s and began her professional career in Gerona where she also founded the magazine *Presencia*. After her magazine failed, she followed her calling to become a journalist in Barcelona, writing for *La Vanguardia*, *Destino*, and *Diario Femenino*, among others. Her combative, liberal prose soon collided with censors; the Franco dictatorship had proscribed such liberal journalism in Spain. Newspaper publishers were reluctant to incur government pressure caused by a journalist, least of all when the writer happened to be a woman they called annoying, communist, and confrontational. Alcalde suffered greatly from the consequences of an apparent conspiracy when directors of the Barcelona press would no longer publish her articles. At that point she could only take satisfaction in knowing that she was among the first to champion and document in writing the conditions of Catalonian and Mallorcan working women. She endured fear and exclusion for several years, and when illness afflicted her, only a few friends came to her aid financially to ensure her survival.

Despite such adversity, her intellectual curiosity did not falter; and she continued to gather data on feminist history and issues. In 1970 Alcalde collaborated with Maria Aurèlia *Capmany in publication of *El feminismo ibérico* (1970; Iberian Feminism). Their intention was to analyze the characteristics of *feminism in Spain: why it arrived so late, why women did not succeed in integrating into Spanish society, why some said that Spain did not have a feminist movement. Capmany and Alcalde did research in Madrid and Barcelona and found material enough to deal with these questions. While they regarded the establishment of a feminist cause and the consciousness of women's alienation as serious problems in Spain, they also observed that previous feminist works and efforts had left a trace and could perhaps represent a point of departure for finally achieving the incorporation of women into Spanish society.

Alcalde's investigation of the causes of women's oppression and alienation continued without pause, and in 1971 she went on to compile another work that was to become *La mujer en la guerra civil española* (1976; Woman in Spain's Civil War). After collecting press clippings and foreign books, she started the difficult task of finding the immediate testimony of Spanish women in newspaper libraries. She searched for forgotten books and pamphlets from used book dealers. She then studied biographies of feminist pioneers of France, Germany, Russia, the United States, and elsewhere, finally assembling the data on all of them in chronological order. Thanks to her research, the names and histories of scores of Spanish feminists totally unknown to present generations were rescued from the obscurity of national and municipal archives.

Alcalde gave this compilation of material a political and feminist interpretation; the history of feminism and of women's struggle is described in a systematic way that goes from Olympe de Gouges of eighteenth-century France to Spain's celebrated *Pasionaria* (Passionflower, epithet given to Dolores *Ibarruri) in 1939. Alcalde concentrates on analyzing the materials in order to extract from them a uniform history of feminism since 1792. Her point of departure comes from her view of the history of women; for her, it is a struggle for liberation, a collective tragedy that cuts directly into the most remote substrata of the human species. In that struggle a conquered front or perceived victory signifies almost nothing. Suffragists believed that once they had obtained the right to vote, they would find the world accessible to them. Later feminists, having secured certain other legal, cultural, or sexual rights, also felt that they had gained some ground. Alcalde concludes, however, that in such instances history has shown that women's chances to gain power lessened; the gap between men and women did not disappear—it widened. Yet her interpretation does not depend solely on the struggle between the sexes. Rather, she asks if the new generation of feminism and its detractors are conscious of history's already defined feminist philosophy. Ultimately, she suggests that the issues of justice, equality, and standard of living cannot be discussed before changing the economic and political structures of a regime based on the oppression of the working class. Alcalde's book was finished in 1973, a time when diverse publications on the topic of feminism began to appear, but she was unable to find a publisher until 1976, the year that marks the end of Franco's dictatorship in Spain.

Three years later Alcalde published a work of an entirely different nature, *Cartas a Lilith* (Letters to Lilith). Her prefatory note claims the book represents a set of circumstances that could have happened to any woman born in 1936, in spite of many similarities to real events and people in her life. Nonetheless, Alcalde traces the course of a woman's life, evidently her own, by blending the personal memoir with monologue and epistolary form. A series of impressionistic chapters cover the death of her father, the mother superior at school, the Falange, the poor and homeless, the Opus Dei, and the Communist Party. Unlike her previous writings, this self-conscious, intimate work makes known the anguish she felt wresting herself from one phase of her personal history to the next in search of authenticity and her own truth.

Recently, Alcalde seems to have found more success in having her work published, but she has received almost no serious critical attention and unfortunately remains almost unknown in North America.

Work by

Cartas a Lilith. Barcelona: Bruguera, 1979.
El feminismo ibérico. With Maria Aurèlia Capmany. Barcelona: Oikos-Tau, 1970.
La mujer en la guerra civil española. Madrid: Cambio 16, 1976.

Glenn Morocco

Aldecoa, Josefina R(odríguez) (1926–)

A member of the Spanish postwar generation who strongly identifies with this group, Josefina Aldecoa's novels characteristically explore the past and feature strong female characters who struggle with some kind of existential conflict.

In 1952 she married the famous novelist Ignacio Aldecoa, and the two collaborated on the *Revista española* magazine with writers such as Alfonso Sastre and Rafael Sánchez Ferlosio. After publication of the short story collection *A ninguna parte* (1961; Going Nowhere), Aldecoa's literary career was interrupted by the untimely death of her husband in 1969. In tribute to him, she kept his surname (something that is not customary for women in Spain). Faced with the need to provide for her daughter, she turned to teaching and founded the Colegio Estudio, which she still directs.

In 1983 she published an anthology on the members of her generation, *Los niños de la guerra* (War's Children). Despite the lyrical tone of the introduction and the book itself, the text also contains an implicit denouncement of Francoist repression. As the title indicates, the writers of this generation were children during the war, and the frustration of their shattered childhoods is evident throughout their fiction. Encouraged by the success of this volume, Aldecoa returned to writing novels, her favorite genre.

Aldecoa admits that she had been harboring the idea for *La enredadera* (1984; The Trellis) for over 20 years. In it, two women from two different centuries make opposite life decisions in regard to the men they love. Because both of them consider the implications of pregnancy, motherhood, love, and marriage, the work invites a wealth of feminist interpretations. *Porque éramos jóvenes* (1986; Because We Were Young) is a more complex narrative with flashbacks and epistolary technique that explores the postwar years and the young people caught in that oppressed society. Annick, a French woman, is the only character who fulfills her expectations, doing so away from Spain when she moves to New York. The protagonist of *El vergel* (1988; The Garden) is reminiscent of female characters in Aldecoa's earlier novels, but her decision to stay with the man she loves is markedly different. Adriana can be interpreted as an archetypal figure that chooses nature (what literary critic Annis Pratt has termed the "green world archetype"), the lost paradise suggested by the title, over a conventional professional life.

Aldecoa's latest novels, *Historia de una maestra* (1990; A Schoolteacher's Story) and *Mujeres de negro* (1994; Women in Black), continue to explore the feminine psyche and the Spanish past. The two texts form a chronological sequence but can be read independently of each other. Aldecoa believes that the historical moment determines people's lives; her purpose in writing these novels, particularly the first one, was to vindicate teachers during the Spanish Republic, a situation Aldecoa experienced firsthand, since her own mother (to whom the book is dedicated) was one of those instructors. This novel can be interestingly compared to *Diario de una maestra* (1961) by Dolores *Medio, for each work deals with a similar experience and historical times.

Mujeres de negro takes place in Spain during the Civil War years, subsequent exile in Mexico, and finally back in Spain during the 1950s. Portrayal of the mother-daughter relationship is of particular interest to feminist readers. The women in black represent the strict, traditional upbringing of the motherland in contrast with the rebellious spirit of youth.

Aldecoa has earned an important place in the literary history of the postwar generation she knows so well. Her five novels in the last 10 years show a wide spectrum of female characters who are an inspiration to the feminist reader.

Work by

A ninguna parte. Madrid: Arión, 1961.
La enredadera. Barcelona: Seix Barral, 1984.
Historia de una maestra. Barcelona: Anagrama, 1990.
Mujeres de negro. Barcelona: Anagrama, 1994.
Los niños de la guerra. Madrid: Anaya, 1983.
Porque éramos jóvenes. Barcelona: Seix Barral, 1986.
El vergel. Barcelona: Seix Barral, 1988.

Work about

Alborg, Concha. *Cinco figuras en torno a la novela de posguerra: Galvarriato, Soriano, Fórmica, Boixadós y Aldecoa.* Madrid: Ediciones Libertarias, 1993.
Leggott, Sarah. "History, Autobiography, Maternity: Josefina Aldecoa's *Historia de una maestra* and *Mujeres de negro*." *Letras Femeninas* 24.1–2 (Spring–Fall 1998): 111–127.
Pérez, Janet. "La madurez narrativa de Josefina Aldecoa." *Alaluz* (Spring 1991): 49–53.
Talbot, Lynn K. "Entrevista con Josefina Aldecoa." *Anales de la literatura española contemporánea* 14 (1989): 239–248.

Concha Alborg

Alfaro, María (1900–?)

Born in Gijón, this poet, novelist, critic, translator, and essayist began writing during the culturally heady days of the Republic as a literary critic for *El Sol*, the major Madrid daily in the prewar years. Travel and residence abroad honed her language skills, and for a time she directed a literary segment for Radio Mundial (World Radio in Paris). She translated some of Corneille's plays from French and rendered novels of Mark Twain to Spanish. Her fondness for theater produced an essay collection, *Teatro mundial* (1961; World Theater). Although she produced no major commercial successes, Alfaro earned respect from other writers for her cultural contributions. Her poetry collections include *Poemas del recuerdo* (1951; Poems of Memory) and *Poemas líricos: Selección, versión y prólogo* (1945; Lyric Poems: Selection, Version, and Prologue). She also published *Memorias de una muerte* (n.d.; Memoirs of a Death). Alfaro's Republican beginnings added to the difficulties facing women writers under Franco and resulted in denial of critical recognition, but her struggle helped to encourage others.

Work by

Memorias de una muerte. Madrid: n.p., n.d.
Poemas del recuerdo. Madrid: Méndez, 1951.
Poemas líricos: Seleccíon, version y prólogo. Madrid: Hispánica, 1945.
Teatro mundial. Madrid: Aguilar, 1961.

Janet Pérez

Alfonso, Pedro, or Alonso, Pedro
See *Disciplina clericalis* (eleventh century)

Alfonso el Sabio (1221–1284): Women in *Las siete partidas*

Alfonso X, more popularly known as Alfonso el Sabio, occupies an important place in the medieval literature of Spain. A prolific writer, his literary efforts spanned multiple disciplines resulting in books as diverse as the *Cantigas de Santa María* (1279; Canticles to Holy Mary), *Grande e general estoria* (1280; Great General History), and *Las siete partidas* (1251–1284; Seven Statutory Divisions), the first compilation of law anywhere to be written in the vernacular. In the preface to his masterpiece, often considered the most important Spanish legal code, Alfonso commanded that his realm be governed by this codex and no other. More than the mere statement of laws, the *Partidas* also include explications that clarify their connotation and offer the reader a unique view of the diversity and complexity of thirteenth-century Spanish society. Alfonso's work is arranged into seven *partidas* (divisions) divided into *títulos* (chapters) and subdivided into *leyes* (laws). Each division focuses on a specific aspect of life, that is, commercial law, marriage, wills, et cetera. In compiling these statutes, Alfonso relied upon many existing bodies of law, among them the Justinian Code, Canon Law, and the *Fuero Juzgo*. As a legal code, the Partidas have survived to the present century as the basis of all Spanish law and comprise basic common law in Hispanic America. More important, they have determined the condition of woman in Spanish-speaking nations with little change until the Spanish constitutional reforms of 1981.

Alfonso alludes to women in almost every division of the *Partidas*, with more frequent mention in the fourth and seventh divisions, which deal with domestic relations and crimes, respectively. The Castilian king's work echoes the underlying concern over the definition of woman noted in early writing and legislation in Spain. He describes woman simply as "a virgin more than 12 years of age, and all others." That is, he defines her in biological terms, omitting any philosophical, religious, or social considerations. He assumes no need to define man, finding him in every way superior to woman.

The fourth *Partida* dealing with betrothals, marriage, divorce, and associated issues of domestic relations offers some of the clearest evidence of the persistence of attitudes from the thirteenth century to the twentieth. Modern Spanish law stipulating that a male may contract marriage at age 14, while a woman may do so at age 12 because of the earlier manifestation of puberty in females finds its precedence in the fourth *Partida*. At the same time, while a female can legitimately marry at 12, Alfonso insists that at that age she cannot legally make a purchase, decide her residence, nor choose what she shall study. Moreover she cannot dispose of any of her real property until she is 25 without prior consent of a guardian or other male responsible for her. Until the 1981 reforms,

Spanish law echoed Alfonso's thinking in that a single woman of legal age (21) could not, between the ages of 21 and 25, live outside of her parents' home without their express permission except to marry or to enter an institution approved by the Church. While the Castilian king maintains that parents cannot promise their daughters in marriage without their consent, he grants parents the right to disinherit any daughter who refuses to marry the mate selected by them.

Until the reforms of 1981, Spanish law allowed only the husband and not the wife to charge a spouse with adultery, reserving the term solely for the wife's transgression. Both the ancient and the modern codes saw only the husband as the aggrieved party in an adulterous relationship.

The notion of an innate weakness in woman that impedes objective direction of her affairs as well as those of others surfaces routinely in the *Partidas*. In both the thirteenth- and twentieth-century codes this impairment is often coupled to a woman's marital status. For example, Alfonso specifically excludes woman from serving as the guardian for dependent children except where "a mother or grandmother has been appointed guardian." However, he insists that she promise the authorities where the children reside that she will not marry as long as she has charge of them. Provided she not remarry, said woman is deemed competent to appoint guardians for those children she "leaves as her heirs." The notion that marriage hampered a woman's judgment persisted in Spain until 1981 to the extent that a woman in business for herself needed her future husband's permission to continue in business once married. Upon dissolution of the marriage for whatever reason, the same woman was considered competent to reassume ownership and direction of her business.

Alfonso's preoccupation with women extended beyond the domestic arena. He forbade a woman from serving as an advocate in court because he considered it improper for a woman to assume masculine duties and to associate publicly with men. A similar rationale informs his ban on a woman's serving as a judge. Furthermore, he prohibited the ordination of women, not because of any lack of qualifications but because Christ, despite placing his mother above the Apostles, chose to confer Holy Orders upon the latter because they were men.

A review of Alfonso's pronouncements concerning woman in the *Partidas* not only suggests his concurrence with much of the religious, social, and philosophical thinking of the time but also reveals numerous inconsistencies. Although she was of such an inferior nature that she could neither control her dowry nor attend an established school, at age 10½, the same age as her male counterpart, she was liable in court for any criminal deeds. Although woman was so fragile that he found it unseemly for her to appear in court, she could, nonetheless, be publicly burned to death if convicted of fornication with her slave. In justifying much of his legislation affecting woman one notes that Alfonso never stated that woman found it difficult to interact with man. Rather, the presence of woman disconcerted man, thus sanctioning the legislation limiting her rights and activities.

To categorize the *Partidas* as biased is unjustified. The Castilian king's work reflects the prevalent attitudes of the time that, in turn, determined the laws promulgated. The tragedy here is not the existence of Alfonso's codex but its persistence essentially unchanged over 700 years, which deprived women on two continents of their legal rights as well as their juridical identity.

Work by

Las siete partidas. 4 vols. Madrid: B. Cano, 1789.
Las siete partidas. Trans. Charles Sumner Lobingier. 3 vols. New York: Commerce House, 1931.

Work about

Bofill, Mireia, M.L. Fabra, Ana Sallés, and Elisa Valles. *La mujer en España*. Barcelona: Cultura Popular, 1968.

González Casanovas, Roberto. "Gender Models in Alfonso X's *Siete Partidas*: The Sexual Politics of 'Nature' and 'Society.'" *Desire and Discipline: Sex and Sexuality in the Premodern West*. Ed. and intro. J. Murray. Ed. K. Eisenbichler. Toronto: U of Toronto P, 1996, 42–60.

Rivera, Olga. "El cuerpo disciplinable de la 'perfecta casada.'" *Cincinnati Romance Review* 15 (1996): 20–26.

Stone, Marilyn MacDonald. *Marriage and Friendship in Medieval Spain: Social Relations According to the Fourth Partida of Alfonso X*. New York: Peter Lang, 1990.

———. "Las Siete Partidas in America: Problems of Cultural Transmission in the Translation of Legal Signs." *Translation and the Law*. Ed. Marshall Morris. Amsterdam: Benjamins, 1995. 281–291.

Francesca Colecchia

Alós, Concha (1922–)

A transitional figure among women writers of the Spanish post–Civil War novel, Concha Alós falls between such authors of the 1940s and 1950s as Carmen *Laforet, Ana María *Matute, Dolores *Medio, Elena *Quiroga, and those of the post-Franco era such as Esther *Tusquets. Her novels published in the 1960s continue the "social novel" and neonaturalism of the preceding decade, with the difference that Alós was able to treat topics previously considered anathema by the fascist regime. Limited freedom in the 1960s did not approach the level attained after Franco's death, but thanks to the new Press Law, it sufficed to allow Alós to criticize the regime and society and develop themes such as women's independence from men (contrary to the fascist image of the family) and women's freedom to abort unwanted pregnancies. For the most part, Alós's heroines challenge the patriarchal regime more openly than those of the previous decade and triumph in their endeavors. Feminist themes and motifs that recur throughout her writing include the war between the sexes; women as sex object; feminine alienation caused by an oppressive environment; and woman as predator. The Spanish Civil War, hunger, and destruction of the environment by unchecked overdevelopment also appear as obsessive themes.

In her first novel, *Los enanos* (1962; The Dwarfs), Alós portrays the crowded living conditions of many people in a small building, pointedly and poignantly reflecting the state in which poor Spaniards found themselves after the Civil War. *Los cien pájaros* (1963; The Hundred Birds) portrays a young woman from the lower classes who, while studying to improve her station in life, is seduced by a young man from a wealthy family. The pregnant heroine must leave the city and find some means of supporting herself and her child since her lover's family refuses to allow him to marry a lower-class woman. *Las hogueras* (1964; The Bonfires), which received the important Planeta Prize, flaunts a feminine eroticism heretofore unseen in Spain as the reactionary Franco regime deemed feminine sexual desire an attribute of prostitutes. *El caballo rojo* (1966; The Red Horse), perhaps Alós's most autobiographical novel, describes the penury experienced by Spaniards during the Civil War and depicts the refugees' struggle for survival with particular emphasis on women and children. *La madama* (1969; The Madam) presents the travails of a middle-class family shortly after the Civil War. With living conditions reduced drastically, and with some of the men in jail, women are forced to prostitute themselves for their children's survival as well as their own.

With the short story collection *Rey de gatos* (1972; King of Cats), Alós begins a new fictional direction, abandoning the social novel and neonaturalism. Following the lead of new novelists in Spain and Latin America, she commences experimentation with time and space, subjectivity and fantasy, and she experiments linguistically. Also notable is what some critics have called "magic realism," showing reality as if it were highly unusual, while the uncanny is treated as a normal part of existence. Much delving into the unconscious of characters to bare their innermost fears results in the frequent dichotomy of hallucination versus reality. *Os habla Electra* (1975; Electra Speaking) continues exploration of the feminine unconscious, offering a fascinating Neofreudian/lacanian study of relations between mother and daughter, ending with a feminist inversion of the proverbial oedipal attraction. The daughter struggles for independence from a phallocentric, patriarchal society as well as from the mother, a collaborator with the system that tries to maintain the status quo. The protagonist must decide whether to identify with the mother and continue as a subservient part of a *machista* (male exalting) society or identify with the father and assume the characteristics of the reigning gender in order to survive as an independent entity. With *Argos ha muerto, supongo* (1982; Argos Is Dead, I Presume), Alós again explores the feminine unconscious, employing mythical and allegorical elements. This novel, unlike the preceding ones, is structurally conventional but employs archetypes—something new in her work. *El asesino de los sueños* (1986; The Assassin of Dreams) continues a preoccupation with Neofreudian/lacanian psychoanalysis, apparently rewriting certain events from her earlier *Os habla Electra*, making the later work as sort of auto-intertext. See also Short Fiction by Women Writers: 1975–1998, Post-Franco

Work by

El asesino de los sueños. Barcelona: Plaza y Janés, 1986.
Os habla Electra. Barcelona: Plaza y Janés, 1975.

Work about

Lee-Bonanno, Lucy. "Concha Alós's *Os habla Electra*: The Matriarchy Revisited." *Anales de la Literatura Española Contemporánea* 12.1–2 (1987): 95–109.
Ordóñez, Elizabeth J. "The Barcelona Group: The Fiction of Alós, Moix, and Tusquets." *Letras Femeninas* 6.1 (Spring 1980): 38–49.
———. "The Female Quest Pattern in Concha Alós's *Os habla Electra*." *Revista de Estudios Hispánicos* 14.1 (1980): 51–64.
Pérez, Genaro J. *La narrativa de Concha Alós: Texto, pretexto y contexto*. London: Tamesis, 1993.
Pérez, Janet. *Contemporary Women Writers of Spain*. Boston: Twayne, 1988.

Genaro J. Pérez

Alvarez de Toledo, (Luisa) Isabel, Duchess of Medina Sidonia (1930–)

Turning her back upon the easy existence of the rich and famous, Isabel Alvarez de Toledo focuses on economic injustice, criticizing the affluent lifestyle and promoting humanitarian issues. She was jailed in 1969 for her campaign defending the villagers following the hydrogen bomb accident in Palomares and published her experience in a series of memoirs that first appeared in the periodical press, then were expanded and translated to English as *My Prison* (1972). The writer comments acerbically on the prison and criminal justice system and treatment of prisoners in addition to recounting her own experiences. Her thesis novel *La huelga* (1967; The Strike, 1971) purports to expose the establishment's unjust and brutal treatment of Andalusian workers—with collusion of the clergy. *La base* (1971; The Air Base) was published in France, as was its predecessor, because of political opposition in Spain. It employs a fictitious family as its focalizing device to portray the ill effects for the community following a treaty establishing a joint U.S.-Spanish base that brings corruption, loss of autonomy, and declining self-esteem. In *La cacería* (1977; The Hunt), the author turns to the decadent aristocracy, denouncing the social injustices of the late Franco era via an account of the annual hunting expedition and attendant depredations by a group of the Madrid elite visiting an Andalusian village. While not specifically or exclusively feminist in her focus, Alvarez de Toledo refused to recognize social prohibitions and instead defied many class and gender restrictions; given her high visibility, she helped to break down barriers enclosing women under the Franco regime.

Work by

La base. Paris: Grasset, 1971.
La cacería. Barcelona/Buenos Aires/Mexico: Grijalba, 1977.
La huelga. Paris: Librarie du Globe, 1967.
My Prison. Trans. H. Briffault. New York: Harper & Row, 1972.
The Strike. A Novel of Contemporary Spain. Trans. W. Rose. New York: Grove, 1971.

Janet Pérez

Ama

See Women's Professions in Early Spanish Literature: *Santas, Rameras, Casadas, Amas,* and *Criadas* (Saints, Whores, Wives, Governesses, and Servants).

Amante invisible

See Invisible Mistress

Amar y Borbón, Josefa (1749–1833)

Born in Zaragoza, Josefa Amar y Borbón was the fifth child of José Amar and Ignacia Borbón, a distinguished Aragonese couple. Her father became court physician when she was five, and the family moved to Madrid, where she received an excellent and unusually liberal education. She married Joaquín de Fuertes Piquer at a young age and moved back to Zaragoza when he was appointed to the Royal Court of Aragon. Amar's intellectual prowess and her active involvement in civic-minded affairs were such that her petition for membership to the powerful Economic Society of Aragon was granted before she was 30. In 1786, Amar entered the debate on the wisdom of admitting women to the Madrid Economic Society with her essay *"Discurso en defensa del talento de las mujeres y de su aptitud para el gobierno, y otros cargos en que se emplean los hombres" (Defending Women's Talent and Aptitude for Government and Other Jobs Employing Men). This text, which antedates Mary Wollstonecraft's famous 1792 treatise on women's rights, answers the essays also published in 1786 in *Memorial Literario* by the two male *socios* (members), Gaspar Melchor de Jovellanos and Francisco Cabarrús, who debated the question. Amar asserted women's equal intelligence and their rights to the same education that men received. She also argued that some women were already prepared to participate as equals in the Societies' work. Although the members of the Madrid Society eventually voted to accept women, the king did not allow it. Instead, he asked the members to create a separate (but obviously not equal) Junta de Damas. Not surprisingly, Amar became one of its first members when she was elected Socia de Honor y Mérito. Amar was also elected to the Medical Society of Barcelona. Her addresses to all these societies have been preserved in their respective acts.

Amar y Borbón published additional writings on a wide variety of topics, demonstrating her almost encyclopedic knowledge and her ability to write clearly and cogently. She was celebrated also for her excellent critical translations from Italian, French, Portuguese, and English. Her translations from Italian are the best known. Not only did she translate the erudite multivolumes of *Ensayo histórico-apologético de la literatura española* (Historical and Apologetic Essay on Spanish Literature), written by exiled Catalan Jesuit Javier Lampillas, she also translated an important *Discurso* (Discourse) on whether parish priests should teach agricultural economy to local farmers, published in Zaragoza in 1783.

Amar was one of that rare breed of enlightened women associated with the reign of Carlos III. She has been called the most erudite Spanish woman of her time, the equal of outstanding Italian, French, German, and Russian women writers and academicians. Additionally, she was an active civil rights leader who defended through her writings and debates the rights of women to equal education and equal participation in public life. *See also* Feminism in Spain: 1700–

1800; Women's Situation in Spain: 1700–1800

Work by

"Discurso en defensa del talento de las mugeres y de su aptitud para el gobierno y otros cargos en que se emplean los hombres: Compuesto por Josefa Amar y Borbón, Socia de mérito de la Real Sociedad Aragonesa de los Amigos del País." Ed. Carmen Chaves McClendon. *Dieciocho* 3.2 (1980): 144–161.

Discurso sobre la educación física y moral de las mujeres. Ed. María Victoria López-Cordón. Madrid: Cátedra, 1994.

Ensayo histórico-apologético de la literatura española. Trans. from Italian. 6 vols. Zaragoza, 1782–1784.

Importancia de la instrucción que conviene para las mujeres. Zaragoza, 1784.

Memorias literarias de varios escritores de la Corte. Madrid, 1787.

Ramillete de escogidos consejos que la mujer debe tener presentes en la vida del matrimonio. Zaragoza, 1784.

Work about

Fernández Quintanilla, Paloma. *La mujer ilustrada en la España del siglo XVIII.* Madrid: Ministerio de Cultura, 1981.

Franklin, Elizabeth M. "Feijoo, Josefa Amar y Borbón, and the Feminist Debate in Eighteenth-Century Spain." *Dieciocho* 12.2 (Fall 1989): 188–203.

McClendon, Carmen Chaves. "Josefa Amar y Borbón: Essayist." *Dieciocho* 3.2 (1980): 138–143.

———. "Josefa Amar y Borbón y la educación femenina." *Letras Femeninas* 4 (1978): 3–11.

Sullivan, Constance A. "Josefa Amar y Borbón (1749–1833)." *Spanish Women Writers. A Bio-Bibliographical Source Book.* Ed. Linda Gould Levine, Ellen Engelson Marson, and Gloria Feiman Waldman. Westport, CT: Greenwood P, 1993. 32–43.

———. "Josefa Amar y Borbón and the Royal Aragonese Economic Society." *Dieciocho* 14.1–2 (Spring–Fall 1992): 95–148.

———. "The Quiet Feminism of Josefa Amar y Borbón's 1790 Book on the Education of Women." *Indiana Journal of Hispanic Literature* 2.1 (Fall 1993): 49–73.

María A. Salgado

Amorós, Amparo (twentieth century)

Best known for her ludic and contemplative poetry, Amparo Amorós has also regularly contributed critical essays on the work of European poets to several leading literary journals of Spain. Her creative texts sustain and embellish the deeply hermetic tradition of Spanish mystics, while her criticism delves into the contours and contexts of the poetic experience. Although her work is not openly feminist, it successfully lobbies for an all-inclusive vision of humanity by examining the quality and limits of human perception and knowledge.

Amorós was born in Valencia (date unknown) and studied journalism and philosophy and letters at Madrid's Universidad Complutense, receiving a degree in Hispanic philology. Afterward she worked as a literature and language teacher at the Instituto "Calderón de la Barca" in Madrid, a position held at publication of this entry. She has written essays for several Spanish periodicals, among them *Insula, Litoral, Los Cuadernos del Norte,* and *Nueva Estafeta. Ludia,* her first book of poetry, won second place in the Premio Adonais in 1982 and was followed by the publication in the 1980s of two additional volumes of poetry: *La honda travesía del águila* (1986; The Eagle's Deep Crossing) and *Quevediana* (1988; Concerning Quevedo). A segment of *La honda travesía del águila* appeared as *Al rumor de la luz* (To the Sound of Light) in 1985, and the entire volume was published in a bilingual French and Spanish edition in 1989. In 1992, Amorós's published and unpublished poetry to date was collected and issued under the title of *Visión y destino. Poesía 1982–1992* (Vision and Destiny. Poetry 1982–1992), and her poetry volume *Arboles de la música* (Trees of Music) appeared in both Spanish and French in 1995.

Amorós has also been quite active on the contemporary critical scene in Spain since the 1980s. Her interests range from the poetry of Paul Celan and Jorge Guillén to the poetics of the Spanish *novísimos* to the philosophy of María *Zambrano. She has edited a volume of essays on Jaime Siles titled *Palabra, mundo, ser: La poesía de Jaime Siles* (1986; Word, World, Being: Jaime Siles's

Poetry), and she recently published her doctoral dissertation, *La palabra del silencio: La función del silencio en la poesía española a partir de 1969* (1991; Words in Silence: The Function of Silence in Spanish Poetry after 1969). As of 1996 Amorós had in press two volumes of poetry and a hybrid collection of essays, criticism, and poems. The latter will also appear in French.

Although Amorós belongs chronologically to the poetic generation of the 1970s, her dates of publication would place her in the subsequent generation of the 1980s. She actively resists inclusion, however, in either poetic generation (hence, her refusal to provide a birthdate) by citing more differences than similarities with her contemporaries. Amorós's poetry frequently explores the dialectic of presence and absence, the metaphysical constraints of reality, and the revelatory power of poetry. Her poetic language derives from an intense intuitive experience, what she calls a "verbal epiphany," and depends heavily on the union between image and concept. Much of her poetry could be called visionary, in that she tries to push her poetic thought beyond the confines of the rational or the real, plumbing the depths of the mystical encounter in order to posit the creative force of silence and the unsayable, and the regenerative possibilities of destruction. Destiny and identity constitute central themes in her poetry, and language offers the link between understanding human existence and achieving individual fulfillment.

Amorós cannot be considered a feminist poet or a feminist scholar, if by these terms one means that she argues in favor of a specific ideological attitude that privileges women's ways of being and knowing. Rather, the feminism of her work resides in her steadfast commitment to a holistic vision of human transformation and a poetics based on the interdependence of intellect and intuition.

Work by

Arboles en la música. Palma de Mallorca: Calima, 1995.

Arbres en la musique. Paris: Jose Corti, 1995.
La palabra del silencio: La función de silencio en la poesía española a partir de 1969. Madrid: Universidad Complutense, 1991.
Visión y destino. Poesía 1982–1992. Madrid: La Palma, 1992.

Work about

Acosta, Marta Elena. "Creation to Apocalypse: Renewal in the Poetry of Amparo Amorós." Diss. U of Miami, 1994.
Hart, Anita M. "Amparo Amorós's Creative Vision." *Revista de Estudios Hispánicos* 29 (1995): 313–333.

Nina L. Molinaro

Andrés, Elena (1931–)

Born in Madrid, Andrés experienced the Spanish Civil War of 1936–1939 as a child; the future poet grew up in the most difficult, repressive years of the Franco dictatorship. Spanish education for women in that period—conservative, patriarchal, and puritanical—was predominantly in the hands of nuns and geared first and foremost to producing faithful, self-abnegating, and obedient wives and mothers, with the inculcation of moral and religious principles taking precedence over career considerations or marketable skills. Andrés managed to complete a *licenciatura* (five-year university degree, somewhere between the U.S. baccalaureate and master's) at a time of pervasive tacit discouragement of higher education for women, which bespeaks a relatively enlightened and privileged background. She studied philosophy and letters (considered the appropriate field for young ladies) and has been a professor of language and literature ("professor" may apply to secondary school teachers in Spain). For many years, Francoist laws forbade married women to work outside the home, and it appears she remained single (very little is known of her personal life, despite the intimate nature of much of her poetry).

Andrés began publishing poetry in literary journals in 1959 and shortly thereafter in books, at the height of the postwar "social poetry" movement—a euphemism for veiled political opposition and "protest literature." Given the failure of Francoist economic policies, most "social" literature targeted economic problems, exposing poverty, hunger, illness, exploitation of the poor, neglect or suffering of women and children, and similar ills. While the regime had its apologists, none attained any convincing critical acceptance, and literary figures achieving renown outside Spanish borders were almost unanimously anti-Franco (to varying degrees). Andrés was by no means an apologist for the regime, but neither was she a "social poet"; her being apolitical was viewed by social poetry's theorists—largely Marxists—as unacceptable, a refusal to accept *engagement*. Not only was Andrés a marginal figure by reason of not belonging to the poetic in-group of the period, but she cultivated styles and themes seen as passé—a continuation of prewar surrealism—or as implicitly challenging the "objective" tenets and collective values associated with social poetry. Her poetry, filled with personal and existential concerns, is often profoundly anguished, frequently philosophical, contemplative, and questioning, but not specifically concerned with the immediate, problematic socioeconomic and political realities of Francoist Spain. Consequently she received little mention during her first two decades of publication, beyond an occasional review.

In her first volume, *El buscador* (1959; The Seeker), Andrés perceives a contradictory dichotomy or separation in humanity and nature and strives for harmony, seeking a kind of Hegelian dialectic or synthesis, humanizing nature and fusing the human being with natural elements. Her poetry seeks via contemplation and meditative introspection to identify what is most essential in human existence, and what she considers of the essence ranges from personal emotions to fundamentals of daily life. There are occasional touches of social concern as she examines ordinary elements of quotidian existence, but echoes of existential irrationality undergird her view of humankind as trapped between an oneiric, mysterious past and a future that is even more unknown.

In *Eterna vela* (1961; Eternal Candle), Andrés appears more optimistic, rejecting existential nothingness and investigating contemporary spirituality more thoroughly, delving deeper into human intimacy, and eventually proclaiming some semblance of ultimate human spiritual victory. Commentators have noted evident development in her technique, more subtle nuances and complex levels of interpretation, an artistic maturation still more visible in her next collection, *Dos caminos* (1964; Two Paths), which looks backward thematically to a major concern of her first book. Meditations again alternate between the mysteries of humanity's ancestral past and an unfathomable future. Andrés once more employs a modified surrealism, paradoxically governed by reason and consequently more accessible to readers. Technical mastery, conceptual depth, and poetic intensity in this collection won for Andrés the distinction of runner-up for the 1964 Adonais Prize (the period's most prestigious award for poetry). Her preoccupations continue to be primarily individual and emotional, and the poetic consciousness centers upon reliving a problematic and painful past, striving to eliminate or otherwise come to terms with the most painful memories, sometimes taking refuge in dreams or fantasy (anathema for the "social poets" and denounced as escapist "evasion").

In *Desde aquí mis señales* (1971; From My Address Here), Andrés pursues her quest for ultimate meaning, continuing her search for human essence, yet paradoxically also focusing more intensely on the here and now, the concrete details of daily existence with its joys and sorrows, as opposed to the universal and abstract. Nevertheless, the collection is simultaneously more metaphysical, and the poet seems less concerned with reader comprehension, becoming more hermetic, visionary, and metaphorical. Paradoxically, it is in these poems that Andrés more closely approaches concerns of the "social poets," combining the personal and collective, proclaiming her oneness with the reality around her, and affirming her solidarity with other suffering human beings, anguished victims of injustice—at a moment when "social poetry" was languishing and had largely been abandoned both by its practitioners and by critical advocates. Obviously, Andrés was never ruled by literary fashion, and the synthesis she achieved in *Desde aquí mis señales* brought her a greater measure of critical acclaim than earlier works; many consider it her best collection.

Trance de la vigilia colmada (1980; Trance of Fulfilled Sleeplessness), published after nearly a decade's hiatus, again examines the mysterious unknown, returning to the search pursued in *Eterna vela* and resumed in *Desde aquí* in order to explore a strange and sinister universe, expressing once more the poet's existential anguish through depiction of nightmarish surroundings and revealing a kind of identity crisis involving her multiple selves, her authentic internal self versus what (or who) others perceive, as well as the conflicts introduced by the need to be more than one self at once. The aspects of social conscience visible in *Desde aquí* decline considerably in importance in this fifth collection, and less concern appears for the here and now than for the eternal dimension. References from the mid- to late 1980s mention an unpublished collection entitled *Paisajes conjurados* (Conjured Landscapes), suggesting a possibly incomplete continuation of her anguished search through nightmarish dreamscapes.

Andrés, obviously not a feminist writer, transcends gendered themes and discourse, much as she skirted sociopolitical rhetoric and poetic trendiness. Her importance for feminist scholars and gender studies may reside precisely in her insistence on treating universal, eternal, philosophical, and metaphysical themes traditionally "reserved" for male writers, refusing to treat topics the conservative regime of the 1950s and 1960s considered appropriate for women when she began writing. Andrés remained true to her self, listening to her inner voice instead of seeking more facile acceptance by writing on love, motherhood, and other themes deemed appropriate for women. Together with philosopher-critic María *Zambrano of the "Generation of 1927" (and Clara *Janés in her own generation), Andrés is one of a very small number of women to focus on the philosophical and metaphysical.

Work by

El buscador. Madrid: Agora, 1959.
Desde aquí mis señales. Salamanca: Alamo, 1971.
Dos caminos. Madrid: Rialp, 1964.
Eterna vela. Madrid: Rialp, 1961.
Trance de la vigilia colmada. Barcelona: Anthropos, 1980.

Work about

Bravo, María Elena. "Ausencias/presencias en la poesía de postguerra: El caso de Elena Andrés." *Letras Peninsulares* 9.2–3 (1996–1997): 377–389.
Fagundo, Ana María. "Realidad e irrealidad en la poesía de Elena Andrés." *Cuadernos hispanoamericanos* 351 (1979): 641–651.
Lacasa, Cristina. "Realidad y alucinación." *Nueva Estafeta* 27 (1981): 101.
Newton, Candelas. "Un interlocutor eclipsado: El discurso femenino en la poesía española actual." *Discurso femenino actual.* Ed. Adelaida López de Martínez. Puerto Rico: U of Puerto Rico, 1995. 161–177.
Valdivieso, L. Teresa. "La poesía de Elena Andrés como una pluralidad de discursos." *Alaluz* 16–17 (Autumn–Spring 1985): 3–11.

Janet Pérez

Andreu, Blanca (1960–)

A Galician native born in La Coruña but schooled in a small town near Murcia, Blanca Andreu moved to Madrid at age 19 and has since then resided in the Spanish capital. Andreu made a dramatic splash on the literary scene with publication of her first book of poetry, *De una niña de provincias que se vino a vivir en un Chagall* (About a Provincial Girl Who Came to Live in a Chagall Painting), which was awarded the prestigious

Adonais poetry prize in 1980. Andreu was a computer science major at Madrid's Universidad Complutense at the time. The book was an immediate success and has since been published in a modified and expanded third edition.

Her second book of poetry, *Báculo de Babel* (1983; Babel's Walking Stick), won the Premio Mundial de Poesía Mística Fernando Rielo. A period of five years passed before publication in 1988 of her third major book of poetry, *Capitán Elphistone*. Work from all three books appears in an anthology titled *El sueño oscuro* (1994; Dark Dreaming), which represents collected writings from 1980 to 1989. While first and foremost a poet, she also writes short stories and in 1981 was the recipient of the Premio de Cuentos Gabriel Miró prize.

In general, Andreu is considered to be a surrealistlike poet because her work, as evidenced in *De una niña de provincias que se vino a vivir en un Chagall*, is characterized by the predominance of striking but often disconnected, apparently unrelated irrational images that in conjunction offer an overall picture that is not fully cohesive to the logical mind but accurately reflects what the poet describes as her "internal chaos." Written exclusively in free verse, the text is a composite of surprising and unsettling images whose unifying theme is that of life's elemental forces and enigmas—love, death, destruction, illusoriness, and irrationality. Process is prominent over product, and startling effect becomes primary.

A similar style is carried further in *Báculo de Babel*, which consists in large part of initially incoherent sections of poetic prose composed of a series of run-on sentences and of images incomprehensible at a rational level, all of which for Andreu responds to a kind of inner delirium. The overall tone is one of anguish and despair, especially when the poet is confronted with the meaninglessness she perceives as permeating life.

Elphistone indicates a return in form and style to Andreu's initial *Niña de provincias* and is inspired by the mythical figure of an unknown sailor (Elphistone), whose presence, mystery, and spirit permeate the work. Both the sea and death figure as prominent themes. Again, imaginative poetic language and vehement force of expression feature strongly.

Overall, Andreu is regarded as an innovative, experimental, and imaginative poet, unique and daring especially in her approach to poetic structure and imagery. Her work is most often likened to that of earlier surrealists and other avant-garde artists for whom the artistic form represents an aesthetic expression of a more complex and often irrational internal struggle.

Work by

Báculo de Babel. Madrid: Hiperión, 1983.
Capitán Elphistone. Madrid: Hiperión, 1988.
De una niña de provincias que se vino a vivir en un Chagall. Madrid: Hiperión, 1981.
El sueño oscuro. Poesía reunida 1980–1989. Madrid: Hiperión, 1994.

Work about

Ugalde, Sharon K. *Conversaciones y poemas: La nueva poesía femenina española*. Madrid: Siglo XXI, 1991.
Wilcox, John. *Women Poets of Spain, 1860–1990: Toward a Gynocentric Vision*. Champaign: U of Illinois P, 1997.

Anne M. Pasero

Ángel del hogar

Taken from the narrative poem entitled "The Angel in the House" (serialized 1854–1863) by British poet Coventry Patmore (1823–1896), this figure has come to symbolize the Victorian ideal—and stereotype—of womanhood in both society and literature of the nineteenth century. The figure was popularized in Spain in María del Pilar *Sinués's (1835–1893) conduct manual, *El ángel del hogar* (1859).

As evidenced by the many reissues of *El ángel del hogar* into the 1890s, the angel-figure came to be used as the model for the indoctrination of countless women into roles of wife and mother in a society devoid of other alternatives for them. The popularity and prevalence of the angel-figure also reflects the development of a new Victorian ideology of gender roles. As wife and mother, the woman was an integral component of the marriage bond that was, from a feminist standpoint, the basis of a conservative hierarchical social order grounded in sexual repression within the patriarchy. Marriage served the function of creating well-defined, religiously sanctioned social roles for both men and women. It also created and endorsed a dichotomization of the sexes that upholds as "natural" a mutually exclusive distinction between masculine and feminine based on male dominance and female suppression.

Nineteenth-century women were constantly reminded by their families and their culture—specifically by prescriptive literature such as *El ángel del hogar* and other such conduct books—of their right and proper role within society. That is, women were relegated to a different, and much more confined, sphere of influence than their husbands. Whereas the man was permitted to enter the public world of business, his wife was limited to a private place within the realm of the family—the house, *el hogar*. The ideal woman, the angel, was to be decent, pious, and dutiful; and she was expected to remain virtuous, pure, and untainted by the dangerous worldly contact with which her husband was necessarily involved. This woman was an asexual being whose task in life was, paradoxically, to produce children. She was also required to maintain a harmonious, orderly, and peaceful atmosphere in the household and to provide spiritual support for her husband.

True, she was granted superior authority in the areas of spirituality, sentiment, and emotion; but despite much rhetoric to the contrary, the angel-woman was in no way equal to her husband. Because she did not share in the man's corrupt material sphere, the woman was viewed merely as a domestic companion, worthy of respect and admiration, but only within her appropriate domain. The angel-woman was a dehumanized male creation devoid of any real legal or personal power or even any sense of identity beyond that of someone's wife or mother.

This process of dehumanization through idealization and elevation does not outwardly degrade women; it is not overtly subhuman or vulgar. On the contrary, a superhuman ideal is created; the woman is placed on a pedestal and perceived, in social and literary settings, as nothing less than a fragile angel embodying pure virtue, defining the feminine. The angel is delicate, compliant, chaste, reticent, and selfless but also helpless, weak, and repressed. Consequently, she is also in need of protection—a protection that leads all too easily to control within this patriarchal system. Certainly, the nineteenth-century woman, the ideal wife of the period, may be an angel, but she is an angel without wings. *See also Encierro*

Work about

Aldaraca, Bridget A. *El ángel del hogar: Galdós and the Ideology of Domesticity in Spain*. Chapel Hill: U of North Carolina P, 1991.

Auerbach, Nina. *Woman and the Demon: The Life of a Victorian Myth*. Cambridge: Harvard UP, 1982.

Christ, Carol. "Victorian Masculinity and the Angel in the House." *A Widening Sphere: Changing Roles of Victorian Women*. Ed. Martha Vicinus. Bloomington: Indiana UP, 1977. 146–162.

Gilbert, Sandra M., and Susan Gubar. *The Madwoman in the Attic: The Woman Writer and the Nineteenth-Century Literary Imagination*. New Haven: Yale UP, 1984.

Jagoe, Catherine. *Ambiguous Angels: Gender in the Novels of Galdós*. Berkeley: U of California P, 1994.

Langland, Elizabeth. *Nobody's Angels: Middle-Class Women and Domestic Ideology in Victorian Culture*. Ithaca: Cornell UP, 1995.

Montabrut, Maurice. "Courtly Manners in a Victorian Home: Patmore's 'The Angel in the House.'" *The Crisis of Courtesy: Studies in the Conduct-Book in Britain, 1600–1900*. Ed. Jacques Carré. Leiden: E.J. Brill, 1994. 145–155.

Pérez, Janet. "Subversion of Victorian Values and

Angel in the House
See Ángel del hogar

Antigua, Sor María de la (1566–1617)

This visionary nun was born near Seville to Baltasar Rodríguez and Ana Rodríguez, who were unmarried. Her impoverished parents took refuge in a series of charitable convents, finally securing work in the convent of Nuestra Señora de la Antigua. They placed their daughter in the care of nuns there at the age of three months; Sor María de la Antigua took her surname from the convent. After a few years, the very young girl left the convent to live with an uncle but returned at age 13, begging her parents not to arrange a marriage for her. Having no dowry, Sor María entered the convent as a nun *de velo blanco* (white veiled) and earned her keep there working as a cook.

Like Santa *Teresa de Jesús (1515–1582), whose writings influenced her, Sor María experienced mystic raptures and visions in the convent kitchen. She relates that God commanded her to write what she experienced; secondarily, her confessor encouraged the same activity. Her writings describe religious visions of all sorts but chiefly concentrate on eucharistic and crucifixion themes. Lacking an extensive formal education, Sor María's poems use simple or traditional verse forms and are often quite conversational in tone. One must consider, however, the possible influences of the humble style adopted by some other women writers as a defense against accusations of presumption and of the influence of Santa Teresa's writing.

Sor María utilizes many of the topoi traditional to mystic writing, including the motif of milk flowing from the wounds in Christ's side at the crucifixion. This motif was not uncommon among mystic nuns in twelfth-century Germany, although there is no evidence that Sor María was aware of the precedent.

Sor María's writings are collected and published by P. Fr. Pedro de la Santa Recolección in the *Desengaño de religiosos y de almas que tratan de virtud* (1678; Disillusion of Religious [Individuals] and Souls Seeking Virtue). Some works had previously been published in *Vida exemplar, admirables virtudes y muerte prodigiosa de la V. Madre, e iluminada virgen Soror María de la Antigua* (The Exemplary Life, Admirable Virtues and Prodigious Death of the Reverend Mother and Inspired Virgin Sister María de la Antigua) by Andrés de San Agustín in 1674–1675. Sor María died on September 22, 1617. *See also* Autobiographical Self-Representation of Women in the Early Modern Period; Nuns Who Wrote in Sixteenth- and Seventeenth-Century Spain

Work by

Navarro, Ana, ed. *Antología poética de escritores de los siglos XVI y XVII*. Madrid: Castalia/Biblioteca de escritoras, 1989.

Tras el espejo la musa escribe: Lírica femenina de los Siglos de Oro. Ed., intro., and notes Julián Olivares and Elizabeth S. Boyce. Madrid: Siglo Veintiuno de España, 1993. 531–618.

Elizabeth S. Boyce and Julián Olivares

Antoñita la Fantástica
See Casas, Borita (1911–1999)

Aragón, Catalina de
See Catalina de Aragón (1485–1536)

Aragoneses Urquijo, Encarnación
See Fortún, Elena, Pseudonym of Encarnación Aragoneses Urquijo (1886–1952)

Aranda, Condesa de
See Padilla Manrique y Acuña, Luisa María de, Condesa de Aranda (1590–1646)

Arcipreste de Hita

See *Libro de buen amor* (1335, 1343): Its Portrayal of Women

Arcipreste de Talavera

See *Corbacho, El* (1438)

Arenal, Concepción (1820–1893)

Born in El Ferrol, Galicia, her family later moved to Madrid, where the precocious young Concepción, a voracious reader, taught herself French and Italian. It was rumored that she even attended the university disguised as a man. Married in 1847 to Fernando García Carrasco, a lawyer and writer, both wrote for the important political newspaper *Iberia*. After Arenal's husband died in 1855, she settled with her children in Santander and subsequently returned to Galicia, where she died.

Concepción Arenal composed fiction, drama, and poetry, but her fame rests on her expository writing. Her treatises on poverty, delinquency, prisons, charity, and social welfare deal with social problems in an unjust, unequal nineteenth-century society. Her most influential books were *El visitador del pobre* (1860; Visitor of the Poor), translated into several languages; *Beneficencia, filantropía y caridad* (1861; Beneficence, Philanthropy and Charity); *Cartas a los delincuentes* (1865; Letters to Delinquents), *El pueblo, el reo y el verdugo* (1867; The People, the Criminal and the Executioner); *El derecho de gentes* (1879; People's Rights); *El visitador del preso* (1891; The Prison Visitor); and *El delito colectivo* (1892; Collective Guilt). She contributed papers and reports to international conferences and founded the journal *La Voz de la Caridad*, for which she wrote 464 articles. Her critical works include studies on Father *Feijóo and Herbert Spencer.

She also expressed concern for society's victims in her actions. Arenal established several charity organizations to help women prisoners and assist poor families; she organized a chapter of the Red Cross and directed one of its hospitals during the Carlist War; she founded La Constructora Benéfica to build houses for working people, was appointed general visitor of female prisons, and presented a *Proyecto de Reglamento de Cárceles* (Proposal for the Regulation of Prisons), among many other worthwhile projects.

As the first Spanish intellectual to address women's issues in a systematic, consistent way, Arenal's feminist discourse was always based on a sense of justice. She dealt with women's condition in Spain in her sociological works on poverty, welfare, education, and delinquency but concentrated on women's rights in two books, *La mujer del porvenir* (1868 [written 1861]; The Woman of the Future) and *La mujer de su casa* (1881; The Housewife), and in three long essays, "Estado actual de la mujer en España" (original version c. 1884, updated 1892; Women's Present Condition in Spain), "La educación de la mujer" (1892; Women's Education), and "El trabajo de las mujeres" (1891; Women's Work). In *La mujer del porvenir*, Arenal examines the contradictions evident in legal matters, religion, public opinion, and scientific research with regard to women. Laws do not grant equal rights to men and women, but they impose equal penalties for crimes. The Catholic Church venerates the mother of God and worships female saints and martyrs but does not allow women to become priests. Arenal devotes a chapter to refuting German scientist Dr. Franz Gall's theories about the inferior intelligence of women and concludes that upper- and middle-class women appear less intelligent than men due to their inferior education, while in poor families and among schoolchildren both sexes perform with equal intellectual capacity.

Arenal finds an explanation for the unfair treatment of women in history. Primitive and war-prone societies highly value physical force, which has contributed to the perception of male superiority. She contends that in modern societies intellect is more important than physical vigor; but women have not been allowed to develop their mental ability. When given the opportunity, as on the throne and in the theater, women have excelled; and she underlines the fact that the number of great queens in proportion to the few who occupied the throne should counter any thought of female intellectual inferiority.

Arenal supports her claim that education affects the development of women by citing the significant changes the U.S. Civil War brought about as women replaced men as teachers. After the war, American women in greater numbers taught in elementary and secondary coeducational schools. And she concludes with the story of the foundation of Vassar College for women, chartered in the state of New York in 1861. Three chapters demonstrate the consequences that lack of education poses for women, men, and society at large. Women are forced into marriages, their only "careers," with negative results for both spouses; and single and widowed women, and even those with a sick or disabled husband, cannot support their families in an honorable way. Prostitution is caused by poverty, compounded by lack of education and job opportunities. Wealthy women suffer from boredom or anger, engage in frivolous shopping, or become religious fanatics because they cannot seek a higher intellectual calling. Arenal proceeds to examine careers that women can successfully pursue. The first one is the priesthood, followed by law, medicine, and pharmacy. She would oppose women as judges or politicians, because she prefers women to console rather than to punish and to avoid the corruption involved in political life. Yet she is quick to refer to American women who sit on juries or vote and participate in politics. Her opposition to women in politics is surpassed only by her rejection of the armed forces as a career for women or men. Arenal makes a case for the compatibility of professional work with household responsibilities and raising children. Finally, she voices a strong plea for respect for unmarried women, an anomaly in nineteenth-century Spanish society, which viewed spinsters as a burden or as persons leading a pointless life after failing to fulfill their most sacred mission, motherhood. Most of Arenal's ideas are still relevant today and constitute a landmark in the history of feminism. However, her opinions of woman as physically weak, more sensitive, compassionate, and religious than men, and loving her children more than her husband, as well as her opinion that men possess a natural hierarchical superiority in the home, have become completely obsolete. Arenal's persuasive, rational approach occasionally gives way to passion, as when she warns eminent contemporary men who proclaim women's intellectual incompetence that future generations will read their works with the same astonishment and disappointment as was then provoked by Plato's and Aristotle's writings in defense of slavery.

La mujer de su casa (1881) is an ironic title for a combative and angry book that responds to the criticism generated by *La mujer del porvenir*. Arenal argues that the idealized view of the perfect woman as a traditional housewife is a farce and an anachronism. She analyzes the evolution of society throughout time and concludes that modern free nations require a strong work ethic and the active participation of an educated citizenry striving for the common good. Countries in which half of the population is excluded by law or public opinion from those activities cannot prosper or succeed. She then reiterates her previous argument that an uneducated woman can be neither a perfect wife nor a perfect mother, because her lack of schooling will hinder her ability to offer appropriate advice. Arenal examines the historical reasons for the low esteem given to traditional work associated with women and revisits the topic of physical strength. Now she claims that women are not really weak; instead, they have a different type of strength—endurance, stoicism, and patience—and they enjoy a longer life span. Arenal seems to modify her opinion about the intellectual capabilities of women, raising the question of whether women have an equivalent rather than an equal intelligence to that of men. She quotes extensively from *The History of Woman Suffrage* (1881–1902), by Susan B. Anthony et al., to prove the competence and success of U.S. women in many fields, including military strategy and politics, and ends with a strong plea for the education and emancipation of women.

"Estado actual de la mujer en España" was Arenal's contribution to *The Woman Question in Europe* (1884), edited by Mr. Staton in New York. Its original Spanish version was published in the *Boletín de la Institución Libre de Enseñanza* in 1895. Arenal presents an analysis of women's situation in the context of the workforce, religion, education, legislation, public opinion, moral values, social condition, and progress. Her thesis is that Spanish society oppresses and belittles women, limiting their opportunities and treating them unfairly as compared to men. The article ends on a more positive note, pointing out some progress made in education, such as the increase in the rate of literacy, the establishment of a new Commerce School, School for Governesses, Telegraph School, and foreign languages and art courses for women.

"El trabajo de las mujeres" was published in the *Boletín de la Institución Libre de Enseñanza* in 1891. Arenal denounces the fact that poor women hold the lowest and least appealing jobs and in the rare cases in which men do the same tasks, their salaries are higher. As in other articles, Arenal strongly advocates equal pay for equal work. She denounces working conditions and long hours in factories. Untrained for better factory jobs and lacking muscular strength, women are assigned menial tasks that depress them psychologically and result in illness and death. She points out that an exhausted mother procreates weak children. For critics who prefer a woman who never leaves the home, she argues that poor women always must work to supplement their husbands' meager salary and observes that if society wants mothers at home, women's education and working conditions should be improved so that women "can earn in six hours what they now earn in 12." Labor laws, old traditions, and prejudices contribute to the limited and inadequate opportunities for working women. Arenal sees hope in the few isolated cases of some factories where women enjoy flexible schedules. In her view, this positive attitude will contribute to abandonment of the erroneous dichotomy "worker *or* mother" so that instead society, laws, and justice will proclaim a new concept of "worker *and* mother."

"La educación de la mujer" was a paper read at the Congreso Pedagógico in 1892. Arenal makes the case for equal education for both sexes; she defines education as the formation of the whole person, the character building of compassionate and productive members of society. Arenal questions the traditional idea that a woman's only mission is that of wife and mother; on the contrary, whether single, married, or widow, a woman has duties, rights, and a dignity of her own; she should take life seriously because otherwise she will become a toy. Arenal advocates preparation to hold a job and earn a living and involvement in social causes. She favors physical education for both sexes, but particularly for women who bear the main responsibility of the household. Intellectual and physical development would enable women to be independent and valuable members of society.

Work by

Obras completas. 22 vols. Madrid: Sucesores de Rivadeneyra, 1894–1902.

Work about

Campo Alange, María. *Concepción Arenal (1820–1893): Estudio biográfico documental.* Madrid: Revista de Occidente, 1973.

Díaz Castañón, Carmen. "Concepción Arenal en su centenario." *Revista de Occidente* 151 (1993): 137–152.

Guillermo, Edenia. *Concepción Arenal: Palabra y ejemplo*. Havana: Centro Gallego, 1943.

Irizarry, Estelle. "Weighing the Evidence: Legal Discourse in the 19th-Century Spanish Feminist Concepción Arenal." *Computers and the Humanities* 29.5 (1995): 363–374.

Juana Amelia Hernández

Atencia, María Victoria (1931–)

In many senses, she is a bridging figure of Spanish postwar poetry. Born in Málaga, María Victoria Atencia would normally be considered part of the "second postwar generation" of Spanish poets, who began to publish in the 1950s. Her work, however, has little in common with the social poetry prevalent during that decade. It is aesthetically more attuned to the poetics of Jaime Gil de Biedma (1929–1990) in its careful form and its relation of interior and exterior spaces and to the later poetry of José Angel Valente (1929–) in its minimalism. It also recalls the *novísimo* (newest) poetry of the 1960s and 1970s in its elimination of anecdotal detail and in its reference to artistic works and symbolic spaces instead of social or personal reality. In fact, although Atencia's earliest major books date from 1961 (*Arte y parte* [Art and Report]; *Cañada de los ingleses* [Canebrake of the British]), most of her poetry has been published in the post-Franco years, coinciding chronologically with some of the most important books of the *novísimos*. Even Atencia's personal and literary friendships—with Vicente Aleixandre, Jorge Guillén, María *Zambrano, Pablo García Baena, Clara *Janés, and Guillermo Carnero, among others—bridge generations.

Atencia's poems forge intricate, occasionally disquieting connections between subjects and objects while maintaining a serene tone. Her early books *Tierra mojada* (1953; Moist Earth), *Arte y parte*, and *Cañada de los ingleses* are linguistically and conceptually simpler than her subsequent work. Her more culturalist books may be divided into two categories. The books written in unrhymed alexandrine verses—*Marta & María* (1976), *El mundo de M.V.* (1976; The World of M.V.), *Los sueños* (1978; Dreams), *Paulina o el libro de las aguas* (1984; Paulina or the Book of Waters), *Trances de Nuestra Señora* (1986; Our Lady's Trances), and *De la llama en que arde* (1988; Of the Flame in Which It Burns)—largely explore an interior world in relation to artistic or domestic objects. Atencia has also written several books of culturalist, often metapoetic, poems of varying line length, including *El coleccionista* (1979; The Collector), *Compás binario* (1984; Binary Rhythm), *La pared contigua* (1989; The Adjoining Wall), *La intrusa* (1992; Female Intruder), and *El puente* (1992; The Bridge).

The categorization of Atencia's poetry within feminist poetics has proved difficult because she seems to conform more to patriarchal poetic and social traditions than to most models of feminism or feminist writing. Thus some critics (Romero Márquez, Ugalde, Wilcox) believe that Atencia is not feminist but profoundly feminine. Her poetry certainly contains conservative elements, from alexandrine verses to religious figures to bourgeois domestic images, and the tone of her work is more serene (Jorge Guillén called her "María Victoria Serenísima") than revolutionary. Nonetheless, some critics (Ciplijauskaité, Coco, Kruger-Robbins, Metzler, Newton) believe that Atencia subtly undermines categorical definitions of men and women from within the limitations of femininity and form through her linguistic ambiguity and doubling techniques, which tend to blur the differences between female and male, interior spaces and the exterior world, artistic objectivity and subjectivity.

Work by

Antología poética. Madrid: Castalia, 1990.

Ex Libris. Sel. of poetry, 1976–1984. Madrid: Visor, 1984.

Marta & María. 2nd ed. Madrid: Caballo Griego para la Poesía, 1984.

Poesía completa. Ed., English trans., notes Victoria León. Málaga: n.p., 1995.

La señal: Poesía 1961–1989. Málaga: Excelentísimo Ayuntamiento de Málaga, 1990.
Tierra mojada. Málaga: Dardo, 1953.

Work about

Ciplijauskaité, Biruté. "La serena plenitud de María Victoria Atencia." *Alaluz* 22 (1990): 7–21.

García Martín, José Luis. Introduction. *María Victoria Atencia: Antologia poética.* Madrid: Castalia, 1990. 7–38.

Jaffe, Catherine. "Gender, Intersubjectivity, and the Author/Reader Exchange in the Poetry of María Victoria Atencia." *Letras Peninsulares* 5 (1992): 291–302.

Kruger-Robbins, Jill. "(Not) Just a [(Wo)Man] Poet: The Dialectic of Identity and Difference in the Poetry of María Victoria Atencia." *Revista de Estudios Hispánicos* 29 (1995): 231–244.

Metzler, Linda D. "Images of the Body in the Poetry of María Victoria Atencia." *Anales de la Literatura Española Contemporánea* 18 (1993): 173–181.

Newton, Candelas. "Representación del sujeto y escritura femenina en los poemas ecfrásticos de María Victoria Atencia." *Revista de Estudios Hispánicos* 29 (1995): 213–229.

Ugalde, Sharon Keefe. *La poesía de María Victoria Atencia: Un acercamiento crítico.* Madrid: Huerga y Fierro, 1998.

———. "Time and Ekphrasis in the Poetry of María Victoria Atencia." *Confluencia* 3.1 (1987): 5–12.

Wilcox, John. "María Victoria Atencia: 'serenísima'—ma non troppo." *Revista de Estudios Hispánicos* 29 (1995): 199–211.

Jill Kruger-Robbins

Autobiographical Self-Representation of Women in the Early Modern Period

After the 1559 *Index of Prohibited Books* deprived *Teresa of Avila (1515–1582) of her most treasured reading material, she starting coping with the loss by turning more intensely inward and began to accept explanations of all she needed to know directly from God. Her obligatory sharing of this infused wisdom and her other extraordinary experiences with her confessor made him anxious about his ability to discern the spirit moving Teresa: Was it diabolical or holy? He requested that she produce an account of her life with God, to help him determine what to do next, and thereafter several priests were consulted. Teresa declared outright that these exchanges among powerful men who did not know her were violations of her privacy. More positively, from the same exchanges were sown the seeds of what developed into her reconstruction of her relationship with God. This document has been reductively but irrevocably labeled her *Vida*, or life itself, although she finished it in 1562 at age 47 and lived 20 years longer, years of literary and reformist activity much greater than that recounted in her "*Life*."

Teresa's "book of God's mercies," as she herself called it, was the founding text in Spain of one of the most prolifically practiced genres of sixteenth- and seventeenth-century Spanish literature, the spiritual life story. Although generally referred to as "spiritual autobiography," this is a type of writing whose explicit purpose is to reveal a team of at least two, God and the pious individual. The voice that narrates represents itself as meaningless except as a vehicle of an otherworldly authority. By the end of the sixteenth century, the human-God duo had developed into an ornate chorus in which the entire heavenly host might play a prominent role alongside the Virgin and Christ. These texts are by no means purely historical; rather, they are based on direct and indirect imitation of hagiographic accounts, whose structure provides the basic framework for the tales.

In early modern Spain, the spiritual life story was a type of text almost exclusively written by women, and over 100 are extant, some published and many in manuscript. Its origins are complex; there is a late-fifteenth-century precedent by the Poor Clare Camilla Battista da Varano, a text that lacks the menaced quality evident in Teresa's account. Varano's work had few imitations in Italy, whereas every spiritual life story written by an early modern Spanish woman invokes the Teresian model, famous and much circulated among female religious well before its first publication in 1588. Thus, although Spanish women seem to have composed little, if any, of the autobiographical accounts such as diaries, family histories, or memoirs at which English and French women excelled during this period, they did represent themselves as God's partners through this religious tool.

The spiritual life story occurs at the nexus of several forms of representation that converge in Spain for the first time in Teresa's narrative: the state *relación* (report), the Inquisitorial trial, the general confession, and the Western tradition of Christian hagiography and vision literature in general, in which women had long played an important role. These forms provided the structure through which each woman filtered her own experience.

As the Spanish empire expanded over the turn of the fifteenth century, its equally expansive state bureaucracy developed a form through which to process petitions to the king and queen. The protocol that emerged was the *relación*, which consists of a brief self-identification, the story of one's case, followed by a rationale and petition. As *relaciones* from the New World make clear, this is a type of writing in which fiction happily meets fact, in which interpretation and presentation are everything; it shares this feature with the spiritual life story.

As an arm of the Spanish state, whose bureaucracy expanded in equal if not superior proportions into the seventeenth century, the Inquisition likewise developed specific methods of collecting information, almost identical to the *relación*: name and identification in history: parents, spouse (in the case of women), birthplace, notable features relative to the inquiry, followed by the body of information collected or interrogation. The trial document, which provided the framework to the picaresque novel as well, lent its structure to the spiritual life story, which is also a response to an inquiry. Worldly power rests outside the narration; the author's task is to immobilize the extratextual threat. In Teresa's use of only the first 10 (out of 40) chapters of her *Vida* to relate her historical past, and her dedication of the other 30, or 75 percent, to descriptive narrative about her method of prayer (which constituted the "problem"), the relative proportions of both the *relación* and the Inquisitorial trial are evident.

The state's growing obsession with written documentation, and the Spanish monarchs' employ of *letrados* (paper-pushers) rather than the nobility as managers of their affairs, combined with increasing ecclesiastic disease over evidence of heresy in the theoretically clean Spanish Catholic community and melded easily with the increased emphasis on local diocesan control in the post-Tridentine Church. All this made it both possible and necessary for confessors to examine their spiritual charges with particular vigor and persistence in cases of extraordinary piety and to insist on written or dictated accounts during those inquiries.

Only spiritually problematic women were required to represent their relationships with God in writing, and many prolific female religious authors were never asked to complete this task (Juliana de Morell [1594–1653], Marcela de *San Félix [1605–1687], for example). As confessors acquired increased responsibility for their confessants, an interdependence developed in which the indictment of one led to the censure of the other, as the glory of one likewise produced fame and good fortune in her counterpart. Many Inquisitorial trials began with an accused woman and led back to her irresponsible spiritual adviser, who was punished (usually with less severity than she) along with his stray sheep.

The Catholic response to Protestantism, a response that accentuated the Church hierarchy and the need for the priest and confessor in the lives of individuals, as well as the increased sophistication in the discernment of spirits facilitated by the printing press, made confessors both wary and aware of the potential latent in exuberantly pious souls. At the same time, the Catholic

Church during this period was sensitive to the benefits to be accrued from evidence that God was alive and well in practicing Catholics and could be directly experienced through the hierarchy of the Church. Orthodox mystics provided this evidence, and there is little doubt that women's voices were actively sought out during this period to testify for Catholic vitality, much the way their voices had been cultivated in the twelfth and thirteenth centuries as weapons against the Cathar heresy and Great Schism.

Heightened awareness of what distinguished Catholic experience from other nascent forms of Christianity increased emphasis on the cult of the saints, Church ceremony, and the productive intervention of confessors in lives of the pious. The general confession, still practiced in the Catholic Church today, was one way used to solidify Catholic practice: It consisted of a complete review of an individual's personal history and was required at turning points of her or his life. After the general confession, which usually took several days, it became the confessor's responsibility to guide the confessant's soul along the proper path. Ignatius of Loyola (1491–1556) built a general confession into the practice of his Spiritual Exercises, which were used widely in Spain as a spiritual tune-up by members of all social classes by the end of the sixteenth century. Teresa de Avila's Vida had its origins in the general confession she was required to prepare so that the events transpiring in her soul could be better examined by her superiors. The turning point consistently represented in the spiritual life story is the direct and obvious intervention of God into the narrator's consciousness. The narrator's challenge was to represent that intervention as the culmination of a long, purifying process that made it clear that the divine presence was authentic and the vessel a worthy one.

All known spiritual life stories of early modern Spain were written with the sanction of, and usually at the insistence of, a confessor; whether they were willingly composed or written under coercion is still debated, but it is difficult to deny Teresa's discomfort over revealing her intimacies with God. Had they been able to do so, it is likely that these authors would have chosen another, less exposing type of writing through which to represent themselves. Most of them did so, and without insisting their confessors made them compose those other documents. However, women and men religious, whether professional religious or holy people living in the world, took vows of one type or another, the first of which was almost always one of obedience to a spiritual superior, without whose permission no writing took place (theoretically) and whose order to write had to be obeyed.

As the avenues for self-expression and public performance in professional and domestic roles diminished for women in the early modern period, they began to direct their substantial energies inward, in proportions that did not occur with men. This enclosure (*encierro) was obviously facilitated by the introspection characteristic of the period, and the newly developed interest in the individual, manifest in the emergence of portraiture and first-person literary works. The closing off of women from the world intensified this inward gaze and was in turn intensified by Tridentine rules of cloister, against whose mandates women inevitably collided when trying to form religious orders that involved work in the world (as did Isabel Roser and Luisa de *Carvajal [1566–1614], for example).

The renewed religious energy produced by the Catholic reform at the end of the fifteenth and early sixteenth centuries made women aware of possibilities for action in spite of attempts to encourage their passivity. This double-edged awareness produced the inward and outward movement typical of the spiritual narration, which reaches to interior depths as it stretches out a hand to the reader. Again the printing press was crucial in the dissemination of heroic female models of behavior, feeling, and knowing, upon which women, in a decidedly quixotic fashion, often based their very lives and certainly their life stories. The writings by and about famous Christian women religious circulated widely during the period in the several, voluminous *Flos sanctorum* published across the sixteenth and seventeenth centuries and in books whose translation Cardinal Cisneros (1436–1517) sponsored specifically for placement in convents in the early 1500s: the *vita* of Catherine of Siena (1347–1380) and works by Angela of Foligno (1248?–1309) and Mechthild von Magdeburg (c. 1212–c. 1282). Echoes and even complete passages from these texts provide the underpinnings for women's spiritual life stories.

There are two types of spiritual life stories: the examination document used for the discernment of spirits, and the recounting of one's life for posterity. Teresa of Avila composed the first type, which was used as a tool for probing her inner life. Once complete, it was passed around a coterie of men who determined the orthodoxy of the relationship it represented, the standard procedure for such texts. Clearly, the burden on these women, almost none of whom had been educated as writers or theologians, was heavy. The "examination texts" offered official sanction to the successful writer and isolation from community and God for those who failed. They were demanded as part of a formal or informal interrogation or trial proceeding, and the women who wrote them were almost always mature individuals at the threshold, not end, of their spiritual careers, usually between the ages of 40 and 50. Consequently, the standard female spiritual life story in first person made possible, but does not contain, the true heights of its author's career. In 1611, Ana Domenge was forced to render her life with God in writing while in the cells of the Barcelona Inquisition, where she spent seven months awaiting the resolution of her trial. Having performed the task satisfactorily, she was released and went on to become the foundress of the Dominican convent in Perpignan; her relationships with the celestial company whose lengthy conversations her manuscript records evidently prospered as well. No texts of the examination type by men have been yet found.

The posterity-serving spiritual life story has its origins in hagiography, which in turn has its roots in classical biography; under this rubric, exemplary individuals were ordered to write a description of their life with God, usually just before death, for the benefit of their community (and glory of their Order, in the event a plan for canonization was on the horizon). The responsibility for recording the life of a holy person had passed from a biographer to the individual him- or herself by the early modern period, and the practice continues to this day in religious orders such as the Carmelites. María Machuca (1563–1638), a spiritual daughter of San *Juan de la Cruz (1542–1591), wrote a posterity-serving spiritual life story at the incredible age of 75. She describes therein how her more youthful spiritual exuberance had led her to compose poetry, which a confessor required that she explicate in prose and hand over to him. Later, she was told the poems had been burned; she says she was ordered to stop writing and did so until a subsequent confessor lifted the ban. In contradistinction to the examination-type life story, the posterity-serving variety was written by women believed to be close to death. Men, on the other hand, were allowed to compose them little by little across their later years, and the end product was handed over to their superiors upon the death of their authors. The obligation to submit the text for an error check did not exist, and presumably only exemplary individuals were asked to carry out this enterprise. Such is the spiritual life story of the Carmelite ecstatic Juan de Jesús María (1560–1644), who worked on his from 1594 to 1635.

Related to the spiritual life story, but having fundamentally different purposes and features, are other types of religious documentation related to matters of conscience, such as spiritual journals, spiritual diaries, and vision literature. Teresa of Avila was writing her accounts of conscience two years before she began her *Vida* text. The *cuentas*, short accounts, are the written counterpart of the daily examination of conscience, just as the general confession is the oral complement to the spiritual life story. Daily accounts and the retelling of specific experiences do not create the vital whole found in the life story, forced as it is to prioritize and order many years of interior life. The same may be said of vision literature, devoted more to messages of other-worldly beings than to the human vehicle of divine expression that carries the life story through time.

The structure of the spiritual life story follows the general pattern of female saints' lives and rarely varies: The introductory chapters, relatively short, present the woman as one chosen by God at an extremely early age, typically in conflict with some member of her earthly family, who eventually submits to divine will by acquiescing to her plan to become a religious or dies. The subject experiences a brush with death that often coincides with the moment of irrevocable commitment to a religious life. Long periods of mortification, conflict, and doubt follow, usually embellished by numerous encounters with Satan. Self-confirming experiences of advanced union with God follow, indicating that the rite of passage into spiritual authority was complete.

Relatively few spiritual life stories went to press as they were written, unedited and without a frame imposed upon them by a man. Fray Luis de *León's (1527–1591) 1558 edition of Teresa's works touched her originals lightly; later editors of other women's works used a much heavier hand. By the beginning of the seventeenth century, most women's manuscripts were not published themselves but rather cited and manipulated by their confessors, who displaced the subjects as authors of their lives and placed themselves, as biographers, in their stead. Spiritual life stories are still composed by women today and still invoke Teresa of Avila as their model. So wrote Dorothy Day in her 1952 life story *The Long Loneliness*, the title of which comes from a quote by Mary Ward, a seventeenth-century reader and imitator of Teresa. *See also* Nuns Who Wrote in Sixteenth- and Seventeenth-Century Spain

Work about

Beasley, Faith. *Revising Memory: Women's Fiction and Memoirs in Seventeenth-Century France.* New Brunswick, NJ: Rutgers UP, 1990.

Efren de la Madre de Dios, Father, and Otger Steggink. *Tiempo y vida de Santa Teresa.* 2nd ed. Madrid: Editorial Católica, 1972.

Herpoel, Sonja. "Bajo la amenaza de la Inquisición: Escritoras españolas en el Siglo de Oro." *España, teatro y mujeres. Estudios dedicados a Henk Oostendorp.* Ed. Martin Gosman and Hub. Hermans. Amsterdam/Atlanta, GA: Rodopi, 1989. 123–131.

La Iglesia en la España de los siglos XV y XVI. Ed. Ricardo García-Villoslada. *La historia de la Iglesia en España, Vol. 3, Parts I and II.* 5 vols. Madrid: Editorial Católica, 1979–1980.

Juárez, Encarnación. "Autobiografías de mujeres en la Edad Media y el Siglo de Oro y el canon literario." *Monographic Review/Revista Monográfica* 13 (1997): 154–168.

Liebewitz, Ruth P. "Virgins in the Service of Christ: The Dispute over an Active Apostolate for Women during the Counter-Reformation." *Women of Spirit: Female Leadership in the Jewish and Christian Traditions.* Ed. Rosemary Ruether and Eleanor McLaughlin. New York: Simon and Schuster, 1979. 132–152.

McGrath, Lynette. "Researching the Early Modern Female Body." *Women in the Renaissance. Newsletter Published by the New York Society for the Study of Women in the Renaissance* 3 (1994): 2–7.

Olin, John C. *Catholic Reform from Cardinal Ximenes to the Council of Trent, 1494–1563.* New York: Fordham UP, 1990.

O'Malley, John W. "Was Ignatius Loyola a Church Reformer? How to Look at Early Modern Catholicism." *Catholic Historical Review* 77.2 (1991): 177–193.

Ortega Costa, Milagros. "Spanish Women in the Reformation." *Women in Reformation and Counter-Reformation Europe: Public and Private Worlds.* Ed. Sherrin Marshall. Bloomington: Indiana UP, 1989. 89–119.

Ozment, Stephen E. *Mysticism and Dissent: Religious*

Ideology and Social Protest in the Sixteenth Century. New Haven, CT: Yale UP, 1973.

Poutrin, Isabel. *La voile et la plume. Autobiographie et sainteté féminine dans l'Espagne moderne*. Madrid: Casa de Velázquez, 1995.

Rapley, Elizabeth. *The Dévotes: Women and Church in Seventeenth Century France*. Montreal: McGill Queen's UP, 1990.

Schizzano Mandel, Adrienne. "Le procès inquisitorial comme act autobiographique: Le cas de Sor María de San Jerónimo." *Actes du Colloque International de la Baume-les-Aix*, May 11–13, 1979. Université de Provence, 1980. 155–168.

Wiesner, Merry E. *Women and Gender in Early Modern Europe. New Approaches to European History*. 1993. New York: Cambridge UP, 1994.

Wogan-Browne, Jocelyn. "Saints' Lives and the Female Reader." *Forum for Modern Language Studies* 27.4 (1991): 314–332.

Elizabeth Rhodes

Azorín (1873–1967): Feminism in His Novel *Doña Inés* (1925)

Born José Martínez Ruiz in Monóvar, Alicante, Azorín took his pseudonym from the title of one of his early novels. He studied law in Valencia and in 1896 moved to Madrid, where he wrote for republican and liberal newspapers, gaining renown as a revolutionary thinker. At that time Spain was experiencing a political, economic, and cultural crisis that intensified with its defeat in 1898 in the Spanish American War. Before and after this climactic event, writers and intellectuals were consumed by this spiritual turning point. It led them to probe Spanish character, history, and cultural tradition in order to assess Spain's identity and place in a rapidly changing modern world. The leading group of writers of this era, the Generation of 1898, derived its name from a 1913 essay written by Azorín.

Azorín's publications produced between 1905 and 1925 embody that crucial search for identity. In *Doña Inés* (1925), as in the hundreds of essays he wrote during this period, Azorín sets aside his earlier radical style and looks back on Spain's literature and spirit in an effort to show what is eternal in the past. As he reexamines his nation's civilization, he views its commonplace landscapes and villages as well as the legendary Don Quixote (see *Don Quijote*). Azorín's novels show little regard for traditional novelistic construction since he composed them in a fragmented, impressionistic fashion dominated by the episode and the vignette. Consequently, his principal novelistic innovation resides in the contemplation of reality as a source of human reactions and sensibilities. In the philosophical domain, one of the concepts closely associated with Azorín remains that of Nietzsche's eternal recurrence.

In the novels *Don Juan* and *Doña Inés*, Azorín evoked one of Spain's most universal literary personages by recasting *Zorrilla's play *Don Juan Tenorio* in two separate prose pieces. In the latter novel, the previously angelic savior of the classic male predator appears as a mature, decisive woman whose identity has been predicated on the failure of her relationships with men. At the novel's onset, she awaits Don Juan. He does not keep his appointment but sends a letter; in a highly dramatic episode she tears up the letter and returns to Segovia, where her uncle, Don Pablo, welcomes her in the family home. There, Inés gradually becomes acquainted with the formidable story of Doña Beatriz de *Silva, her fifteenth-century ancestor through her uncle. Don Pablo is composing the biography of Beatriz, and he relates the story of their noble medieval relative to his niece. Inés and Beatriz resemble each other physically, and the life of each woman is suffused in romantic involvement. Beatriz, married to Esteban de Silva, deceives her husband by falling totally in love with Guillén de Treceño, a fair, blue-eyed poet. Her husband, depicted as a man of action and master of his domain, discovers his wife's infidelity. To exact revenge and punish his unfaithful wife, he plans a ruse by announcing a day of celebration in his wife's honor. As she prepares for the festivities in her chambers, one of her maids delivers a small box. When she opens it, she discovers a lock of her beloved poet's blond hair; her husband had her lover killed. Subsequently, Don Esteban has Beatriz confined by force in a country house where she eventually dies of madness, unable to live without her cherished poet.

As *Doña Inés* progresses, the ancestor's story seemingly entwines with the life of the living relative. Inés develops a romantic interest in Diego, a much younger poet who physically resembles Guillén, behaving in moderately aggressive fashion. The love story and the mingling of identities culminate late in the novel when Inés goes to the cathedral in Segovia to visit Beatriz's tomb. There, as if in a previous life, Inés feels that she had already lived the present moment, and on touching the cold marble of her ancestor's tomb, she experiences a profound sensation that the narrative describes as "undefinable." Inés deepens the bond with her relative by placing an imploring kiss on Beatriz's tomb. Inés then senses a presence and hears a voice calling her. Turning to look behind her, she discovers that the poet Diego has been nearby, watching her. The ensuing events are vast and cinematic—the would-be lovers fall into each other's arms, and as they kiss, their embrace reverberates throughout the city of Segovia. A scandal follows, town and church officials admonish both parties, and Inés departs for Argentina, but not before leaving a dowry for Diego's former girlfriend. The novel closes as an even older Inés presides over the school she founded for children of poor Spaniards. As the children call to "Mamá Inés," the narrative infers that another poet may be waiting in the wings of this cyclical drama.

Interpreters of this novel have often found that the concept of eternal recurrence constitutes its form and substance. For others, the organization of the chapters and the linkage of motifs form a symmetrical and cyclical architecture. Such recurrences abound: the victimization of women at the hands of cruel men, the cyclical nature of thwarted love, and the physical resemblances between medieval and present-day lovers, both men and women. Such commentaries affirm the novel's dependence on the philosophical concept of eternal recurrence, as if governed by the principle of unchanging content that repeats its essence as time passes.

There are, however, clear and remarkable indications at the start of the text that distinguish Inés and her ancestor Doña Beatriz. Although Inés finds only unhappiness in love, she does enjoy freedom from the social rigors that imposed passivity and male domination on Beatriz. Inés's symbolic gesture of shredding Don Juan's letter and her subsequent departure for Segovia demonstrate her independence and autonomy. Unlike Beatriz, Inés is no man's property, nor does she perish from the wrongs inflicted on her by love's adversities. She does suffer abandonment by Don Juan, yet she turns the tables after the thrilling incident with Diego at her predecessor's tomb. Her reversal materializes as a letter. Inés writes to her uncle and assumes authority by making her own conscious and wise decision to renounce happiness that one pursues but seldom finds. The amorous relationships that dominate the novel suggest the eternal recurrence of women's traditional role in society. Nonetheless, the instances of the two letters handled by Inés manifest her willpower to rise above the pain she once tolerated as a near victim of Don Juan. Thus, the novel of Doña Inés is formally determined by *her* actions.

In terms of overcoming the traditional role inflicted on women by patriarchal society, the theme of the journey is just as significant as the letters. Inés has the freedom to transport herself from one geographical place to another, quite unlike Beatriz, who endured incarceration. Inés travels to Segovia and Argentina, and her journeys, foreshadowed early in the novel, symbolize her inner conflict. During the long wait for Don Juan, Inés repeatedly stares at a yellowed map of Argentina, and the narrative converts her gaze into a metaphorical geography of her inner anguish. She recognizes her own vulnerability for betrayal by Don Juan, and that perception becomes a spiritual region of despair, a river flanked by banks of health and sickness, a land of pain and tears. Yet it is here that the narrative explicitly marks Inés's incipient transcendence and eventual triumph over such passivity; her affective geography turns to the contemplation of the peaceful and delightful shore of health, her final destination. That goal on her inner map is directly bound to the ultimate Inés who travels, leaving behind an erstwhile willingness to suffer from love. Her resolve to break the preordained patterns dictated to women results in her letter of farewell, a safe passage written in her own hand.

Azorín wrote several essays that disclose his condemnation of the patriarchal attitudes that oppressed women in Spain. His feminist stance has not garnered frequent comment since critical attentions have more often concentrated on the aesthetics of the unchanging aspects of eternal recurrence. However, by calling attention to cyclical recurrence of *similar* events and situations in *Doña Inés*, Azorín's preoccupations acquire richer significance. The route Inés has traveled diverges markedly from her ancestor's, for even though she has not found personal contentment in love, she has altered the metaphorical map that once hampered her self-fulfillment. Not only has she revised the map, but she has crossed the boundaries of life confined by heterosexual relationships, taking charge of herself, defining her own identity, or, as it were, writing her own ticket. *See also* Sáenz-Alonso, Mercedes (1917–): *Don Juan y el donjuanismo*

Work

Doña Inés. Ed. Elena Catena. 2nd ed. Madrid: Castalia, 1984.

Work about

Glenn, Kathleen M. *Azorín (José Martínez Ruiz)*. TWAS 604. Boston: Twayne, 1981.

Pieropán, María Domenica. "Una re-visión feminista del eterno retorno en *Doña Inés* de Azorín." *Hispania* 72 (May 1989): 233–240.

Risco, Antonio. "La mujer en la novela de Azorín." *Cuadernos Hispanoamericanos* 385 (1982): 172–196.

Glenn Morocco

Badell, Ana María (1932–)

Born in Santander, this novelist and journalist is an independent and self-directed figure who has defied traditional Spanish gender restrictions in her choice of profession, becoming a landscape architect and agronomist. Badell is better known, however, for her numerous articles and novels, whose titles often indicate her interest in feminine subjects and women's lives. These include *Las monjas: esas mujeres* (1966; Nuns: Those Women), *Las nuevas colegialas* (1968; The New Schoolgirls), *Historia de un perro* (1969; Story of a Dog), *Monte de piedad y caja de ahorros* (1977; Pawnshop and Savings Bank), and *¡Hasta mañana, dolor!* (1997; See You Tomorrow, Pain).

Work by

¡Hasta mañana, dolor! Madrid: Dólar, 1997.
Las monjas, esas mujeres. Madrid: n.p., 1966.
Las nuevas colegialas. Madrid: Iberoamericanas, 1968.
Sor Ada. Madrid: Iberoamericanas, 1967.

Janet Pérez

Ballesteros, Mercedes (1913–)

The daughter of titled aristocrats, both of whom were well-known historians, scholars, and academicians, Mercedes Ballesteros de Gaibrois was born in Madrid in 1913 (her birthdate was erroneously reported as 1891 in Galerstein et al., *Women Writers of Spain*). As daughter of the count of Beretta, she enjoyed a privileged, relatively enlightened upbringing, with extensive exposure to the culture of Spain and Colombia (her mother's homeland). Little is known of her life prior to 1939, when she published her first three works of fiction: *Paris-Niza* (From Paris to Nice), *La extraña boda de Glori Dunn* (The Strange Wedding of Glori Dunn), and *La aventura de una chica audaz* (The Adventure of an Audacious Girl). The timing of their publication—the year that saw the end of the Spanish Civil War of 1936–1939—suggests that Ballesteros may have written these works as a means of whiling away the hours during wartime. All are out of print and inaccessible, but the titles indicate either juvenile fiction (intended for adolescent girls) or the *novela rosa*, sugar-coated romances aimed at female audiences. According to Eugenio G. de Nora (*La novela española contemporánea*), Ballesteros published various collections of poetry; she has also written plays and critical essays, plus a biography of the nineteenth-century Cuban Spanish writer Gertrudis *Gómez de Avellaneda, of special interest for women's studies. In addition, Ballesteros became well known on the lecture circuit. She has written under several pseudonyms, including Silvia Visconti, Rocq Morris, and most frequently, Baronesa Alberta.

Other publications aside, Ballesteros is best known for her fiction, both novels and short stories. She is one of very few Spanish women to have scored successes as a humorist, authoring numerous brief, ironic, subtly comedic essays on topics ranging from social rites and rituals to vacations and cocktail parties, modern shortcomings, and the most varied people, places, and situations, as seen in collections such as *Este mundo* (1950; This World, reprinted in 1959 in two parts entitled *Invierno* [Winter] and *Verano* [Summer]); *Así es la vida* (1953; That's Life), a collection of articles first appearing in periodicals; and *El personal* (1975; Personnel).

Ballesteros's narrative strengths include her facility for capturing subtle psychological shadings and nuances, an eye for detail, and smiling, tolerant, but incisive humor. A gifted narrator, she creates situations of tremendous credibility, endowed with a certain sense of timelessness. Time as eternal, universal structure, encompassing life and death, constitutes a recurring preoccupation of her fiction. *La cometa y el eco* (1956; The Kite and the Echo) expresses the notion that time does not pass, even though the novel spans some 20 years in the life of the orphaned Augusta and the family with which she lives, alternating between a Valencian fishing village (the family's summer home) and the provincial capital, where they spend their winters in an old-fashioned, genteel mansion. In this novel, as in several other works, Ballesteros focuses primarily upon women. The protagonist Augusta, although only a teenager, is well acquainted with death and loneliness before being taken in by distant relatives. Two Platonic, intellectual relationships end prematurely with the man's death, and at novel's end, Augusta in her midthirties is well on her way to spinsterhood. The grandmother, a fragile but strong, generous character, is nevertheless a product of the past century, a partisan of the patriarchal establishment who sympathizes with the men when their wives complain about husbandly shortcomings and infidelities. Varying portraits of women in the novel run the gamut of ages and social classes, none of them being feminist (the most natural and authentic is Augusta who, although deprived of higher education, devotes her life to reading and study).

Eclipse de tierra (1954; *Nothing Is Impossible*, 1956), a novelette, blends fantasy and reality, employing a child protagonist whose escapades occasionally recall the picaresque. Because of its lyrical tone and similar ages of the boy protagonists, *Nothing Is Impossible* has been compared with another Ballesteros novel, *El chico* (1967; The Kid), but such comparisons overlook the archetypal nature of the child in *Eclipse de tierra* (whose title literally means Eclipse of the Earth). This boy, an improved descendant of the "sorcerer's apprentice" or perhaps Till Eulenspiegel, both innocent and worldly-wise, possesses an instinctive wisdom bordering on the magical, making him quite unlike the nameless boy in *El chico*, a 12-year-old from a squalid proletarian background, raised by a putative aunt who struggles to support him, running a produce stand. Upon her death, he learns she was his birth mother. His goatherd father comes from a rural hamlet, taking him to live with a retarded younger daughter and his wife, Andrea, who sets the hut afire, eloping with her lover and leaving the retarded child inside. The boy is severely burned in rescuing her, and both drown when he rushes to a nearby pond to extinguish their burning flesh. The religious symbolism of the ending is fully consonant with the story tone and with repetitive aspects of Ballesteros's thematics, including her long-standing interest in the orphan and a conviction that life is wonderful, no matter how painful individual experiences may be.

Taller (1960; The Workshop) depicts the life of seamstresses, well represented in Spanish fiction, as this occupation continued to employ many women as dressmakers up through the end of the 1960s. A considerable popular success, it was adapted for the stage as *Las chicas del taller* (1963; The Girls in the

Workshop). Set in a fashionable Madrid salon, this neorealist novel examines the private lives of a group of characters who temporarily occupy the same space and time but is less identified with socialist sentiment than other such "social novels," emphasizing psychological rather than economic problems and focusing on frustration, despair, homosexuality, rejection, abortion, loneliness, and feelings of inadequacy. *Taller* thus more closely approaches feminist thematics than most of Ballesteros's narratives, although she is in no sense militant.

Mi hermano y yo por esos mundos (1962; My Brother and I Around Those Parts of the World) employs the first-person narrative perspective of an anonymous girl who is perhaps 10 years old. It is divided in two parts, the second of which appeared separately as *El perro del extraño rabo* (1953; The Dog with the Strange Tail). Although not strictly juvenile fiction, it lacks real character development, reaches no psychologically mandated conclusions, and has no perceptible plot structure. Ballesteros compares it to life; it belongs vaguely to literature governed by the journey topos (with the journey being a conventional symbol of life). The first part, symbolically entitled *La sed* (1965; Thirst) presents Justa's thirst for her self—her search for identity and meaning in her life, as she suffers frustration both from her inability to bear children and from a lack of existential fulfillment—a need to feel that her life amounts to something. Justa exists in function of other persons in her life, primarily men: her grandfather, her husband Carlos, her former sweetheart Juan, and her cousin Lorenzo, each representing different forms of love and potential paths for self-development that Justa does not decisively commit herself to explore. Here again, Ballesteros treats themes often addressed by feminists but does not employ a clearly feminist discourse.

Ballesteros, feminine rather than feminist, produces fiction that holds reader interest, is well told, and is often elegantly written. Her emphasis on women and children results in thematics that are predominantly feminine gendered, and it is with the characterization of women and children that her psychological penetration reaches its apogee, as well; men, by comparison, are less developed and often shadowy. However, she tends to uphold traditional values of marriage and family, and ideologically she is generally conservative, occasionally moderate. Aesthetically, also, she is relatively conservative but occasionally experiments with plotless fiction. Neither her techniques nor ideas are innovative, but the consistently high quality of her writing undoubtedly has contributed to enhancing general perceptions of women writers in Spain.

Work by

El chico. Barcelona: Destino, 1967.
La cometa y el eco. Barcelona: Destino, 1956.
Eclipse de tierra. Barcelona: Destino, 1954.
Mi hermano y yo por esos mundos. Barcelona: Destino, 1962.
Nothing Is Impossible. Trans. Frances Partridge. London: Harvill, 1956.
La sed. Barcelona: Destino, 1965.
Taller. Barcelona: Destino, 1960.

Work about

Friedman, Edward. " 'Dos veces bueno': The Art of the Miniature in Mercedes Ballesteros's *Pasaron por aquí*." *Romance Languages Annual* 5 (1993): 387–391.
Merrill, Judith. "Las chicas del taller: A Dramatization of the Novel 'Taller.' " *Language Quarterly* 24.3–4 (1986): 49–50, 53.
O'Connor, Patricia W. "Mercedes Ballesteros' Unsung Poetic Comedy: *Las mariposas cantan*." *Crítica Hispánica* 7.1 (1985): 57–63.

Janet Pérez

Baltasara, La (seventeenth century)

This actress was well known to seventeenth-century Spanish theater audiences, especially for her roles as a *mujer vestida de hombre* (woman dressed as a man). After Francisca Baltasara retired from acting, she lived the life of a religious woman in a hermitage where several miracles ascribed to her occurred. McKendrick classifies her as an amazon type, in part because of references to her within the play about her life, *La Baltasara*, as Palas. Pellicer mentions her as a famous actress and no less famous religious figure. She was a leading lady in these and other parts but especially in roles where she dressed as a man, brave and fierce, mounted on horseback, brandishing a sword. Carmen *Bravo-Villasante also cites her as famous for these roles and classifies the play bearing her name as typically popular, a combination of *comedia* (play) with a religious focus (*comedia a lo divino*).

Work about

Bravo-Villasante, Carmen. *La mujer vestida de hombre en el teatro español*. Madrid: Revista de Occidente, 1955.

McKendrick, Melveena M. *Woman and Society in the Spanish Drama of the Golden Age. A Study of the Mujer Varonil*. Cambridge: Cambridge UP, 1974.

Pellicer, Casiano. *Tratado histórico sobre el origen y progresos de la comedia y del histrionismo*. Madrid, 1804.

Shergold, N.D. *A History of the Spanish Stage from Medieval Times until the End of the Seventeenth Century*. Oxford: Clarendon P, 1967.

Stoll, Anita K. "La Gran Comedia de La Baltasara by 'Tres Ingenios de la Corte.'" *Bulletin of the Comediantes* 48.2 (Winter 1996): 214–215, 329–338.

Vélez de Guevara, Antonio Coello, and Francisco de Rojas. *La Baltasara. Primera parte de comedias escogidas de los mejores de España*. Ed. Domingo García y Morras. Madrid, 1652.

Anita K. Stoll

Barberá, Carmen (twentieth century)

Born in Castellón de la Plana, Carmen Barberá has written novels, poetry, essays, short stories, and at least one play, but she is best known for her novels, most of which are starkly social-realist. Like Carmen *Laforet, her work presents an unflinching look at Franco's Spain from a strong feminine viewpoint. She was a finalist in the Barcelona City Prize competitions and won the Ondas Prize in 1958 and the Ateneo de Tortosa Prize in 1963.

Barberá's novels span two decades and, while sharing the common tie of a female viewpoint or protagonist, also show variety and experimentation. Her early novel *Adolescente* (1957; The Adolescent) studies a woman remembering pivotal experiences through her early teens to young adulthood in the years after the Civil War. It has been considered a startling work for its vivid portrayal of the narrator and her surroundings and for the remarkable parallel alignment to psychological theory found in its structure.

Barberá's last novel, *Tierras de luto* (1976; Land of Mourning), is a much more complex book. Not only does it deal with the problems particular to women and show a detailed portrait of daily life, but it also explores the passionate conflicts that can erupt within families and how the survival instinct can create an inspiring strength in the face of tremendous difficulties. The only oddity in this rich work is the author's decision to set the novel in Holland rather than in Spain, where her readers could identify with the characters with even more ease.

Work by

Adolescente. Barcelona: J. Janés, 1957.
Debajo de la piel. Madrid: Cid, 1959.
Despedida al recuerdo. Barcelona: Rubos, 1955.
Tierras de luto. Barcelona: Planeta, 1976.

Shannon W. Sudderth

Barbero, Teresa (1934?–)

A prolific poet, novelist, and essayist, Teresa Barbero has been writing for more than four decades, and her work represents a sustained effort to foreground women's experiences in postwar Spain. Barbero consistently frames her literary texts in terms of the feminine voice and its exploration of the universal themes of solitude, the search for authenticity, and the perils of romantic love, while also occasionally experimenting with the formal properties of poetry and narrative.

Barbero was born in Avila and participated during the 1950s in creating the literary group "El Cobaya," as well as the poetry magazine of the same name. She published her first collection of poetry, *La muchacha en el exilio* (1952; The Little Girl in Exile), before age 20, and her first novel, *Una manera de vivir* (1965; A Way of Living), won the prestigious Premio Sésamo the year of its publication. After marrying writer Joaquín Fernández, Barbero moved to Madrid in 1959 where she was employed by a Centro Cultural Experimental and by several daily newspapers. She also wrote scripts for Radio Nacional Español and directed the series *La mujer protagonista* in the 1980s. More recently she has worked as a librarian for the Instituto Nacional de Industria, while concentrating on her artistic vocation.

Barbero's literary career borders on the prodigious, as evidenced by the publication of some six volumes of poetry, seven novels, two book-length essays on the work of Gabriel Miró, and numerous short stories. Two collections of her poetry, *Presencia ajena* (n.d.; Alien Presence) and *El delito secreto* (1990; Secret Crime), have received the Premio "Rafael Morales" and the Premio "Angaro" de Sevilla, respectively. She has received five "Huchas de Plata" and one "Hucha de oro" award from the Confederación de Cajas de Ahorro for her short stories. In addition to winning the Premio Sésamo for *Una manera de vivir*, Barbero was awarded the Premio de Asturias de Novela for her novel *Y no serás juzgado* (1984; And You Will Not Be Judged) and the Premio de Novela "Casino de Mieres" for *Reencuentro* (1985; Chance Meeting).

Barbero's poetry often explores losses that keenly affect women: the loss of emotional attachments, the loss of youth and physical attractiveness, the loss of opportunities, real and imagined. In recent volumes, such as *Ciudad de ceniza* (1991; City of Ash) and *Un lugar en la memoria* (1994; A Place in Memory), the poetic speaker identifies nature as a possible source of salvation in spite of these losses. The speaker also treats the topics of abandonment and absence by tracing how women receive no acknowledgment for the multitude of ways in which they nurture and comfort others. Many of Barbero's later poems are filled with images of return and arrival, suggestive of the manner in which women become aware of their places in the world. One particularly salient example of this process occurs in the poems collected in *En las manos de Albertina* (1984; In Albertina's Hands), a text that openly dialogues with the work of Marcel Proust (1871–1922) and shuttles back and forth between imagined scenes from his multivolumed *A la recherche du temps perdu* and the emotions these scenes evoke in the speaker.

Barbero's narrative engages many of the same issues while playing with perspective and narrative voice. In her short story "Un espacio oscuro" (A Dark Space), the friendship between two women provides a backdrop for their individual crises and offers commentary on the ways in which women are forced to make choices that destroy their ability to construct an identity. These choices may be linked to the economic realities of postwar Spain, as presented in *Una manera de vivir*, or they may be produced by the paucity of educational opportunities, as Barbero suggests in *El último verano en el espejo* (1967; Last Summer in the Mirror). Whereas her earlier novels emphasized the impact of material forces on the establishment and maintenance of gender roles that disable women, Barbero's more recent narratives have focused on the psychological nature of women's oppression. In texts such as *Reencuentro* (1985) and *Al final del laberinto* (1995; At the End of the Labyrinth), the women protagonists who narrate their stories exhibit profound psychological trauma over their intimate relationships. They narrate from a moment of extreme internal conflict in which their connections with male characters jeopardize their emotional and physical well-being. In *La larga noche de un aniversario* (1982; The Long Night of an Anniversary), this same conflict expands to include both the female protagonist's lover and her mother. More often than not, women in Barbero's novels experience alienation, confusion, and ultimately, some form of emotional or physical damage.

Although Barbero relies heavily on the techniques of first-person narrative, she has also probed the possibilities of dual perspective in novels such as *La larga noche de un aniversario* and the dynamics of suspense in texts including *Una manera de vivir*. Her novels tend to unfold in a limited time and space, they employ accessible language, and the progression of the plot is straightforward.

Barbero's contribution to women's literature in postwar Spain is significant insofar as her literary texts inevitably focus on the limitations that women encounter in their physical and imaginary realities. Her work is both woman centered and woman specific, testifying to the struggles that women as a class encounter when they try to realize their potential in a hostile and inflexible society.

Work by

Al final del laberinto. Madrid: Libertarias/Prodhufi, 1995.
En las manos de Albertina. Madrid: Asociación de Escritores y Artistas, 1984.
Las figuras femeninas en la obra de Gabriel Miró. Alicante: Instituto de Estudios Alicantinos, 1981.
Gabriel Miró. Madrid: Espesa, 1974.
La larga noche de un aniversario. Madrid: Ibérico Europeo de Ediciones, 1982.
Un lugar en la memoria. Madrid: Libertarias/Prodhufi, 1994.
Una manera de vivir. Madrid: Ediciones A.U.L.A., 1965.
Y no serás juzgado. Gijón: Noega, 1984.

Nina L. Molinaro

Baroja, Pío (1872–1956): Women Characters in His Works

Of the more than 60 novels by Pío Baroja that feature a variety of women characters, four possess a female protagonist whose characterization represents a modern and atypical exploration of woman's role possibilities during the first half of the twentieth century. María Aracil and her father are coprotagonists of *La dama errante* (1908; The Wandering Lady), and María continues as protagonist of the 1909 sequel, *La ciudad de la niebla* (1909; City of Mist); the Russian Sacha Savarof is protagonist of *El mundo es ansí* (1912; Such Is the World), and Laura Monroy plays the leading role of *Laura o la soledad sin remedio* (1939; Laura or Unavoidable Loneliness). Through the characterizations of these three young women, and to a lesser extent other female characters in the novels, Baroja examines the much-debated woman question and its consequences. He explores fictionally what Morgan in *Men Writing the Feminine* calls the "historical specificity" of being "culturally encoded as 'woman.'"

While some critics have either ignored or oversimplified Baroja's treatment of women as characters (Granjel; Bergasa; Sender), Shaw considers his characterization of María to be the first treatment by a major Spanish novelist of the struggle of modern woman. Likewise, Bretz, Durán, and Eller contend that some of Baroja's female characters are both convincing and complicated. Smith sees *El mundo es ansí* as relating to the woman question in regard to deeply rooted social problems. He explores how the three above-mentioned female protagonists are representative of woman's problems and needs within an emerging feminist framework. In these four novels, Baroja does not romanticize the woman question but rather engages in the polemic of traditional (submissive *ángel del hogar, "biology is destiny") versus modern (liberally educated, independent) views in discourse about woman and her roles in society. The result cannot be completely satisfactory, because within a society dominated by traditional patriarchal discourse, the female remains limited in her choices. In addition, the promoters of the late-nineteenth- and early-twentieth-centuries equal rights discourse, consumed with specific efforts to achieve education, suffrage, and legal rights for women, do not fully confront the broader issue of female empowerment, especially within the female/male dyad. Likewise, Baroja's female protagonists illustrate the frustrations of the increasingly aware and educated woman who is fundamentally unable to make significant personal choices.

Baroja's characterizations also illustrate his personal rejection of extreme positions representative of both traditional and modern discourses. His reputation as a misogynist (Torrente Ballester and others) arises primarily from his view of the typical female product of traditional Spanish society as false, affected, and interested only in ensnaring a man who will maintain her materially and advance her socially. Dolores *Medio affirms that Baroja's purported aversion to women is not to all women but to the bourgeois female. In the nonfiction work *Las horas solitarias* (1918; Solitary Hours), Baroja deals caustically with these women who neither read nor wish to learn and use all their wiles to pursue rich young men. María's female cousins in *La dama errante* are fictional counterparts, totally lacking in curiosity and pushed by their mothers to search for the perfect man; they are "algo tontas, de una ignorancia terrible" (rather foolish, terribly ignorant), and they dedicate themselves to the "legalized hunting of men," failing to realize their own ability to live independently. The same type of Spanish woman is described in *El mundo es ansí* as a woman devoid of any intellectual or moral personality.

Also generally rejected by Baroja is the stridently feminist woman whom he portrays negatively as the *cursi* (affected, tasteless) product of bourgeois society. His disapprobation of this type as representative of female freedom carried to excess is evident in the depictions of Julia Garchin of *La ciudad de la niebla*, the libertarian women in *El mundo es ansí*, and Irene, the poetess and sexual devourer of men in *Laura o la soledad sin remedio*. While Baroja is less judgmental about the feminist Swiss narrator of part of *El mundo es ansí*, his description of her is sardonic.

While extreme representations of either traditional or modern discourse lie outside the parameters of Baroja's positive portrayal of women, his characterizations in the novels mentioned above produce two versions of a sociologically viable and affirmatively esteemed woman, one exemplified in each case by the best friend of the protagonist, in which the traditional discourse dominates over the modern. The other, more developed in the text is embodied by each of the female protagonists. In this instance, the modern discourse dominates for a time but then breaks down before the character can achieve self-determination. The protagonists María, Sacha, and Laura are three variations of a single paradigm of modern woman: educated, well traveled, experienced in the dangers and challenges of life, and independent until each marries and has a child. Then there is a reversion to patriarchal authority and a concomitant loss of independence and sense of self.

In his 1904 essay "La secularización de las mujeres" (The Secularization of Women), from the collection *El tablado de Arlequín*, Baroja argues that females must receive a secular education if they are ever to participate fully in society. It is interesting that the two novels about María were published shortly after this essay, in 1908 and 1909, and, as reported by Fox, in 1910 Baroja participated in a campaign in Valencia supporting secular schools. In *La dama errante* María's father insists that his daughter receive only a secular education, and in this novel she is compared positively to her *primitas tontas* (silly cousins) described above.

All three protagonists are portrayed as modern women who initially receive a substantial education and work toward personal independence. María declares to her father that her independence comes before everything else. The Russian Sacha desires to study medicine and seek justice for her downtrodden compatriots; in so doing she successfully resists the opposition of a father who rants that he'd sooner hang her by the neck than let her pursue such nonsense. Laura studies medicine against the wishes of her mother who worries about a daughter who wants to study instead of socialize, risking spinsterhood.

Along with an unconventional education, each female protagonist gains life experience through travel; all three are representative Barojan vagabonds in female form. The journey abroad that each woman makes is forced by a political situation. As they travel, each woman gains valuable life experience; none is unable to face life's challenges because she is provincial or protected.

Finally, each woman achieves a degree of independence, later to be viewed as more symbolic than substantial. Although none of the three practices a profession, María supports herself in London after her father remarries and leaves for Argentina. Sacha never attains complete financial self-sufficiency but achieves some independence by dedicating herself to revolutionary goals and studying medicine. Laura earns a living in Paris and provides for her mother. However, in each case independence is but an interstice between parental control and marriage.

Becoming a wife and mother is crucial in marking an end to personal freedom for these three protagonists, and except for Sacha's decisions to separate from her husbands, there is no return to self-determination in the texts. In *La ciudad de la niebla* María is advised to accept the patriarchal solution of submitting to *un buen amo* (a good "master of the house") rather than living independently and probably failing. The epilogue to *La ciudad de la niebla*, "Epílogo feliz, casi triste" (Happy, Almost Sad Epilogue), indicates Baroja's ambiguous feelings about his "solution," the only one he can envision for a turn-of-the-century woman. It points to the collapse of choice as envisioned by modern discourse in favor of an "updated" patriarchal discourse—María, married and a mother, appears as an evolutionarily more advanced woman, the enlightened wife and mother who in actuality has become a modernized, secularized Madonna.

Sacha in *El mundo es ansí* contracts two disastrous marriages in part because of her cultural illusions about romantic love. She is a divorced mother when she marries a man who completely dominates her. When she finally rebels and leaves Juan, she has been broken by the experiences of marriage and is incapable even of caring for her own daughter. She cannot successfully couple her romantic illusions and emergent independence with her husbands' traditional marriage expectations.

Unlike Sacha, Laura of *Laura o la soledad sin remedio* is not disillusioned by a romantic love she does not believe in. Even though she marries an intelligent, sensitive, nonthreatening man, she entrusts herself completely to his care and surrenders her independence in a seemingly voluntary act that in reality is conditioned by societal tradition. At the end of the novel, dependent and passive, she cries as she gazes at her newborn son, feeling a complete failure in life.

In contrast to María, Sacha and Laura are the close friends of these protagonists, Natalia, Vera, and Mercedes, respectively. Each is practical, intelligent but not intellectual, and accepts and relishes her biological and social lot as a woman. In addition, each of these women possesses a natural feminine strength, a resilience and endurance that allow her to suffer but not be overcome by circumstances. These three, much like Dolores of *Camino de perfección* (The Way of Perfection), are ideal adaptations of the female within patriarchal discourse. Nevertheless, while they are more balanced characters than María, Sacha and Laura, the latter as protagonists are more developed and complex; they intellectualize and possess a deeper sensitivity to life. This complexity makes them suffer more but also makes them the subject, or protagonist, of an individual, feminine search for meaning in life, just as Fernando de Ossorio and Andrés Hurtado are among Baroja's male protagonists. Baroja has grasped the dilemma of being female within a traditional society increasingly challenged by the justice of modern equal rights discourse that would allow woman as well as man to be the creator of individual destiny.

Evidence from Baroja's fiction and nonfiction bolsters the view that he favored an enlightened posture toward woman. However, caught culturally between the conflicting traditional and modern discourses, his progressively educated female characters lose the prerogative to choose when they enter the relatively unchanged institution of marriage. Patriarchal patterns resume as adaptation to the traditional roles of wife and mother, not individual choice, determines whether or not they succeed. Rather than expressing the author's exasperation or reluctant acceptance of biological determinism, María, Sacha, and Laura appear as fictional precursors consistent with Baroja's evolutionary, rather than revolutionary, stance, much as is Andrés Hurtado of *El árbol de la ciencia* (*The Tree of Knowledge*, 1974). Baroja's originality lies in his conception of possibilities for early-twentieth-century women along with a consideration of the reality of existing sociological conditions that dictate the probable initial failure of the ideal. In *La ciudad de la niebla*, María's male adviser declares that many tests and trials will be needed to allow contemporary women to emancipate themselves and create an identity. Nevertheless, Baroja's willingness to bring the woman question to the forefront and explore its implications opens new ground in male-authored Spanish letters.

Work by

Obras completas. 8 vols. Madrid: Biblioteca Nueva, 1947.

Work about

Bergasa, Francisco. *Baroja, las mujeres y el sexo*. Madrid: Nacional, 1973.

Bretz, Mary Lee. *La evolución novelística de Pío Baroja*. Madrid: José Porrúa Turanzas, 1979.

Durán, Gloria. "¿Baroja antifeminista?" *Insula* 7–9. 308–309 (1972): 8.

Eller, Kenneth G. "Favorable Portrayals of Women in Pío Baroja's Novels." *USF Language Quarterly* 23 (Fall–Winter 1984): 17–21.

Fox, E. Inman. "Spanish Writers as Political Intellectuals (1905–1914)." *Romance Quarterly* 36 (August 1989): 299–306.

Granjel, Luis S. *Baroja y otras figuras del 98*. Madrid: Guadarrama, 1960.

Medio, Dolores. "Pío Baroja y las mujeres." *Encuentros con Don Pío: Homenaje a Baroja*. Ed. Manuel Andújar et al. Madrid: Al-Borak, 1972.

Morgan, Thais E. "Two Conversations on Literature, Theory, and the Question of Genders." *Men Writing the Feminine: Literature Theory and Questions of Gender*. Ed. Thais E. Morgan. Albany: SUNY P, 1994. 189–199.

Sender, Ramón. *Los noventayochos*. New York: Las Américas, 1961.

Shaw, Donald L. *The Generation of 1898 in Spain*. London: Ernest Benn, 1975.

Smith, Gilbert. "Feminism and Decadence in Baroja's *El mundo es ansí*." *Romance Quarterly* 36.3 (August 1989): 361–368.

Torrente Ballester, Gonzalo. *Literatura española contemporánea (1898–1936)*. Madrid: Afrodisio Aguado, 1949.

Sally Webb Thornton

Basque Women Writers: 1804–1997

Because Basque literature has usually been perceived as a male domain, women's contributions to the Basque literary corpus have been consistently neglected. However, recent research such as Oxtoa's *Emakume Olerkariak/Poetas Vascas* (1990), McNerney and Enríquez de Salamanca's *Double Minorities of Spain* (1994), and White's "Emakumeen hitzak euskaras: Basque Women Writers of the Twentieth Century" (1996) attests to Basque women's active and productive role in the creative process. Written literature in Basque is almost nonexistent before the nineteenth century. Three publications by nineteenth-century Basque women have been identified. Bizenta Moguel's *Ipui onak* (1804; Good

Tales) is the first extant fictional book in Basque written by a woman, and it also holds significant linguistic importance. Mogel presents five fables in prose and eight in verse, following the Aesopian model. She includes Spanish translations of Basque animal names used in her book and also their Basque etymology. The second publication, titled "Euskal Herriak Aita Santuary" (1887; The Basque Country to the Holy Father), is a collective poem written by 10 nuns upon the visit of Pope Leo XIII to the Basque country. Rosario Artola's two poems, "Nere guitarchoari" (1889; To My Little Guitar) and "Naigabea eta atsegiya" (1889; The Unwanted and the Unpleasant), complete this short list of published nineteenth-century literary works by Basque women.

This situation changes dramatically in the twentieth century. Linda White's earlier-mentioned dissertation demonstrates that both before and after the Spanish Civil War (1936–1939) Basque women wrote extensively, publishing in magazines, newspapers, and collections, and also producing individually authored books. These works have received little critical attention, perhaps because they appeared primarily in literary magazines and newspapers. Unless translated to French or Castilian, however, women writing in Basque will continue to be even more marginalized than counterparts writing in Spanish, given the very limited numbers of Basque speakers and readers. Most of the information that follows is taken from White's groundbreaking research.

One of the most important pre–Civil War magazines was *Euskal-esnalea*, which from 1908 to 1930 organized literary competitions, many of which were won by women. In 1923, Karmel Gizkarbiaren Modesta Ana Begoña won, and the following year top honors went to *Txindokiko Marie* (1924; Mary from Txindoki), a children's story by Margarita Unzalu. In 1928, Rufina Azkue, Joakina Garayalde, and Miren Pilar Lekuona garnered prizes; in 1929, Azkue and Garayalde were honored again; in 1930, Julene Gabilondo and Azkue won. The majority of their writings was composed of articles on topics chosen by the magazine, but they also wrote stories for children. María O. Artiñano received an honorable mention in *Euskal-esnalea* for her story "Ezin aztu" (1909; Impossible to Forget), and Petra Belaustegi won the same distinction for her story "Ametsa" (1909; The Dream).

Mayi Elissague (1899–1941), author of novels, articles, and short stories, wrote primarily in French but also experimented with Basque. Using the pen name "Intza," Erromana Elustondo Otaño contributed to the weekly *Argia*. Karmele Errazti Saratxo (1885–1954; pen name "Etxakin") collaborated with Ceferino Jemein on the play *Oleskary biyak* (The Two Callers), which won the "Euzkalzaleen Bazkuna" Prize in 1917. Mlle. Hillau wrote two plays, *Egiazko eskualdunak* (1935; True Basques) and *Vichy ala Ahuzki* (Vichy or Ahuzki). Miren Maortua Garitazelaia took the pen names "Aberrilore" and "Aldakaitz" for her contributions to *Karmel*, *Agur*, *Euzkadi*, *Euzko*, and *Ekin*. Josefa Olaizola published the poem "Goyan bego, bego" (May He Rest in Peace) in *Euskal-esnalea* in 1906. Ignacia Pradere published some nonfiction pieces in the same magazine between 1912 and 1915.

The years prior to the Civil War were ones of intense literary activity. White's dissertation lists the following writers and works. Julene Azpeitia (1888–1980) started her career in Mexico where she lived for nine years, writing under the pen name "Arritokeita." She composed articles for several magazines, including a weekly column titled "Euskotar umien alde" (In Favor of the Basque Children) for the magazine *Euskadi*. In 1922 she published *Osasuna, merketza eta yanaritza* (Health, Economy and Nutrition). She subsequently dedicated herself to writing children's stories, publishing the collection *Irakurri, maite* (Read, Darling) in 1932. The following year she won the Kirikiño Saria prize for her story "Euli baten edestia." Her postwar production includes *Azeri jauna*

(1960; Mr. Fox), *Amandriaren altzoan* (1961; On Grandmother's Lap), *Umien adizkaia* (1962; On Behalf of Children), and *Zuentzat. (Aurrentzako ipui ta irakurgaiak)* (1974; For You: [Stories and Readings for Children]). In 1959, Azpitia won another literary prize for her story "Goizeko izarra" (The Morning Star). Other stories by her include "Odolak odolari dei" (1969; Blood Calls Blood), "Martxela" (1969), and "Krabelin Gorriak" (1970; Red Carnations).

Dramatist Madelaine (Magalena) Jauregiberry (1884–1977) wrote in Basque and French for *Gure Herria, Herria, Basque-eclair,* and *Sud-ouest* and was head of the "Begiraleak" theater group in Donibane Lohitzun (St. Jean de Luz). Three of her works were staged as puppet shows with marionettes: *Mirakuilu bat* (A Miracle), *Zikoitza* (The Miser), and *Eskualdu jantzia* (Basque Clothes).

Tene Muxika, also known as Errobustiana Mujica (1888–?), wrote poetry: *Miren Itziarri dazkiak eta olerkiak* (1923; Poems and Writings to Miren Itziar) and *Udaskenala* (1928; As It Was Autumn); plays: *Gogo-oñazeak* (1934; Spiritual Suffering), *Gabon* (1935; Christmas), and *Joan-Joxe* (1936); and a collection of stories and anecdotes: *Nekazari bizitza* (1964: Rural Life). She won prizes for her plays and her collection of stories.

Mayi Ariztia (1887–1972) wrote for *Gure herria, Herria, Egan,* and *Annuario de eusko folklore* and published a collection of tales, *Amattoren uzta: La Moissen de Grandmere* (1934; Grandmother's Harvest).

Errose Bustintza Ozerin (1899–1953) used the pen names "Mañariko" and "Mañarko Errose," writing short stories and poetry for several publications. One of her poems is included in the collection *Mila euskal olerki eder* (1954; One Thousand Beautiful Basque Poems), and her stories were compiled in 1991 under the title *Ipuiak* (Stories). Her sister, Basilia Bustintza Ozerin (1889–1973), wrote poetry that appeared in the magazine *Olerti* under the pen name "Karmel."

Eustakia Altzola (1899–?) wrote in letter form on topics ranging from language, ethnography, and everyday life to family, friends, religion, and mysticism. Most of her work is unpublished.

Maria Dolores (Agirre) Lasheras (1903–?) wrote short plays such as *Aukeraren maukera. Azkenean okerra* (1949; The Impertinence of Choice. Wrong in the End), *Bear-bearra* (1956; Absolutely Necessary), and *Amal* (1962). She also translated Alejandro Casona's *La barca sin pescador* and Federico *García Lorca's *Yerma* to Basque.

Playwright Katalina Elizegi (also spelled Eleízigí and Eleizegui) Maiz (1889–1963) was drawn to historical topics. Set in the thirteenth century, her play *Garbiñe* (1916) won the Ayuntamiento de Sebastián Prize; *Loreti* (1918), which treats the wars between Cantabrians and Romans in the first century A.D., won the same award two years later. Her play *Yatsu* (1934, also spelled Jatsu) is a two-act drama on the conquest of Navarre. Maiz also left an unpublished play about the Golden Age transvestite Catalina de *Erauso.

Sorne (Concepción) Unzueta (1900–?) wrote poetry; two of her poems, "Gomutakiak" (Reminders) and "Gogo ituna" (Sadness of Spirit), were included in *Mila euskal olerki eder* (1954). Joakina Garayalde, mentioned earlier as an *Euskal-esnalea* magazine prizewinner, also wrote essays and the short story "Bejundaizula, Mañaxi!" (1930; May You Enjoy It, Mañaxi!). Five women (Victorina Arrieta, M. Aristegieta, J. Aranburu, E. Olaso, and C. Aranburu) collaborated on the one-act comedy *Rotxil'en sakeltxoa* (Rotxil's Little Bag), which won the 1917 Ayuntamiento de San Sebastián prize.

Following the Spanish Civil War, literary activity declined markedly in the Basque region, but it slowly revived, and by the 1960s it was flourishing. White's dissertation registers the names of 78 women writers, 42 of whom composed literary works.

One of the most prolific contemporary Basque women writers is Itxaro Borda. In 1984, she published the novel *Basilika* (The Basilica), followed by the play *Infante zendu batendako pavana: Maurice Ravelen musika* (1986; Pavanne for a Dead Princess: The Music of Maurice Ravel). She then tried her hand at poetry with *Just Love* (1988) before returning to the novel with *Udaran betaurreko beltzekin* (1987; In the Summer with Dark Glasses). *Urtemuga lehorraren kronika: Allegro ma non troppo* (1989; The Chronicle of a Mixed Anniversary) mixes narrative and poetry. Her most recent works include the poetry collection *Bestaldean* (1991; On the Other Side) and the novel *Bakean utzi arte* (1994; Until Left in Peace). In summer 1995 her short story "Atom Heart" was included in the collection 9508 *Narraziok*. Borda also is the author of *Hogoigarren mendeko emakumeak idazle* (1984; Women Writers of the Twentieth Century), one of the few existing studies about Basque women writers.

Enkarni Genua, pen name "Txotxongilo," writes poetry and stories for children, including *Erreka Mari* (1979; Mary River), *Zezena plazan* (1981; The Bull in the Square), *Hondarrezko gaztelua* (1986; Sandiest), *Txori txiki polit bat* (1986; A Pretty Little Bird), and *Altxor bat patrikan* (1988; A Treasure in a Pocket). She is coordinator of the puppet group "Txotxongilo Taldea" and author of *Amonaren ipuinak: Haurrak euskalduntzen bideoaren bidez* (1984; Grandmother's Tales: Children Learning Basque through Video Tapes).

Lurdes Unzueta Zamalloa started her writing career through contributions to *Idatz and mintz*. She has written a collection of short stories, *Argilunak begietan* (1991; Lights and Shadows in the Eyes), considered by critics as easy narratives for young readers. Edurne Urkiola also writes novels for young adults, among them *Inortxok ezer baleki* (1992; If Anyone Knew Anything). Winner of several prizes in the *Idatz and mintz* competitions, she also published the illustrated children's book *Ibanentzako argi apur bat* (1984; A Little Light for Ivan).

Arantxa Urretabizkaia (1947–) showed an interest for poetry in her early works, with "San Pedro Besperaren ondokoak" and "Maitasunaren Magalean" winning local recognition. Subsequently, she has become widely regarded as a talented novelist whose titles include *Zergatik, panpox* (1979; Why, Darling), *Aspaldian espero zaitudalako ez nago sekula bakarrik* (1984; I Am Never Alone Because I Have Been Waiting for You for a Long Time), *Saturno* (1987; Saturn), and *Aurten aldatuko da nere bizitza* (1992; This Year My Life Will Change).

Poet Teresita Irastorza (1961–) won the Premio Nacional de la Crítica Literaria for poetry in Basque with *Gabeziak* (1980; Wants). Other works by Irastorza include *Gaia eta gau aldaketak. Hostoak* (1983; Gaia and the Night Changes. The Leaves), *Alkolaren poemak* (1984; Poems of Alcohol), *Derrotaren fabulak* (1985; Fables of Failure), and *Osinberdeko khantoriak* (1986; Songs of the Green Abyss).

Amaia Lasa has composed several books of poetry—*Poema bilduma* (1971; Poetry Collection), *Hitz nahastuak* (1977; Jumbled Words), and *Nere paradisuetan* (1979; In My Paradises)—and a collection of short stories—*Malintxeren gerizpean* (1988; In the Shade of the Malinche Tree). She was included in *21 poetas vascos* and has written for many magazines and newspapers.

Publications by Basque women writers in the last decade also include the following authors and works. Playwright Yolanda Arrieta captured the 1992 Pedri I Barrutia Antzerki Saria prize for *Badago ala es dago . . .* (Is There or Isn't There . . .) and collaborated with Miriam Etxabe and Rosa Mari Etxabe on *Hamalau heriotzarena* (1989; [The Story of] the Fourteen Deaths). Ana Arruza's children's book *Frakote ikerlari* (Frakote the Investigator) won a local prize in 1992. Maite González Esnal (1943–) is a translator and writer of children's stories, which include *Bertan ikusia* (1983; I Saw It Right There), *Lapitz baten ibilerak* (1996; The Adventures of a Pencil), and *Mari-Marietta* (1996). Arantxa Iturbe Maiz has published two books of short stories: *Ezer baino lehen* (1992; Before Anything Else) and *Lehenago zen berandu*

(1995; Earlier Was Late). She has also written a radio serial, "Maite, maite, maitea" (1992). Amaia Iturbide (1961–) has published three books: *Eskaileraren bi aldeetan* (1986; On Both Sides of the Staircases), *Itzulbidea* (1992; The Way Back), and *Gelak eta zelaiak* (1994; Rooms and Meadows).

The list of Basque women writers grows daily, and their names are beginning to be well known not only in the Basque country but also in Spain. Mariasun Landa's reputation as a writer now parallels that of male author Bernardo Atxaga. Novelists such as Itxaro Borda and Laura Mintegi and poets like Amaia Lasa show a strong commitment to Basque literature, and younger writers such as Tere Irastorza are being heard and read. It is now the task of critics and readers to give these women writers the attention they have been denied for so long.

Work about

Gabilondo, Joseba. "Del exilio materno a la utopía personal: Política cultural en la narrativa vasca de mujeres." *Insula* 623: (Nov. 1998): 32–36.

McNerney, Kathleen, and Cristina Enríquez de Salamanca, eds. *Double Minorities of Spain. A Bio-Bibliographic Guide to Women Writers of the Catalan, Galician and Basque Countries.* New York: Modern Language Association, 1994.

Molina Gavilán, Yolanda. "Magdalena Moujan Otano's 'Gu Ta Gutarrak' (We and Our Own): A Science Fictional Look at the Basque Nationalist Myth of Pure Racial Origins." *Romance Languages Annual* 10.2 (1998): 600–605.

Otxoa, Julia. *Euskal olerkariak/Poetas Vascas.* Madrid: Torremozas, 1990.

White, Linda. "Discovering the Basque Woman Writer: Her Contributions prior to the Spanish Civil War." *Letras peninsulares* 13.2-3 (Fall-Winter 2001): 677–693.

———. "Emakumeen hitzak euskaras: Basque Women Writers of the Twentieth Century." Diss. U of Nevada–Reno, 1996.

Zárate, Martha. "Bibliography of Basque Linguistics and Literature Resources." *Humanities-Collections* 1.1 (1998): 67.80.

Maite Núñez-Betelu

Beata

Originally designating a person who had successfully completed one of the stages en route to sanctification (beatification), the term *beata* (pious woman) came to designate a negative social and literary stereotype, almost always female. It refers not merely to one's being devout but to living in excessively pious and/or ostentatiously sanctimonious fashion, often (it would seem) as a sublimation for the absence of more normal human interests and activities. Hence, writers often combine the stereotypes of *beata* and "old maid," creating a busybody or goody-goody prone to criticizing and interfering in others' lives, one who is frequently hypocritical and usually embittered. Although the character type is not new, it appears especially in nineteenth- and twentieth-century works, whose authors repeatedly suggest that the *beata* suffers vital or erotic frustration and consequently wants others to suffer likewise. While not unknown to metropolitan areas, literary *beatas* abound in small towns and villages, where traditionalism is strongest and individual anonymity most difficult. The crippling limitations imposed upon women's lives and activities by patriarchally inscribed norms in such environments inevitably produced real-life models of the stereotype.

Janet Pérez

Beauvoir, Simone de (1908–1986): Her Influence in Spain

After World War II, Simone de Beauvoir's *Le deuxième sexe* (1949; *The Second Sex*, 1952) brought international recognition to the status of women. According to de Beauvoir, women occupy a secondary place in the male-dominated world; consequently, the author sets forth two fundamental and unorthodox theories. First, she states that woman's condition is determined more by culture than by nature. One of the most famous declarations from *The Second Sex* asserts that one is not born but rather becomes a woman. Second, she portrays woman as existing in a state of alterity—as the Other—in relation to the dominant figure of man. De Beauvoir's theoretical position was so unconventional that on publication her book was not immediately understood. However, in the 1950s, *The Second Sex* became a major document that inspired other important writings and still emerges in citations and bibliographies of essays and scholarly articles.

In the matter of influences, Spain made the initial impression on the young de Beauvoir when she first traveled there with Jean Paul Sartre in 1931. By 1939 de Beauvoir would experience a major change directly caused by events in Spain. The first and subsequent trips moved her greatly, and she later incorporated her travels to Spain in her memoirs, particularly in *La force de l'âge* (1960; *The Prime of Life*, 1962). She recalled how immersed in the Spanish exoticism she and Sartre felt after their very first stop in Figueras; also she commented frequently on the quality of Spanish food as a measure of culture. According to de Beauvoir, they traveled as tourists, and thus visiting museums and monuments interested them more than the signs of unrest they saw. Yet those signs soon gathered historical magnitude as the Spanish Second Republic headed toward a communist regime. In Barcelona during their first journey, en route to see the cathedral the couple passed by an attempted general strike by an anarchist union. The following year, in Seville they coincided with Sanjurjo's attempted military coup, one of the first strikes against the Second Republic. She later recalled how the monuments, museums, and cafés serenely welcomed tourists just after she and Sartre watched firemen and communist sympathizers stand by as an affluent neighborhood burned down.

Despite their liberal political leanings, at that time Sartre and de Beauvoir did not join in political action in France or elsewhere, for their most vital enterprise was intellectual cultivation and writing. While they were convinced that they could serve the political domain through literary channels, Spain's Civil War delivered the blow that crushed these notions and others of Europe's intellectual Left. The increasing Nazi menace in Europe impelled de Beauvoir and Sartre to perceive Spain's conflict as a call to action. As advocates for the Spanish Republic, they tried unsuccessfully to persuade the French government to defy the nonintervention policy by sending weapons to the Republican forces. At the end of the war, de Beauvoir judged France's policy as neglectful when she learned that military aid in 1936 might have saved the Second Republic. When Madrid fell to Franco's troops in 1939, de Beauvoir felt guilty for her country's and her own inaction. She underwent a personal crisis, a turning point that brought about a conversion in her. She renounced what she called her "antihumanism" and advocated solidarity, above all for the poor and the victims of fascism.

For all her belated sympathy, some Spanish critics find, even after her death, that de Beauvoir's focus on the Civil War remained one-sided. She presented only the Republic's cause and did so with factual inaccuracy and deficient analyses. Also, like nineteenth-century French romantic writers, the seemingly frank and well-intended de Beauvoir presented a skewed image of Spain in her memoirs. In her observations from a postwar visit, de Beauvoir reported what she wanted to see: poverty-stricken areas, anti-Franco factions, and food supplies. She cut a superficial profile of Spain, using pathetic or exotic details as if its people and customs had not yet signed on to the changing times of the postwar world. Given the wide range of past and present political viewpoints in Spain, such reproaches merit understanding and respect.

However, in cultural and literary movements of postwar Spain, Europe, and America, few deny the influential presence of major proportions that de Beauvoir has imposed as feminist, essayist, novelist, and intellectual. Male and female Spanish writers, feminists, scholars, and intellectuals such as Carmen *Martín Gaite, Rosa *Chacel, María Aurèlia *Capmany, Elena Soriano, and José Luis L. Aranguren, to name a few, have understood and recognized de Beauvoir's importance. Not all admire her totally, but each sees her as part of a societal and cultural shift that energized change in common attitudes.

Spain, however, presents special characteristics regarding women writers. Even today, many of Spain's leading women writers do not want to be known as feminists, for a variety of reasons. Often they do not wish to be classed with militancy, or they have philosophical differences with French theorists. The influence exercised by authors such as Simone de Beauvoir (or Virginia Woolf, Doris Lessing, or Mary McCarthy) has contributed to the transformation of the feminine personality and has affected the woman writer. More than the women of the immediate post–Civil War era, Spanish women authors of subsequent generations became susceptible to foreign literary theory and tendencies, such as French, American, and English authors (female or male).

By the mid-1960s, de Beauvoir's writings were known in Spain. After publication of her *Memoires d'une fille rangée* (1958; *Memoirs of a Dutiful Daughter*, 1959), female authors began to inscribe their life experiences as part of a wave of new feminist writing emerging at that moment, that is, literature as a confessional instrument. A Spanish woman who reviewed *Dutiful Daughter*, *The Prime of Life*, and *La force des choses* (1963; *The Force of Circumstance*, 1965) classified these books as a trilogy of confessions of a twentieth-century woman. De Beauvoir looms large, *un caso*, a "character," as one says commonly, because of her unusual life but nonetheless merits interest and attention, according to the reviewer.

In *Usos amorosos de la postguerra española* (1987; *Amatory Customs of Postwar Spain*), Carmen Martín Gaite points out the importance of what transpired in Spain during the 1950s. In September 1950, the first agreements between the United States and Spain were signed, allowing for the establishment of American military bases on Spanish soil. In their wake, the first signs of change in economic policy began to appear in Spain, encouraging the development of tourism and a timid opening of cultural and religious issues. As the decade of the 1950s passed and the immediate penury of postwar times disappeared, a change in the mentality of the new adolescents could be noticed; for these young people the memory of the Civil War held no vital significance.

In the 1960s, young, trendy Spanish women who felt modern devoured the Spanish translation of *The Second Sex* in a craze that coincided with the highpoint of the Beatles' popularity. Concurrently, deeper changes started to relax Spain's conservative sexual mores and outlook on life. Unlike previous generations of dutiful daughters, the kind of young woman who went out dancing in clubs began to emerge. She came home late for supper, made a show of using crude language, stopped wearing a girdle, and would not consider having more than two children. Furthermore, entering marriage a virgin seemed old-fashioned or indicative of a lack of sanity. Unlike Martín Gaite, Aranguren expressed another view on the matter. In 1963 after he observed that some young university women adopted airs of liberation after reading de Beauvoir, he noted that the traditional social pressure that prevailed repressed liberated behavior in public life, mostly in the provinces. Aranguren also perceived that the problem of women in the professions had become a matter of social class since young women of money had greater access to professional status.

Rosa Chacel takes another point of view. In her essay "Comentario tardío sobre Simone de Beauvoir" (1956; Late Commentary on Simone de Beauvoir), Chacel wrote ostensibly on one of de Beauvoir's novels but also discussed *The Second Sex*. Throughout her long career, Chacel opposed any feminist stance; as she put it, she had an account to settle with the French author. Chacel questioned de Beauvoir's combative attitude toward man and also the timorous respect for him that coexist in her work. Chacel finds reason to doubt the French writer's choice of authoritative voices when de Beauvoir supports her feminist argument against man with a long string of citations from second-rate thinkers. Similarly, Chacel acknowledges that she does not understand the business of "the Other" since de Beauvoir discusses and derives the complex concept of alterity from a rather unknown source that Chacel calls gibberish. Chacel had consistently refused categorical classifications and sought means to transcend biological necessity. Thus, Chacel states, to place all blame for the inferior condition of the female on the male is to think like a woman; destiny has been hard on women throughout history. Another point of disagreement resides in de Beauvoir's refusal of motherhood because it represents a personal burden and a deterrent to the intellect. Chacel is not the only Spaniard to question this attitude.

Chacel recognizes the correctness of facts that de Beauvoir presents in *The Second Sex* but disagrees with the meaning that de Beauvoir assigns them. For example, the principle of the history of humankind is more complicated than the materialistic sense that de Beauvoir attaches to property in her approach to that topic's history. In the final analysis, however, Chacel believes that de Beauvoir's purpose of finding independence in the bosom of dependency is irreproachable.

A few years later, Chacel deals with what she and de Beauvoir have in common. Eighteen years before publication of *The Second Sex*, Chacel published a long article in *Revista de Occidente*, "Esquema de los problemas prácticos y actuales del amor" (1931; Schema of the Practical and Current Problems of Love). In this piece she set out to study love in its elemental form of relationship of the sexes in order to discern clearly whether there are differences that essentially separate the existential bases of man and woman. Chacel indicated that because she had chosen her own daring mode of scrutinizing the problem, she differs from de Beauvoir's prophetic character. Chacel's retrospective stayed in the boundaries of love's historical fortunes, whereas de Beauvoir's social concerns, fused with her extensive scholarship, situate the latter in the fashion of her generation. The gap in time that separates these two works dressed de Beauvoir in the new look of existentialism, thereby giving her greater prominence. Chacel's comments demonstrate a keen understanding of de Beauvoir's work and the reality of being a woman writer in Spain. For centuries, Spanish women writers have found it necessary to work on their own in solitude, often in secret. Much of what Chacel wrote on de Beauvoir emanated from her time in exile, a result of the Spanish Civil War.

Although they argued from distinct viewpoints, Chacel still found a kindred spirit in de Beauvoir. Chacel's point of departure reflected Christian morality, as she pursued the ageless intangible of all cultures that represents, incontestably and absolutely, the idea of *el prójimo* (fellow creature). For Chacel, de Beauvoir's conscientious and gigantic work *The Second Sex*, along with her own essay written 18 years earlier, both deal with the analysis and implacable censure of all morality or theory that impedes woman from taking her place next to man.

Elena Soriano penned a short tribute to de Beauvoir after her death, a farewell to "Castor," as Sartre had dubbed her. Soriano described the French author as a natural figure of her times, although many thought her abnormal since she did not fit the pattern of woman in the Judeo-Christian tradition. Soriano credits de Beauvoir for defying the passivity of her sex, for knowing how different and out of the ordinary she was, destined to be someone important whose life served a purpose. Soriano also stresses the bold honesty of de Beauvoir's goal throughout her life: to be the perfect intellectual woman and attain world recognition for it. Soriano herself backed women's causes and, after some rights had been won on the public front, had written on what she called "small rights."

Habitually granted to men, such rights as intellectual credibility or the right to have friends of both genders had been denied to women for centuries. By dint of study, tenacity, and the will for power, de Beauvoir was one of the first women to earn such rights and show other women how to follow her example.

In 50 years de Beauvoir produced an important body of literary work, uneven in quality and ideologically controversial but all the same admirable and unequaled by any woman: narrative, political journalism, sociological essay, memoirs (the most interesting for Soriano). Inspired by Sartre, but bringing her own intellectual commitment to the existentialist tenet of word and act, de Beauvoir participated in radical political militancy, revolutionary causes, as well as numerous activities in defense of freedom, social justice, and human rights. For Soriano, de Beauvoir and Sartre represented the most perfect model of the intellectual, leftist couple, a marriage of minds in the true Platonic sense. Soriano bids farewell to "Castor," attributing greater influence to de Beauvoir than to Sartre, saying all women should continue fighting in order not to remain the second sex but to claim their rights, even the smaller ones.

Work by

Le deuxième sexe. Paris: Gallimard, 1949.
La force de l'âge. Paris: Gallimard, 1960.
The Prime of Life. Trans. Peter Green. Intro. Toril Moi. New York: Paragon House, 1992.
The Second Sex. Trans. H.M. Parshley. New York: Knopf, 1952.

Work about

Chacel, Rosa. "Comentario tardío sobre Simone de Beauvoir." *Obra completa*, Vol. IV: *Artículos II.* Ed. and prol. notes Ana Rodríguez Fischer. Valladolid: Excma. Diputación Provincial de Valladolid, Centro de Estudios Literarios Fundación Jorge Guillén, 1993. 501–529.
———. "Esquema de los problemas prácticos del amor." *Revista de Occidente* 92 (1931): 129–180.
———. "Volviendo al punto de partida." *Revista de Occidente* 2.17 (August 1964): 203–225.
Cismaru, Alfred. "Simone de Beauvoir and the Spanish Civil War: From Apoliticism to Commitment." *The Spanish Civil War in Literature.* Ed. Janet Pérez and Wendell Aycock. Lubbock: Texas Tech UP, 1990. 67–73.
Cuenca Torribio, J.M., and Soledad Miranda García. "España en la obra de Simone de Beauvoir." *Cuadernos Hispanoamericanos* 462 (1988): 117–123.
Soriano, Elena. "El castor." *Insula* 41.475 (1986): 5.

Glenn Morocco

Bécquer, Gustavo Adolfo (1836–1870): Women in His Works

This was the most recognized pseudonym of Gustavo Adolfo Domínguez Bastida, a poet, prose writer, and librettist of *zarzuelas* (vaudevillesque operettas), which he signed as Adolfo García or Adolfo Rodríguez. The idea of woman is central to the works of Gustavo Adolfo Bécquer, but not woman in her usual roles as mother, wife, daughter, or sister. Instead, as García-Viñó suggests in *Mundo y trasmundo de las leyendas de Bécquer*, she is the essence of woman as defined by José Ortega y Gasset (1883–1955) and not a flesh-and-blood woman.

Bécquer's life was bohemian, lonely, penniless, and short. His loneliness began with the 1841 death of his father, a mediocre painter descended from a noble Flemish family, and that of his mother in 1845. He and his six brothers were taken in by an uncle, and his childless godmother, Manuela Monnehay, assumed responsibility for his schooling at the Colegio de San Telmo, a naval school for orphans of noble families. When San Telmo was closed by the government, he went to live with Monnehay, in whose personal library he began his literary readings. His uncle, a painter himself, apprenticed him to a former student of his but soon advised him to put away his brushes and devote himself to literature.

At age 18, Bécquer left Monnehay's home in Seville, forfeiting an inheritance she had made conditional on his entering a career in business, and went to Madrid. His financial troubles and the need to engage in clerical work to survive soon dampened his hope of fame and fortune in the capital. Symptoms of the tuberculosis that would claim his life first appeared in 1857. A friend, Ramón Rodríguez Correa, found the manuscript of "El caudillo de las manos rojas, tradición india" (The Chief with Red Hands, Indian Story) while caring for Bécquer during his convalescence and encouraged him to publish it; it appeared in the newspaper *La Crónica* in 1857. That same year, enjoying the patronage of Isabel II (1830–1904), he began work on *Historia de los templos de España* (1857; History of Temples in Spain). Parts of this tome appeared in installments and later were published in book form, the only part of his writings to be published as a book during his lifetime. This work focused on the churches, mosques, and synagogues of Toledo and is important because in it can be found the seeds for much of his verse and prose writings. Other volumes projected for this ambitious work were never published due to legal problems.

The hand-to-mouth poverty and illness that tormented his life in no way blunted Bécquer's romantic nature. He became infatuated with Julia Espín, a young woman who remained unaware that he wrote poetry for her while adoring her from afar. Later he gravitated to the radius of Elisa Guillén, a successful singer who, because of her social position, insisted on persisting to be merely an acquaintance. After a brief courtship orchestrated by his friends, he married Casta Esteban Navarro, his doctor's daughter, in 1861. With Rodríguez Correa as intermediary, he was hired by *El Contemporáneo*, a newspaper in which he published many prose writings as well as the epistolary collection *Desde mi celda* (From My Cell). One year after the wedding, his older brother Valeriano Domínguez Bastida (1833–1870) moved in with the couple, following his own failed marriage. Perhaps as a result of the strain of the elder brother's constant presence, the couple separated, and from then until the older sibling's death, the brothers lived together. The couple had three sons: Gregorio G. Adolfo, born in 1862, Jorge in 1865, and Emilio Eusebio in 1868. Nothing is known of the lives or dates of death of any of them.

Things looked brighter for the author when, in 1864, Luis González Brabo, prime minister under Isabel II, took an interest in his work and named him censor of novels. However, the Revolution of 1868 forced Brabo to flee from Spain, and the manuscript of Bécquer's *rimas* (poems), which he had offered to publish, was lost. Fortunately, the poet was able to rewrite many of his *rimas* from memory. Political conviction forced him to renounce his position as censor, and he was once again reduced to penury. During 1869 he spent time in Toledo and, on his return to Madrid, worked as translator of the *Biblioteca de grandes autores*, a position that, along with his publication of the *Ilustración de Madrid*, provided a slightly more comfortable livelihood.

Bécquer's older brother died on September 23, 1870; before his own death three months later, the author and his wife were reconciled briefly. After the poet's death on December 22, 1870, Rodríguez Correa collected his works and published them in 1871 under the preferred pseudonym, Gustavo Adolfo Bécquer.

The treatment of woman in Bécquer's works is influenced by his romantic temperament and the longing he always felt for the love of a woman. In his writings women are, almost without exception, beautiful—a preference he puts in his narrator's mouth in "Tres fechas" (Three Dates) when the latter states that when he says *woman* it is understood that she will be young and beautiful. Taken as an aggregate, the women in Bécquer's writings project an image of idealized, European feminine beauty: long blond or black hair; fair skin; blue or green eyes; delicate, rosy lips; expressive hands with slender fingers; tall, slender bodies. Individually, many of the women are illusive; they lack corporeality. Their eyes, as is the case in "Rima XIII," are only a pupil, their mouths, as in XVII, only a lip or a smile, their body, as in "Rayo de luna" (Moonbeam), only the hem of a floating garment. They are beyond the reach of the male narrators or poetic persona. In "Rima XV" the woman addressed by the poetic voice is described as an aerial shadow that disappears like a flame, like a sound, like a mist, like a whimper. Despite the women's incorporeality, male characters fall obsessively in love with them. In the previously mentioned "Tres fechas," the narrator falls in love with a mere figment of his imagination, a woman he *imagines* is standing behind momentarily raised curtains, a snowy-white hand glimpsed in a convent tower, a novice whose face is obliterated by the light of a ceremonial candle. He never sees her but is, nevertheless, driven by his obsession with her. In "El beso" (The Kiss), the protagonist's passion is excited by an equally incorporeal woman, a white marble statue of Doña Elvira set upon her tomb. His passion for the idea of woman made visible in the statue leads to his death when he attempts to kiss the statue before the stony eyes of her husband's jealous effigy that guards the grave next to hers. The most incorporeal and illusive of the women in the prose writings is found in "Rayo de luna." In that legend a man fixated on finding his ideal love glimpses, by the dim light of midnight, something white floating in the woods and is convinced that it is the beautiful woman he has been seeking. After pursuing the vision through the dark forest for several nights, he finally realizes that what he has seen is merely a moonbeam. He goes mad, convinced that love is as illusive as a moonbeam.

Many of Bécquer's female characters are beautiful but perfidious. The woman in "Rima XXXIX," despite her beauty, has a heart composed of a nest of serpents. Women like these lure the men who love them to evil ends. A few cause the men who love them tremendous emotional trauma, driving them to madness. María Antúnez in "La ajorca de oro" (The Gold Bracelet) is a woman of "diabolic beauty" who weeps with despondency because she covets the diamond bracelet she saw on the Virgin's arm in the Toledo cathedral. Her husband Pedro, wishing to placate her, goes to the cathedral at night and steals the bangle, whereupon all the statuary in the church moves toward him, causing him a seizure that drives him insane. In "La corza blanca" (The White Doe), the love of Constanza causes Garcés unwittingly to commit a crime when, in order to present her with it, he kills a white roe deer that talks and laughs. Sadly, the white deer he kills for her is her magical incarnation, and his arrow slays her, the woman he loves. When he realizes what he has done, he goes mad.

Other feminine characters cause the men who love them to go willingly to their deaths as a result of their love. In "¡Es raro!" (It's Strange!), the femme fatale is the wife of a gentle man who, although born poor, prospers with the help of the animals he has rescued from sure death. He had married her to make his happiness complete. After a time, however, she betrays him and flees with her lover. In the mistaken belief that she has been kidnapped, he tracks them, only to learn the truth as he becomes the butt of people's jokes. Discovering the truth causes a seizure, and he also becomes mad before he dies. Another perfidious woman is Beatriz, the beauty who captivates the protagonist of "El monte de las ánimas" (Forest of the Spirits) and requires him, as proof of his devotion, to visit a haunted wood on All Souls Night to retrieve a blue ribbon she dropped there during the day's hunt. Although he fears the restless souls who are said to be abroad that night and the killer wolves that infest the woods, he obeys. After being mauled and killed by the wolves, his ghost leaves the bloody ribbon on her prie-dieu. One more example is the apparition in "Los ojos verdes" (Green Eyes), who first reveals herself to Fernando as a pair of beautiful eyes at the bottom of a pool. He becomes possessed by these eyes and returns repeatedly to the pool, until one day a beautiful woman appears to him and, with promises of perfect love, lures him to his death in the pool.

On one hand, Bécquer's romantic temperament and the loneliness he bore since his mother's death caused him to idealize women, as can be seen in "Rima IV" where he acknowledges that as long as beautiful women exist, there will be poetry; or, as he says in his most often quoted line addressed to a woman: "Poetry... is you" ("Rima XXI"). The exaggerated, idealized beauty of his feminine characters or their incorporeality makes them unreal, illusive. No flesh-and-blood woman could measure up to the magnified standards set by this author. On the other hand, he allows his own disappointments brought on by his unattainable objectives in love and the beloved to color the portrayal of women in his writing. In "Rima XXXIV," he portrays the woman as beautiful and expressive but inane. The woman in "Rima XL," too, has a beautiful face, but that face is a mask to hide her deceitfulness.

Work by

Historia de los templos de España. Ed. and intro. J.R. Arboleda. Barcelona: Puvill, 1979.
Obras Completas. 13th ed. Madrid: Aguilar, 1969. (Contains incomplete *Historia de los templos de España* and no theater)
Romantic Legends of Spain, by Gustavo Adolfo Becquer. Trans. C. Bates and K.L. Bates. New York: Crowell, 1909.
Symphony of Love, Las Rimas, by Gustavo Adolfo Becquer. Trans. David F. Altabe. Long Beach and New York: Regina, 1974.
Teatro de Gustavo Adolfo Bécquer. Ed. and study J.A. Tamayo. Madrid: Consejo Superior de Investigaciones Científicas, 1949.

Work about

Benítez, Rubén. *Leyendas, apólogos y otros relatos*. Barcelona: Labor, 1974.
Billick, David, and Walter A. Dobrian. "Bibliografía selectiva y comentada de estudios becquerianos, 1960–1980." *Hispania* 69 (1986): 278–302.
Díez Taboada, Juan María. *La mujer ideal: Aspectos y fuentes de las Rimas de G.A. Bécquer*. Madrid: Consejo Superior de Investigaciones Científicas, 1965.
Entrambasaguas, Joaquín de. *La obra poética de Bécquer en su discriminación creadora y erótica*. Madrid: Vasallo de Mumbert, 1974.
García Viñó, Manuel. *Mundo y trasmundo de las leyendas de Bécquer*. Madrid: Gredos, 1970.
Montesinos, Rafael. *La semana pasada murió Bécquer*. Intro. Juan Barcelo. Madrid: Museo Universal, 1992.
Risco. Antonio. *Literatura y fantasía*. Madrid: Taurus, 1982.
Sebold, Russell P. *Gustavo Adolfo Bécquer*. Madrid: Taurus, 1982.

Oralia Preble-Niemi

Belisarda, Marcia (seventeenth century)

Sor María de Santa Isabel took the pseudonym Marcia Belisarda when she wrote her poems and collected them for publication, a book that never came to be for unknown reasons. As an adult, she was a nun in the Real Convento de la Concepción in Toledo. The date of her birth, like that of her death, is unknown. A note on one of her poems indicates that she wrote her first verse at the age of 27; an annotation to a subsequent poem indicates that she was still alive in 1646.

Belisarda wrote both secular and religious poems; some 140 compositions are preserved in ms. 7469 of the Biblioteca Nacional in Madrid. Many of the poems appear to have been solicited by others, for particular purposes or on particular themes. Some are poetic exercises or exhibitions of poetic skill (glosses, for example; an *a lo divino* [religious] version of a Lope de *Vega poem; and one double poem in which parallel verses offer a love complaint and its answer side by side). There are satirical poems, especially ridiculing lovers or ill-matched spouses. Like many other nuns who wrote poetry, Belisarda's religious verse concentrates (although not exclusively) on nativity and crucifixion themes and includes a poem to Sta. *Teresa. *See also* Nuns Who Wrote in Sixteenth- and Seventeenth-Century Spain

Work about

Olivares, Julián, and Elizabeth S. Boyce, eds. *Tras el espejo la musa escribe: Lírica femenina de los Siglos de Oro.* Madrid: Siglo Veintiuno de España, 1993.

Serrano y Sanz, Manuel. *Apuntes para una biblioteca de escritoras españolas desde el año 1401 al 1833.* Madrid: Rivadeneyra, 1903–1905. 2: 362–382.

Elizabeth S. Boyce and Julián Olivares

Beltraneja, Juana la (1462–1530)

She was daughter of Juana de Portugal, the wife of Enrique IV *el Impotente* (1425–1474; the Impotent). Since Enrique's doctors considered him incapable of having children, the rumor spread that Juana de Castilla, his only progeny, was the daughter of Beltrán de la Cueva, a favorite of the king who, it was said, was encouraged by Enrique to sleep with Juana. Under these circumstances, *Isabel I de Castilla (1451–1504), the king's half sister, prepared for her own ascension to the throne of Castile by marrying Fernando de Aragón (1469) and recruiting the help of important grandees for her cause. Nevertheless, some of the nobles (in particular the archbishop of Toledo and the marqués de Villena) feared they could lose control over the crown if Juana were disinherited by the crown. They therefore arranged for her to marry the aging King Alfonso of Portugal (1432–1481) shortly after Enrique's death and then used Portuguese troops to seize a number of Castilian cities for Juana. The ensuing civil war lasted five years and forced Juana and her allies to retreat to Portugal and to sue for peace. Juana then became a pawn for both sides. After Alfonso's death, the Portuguese tried to create a new alliance with Castile by marrying her to Isabel's son Juan; but the Castilian queen adamantly refused to consider any political role for Juana and forced the Portuguese to put her in a nunnery and to promise they would never permit her to marry or to leave Portugal. Juana entered the elegant Convent of Santa Clara in Coimbra and for the next half century spent a life totally devoid of the greatness and influence that had characterized her first 18 years.

Work about

Liss, Peggy K. *Isabel the Queen: Life and Times.* New York: Oxford UP, 1992.

Sarasola, Modesto. *Isabel la Católica y el destino de doña Juana la Beltraneja.* Valladolid: Casa Martín, 1955.

David H. Darst

Benavente, Jacinto (1866–1954): His Portrayal of Women in *La noche del sábado* and *La malquerida*

During the first half of the twentieth century, Jacinto Benavente, recipient of the 1922 Nobel Prize for Literature, dominated the Spanish stage, composing 172 theatrical pieces within a 60-year period. Of his three major works, *La noche del sábado* (1903; The Witches' Sabbath), *Los intereses creados* (1907; *The Bonds of Interest*, 1967), and *La malquerida* (1913; The Ill-Beloved), women play the principal role in two of the three, as well as in the majority of Benavente's other plays. Besides being the central figure, they frequently have the strongest, most well-defined personality among the cast, overshadowing the men in their lives. In spite of their dominant portrayal, women are cast in traditional roles, dependent upon men for their economic well-being and social status. Furthermore, their principal source of personal identity is derived from their role as wife and/or mother.

Benavente's characterization of Imperia, the principal female figure in *La noche del sábado*, and Raimunda, her counterpart from *La malquerida*, captures various facets of women that he will develop throughout his theatrical career. On one level, the two protagonists initially appear to be in stark contrast, given the divergent worlds the two plays portray. *La noche del sábado* takes place in the cosmopolitan world of royalty, circus entertainers, and rogues, where characters attempt to escape from society's conventions, while *La malquerida* depicts the conservative environment of a rural Castilian town controlled by public opinion and rumor. In spite of these superficial differences, Imperia and Raimunda present a similar view of women.

Imperia is a strong-willed woman who bridges the two extremes of the social spectrum depicted in the play. Driven by the basic need for survival and a desire to break away from her humble roots, she first becomes a model of the artist Leonardo, her confidant in the play, and then mistress of Prince Florencio, the decadent heir to the throne of Suabia. At the time of the play, Imperia is the mistress of Prince Florencio's uncle, Prince Miguel, whom she dominates. In two different conversations, she clearly indicates that for her the relationship provides economic stability when she confides that her dream in life is to have money because it affords power and freedom, both of which she owes to Prince Miguel. According to Imperia, her only true love was the imprisoned father of her daughter, Donina. Imperia's portrayal should not be misinterpreted as one of a social climber. In describing the symbolism of the sculpture (inspired by a young Imperia) that provided him fame and fortune, Leonardo defines one aspect of her character, the power of human will to acquire its dreams. He identifies this power with Imperia the woman. Benavente develops this idealized view of women as inspiration as a central theme in the farcical *Los intereses creados*, where Leandro's love for Silvia causes him to disclose the fraudulent plot that Crispín has masterminded to swindle Silvia's father.

Like Imperia, Raimunda is also a forceful woman who overshadows her second husband, Esteban. Unbeknownst to Esteban, she initiates an investigation of her nephew Norberto's role in the murder of Faustino, their future son-in-law, which leads to her discovery of rumors surrounding the alleged incestuous relationship between Esteban and his stepdaughter Acacia (child of Raimunda's late husband). This "forbidden" love is the real cause of the murder. Although her actions reflect an independent, self-sufficient woman, Raimunda reinforces the patriarchal stereotype of women's dependence upon men when she justifies to friends her marriage to Esteban, against her daughter's will, by citing the need for a man to provide stability in their lives. Thus, the romanticized view of love and marriage presented in *Los intereses creados* is contrasted with a demythified view of love and marriage as a social convention in *La noche del sábado* and *La malquerida*.

Although Imperia and Raimunda live worlds apart, both view their roles as mother to be paramount, resulting in external and internal conflicts for each of them. Even though Imperia's relationship with her daughter is unconventional in that Donina does not live with her, Imperia never loses the basic instinct to protect her offspring. In the play, Donina's boyfriend Nunú attempts to use her for his own profit by creating a scheme to bribe Prince Florencio for seduction of a minor. When Donina defends herself and murders the prince, Imperia intercedes to protect her, which results in her own personal conflict—whether to pursue her dream of becoming an empress and accompany Prince Miguel or to fulfill her social obligation and remain with her daughter. Initially, Imperia decides to dedicate herself to Donina, but Donina's approaching death absolves Imperia from the difficulty of making the final choice, and she decides to accompany Prince Miguel to Suabia to become the empress.

In *La malquerida*, Raimunda must confront a similar choice. Upon learning of Esteban's role in the murder of Faustino, Raimunda's initial concern is to protect her daughter, but the conflict immediately changes into a personal struggle between her role as mother and her role as wife. On the one hand, she cannot dismiss the charges, but on the other, she cannot reconcile them with the Esteban that she knows. After hearing Esteban's confession, Raimunda decides to take actions that will protect Esteban, allowing her to maintain her marriage. Only when Acacia reveals her own love for Esteban does Raimunda realize she has lost them both, eliminating the need for her to resolve her personal conflict, as in La noche de sábado. Her final, passionate attempt to stop their sudden departure results in her death at the hand of Esteban.

Benavente's facile resolutions to such dramatic conflicts may suggest his acceptance of traditional role models; however, an examination of his lesser-known plays indicates the contrary. In El hombrecito (1903; Little Man), the protagonist Nene decides to follow her true feelings and maintain her relationship with a married man she loves, rather than enter into a loveless marriage in order to receive society's approval. When Eugenia, the central figure of Vidas cruzadas (1929; Crossed Lives), finds herself an expectant mother, she opts to work to support herself and her child rather than marry the child's father solely to preserve her *honor and gain society's approval. In sum, although Benavente portrays women in traditional roles, his works often question to varying degrees the established social conventions of his time.

Work by

Obras completas. 11 vols. Madrid: Aguilar, 1969.
Plays of Jacinto Benavente. Trans. John G. Underhill. 4 vols. New York: Scribner, 1917–1924.

Work about

Martínez Tolentino, Jaime. Literatura hispánica e hispanoamericana: Tres autores revalorados: Ricardo Palma, Julián del Casal y Jacinto Benavente. Kassel: Reichenberger, 1992.
Peñuelas, Marcelino C. Jacinto Benavente. New York: Twayne, 1968.
Sánchez Estevan, Ismael. Benavente y su teatro. Barcelona: Ariel, 1954.
Tzitsikas, Helene. La supervivencia existencial de la mujer en las obras de Benavente. Barcelona: Puvill, 1982.

Linda S. Glaze

Beneyto Cunyat, María (1925–)

Author of novels, short stories, and literary criticism, María Beneyto Cunyat is especially known for her poetry. Beneyto spent her early childhood in Madrid but returned to her native Valencia during the Spanish Civil War (1936–1939), which interrupted her early schooling and precluded her plans to pursue a university career. These frustrated dreams imbue her poetry with an elegiac longing for things that never were but should have been. In 1992, Beneyto received the Valencian Literary Prize, the highest honor awarded to a writer in her region.

The romantic young speaker of Beneyto's first book of poems, Canción olvidada (1947; Forgotten Song), expresses the culturally forgotten or repressed voice of dreams and the unconscious. In Eva en el tiempo (1953; Eve in Time), Eve is the representation of that primitive life or forgotten song suppressed by civilization. Eve also depicts woman's self divided between the romantic *ángel del hogar ("La que está en sombras" [The One in the Shadows]) and the freedom seeker of "La peregrina" (The Pilgrim). Criatura múltiple (1954; Plural Creature) attributes the absence of a unitary female subjecthood to a division from an original state of fullness with a(n) (m)other or primitive life. The myth of that original life is developed in Poemas de la ciudad (1956; City Poems), Tierra viva (1956; Living Earth), and Vida anterior (1962; Life Before). The earth has been buried under the city asphalt. Several poems depict the mother as the representation of original values, from which the speaker was torn by history.

Poems from El agua que rodea la isla (1974; The Water Surrounding the Island) reveal Beneyto's romantic aesthetics: a distinct preference for the spoken over the written word, for the direct expression of feelings, and for poetry as the re-creation of the first unity with the (m)other. In Biografía breve del silencio (1975; Brief Biography of Silence), Beneyto retells a series of historical events from her mother's perspective. External history is thus fused with the mother's personal history, or intrahistory. Vidre ferit de sang (1977; Glass Wounded with Blood), a poetry collection in Catalan, marks a shift in Beneyto's imagery from romantic ideals to their irremediable loss. Equally, in *Nocturnidad y alevosía* (1993; Nocturnal World and Treachery), romantic dreams have turned into nightmares: The composed face of the man roaming the streets represses the woman he would like to be, and the virginal maidens of romantic stories are now prostitutes and drug addicts performing phantasmagoric dances under the moon. Similar disenchantment imbues *Hojas para algún día de Noviembre* (1993; Leaves for Some November Day). The uncertainty of the word *hojas* (pages of a book and leaves from trees or plants) fuses the process of writing with the passage of time. The hope for a fuller life is now perceived as a treacherous fraud primarily victimizing women (see "Madre" [Mother], "La indecisa" [The Undecided], "Mujer aherrojada" [Woman in Irons]). The reference to November is followed by one to springtime in *Para desconocer la primavera* (So as Not to Recognize Spring), published the following year. Winter and spring represent the cyclical passage of time that romantic poet Gustavo Adolfo *Bécquer describes in his famous poem "Volverán las oscuras golondrinas" (The Dark Swallows Will Return), the main source of inspiration for Beneyto's book. Various poems depict female types (George Sand, Ophelia, Madame Bovary) caught within the trappings of romantic ideals. This book is filled with the sense of *ubi sunt?* (where are they now?) for romantic ideals that now rest dead in the laps of old, solitary women. Bécquer's swallows will return with spring, but their message is a fraud.

Beneyto's narrative works in Castilian and Catalan share some themes with her poetry: the war, human loneliness (woman's in particular), and social concerns (*La gent que viu al món* [1966; People Who Live in the World]; *La dona forta* [1967; The Strong Woman]). *La promesa* (1958; The Promise), a collection of six short stories, is ironic because the promise of life is limited by society and time. In *Antigua patria* (1969; Ancient Fatherland), an autobiographical narrative, the main character, Luz, is the "light" through which the humanity of various social types is revealed.

Work by

Antigua patria. Valencia: Prometeo, 1969.
Antología general. Caracas: Lírica Hispana, 1962.
Archipiélago. Poesía inédita 1975–1993. Valencia: La Buhardilla, 1993.
Hojas para algún día de Noviembre. Valencia: Ajuntament, 1993.
Nocturnidad y alevosía. Valencia: Pre-Textos. Generalitat Valenciana, 1993.
Poesía 1947–1964. 2nd ed. Barcelona: Plaza y Janés, 1972.

Work about

Albi, José. "Introducción al conocimiento de la nueva poesía de María Beneyto." Intro. to *Hojas para algún día de Noviembre*. Valencia: Ajuntament, 1993. 10–25.
Fisher, Diane R. "Negotiated Subjects: Multiplicity, Singularity, and Identity in the Poetry of María Beneyto." *Symposium* 51.2 (Summer 1997): 95–109.
Manegat, Julio. "Prólogo." *Poesía 1947–1964*. By María Beneyto. Barcelona: Plaza & Janés, 1976. 13–33.
Newton, Candelas. "Voces silenciadas: La poética de María Beneyto." *Alaluz* 1–2 (Spring–Fall 1989): 21–38.

Candelas Gala

Berenguela de Castilla la Grande (1181–1246)

Queen of Castile and León, as daughter of Alfonso VIII and Leonor of England, she was carefully educated by her parents for rulership. In 1197, she married Alfonso IX of León and moved to that city, which she helped rebuild after the destructive incursions of Almanzor. However, Pope Innocent III declared her marriage to Alfonso void for reasons of consanguinity, and Berenguela was forced to leave her husband and son Fernando and return to Castile. In 1214, both her parents died within a month, and Berenguela was named regent for her 11-year-old brother Enrique. Her nomination infuriated many of the nobles, especially the Lara family, and she was forced to step down as regent and flee to Antillo. Her absence initiated a civil war among the nobles that lasted until Enrique's death in 1217. Berenguela then convinced the Council of Valladolid to declare her queen of Castile. At the ceremony, when the crown was placed on her head, she immediately removed it and crowned her young son Fernando, who was recognized by all as the legitimate ruler of Castile. When Alfonso IX died in 1230, Berenguela helped gain the crown of León for her son, thereby uniting the two kingdoms definitively. During the next 15 years, Berenguela continued to perform important roles in Spanish politics because Fernando III was continually occupied with the reconquest of Andalusia.

Work about

O'Callaghan, Joseph F. *A History of Medieval Spain.* Ithaca: Cornell UP, 1975.
Suárez Fernández, Luis. *Historia de España: Edad media.* Madrid: Gredos, 1970.

David H. Darst

Biedma y la Moneda de Rodríguez, Patrocinio de (1848–1927)

Born in Begíjar (Jaén), Patrocinio de Biedma received a very thorough education. She was married at age 15, a rather common occurrence in nineteenth-century Spain. Ten years later, already a widow, she became a writer. In 1877, Biedma founded the magazine *Cádiz*, which she also directed. *Cádiz* was the official publication of an Andalusian literary federation. Biedma wrote for numerous magazines and newspapers, including *El ángel del hogar*, *Revista de España*, *La ilustración ibérica*, *La fé católica*, *La época*, *El correo de la moda*, and *El renacimiento*. Some of her articles appeared with the anagram of her name, Ticiano Imab.

Work by

El mejor castigo. Leyenda dramática en tres actos y en verso. 2nd ed. Cádiz: Tip. La Mercantil, 1884.

La muerta y la viva. 2nd. ed. Cádiz: Tip. La Mercantil, 1883.
Romances y poesías. Cádiz: Tip. La Mercantil, 1881.

Work about

Ferreras, Juan Ignacio. *Catálogo de novelas y novelistas españoles del siglo XIX.* Madrid: Cátedra, 1979.
Simón Palmer, María del Carmen. *Escritoras españolas del siglo XIX: Manual bio-bibliográfico.* Madrid: Castalia, 1991.

Carmen de Urioste

Blasco Ibáñez, Vicente (1867–1928): His Portrayal of Women

In the author's 1919 novel *Los enemigos de la mujer* (*The Enemies of Women*, 1920), the main character, Prince Lubimoff, attempts to conquer his primordial instinct and establish a society where no women are allowed. His reasoning is that although there may be an occasional *Mater dolorosa* (sorrowful Mother), the majority of females are simply a *Venus dolorosa* (sorrowful Love Goddess), and he wishes to establish a sanctuary free of such influences. The experiment soon collapses, however, when his monastic friends are unable to continue their celibacy, and he himself is captivated by his previously much-despised cousin. This characterization of women as either submissive, domestic servant or manipulative seductress is quite prevalent throughout Vicente Blasco Ibáñez's literary corpus.

The novelist's most recognized works, the Valencian cycle (1894–1902), reveal this same stereotypical tendency. In *Arroz y tartana* (1894; *The Three Roses*, 1932), Manuela, after exploiting her own son Juanito's finances and pawning the family's possessions, finally resorts to selling herself in order to maintain her lavish lifestyle. Antonia, Juanito's friend, is the suffering one who sees both her and Juanito's savings disappear with the stock market crash and his subsequent death. *Flor de Mayo* (1895; *The Mayflower*, 1921) revolves around the wives of two brothers: Dolores, who betrays her husband Pascual by bringing his brother to her bed while Pascual is out fishing, and Rosario, who bears the shame, obtaining a job and financially supporting her household when her husband forsakes her for Dolores.

La barraca (1898; *The Cabin*, 1917) has more male than female characters. However, Teresa, the farmer Batiste's wife, exhibits the long-suffering characteristics of the *Mater dolorosa*; her son is murdered by the locals, her home is burned down, her daughter is assaulted by other girls, and her husband is ambushed by the local bully. *Entre naranjos* (1900; *The Torrent*, 1921), portraying the ruling class, has as a principal character Leonora, a worldly-wise operatic soloist who instills strong desires in Rafael, the local political boss.

Sónnica, in *Sónnica la cortesana* (1901; *Sonnica*, 1912), displays a similar control over her masculine counterpart Acteon; he, however, manages to conform to societal codes because of Sónnica's control over all of Sagunto. Tonet, in *Cañas y barro* (1902; *Reeds and Mud*, 1928), is not necessarily a weak man; his inability to convince Neleta to marry him results in his downfall. Her venus attraction and avarice lead to both his and their child's deaths.

In 1922, at the request of a U.S. movie company, Blasco Ibáñez wrote the screenplay for *El paraíso de las mujeres* (Women's Paradise). This novel, owing in part to its intended audience, is perhaps the work that most favorably portrays the female character. Here, Edwin Gillespie is shipwrecked where Swift's Gulliver had sojourned two centuries earlier. The land is ruled by women because the men have become too bellicose to govern properly. With women's rule comes peace, social stability and a federation called the *Estados Unidos de la Felicidad*, the United States of Happiness.

Although women other than those named are present in the aforementioned novels, the author's treatment of female characters typically follows the outlined formula. The woman is either a suffering, to-be-pitied member of the weaker sex or a manipulative, controlling seductress. Her place in society, stereotypically following the cultural norm of the period, is not that of even a few short years later; her positive value as a role model outside of the home is negligible.

Work by

Blood and sand. Trans. F. Partridge. New York: Ungar, 1974.
Cuentos medievales. Madrid: Clan, 1996.
Cuentos valencianos. Buenos Aires/Mexico: Espasa-Calpe, 1953.
The Enemies of Women. Trans. Irving Brown. New York: Burt, 1920.
The Holding/La barraca. Trans. L. Clark and E. Farrington Birchall. Intro. and notes Patricia McDermott. Warminster: Aris and Phillips, 1993.
El intruso. Intro. Javier Corcuera. Bilbao: El Tilo, 1996.

Work about

Anderson, Christopher L. *Primitives, Patriarchy, and the Picaresque in Blasco Ibáñez's* Caño y Barro. Potomac, MD: Scripta Humanistica, 1995.
Iglesias, Concepción. *Blasco Ibáñez, un novelista para el mundo.* Madrid: Silex, 1985.
Medina, Jerry. *The "Psychological" Novels of Vicente Blasco Ibáñez.* Valencia: Albatros, 1990.
Oxford, Jeffrey. *Vicente Blasco Ibáñez: Color Symbolism in Selected Novels.* New York: Lang, 1997.
Trau, Aida. *Arte y música en las novelas de Blasco Ibáñez.* Potomac, MD: Scripta Humanistica, 1994.

Jeffrey Oxford

Bodas de sangre

See García Lorca, Federico (1898–1936): Women in His Rural Trilogy

Böhl de Faber, Cecilia, Pseudonym Fernán Caballero (1796–1877)

Like her counterparts "George" Eliot in England and "George" Sand in France, Cecilia Böhl de Faber wrote under a male pseudonym that enabled her to appeal to a generation of readers not yet ready for female authors. Böhl de Faber is credited with introducing the modern novel to Spain. By background and birth she was ideally suited for this task. Though Cervantes, with his *Don

Quijote, had first introduced the novel to Spain with Part I of that great work in 1605, writers following him for some 200 years until publication of de Faber's pace-setting *La gaviota* (*The Sea Gull*, 1965) in 1849 had preferred to follow French models. De Faber, born of a German father, with his great love and knowledge of Spanish Golden Age literature, and of a conservative Roman Catholic Spanish mother, was poised to express the best of the Spanish realistic tradition. A cosmopolitan woman whose family shuttled between Germany, Paris, and Spain, she attended a French boarding school in Hamburg from age 6 through age 16. While she respected French culture—she wrote her first novel in French and then translated it into Spanish—she was not in awe of it. She was, however, enamored of Spanish culture and society and saw the Spanish countryside—particularly in Andalusia—as the appropriate corrective to what she viewed as the evils of advancing city life. In this regard, de Faber is a romantic, but in all other ways she strives for realism. Critics deem her a transitional figure and a regionalist.

Böhl de Faber helped to inaugurate *costumbrismo*, a nineteenth-century literary movement that flourished in Spain and Latin America and corresponds to regionalism or local color in English/American literature. Her first novel, *La gaviota*, which was serialized in a Madrid daily newspaper and became an instant success, traces the rather romantic story of a peasant woman who rises to be an opera star. In this work Böhl de Faber provides lyrical and detailed descriptions of Spanish provincial life and also duplicates the inconsequential prattle of the upper classes, in whose circles she moved. Thus, she further rebels against the artificial descriptions and dialogue of the then-popular historical romantic novel by striving to accurately depict the life and speech of the Spain of her day.

Böhl de Faber's own life was a colorful one. Born in Switzerland, after her early education in Hamburg, she moved to Cádiz with her parents, married at 17, and settled permanently in Spain in about 1813. Widowed within a short time, five years later she married the wealthy Marquis de Arco-Hermoso and lived in his palace in Seville, where she was known as a beautiful, witty, and accomplished cultural and social leader. Widowed by him in 1835, two years later she married the lawyer De Arrom, who proceeded to lose his and her money and eventually left Spain to be Spanish consul in Australia. Böhl de Faber never joined him there; she instead turned to other pursuits, including writing, and retreating, when possible, to her beloved Spanish countryside. She actually began to publish after age 50. Between 1857 and 1863, she lived in the splendid Moorish palace, the Alcazar in Seville, and was tutor to the royal children of Spain. Her husband died in Australia in 1863.

Böhl de Faber never duplicated the literary success of her first work, but she continued to publish other novels that stressed local color, such as *Clemencia* (1852) and *La familia de Alvareda* (1856; *The Family of Alvareda*, 1872). Washington Irving, who served as U.S. ambassador during this era, saw the manuscript of the latter work and encouraged her to continue writing. She also published *Un servilón y un liberalito* (*A Loyalist and a Liberal, or Three Souls of God*, 1882) in 1857 and continued to write short stories and to compile several volumes of folktales.

Unfortunately, Böhl de Faber's work does not translate well because of the difficulties in reproducing the earthy speech of the peasants, the constant plays on words, and the folk sayings and snatches of songs and ballads that she interweaves throughout her text. Further alienating her from some readers is her occasionally moralistic tone and staunch conservatism that caused her and others of her generation and background to fear the changes in Europe after the revolutions of 1848. Still de Faber was an original for her time, engaging successfully in an occupation virtually closed to women and inaugurating not only the modern Spanish novel but also an entire literary movement spanning two continents. *See also* Short Fiction by Women Writers: 1800–1900

Work by

La familia de Alvareda. Ed., intro., and notes Julio Rodríguez-Luis. Madrid: Castalia, 1979.
La gaviota. Ed. Carmen Bravo Villasante. Madrid: Castalia, 1979.
The Sea Gull. Trans. and intro. Joan Maclean. Woodbury: Barron's Educational Series, 1965.

Work about

Herrero, Javier. "The Castrated Bull: Gender in *La gaviota*." *Revista Canadiense de Estudios Hispánicos* 21.1 (Fall 1996): 155–165.
Klibbe, Lawrence H. *Fernán Caballero*. New York: Twayne, 1973.

Jeanne J. Smoot

Boixadós, María Dolores (1919?–)

She is not well known in her native Spain, despite the fact that her novel *Aguas muertas* (Stagnant Waters) was a finalist for the first Nadal prize in 1944, and because she left Spain in 1949, she has not been considered part of the group of exiles who left 10 years earlier, either. Nevertheless, during some 20 years of college teaching in exile, María Dolores Boixadós has continued writing novels to the present, even though not all of her works have been published.

Balada de un músico (1968; Ballad of a Musician) and the already mentioned *Aguas muertas* (1970) deal with life in Spain during the years before and after the Civil War (1936–1939). The first is noteworthy for characterization of its male protagonist, Señor Mases, and his submissive wife, typical of the patriarchal society depicted. The latter deals with the coming of age of Elena Just, in striking resemblance to Andrea, protagonist of Carmen *Laforet's *Nada*, which won the 1944 Nadal prize.

Boixadós's most successful novel is *Retorno* (1967; Return). Published in Mexico, it was not allowed in Spain during Franco's censorship. It incorporates all the characteristics of the "structural novel" as defined by Sobejano: an emphasis on structural elements; exploration of protagonist's conscience in relation to social context; discontinuity in the narrative point of view; innovations and complexity in the language and its representation. In its themes, *Retorno* resembles the exile novels written by her contemporaries.

Her two remaining novels, *Gabriel: Coda final* (1991; Gabriel: Final Coda) and *Apocalipsis en tiempo de rock* (unpublished; Apocalypse in Rock Tempo), both deal with the Spanish past (particularly the Civil War), with life in the new country of exile, and with the problems involved in a symbolic or real return to the homeland.

As of 1997, Boixadós lived in Florida in semiretirement and continuing to write. There, she was working on two novels, an exposé about scientific research in the United States and a journal-type account of her husband's illness and the impact it was having on her and her family. Subsequent to his death, she returned to Sort, Lerida, Catalonia, to be close to her brother. The fact that her last works have not been published has not deterred her from this true vocation of writing.

Work by

Aguas muertas. Madrid: Punta Europa, 1970.
Balada de un músico. Madrid: Quevedo, 1968.
Gabriel: Coda final, Barcelona: Hogar del Libro, 1991.
Retorno. Oaxaca: España Errante, 1967.

Work about

Alborg, Concha. *Cinco figuras en torno a la novela de posguerra: Galvarriato, Soriano, Fórmica, Boixadós y Aldecoa*. Madrid: Ediciones Libertarias, 1993.

Concha Alborg

Boss, Carolina del

See Ríos Nostench de Lampérez, Blanca de los (1862–1956)

Bravo-Villasante, Carmen (1918–1995)

Born in Madrid where she studied philosophy and letters at the university, biographer of literary figures, and author of children's literature, Carmen Bravo-Villasante was also a translator of German writers (Goethe, Heine, Hoelderling). She traveled extensively in Europe and America and taught literature in courses for foreign students in Madrid.

The interest of Bravo-Villasante in feminine topics was manifest in the theme of her doctoral dissertation, which studied the role of women disguised as men in the Spanish *comedia*, or theater. That work later became *La mujer vestida de hombre en el teatro español. Siglos XVI y XVII* (1955; Woman Dressed as a Man in Spanish Theater. Sixteenth and Seventeenth Centuries). Subjects of her biographies include women writers (*Pardo Bazán, Gertrudis *Gómez de Avellaneda) and male writers who created memorable feminine characters that were powerful, determined, modern women: (Juan *Valera, Benito Pérez Galdós). Other biographical subjects include Bettina Brentano, the young girl who fell in love with Goethe, and German writers Heinrich von Kleist and E.T.A. Hoffman. Bravo-Villasante worked extensively on children's literature as a historian, anthologist, compiler, and author and was a board member of the International Committee on Books for Young People. Her contributions in this field include anthologies of Spanish, Ibero-American, Chinese, and World children books.

Although she herself never created any feminine character, her work indicates a marked interest in feminine concerns. She chose to edit texts of women writers—*La gaviota* by Cecilia *Böhl de Faber, Emilia Pardo Bazán's *La cuestión palpitante* and *La vida contemporánea*—and compiled a collection of women's letters as *Veinticinco mujeres a través de sus cartas* (1975; Twenty-five Women through Their Letters). In her biography *Vida y obra de Pardo Bazán* (1973), Bravo-Villasante considers Pardo Bazán to be a feminist, because of her strong participation in the literary life of her day and also because of her incarnation of the image of a new woman, similar to some of her feminine characters, as in Pardo Bazán's *Memorias de un solterón* (1896; Memories of a Bachelor).

In *Una vida romántica: La Avellaneda* (1967; A Romantic Life: Avellaneda), Bravo-Villasante finds Gertrudis Gómez de Avellaneda to be a woman of impulse, rebellious to prejudice, very independent, and able to set aside society's conventions. An avid reader given totally to her work, her defiance of convention included an illegitimate child and several marriages. She is depicted by Bravo-Villasante as strong, of great beauty, energetic, exuberantly creative, and able to follow the drive of her mind and the dictate of her heart.

When the subject of the biography is a male, Bravo-Villasante still relates her subject to women's concerns. Juan Valera, in *Vida de don Juan Valera* (1974), is depicted as a defender of women's freedom through characters created in his novels at a time when women's "liberation" was unattainable in Spanish society. He is recognized as creator of memorable feminine figures such as the heroines of *Pepita Jiménez* and *Juanita la Larga*, representing a feminine canon that precedes his own time through women portrayed as independent, free of convention, able to create their own destiny and manage their own lives. Those characters are viewed by Bravo-Villasante as embodying an ideal of freedom and human dignity, acting according to their own conscience regardless of the dictates of the world and society. They represent a triumph of sincerity and appear guided by individual principles that are not sacrificed on behalf of a preestablished social code. Bravo-Villasante does not fail to record that Valera defends women writers and their right to the pen in *Cartas americanas* (of course, he also acerbically attacked Pardo Bazán).

In *Galdós visto por si mismo* (1976; Galdós as He Saw Himself) Bravo-Villasante finds a wealth of feminine characters in Galdós's novels, observing a preference for the portrayal of women as practical, active, dynamic, more given to action than to introspection. She also observes that when women are presented as selfless, they are noted for their generosity and goodness toward humanity and for their orderliness, tenacity, and diligence in tending to details of everyday life. She perceives in Galdós an interest in feminism and a concern for women's education, initially limited to that afforded by institutions such as the Escuela de Institutrices and the Asociación para la Enseñanza de la Mujer. Changes in his attitude emerge at the turn of the century when Galdós's feminine characters become strong emancipated women, full of energy and vitality, who confront life by themselves and later choose their own husband. Thus Galdós's awareness of the work of contemporaries such as Concepción *Arenal and Pardo Bazán is brought to light.

Bravo-Villasante was a professional woman who benefited from a progressive education during the pre–Civil War era at the Instituto Escuela, a Madrid coeducational school that followed the principles of education advocated by the Institución Libre de Enseñanza. There children, both female and male, received equal instruction that prepared them to study later on at the university. She thus enjoyed access to an excellent education and faced no social impediments to engage in her work. Married and with a family, she nonetheless was able to pursue her literary interests to an extent available to few Spanish women during the Franco era.

Work by

Galdós visto por si mismo. Madrid: EMESA, 1976.
Historia de la literatura infantil española. Madrid: Doncel, 1972.
La mujer vestida de hombre en el teatro español. Siglos XVI y XVII. Madrid: SGEL, 1976.
Veinticinco mujeres a través de sus cartas. Madrid: Almena, 1975.
Vida de Bettina Brentano. Madrid: Aedos, 1957.
Vida de don Juan Valera. Madrid: EMESA, 1974.
Una vida romántica: La Avellaneda. Barcelona: EDHASA, 1967.
Vida y obra de Pardo Bazán. Madrid: EMESA, 1973.

Pilar Sáenz

Bridoux y Mazzini de Domínguez, Victorina (1835–1862)

A poet and short story writer born in Manchester, England, to a French businessman and Italo-Spanish woman, she owed her literary bent to her mother, a poet who taught French, English, and German in the private religious school where Victorina Bridoux y Mazzini de Domínguez was educated. Following her father's death, mother and daughter moved to Cádiz, then to Gibraltar, and later to Tenerife, Canary Islands, where Victorina's poems appeared (1852–1862) in the local press. Her early death was due to yellow fever, after which her husband gathered and published her poems as *Lágrimas y flores* (1863; Tears and Flowers). Notwithstanding the late date, Romantic traces linger in her poetry, which employs Romantic meters and consonant rhyme; similarities have been noted between her poems and those of Gustavo Adolfo *Bécquer, although most of her poems were published earlier. Her friendship with Pilar *Sinués and other women writers in Spain provides a major poetic theme; other poetic traits include her strong sense of mystery, her vision of the poet as creator of a magical subjective world, and the search for an evasive, transcendent presence. Although she died too young to become a major figure, and is a relatively traditional writer, she is paradigmatic of the growing body of writing women of the mid-nineteenth century.

Work by

Lágrimas y flores. Producciones literarias. 2 vols. Santa Cruz de Tenerife: n.p., 1863.

Work about

Alonso, María Rosa. *En Tenerife, una poetisa. Victorina Bridoux y Mazzini (1835–1862)*. Santa Cruz de Tenerife: Librería Hesperides (Canarias), 1940.

Janet Pérez

Buero Vallejo, Antonio (1916–2000): His Vision of Women

The theater of Antonio Buero Vallejo is compelling for many reasons. Both the realistic and spiritual dimensions of the human condition lie at the heart of Buero's dramaturgy. His theater dramatizes the hopes and aspirations of humanity in the universal sense of the word and invites us to ask probing questions about ourselves and the reality that surrounds us. It sensitizes us to aspects of our day-to-day existence that we have lost sight of. It forces us to recognize characteristics, both good and bad, about ourselves; to face our most deep-seated fears; to confront our most cherished needs and wants; to raise our consciousness as individuals of worth regardless of our shortcomings. Buero's intent, as personified by his protagonists, is to stir in us something of a reawakening. Like his protagonists, we are asked to become engaged in a deep inner struggle and rebel against and overcome limitations thrust upon us by fate. Buero's theater is nothing short of a lesson in reasserting the self.

The role of women is pivotal to the evolution of Buero's dramaturgy. His female characters are remarkable individuals both in a social and in a symbolic context. They are generally strong and implacable and always inflexible in their determination to speak their mind or make their feelings known. Buero's women characters, though often morally superior to their male counterparts, are not always depicted in a positive light. At times they resort to drastic measures to attain their goals. Whether represented positively or negatively, whether principal or secondary characters, Buero's women function as a means of gaining a deeper understanding of the objective world and how we function in it.

The women in Buero's early plays, such as *Historia de una escalera* (1949; *The Story of a Stairway*), *En la ardiente oscuridad* (1950; *In the Burning Darkness*, 1985), *La tejedora de sueños* (1952; *The Dream Weaver*, 1967), and *La señal que se espera* (1952; *The Awaited Sign*), are fundamental catalysts both for dramatic tension and for his ideological premise. They represent individuals who bring about the necessary confrontation with reality and provide the means toward action. In the closing moments of *Historia de una escalera*, for example, when Fernando decides to attempt to overcome his sordid existence, he openly admits that he cannot bring about change without Carmina at his side. It is Juana's involvement with Carlos and Ignacio in *En la ardiente oscuridad* that brings the former to a vital recognition of his physical blindness yet spiritual superiority. In *La tejedora de sueños*, Penelope's irresolute waiting for the return of Ulysses and her methodical weaving of the tapestry imply that we as individuals possess the power to construct our own realities. The same is true of Susana, who in *La señal que se espera* instills in Luis a renewed hope in his artistic endeavors as a composer.

The pattern becomes more defined in later works as women characters embody more explicitly the tension between poetic reality (false reality) and reality itself. In *Casi un cuento de hadas* (1953; *Almost a Fairy Tale*), Buero pits the inner struggle of the individual within a female protagonist. Leticia displays incomparable valor and courage when at the end of the play she accepts reality over illusion, knowing full well that with her decision comes undue suffering. Amalia in *Madrugada* (1953; *Dawn*), widowed and desolate after her husband's death, finds the strength to go in search of answers about herself and her husband's past. Irene, in *Irene, o el tesoro* (1954; *Irene, or the Treasure*), suffers and lives a deprived reality, yet she endures in ways that only make her stronger in transcendental terms.

The role of women in Hoy es fiesta (1956; Today Is a Holiday), Las cartas boca abajo (1957; The Cards Face Down), and Aventura en lo gris (1963; Adventure in Gray) signifies a consolidation of women as the source of moral strength, hope, change, and a greater knowledge of the self. Pilar in Hoy es fiesta and Ana in Aventura en lo gris provide the necessary source of encouragement for Silverio to rise above his squalor and Silvano to take a stand, respectively. In Las cartas boca abajo, Buero uses two female figures, Adela and Anita, to convey his message of hope and a renewal of self.

As the conflict between inner vision and outer reality intensifies in subsequent plays, the spiritual symbolism of Buero's women characters increases accordingly. Fernandita in Un soñador para un pueblo (1959; A Dreamer for a People), for example, is a means toward consciousness for Esquilache as he proposes his social reforms. Juana's refusal to serve as Velázquez's model in Las Meninas (1960; The Ladies in Waiting) in many ways forces the painter to excel in his art. David's dilemma in El concierto de San Ovidio (1962; The Concert at Saint Ovide, 1967) has to do with his compelling desire to overcome the physical limitations thrust upon him by his blindness and provides the best example of the increased importance of Buero's female characters. David has struggled with his blindness since childhood. The motivating force for his desire to become an accomplished musician in spite of his handicap comes from Melania de Salignac, herself a blind woman who learned to read music.

Women are negatively portrayed in a number of Buero's plays. Mary in La doble historia del doctor Valmy (1964; The Double Case History of Dr. Valmy, 1967), for example, attempts to shoot her husband Daniel in order to precipitate the necessary encounter of inner and outer reality, while Encarna in El tragaluz (1966; The Skylight) prostitutes herself as a means to take control of her life. In similar fashion, in Jueces en la noche (1979; Judges in the Night), Julia's suicide underscores the need to equate action with principles. The women of Caimán (1981; Alligator), Rosa, Rufina, and Charito, are self-serving and egotistical. Their characterization implies that heightened self-awareness is not always a matter of conflict between two individuals but also between the individual and society. Some women are also portrayed as insensitive. The inability of Larra's wife and lover to understand him, for example, is one factor in Larra's suicide in La detonación (1977; The Detonation). The portrayal of women as victims also proves a useful technique for Buero. In El sueño de la razón (1970; The Sleep of Reason, 1985), Goya's conscious recognition of the frailty of humankind comes only after Leocadia is raped. In Llegada de los dioses (1971; Arrival of the Gods), Nuria is killed before her father Felipe can undergo a consciousness-raising experience.

In other plays, women function as the alter egos of male protagonists, what they deny within themselves and must forcibly confront. Tomás of La fundación (1974; The Foundation, 1985), for example, is unable to accept responsibility for the capture and incarceration of his comrades and fantasizes that the prison in which he finds himself is a research center for artists and scientists. He converses with Berta, an imaginary figure, who facilitates Tomás's evolution from a state of mental illness to one of lucidity and responsibility for the situation he and his comrades now face in prison. Similarly, in Diálogo secreto (1982; Secret Dialogue) Aurora represents the crucial link between her color-blind art critic father's refusal to accept his handicap and his recognition of the fact that he has lived a lie. Berta and Aurora are intimately linked to the inner vision of the male protagonists at a subconscious level and thereby facilitate the necessary exploration of their intuitive side.

In Buero's more recent plays, women function as a means of atonement between past and present. The past and the present are eerily linked in these plays to provide a vehicle for exploring the full potential of human existence by dispelling false hope and authenticating personal aspirations. Amparo in *Lázaro en el laberinto* (1986; Lazarus in the Labyrinth), Lorenza, Sandra, and Isolina in *Música cercana* (1989; Music Nearby), and Matilde in *Las trampas del azar* (1995; The Traps of Chance) all in some way force a rapprochement of the past and present lives of the plays' respective protagonists. They add a new dimension to Buero's image of women by awakening in the male protagonists of each play a consciousness of the self with definite temporal connotations as if to suggest that we are the product of tensions not only in a given moment of our existence but between various stages of our existence as well.

Women play an unquestionably important role in Buero's design of reality and strategy for personal survival. His female characters, like his frequent and varied use of symbols, bear transcendental significance within his dramatic narrative. They serve as an effective means for conveying dramatic tension and representing on the stage the complex interaction between an individual's inner reality and the external world. Given Buero's focus on the human elements of his art, it is not at all surprising that women are of intrinsic value to his dramatic craft.

Work by

Antonio Buero Vallejo's Today's a Holiday. Trans. and intro. James A. Dunlop. Lanham, MD: UP of America, 1987.
A Dreamer for the People. Trans., intro., and notes Michael Thompson. Warminster, England: Aris and Phillips, 1994.
Las Meninas: A Fantasia in Two Parts. Trans. Marion Peter Holt. San Antonio: Trinity UP, 1987.
The Music Windows. Trans. Marion Peter Holt. University Park, PA: Estreno, 1994.
Obra completa. Vol. 1. Madrid: Espasa Calpe, 1994.
The Shot. Trans., intro., and notes David Johnston. Warminster, England: Aris and Philllips, 1989. Spanish and English.
Three Plays/Antonio Buero Vallejo. Trans. M.P. Holt. San Antonio: Trinity UP, 1985.
Las trampas del azar. Madrid: Espasa Calpe, 1995.

Work about

Halsey, Martha T. *Antonio Buero Vallejo*. New York: Twayne, 1973.
———. *From Dictatorship to Democracy: The Recent Plays of Buero Vallejo (from "La Fundación" to "Música cercana")*. Ottawa: Dovehouse, 1994.
Iglesias Feijoo, Luis. *La trayectoria dramática de Antonio Buero Vallejo*. Santiago de Compostela: Universidad de Santiago de Compostela, 1982.
Ruggeri Marchetti, Magda. "Aspectos feministas del teatro de Antonio Buero Vallejo." *Boletín de la Asociación Europea de Profesores de Español* 34–35 (1986): 31–35.
Sollish Sikka, Linda. "Buero's Women: Structural Agents and Moral Guides." *Estreno* 16.1 (1990): 18–22, 31.

John P. Gabriele

Burgos, Carmen de (1867–1932)

A teacher, feminist, lecturer, translator, and tireless traveler, Carmen de Burgos scandalized Spanish society with her lifestyle and her progressive political ideas. She spent her life fighting for equal opportunities for women, focusing on the importance of education for women from her earliest writings.

Born into a wealthy family in Almeria, Spain, her birthplace was to play an important role in her novels and articles. Her father, José de Burgos Cañizares, was vice consul of Portugal; her mother, Nicasia Seguí Nieto, bore nine more children after Carmen. Of these siblings, de Burgos was especially close to her sister Catalina, who often lived with her and helped her rear her own daughter. At a very young age and much against the wishes of her family, de Burgos wed the Almerian poet Arturo Alvarez Brito. The marriage went badly, and out of necessity de Burgos went to work for her father-in-law at the family paper *Almería Bufa*. After losing three children, and with the goal of gaining economic independence, she studied to become a teacher. Throughout the memoirs she wrote for her exams, one sees the influence of the Krausist movement and the teachings of the Institución Libre de Enseñanza. Upon securing her diploma, in a climate of extreme hostility she left her husband and moved to Madrid with her young daughter.

In Madrid she found a rich intellectual environment that stimulated and encouraged her. Here too her life was replete with challenges, and her views on the world and the status of women underwent many changes that at times appear contradictory. De Burgos taught at schools in Guadalajara and Toledo but spent more of her academic life in Madrid at La Escuela Normal de Maestras. School scholarships allowed her to travel and broaden her understanding of educational systems in Switzerland and France. A supporter of coeducation and religious tolerance in schools, she used her classroom to teach women students the importance of productive work, communicating also her vision of a future world in which convenience food would free them from wasting time on household chores. Like Concepción *Arenal, she felt that even prisons should be made into centers for learning, especially in the case of incarcerated adolescents and young women.

Parallel to her teaching, and as a way to support herself and her child, de Burgos began to work for two newspapers, *El Sol* and *El Heraldo de Madrid*. Using the pseudonym Colombine, she also wrote a daily column for *El Diario Universal* titled "Lecturas para la Mujer" (Readings for Women). In these articles she discussed current events, child rearing, health, home management, and other women's issues. She received much notoriety in 1904, as the first person in Spain to publish a survey on divorce in a newspaper, and became the target of a slur campaign in Catholic journals. A survey she took in 1906, again using newspapers, to solicit public opinion on the vote for women was passionately attacked and defended by those on both sides. Nicknamed "La dama roja" (The Red Dame), she continued to fight for these social causes throughout her life.

Over the years de Burgos wrote for many newspapers and magazines, often having her own column on topics for women. She additionally published numerous practical guides on children's health, various cookbooks, writings on the art of beauty and love, all of which brought her recognition but insufficient economic security. De Burgos also continued to discuss the status of women as part of her vision of a better society. As the first female "roving" reporter in Spain, she traveled throughout Europe and North Africa during World War I, meeting intellectuals and interviewing theater personalities, former queens, and even Pope Pius X.

As an internationalist and activist, de Burgos founded the Alianza Hispano-Israelita in 1908. The same year, she founded the journal *Revista Crítica*. Both the organization and the journal became vehicles for connecting with and supporting the Jewish community worldwide. One of her magazine's greatest innovations was a section called "Lecturas Sefarditas" (Sephardic Readings), an open tribune on Jewish issues. De Burgos had become interested in Jewish culture after meeting French philosopher Max Nordau in 1905, frequenting the literary gatherings that took place at Nordau's house in Paris. Her socialist ideas evolved during this period as she became interested in Zionism and the creation of a Jewish State. Together with Angel Pulido she became a spokesperson for the Sephardic Jews, believing that Spanish history needed to be reviewed in the light of injustices perpetrated against the Jews since 1492. In the pages of her *Revista* she campaigned against popular stereotypes of Jews, considering it essential to educate Spanish people about them. Supported by many intellectuals, including Pulido, José Francos Rodríguez, and José Nakens, her campaign against anti-Semitism was well received in various parts of Europe. The German newspaper *Israelitsches Familienblat* of Frankfurt and *The Daily Telegraph* of London published articles praising Colombine's work. In 1909, Burgos faced economic difficulties that prevented publication of the *Revista Crítica*. Around this time she met writer Ramón Gómez de la Serna with whom which she developed a relationship of mentor, friend, colleague, and lover. Together they created *Prometeo*, a literary review that served as a platform for de la Serna's avant-garde writings. Burgos again dedicated a section of that magazine to Jewish issues. *Prometeo* lasted four years. Gómez de la Serna betrayed the amorous relationship, but the friendship between the two lasted until de Burgos's death. Some of the best descriptions of de Burgos are found in Gómez de la Serna's introductions to several of her books.

Her travels with Gómez de la Serna often took her to Portugal and familiarized her with the political situation there. For her support of the Portuguese revolution and her work on behalf of Portuguese women, she became the only woman to be awarded the Medal of Order of Santiago. Portugal also became the site for two novels by de Burgos that treat religious intolerance: *El retorno* (1921; The Return) and *Los espiritados* (1923; The Spiritists).

A prolific writer, de Burgos produced novels and short stories initially published by Sempere publishing house with the support of her friend Vicente *Blasco Ibáñez. She also formed a literary circle, later known as Colombine's Salon, frequented by intellectuals such as Gabriel Miró, Juan Ramón *Jiménez, Consuelo Alvarez, Rafael Cansinos Asséns, and Sofía Casanova. De Burgos also brought in ideas from abroad through her own translations and through those of other young writers she supported to translate the works of Oscar Wilde (1856–1900), John Ruskin (1819–1900), Leo Tolstoi (1828–1910), Colette (1873–1954), and Giacomo Leopardi (1798–1837).

As part of Madrid's cultural explosion, de Burgos contributed dozens of short stories to the flood of magazines that began to appear in 1907 when Eduardo Zamacois founded *El Cuento Semanal*. With Emilia *Pardo Bazán, Sofía Casanova, Concha Espina, and others, de Burgos thrilled the reading public with tales of romance, exotic locales, and themes of social significance. One of her most well-known and controversial stories, "El artículo 438" (Article 438), deals with the Spanish penal code and its treatment of women who, because of their economic vulnerability, are victimized in cases of adultery.

Like Pérez Galdós, de Burgos chronicled the developing, rapidly changing city of Madrid. In hundreds of articles, stories, and particularly in her novels, she focused on the status of women and their treatment by traditional and newly developing institutions and classes. *La rampa* (1917; The Ramp) studies the descending trajectory that lower-middle-class women experience due to their lack of economic independence, and *Quiero vivir mi vida* (1931; I Want to Live My Life) analyzes the institution of marriage and the unnatural demands it places on women. Her nonfiction study *La *mujer moderna y sus derechos* (written 1927, pub. 1929; Modern Woman and Her Rights) surveys the status of women internationally and examines their progress in achieving legal equality and the right to vote. The study, which shows the influence of August Bebel's *Women under Socialism* (1993) as well as the views of Havelock Ellis and Gregorio Marañón, can clearly be considered a precursor to Simone de *Beauvoir's *The Second Sex* (1949).

Other travels took her throughout Latin America, where she gave speeches on women's causes and studied social systems around the world. She served as president of the Cruzada de Mujeres Españolas (Spanish Women's Crusade) and late in life joined the Masons. At the end of this life of committed political activity, with the advent of the Second Republic she joined the Partido Republicano and was elected a provincial delegate. She disagreed strongly with party colleague Victoria *Kent, who was not ready to support giving the vote to women.

De Burgos died while giving a speech at the Círculo Radical Socialista. Recognized in her day as a precursor of feminism and indefatigable activist for social change, her vast, varied literary production and her radical political and social stances were lost to history for decades, with the ensuing Spanish Civil War and the years of Franco's dictatorship. *See also* Short Fiction by Women Writers: 1900–1975; Women's Education in Spain: 1860–1993

Work by

Los anticuarios. Ed. José María Marco. Madrid: Biblioteca Nueva, 1989.

La Flor de la Playa y otras novelas cortas. Ed., intro., and sel. Concepción Núñez Rey. Madrid: Castalia, Instituto de la Mujer, 1989.

Obras completas. Madrid: Compañía Ibero-Americana, 1929.

Pasiones: novela inédita. Madrid: Novela Corta, 1917.

"El triunfo de Israel." *Raíces* 19 (1994): 55–56.

Work about

Bieder, Maryellen. "Self-Reflexive Fiction and the Discourses of Gender in Carmen de Burgos." *Bucknell Review* 39.2 (1996): 73–89.

Castañeda, Paloma. *Carmen de Burgos, "Colombine."* Madrid: Comunidad de Madrid, Dirección General de la Mujer, 1994.

———. "Carmen de Burgos y los judíos." *Raíces* 19 (1994): 52–54.

Rodríguez, María Pilar. "Desviación y perversión en 'El Veneno del Arte' de Carmen de Burgos." *Symposium* 51.3 (Fall 1997): 172–185.

Starcevic, Elizabeth. *Carmen de Burgos, defensora de la mujer*. Almeria: Cajal, 1976.

Urioste, Carmen de. *Narrativa andaluza (1900–1936): Erotismo, feminismo y regionalismo*. Seville: Secretariado de Publicaciones, 1997.

Elizabeth Starcevic and Carlota Caulfield

Burlador de Sevilla, El (1627–1629): Its Women Characters

Traditionally, we have considered only the four female characters (deceived by Don Juan) who have speaking parts in *El burlador de Sevilla y convidado de piedra*—Isabela, Tisbea, Ana, and Aminta—however limited those parts may be (e.g., Doña Ana). Susana Pendzik has recently deployed some very effective feminist reading strategies, however, to call attention to a series of marginalized women—some anonymous, all invisible—who are alluded to in the course of the action. Among these are the Spanish noblewoman victimized by the trickster prior to his Italian interlude, several prostitutes of the section of Seville known as Little Lisbon, and Beatriz, who may be Mota's mistress. Collectively, these invisible women are said to stand for the multitude of suppressed and unheard female voices that tend to be ignored under the patriarchal system of justice. They serve to remind us that this system is not likely to distribute justice evenly, and certainly not universally. Pendzik wisely considers the queen and the absent mother figure separately, since neither would qualify as a victim in any meaningful sense. Her study stresses the importance of absences, silences, and gaps as dimensions that must be taken into account in arriving at a full appreciation and understanding of this seminal text. This is a sympathetic and subtle reading, although it overstates the case in claiming that the women characters constitute the most powerful source of dramatic energy in the text—a patent example of reading against the grain. The central source of dramatic energy is adumbrated in the title itself, and while that focus may waver, it gains in clarity throughout and becomes crystal clear in the climax.

Three readers who offer a less benign perspective on the female characters are Ruth Lundelius, Armand Singer, and Carlos Feal. Lundelius was one of the first to question the received wisdom of Blanca de los *Ríos, Esmeralda Gijón, and other defenders of Tirso as a defender of women. Taking her cue from A.A. Parker's remarks in his well-known approach to the *comedia* (theater), Lundelius proceeds to detail the transgressions of Isabela, Tisbea, Ana, and Aminta, maintaining that each is, if not equally guilty, at least complicit in the loss of life and/or *honor left in their wake. She sees Tirso as being very much a product of his time and place, someone who could therefore be expected to express Scholastic/Aristotelian *misogyny in his work. Singer speaks highly of Lundelius's effort but refuses to view the play as a misogynist tract, arguing instead that it expresses a love of women, albeit in their subordinate, pleasure-providing place. Feal is more psychologically oriented and more speculative. He speaks, for instance, of an unconscious attraction on the part of Aminta toward Don Juan. He agrees with Arturo Serrano Plaja that Isabela, somewhere deep within her, wishes to be seduced by Don Juan. He seems to applaud the fact that Tisbea is served a dose of her own medicine and put in her place by Don Juan.

The dynamics of the play are such that only a partial or truncated explanation will result from an excessive concentration on either the male or the female roles. Each depends on the other. The *Burlador* cannot be understood without the *burlados* (duped ones), both male and female, nor can these subordinate roles be properly appreciated without an awareness of their connections to the protagonist. The original Don Juan is a trickster, not a lover. He delights in deceiving both men and women. Three of the four documented escapades entail treachery or deception involving both a man and a woman (Isabela/Octavio; Ana/Mota; Aminta/Batricio). Sexuality and seduction are certainly factors, but they pale in comparison to the imperative of the *burla* (the trick or deception). An insightful study by Raymond Conlon argues that there is an odd sort of complicity among Don Juan and the male *burlados*, all of whom seem to be similarly misogynistic.

Attention to the generic dominant of Tirso's text can aid in developing a proper perspective on both the male and female characters. The work is, without doubt, a social satire, and as such, its commentary on the human condition is more than slightly slanted. The situations it presents are exaggerated in such a way that we are led to the following pessimistic inferences, at a bare minimum: There is little prospect of human justice, of harmony between the sexes, of respect for authority, or honor among friends. Tirso's pessimism is directed toward the foibles and false values of the men and women who make up society; it is pessimism *de tejas abajo* (with no help from above), as literary critic Otis Green defines it, and it carries with it the implication of a corresponding optimism *de tejas arriba* (with divine intervention). The implication becomes a statement through the supernatural intervention that ends the career of Don Juan, making explicit the idea that God is not mocked and that order and justice do exist, albeit on a higher plane. Within the world of the play, both men and women are shown to be seriously flawed. Tirso's satiric depiction of the society of the day is all-encompassing.

Of the four women Don Juan attempts to dupe, two are nobles and two are commoners. The sequence is a contrapuntal one, alternating between higher and lower classes: first, Isabela, a duchess; second, Tisbea, a fisherwoman; third, Doña Ana, a noble; finally, Aminta, a peasant girl whose marriage to Batricio is ungallantly interrupted. All are married off during the denouement, as the king belatedly restores a semblance of order, allowing the tragic isolation from society of Don Juan to be replaced by the comic muse of integration, with its promise of parturition and the perpetuation of the species. Whether it is a species worth perpetuating remains a suggestive open topic. *See also* Sáenz-Alonso, Mercedes (1917–   ): *Don Juan y el donjuanismo*; Zorrilla y Moral, José (1817–1893): His View of Women

Work

El burlador de Sevilla y convidado de piedra. Ed. James A. Parr. Binghamton: Medieval and Renaissance Texts and Studies, 1994.

Work about

Conlon, Raymond. "The *Burlador* and the *Burlados*: A Sinister Connection." *Bulletin of the Comediantes* 42 (1990): 5–22.

Feal, Carlos. *En nombre de don Juan: Estructura de un mito literario*. Amsterdam/Philadelphia: Purdue U Monographs in Romance Lges., 1984.

Lundelius, Ruth. "Tirso's View of Women in *El burlador de Sevilla*." *Bulletin of the Comediantes* 27 (1975): 5–14.

Parker, Alexander A. "The Spanish Drama of the Golden Age: A Method of Analysis and Interpretation." *The Great Playwrights*. Ed. Eric Bentley. Garden City, NY: Doubleday, 1970. 679–707.

Pendzik, Susana. "Female Presence in Tirso's *El burlador de Sevilla*." *Bulletin of the Comediantes* 47 (1995): 165–181.

Singer, Armand E. "Don Juan's Women in *El burlador de Sevilla*." *Bulletin of the Comediantes* 33 (1981): 67–71.

James Parr

Bursario

See Rodríguez del Padrón (de la Cámara), Juan (1399?–1450)

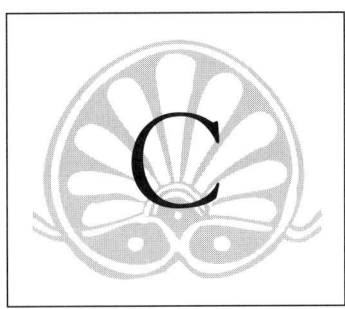

Caballerías, novelas de: Their Treatment of Women

A *novela de caballerías* (chivalry novel) is an adventure book where one or a group of protagonists travels far and wide in a fantastic world, encountering wizards, monsters, and the like and waging endless battles with other knights. Condemned by the Church as unrealistic and frivolous, they were extremely popular during the fourteenth and fifteenth centuries and avidly read by men and women of all ages and social classes—King Carlos I/V and Santa *Teresa de Jesús were two such readers. The most famous chivalry book in Spain was *Amadís de Gaula* (before 1508; Amadis of Gaul). The *Amadís* was one of the few chivalry novels that Cervantes saved from the fire in *Don Quijote de la Mancha*'s (Part I, 1605) symbolic "book inquisition." Indeed, Cervantes took the *Amadís* as a model and an inspiration for his writing. Other chivalry books of the day include continuations of the *Amadís* cycle, numerous novels in the *Palmerín* series, and others. Eisenberg notes that during Carlos V's reign (1517–1556) new chivalry books were published at the rate of nearly one per year. Chivalry books accompanied the first sailors from Spain to the New World and influenced the style of writers describing the lands and peoples of the New World.

Women enjoyed reading chivalry books and were an essential component of the chivalric world. Women were the cause of all adventures, and knights listened to their words of wisdom. Female characters span all ages and a variety of relationships and positions: As ladies of the knights, they are patient and beautiful; as queen mothers, they are women of authority; as sisters, they are trusted and strong. There are also magic women whose powers reach far beyond the authority of queens or the strength of the knights. Chivalry novels divinized women as supreme beings who had to be satisfied. Although presented as fragile maidens, they also constituted powerful forces that moved and influenced the knights.

Women in *Amadís de Gaula* are present from the opening moments of the novel when the author introduces the hero via his lineage. The description of Amadís's mother, her shyness, spirituality, and beauty, is notable in comparison with the description of the father, a mature king. The Sin-par Oriana (Oriana Matched by None), Amadís's lady, is likewise introduced by her lineage. A beautiful creature, she possesses her own voice in the narrative and maintains her ability to control her life and feelings. Oriana appears as a loving admirer of Amadís, but when she becomes unsure of his fidelity to her, she reacts with pain and anger and composes "Oriana's letter," which changes the course of the story. Urganda la Desconocida is another very important determinant. As the all-powerful magic woman who controls the destiny of Amadís and his descendants, she functions as Athena does in monitoring Ulysses's journey in the *Odyssey*. Traditional negative characteristics are also assigned to women in *Amadís de Gaula*. Women are presented as distractions that can provoke a knight's defeat—Oriana can be criticized for reacting hastily with insufficient information. Some women constitute a temptation to knights, such as Queen Briolanja, the cause of Oriana's anger toward Amadís. Together, these characters comprise the familiar women whose presence constitutes a network of characters repeated in all the chivalry novels.

Chivalry novels also include other women whose roles depend on the adventures. Some are damsels in distress who need a knight's protection. Others are introduced as elements of surprise, to amuse the reader. To this category belong Queen Calafia and the witch Melia, both in *Las sergas de Esplandián* (before 1510; Esplandián's Exploits). Calafia is queen of the island of California, which is inhabited by black women warriors of great strength and ferocity who share the island with griffins, monstrous birds who eat men but not women. Melia is an old enchantress whom Esplandián and his cohorts want to capture and bring to Amadís; in the course of the episode, she engages in a highly undignified fistfight with the younger magic woman Urganda.

To conclude, chivalry novels included women in their plot and did not limit their role to that of spectator but rather involved them in the action in a variety of important ways.

Work

Amadís de Gaula. Ed., intro., and notes V. Cirlot and José Enrique Ruiz Doménec. Barcelona: Planeta, 1991.
Amadís de Gaula. Ed. and prol. Jesús Rodríguez Velasco. Madrid: Fundación José Antonio de Castro, 1997.
Amadis of Gaul. English trans. E.B. Place and H.C. Behm. Lexington: UP of Kentucky, 1974.

Work about

Eisenberg, Daniel. *Castilian Romances of Chivalry in the Sixteenth Century: A Bibliography*. London: Grant and Cutler, 1979.
———. *Romances of Chivalry in the Spanish Golden Age*. Newark, DE: Juan de la Cuesta, 1982.
Orduna, Lilia E.F. de, ed. *Amadís de Gaula: Estudios sobre narrativa caballeresca en la primera mitad del siglo xvi*. Kassell: Reichenberger, 1992.
Pierce, Frank. *Amadís de Gaula*. Boston: Twayne, 1976.
Riquer, M. de. *Estudios sobre el Amadís de Gaula*. Barcelona: Sirmio, 1987.

María Luisa García-Verdugo

Caballero, Fernán

See Böhl de Faber, Cecilia, Pseudonym Fernán Caballero (1796–1877)

Cadira del honor

See Rodríguez del Padrón (de la Cámara), Juan (1399?–1450)

Cajal, Rosa María (1920–)

Feminist and existentialist themes are developed in several of Rosa María Cajal's novels, especially *Juan Risco* (1948), *Primero, derecha* (1955; First Floor, Right), and *Un paso más* (1956; One Step Further), with the latter presenting an unconventional female protagonist and her quest for independence. Cajal was born in Zaragoza and from an early age felt that writing was her true vocation, but financial constraints forced her to work in an office and delay her literary career. Nevertheless, by the time she was 17, Cajal had already written a novel and soon afterward started collaborating in several literary journals. She has since published hundreds of short stories and articles, as well as over a hundred novels.

The existentialist novel *Juan Risco* is her

first published work and was a finalist in 1948 for the Premio Nadal. The novel is centered around a male protagonist, Juan Risco, and his failed relationships with women. At the beginning of the novel, Risco tries to help a young woman down on her luck but is compelled to reject her when she falls in love with him. He then arranges for her to meet an editor who becomes her lover. When the editor's wife dies, Risco's past comes to light—he was her first husband, a famous journalist who faked his own death and took on a new identity. Throughout the novel, Risco manipulates his relationships with women in order to free them, but in turn he ends up consumed by feelings of emptiness and despair in his own life.

Primero, derecha portrays a traditional female character who lives only for her family and home. She is always situated within the confinements of her house, the only universe where the protagonist can exist. Her identity is defined exclusively in terms of her role as mother and wife.

With *Un paso más*, Cajal presents for the first time a nontraditional female character. Protagonist Alejandra leaves the security of her home village to find a career and new future in the city. The experiences of her new life slowly shape her character and help her find strength and courage to gain her independence. Throughout the novel Alejandra proves to be of stronger character than the men and women that surround her and transcends them all in her journey toward freedom and independence.

Most of Cajal's novels deal primarily with the psychological aspect of characters and their actions. Her aim is to portray female characters as ordinary women that readers can recognize, understand, and identify with.

Work by

El acecho. Madrid: Bullón, 1963.
Juan Risco. Barcelona: Destino, 1948.
Un paso más. Barcelona: Garbo, 1956.
Primero, derecha. Barcelona: Caralt, 1955.

Work about

Calvo de Aguilar, Isabel. "Rosa María Cajal." *Antología biográfica de autoras españolas*. Madrid: Biblioteca nueva, 1954. n.p.
Díaz, Janet. "Rosa María Cajal." *Hispania* 58 (1975): 555–556.
"Rosa María Cajal." *Women Writers of Spain: An Annotated Bio-Bibliographical Guide*. Ed. Carolyn L. Galerstein and Kathleen McNerney. Westport, CT: Greenwood P, 1986. 55–56.

Delmarie Martínez

Calderón de la Barca, Pedro (1600–1681): His Representation of Women

This Golden Age playwright represents the culmination of roughly 100 years of remarkable dramatic production and richness in Spain, and his name has become virtually synonymous with Spanish Baroque drama. Calderón's work is generally characterized by complex language combining *gongorista* (euphuist) formal tendencies infused with ingenious *conceptista* meaning (full of conceits or puns). An intellectual of the noble class, Calderón was appointed court dramatist for Felipe IV, and during his career he wrote approximately 100 *comedias* (three-act tragicomedies) conventionally subdivided into *comedias de capa y espada* (plays of intrigue), *comedias mitológicas* (mythological plays), *comedias de honor* (honor plays), and *comedias filosóficas* (philosophical plays). Calderón also wrote an opera and several *autos sacramentales*, a genre exclusive to Spain in which specific aspects of Catholic faith are dramatized in a one-act piece culminating in the Eucharist. Most of Calderón's plays deal with moral and religious philosophy, often dramatizing human beings' struggle to dominate instinct through intellect. Traditionally, Calderón's work has been characterized as rigidly affirming seventeenth-century Spain's Counterreformation religious and philosophical points of view, as well as the country's social and moral codes. Perhaps most significant for a feminist reading of Calderón's work is his treatment of the *honor theme and the role women played as instruments to test and prove men's ability to control passion by means of reason in order to uphold social and moral values.

A necessary first step toward understanding Calderonian drama and its relationship to feminist scholarship is an examination of the role of women in the historical context in which Calderón wrote. Golden Age Spain was a period of contrasts; rigid conservatism, which sometimes manifested itself through antitheater moral tirades and bans, coexisted with bawdy, raucous humor celebrating the baser elements of human nature. Women writers such as dramatists María de *Zayas and Ana *Caro negotiated for a space from which their right to write (and to participate in the intellectual activities of their era) could be exercised, despite their repressed status. Not surprisingly, such contrasts became the stuff from which plays were made as Golden Age drama imitated and shaped life.

A major theme of sixteenth- and seventeenth-century Spanish drama that is also reflective of social institutions was honor. Although scholars are unsure of the exact relationship between honor as a literary phenomenon and as a social code, its significance for feminist scholars is paramount since women were considered the vessels in which men's honor was stored. Evidence does exist that in Golden Age Spain a husband could kill an unfaithful wife, provided that he kill her lover, too. In drama of the period, wives, daughters, and sisters who transgressed society's rules regarding sex caused a loss of honor for male family members; such transgressions were in the theater often punished by death at the hands of the female character's male relatives.

Many of Calderón's plays treat the theme of honor, but with different outcomes. *El alcalde de Zalamea* (1642; The Mayor of Zalamea) portrays the rape of Isabel at the hands of Don Alvaro, a military captain of noble birth. After the incident, Isabel, aware of the exigencies of the honor code, asks that her father, Pedro Crespo (the mayor), kill her. Her brother Juan pursues Isabel with precisely that intent, but Isabel's father spares her life and demands satisfaction from the captain. Pedro gives Don Alvaro the choice of marrying Isabel, but the captain refuses because Isabel is not of noble blood. Though of an inferior social class, Pedro Crespo then has the captain garroted, and his actions as mayor are supported by the king in spite of their transgressive nature. Isabel is sent to a convent and, though spared death, is relegated to a life of shame at the margins of society.

Another play that deals with the theme of the honor code and its effects on women is *El médico de su honra* (1635; Physician to His Honor). The protagonist Gutierre kills his wife because he suspects she has been unfaithful, even though his suspicions are unconfirmed. Throughout the play, Gutierre struggles with his professed love for Mencía and with what he perceives as his obligation to respond to and uphold an inflexible social code. In the end, Gutierre's actions are supported by the king, and he is married to Leonor, a woman to whom he owes an obligation due to a previous relationship.

Both plays reflect the characteristic ambiguity of Baroque literature through their problematic stance regarding honor. In one respect, Pedro Crespo spares his daughter's life and kills her rapist; this would suggest placing proper blame in its proper place. Nevertheless, Isabel is still a social outcast through no fault of her own: She in unmarriageable (unless she marries her rapist) and joins a religious order as a means to distance herself from a society that would punish the victim of a crime. Perhaps most troubling is Isabel's willingness to accept death in apparent support of a repressive system that deems her valuable in terms of her effect on the lives of male relatives and her virginal purity. Isabel functions similarly on a structural level, for she is little more than a mechanism whereby Pedro Crespo asserts his autonomy and the privileges and responsibilities of the noble class are scrutinized.

Whether or not the text affirms or censures Gutierre's actions in *El médico de su honra* is also difficult to ascertain with certainty. Mencía's murder could be viewed as a triumph of reason over passion. In spite of his love for his wife, Gutierre kills her in order to fulfill his social obligation to maintain his honor. Still, his questionable conduct with Leonor, coupled with Mencía's apparent innocence, may well prompt readers and spectators to ask themselves just how honorable he was. Perhaps the text can in fact be read as a criticism of rigid conformism and the extremes to which the honor code may lead people.

In some plays, women avenge their own honor and often resort to disguise in order to pass through the world unnoticed. The role of disguise leads to a discussion of another feature of Calderonian drama (and Golden Age theater in general) significant to feminist readings, the convention of the *mujer vestida de hombre* (woman dressed as a man) or the *mujer varonil* (masculine woman). The latter is seen in *La hija del aire* (1653; Daughter of the Air) in which Calderón dramatizes the myth of Semiramis. Semiramis's cross-dressing has been read as an expression of her masculine side, since she is characterized as having somewhat manly interests and tendencies. Power hungry, Semiramis dresses as a man as part of a strategy whereby she usurps the throne from the king.

La vida es sueño (1635; Life Is a Dream, 1970), perhaps Calderón's best-known play, also employs the *mujer vestida de hombre* in the character of Rosaura. The drama presents the story of Segismundo, prince of Poland, who has been exiled to a lonely tower in infancy by his own father because of astrological predictions that the infant would become a monster. Rosaura appears at the Polish court dressed as a man in an attempt to avenge her own lost honor from Duke Astolfo. History seems to repeat itself as it is revealed that Segismundo's tutor Clotaldo is none other than Rosaura's father who had seduced and left Rosaura's mother without husband or honor. Although criticized by some as a mere subplot, with no relationship to the theme of Segismundo's rebirth into society, Rosaura's story functions as a means for Segismundo to prove that he has learned to regulate instinct with reason. Upon their first meeting in the palace (with Rosaura dressed as the lady-in-waiting Astrea), Segismundo attempts to attack her. Eventually he learns that in order to be a good prince, he must sacrifice emotions to social organization. After Segismundo's development into a just ruler, he unites Astolfo and Rosaura in marriage, forsaking his own love for her in order to uphold social values.

For feminist scholars, cross-dressed characters like Semiramis and Rosaura represent the potential for theater to examine the constructedness of gender roles, problematizing essentialist notions of feminine and masculine. Although Spain did not have a tradition of cross-dressed actors (as did England), numerous *comedia* characters appropriate the clothing of the opposite sex, and much recent criticism centers on the ability of these characters to invert cultural norms. Perhaps a Renaissance woman described as manly in deference to patriarchal values was merely being paid the highest compliment in a sexist society. Assuredly, Golden Age gender play often resulted in affirmation of seventeenth-century Spain's rigidly defined categories of male and female, as marriage always provided social and dramatic closure. Additionally, scholars have observed that male costumes revealed more of the actress's body, a decidedly unfeminist objectification of women. However, the *mujer vestida de hombre* could have a subversive potential since the simple act of casting doubt on the notion of gender as essential undermines the repressive social systems within which the dramas unfold.

Conventionally viewed as having less philosophical content than other subgenres, Calderón's *comedias de capa y espada* (cloak and sword plays), like the plays in which female characters dress as men, often afford readers and spectators the opportunity to see women assume an active role outside the domestic sphere. *La dama duende* (1629; The Phantom Lady) belongs to this category. In the play, Doña Angela uses her ingenuity (and fortuitous architectural details of her house) to escape the watchful eye of her brother and pursue a marriage between herself and Don Manuel, a house guest in her home. A mysterious figure from the first scene, Angela discovers a door connecting her room to that of Manuel and uses it secretly to enter his room, rifle through his things, and leave him notes. Unsure of exactly who has been entering his room, Manuel parallels the text's ambiguous characterization of Angela; he does not know if she is a woman, an angel, or a demon. Similarly, readers and spectators must wonder if Angela's efforts are really rewarded when she marries Manuel and must presumably renounce the freedom offered by her secret evening excursions.

Feminist approaches to Calderón's comic plays such as *La dama duende* explore the liberating qualities of comedy, which allows female protagonists liberty to explore different identities, spaces, and discourses. Female protagonists of *comedias de enredo* (plays of complicated plot), characterized by their use of self-conscious language, play, and role-playing, control their own lives and destinies through their ability to manipulate linguistic and theatrical conventions. However, this freedom is short-lived, for women are invariably reinscribed into the patriarchal order through marriage at the play's conclusion. Ironically, the subversive potential of their actions is only alluded to, and their newfound power is used to support the very social institutions that curtail their rights of self-determination.

Such ironies are characteristic of Baroque literature in general and of Calderonian drama in particular. In Calderón's plays, women are often relegated to a secondary position with respect to men. Nevertheless, these same female characters are crucial to the development of the work's thematic content, be it an honor play, a philosophical play, a mythological play, or a play of intrigue. As an example of Calderón's conformity to his society, he is cited as having written plays "por mi Dios, por mi rey, por mi dama" (for my God, my king, and my lady). Curiously, the first two categories usually revolve around that of the lady. As his plays support Catholic doctrine, they tacitly affirm the Church's teachings about women's social roles and the mythology of the Virgin Mary and Eve, a damaging binary that pretends to categorize women as either saints or sinners. Further, Calderón's allegiance to the king and to social order, chiefly manifested by his treatment of honor, may well result in the degradation of his female characters, be they innocent or guilty. In their affirmation of the supremacy of reason over emotion, as well as the use of female characters to undermine or test such rational orders, Calderón's texts seem to posit a relationship between passion and the feminine and logic and the masculine, with an emphasis on erasing the former. Even when characters such as Rosaura or Isabel attempt to uphold the honor code, their actions must be confirmed by official (male) representatives of social power. Nevertheless, this potential erasure in Calderón's plays is incomplete, as feminist scholars are discovering in their analyses of the significant, though sometimes faint, traces of the feminine, all too often at the margins of Calderonian drama. *See also* Sexuality in the Golden Age: Fray Manuel de Guerra y Ribera (seventeenth century).

Work by

Four Comedies by Pedro Calderón de la Barca. Trans. K. Muir and Ann L. Mackenzie. Lexington: UP of Kentucky, 1980.

Life Is a Dream. Trans. E. Honig. New York: Hill and Wang, 1970.

Obras completas. Ed. Angel Valbuena Briones. Madrid: Aguilar, 1973.

Work about

Dunn, Peter N. "Honor and the Christian Background in Calderón." *Bulletin Hispanique* 17 (1960): 75–105.

Durán, Manuel, and Roberto González Echeverría. *Calderón y la crítica: Historia y antología*. Madrid: Gredos, 1976.

Ganelin, Charles, and Howard Mancing, eds. *The Golden Age Comedia: Text, Theory and Performance*. West Lafayette: Purdue UP, 1994.

Hildner, David Jonathan. *Reason and the Passions in the Comedias of Calderón*. Amsterdam: Benjamins, 1982.

McKendrick, Melveena M. *Woman and Society in the Spanish Drama of the Golden Age: A Study of the Mujer Varonil*. Cambridge: Cambridge UP, 1974.

Salstead, M.L. *The Presentation of Women in Spanish Golden Age Literature: An Annotated Bibliography*. Boston: G.K. Hall, 1980.

Stoll, Anita K., and Dawn L. Smith, eds. *The Perception of Women in Spanish Theater of the Golden Age*. Lewisburg, PA: Bucknell UP, 1991.

Wiltrout, Ann E. "Murder Victim, Redeemer, Ethereal Sprite: Women in Four Plays by Calderón de la Barca." *Hispanófila* (1979): 103–120.

Mindy Badía

Calvo de Aguilar, Isabel (1916–)

Author of short stories, novels, and articles, Isabel Calvo de Aguilar was born in a traditional family; her father was a Navy physician, and she herself married a military officer. She belonged to women's voluntary organizations such as Damas de la Cruz Roja y de Sanidad Militar, and she founded and presided for six years over the Asociación de Escritoras Españolas. Her work was recognized with several Portuguese and Italian honorable mentions, and she won the Costa del Sol journalism prize in Portugal.

Calvo de Aguilar is best known for her *Antología biográfica de escritoras españolas* (1954; Biographical Anthology of Spanish Women Writers), a volume written with the intention of dispelling the opinion that Spain had no important contemporary women writers. In addition to her anthology she wrote short stories and several novels, published within a very short period of time, the most important being *Doce sarcófagos de oro* (1951? Twelve Gold Sarcophagi), *El misterio del palacio chino* (1951; The Mystery of the Chinese Palace), *La danzarina inmóvil* (1954; The Motionless Dancer), and *La isla de los siete pecados* (1952; The Isle of Seven Sins). Other novels are *El monje de los Balcanes* (n.d.; The Monk from the Balkans) and *El numismático* (n.d., The Numismatist).

Calvo's novels combine suspense, mystery, and imagination and often include exotic places. There are psychological observations in her characters and an inclination to incorporate pathologic elements. *Doce sarcófagos de oro* combines the reality of known places—Granada—with elements of fantasy reminiscent of the *Arabian Nights* and a pseudohistoricism with references to medieval history, bibliographic data, and an anachronistic passing mention of Maximilian and Charlotte, emperor and empress of Mexico. The female character embodies the traditional stereotype of a feminine figure, who is romantic and capricious and whose essence of femininity is based on modesty and convention, where weakness does not exclude shrewdness. *La danzarina inmóvil* also combines mystery and the Gothic novel. Female characters are portrayed as fragile, infirm, and incapable of escaping a destiny that traps them. Calvo de Aguilar calls this work a mystery and a love story. Critics have compared her work to Simenon's, and some have called her an Agatha Christie of Spain.

Calvo de Aguilar's writings belong to the feminine phase advocated by critic Elaine Showalter that presupposes imitation and internalization of the prevailing modes of the dominant tradition. However, there is an incipient feminist conscience in Calvo that is conciliatory with codes of the established canon, manifested in her assertion in *La danzarina inmóvil* that a female can be a very good writer and also be adept in the use of the thimble. The motivation for writing her *Antología* clearly signifies a stand toward feminism.

Work by

Antología biográfica de autoras españolas. Madrid; Biblioteca Nueva, 1954.

La danzarina inmóvil. Madrid: Rumbos, 1954.
Doce sarcófagos de oro. Madrid: Escelicer, 1951?
El misterio del palacio chino. Madrid: Reus, 1951.

Work about

Bleiberg, Germán, Maureen Ihrie and Janet Pérez. *Dictionary of the Literature of the Iberian Peninsula*. 2 vols. Westport, CT: Greenwood P, 1993.

Galerstein, Carolyn L., and Kathleen McNerney, eds. *Women Writers of Spain. An Annotated Bio-Bibliographical Guide*. Westport, CT: Greenwood P, 1986.

Pilar Sáenz

Campo Alange, Condesa de (1902–1986)

María de los Reyes Laffitte y Pérez del Pulgar, better known as Condesa de Campo Alange, is one of the major Spanish gender scholars of the postwar period (1939–1975). Her activity reached well into democratic Spain from 1961 to 1987 through the Women's Studies Sociology Seminar (SESM) founded by her. She began her work as a theorist of feminism with the lesser-known *La secreta guerra de los sexos* (1948; The Secret War between the Sexes) and *La mujer como mito y como ser humano* (1961; Woman as Myth and as Human Being) and continued as a historian with the widely read *La mujer en España. Cien años de su historia, 1860–1960* (1964; Woman in Spain: One Hundred Years of History, 1860–1960), together with a biography of the first Spanish feminist, *Concepción *Arenal, 1820–1893* (1973). She also became a sociologist as director of the Women's Studies Seminar. Laffitte's scholarly work started rather late, when she was in her forties. Her childhood, adolescence, and early adulthood groomed her to be an aristocrat strongly linked to traditional values. The advent of the Second Republic (1931), however, changed her perspective, and as a consequence, she accompanied her husband, the count of Campo Alange, to exile in Paris until 1934 and thereafter in their Biarritz home, near the Spanish border. The family returned to Madrid at the end of the Civil War in 1940, and at that point, Laffitte entered the rarefied Spanish intellectual scene.

Laffitte wrote two books of personal recollections. The first, *Mi niñez y su mundo* (1954; My Childhood and Its World), published when she was 54, is a portrayal of her childhood that offers valuable insights for understanding the later emergence of a feminist writer. The second, *Mi atardecer entre dos mundos* (1981; My Sunset between Two Worlds), was written when she was 75 and deals with her adult years but also provides interesting information about her adolescence and early youth. The link connecting an aristocratic Sevillian and a feminist intellectual is found in the inquisitive, courageous little girl who climbed orange trees and fought and killed a large lizard that attacked her; a little girl curious about things surrounding her. She did not attend school; her education, directed by a nanny, depended on everyday experiences and her creative attitude toward toys, pets, songs, and random readings. At age 12, nevertheless, she consciously but unwillingly gave up her drive to learn and her natural creativity, making room for the conventional behavior expected of an upper-class young Seville woman. Two turning points in the first part of *Mi atardecer entre dos mundos* indicate her future career. The first one is her wedding night when she discovers women's assigned sexual role as rape victims of male voracity. The second incident takes place upon presentation of her first child to the Church. She was outraged when not allowed to enter the temple until she was "purified," unlike her husband who required no such purification.

Nevertheless, it took creation of a Spanish Republic and a departure from Spain for her to become an independent woman. Laffitte seemed to know little about the debate for women's franchise in Spain in the 1910s and 1920s; she was, instead, introduced to the queen as a Grandee of Spain. Her French exile experience afforded her private space and time, circumstances she used to attend art school and become acquainted with painting. In that study, she discovered a great woman painter who served as a model, an ideal; thereby she also discovered herself. Her first book was the biography of Spanish painter María Blanchard (1881–1932). It was 1939, and with France preparing for World War II, Laffitte and her family returned to postwar Spain.

Back in Madrid she began her research on the life of Blanchard, not even realizing that her subject's death had been mourned and her work celebrated in the Madrid Ateneo in 1932 by Clara *Campoamor (1888–1972) and other Republican feminists. She wrote her manuscript with the fervor of a convert. When she found that publishers had no interest in a woman painter, and suggested that she write about Goya instead, she decided to finance the book herself. Signed under her aristocratic title, the book was well received and opened doors to intellectual circles of the early 1940s, which were led by people who had not left in exile and thus recalled the prewar vanguard. Eugenio d'Ors (1881–1954) headed this cultural elite that had managed to survive, despite the pervading ideological supremacy of the Church and the nationalist party, Falange. La Academia Breve de las Artes was founded by Enrique Llosent, husband of feminist writer Mercedes *Fórmica (1918–). The Academy's president, whose role was to keep innovative trends alive, was Eugenio d'Ors, and he invited Laffitte to join. She accepted and was the only woman among 10 men.

At this time Laffitte decided to write on the topic that had been, on and off, a constant preoccupation in her life; the result was *La secreta guerra de los sexos*. A product of her readings in history and anthropology, and her own experience of constant crashes against the gender wall, the title came from German philosopher Oswald Spengler (1880–1936), and the word *sex* became an issue in itself. Produced by Revista de Occidente publishing house in 1948 (almost a year before de *Beauvoir's *The Second Sex*), publisher José Ortega Spotorno accepted the manuscript and its title on condition that she continue to sign her name as Countess of Campo Alange rather than as María Laffitte, the name she would have preferred. The reception of the book was rather warm, with two more editions (1950 and 1958), but its role in feminist thought went unnoticed even to this day. The Women's Studies Sociology Seminar later characterized its reception as amazing many, prompting enthusiasm and inspiration among a male and female elite and being silenced by the traditional, reactionary majority. Even her mentor, d'Ors, opposed her writing the book and tried to bribe her to forget the topic with the promise that he would make her "the best art critic in Spain." She declined, being utterly convinced that in Madrid of the 1940s the topic of women's social predicament, although nothing new, needed revision—the time was right.

Following contemporary findings in anthropological and historical research, the book explores essential aspects of feminist and gender studies such as equality and difference, myth and maternity. Laffitte touches myriad aspects of Western culture to find hidden explanations of female invisibility in its construction. For this work she must be given first place among Spanish postwar feminists, and she also deserves recognition as a pioneer of international modern feminism. Her contributions open avenues of thought similar to those found in de Beauvoir's *The Second Sex*. Peculiar Spanish circumstances caused her work to be ignored or rejected by militant postwar feminists, most of whom were working within Marxist parameters. Her eclectic approach is made clear in the book's prologue, where she declares the work to be an incomplete approach to what she considers the origin of most evils that presently stalk society, namely, the almost total annihilation of the "feminine."

Laffitte considers feminism's emergence a true revolution provoked by women's dissatisfaction. In the essay "What Is Feminine" she asks whether woman has ever, at any time, been able to be what she wanted. She observes that since nothing was really given willingly to women, the feminist fight was essential; she further comments that if a woman's hand were really too white or too weak, it could never have opened so many heavy, closed doors. Laffitte probes questions regarding the ownership of culture and woman's identity as a human being. Her thesis is that women in the past who wanted to enter the cultural or scientific world either had to disguise themselves as men or suffer being considered abnormal sharers of masculine characteristics. Laffitte centers her discussion upon Concepción *Arenal (1820–1893) who, in order to attend the university, was forced to adopt masculine dress. For Laffitte, Arenal is a heroic fighter who in spite of her disguise possessed one of the strongest motherly powers ever known. Laffitte also recognizes that there were women who rejected their own sex. Laffitte sees that this second position has been more easily accepted by the patriarchy that allows exceptions to those women who deserted other women, for they become "rare exceptions" that confirm the traditional gender rule of women's innate inferiority. She goes on to analyze gender stereotypes that have prevailed historically, quoting frequently from Fray Luis de *León's *La perfecta casada* (1583) in which "feminine" stands for a lack of intellectual strength and discipline, oscillating will, that which is superficial, insignificant, routine, fearful, dilettantelike, and antieconomic. Conversely, argues Laffitte, men attribute to themselves all positive qualities and yet brand as manlike and pathological any woman who, possessing "so-called male attributes," would use them rather than suppress them as shameful.

Working with a bibliography still valid in studies of the origin of social and family structures, one of Laffitte's objectives is to identify traces left on culture by women. Using the classic interpretation of Joan Jacobus Bachofen's *Matriarchy* (1861), she is attracted to Greek works such as Aeschylus's *The Orestiade*, which (as many current feminists also think) offers vestiges of the transition from old matriarchal to modern patriarchal structures. This tragedy illustrates the step that initiates submission of the female when Apollus exonerates Orestes from his crime by saying that it is not the mother who engenders what is called her son. The concept came from Bachofen, but Laffitte (precociously so for postwar feminism) considers it an essential one for understanding the historical and anthropological evolution of women. She also points out that Bachofen provided the groundwork for later studies by P. Krische and Henry Lewis Morgan, who in turn were essential to Marxist approaches to gender and family as seen in Auguste Bebel's *Women and Socialism* (1883) and Frederick Engels's *The Origin of Family* (1884).

Laffitte realized that much research useful for advancing gender interpretations had been carried out in archeological studies, comparative ethnology, and particularly modern anthropology. For instance, after Levi Bruhl's (1857–1939) theories, a perspective is offered on women's contributions to culture as soothsayers, mediators between the divine and the unknown. Laffitte is interested as well in the evolution of women under the patriarchy, and following John Lubbock, Levi Bruhl, and Gaston Richard from a sociological and historical stance, she underscores the importance of the institution of the dowry as protection given by father to daughter instead of as purchase of the wife/wives. She sees that patriarchy, once settled, is to this day the site of male dominance and subjugation of women. Throughout the work, Laffitte touches questions of enduring concern to feminist and gender theories: motherhood, medieval concepts of femininity, love, myths and symbols, traditional feminine power. These essays comprise an early, valuable study of gender that deserves to occupy a position among world classics.

La mujer como mito y como ser humano (1961) consists of five articles with perspectives ranging from the anthropological and biological to the philosophical, literary, sociological, and artistic. Staying abreast of current research, Laffitte refers to Merleau-Ponti, Simone de *Beauvoir, Teilhard de Chardin, Margaret Mead, Julian Huxley, and F.J.J. Buytendijk. Once again, the common denominator for the articles is that culture as it is known does not allow for knowledge of what truly defines women. If, according to Merleau Ponti, man is in the process of permanent self-creation, one's lifestyle can impress new characteristics upon the person, and since biological findings confirm that a vital project is enough to modify hormonal secretions, then what we know as woman is an answer to constraints set by a patriarchal society. For instance, while men have double the number of male versus female hormones, women have over 40 to 50 times more female than male hormones. The disproportion is not "natural" but acquired and apparently results from the age-old acceptance of sexist concepts forced upon women. Women, Laffitte argues, are very similar to men but have been trained to be dependent, illiterate, and irresponsible. If social environment produces a certain type of individual, we don't really know what woman is. Laffitte thus embraces Dutch biologist Buytendijk's concept of human plasticity to explain the absence of women from the historical project, and she concludes that women, like dinosaurs, disappear for lack of brains. In women's place is the feminine human being, useless, unsatisfied, perplexed. Placing much confidence in science and very little in culture, Laffitte believes that if Margaret Mead's findings in New Guinea are set within broad limits, it is clear that anything can be achieved by either men or women. She concludes that the man-woman couple is the authentic human being, but this truth has been forgotten for millennia.

On the contemporary cultural scene, Laffitte refutes Ortega y Gasset's "For a History of Love" (in *Studies on Love*, 1927) on the role that women play in Plato's *Banquet*. According to Ortega the only woman who has any role in this first essay about love is Aspasia, who, because she has a man's knowledge, has become masculine. For Laffitte, however, Aspasia is totally feminine because, like all women of her class (*hetairas*), she is free, exquisitely educated, and close to Pericles, her adviser and friend. What is more, Ortega does not even mention Diotima, teacher of Socrates, through whom he defines love. As Ortega continues his account of love, in "Notes on Courtly Love," Laffitte finds another fallacy, that real women have nothing to do with the fantasies that men dream about, which are sentimental fictions of love that hide an underlying lack. Men have again maintained a monopoly on the configuration of love, pushing women aside, out of all possibility of action. As for romantic love, she agrees with Ortega that it is a lie; the difference between them is that what lies behind the fallacy can either be another fallacy or an honest approach between two persons. For Laffitte, if it is another fallacy, as in the case of a society that has caused women to embrace Jacinto *Benavente's Dominica of *Señora ama* (1908) and to reject Henrik Ibsen's Nora of *A Doll's House* (1879), then women will be condemned to assume the role of second-class citizens.

Male conceptions of women from an artistic stance are also elucidated in Laffitte's analysis of painter José Gutiérrez Solana's (1886–1945) work. While women are obsessively the subjects of his paintings, they always appear void of real entity; instead, they are seen through carnivallike stereotypes men have devised for them. Laffitte detects three such categories in his work: the prostitute who embodies fear of sex by men and is a grotesque representation of venereal dangers; the *destrozona* (female destroyer), which is a mixture of bestiality and witchcraft representing fear of symbolic feminine power and caricaturing feminine morphology (the mask bearer is always a big man disguised as woman). Finally, there are mannequins, which represent fear of women's autonomy and intelligence.

Laffitte courageously refuted several other Spanish intellectuals who approached the topic of gender from a masculine perspective: Fray Luis de León (*The Perfect Wife*), Gregorio Marañón (*Three Essays on Sexuality*, 1926), and Roberto Novoa Santos (*Woman, Our Sixth Sense*, 1928). She also took into account the works of Jerónimo *Feijóo (1676–1764), Concepción Arenal, Santiago Ramón y Cajal (1851–1934), Margarita *Nelken (1896–1968), and Pilar Oñate. She provided an insightful analysis of patriarchy, and cultural criticism that places her in the vanguard of Spanish feminist thought (among philosophers such as Celia Amorós or historians such as María Remedios *Rivera Garretas) and of international feminism, in the company of Hélène Cixous, Luce Irigaray, Susan Gubar and Sandra Gilbert, and Elaine Showalter.

The last chapter of *La mujer como mito* deals with the situation of contemporary Spanish women. As a consequence of the Civil War, in the 1940s many were either widows or single after the death of 1 million men. These mature women were thrown utterly unprepared into decision-making situations, while younger women followed the trend toward internationalization of uses and customs imposed mostly through the cinema. For Laffitte, women were freely given the same privileges as men, with the difference that they were not ready for it. Laffitte fails to acknowledge that before the war there had been a strong feminist debate promoted by women activists, even though she recognizes that Franco's restoration of the 1889 Civil Code was a brutal setback and that in spite of an apparent autonomy, women had no real prospects professionally, due to the misogynist atmosphere and misogynist legislation. Her research for subsequent works better acquainted her with both the past and the present of her compatriots.

Laffitte was commissioned by Aguilar publishers to write her best-known work, *La mujer en España. Cien años de su historia* (1964; Women in Spain: One Hundred Years of Their History). This study covers Spanish women's emancipation in comprehensive fashion for the first time. Ironically, the year of its publication coincided with the celebration of 25 years of Franco's regime. At this time the general perception was that women in Spain were fairly independent, modern, and integrated into international trends, making feminism and vindication appear unreal. In her prologue Laffitte passes judgment on Spanish feminism and in a way creates anticipation, but the book does not give adequate recognition to previous women and men who consistently engaged in the franchise of women. She identifies and introduces these men and women to her reader but then observes that Spain experienced nothing comparable to the aggressive, heroic impulse of the British suffragettes, for Spanish feminism never became a movement and always possessed a furtive character, since conformity was the dominant trait of its women. Yet the entire book refutes such a stance. This lack of clear appreciation of Spanish women's achievement has been traditionally shared or quoted by later feminists such as Lidia *Falcón, Maria Aurèlia *Capmany, Imelda Navajo, and even Geraldine Scanlon, all of whom assert that in Spain there was no true feminist debate. Laffitte reiterates that postwar women had been given *the gift* of a progressive history, and she does not emphasize the fight and achievements of her predecessors.

Thus, for Laffitte in the 1950s, Spanish women were quite passive compared to women in other societies who underwent sharp identity crises. Even though the book deals with groundbreaking authors such as Emilia *Pardo Bazán, Concepción *Sáiz, Adolfo Posada, Margarita *Nelken, María Martínez Sierra, and Carmen de *Burgos, it maintains a very conservative approach, based on peace, evolution, and progress. The book does not quite denounce the setback that the postwar entailed. In the conclusion, after 385 pages of exciting data and constant discoveries, Laffitte fails to see that during the postwar period total regression was made impossible due to the advances of the first third of the century; even if women's legal status was reversed with the restoration of the 1889 Civil Code, regarding education and social status, some achievements were irreversible.

Curiously, her biography makes very little reference to *La mujer en España*. The most relevant one is the sense of surprise and delight, as well as discomfort, during the research process. It is clear that in spite of the fact that she encountered unexpected vitality, she also found material that was difficult from a political perspective. But she did not voice an opinion. She accumulated data but failed to analyze or draw conclusions from it. Paradoxically, for a book on which she probably labored more than any other, it does not leave her imprint as a feminist in the same way her two previous works did. Perhaps we can find an explanation in the fact that the book was commissioned for celebration of 25 years of Franco's rule, and she never felt real ownership of it. Also, in spite of her feminism, Laffitte was looking at past situations from the sheltered perspective of an intellectual aristocrat of the Spanish 1960s, one who had gone into exile when other women were at the peak of their struggles and achievements. This docile attitude probably shocked young radical feminists of the late postwar period and alienated her from the very militant feminist groups that emerged after 1974.

On the other hand, Laffitte founded the Women's Studies Sociology Seminar in 1961, just as she was writing *La mujer en España*. The seminar set as its mission a scientific approach to the feminist question touching all of society: education, family, work, politics. At the time this Seminar was the only legally constituted feminist group, and it had as its site Laffitte's home; it met weekly to study specific topics concerning women's issues. The members were a permanent team of professionals invited by Laffitte: Lilí Alvarez, Concha Borreguero, Elena Catena, Consuelo de la Gándara, María de Salas, and Pura de Salas. The team worked on specific aspects of women's studies, conducted intensive research, and asked experts (among them several feminists, particularly after the arrival of democracy) to contribute papers or colloquia for the group. Several papers and articles were written, besides the following books: *Habla la mujer. Juventud femenina actual* (1967; Woman Speaks. Today's Young Women); *Mujer y aceleración histórica* (1970; Woman and Historical Acceleration); *Diagnosis sobre el amor y el sexo* (1977; Diagnosis of Love and Sex); and *La mujer española: De la tradición a la modernidad, (1960–1980)* (1986; Spanish Women: From Tradition to Modernity, 1960–1980). The seminar continued for some time after Laffitte retired, although she continued as its honorary president. It was dissolved in 1987, after 25 years of activity. It would appear, nevertheless, that by the time she founded SESM her anger as a woman had disappeared. She was more interested in objective, documented analyses about the essence of women.

Comparing this eclectic thrust to the activism of the feminist groups that surfaced during the transition to the democracy, the silence or hostility shown by them toward Laffitte can be understood. To this day Laffitte's work is practically ignored or even unknown by Spanish feminists. Nevertheless, the material uncovered reveals a much more complex situation, and Maria Laffitte is by right the first feminist of the postwar period, granting that her struggle was intellectual and not political. Her gender inquiries were not prompted by a specific social situation; they were hermeneutic and universal, more philosophical than militant, and for that reason, she did not quite perceive the revolution in Spain, only the evolution. Perhaps for this reason she was not duly acknowledged by younger militants of the 1970s and 1980s. Similar to what happened to her, there was a complete "generation gap," a kind of fracture, a constant reinventing of the wheel by Spanish feminism that now appears to have been definitively overcome. See also Feminism in Spain: 1900–2000; Short Fiction by Women Writers: 1900–1975.

Work by

Concepción Arenal (1820–1893). Estudio biográfico documental. Madrid: Revista de Occidente, 1973.
Diagnosis sobre el amor y el sexo. Barcelona: Plaza y Janés, 1977.
Habla la mujer. Juventud femenina actual. Madrid: Edicusa, 1967.
María Blanchard, Biografía crítica. Madrid: n.p., 1944.
Mi atardecer entre dos mundos: Recuerdos y cavilaciones. Madrid: Planeta, 1983.
Mi niñez y su mundo. Ed. and intro. María de Salas Larrazabal. Madrid: Castalia, 1990.
La mujer como mito y como ser humano. Madrid: Taurus, 1961.
La mujer en España. Cien años de su historia, 1860–1960. Madrid: Aguilar, 1964.
La mujer española: De la tradición a la modernidad, 1960–1980. Madrid: Tecnos, 1986.
Mujer y aceleración histórica. Madrid: Edicusa, 1970.
La secreta guerra de los sexos. Madrid: Revista de Occidente, 1948.

Work about

Salas Larrazábal, María de. "Introducción." Mi niñez y su mundo, by María Campo Alange. Madrid: Castalia, 1990. 7–42.

María Elena Bravo

Campoamor, Clara (1888–1972)

This feminist lawyer and head figure of the Spanish suffragists is of utmost importance to the Spanish political scene during the 1920s and 1930s. She symbolizes the social change made possible for women through education and different organizations that began to appear in the 1870s. Campoamor rose from the position of seamstress to become a lawyer who fought for and won women's suffrage. As a member of the commission in charge of drafting the 1931 Republican Constitution, she helped place women on the same legal level as men, making possible a kind of legislation among the most progressive in the world. Her independent political views made her one of many political casualties that strict party militancy imposed on its members during the Second Spanish Republic. And she embodies the exiled politician who could not return to Spain after the war despite repeated attempts to do so. It is clear that Campoamor paid dearly for her ideals; it is also clear that to this day she has not yet been fully vindicated by Spanish feminism.

In 1981 Concha Fagoaga and Paloma Saavedra edited her work Mi pecado mortal. El voto femenino y yo (1936; My Mortal Sin. Women's Suffrage and I) as part of the fiftieth-anniversary celebration of women's vote. In the same year, they also published the only biography to date, Clara Campoamor. La sufragista española. The postwar period was notorious for a collective amnesia that only recently has begun to be conquered. Even in the prologue to her biography, the Sub-Director General for Women Affairs of the Ministry of Culture repeats assumed generalizations about Spanish feminism, stating that women's *suffrage in Spain was granted more as a gracious concession than as the privilege won by repeated petitions, thereby denying Campoamor's specific contribution to suffrage, as well as the contributions of an entire generation of women.

Two books written by Campoamor provide autobiographical data: Mi pecado mortal (My Mortal Sin) and one published in French, La revolution espagnole vue par une republicaine (1937; The Spanish Revolution as Seen by a Republican Woman). In a letter written to Consuelo Bergés, one of the feminists who stayed in Spain after the war, Campoamor described a book of memoirs she was writing in 1957, but the manuscript was never found. Campoamor was born in Madrid to a working-class family where women had consistently worked. Her grandmother, Clara Martínez, was a janitor/doorkeeper and her mother, Pilar Rodríguez, a seamstress. Her father, Manuel Campoamor, worked in the administration of a newspaper, dying when Campoamor was 10. She abandoned formal studies and began to work at 13, first helping her mother with the seamstress business, then as a salesperson in the shop. She continued her education on her own, and at 21, in 1909, she obtained a position as telegraph operator in the Spanish Post Office and Telegraph Organization through a national examination. Sent to San Sebastián, she continued to work and study, and in 1914 she returned to Madrid, having won yet another position in the Spanish administration as a shorthand and typing teacher in the School for Adult Women of the Ministry of Public Instruction.

Back in Madrid teaching, she entered the cultural and political scene through a second job as secretary for the liberal newspaper *Tribuna*. Thus she continued to be immersed in the workforce from a feminist perspective, never losing sight of the real working woman. She rejected the temptation to join the privileged ranks of men as a glorious exception to her gender—rejecting the idea of a superior, especially deserving female, so outstanding, she is actually allowed to participate in male affairs. Like other women of the period, she felt the call to fight for equal rights. At this time she decided to further her studies to the highest level and registered to complete a secondary education degree, then study law at the university. During these years of study, she was also intensely engaged in feminist projects such as the fight against legal prostitution, along with two notorious socialist women, María Martínez Sierra (1874–1974; pen name María Lejárraga) and Elisa Soriano. She registered at the University of Madrid School of Law and, while studying, continued to work as teacher in the School for Women, secretary of *La Tribuna*, and also in another job as typist for the Ministry of Public Instruction. At the same time she wrote for widely read papers, such as Ortega y Gasset's (1883–1955) *El Sol*. Above all, she continued her commitment to the advancement of women through participation in militant feminist associations such as the Juventud Universitaria Femenina de Madrid (Madrid's University Women Association) and Casas de Pueblo (Houses for the People).

Campoamor received her law degree in December 1924 when she was 36. While continuing her teaching duties, she immediately opened an office and began to work on behalf of women. One of her specialties was defending the vulnerability of married women. The speech she gave when she was admitted to the Academy of Juridical Sciences discussed this particular problem. Entitled "The New Woman before Law," using a feminist stance she defied Marañón's theories on women's inadequacies concerning work. Again in 1928 she gave a lecture in the Academy on this topic, recommending that women endorse a marriage contract that would insure their legal solvency. Both these works are published in *El derecho de la mujer*. Another field of expertise for Campoamor was paternity investigation. In 1926 she opposed the future president of the Republic, Niceto Alcalá Zamora, before the Supreme Court on this issue. She was appointed as professor of the Academy of Juridical Sciences in 1928. Campoamor was also an active member of the Colegio Oficial de Abogados where she requested admission the same day she got her law degree.

Campoamor frequently worked with other feminist fighters from all areas of professional life, including lawyers (Matilde Huici, Concha Peña, Victoria *Kent), writers (María Martínez Sierra and Isabel Oyarzábal), educators (María de *Maeztu), physicians (Elisa Soriano), and many university women affiliated with the Juventud Universitaria Femenina, and the women workers who were also her students in the School for Adults and in the Casas del Pueblo, where she lectured. Her public work was closely followed by the feminist publication *La voz de la mujer*. At the same time Campoamor never lost sight of women's situation on the international front. In 1928 she and three other European lawyers founded the International Federation of Women Lawyers (in Paris), which still exists. After approval of the divorce laws, which she helped draft as a member of the commission charged with writing the 1931 Republican Constitution, she defended women in these kinds of litigation. She was offered, but declined to receive, the Gran Cruz de Alfonso XII for her outstanding performance. Being an active member of the Ateneo, she was offered a position on the board of directors by Primo de Rivera, which she likewise rejected. Campoamor considered herself a mouthpiece for women in general, as she said in her first speech before the Academy of Jurisprudence, and this was her real and only loyalty. All other party and political commitments held less importance. This loyalty to women brought her political isolation and made necessary her flight from the revenge-ridden Republican Madrid at the outset of the war in the summer of 1936.

The question of women's suffrage in Spain had long been on the table when Campoamor appeared on the political scene. In 1921, a decade before Campoamor's defense of women's franchise in the Parliament, after a campaign on behalf of suffrage La Liga Internacional de Mujeres Ibéricas e Iberoamericanas (led by Carmen de *Burgos) and the Cruzada de Mujeres gathered thousands of signatures in the streets and took them to President Allende Salazar. On April 12, 1924, women were granted the right to vote by Primo de Rivera, with the *exception* of married women and prostitutes. When the Asamblea Consultiva was appointed in 1927, 13 women were included, some of whom had been indirectly elected for municipal positions. After the triumph of the Republic, the question of women's suffrage was logically considered, and in 1931, a decree granted women the possibility of running for Congress despite the fact that they themselves were *not* allowed to vote. Campoamor joined the Radical Party slate and won a place in the Chamber with 52,731 votes, ahead of Victoria Kent, who belonged to the Partido Radical Socialista. Both represented Madrid. Socialist Party member Margarita *Nelken was also elected.

Even though the Radical Party, like the other republican parties, had in principle supported women's suffrage, the radicals, radical socialists, and Republican Action Party decided to oppose women's suffrage in June 1931. At this point, Campoamor chose to fight on her own, following no loyalty other than her own principles. Nelken, as a socialist, opposed granting the vote and did not attend the key sessions. Most socialists, the CEDA (Catholic Federation of Autonomous Right) and small republican Catalan and Galleguista nuclei were in favor of suffrage. Campoamor's eloquence and the strength of her arguments created tremendous tension in the debate. Women in the gallery followed it in support of Campoamor. Benita Asas Manterola, president of the Asociación Nacional de Mujeres Españolas, representing also the Agrupación Republicana Femenina, the Asociación Universitaria Femenina (to which Campoamor belonged), and the National Association of Spanish Women Physicians, distributed flyers supporting equal rights for women to chamber members. Eventually Kent and Campoamor fiercely confronted each other. For Kent, follower of her party's instructions, the time was wrong and the Republic would suffer with the gained strength of the right for which most women were expected to vote. For Campoamor the right to be free could not be denied in order to gain an ulterior benefit; for her, freedom is secured by its use. Forty votes made the difference, and Article 34 of the Constitution granting equal rights to men and women was approved with 161 in favor and 121 against.

What makes Campoamor's thoughts concerning feminism most compelling is the clarity of her principles and loyalty to her gender. She defended the vote by arguing that regardless of political consequences, women had as much a right to political opinions as men. She clarified repeatedly that feminism, far from denoting something extravagant, sexless and grotesque, really signified the complete realization of woman in all her capabilities, so that feminism should be called humanism. After the vote for women was won, she began to pay for this loyalty with increasing ostracism from all political venues. She founded and promoted the Unión Republicana Femenina to win women's votes for the Republic in the following elections of 1933. She was appointed part of the Spanish Delegation before the Society of Nations, and she continued to work fervently in divorce cases. Nevertheless, she lost her seat in the Parliament in the 1933 elections, won as it were, by the conservative parties. At this point she was appointed by radical Prime Minister Alejandro Lerroux to the position of Director General de Beneficencia but resigned when the intervention of the conservative CEDA was made quite apparent. In order to run for the elections of 1936, she tried to enter the electoral fight with the Frente Popular, representing her own group, Unión Republicana Femenina, but her application was rejected. In 1936 after the triumph of Frente Popular and the uprising of the military she left Madrid, expecting to return.

Campoamor arrived in Argentina from Paris where she had written a personal assessment of the political situation in Spain, published in French with the title *La revolution espagnole vue par une republicaine*. During her exile years in Buenos Aires, Campoamor wrote a biography of Concepción Arenal and another one of Sor Juana Inés de la Cruz (1651–1695). In the 1930s she had undertaken the task of erecting a monument in the Parque del Oeste to Arenal, which was inaugurated in 1934. The biography written in Argentina completed Campoamor's homage to the most outstanding woman in the history of Spanish feminism, a woman who, like herself, had been heroically lucid, independent, and loyal to her own ethical vision. Sor Juana, on the other hand, represents another woman toward whom Campoamor felt a notable kinship. The biography she wrote and her critical interpretations of Sor Juana's work by far predate any other feminist reading of this writer, so abundant in recent years. Campoamor's analysis shows profound understanding both of Sor Juana's passion for knowledge and of her fight to be allowed to write as a woman in *La respuesta a Sor Filotea*. Another aspect explored by Campoamor is Sor Juana's less-documented renunciation of humanistic ideals, forced by insurmountable moral pressure during the nun's last years, a period that Campoamor interprets as spent in torture and self-destruction. This perspective may be Campoamor's own identification with the Mexican feminist because of her own regrets and sense of loss following exile from Spain.

Campoamor wanted to return to Spain. She probably could not quite accept the fact that when she left Madrid in 1936, she exited the most important period of her life. She actually returned to the city of her passion for a few weeks during Christmas 1947 and again once after 1950, just before establishing residence in Lausanne. The conditions imposed upon her by the Franco regime made return impossible; as critic Fagoaga reports, she would have had to reveal names of freemason colleagues and abjure all past anticlerical statements or be incarcerated 12 years. While in Lausanne she tried to recover part of her energetic past. To friends she wrote that she was ready to found associations, give lectures, fight in debates. She missed the Spanish vitality of her prime as compared to the bland Swiss mode of the 1950s, where women's associations' meetings were irritatingly useless and boring. Only her ashes were repatriated for burial in Polloe cemetery in San Sebastián on May 17, 1972.

Clara Campoamor deserves a position among the most significant Spanish women. Even if her writings, her person, and her history have been erased from such iconography, all Spanish women have inherited the fruits of her idealistic, generous labor. Those fruits that other women, Campoamor companions, also struggled to secure have been nevertheless systematically credited to an abstract, self-generated "gracious concession." See also Feminism in Spain: 1900–2000.

Work by

Concepción Arenal. Buenos Aires: Losada, 1943.
El derecho de la mujer. Madrid: Beltrán, 1936.
La revolution espagnole vue par une republicaine. Paris: Plom, 1937.
Sor Juana Inés de la Cruz. Buenos Aires: Emecé, 1944.
El voto femenino y yo. Mi pecado mortal. Intro. Concha Fagoaga and Paloma Saavedra. Barcelona: LaSal, 1981.

Work about

Fagoaga, Concha and Paloma Saavedra. Clara Campoamor. La sufragista española. Madrid: Dirección General de Juventud y Promoción Social, 1981.

María Elena Bravo

Cancionero

See Isabel I, Queen of Castile: The Vision of the Queen in Converso Poetry (c. 1474–c. 1480)

Canelo Gutiérrez, Pureza (1946–)

Born in Moraleja (Cáceres) and educated to be a teacher, poet Pureza Canelo Gutiérrez has served as Head of Cultural Activities, Information and Attendance of Madrid's Universidad Autónoma. Her poetry has been supported by the Ministry of Culture (1982) and the March Foundation (1975) and has received prestigious awards such as the Premio Adonais (1970) and the Premio Juan Ramón Jiménez (1975). Gustavo Correa selected several of her poems for inclusion in his Antología de la poesía española (1900–1980), and her work has appeared in numerous other anthologies and has been translated to English, German, French, and Italian.

Canelo wrote her early collections, Celda verde (1971; Green Cell), Lugar común (1971; Commonplace), and El barco de agua (1974; The Water Boat), under the whimsical sign of a creacionista (creationist) aesthetic. With poems that burst into the preexisting realm of language, Canelo moves past the modernist achievements of her mentors, poets such as Federico *García Lorca and Gerardo Diego, to reconfigure the feminine subject and to privilege contradiction. At a decisive oedipal moment, the subject of the poem remains fragmented, resisting conventional conceptualizations of the feminine.

In Habitable (Primera poética) (1979; Habitable [First Poetics]), a reasoned treatise on poetry displaces the spontaneous monologue of Canelo's early verse. Yet the semiotic language, fragmented voice, and focus on artistic creation remain constant. No less difficult than her creacionista verse, Habitable inclines toward the recurrent symbolist trend followed by various poets of the 1970s generation. In Tendido verso (Segunda poética) (1986; Extended Verse [Second Poetics]), Canelo uses poetic prose to portray a nostalgic return to nature and to Moraleja, the place of her youth. These "love poems" are not unlike the allegorical poems of the Spanish mystics, but in this instance the Amada (Beloved) is not God but the word.

Pasión inédita (1990; Unpublished Passion) hones the essence of Canelo's verse into a definitive statement on poetry, love, and nature. Approached intuitively and passionately, the poems recall the mature works of Juan Ramón *Jiménez, to whom Canelo paid homage in Espacio de emoción (1981; Period of Emotion). Like Jiménez, Canelo views poetry as a path to the divine. In "De verdad oración" (True Prayer) she asks for help in believing that poetry is the one way to heaven. Here the style is more lucid and the concepts more humanized, but the lover, nonetheless, remains amorphous, signifying either another human being or poetry. Although Canelo has not allied herself to a feminist cause, her poetry remains an artifact of the feminine voice in formation. Of particular interest to feminists is the fact that her earliest poems evoke the voice of the young girl, rarely heard in Spanish literature.

Work by

El barco de agua. Madrid: Cultura Hispánica, 1974.
Celda verde. Madrid: Nacional, 1971.
Habitable (Primera poética). Madrid: Rialp, 1979.
Lugar común. Madrid: Adonais, 1971.
Pasión inédita. Madrid: Hiperión, 1990.
Tendido verso (Segunda poética). Madrid: Caballo Griego para la Poesía, 1986.

Work about

Brown, Bonnie M. "Entrevista con Pureza Canelo." *Anales de Literatura Española Contemporánea* 5 (1981): 267–270.
Hiriart, Rosario. "Pureza Canelo: Su entrega a la palabra." *Revista de Estudios Extremeños* 42 (1986): 585–593.
Janés, Clara, ed. *Pureza Canelo*. Madrid: Ministerio de Cultura, 1981.
Ugalde, Sharon Keefe. *Conversación y poemas. La nueva poesía femenina española en castellano*. Madrid: Siglo XXI de España, 1991. 95–110.

Kay Pritchett

Cantiga de amigo

A traditional song with female protagonist and voice, the earliest examples of the genre appeared in the south of Spain as *jarchas (refrains in Mozarabic Spanish at the end of Arabic or Hebrew poems), then flourished in Galician-Portuguese forms in the twelfth and thirteenth centuries and in Castilian forms in the Renaissance and Golden Age.

The early Galician-Portuguese *cantigas de amigo* have been preserved in three "songbooks" known as the *Cancionero de Ajuda, de la Vaticana*, and *Colocci Brancuti*. The lovesick female speaks of her beloved to her mother, to a girlfriend, to herself, or to the beloved himself and complains of his absence or tardiness in coming to see her or his having to leave her. In a few rare cases the voice will be that of a shepherd girl who speaks to the birds and animals about her loneliness. The popular tone of these songs is manifested in simple form with two or three lines of narrative repeated in parallel patterns, the elemental features of speaker/listener, the absence of spatial or temporal references, and the use of identical short refrains at the end of each strophe. Another example of the autochthonous nature of the *cantiga de amigo* is that the girl's love is always expressed in the most elemental terms of physical desire, without any kind of religious, parental, or socioeconomic restrictions.

The particular situation of the female voice is limited to only a handful of chthonic structures. The girl may be on a pilgrimage to meet her beloved at a hermitage, and he doesn't appear; she may be at a dance, in which case she urges her beloved to enjoy her presence; she may be at the window of her bedroom at dawn, calling for the man to enter her bed or to leave because the day approaches (a large group of songs known as *albas).

These female songs so popular in Galician-Portuguese songbooks of the Middle Ages were not incorporated into contemporary Castilian songbooks such as the *Cancionero de Baena*. They first appear in Spanish around 1450 as verses sung by shepherd girls in the *serranías* collected and reworked by Iñigo de Mendoza, Marqués de *Santillana (1398–1458). They then become integral parts of the many songbooks collected during the reign of *Isabel and Fernando (1474–1516), often with the music included. Most of the Castilian songs present the young girl speaking of her desires either to her mother (*madre*) or to the beloved himself (*amigo*). In the sixteenth century the situation expressed in the *cantiga de amigo* merges with the *villancico* (carol) form of an initial refrain (*glosa*) and a series of strophes elaborating the refrain. It then spreads to all the literary forms of the time and in particular the *comedia nueva* (new theater). Today, the *cantiga de amigo*, with its distinct female voice directed to her mother or the beloved expressing uninhibited sexual emotions, is an integral part of the *cante jondo* form of flamenco music popularized by Federico *García Lorca (1898–1936) and others.

Work

Frenk, Margit. *Corpus de la antigua lírica popular hispánica*. Madrid: Castalia, 1987.

Work about

Alvar, Carlos, and José Manuel Lucía Megías, eds. *La literatura en la época de Sancho IV*. Alcalá de Henares, Spain: U de Alcalá de Henares, 1996. Contains several articles.

Menéndez Pidal, Ramón. "La primitiva poesía lírica española." *Estudios literarios*. Madrid: Espasa-Calpe, 1938. 197–269.

Wright, Janice. "Nature and the 'Amiga' in the Galician Portuguese 'Cantigas de Amigo.'" *La CHISPA '89: Selected Proceedings*. Ed. Gilbert Paolini. New Orleans: Tulane U, 1989. 345–355.

David H. Darst

Capmany i Farnés, Maria Aurèlia (1918–1991)

As a novelist, playwright, and essayist, Maria Aurèlia Capmany was deeply concerned with the social condition of women, a theme she explored in most of her works and in articles she wrote for newspapers and magazines. Born in Barcelona in 1918, this daughter of Catalan folklorist Aureli Capmany was brought up in an intellectual and political environment that strongly affected her later life. Capmany received a liberal, progressive education at the Institut-Escola de la Generalitat and had just started to study philosophy at the Universidad Autónoma in Barcelona when the Civil War began in 1936.

Capmany taught at the university and other schools until 1960 when she decided to devote herself entirely to writing. During these years she consolidated her reputation as a leading feminist figure in Catalonia and all Spain and was very active politically. Her essays examine the behavior of women of different classes and their position within the women's movement: *De profesión mujer* (1970; Woman by Profession); *El feminismo ibérico* (1970; Iberian Feminism), an essay that denounces society's assimilation of dissident positions; *Carta abierta al macho ibérico* (1973; Open Letter to the Iberian Male), part of open letters by various authors to different Spanish groups and institutions; *El comportamiento amoroso de la mujer* (1974; The Amorous Behavior of Women); *Antifémina* (1977; Antifeminist). Capmany felt strongly that women cannot be passive when oppressed by a sexist society. Her writings challenge women to examine their behavior and roles.

The authors that influenced her most were modern writers such as James Joyce, Katherine Mansfield, and Virginia Woolf. Capmany addresses to Woolf the prologue of her narrative *Quim/Quimá* (1971) as a letter in which she admits to imitating Woolf's *Orlando*. Capmany's first published work, *Necessitem morir* (We Need to Die), dates from 1952. Her works, though, remained unpublished for years because of Francoist censorship of the Catalan language and culture. In 1948 she was awarded the Joanot Martorell Prize for *El cel no és transparent* (The Sky Is Not Clear), an epistolary novel that deals with the lives of two women and the destructive effects of the Civil War. In *Necessitem morir*, the main character, Georgina, is depicted as a woman who fails in life because of a traditional upbringing that makes it impossible for her to have a life of her own. Capmany's best-known novel, *Un lloc entre els morts* (1967; A Place among the Dead), which won the 1969 Sant Jordi Prize for the Novel in Catalan, strongly criticizes the men and women who belong to "bourgeois" society. Among her best works are *L'altra ciutat* (1955; The Other City); *Betúlia* (1956); *Tana o la felicitat* (1956; Tana or Happiness); *La pluja als vidres* (1963; Rain on the Windows); and *Vitrines de Amsterdam* (1970; Showcases of Amsterdam).

Capmany also wrote a number of plays, alone or in collaboration with other writers: *Tu i l'hipòcrita* (1959; You and the Hypocrite); *El desert dels dies* (1966; The Desert of the Days); with the historian Xavier Romeu, *Preguntes i respostes sobre la vida i la mort de Francesc Layret, advocat dels obrers de Catalunya* (1971; Questions and Answers about the Life and Death of Francesc Layret, Advocate of the Workers of Catalonia); and *L'alt rei Jaume* (1977; The Other King James); *Ca, barret!* (1984; Nonsense, Chapeau!), with Jaume Vidal Alcover. Capmany founded the Escola d'Art Dramátic Adriá Gual (School of Drama Adriá Gual) with Ricardo Salvat where she directed and acted.

She also wrote scripts for radio and television and was in the last years of her life Cultural Counselor for the City of Barcelona. *See also* Catalan Women Writers: A Brief History; Feminism in Spain: 1900–2000

Work by

La color més azul. Spanish trans. Carolina Roses. Barcelona: Planeta, 1984.

De profesión mujer. Esplugas Llobregat, Barcelona: Plaza y Janes, 1970.

El feminismo ibérico. Barcelona: Oikos-Tau, 1970.

Un lugar entre los muertos. Barcelona: Nova Terra, 1970.

Obra Completa. 4 vols. Barcelona: Nova Terra, 1974.

Work about

Marín, Marta. "Barcelona, geografía iniciativa." *Catalan Review* 7.2 (1993): 57–69.

Martí Olivella, Jaume. "Woman, History and Nation in the Works of Montserrat Roig and Maria Aurèlia Capmany." *Catalan Review* 7.2 (1993): 11–18.

May, Barbara Dale. "The Power Dynamics of Woman's Anger in Maria Aurèlia Capmany's 'La color más azul.'" *Letras Femeninas* 12.1–2 (1986): 103–113.

Pérez, Genaro. "La poética feminista del género noire: Pottecher, Ortiz y Capmany." *Explicación de Textos Literarios* 24.1–2 (1995–1996): 149–158.

Pérez, Janet. *Contemporary Women Writers of Spain.* Boston: Twayne, 1988.

———. "Maria Aurèlia Capmany's *Quim/Quima*; Apocalyptic and Millennial Context, Text and Subtext." *Catalan Review* 7.2 (1993): 91–103.

Soler i Marcet, Maria Lourdes. "Bibliography: Maria Aurèlia Capmany." *Catalan Review* 7.2 (1993): 215–219.

Nereida Segura-Rico

Cárcel de amor
See San Pedro, Diego de (fifteenth century)

Caro Mallén de Soto, Ana (1565?/1600?–1652?)

This Golden Age poet and playwright was praised by many of her contemporaries, including Alonso de Castillo Solórzano (1584–1648), Rodrigo Caro (1573–1647), Matos Fragoso (1508?–1689?), Luis Vélez de Guevara (1579–1644), and María de *Zayas y Sotomayor (1590–after 1647?). Yet she was virtually forgotten from the 1670s to the 1970s. In spite of recent critical interest, very little is still known about her life. Some believe that Ana Caro Mallén de Soto (d. 1652?) was born in the latter third of the sixteenth century (1565/1569), while others argue that her birth took place around 1596/1600. Her place of birth is also in doubt. Arguments have been made for Granada, Seville, and Utrera. Caro spent her early years in Seville, where she became known as a poet. Here she wrote accounts of religious festivals such as the *Relación . . . de las grandiosas fiestas . . . a los Santos Mártires del Japón* (1628; Account . . . of the Grand Festival . . . for the Sainted Martyrs of Japan) and the *Relación de la grandiosa fiesta, y octava, que en la iglesia parroquial de el glorioso san Miguel de la Ciudad de Sevilla, hizo don García Sarmiento de Sotomayor . . .* (1635; Account of the Grand Festival, and Octave Which Don García Sarmiento de Sotomayor Gave in the Parish Church of Glorious St. Michael in the City of Seville). Wanting to attend the festivities at the Palace of the Buen Retiro for the crowning of Ferdinand III of Hungary as king of the Romans (a prelude to his succession as emperor), she traveled to Madrid in 1637. On her return to Seville, Caro wrote an account of what transpired at the fiesta: *Contexto de las reales fiestas que se hizieron en el Palacio del Buen Retiro a la coronación del Rey de Romanos, y entrada en Madrid de la Señora Princesa de*

Cariñán en tres discursos (1637; Context of the Royal Festivities Celebrated in the Palace of the Buen Retiro for the Coronation of the Roman King and Princess Lady Cariñán's Arrival to Madrid in Three Essays). She dedicated the second part of this account to the count-duke of Olivares, thus showing her alignment with Philip IV's minister, who gathered around him a number of poets and architects to host ostentatious feasts for the king. Olivares used these festivities to dazzle the world, to exhibit the power and glory of the Spanish Empire, and to bolster his policies and the king's power. Indeed, Philip's minister was always ready to embrace poets from his native Seville and help them to gain fame at court. Knowing this, Caro strives to please the minister in her *Contexto*. Laudatory commonplaces abound in her text. She refers to Philip IV as the sun king and to his minister as a new Atlas.

During her visit to Madrid, Caro must have met María de Zayas since she writes some prefatory *Décimas* for Zayas's *Novelas amorosas y ejemplares* (1637), calling her a new Sappho. Castillo Solórzano, who also wrote prefatory verses to Zayas's volume, will later praise Zayas's *novelas* and Caro's account of the 1637 feast in his novel *La garduña de Sevilla* (1642). In 1639, Caro turns to the theater and writes a *loa sacramental* (short religious panegyric) for the Corpus Christi festivities. And in the early 1640s she is busy composing *autos sacramentales* (religious plays) for the *cabildo* (town council) of Seville. Both *La puerta de la Macarena* (1641; The Macarena Gate) and *La cuesta de Castilleja* (1642; The Slope of Castilleja) have been lost. Three other theatrical works by Caro are known today: a *Coloquio entre dos* (Colloquy between Two) and two plays, *El conde Partinuplés* (Count Partinuplés) and *Valor, agravio y mujer* (Valor, Insult, and Woman). Although she is said to have composed other plays, her fame today rests on these two works of uncertain date.

Valor, agravio y mujer strives to create wonderment through a series of astonishing situations. The play utilizes a typical *comedia* plot, that of the woman who, in order to vindicate her *honor, dresses as a man and searches for the lover who abandoned her. In the hands of a woman playwright, this motif acquires even greater significance since it allows her to depict the constrictive mores of society and to ascribe to the male character a fickleness often associated with woman. As one critic asserts, the notion of role-reversal is already apparent in the title since Golden Age society related valor to male behavior. Indeed, the valorous heroine of this play follows her lover to Flanders, where Spain is fighting to preserve its own honor. Here, Leonor disguised as Leonardo poses as a boastful and bellicose soldier in a way that satirizes male conventions. "Leonardo" asserts that "he" is in love with Leonor and wishes to kill the man who dishonored her. Thus, she creates her own stage where she can act out the role she has created and involve the fickle Don Juan in her schemes. Leonor thus represents the playwright who, through her imagination, can transform social perceptions. Duels in the night and intricate scenes of mistaken identities prove her control over this male-dominated genre, although for some critics Caro may be carrying theatricality to the limits of parody.

El conde Partinuplés is a spectacle play that could well have been performed at court. It uses the *Invisible Mistress plot and in particular the French chivalric romance, *Partonopeus de Blois* (which had been translated into Spanish), to develop the problematics and limits of woman's power in a patriarchal society. Here, Rosaura, princess of Constantinople, is given a deadline for choosing a marriage partner. But her decision must be made under the threat of a dire astrological prediction. If she does not choose properly, her future husband will most probably deceive her and destroy the kingdom. To test her chosen partner, she utilizes the plot of the Invisible Mistress. Partinuplés is taken to reside in an enchanted palace where he is provided with every comfort, but he is not allowed to gaze at his female jailer nor is he permitted to guess her identity. He is forever in the dark, controlling his curiosity and hoping for the time when she will release him from this injunction. Like Psyche in the classical myth, Partinuplés eventually fails to control his curiosity and takes a light in order to behold his beloved. In this reversal of roles, the woman is the beautiful Cupid, while the male is the one guilty of the "sin" of Psyche. When Partinuplés breaks his promise by lighting a candle, she understands him to be a threat to the empire. Disaster is averted by Aldora, the female magician, who represents the magical powers of playwriting and serves to foreground the creativity of woman. In the end, the humanity of woman's power triumphs over male curiosity and suspicion.

With style, imagination, and exuberance, Caro creates engagingly complex plots, exciting conflicts, and amazing dramatic situations. Clever manipulations of gender stereotypes and intriguing role reversals serve to problematize the role of women and men in society. Political contexts further enrich the texture of these plays that are beginning to emerge from undeserved oblivion.

Work by

El conde Partinuplés. Ed. Lola Luna. Kassel: Reichenberger, 1993.

Contexto de las reales fiestas que se hizieron en el Palacio del Buen Retiro a la coronación del Rey de Romanos, y entrada en Madrid de la Señora Princesa de Cariñán en tres discursos. Madrid: Imprenta del Reino, 1637; Facs. ed. Antonio Pérez y Gómez. Valencia: Tipografía Moderna, 1951.

Valor, agravio y mujer. Ed. Lola Luna. Madrid: Castalia, 1993.

Work about

De Armas, Frederick A. The Invisible Mistress: Aspects of Feminism and Fantasy in the Golden Age. Charlottesville: Biblioteca Siglo de Oro, 1976.

Lundelius, Ruth. "Ana Caro: Spanish Poet and Dramatist." Women Writers of the Seventeenth Century. Ed. Katharina M. Wilson and Frank J. Warnke. Athens: U of Georgia P, 1989. 228–250.

Ordóñez, Elizabeth. "The Woman and Her Text in the Works of María de Zayas and Ana Caro." Revista de Estudios Hispánicos 19 (1985): 3–15.

Soufas, Teresa S. "Ana Caro's Re-Evaluation of the Mujer Varonil and Her Theatrics in Valor, agravio y mujer." The Perception of Women in Spanish Theater of the Golden Age. Ed. Anita K. Stoll and Dawn L. Smith. Lewisburg, PA: Bucknell UP, 1991. 85–106.

Stroud, Matthew D. "La literatura y la mujer en el Barroco: Valor, agravio y mujer de Ana Caro." Actas del VIII Congreso de la Asociación Internacional de Hispanistas. Ed. David Kossoff et al. Providence: Brown U, 1983. 2:605–612.

Williamsen, Amy R. "Re-writing in the Margins: Caro's Valor, agravio y mujer as Challenge to the Dominant Discourse." Bulletin of the Comediantes 44 (1992): 21–30.

Frederick A. de Armas

Cartagena, Teresa de (c. 1420–after 1460?)

Afflicted with deafness as a child, Teresa de Cartagena was for that reason apparently shunned by her illustrious and aristocratic, learned converso (converted Jewish) family. Nonetheless, as Seidenspinner-Núñez notes, she must have received the same excellent education her siblings enjoyed and access to several family libraries. By 1453 she had professed as a nun, probably with the Franciscan order.

Two works by Cartagena have survived: Arboleda de los enfermos (n.d.; Grove of the Infirm) and Admiraçión operum Dey (n.d.; Admiration for the Work of God). The Arboleda narrates how physical illness or infirmities are better understood as opportunities for cultivating virtues and habits that may secure one's spiritual health. Surtz has shown how the Arboleda combines a commentary of Psalm 45:10 and Psalm 32:9 with the personal experiences of how deafness affected her. It circulated in manuscript form, receiving at least in part a negative reception as it violated the accepted practice that only men were capable of offering spiritual instruction. Her detractors deemed it entirely inappropriate for a woman to compose a spiritual text. In the Admiraçión Cartagena vigorously responds to her critics, attributing the text entirely to God's miraculous intervention but also indirectly defending the intellectual ability of women. She argues that male and female complement each other: Both are equally necessary parts of humankind and therefore equal in their humanity.

Although neither work challenges accepted gender roles, Cartagena does defend female intellect in each and questions the value of intellectual activity—the traditional male sphere. The *Admiraçión* was dedicated to the wife of poet Gómez Manrique, who may well have also been the "virtuous lady" to whom the *Arboleda* was dedicated. In her study of Cartagena's narrative voice, Seidenspinner-Núñez finds that in the course of composing the two essays Cartagena begins as an emasculated reader/writer but evolves to a self-conscious and critical reader/writer who ultimately is able to subvert patriarchal control and contemporary definitions of literary authority and authorship.

Work by

Arboleda de los enfermos. Admiraçión operum Dey. Ed. Lewis J. Hutton. Madrid: Anejos del Boletín de la Real Academia Española, 16. Madrid: Real Academia Española, 1967.

The Writings of Teresa de Cartagena. English trans., intro., notes, and essay Dayle Seidenspinner-Núñez. Rochester, NY: D.S. Brewer, 1998.

Work about

Ellis, Deborah S. "Unifying Imagery in the Works of Teresa de Cartagena: Home and the Dispossessed." *Journal of Hispanic Philology* 17.1 (1992): 43–53.

Surtz, Ronald E. "El llamado feminismo de Teresa de Cartagena." *Studia Hispanica Medievalia III.* Ed. Rosa E. Penna and María A. Rosarossa. Buenos Aires: Universidad Católica Argentina, 1993. 199–207.

Vicente García, Luis Miguel. "La defensa de la mujer como intelectual." *Mester* 18 (Fall 1989): 95–103.

Maureen Ihrie

Carvajal y Mendoza, Luisa de (1566–1614)

Few figures of seventeenth-century Spain can vie with Carvajal as a portrait of high drama and disturbing, zealous piety, documented in a rich panorama of autobiographical and historical texts by and about her. Singular Catholic missionary, expert Latinist, comparative theologian, and prolific writer, Carvajal accomplished all of her impressive life's work in the post-Tridentine period whose restrictive mandates may have dictated her formal self-expression but seem to have only fomented her activist vocation. Neither married nor a nun, Carvajal challenges present-day formulas about the limited roles and spaces of female activity in Early Modern Europe.

Carvajal was born into wealth and privilege in Jaraicejo, a small town in eastern Cáceres (Extremadura), and went with her family to León. Her mother, María Hurtado de Mendoza y Pacheco, and father, Francisco de Carvajal y Vargas, both died when she was 6. She was sent to live with a maternal aunt, María de Chacón, governess of Philip II's children in Madrid. As her aunt's charge, Carvajal spent four important years, until she was 10, in the household of Princess Juana de Austria, whose status as the only woman ever admitted to the Jesuits was at that time a well-kept secret but absolutely formative of Juana's strict, pious domain. The devout queen, Margarita de Austria, also visited her often. Carvajal grew up in her apartments, then attached to the Convent of the Descalzas Reales, which the princess had recently founded. Under the tutelage of her own abusive governess, Isabel de Ayllón, Carvajal was exercised in severe formalistic piety and the strictest of female propriety; at the same time she enjoyed the resources of the best-educated children in Spain, the royal offspring, and the support of Princess Juana herself.

In 1576, Carvajal was again struck a heavy blow when her aunt died suddenly, leaving the 10-year-old girl in the hands of an uncle, the important diplomat Francisco de Hurtado y Mendoza, marquis of Almazán. Carvajal lived with his family, often his wife and three children, on their various estates, learning Latin with his daughters and a very peculiar form of piety from the marquis himself. Luisa's penitential excesses, perhaps the response of a lonely child observing a string of family members die around her, doubtless called her to the marquis's attention. For whatever reason, he singled out his young niece as his own spiritual charge and exercised her in perverse, exaggerated piety, most notably reenactments of the Passion in which two servants were paid to undress, mortify, and physically abuse the adolescent girl in remote rooms of the mansion. Carvajal's letters relate a great deal of physical suffering. Similarly, her uncle had her kneel before him for several hours in his private apartments while he lectured and read from pious books. This and other excesses, the true extremes of which can only be imagined, produced in Carvajal an impeccably controlled will of iron, an exquisite familiarity with the theological texts of her day, and an obsessive esteem for sacrificial ethics, which played their contradictory natures out throughout her adult life.

In 1591, when Carvajal was 25, she obtained her uncle's permission to live apart from the family in the company of a few servants, enacting in a decidedly quixotic way the life of Catherine of Siena as described in her confessor's fourteenth-century *vita*, a book read by Carvajal and most religious women of her day. The next year both the marquis and his wife died, leaving Luisa, as she herself said, "free at last." She moved to Madrid and then to Valladolid with the court to supervise the lawsuit she filed to win rights to the sizable fortune left her in her father's will, a document whose execution was made difficult by her neither marrying nor taking the veil, the only possibilities provided for by her father. During these years in Madrid and Valladolid, Carvajal enacted social reversals that she continued throughout her life: While under the formal spiritual supervision of the Jesuits, she vowed obedience to an abusive, ignorant servant and began to mingle with the poor of the city, going so far as to beg for food with the truly needy at the portals of selected churches. Under these circumstances, her physical condition began to deteriorate, and she acquired the poor health that had become a hallmark of Catholic holy women centuries before. Between 1593 and 1598 she took four vows, of poverty, obedience, to pursue perfection, and finally the extraordinary promise to "pursue all avenues of martyrdom which are not repugnant to the laws of God."

Carvajal's vow of martyrdom proved to be an ironic door to self-realization, for it was probably this act of complete renunciation of her own life for that of God that convinced her superiors and her king to permit her to realize a vocation only dreamed of by many female religious women of her day: missionary work. In 1604 she made the Spiritual Exercises related to election and committed herself to go to England, where she believed she could best attain her heroic goal of dying for God. Persecution of Catholics by Anglicans was at a frenzied pitch at that time, and stories of martyred men, particularly Jesuits, had circulated around the Jesuit centers with which Carvajal was closely associated during the years she was formulating her plan. Willing her entire fortune to the Jesuits and persistently but humbly maintaining that God called her to England, she managed to convince the necessary authorities to let her cross the Channel, in the company of servants only, and live out her life's dream of dying for Christ.

Carvajal's years in England were characterized by high intrigue, secrecy, and drama. Many of her letters are written in code to mask the identity of those about whom she wrote, and she received support for her apostolic work from a wide network of powerful people throughout Europe, many of whom were women. Arriving in England in 1604, she learned English within a year (correcting what she believed was an error the female Carmelites in France had made in not learning the language of the country where they were working) and, after acquainting herself with the political layout of the London area, set herself to proselytizing until her death in 1614. After some struggle, she attained independence from the Spanish ambassador in whose palace she took frequent refuge but resisted living. Instead, she rented first one, then two houses in which she began what she eventually named the Company of the Holy Virgin, a group of Catholic women for whom she wrote a constitution and a draft Rule in clear imitation of the Ignatian mission for men. Taking advantage of the Jesuit model and the political situation that made cloister impossible, given the need to disperse in a matter of minutes to avoid suspicion and arrest, Carvajal laid out a daily routine based on her own activities. Although prayer, needlework, and domestic chores form the core of the formal day, there is room left for Carvajal's more activist schedule: service to others, specifically consolation of the Catholics in prison and other social outcasts, disinterring the drawn and quartered bodies of executed Catholics and secreting those "relics" to Catholic lands, and teaching Catholic dogma to anyone on the street who would listen. Income for the Company was to come from donations only, although Carvajal received a pension from Philip III throughout her stay in England.

Carvajal's womanhood protected her from immediate arrest, since the powerful men around her seem to have doubted that a "little woman" could pose much danger to English politics, but the day arrived when the authorities could no longer turn their backs on the individual who managed to convince innumerable Catholics to die true to their faith rather than take the Oath of Fidelity to the English crown. Carvajal was famous as a preexecution consoler, and her edifying conversations with Catholic martyrs just before their torments and death have survived, although in a hagiographic haze. She was also probably responsible for the exemplary death of the scandalous royal favorite in Spain, Rodrigo de Calderón, whose correspondence with Carvajal while she was in England survives.

In 1608, Carvajal was imprisoned for four days for talking about religion in a store where she had gone to buy fabric for an altar cloth, and it is in relationship to this episode that documents were written testifying to how she preached in the street and bought antipapal posters then being sold in London and ripped them up in public. She was ushered to prison, at that time the local sheriff's house, where a coterie of women sympathizers, including two important ambassadors' wives, clustered around her immediately and refused to leave her side. Pressure was put on the Spanish ambassador to send her back to Spain, pressure that Carvajal, thanks to her important political and religious connections, was able to mitigate temporarily. Documents written by the women living with Carvajal after her release from prison reveal a tension-filled existence during the final six years of her life, living under constant surveillance by the English authorities. Several attempts were made to enter her house under deceitful tactics, but Carvajal nimbly avoided them, in part by setting up her little company of women with two locking front doors, water piped directly into the house, and instructions to stay away from the windows at all times. In spite of the danger, however, she did not cease her missionary activities, and in 1613 the archbishop of Canterbury himself had her house broken into and Carvajal imprisoned for three days, and this time her dismissal was contingent upon the Spanish ambassador's promise to have her removed from England. Her presence had finally acquired dimensions that reached well into the domain of delicate diplomatic and political business, and had she not died shortly after her second prison sentence, she would have received the orders sent by the Spanish king to return to Spain.

Catholics, particularly Jesuits, are wont to make a martyr of Carvajal, out of respect for her vow, although technically she does not qualify; that vow's delicate balance with sinful suicide was ever on her mind, and she took pains to represent herself as following God's will in every step she took. Her life probably ended because she caught the disease that killed one of her companions (whom pious records have converted into the servant who died on the spot from the shock of her mistress's second imprisonment). Likewise, Carvajal's own insistence on her ill health must be tempered with her relatively long life of physical hardship in close contact with people from all walks of life in her missionary work, which would have overcome a person of lesser constitution much sooner.

Carvajal's writings consist of an autobiography, *Vida y virtudes* (1632; Life and Virtues), which includes spiritual poetry, and many letters, which have been edited under the title *Epistolario y poesías* (1965; Epistolary and Poems). One of her best poems is a dialogue between the soul and God, imitative of the Song of Songs, with rich and sensuous imagery. Her 180 letters reveal a woman who, from a very early age, was dissatisfied with the options open to her and persisted in creating new ones. She also relates a great deal of physical suffering—hardships of travel, persecutions of the English government, and her own "penances," which included not eating and eschewing basic body comforts such as heat in her rooms. The writings as a whole provide a glimpse into the psyche of a complex, intriguing woman, one expressing a bountiful desire for self-destruction but one who nonetheless managed to carve a life of great agency and independence for herself in England, with much greater freedom and empowerment than any profession she could have practiced in Spain.

Critical estimation of Carvajal's work generally falls into one of two categories: those who view her life and writings as examples of the negative influences religion could have on women in seventeenth-century Spain (Arenal and Schlau; El Saffar) and primarily religious writers who believe she is a candidate for beatification (e.g., Camilo Abad, S.J., editor of her letters). El Saffar views her "penances" as examples of women (in this case, nuns and visionaries) interiorizing the hostility directed toward them and uses Carvajal as an example, describing the severe penances her uncle designed for her. It seems possible that hagiographies figured prominently in Carvajal's library, as they did in the libraries of many educated women of the day, as they influenced the lives of women writers' fictional characters. *See also* Autobiographical Self-Representation of Women in the Early Modern Period; Nuns Who Wrote in sixteenth- and seventeenth-Century Spain

Work by

Epistolario y poesías. Ed. Camilo María Abad. Vol. 179 of *Biblioteca de autores españoles*. Madrid: Atlas, 1965.

Escritos autobiográficos. Ed. Camilo María Abad. Barcelona: Juan Flors, 1966.

Poesías completas. Ed. María Luisa García-Nieto Onrubia. Badajoz: Diputación Provincial de Badajoz, 1990.

Work about

Abad, Camilo María. *Una misionera española en la Inglaterra del siglo XVII. Doña Luisa de Carvajal y Mendoza (1566–1614)*. Comillas: Universidad Pontífica, 1966.

Arenal, Electa, and Stacey Schlau. *Untold Sisters: Hispanic Nuns in Their Own Words*. Albuquerque: U of New Mexico P, 1989.

Barbeito Carneiro, María Isabel. *Escritoras madrileñas del siglo XVII*. 2 vols. Madrid: Universidad Complutense de Madrid, Depto. de Bibliografía, Facultad de Filología, 1986.

Cruz, Anne J. "Chains of Desire: Luisa de Carvajal y Mendoza's Poetics of Penance." *Estudios sobre escritoras hispánicas en honor de Georgina Sabat-Rivers*. Ed. Lou Charnon-Deutsch. Madrid: Castalia, 1992. 97–112.

El Saffar, Ruth. *Rapture Encaged: The Suppression of the Feminine in Western Culture*. London: Routledge, 1994.

McNamara, Joann. "The Need to Give: Suffering and Female Sanctity in the Middle Ages." *Images of Sainthood in Medieval Europe*. Ed. Renate Blumenfeld-Kosinski and Timea Szell. Ithaca, NY: Cornell UP, 1991.

Muñoz, Luis. *Vida y virtudes de la venerable virgen doña Luisa de Carvajal y Mendoza*. 1631. Madrid: Sucesores de Rivadeneyra, 1897.

Ortega Costa, Milagros. "Spanish Women in the

Reformation." *Women in Reformation and Counter-Reformation Europe: Public and Private Worlds.* Ed. Sherrin Marshall. Bloomington: Indiana UP, 1989. 89–119.

        Elizabeth Rhodes and Nancy Cushing-Daniels

Casada

See Women's Professions in Early Spanish Literature: *Santas, Rameras, Casadas, Amas,* and *Criadas* (Saints, Whores, Wives, Governesses, and Servants)

Casa de Bernarda Alba, La

See García Lorca, Federico (1898–1936): Women in His Rural Trilogy

Casas, Borita (1911–1999)

One of the best-known writers of fiction for children and young adults of the post–Civil War period, Borita (Liboria) Casas created the popular radio character Antoñita la Fantástica (Fantastic Antoñita). She went on to publish weekly Antoñita stories in the magazine *Chicas* (Girls) and later a collection of 12 books between 1948 and 1958 in which the young Antoñita eventually grows up and marries but never gives up the active imagination and writing talents that had earned her the epithet *Fantástica*.

Casas began her career as a radio broadcaster at age 30, reading anything that was handed to her. Raised in a middle-class household ruined by Spain's Civil War, like so many Spaniards she lost both loved ones (a Falangist brother died in the war, while a Republican brother fled to France in exile) and her own dreams for the future (the war interrupted studies with a university group in Germany and her education as a whole). Casas was forced to learn to survive and find happiness in the new repressive climate. When she invented the cheerful, innocent, and naughty Antoñita who visited Radio Madrid once a week accompanied by her nanny Nicerata, Casas found an outlet for her incredible creativity and for a subtle critique of Spanish society. While politics are never mentioned, through the comments of the child Spaniards shared their worries about food shortages, constant threats of childhood diseases caused by improper sanitary conditions and malnutrition, and the middle-class obsession with keeping up appearances when they lacked so much. But mainly the audience was amused by Antoñita. Soon whole families, not just girls, gathered around the radio to hear stories that reflected the middle class in comical fashion, making listeners forget the frustrations of their daily lives. Meanwhile, Casas became a star, frequently interviewed in major journals of the time and publicly congratulated by such fans as Ramón Gómez de la Serna and Jacinto *Benavente for her insights into the world of children.

In 1947 Casas began to publish her weekly stories in the popular magazine *Chicas*. Thus, when the first *Antoñita la Fantástica* book was published in 1948, it had a ready-made audience eager to make it a bestseller. Antoñita even influenced colloquial language as children with vivid imaginations were commonly told "tienes más pájaros en la cabeza que Antoñita" (you are more featherbrained than Antoñita). Casas's tales preserved an invaluable realistic portrait of Madrid's middle class in the 1940s and 1950s, an image made all the more poignant through its female child's perspective.

Antoñita la Fantástica has been unfavorably compared to Elena *Fortún's Celia by those seeking signs of female rebellion. While it is true that Antoñita is much less openly hostile to her environment than any of Fortún's creations, the changed political and social atmosphere must be considered. Antoñita first appeared in *Chicas* surrounded by articles that openly pushed its young, female target audience to conform to a rigid model of ultraconservative Spanish womanhood. Serialized romance novels such as those of Carmen de *Icaza encouraged girls to always appear cheerful as they suffered in silence waiting for a husband, and they strongly discouraged any sort of intellectual activity. Each issue included optimistic articles describing every possible type of husband. No matter what his flaws might be, girls were taught that they must accept him. Complementary articles issued very stern warnings about female lapses or defects. Girls could not be depressed, intellectual, untidy, flirty, et cetera, since any perceived flaw would lead to the terrible punishment of spinsterhood.

In contrast, the character Antoñita is above all a writer who takes her responsibilities as such very seriously. The various stories and individual chapters of her books are in the form of a diary meant to be read by the public she frequently addresses directly. From the very first stories, Antoñita is always conscious that writing will provide an outlet for her creativity and that without this mode of expression an important point of view will be silenced. Who else will tell the world of the difficulties, and joys, of being young and female in Franco's Spain? Unlike Celia, Antoñita may be a favorite with the nuns at school, but she does not internalize their restrictive teachings even as she is not as openly critical as Celia, who appeared in a more relaxed intellectual climate.

Included in Antoñita's overall positive worldview are her portraits of sincere female friendships, a type of relationship missing from much literature. Antoñita typically begins each new encounter with a female character with a detailed physical description in which all types, no matter how removed from the norms of classical beauty, are deemed attractive. Beneath the portrait of a stylish girl who worries more about whether she should wear a beret to a conference on modern poetry more than the actual poetry itself (perhaps a comment on the status of poetry during the dictatorship) lie severe critiques of the role assigned to women in literature. Thus the above-mentioned incident in *Antoñita la Fantástica se pone de largo* (1951; Fantastic Antoñita Wears a Long Dress) is followed by criticism of romance novels that only serve her as sleep aids. In this same work, she gains a secret admirer who falls in love with her precisely through her writings and later as her husband encourages her to continue writing.

As the series continued over a decade, Antoñita grew into a married woman with a child. Her new station in life never curtailed her creative activities. It is as a married woman that Antoñita writes a collection of what must be considered feminist fairy tales as a birthday gift for her sister Titerris. In *Antoñita la Fantástica en el País de la Fantasía* (1952; Fantastic Antoñita in Fantasy Land) she parodies bourgeois women who are overly concerned with material goods and physical beauty through the characters Snow White and Cinderella whom she meets on her journeys through the land of fairy tales. The centerpiece of this volume is the story of Graciella who, like Sleeping Beauty, suffers a terrible punishment when her parents omit one of the fairies from the guest list of her baptism. Graciella's plight is that she cannot smile or laugh. Before she agrees to marry the prince, she sets out alone on a quest to find the fairy who has her smile. Antoñita accompanies her on this perilous journey, stating that the typical quest-motif journey should be undertaken by the feminine sex since, contrary to popular belief, girls are much braver. In this and other tales, the reader is told repeatedly that physical beauty is worthless unless accompanied by more important traits. In a 1983 reedition by Andina publishing house, Antoñita also encounters Bluebeard's last wife who is organizing summer writing workshops. Unfortunately, the later editions were updated to eliminate the slang associated with previous decades and in the process lost much of their engaging style.

In one of the last books of the series, *Las amigas de Antoñita la Fantástica* (1954; Fantastic Antoñita's Girlfriends), Antoñita prepares to write about her infant son, Cascabel. Instead she is interrupted when readers from two different generations visit Borita Casas herself to sternly reprimand her for having Antoñita marry so young and for having lived such a pampered life. They patiently explain that modern young women prefer to enjoy their youth through travels and studies and then perhaps marry after they have developed a stronger personality. Unlike readers of romance novels, Antoñita's interlocutors are not interested in her adventures in motherhood but rather prefer news of Antoñita's friends who have become independent, well-educated professionals. These female readers of the 1950s who grew up with Antoñita prefer their heroines to live lives more like that of Borita Casas herself: an intelligent, independent woman who broke the rules of traditional Spanish society. See also Fairy Tales in Novels by Spanish Women

Work by

El álbum de Antoñita la Fantástica. Madrid: GILSA, 1958.
Antoñita en México. Madrid: GILSA, 1957.
Antoñita la Fantástica cumplió diez años. Madrid: GILSA, 1955.
Antoñita la Fantástica en el País de la Fantasía. Madrid: GILSA, 1952.
Antoñita la Fantástica se pone de largo. Madrid: GILSA, 1951.
Antoñita la Fantástica y su tía Carol. Madrid: GILSA, 1950.
Más historias de Antoñita la Fantástica. Madrid: GILSA, 1949.

Work about

Cristóbal, Ramiro. Introducción. Antoñita la Fantástica. By Borita Casas. Madrid: Castalia, Instituto de la Mujer, 1989.
Moix, Ana. "Erase una vez... La literatura infantil a partir de los años 40." Vindicación Feminista 5 (November 1976): 28–39.

María Elena Soliño

Castillejo, Cristóbal de
See Diálogo de mujeres (1544)

Castillo Solórzano, Alonso
See Niña de los embustes, Teresa de Manzanares, La (1632)

Castro, Inés de (1325?–1355)

One of the most famous legendary romantic figures of the Middle Ages, Doña Inés de Castro has become immortalized in Spanish literature by the popular Golden Age play Reinar después de morir (To Rule after Dying) by Luis Vélez de Guevara (1579–1644).

Inés de Castro was reared in the court of Don Juan Manuel (1282–1348; author of *Conde Lucanor) and in 1340 moved from Galicia to Portugal with Juan Manuel's daughter Costanza to serve as her lady-in-waiting when she became the wife of Prince Pedro, son of Alfonso IV of Portugal (1291–1357). Pedro immediately fell in love with Inés, and they began a relation that produced several children. When Costanza died in 1345, Pedro brought Inés to the royal court in Coimbra and began living with her as if she were his wife. As time progressed, the nobles began to object to this nonpolitical liaison; and finally, in 1355, shouting the now-famous slogan "que não se perca Portugal por uma mulher" (Portugal shall not be disgraced by a woman), they murdered Inés at the "Quinta de las Lágrimas" (Country House of Tears) in Coimbra. Legends relate that when Pedro became king upon his father's death, he ordered Inés disinterred, dressed in royal garb, and crowned queen of Portugal. Today their bodies and those of their children supposedly lie together in the royal monastery of Alcobaça, and the Portuguese celebrate April 24 as Inés's coronation day.

Besides the Vélez de Guevara masterpiece, there are over 40 dramatic versions of the Inés de Castro legend, from Antonio Ferreira's Dona Ignez de Castro (1565) to the recent Corona de amor y muerte (1955; Crown of Love and Death) by Alejandro Casona.

Work about

Botta, Patrizia. "El romance del Palmero e Inés de Castro." *Medioevo y literatura, I–IV.* Ed. Juan Paredes. Granada: U of Granada, 1995. 379–399.

Cornil, Suzanne. *Inés de Castro.* Bruxelles: Memoires de la Classe des Lettres, 1952.

Induráin, Francisco, ed. *Luis Vélez de Guevara: Reinar después de morir.* Zaragoza: Ebro, 1963.

Johnson, Neal. "Parodies of French Tragedy: Agnes de Chaillot as Parody of Inés de Castro." *Studies on Voltaire and the Eighteenth Century.* Vol. 304. Oxford: Voltaire Foundation, 1992. 1232–1235.

Lapaire, Pierre J. "Power and Innocence: Montherlant's Inés de Castro Revisited." *Language Quarterly* 28.3–4 (1990): 41–47.

David H. Darst

Castro, Juana (1945–)

Born in Villanueva de Córdoba, Juana Castro is a teacher, poet, and translator of Italian verse. She has received prestigious awards for her poetry including the Premio Juan Ramón Jiménez in 1987 and 1989. A vocal feminist among her generation of Spanish poets, she began her impassioned reclamation of women's rights in *Cóncava mujer* (1978; Concave Woman). In subsequent volumes such as *Del dolor y las alas* (1982; Of Pain and Wings), *Paranoia en otoño* (1985; Paranoia in Autumn), *Narcisia* (1986), *Arte de cetrería* (1989; Art of Falconry), and *No temerás* (1994; You Will Not Fear), her feminism has evolved from an early embrace of women's issues within the rational, clearly defined framework of Spanish Marxism to a poetic and multifaceted vision of feminine subjectivity illustrated by her more recent poems.

By gathering together the many vestiges of a supremely complex Feminine, which in Castro's estimation must also include "masculine" elements, she creates a new symbolic representation of the Great Goddess in *Narcisia*. In this regard, *Arte de cetrería*, which some critics have considered a radical departure from her previous feminist posture, continues in the vein of the former volume: Both recast the feminine within archetypal rather than purely social confines and both seek a reconciliation of feminine and masculine qualities, that is, an androgynous Feminine.

In *Arte de cetrería*, Castro embellishes her topic with epigraphs quoted from early Castilian and Hispano-Arabic sources. Although the speaker, depicted as a falcon, embodies classist and sexist servitude, it also symbolizes the contradiction of dependence and independence: In spite of its chain, the falcon achieves flight. The poems imply that an instinctive approach may enable women to reach wholeness, and like Castro's falcon, they may move through instinct toward transcendence.

While treating the erotic and artfully blending it with the spiritual, *No temerás* also makes women's issues its primary focus. Ambiguity, a salient feature of her 1989 volume, occurs again in relation to the speaker and listener of the poem. The poematic *you* is kept in a state of flux, which prevents the poem from resolving into a clear statement. This facet of Castro's recent art departs from her early poems, which, to a degree, adhered to a social realist aesthetic. In essence, while remaining faithful to her exploration of feminine subjectivity, in the 1980s and 1990s Castro has engaged in an unencumbered elaboration of feminist issues, one that integrates many styles and iconologies.

Work by

Arte de cetrería. Huelva: Colección de Poesía "Juan Ramón Jiménez," 1989.
Cóncava mujer. Córdoba: Zubia, 1978.
Del dolor y las alas. Villanueva de Córdoba: Ayuntamiento, 1982.
Narcisia. Barcelona: Taifa, 1986.
No temerás. Madrid: Torremozas, 1994.
Paranoia en otoño. Valdepeñas: Ayuntamiento, 1985.

Work about

Coco, Emilio. *La poesía de Juana Castro.* Córdoba: Trayectoria de Navegantes, 1992.
Miró, Emilio. "El 'arte de amar' de Juana Castro." *Insula* 45 (1990): 29–30.
———. "Continuidad y comienzo de dos poetas cordobesas." *Insula* 42 (1987): 6.

Ugalde, Sharon Keefe. *Conversación y poemas. La nueva poesía femenina española en castellano.* Madrid: Siglo XXI de España, 1991. 55–73.

Kay Pritchett

Castro, Rosalía de (1837–1885)

This poet and prose writer who composed in both Spanish and Galician was considered a minor author during her lifetime, but she is now recognized as a precursor of the Spanish American modernist movement and the Generation of 1898. Some themes in her prose and poetry have come into their own in the second half of the twentieth century.

Born out of wedlock in Santiago de Compostela to a mother from the Galician aristocracy and a seminarian, she lived in the country with her father's relatives until age 10, when she went to live with her mother in Santiago. Despite their early separation, mother and daughter developed a close relationship. Her days in the Galician countryside nurtured a love of nature that is reflected in her writings. Her education, although not very academic, was one considered appropriate for a young lady of her day. It is believed she began writing poetry as early as age 11. Her first book was favorably reviewed by Manuel Martínez Murguía (1833–1923), the man she would marry a year later. After their marriage, the couple left Madrid for Santiago de Compostela. A scholar and writer himself, Martínez Murguía supported Castro's literary efforts and often wrote in praise or defense of her work. Details about their life as a couple are scant because he honored her wish that all letters and unfinished manuscripts be destroyed after her death. Castro died in Padrón on July 15, 1885, and was buried in the cemetery of Andina. In 1891, her remains were moved back to Galicia and interred at the Convent of Santo Domingo de Bonaval in Santiago de Compostela.

Her poetic works are considered the more important. *La flor* (1857; The Flower), her first published work, was a youthful collection of six poems that reflect the influence of European romantic writers. Her second collection, *A mi madre* (1863; To My Mother), was a privately distributed, limited edition of deeply personal poems written at the death of her mother in 1862. Published the same year was the first of two poetic compilations in Galician. Titled *Cantares gallegos* (Galician Songs) and containing poems inspired by her native Galicia, it was taken to the bosom of the Rexurdimento Gallego, the Galician Restoration movement. The brighter poems in this book are glosses of popular Galician songs, sayings, or vignettes of local color. The darker poems movingly recount the hardships endured by Galician men who emigrated in order to support their families as well as the loneliness and suffering of the strong, resilient women left behind.

Between 1869 and 1877, Castro gave birth to the last six of her seven children, left Galicia to accompany her husband in Castile, and apparently devoted her time to care of the family. She still found time to write poems that later were included in *Follas novas* (1880; New Leaves), her second book of poetry in Galician. Published three years after the death at birth of her last child, this volume is characterized by the theme of *dolor*, the pain and sorrow for which her work is so well known. Facets of this theme include the sadness and nostalgia she felt away from her beloved Galicia, mourning and grief for her two children who died in infancy, the sting of being labeled pejoratively for being a woman who dared exercise her artistic or intellectual talents, and her mourning for the nature of Galicia being wantonly destroyed. A degree of social consciousness expressed in a minor key is heard in poems that repeat the concern voiced in *Cantares* for the Galician emigrés and the women they abandoned in their quest of a livelihood. Her search for a suitable poetic expression led to innovative forms of versification that make these poems very effective lyrically.

Castro's last poetry book, *En las orillas del Sar* (1884; *Beside the River Sar*, 1937), was published just months before her death from cancer. The volume includes poems written between 1878 and 1884, including a final appraisal of the poetic *métier*, and is considered by critics to be her finest lyric expression. Her themes are universal, and certain poems suggest the religious questioning of Miguel de *Unamuno (1864–1936) or existentialist writers. The *dolor* theme permeates this collection as it did *Follas*, but now there is a sense of serenity and acceptance absent in *Follas*. Death, which she knew was imminent, is accepted, even welcomed. Perhaps the serenity in these poems is best explained in an epiphany depicted in the poem "Santa Escolástica" (Saint Scholastica), in which her lifelong creative struggle is vindicated as she senses a link between art, poetry, and the divine.

Castro's novels are less known and reflect less mastery in their writing. She completed her first novel, *La hija del mar* (1859; *The Daughter of the Sea*, 1995), shortly after returning to Santiago as a young bride. This novel is preceded by a prologue in which the author recognizes her audacity as a woman in publishing it but justifies the act by naming acclaimed women writers of other epochs and citing contemporary male authors who endorse the intellectual empowerment of women. The plot of this first novel is a romantic tangle in which good plays against evil in absolute terms, rather than in the prevailing terms of contemporary society. Critics have hypothesized that the illegitimate protagonist of this novel is an alter ego of the author.

Her second novel, *Flavio* (1861), tells the romantic story of two mismatched and star-crossed lovers. Character flaws define both Mara and Flavio: She is proud; he is inconstant. Castro posits the idea of a woman's right to an intellectual life by having Mara judged prideful for writing poetry, an activity unbecoming to decent women of the day. True to her vocation, Mara forfeits Flavio's love.

Her short story "El cadiceño: Descripción de un tipo" (1866; The Cadiceño: Description of a Type) and the novella *Ruinas: Desdichas de tres vidas ejemplares* (1866; Ruins: Misfortunes of Three Exemplary Lives) are brief character sketches. The former is a critique of Galician men who migrate to other parts of Spain or immigrate to America to earn a livelihood, then return, flaunting riches of questionable origin and proportions and disdaining their motherland. The latter sympathetically presents three anachronistic misfits unable to adapt to modern times.

El caballero de las botas azules: Cuento extraño (1867; The Gentleman with the Blue Boots: Strange Tale), published the following year, is a novel whose most engaging aspect is an introductory dialogue titled "Un hombre y su musa" (A Man and His Muse). Contrary to traditional muses, the one summoned by this man is hideous and disparages and insults him for being in thrall to old precepts and exhibiting no imagination in his writing. Calling herself "Novedad" (Novelty) and urging him to try new ways of writing, this muse presages tenets of the soon-to-arrive modernists. The gentleman of the title is an extremely strange character who caricatures and ridicules every social type, including women, who are portrayed as rebelling against male domination but unwilling to give up their leisure or the luxuries men bestow on them.

Castro's last novel, *El primer loco: Cuento extraño* (The First Madman: Strange Tale), was published in 1881. Unlike *El caballero*, her other "strange tale," this novel is soul-searching and contemplative. Like *Flavio*, it delves into the nature of the poetic temperament. In Luis, the principal male character, critics have identified Castro's alter ego, when he advises a friend to do as Castro herself had done in her Galician works: Look for the essential truths of life in the traditions of his country, not in science and reason.

A woman's heart and sensitivity are discernible in all of Castro's works. Love or sorrow mold her expression, her images, and most of her plots. The delicacy and purity of her poetic expression link her to Gustavo

Adolfo *Bécquer (1836–1870) and to modernist poets and writers of the Generation of 1898. Besides the theme of sorrow in her poetry, there are also themes of social justice, existential questioning, and the intellectual rights of women, which along with ecological concerns make her a topical author of the moment. *See also* Galician Women Writers: A Brief History

Work by

Beside the River Sar; Selected Poems from En las orillas del Sar. Trans. S. Griswold Morley. Berkeley: U of California P, 1937.
The Daughter of the Sea. Trans. Kathleen N. March. New York: Peter Lang, 1995.
Obras completas. Ed. V. García Martí. Madrid: Aguilar, 1952.
Poems. Trans. Anna-Marie Aldaz, Barbara N. Gant, and Anne C. Bromley. Albany: State U of New York P, 1991.

Work about

Alberto Robatto, Matilde. *Rosalía de Castro y la condición femenina*. Madrid: Partenon, 1984.
Courteau, Joanna. *The Poetics of Rosalía de Castro's Negra sombra*. Lewiston: E. Mellen, 1995.
Kulp, Kathleen K. *Manner and Mood in Rosalía de Castro: A Study of Themes and Style*. Madrid: José Porrúa Turanzas, 1968.
Kulp-Hill, Kathleen. *Rosalía de Castro*. Boston: Twayne, 1977.
Poullain, Claude Henri. *Rosalía Castro de Murguía y su obra literaria (1836–1885)*. Madrid: Nacional, 1974.

Oralia Preble-Niemi

Castroviejo Blanco-Cicerón, Concha (1912–   )

Novelist, journalist, and critic, Concha Castroviejo Blanco-Cicerón was born in Santiago de Compostela, Spain, where she studied at the university and received a degree in philosophy and letters. In 1937–1938 she attended the University of Bordeaux, and at the end of the Spanish Civil War (1936–1939), she left Spain with her husband Joaquín Seijo Alonso and went to Mexico. There both taught at several institutions, including the Lyceum in Campeche, and participated in archaeological excavations in the Yucatán peninsula. Castroviejo returned to Spain in 1950, and after receiving a degree in journalism, she entered the new career and started to contribute articles on literary criticism to *La Noche* in Santiago de Compostela and later to *Informaciones* as well as *La hoja del Lunes* in Madrid.

The two novels written by Castroviejo thematically deal with the Spanish Civil War and its consequences of life in exile and in postwar Spain, focusing on the conflicts faced by feminine characters. The experiences of exile, first in Paris, then in México, confront characters in *Los que se fueron* (1957; Those Who Went Away). The conflict resolves itself in acceptance of the new environment by the feminine character Tiche, center of the story. She does not seek the traditional solution of a new marriage, or the useless bemoaning of the lost homeland, but instead relies on her own strength and creates a career by her own effort, establishing a new and fruitful life for herself and her son.

In the second novel, *Víspera del odio* (1959; Eve of Hate), war engulfs the life of the main character Teresa, who tries to escape an unhappy marriage by joining the man she loves during a hazardous life in war. Teresa fails to gain her freedom; her husband takes revenge on the lover by denouncing him as a "red" to the victorious Francoist troops, condemning him to a fatal end, and Teresa also loses the child that was fruit of their love. Her valiant attempt to escape the system is in vain.

Castroviejo wrote several collections of children's short stories: *El jardín de las siete puertas* (1961; The Seven-Gated Garden), *El zopilote presumido* (1964; The Presumptuous Buzzard), and *Los piratas de "la terrible"* (1964; The Pirates of "The Terrible"). The collection *Los días de Lina* (1971; Lina's Days) is a group of narratives dedicated to children but equally suited for adults because of the sensitivity of its prose. Through the perceptive eyes of a young girl spending her summer vacation in a village where some relatives live, simple episodes of daily rural life are captured, be it nature (the moon, the river), animals (domestic or wild), or people (the parish priest, the apothecary, other villagers).

Like her heroines Tiche and Teresa, Castroviejo suffered from the consequences of the Civil War, going into exile, trying to assimilate herself to a new homeland, and finally resorting to her inner strength to resolve her life through a professional career as a writer.

Work by

Los días de Lina. Madrid: EMESA, 1971.
El jardín de las siete puertas. Madrid: Doncel, 1961.
Los que se fueron. Barcelona: Planeta, 1957.
Víspera del odio. Barcelona: Garbo, 1959.

Work about

Bravo Villasante, Carmen. "Concha Castroviejo: *Los que se fueron.*" Insula 144: 6.
Domínguez Rey, Antonio. "Concha Castroviejo." *La Estafeta Literaria* 528 (1973): 5–17.
Galerstein, Carolyn. "The Spanish Civil War: The View of Women Novelists." *Letras Femeninas* 10 (Fall 1984): 12–18.
Valdivieso, Teresa. "El drama de lo tangencial en *Víspera del odio* y *Una mañana cualquiera.*" *Letras femeninas* 12 (Spring–Fall 1986): 24–33.

Pilar Sáenz

Catalan Women Writers: A Brief History

Beginnings

Catalan literature by women is as old as medieval troubadour poetry: The first female poet whose identity we can document is the Reina de Mallorques from the first half of the fourteenth century. Her one extant poem, known by its first line "Ez yeu am tal qu'es bo e bel" (I Love One Who Is Good and Lovely), is contained in the Miscellaneous Medieval Poetical Manuscript 8 of the Biblioteca de Catalunya and included after the first *giornata* (day) in the Catalan translation of Boccaccio's *Decameron* (1429). The love song laments the absence of the beloved husband gone to France. The writer has been identified as either Constança d'Aragó (1313–1346), sister of King Pere el Ceremoniós, or Violant de Vilaragut, both of whom were wives of King Jaume III of Majorca (d. 1349).

Other women also belonged to the troubadour or posttroubadour tradition. The same Manuscript 8 includes "Axí cant és en muntanya deserta" (Song on a Lone Mountain), an anonymous rhetorical poem belonging to the late fourteenth century that was presented in Toulouse's annual poetry competition. Manuscript 1744 of the series includes the anonymous poem from the late fifteenth century "Ab lo cor trist envirollat d'esmay" (With a Sad Heart Wrapped in Grief), written by a woman who has lost her beloved. Tecla Borja (1435–1459), niece of Pope Calixtus III and sister of Pope Alexander VI, was a singer, poet, and scholar praised by poets of Valencia and Italy. Her only surviving work is a debate with her great Valencian compatriot, the poet Ausiàs March.

The fourteenth century also saw continuation of a long tradition of poetry by nuns unhappy with their state in life. Known as the *Malmonjades*, the cycle goes back to the Latin Middle Ages and appears in various Romance languages. The female poetic voice addresses her mother or sisters, a girlfriend, or Nature, and speaks of griefs, fears, hopes, and passions in the soul of a woman. Examples in Catalan can be found in the "Cançoneret de Ripoll," Ms. 129 of Ripoll.

As in Castilian literature, much early writing was done in convents. The first female prose writer in Catalan was Isabel de Villena (1430–1490), illegitimate daughter of Enric de Villena and abbess of the Trinity Convent of Valencia. Her only known work is a *Vita Christi* (1487; Life of Christ), written for the nuns in her convent and printed by her successor. While she follows in outline the tradition of other religious writers, her *Vita* foregrounds women: the Virgin Mary, Mary Magdalene, Saint Anne, and other women who appear in the Gospels. Villena emphasizes such tasks as washing, sewing, child care, and such courtly activities as dancing and music. She also takes part in the medieval debate on the good or evil nature of women, challenging misogynistic arguments and holding up Mary as the symbol of female virtue (*Marianism).

After the brilliance of the fifteenth century in Catalan literature, represented by the two great Valencians, the poet Ausiàs March and the novelist Joanot Martorell, a long period ensued in which little was written in Catalan. Traditionally known as the "Decadència," the negative depiction is now undergoing revision by specialists, but the fact remains that it is not a rich period in Catalan literature. The only examples of writing by women are religious treatises or poetry, and letters. While Isabel de Villena was writing for her nuns, a contemporary Valencian, Isabel Suaris, wrote letters to poet Bernat Fenollar. The sixteenth century also saw one poet and one epistle writer: Estefania de Requesens (1501/1508–1549) wrote letters to her mother from the court at Madrid, describing her life in the capital, her duties as administrator of properties and the home, and of course, her children. The letters offer a woman's perspective on many historical events as well as a chronicle of daily life of the period. At the same time but writing from the Royal Monastery of Santa Maria at Vallbona de les Monges in Lleida, Jerònima de Boixadors (?–1562) wrote poems in praise of the Virgin and devotions for her convent. Two religious writers appear in the seventeenth century: Maria de Llúria i de Margola (1630/1632–1701), also from Vallbona de les Monges in Lleida, wrote a book of reflections and prayers, her thoughts on a variety of subjects, and her passion for God, following orthodox Catholic teachings of the time. A more philosophical writer of the period is the Majorcan Margalida Baneta Mas Pujol, also known as Sor Anna Maria del Santissim Sagrament (1649–1700). In addition to her own poetry, she commented and glossed certain works of the Majorcan writer par excellence Ramon Llull. In the eighteenth century, we find two more religious writers and a sonneteer. Margarita Esplugues (1738–?), a Franciscan Tertiary Virgin from Majorca, wrote poetry and theological papers. Maria Angela Giralt (active 1730s) was a widow who wrote devotional work to be sung in the missions. To close this difficult period for those who would write in Catalan, we find reference to Narcisa Torres, about whom we know nothing except that she wrote two sonnets.

Nineteenth Century

Parallel to the romantic movements in other western European literatures, the Catalan *Renaixença* (Renaissance) of the nineteenth century had the added impact of a resurgence of the autochthonous language. The publication in 1833 of Carles Aribau's ode "A la patria" (To the Homeland) in Catalan was the wellspring of modern literature in that language and harbinger of canonical poets Jacint Verdaguer (1845–1902) and Joan Maragall (1860–1911). This literary movement was nourished by publication of numerous periodicals and anthologies and by restoration in 1859 of the medieval poetry contests known as the *Jocs Florals* (Floral Games). Both activities facilitated the inclusion of women writers in the *Renaixença*, and indeed a number of women participated in the contests and published their work in various poetry journals and collections. Poems by Isabel de Villamartín (?–1877) won awards in the *Jocs* of 1859 and 1861 and were included in the first two collections of Catalan poetry, *Los trovadors nous* (1858; The New Troubadours) and *Los trovadors moderns* (1859; The Modern Troubadours). A group of roughly contemporary women friends with focuses in Barcelona and Majorca formed around writing activities and mutual support; the capital was central to the work of Maria Josefa Massanés (1811–1887), Maria del Pilar

Maspons (Maria de Bell-Lloch, 1841–1907), Dolors Monserdà (1845–1919), Agnès Armengol (1852–1934), Joaquima Santamaria (Agna de Valldaura, 1854–1930), and Antònia Gili (1856–1909). Working from Majorca but in contact with the Barcelona group were Victòria Penya (1823/1827–1898), Margarida Caimarí (1839–1921), and Manuela de los Herreros (1845–1911). In Valencia, Magdalena García Bravo (1862–1891) wrote in both Catalan and Castilian, participating vigorously in the Valencian counterparts of the contests and journals. While this movement was essentially a poetic one, with patriotic, religious, and popular themes abounding, several of these writers contributed other activities to the cultural and political life of the time. Herreros, for example, espoused such causes as protection of workers and children, as well as the abolition of trafficking in women. Monserdà supported similar causes and also advocated education for women. In addition to poetry, the prolific Monserdà wrote short stories, novels, essays, plays that were performed in Barcelona theaters, and a biography of her much-admired predecessor Josefa Massanés.

Twentieth Century: Before the Civil War

The poetic tradition of the previous century carries over into the early 1900s in the work of Maria Antònia Salvà (1869–1958), transformed into the Majorcan counterpart of Catalan *Modernisme* and *Noucentisme*. Her poetry is deeply rooted in her Mediterranean environment and influenced by its customs, including the oral tradition of the *glosadors*, or popular country poets. She was well known as a translator of poetry from English, Italian, Castilian, and French. However, the writings of women of this period are mainly narratives, with a few incursions into theater. Palmira Ventós (pseud. Felip Palma, 1862–1917) lived in Barcelona but set her stories, novel, and plays in rural Catalonia. Carme Karr (pseud. L. Escardot, 1865–1943) wrote in all genres: short story, novel, drama, and essay, as well as composing songs. A major figure in the women's movement of the period, she was considered by Dolors Monserdà to be the first Catalan feminist. Carme Montoriol (1893–1966) also began with music but became known for her translations of Shakespeare, including the complete Sonnets and the plays *Cymbeline*, *Twelfth Night*, and *As You Like It*. Her own writing focused on theatrical works with themes of family tensions. Her prose works, a novel and a collection of short stories, feature marginal characters as well as criticism of hypocrisy and a closed society. Montoriol was a social and political figure as well, and during the Civil War she devoted herself to cultural activities on behalf of the Republic. Another prolific novelist, poet, and translator of the period was Maria Teresa Vernet (also Barnet, 1907–1974), whose novels deal with female psychology and family conflicts. Her literary production stopped during the Civil War.

The towering figure of the first half of the century, however, is that of Caterina Albert (pseud. Víctor Català, 1869–1966). Born in L'Escala, a small coastal town in the province of Girona, Albert alternated between the city life of Barcelona, keeping abreast of innovations in the literary and theatrical scenes, and the rural environment of her birthplace. After a traditional, basic education, she set up her own disciplined program of reading and study at home, hiring tutors for art classes. Like many other women writers of the time, Albert began by writing poetry, contributing to *Renaixença* journals and winning a prize in the 1898 *Jocs Florals* of Olot. Her masculine pseudonym, along with the themes of violence and brutality in her work, not to mention the prejudices of the time, contributed to assessment of Albert as a "masculine" writer. She was prolific in all genres, but her best-known work is the novel *Solitud* (1905; Solitude), whose female protagonist struggles for survival in an isolated rural environment. This work is representative of Albert's production in its use of *costumisme* (local color), with elements of realism, naturalism, Romanticism, and a rich regional vocabulary. In 1923, Albert became the first woman to be elected to the Reial Acadèmia de Bones Lletres de Barcelona (Barcelona Royal Academy of Fine Arts).

Born into a literary and artistic family, Aurora Bertrana (1899–1974) was already a professional musician when she began her writing career as a journalist. She wrote essays and chronicles for Catalan and Swiss periodicals but turned to fiction, often using characters and situations drawn from her travels to exotic places. In the early 1930s, she failed in her efforts to found a university for women workers; she claimed to be apolitical but embraced a pacifist stance that she maintained throughout her life.

The Postwar Era

Three important poets whose work spans the war years are Clementina Arderiu (1889–1976), Rosa Leveroni (1910–1985), and Simona Gay (1898–1969). They had strong ties with the literary scene in Barcelona and were influenced by the earlier movements of *Modernisme* and *Noucentisme*. Arderiu and Leveroni participated in the *tertulias* (cultural social gatherings) and publishing activities alongside their male counterparts in Barcelona such as Carles Riba (1893–1959) and Josep Carner (1884–1970). Gay was also in contact with these poets from the French side of the Catalan-speaking area, the Roussillon. Working in prose at about the same time are novelists/journalists Anna Murià (1904–   ) and Rosa Maria Arquimbau (pseud. Rosa de Sant Jordi, 1910–   ). Both went into exile, like so many intellectuals, as a result of the Civil War.

In 1980, Mercè Rodoreda (1908–1983) won the prestigious Premi d'Honor de les Lletres Catalanes (Prize of Honor in Catalan Letters). Granted for her entire literary production, it was a rather belated recognition of her peerless talent and impressive body of work. Considered by many to be the greatest narrator of twentieth-century Catalan literature, she is the only woman to have achieved such high regard in the world of Catalan culture. Rodoreda began writing before the outbreak of the Civil War (1936–1939), but she later disclaimed four of the five novels she published in her youth. Like so many others, she spent years in exile, returning to Barcelona after Franco's death in 1975. She won prizes for her poetry in the late 1940s and for short stories in 1957; she also wrote several plays and tried her hand at painting. But her major work is fiction, and most critics consider her masterpiece to be *La plaça del Diamant* (1962; *The Time of the Doves*, 1981), a novel set in wartime and postwar Barcelona. This tragic setting is seen through the eyes of a lower-class woman whose narration is only apparently simple; in fact Rodoreda creates an exquisite idiom, full of lyricism and vitality. Other Rodoredan novels also use female protagonists: *Aloma* (1938) features a young woman trying to make the best of the few choices she has in life; in *El carrer de les Camèlies* (1966; *Camellia Street*, 1993), the orphaned Cecília C narrates her horrendous existence as a brutalized kept woman; and Teresa Goday of *Mirall trencat* (1974; Broken Mirror) is the focal point of several generations of a well-to-do Barcelona family. Rodoreda's short fiction begins with grotesque tales of war and exile and then moves to the fantastic with experimentation in various narrative techniques. Her work was admired and praised by Colombian Nobel Laureate Gabriel García Márquez.

Maria Aurèlia *Capmany (1918–1991) and Teresa Pàmies (1919–   ) are both prolific writers with a lifetime commitment to social change and political activities. Capmany, author of 59 books, served as cultural counselor for the city of Barcelona toward the end of her long career. A strong feminist, many compared her to Simone de *Beauvoir for her tireless striving for equal rights for women, both in her writing and in direct action. Also a strong Catalanist, she served as mentor and inspiration for younger women writers such as Montserrat Roig and Maria-Antònia Oliver. Capmany's early novels are psychological, and later themes become more philosophical, including a growing obsession with the passage of time. Her work is characterized by a healthy optimism and good humor. Pàmies's writings are dominated by novelized chronicles that document her experiences as a militant activist during the Republic, the war, and its aftermath. Her work contains much social criticism done with a great deal of humor and delightful irony.

Angels Anglada (1930–1999) and Olga Xirinacs (1936–) are both known as accomplished poets and novelists, with their musical training showing in both genres. Anglada is a classicist, translator of Greek poetry and retired from teaching Latin and Greek. Her work shows this influence but also includes many Catalan themes, such as a novelized account of a political crime in her native Figueres. Xirinacs also uses her birthplace, Tarragona, as backdrop for much of her adventure-filled fiction. Some of her poetry is love poetry and is also informed by classical writers such as Vergil.

Although both Marta Pessarrodona (1941–) and Maria-Mercè Marçal (1952–1998) have written some fiction, they are known mainly as poets and are perhaps the best-known women poets writing today. Pessarrodona has been greatly influenced by her lengthy stays in England and Germany and her frequent return trips to those countries. She is also a literary critic and strong feminist. Marçal, as well, is known for her insightful criticism and for her feminist activism. Her early poetry shows mastery of technique, particularly the medieval sestina. Some of her poems have been set to music and sung by the masters of the *Nova cançó*. Marçal's themes include female sexuality, motherhood, solidarity among women, and recovery of women's history. Other important poets of the postwar period are Montserrat Abelló (1918–), well known as a translator; Felícia Fuster (1921–), a visual artist working in France; Renada-Laura Portet (1927–), another representative of *Catalunya nord*, the Catalan-speaking area of southern France; and Maria Oleart (1929–), who also writes children's literature.

The post-Franco era is especially rich in prose fiction. In addition to those mentioned above, a number of women have produced an important body of literature featuring such subgenres of the narrative as detective novels, eroticism, family chronicles, and science fiction. One of the most prolific and varied is Isabel-Clara Simó (1943–), whose work includes such difficult subject matter as perversity among children and dissections of power, control, and manipulation among adults. Simó is, at the same time, capable of great lyricism and good humor. Helena Valentí (1940–1990) produced a smaller opus of finely chiseled, elegantly composed narrations, exploring a variety of nontraditional relationships and creating striking images of tightropes and balancing acts, with the constant presence of the sea. Maria-Antònia Oliver (1946–) uses the detective novel to create strong female protagonists and to explore relationships, both traditional and marginal. Her native Majorca serves as more than a background for her work: The island's magical folklore often enriches both plot and imagery. Margarida Aritzeta (1953–) delves into science fiction and politics to explore changing gender roles, aging, powerless minorities, and language control.

Among the most popular recent writers, both with book sales and critical notice, are Montserrat Roig (1946–1991), Carme Riera (1946–), and Maria-Mercè Roca (1958–). Roig's untimely death cut short a brilliant career that began with hard-hitting journalism and went on to great literary production. She never left her work in periodicals, and some of her fiction is informed by that journalistic experience. She creates a family chronicle spanning several generations and narrated by women; an Andalusian maid transformed into a Catalan militant; an ugly, overprotected young man who brings his impeccable education into the student movements of the 1960s. Roig's work often quotes the great Catalan writers of the past, particularly the poets. Carme Riera's fiction is characterized by intertextuality and epistolarity as she weaves real and imagined documents into her stories and novels, several of which take place in Majorca. Her themes range from female sexuality to the creation of writing; her imagery is replete with artistic and literary allusions and nature, especially the sea. Maria-Mercè Roca began a meteoric career with the publication of five books in 1986 and 1987, and she has continued a steady production. Her collections of stories and vignettes range from traditional to whimsical, often unified around some ordinary object or circumstance: a wine list, an apartment building, ads in a newspaper, the recounting of dreams. Her novels include a family chronicle, psychological studies of both female and male protagonists, recreations and/or reinterpretations of biblical scenes, and the post-1492 explorations. Her work shows keen observation and insight and often becomes delicately sensual and lyrical. Roca has also written scripts for Catalan television programs.

While the traditional problems that besiege women writers in all times and places cannot be said to have been solved, so many talented new voices have entered the literary scene in the 1980s and 1990s that, with respect to both quantity and quality, Catalan women writers are reaching the threshold of no longer being marginalized within their cultural milieu. *See also* Drama by Spanish Women Writers: 1970–2000.

Work by

Albert, Caterina [Víctor Català]. *Obres completes.* 1951. 2nd ed. Barcelona: Selecta, 1972.

——. *Solitude.* Trans. David Rosenthal. London: Readers International, 1992.

Capmany, Maria-Aurèlia. *Obra completa.* Barcelona: Nova Terra, 1974.

Catalan Review 3.2 (December 1989): 224–251. Trans. Kathleen McNerney. Contains Fuster and Portet.

Cortijo Ocaña, Antonio. "Women's Role in the Creation of Literature in Catalonia at the End of the Fourteenth and Beginning of the Fifteenth Century." *La corónica* 27.1 (1998): 7–20.

Marçal, Maria-Mercè. "Witch in Mourning" (Selections from *Bruixa de dol*). Trans. Kathleen McNerney. *Catalan Review* 1.2 (1986): 180–181; *Seneca Review* 16.1 (1986): 45–48.

Oliver, Maria-Antònia. *Antipodes.* Trans. Kathleen McNerney. Seattle: Seal Press, 1989.

——. *Study in Lilac.* Trans. Kathleen McNerney. Seattle: Seal Press, 1987.

On Our Own Behalf: Women's Tales from Catalonia. Ed. Kathleen McNerney. Lincoln: U of Nebraska P, 1988. Includes Riera, Valentí, Oliver, Simó, and Roig.

Rodoreda, Mercè. *Camellia Street.* Trans. David Rosenthal. Saint Paul: Graywolf, 1993.

——. *My Christina and Other Stories.* Trans. David Rosenthal. Port Townsend: Graywolf, 1984.

——. *Obres completes.* 3 vols. Barcelona: Edicions 62, 1976–1984.

——. *The Time of the Doves.* Trans. David Rosenthal. New York: Taplinger, 1984. Saint Paul: Graywolf, 1986.

Simó, Isabel-Clara. *A Corpse of One's Own.* Trans. Patricia Hart. New York: Peter Lang, 1993.

Survivors. Sel. and trans. D. Sam Abrams. Barcelona: Institut d'Estudis Nord-Americans, 1991. Includes Salvà, Arderiu, Leveroni, Abelló, Fuster, Anglada, Pessarrodona, Ballester, and Marçal.

Work about

Martí-Olivella, Jaume, ed. *Catalan Review* 2.2 (1988). Special issue devoted to Rodoreda.

——. *Catalan Review* 7.2 (1993). Special issue devoted to Roig and Capmany.

McNerney, Kathleen, and Cristina Enríquez de Salamanca, eds. *Double Minorities of Spain: A Bio-Bibliographic Guide to Women Writers of the Catalan, Galician and Basque Countries.* New York: Modern Language Association, 1994.

McNerney, Kathleen, and Nancy Vosburg, eds. *The Garden across the Border: Mercè Rodoreda's Fiction.* Selinsgrove: Susquehanna UP, 1994.

Riquer, Martí de, et al. *Història de la literatura catalana.* 11 vols. Barcelona: Ariel, 1964–1988.

Roca Pons, Josep. *Introduction to Catalan Literature.* Bloomington: Indiana UP, 1977.

Zubatsky, David S. *Spanish, Catalan, and Galician Literary Authors of the Twentieth Century: An Anno-*

tated *Guide to Bibliographies*. Metuchen, NJ: Scarecrow P, 1992.

Kathleen McNerney

Catalina de Aragón (1485–1536)

The eldest child of Isabel I and Fernando, the *reyes Católicos* (Catholic Monarchs), Catalina de Aragón was the first wife of Henry VIII of England. Her refusal to accept an annulment of her marriage and Pope Clement's support of her claim led to England's break with the Roman Catholic Church. She had married Prince Arthur in 1501, but he died the following year, and she then married Henry in 1509. A well-read, competent queen, she served as regent from 1512 to 1514 while Henry was in France. Catalina became a patron of humanistic study, supporting scholars and contributing to lectureships at Cambridge and Oxford. Her court was an illustrious one, frequented by Erasmus, Thomas More, and Luis *Vives, among others. Erasmus commented on her exceptional learning. Vives, who first came to England in 1523, dedicated his treatise *De institutio christiana feminae* (On the Education of a Christian Woman) to Catherine, assisted her in planning her daughter's education, and served as her tutor. Both Vives and More supported a higher degree of education for young girls.

Catherine bore her husband six children, but only Mary survived infancy. Henry's desire for a male heir prompted him to seek an annulment of the marriage in 1527 and to unilaterally divorce Catalina in 1531. In 1533, when he married Anne Boleyn, Henry convinced Parliament to pass the Act of Supremacy repudiating papal authority in England and making him head of the Church. Catalina was forced to retire completely from public life and lived as a virtual prisoner until her death.

Work about

Luke, Mary M. *Catherine, the Queen*. New York: Coward-McCann, 1967.

Mattingly, Garrett. *Catherine of Aragon*. New York: Vintage, 1941.
Travitsky, Betty S. "Reprinting Tudor History: The Case of Catherine of Aragon." *Renaissance Quarterly* 50.1 (Spring 1997): 164–174.

David H. Darst

Cela, Camilo José (1916–2002): Women in His Works

Spain's most recent recipient of the Nobel Prize for Literature (1989) was the author of "more than 100 books" (according to numerous attributions published following the award)—some 14 long novels and several collections of novelettes, at least half a dozen story collections, and many volumes of unclassifiable brief fiction and artistic essays variously termed sketches, notes, vignettes, and scenes. He also published poetry, autobiography and memoirs, theater, and assorted scholarly essays, in addition to many volumes of collected journalistic articles. Cela's output includes a four-volume, truncated *Diccionario secreto* (1969–1974; Secret Dictionary), an erudite, lexicographical, and morphological compilation of obscenities (primarily related to human sexual organs) with corresponding slang, euphemisms, and learned equivalents; plus a two-volume *Enciclopedia del erotismo* (1976; Encyclopedia of Eroticism)—a lavishly illustrated, glossy collector's edition that concentrates on sexual deviance, oddities, abnormalities, and otherwise little-known aspects of human sexuality, along with eroticism's less esoteric facets.

The foregoing obviously bears upon Cela's treatment of women in his creative writing, especially the fiction for which he is best known, the more so because similar emphasis upon eroticism and deviant sexuality pervades his fiction, long and short. The relatively small percentage of women in his works who are not prostitutes or sexual predators are usually very young, very old, or not very bright—neglected housewives who struggle with insufficient food allowances, remaining faithful and submissive to an inept husband who puts his teeth in a glass of water beside the bed, for example, as seen in one characteristically ironic or cynical portrayal of conventional matrimony. In fairness, it must be noted that Cela's male characters are no better than the females, and are usually worse, but his fiction unquestionably portrays a *machista* (male-exalting), phallocentric vision of human relationships in which women are not merely sex objects but pawns.

Cela has been controversial throughout his career, from publication of his first novel in 1942 through the 1989 Nobel Prize and 1997 Premio Cervantes. Critics consider him the founder of *tremendismo*, a grotesque, expressionistic variant of neonaturalism, deemed Spain's first postwar "movement" (Cela always denied its existence). Aspects of naturalism (sordidness, illness and deformities, lower-class environments, violence, and repulsive characters) combine with expressionist techniques (deformation, caricature, exaggeration) producing a "tremendous" effect on readers. It is important to remember that these negative aesthetics inform Cela's worldview, not only his portrayal of women. He depicts a world populated by the crippled, ugly, retarded, mutilated, blind, and deformed, on the one hand, and on the other, those of sound body tend to be psychologically negative: sadists, fanatics, pedophiles, misers, pimps, criminals, wife beaters and child abusers, degraded, slothful, drunken. These include few rounded characterizations: Cela's personages are largely caricatures, superficially sketched, with little or no psychic development.

Cela's two most celebrated novels, *La familia de Pascual Duarte* (1942; *The Family of Pascual Duarte*, 1946) and *La colmena* (1951; *The Hive*, 1953) are also the most studied; close to three-fourths of all critical investigations privilege these two titles and the majority mention the presence of crimes, murders, and atrocities, existential alienation, solitude, absurdity, and despair. The variety and number of exotic, horrible forms of violent death are exceeded only by the range of sexual aberrations and perversions, contributing to a seemingly endless portrayal of hunger, misery, moral bankruptcy, and man's inhumanity to man (and women and children). Prefaces to *La colmena* contain such authorial statements as "Life isn't good; neither is man" and "All I've done is take my camera into the streets; if the models are ugly, too bad." A critical commonplace divides Cela's characters into victims and executioners, or exploiters and the exploited, and exceptions are rare, indeed.

La familia de Pascual Duarte, allegedly the most translated work of Spanish literature after *Don Quijote, paints a dark vision of the world and humanity that provoked widespread shock and revulsion. Cela's preface to an edition for American students of this autobiographical "confession" of a convicted criminal awaiting execution affirms that society as a whole bears a "pro rata of guilt" in the crimes of individuals such as Pascual. Despite the title, Cela is in no way a novelist of families or domestic life; not even *Mrs. Caldwell habla con su hijo* (1953; *Mrs. Caldwell Speaks to Her Son*, 1968), his first novel with a feminine protagonist and feminine narrative consciousness, involves any semblance of family life. Pascual Duarte's reconstruction of his life in relation to his family and his home, both cruel caricatures of the ideal, subversively parodies the Holy Family or the Franco regime's promulgation of "family values." Pascual's mother resembles a witch—tall, unhealthily thin, with yellowish skin and sunken cheeks, suggesting tuberculosis or some terminal illness. She dresses always in filthy black, hates water, has a thin gray mustache, various scars, warts, and sores—Pascual compares her with a scarecrow; she has a violent temper, permanent bad mood, drinks to excess, is ignorant and blasphemous, and (worse for readers of the day) is an adulteress with little or no love for her children. His sister Rosario's early fondness for alcohol stimulates her precocious talent for thievery; after stealing the family's few objects of value, she leaves home to become a teenage prostitute. Her redeeming quality is her love for her brother. Pascual's first wife, Lola, whom he raped atop his brother's fresh-dug grave and married months later when she became pregnant, is an archetypical sex object: tall, dark, with long black hair and deep eyes, a voluptuous body, and instinctive sensuality. Mainly body, Lola has little subjectivity and, lacking education, no way of supporting herself when Pascual is imprisoned for knifing a man in a barroom brawl; she becomes the lover of "El Estirao," Rosario's pimp, and dies when Pascual strangles her in a knee-jerk reaction upon hearing that Estirao fathered the child she is carrying. Esperanza, his second wife, is older, and less emphasis falls upon her body (her rosy cheeks and slenderness are the principal details); she is an orphan, timid and reserved, quite religious, clean and modest—much closer to the feminine model promulgated by the regime, she is resigned and submissive. Nowhere in *La familia de Pascual Duarte* is there a woman with an individual personality, although his mother's portrait is unforgettably etched on the reader's memory by the scene in which she fights her son like an animal upon awaking to discover him standing over her with an axe. Pascual's mother is one of Cela's most repugnant creations, although Doña Rosa in *La colmena* must be deemed a close second.

Ranking only slightly behind *Pascual Duarte* with readers, and first with many critics, *La colmena* is a long experimental novel, lacking plot, sustained action, and protagonist (unless it be the city of Madrid). The number of shadowy characters varies, with critical counts ranging from 200 to 360+ (many are little more than caricature outlines with various names or nicknames). One of the most extensively developed is Doña Rosa, who owns the cafe frequented by the remaining characters. Obese, with an enormous behind, tremendous breasts, swollen belly, and abundant facial hair, she smokes, swears, drinks constantly, coughs and sweats profusely, and reads pulp novels continually (preferring gore). She is compared to a "civil governor" and her appearance evokes political cartoons. Her face, covered by blemishes, features "little rat's eyes," blackened teeth full of garbage, and skin hanging in strips, as she is "constantly changing it like a lizard." Filthy, tyrannical, miserly, she admires Hitler and is characterized with numerous dehumanizing epithets: sow, pig, witch. Cela attributes to her many traits of the stereotypically masculine spinster, and he insinuates maliciously that she is lesbian. The ferocious caricature appeals to misogynist readers (incorporating the Falangists' hatred of homosexuality), creating a character sufficiently repulsive for the Spanish reading public that she functions to undermine any cause with which she is associated.

The second most memorable female character in *The Hive* is "Miss Elvira," a title suggesting some degree of social standing and refinement, both of which are absent. An aging prostitute, she has so few clients that she seldom eats; her sunken teeth, reddened eyelids, mouthful of cavities, and eyes surrounded by crows' feet all reduce the saleability of an unfortunate woman who never was especially attractive. She clearly belongs to the class of victims: an orphan whose father killed her mother and was executed, she is docile, weak, sentimental, good-hearted, compassionate, passive, and eager to please. Even after a long life of prostitution, she retains certain scruples; like most of the multitude of prostitutes thronging Cela's pages, Elvira suffers from the generalized lack of viable alternatives for women in need of work, educated not for a career or any form of "employment" other than matrimony. Another victim, in a lesser degree, is Filomena, a 34-year-old housewife whose husband describes her mentality as that of a 6-year-old; she is romantic, sentimental, and cried all night because her husband and brother forgot her birthday. With five small children and little food in the house, she starves herself (despite being under a doctor's care) in order to feed her brother, who cannot obtain work because of his political background. She is the stereotyped "good wife and mother," self-abnegating, faithful, affectionate, devout, hardworking, and utterly boring, surely never having had an original idea in her life. Filomena belongs to a small minority of "good" characters in Cela's work, most of whom are neither fortunate nor clever. Petra, an 18-year-old maid, is exceptional and perhaps unique, not only in *La colmena*, but in the vast majority of Cela's fiction, in that she is capable not only of an unselfish, disinterested sacrifice but also of concealing it from the beneficiary. This strangely beautiful girl with wild hair and shining eyes, enamored of Filomena's destitute brother Martín, neither reveals her feelings nor permits him to return her love, avoiding his attempts at intimacy. Upon learning that Martín has a debt neither he nor his sister can repay, she pays the repulsive usurer with her body. Although Spain's puritanical, patriarchal society of the day would condemn a virgin's "selling herself" for any reason, she acts out of pure altruism, avoiding even the possibility of gratitude. Counterbalancing this rare generosity are innumerable cases of venality, such as the grandmother who sells her little granddaughter to an aging pedophile. Most women in *La colmena* are negative caricatures, lacking substance. Age and social class vary, but the most numerous groups include the mistresses of wealthy men (usually young, attractive, and scatterbrained); and gossipy old ladies, wives, or widows, whose primary activity appears to be criticizing others for the most trivial reasons. These figures would have to be somewhat further developed to qualify as stereotypes; they are unfinished sketches, skeletal caricatures (as are the majority of female characters in the remaining works of Cela). All too often they are victims of abuse, rape, torture, and murder. Occasional shadings appear in novels of Cela's "second period" (the 1980s and 1990s), but exceptions to the general pattern are rare.

Two novels by Cela have women's names in their titles, *Mrs. Caldwell habla con su hijo* and *La Catira* (1955); both women may be considered protagonists. Mrs. Caldwell is essentially the only character as others appear only as her recollections or fantasies, filtered through her consciousness. There being no antagonist other than her own hallucinations and exacerbated sexual appetites and frustrations, she is not a true protagonist. In years past, she was an unfaithful wife (her son was sired by a neighbor), and she alludes to her daring dress when younger. Now a vagabond white-haired lady whose body evinces the ravages of aging, she is a victim of her own incestuous fantasies. "La Catira," compared by critics with the protagonist of Rómulo Gallegos's *Doña Bárbara*, shares several traits with Bárbara: Both are characterized as powerful, semicivilized women of the Venezuelan ranchlands. Although Catira departs from typical Cela models, she seems not to be primarily his invention.

With rare exceptions, women in Cela's works fall into a few groups: prostitutes, adulteresses, and the promiscuous (portrayed as having exorbitant sexual appetites); faithful wives and mothers, usually colorless, altruistic, self-abnegating, and not very bright; middle-aged gossips, with more economic means and little to occupy their time; older women who are frustrated, doddering, or both; the occasional bad-tempered bitch; and the very rare, very young virgin, whose innocence is invariably sacrificed. As may be deduced, Cela's works contain evident *misogyny, a good deal of complacent *machismo*, and abundant eroticism (from straightforward heterosexuality to the most bizarre deviations). "Progress" in later works takes the form of increasingly more explicit sexuality, with liberated women allowed more freedom to indulge their sexuality, but without Cela's portraying other significant advances for women. Following the demise of the Franco-era censorship, later works include explicit incest, torture, and sexual mutilations, among other things hardly calculated to endear Cela to feminists.

Work by

El asesinato del perdedor. Barcelona: Seix Barral, 1994.
La colmena. Buenos Aires: Emecé, 1951; Barcelona: Noguer, 1955.
Cristo versus Arizona. Barcelona: Seix Barral, 1988.
La cruz de San Andrés. Barcelona: Planeta, 1994.
La familia de Pascual Duarte. Burgos: Aldecoa, 1942.
Historias de Venezuela: La Catira. Barcelona: Noguer, 1955.
The Hive. Trans. J.M. Cohen and Arturo Barea. New York: Farrar, Straus and Young, 1953.
Mazurca for Two Dead Men. Trans. Patricia Haugaard. New York: New Directions, 1992.
Mazurca para dos muertos. Barcelona: Seix Barral, 1983.
Mrs. Caldwell habla con su hijo. Barcelona: Destino, 1953.
Mrs. Caldwell Speaks to Her Son. Trans. J.S. Bernstein. Ithaca: Cornell UP, 1968.
Nuevas andanzas y desventuras del Lazarillo de Tormes. Madrid: La Nave, 1944.
Pabellón de reposo. Madrid: Afrodisio Aguado, 1944.
Pascual Duarte and His Family. Trans. Herma Briffault. New York: Las Américas, 1956.
Rest Home. Trans. Herma Briffault. New York: Las Américas, 1961.
San Camilo, 1936: The Eve, Feast, and Octave of St. Camillus of the Year 1936 in Madrid. Trans. John H.R. Polt. Durham: Duke UP, 1991.
Tobogán de hambrientos. Barcelona: Noguer, 1962.
Víspera, festividad y octava de San Camilo del año 1936 en Madrid. Madrid: Alfaguara, 1969.

Work about

Blanco Vila, Luis. *Para leer a Camilo José Cela*. Madrid: Palas Atenea, 1991.
Cela Conde, Camilo José. *Cela, mi padre*. Madrid: Temas de Hoy, 1989.
Charlebois, Lucile. *Understanding Camilo José Cela*. Columbia: U of South Carolina P, 1998.
Foster, David W. *Forms of the Novel in the Works of Camilo José Cela*. Columbia: U of Missouri P, 1967.
Giménez-Frontín, José Luis. *Camilo José Cela. Texto y contexto*. Barcelona: Montesinos, 1985.
Ilie, Paul. *La novelística de Camilo José Cela*. Madrid: Gredos, 1971.
Kirsner, Robert. *The Novels and Travels of Camilo José Cela*. Chapel Hill: U of North Carolina P, 1963.
McPheeters, D.W. *Camilo José Cela*. New York: Twayne, 1969.
Pérez, Janet. "Text, Context and Subtext of the Unreliable Narrative: Cela's *El asesinato del perdedor*." *Anales de la Literatura Española Contemporánea* 21.1 (1996): 103–118.
Suárez Solís, Sara. *El léxico de Camilo José Cela*. Barcelona: Alfaguara, 1969.
Zamora Vicente, Alonso. *Camilo José Cela*. Madrid: Gredos, 1962.

Janet Pérez

Celestina, La. Comedia o tragicomedia de Calisto y Melibea

Celestina is the principal female character in Fernando de Rojas's (1465?–1541) play of the same name (*Comedia*, 1499; *Tragicomedia*, c. 1502). Portrayed as a traditional Spanish *alcahueta* (procuress), the character confirms the craftiness and manipulative skill associated with go-betweens by arranging for the nonmarital liaison of the young Calisto and the object of his desire, Melibea, at the former's request. The process leads to a path of murder and corruption involving the lovers, Melibea's family, and various servants and accomplices. Shortly after the lovers finally consummate their passion, the old woman herself is killed by Calisto's servants who are her greedy accomplices, Calisto falls to his death on his way out of Melibea's bedroom, his servants are executed by the authorities, and Melibea commits suicide.

Due to society's negative view of her profession, Celestina inspires much hatred and diatribe throughout the play. Not only do her own accomplices consider her to be corrupt, but also the lovers themselves—in moments of anger—accuse her of covetousness and immorality, in spite of her immeasurable help in bringing about their sexual union. At first sight, therefore, her character reinforces the traditional spite and disapproval aimed at the figure of the procuress in all of literature. Her portrayal is on one level informed by the well-known misogynist notion of the old crone who facilitates the fruition of illicit love and whose aims are nothing but financial greed and the perpetration of intrigue.

Yet the representation of this go-between is not limited to the familiar parameters of medieval *misogyny. Celestina is the most complex literary manifestation of the procuress, appearing at the end of a long tradition of go-betweens and *alcahuetería* (pimping) in medieval literature. In medieval Spanish literature alone, various genres make use of the figure of the *alcahueta* to drive home the notion of the moral dangers and craftiness associated with old women: Legal, narrative, and didactic texts mention the figure as early as the thirteenth century, culminating in the lively and jovial portrayal of the sly go-between Trotaconventos (convent-trotter) by Juan Ruiz, archpriest of Hita (1283?–1353?) in his *Libro de buen amor* (1335, 1343). With Trotaconventos, medieval Spanish literature confirms the indispensability of the third party for facilitation of illicit love affairs and establishes the significance of the old woman in this role. Able to communicate with both men and women, experienced in matters related to love, and highly skillful in translating the young lovers' clumsy attempts at communication into colorful and seductive language, Trotaconventos transcends the usual negative image associated with the go-between.

Rojas's creation harks back in many ways to Trotaconventos, especially in reinforcing the concept that illicit love and seduction are not possible without the mediation of a skilled and linguistically talented third party. At the same time, Celestina's portrayal is reminiscent of numerous other literary traditions, all of which contribute to the complexity of her characterization. To a limited extent, this Spanish *alcahueta* recalls the traits of the Latin "lena," the drunken old procuress encountered in many works from antiquity. From the theater of Titus Maccius Plautus (250?–184 B.C.) to the elegies of Publius Ovidius Naso, better known as Ovid (43 B.C.–A.D. 17), the literature of antiquity contains many examples of old crones who attempt to lure young courtesans into pairing off with wealthy lovers at the expense of true love and monogamy. In medieval Europe, the literatures of France, England, and Italy make use of this basic model: Scattered across prose, narrative poetry, and didactic works, the old woman continues to appear in her capacity as a corrupting third party who laments the loss of her own youth and encourages young wives or unmarried women to benefit from their youth and beauty while they can. One of the most prominent examples of this portrayal is the *Vieille* found in the continuation to the *Roman de la Rose* (c. 1290) by Jean de Meun (?–1305?).

However, contrary to what some critics have always assumed, the similarities between Celestina and her counterparts in antiquity and medieval European literature are not substantial, even if Rojas was familiar with these sources. The European and Latin versions pale in comparison to the vigor and force of Celestina; whereas the latter creates significant impact on the text in both thematic and structural ways, her Latin and European counterparts are largely portrayed as pathetic stock figures who make episodic entrances into the works, repeat a number of used clichés, and disappear without any impact or consequence on the outcome of the work.

Recent research has shown that the literary traditions exhibiting a much closer affinity with the Spanish go-between are found in the East. The early Spanish *alcahuetas*, as well as Trotaconventos and Celestina, derive many significant traits from their Muslim counterparts, as seen in numerous genres in medieval Persian and Arabic literature. Whereas the Latin and medieval European procuresses occupy the text in essentially unimportant and episodic ways, the Near Eastern go-between, often referred to in Arabic as the *ajuz* (old woman), is a crucial element in the seduction of young lovers on behalf of one another. Many genres, including narrative poems, short tales, and treatises on love and sexuality, refer to the old go-between as one of the most common players in the game of seduction, showing that she is an absolute necessity for the realization of an illicit love affair. The *Perfumed Garden* of Sheikh Umar ibn Muhammad al-Nafzawi, written in the sixteenth century, the *Delight of Hearts* (thirteenth century) by the Tunisian Ahmad al-Tifachi (?–1253), and the narrative poem *Vis and Ramin* (1055) by Fakhreddine Gorgani (1048–?) are among the numerous texts in which the go-between plays a crucial role for the lovers, using a wide range of devices, from magic and witchcraft to dazzling verbal skill.

It is not difficult to see how these texts made their way into the literary traditions of medieval Spain. Islamic influences entered medieval Spanish literature through a wealth of translations as well as the work of Muslim writers and scholars in the Peninsula itself. Given the cohabitation of Muslims and Christians for over seven centuries in Spain, the very nature of much of medieval Spanish literature was often marked by a strongly *mudéjar* quality; that is to say, it was informed by Hispano-Oriental traits that recalled Arab and other Eastern sources much more than their Latin counterparts from antiquity. Motifs, subject matter, and significant themes moved freely from the east to Spain. Harking back only superficially to the Latin *lena*, but drawing substantially on the Muslim version of the go-between, the Spanish *alcahueta* is one such motif, going on to assume her own unique identity in works such as *El libro de buen amor* and *La Celestina*.

It is also appropriate to note that the *alcahueta* in literature also reflects the preoccupation of society with the mercenary activities of the third party. Spanish society itself was no stranger to the phenomenon of proxenetism (that is, pimping) at almost every walk of life. The laws of King *Alfonso el Sabio (1221–1284) on the wrongdoings of the go-between and references to the evils of the *alcahueta* in the misogynist writings of the *Corbacho, by Archpriest of Talavera, Alfonso Martínez de Toledo (1398?–1482?), are prominent examples of nonfictional texts that warn the reader against the wiles of the procuress. In the literary portrayal of the figure, elements such as the use of potions, the links with non-Christian religions, and the restoring of virginity to young women are reflective of Spanish society's perceptions of the activities of the old woman.

Rojas does not depart from the norm in his depiction of the *alcahueta*: Like other go-betweens, Celestina is driven by financial greed and her close links with the world of prostitution. Yet the author subjects his go-between to a depth of scrutiny hitherto unknown in the treatment of this character. He explores her motivations, her fears, and her problematic relationship with the law and society. Contrary to other go-betweens from both Western and Eastern traditions, Celestina possesses a strong sense of self and understands the precarious nature of her status in society. When she is defensive, for example, she justifies this attitude in terms that are difficult to refute: In one of the most moving passages of the work (Act III), she indicates that like all others, she too must make a living, and as an old woman with no independent wealth or support, society leaves few options for her. Also, she subtly points out that the entire community knows her, that ambassadors and noblemen are among her clients, and that society nurtures the need for go-betweens. In this way she underscores the blatant hypocrisy at work in a society that simultaneously requires and admonishes her services. No other procuress in medieval or Latin literature draws attention to the problematic attitudes of society in this perceptive manner.

Celestina also articulates her deep fear of failure, which endows her with a markedly human quality. In Act IV of the play, as she embarks on her mission to talk Melibea into meeting Calisto, the old woman expresses her anxiety and imagines Calisto's wrath at her failure, trembling at the thought of the consequences of his anger. At this point the reader becomes aware of the extent to which the old woman is at the mercy of her clients' whims and how she must operate against the constant fear of authority and punishment. This leads to the problematization of the fixed notion that the *alcahueta* is a relentlessly corrupt, unscrupulous, and brazen individual.

By delving deep into Celestina's fears and motivations, Rojas challenges the traditional and essentially limited view of the old crone as an evil influence in an otherwise pure society. Celestina guides the reader through an intricate network of tangled loyalties involving the financial dependence of servants on masters (which invariably leads to resentment), the fear and curiosity of Melibea vis-à-vis Calisto's desire, and the young woman's confused notions regarding the preservation of her own *honor. The men and women who aid Celestina in her tasks are also driven by fear and greed, and the procuress does not stand alone in her immoral doings. Rojas is careful to show that society is so far gone in its own double standards that the procuress is only another player in the dark game of avarice and secret sexual desire. Rojas's attitude stems from his essentially pessimistic outlook as a *converso*, a new Christian living in fear of exposure under the fierce Catholic regime. As such, some *conversos* felt that the communities in which they lived had lost all support and guidance from a higher moral power and that life was governed by cruel and random factors. Celestina is one among many examples of society's lack of a grasp on its own immorality.

But the greatest impact of the old woman is exerted at the level of discourse and language. Reinforcing the notion that women are crafty, skillful, and highly manipulative in the domain of verbal seduction, Celestina first brilliantly seduces Pármeno—the only servant reluctant to commit any transgressions—into seeing the benefits of money and sexual success. Her verbal skills of seduction reach a new height when, after a series of violent rejections, she finally convinces Melibea to initiate and consummate the relationship with Calisto. Both cases highlight the hypnotic and mesmerizing quality of her discourse. She substantiates her arguments with religious, philosophical, and medical authority, proposing in a highly convincing manner that the human being cannot escape the grip of sexual desire and therefore must succumb to it without resistance. The registers she employs in this process cover an impressively wide range, from the most vulgar and graphic references to intercourse to deep philosophical convictions on the nature of male-female relationships. The passages in which she seduces Pármeno and Melibea into changing their minds contain some of the most superb examples of persuasive discourse in medieval literature.

A subtle paradox governs this aspect of her portrayal: The reader is made to hover between admiration and horror at her talent to pursue and corrupt. This is one of the continuous inconsistencies of medieval misogyny, skillfully problematized by Rojas: Discourse is the magic exercised by the experienced older woman, simultaneously stating an irrefutable fact—that sexuality is not a force to be denied—and inspiring moral reservation and fear.

Celestina occupies a significant place in Spanish letters of all ages: A uniquely Spanish creation like Don Quijote and Don Juan, as indicated by writer Ramiro de Maetzu (1875–1936), she draws upon a wealth of traditions to posit problems that are ultimately of a universal nature. She raises questions on the awkward relationship of society with sexuality and on the place of marginal figures in a community plagued by double standards. The play was followed by a number of continuations and has been performed on the stage and on film. Yet the creation of Rojas remains the most complex literary portrayal of the procuress, breathing new life into an otherwise predictable and tired misogynist cliché. *See also* Pícaras and Pícaros: Female and Male Rogues in the Spanish Picaresque Canon; *Tercera*

Work

Celestina: A Play in Twenty-One Acts Attributed to Fernando de Rojas. Trans. Mack H. Singleton. 1958. Rpt. Madison: U of Wisconsin P, 1968.

La Celestina. Comedia o Tragicomedia de Calisto y Melibea. Ed. P.E. Russell. Clásicos Castalia 191. Madrid: Castalia, 1991.

The Spanish Bawd: La Celestina. Being the Tragi-Comedy of Calisto and Melibea. Trans. J.M. Cohen. New York: New York UP, 1966.

Work about

Gilman, Stephen. *The Spain of Fernando de Rojas: The Intellectual and Social Landscape of La Celestina.* Princeton, NJ: Princeton UP, 1972.

Lida de Malkiel, María Rosa. *Two Spanish Masterpieces: The Book of Good Love, and The Celestina.* Urbana: U of Illinois P, 1961.

Márquez Villanueva, Francisco. *Orígenes y sociología del tema celestinesco.* Barcelona: Anthropos, 1993.

Shipley, George. "Authority and Experience in *La Celestina.*" *Bulletin of Hispanic Studies* 62 (1985): 95–111.

Snow, Joseph T. *Celestina by Fernando de Rojas: An Annotated Bibliography of World Interest, 1930–1985.* Madison: Hispanic Seminary of Medieval Studies, 1985.

Leyla Rouhi

Celia

See Fortún, Elena, Pseudonym of Encarnación Aragoneses Urquijo (1886–1952)

Cepeda y Ahumada, Teresa

See Teresa de Jesús, Santa (1515–1582)

Cervantes, Miguel de

See Don Quijote de la Mancha (Part I, 1605; Part II, 1615): Its Representation of Women

Chacel, Rosa (1898–1994)

Born in Valladolid, Rosa Chacel was a follower of the philosopher-critic-publisher José *Ortega y Gasset (1883–1955) and a member of the Generation of 1927. Unlike the "dehumanized" literature of some of her contemporaries, Chacel managed to balance the exploration of her protagonists' psyches with polished writing and emotion. Chacel initially intended to be an artist; she began studying art at age eight, and after moving with her parents to Madrid in 1908, she continued her studies, first at the Escuela de Artes y Oficios and later at the prestigious (but unheated) San Fernando fine arts school. There she met her future husband, painter Timoteo Pérez Rubio. Only after fragile health forced her to abandon art studies did she begin her lifelong association with the literary world, becoming a member of the Madrid Ateneo, meeting Ortega and Ramón Gómez de la Serna (1888–1963), who invited her to collaborate in the leading journals of the day. Chacel and her husband spent 1922 to 1929 in Rome at the Spanish Academy. There she read Ortega's theories of the novel in *Ideas sobre la novela* (1925) and *La deshumanización del arte* (1925) and wrote her first novel, *Estación, ida y vuelta* (1930; Station, Round Trip), a *Küntslerroman* ("formation of an artist" novel) influenced by James Joyce's *Portrait of the Artist* as well as Ortega and Proust. Chacel insisted that her intention was to write a novel following Ortega's theories. She remained Ortega's most faithful follower during her entire career; nonetheless, as Scarlett and others have shown, Chacel also reacted against his ideas on male superiority and woman as the weaker sex intellectually. The word *estación* in the title of this first novel means both train station and season; thus the title refers both to the male protagonist's train voyage Madrid-Paris-Madrid and the cycles of the seasons. *Estación* proved to be seminal, resulting 30 years later in the profound confessional novel *La sinrazón* (1960; Beyond Reason). The protagonist Santiago studies existence, God's will, and his own reasons for being. His search for meaning leads him beyond reason (*la razón*) to *la sinrazón*, literally "without reason," but also connoting injury and injustice. The work was not published in

Spain until 1970 and won the Critics' Prize in 1977.

In the 1930s Chacel also published a collection of vanguard sonnets, *A la orilla de un pozo* (1936; Beside a Well). She was writing a biographical novel of *Espronceda's poetic muse, Teresa Mancha (to be included in Ortega's series Extraordinary Lives of the 19th Century), when the Spanish Civil War broke out. During and after the war, Chacel lived and traveled in several European capitals, finally immigrating in 1940 to Rio de Janeiro with her husband and young son Carlos. While her husband worked in Brazil, Chacel and her son resided in Buenos Aires much of the year, as Carlos attended school and she collaborated on several Argentinean journals, especially *Sur* and *La Nación*. Finally, in 1941, *Teresa* was published in Buenos Aires. The novel treats both political and social exile experienced by the revolutionary Romantic Espronceda and his mistress, who dared defy nineteenth-century society by leaving her husband and young child to life with Espronceda first in Paris and later in Madrid. The Franco regime prevented publication of all of Chacel's novels between 1930 and 1963, when *Teresa* was published there.

Chacel's third novel, *Memorias de Leticia Valle* (Memoirs of Leticia Valle, 1994), was begun in Italy in 1930 and published in Argentina in 1945. This diary presents the themes of artistic education, and possible child molestation or a child seducing a man, from the perspective of the precocious adolescent Leticia. During this same period, Chacel's first collection of short stories, *Sobre el piélago* (1951; On the High Seas), appeared. These were combined with *Ofrenda a una virgen loca* (1961; Offering to a Crazy Virgin) in the 1971 anthology *Icada, Nevda, Diada* (Three Variations on Nothing). These again were incorporated into a new collection, *Balaam y otros cuentos* (1989; Balaam and Other Stories). In 1972, Chacel published an autobiography of her first 10 years, *Desde el amanecer* (1972; Since Dawn) wherein she explains her early vocation for art and literature.

Chacel's next novel, *Barrio de maravillas* (1976; The Maravillas District, 1992) won the 1976 Critics' Prize. It is the first work of the "Platonic School" (*La escuela de Platón*) trilogy, which chronicles the history of Chacel's literary generation. *Barrio de maravillas* covers the period from the turn of the century to 1914 and is followed by *Acrópolis* (1984; Acropolis), which narrates events from 1914 to the Civil War. *Ciencias naturales* (1988; Natural Sciences) begins with the period of exile in Argentina and concludes with the protagonist's airplane trip home to Spain after Franco's death. The trilogy is a *Bildungsroman* of several young artists/writers but concentrates on two young women, Isabel and Elena (the latter being a sort of alter ego of Chacel). The reader sees the struggles of young women attempting to become artists and overcome the prejudices of the male artistic community. The third volume vividly portrays the problems of being a female writer, particularly one in exile. Chacel's prose reaches its zenith in this series, combining interior monologue, omniscient narrative, Platonic dialogue, brilliant descriptions, and the narrator's philosophical/ethical discussion. The long time period between volumes one and two includes Chacel's definitive return to Spain and her husband's death in 1977. Her first works published after the tragedy were the poetry collection *Versos prohibidos* (1978; Forbidden Verses) and *Timoteo Pérez Rubio y sus retratos del jardín* (1980: Timoteo Pérez Rubio and His Portraits of the Garden), an homage and study of her husband's paintings, which also contains much autobiographical information. In 1984 she published the two-volume diary *Alcancía* (1984; translated as Penny Bank by Johnson). Volume one bears the title *Ida* (Departure), covering her more than 30 years in exile; the second, *Vuelta* (Return), begins with Chacel's return to Spain.

Yet another genre at which Chacel excelled was the essay. *La confesión* (1971;

Confession) is a comparative study of the confessional essays of Kierkegaard, Rousseau, and St. Augustine. Her book-length essay *Saturnal* (1972; Saturnalia), written during two years that Chacel spent in New York City on a Guggenheim Fellowship, treats love, philosophy, and films. In *Rebañaduras* (1986; Gleanings) and other collections of her previously published essays, Chacel challenges the *machista* (male-exalting) ideas of her mentor Ortega and her contemporary Julián *Marías.

At age 83, Chacel published an anthology of unfinished works, *Novelas antes de tiempo* (1981; Novels before Their Time), discussing the ideas and techniques used in each novel she had started and explaining how she intended to finish each, should she live long enough. Her aesthetics remained unchanged over more than 60 years of writing. Had she been able to reside in Spain and written uninterrupted by politics and war, she would have been one of the most respected Spanish novelists of her day; had she not suffered the financial deprivations of exile, she almost certainly would have been more prolific. Nonetheless, Chacel was a perennial nominee for the Cervantes prize, Spain's equivalent of the Pulitzer or Nobel Prize. The many honors bestowed on Chacel in her later years include the National Spanish Literature Prize (1988), the Castile and León Prize (1991), and a Gold Medal in Fine Arts, personally bestowed by King Juan Carlos I shortly before Chacel's death in 1994. Chacel was one of the best novelists of the Generation of 1927 and its only woman member. *See also* Beauvoir, Simone de (1908–1986): Her Influence in Spain; Short Fiction by Women Writers: 1900–1975

Work by

De mar a mar: Epistolario Rosa Chacel-Ana María Moix. Prol., ed., and notes Ana Rodríguez Fischer. Barcelona: Península, 1998.

The Maravillas District. Trans. D.A. Démers. Intro. Susan Kirkpatrick. Lincoln: U of Nebraska P, 1992.

Memoirs of Leticia Valle. Trans. and afterword Carol Maier. Lincoln: U of Nebraska P, 1994.

Obra completa [vol.] 1. La sinrazón. Study, Ana Rodríguez Fischer. Valladolid: Centro de Creación y Estudios Jorge Guillén—Excelentísima Diputación Provincial de Valladolid, 1989.

Obra completa [vol.] 2. Ensayos y Poesía. Study, F. Pardo Vallejo. Valladolid: Centro de Creación y Estudios Jorge Guillén—Excelentísima Diputación Provincial de Valladolid, 1989.

Obra completa [vols.] 3–4. Artículos. I-II. Ed., prol., and notes Ana Rodríguez Fischer. Valladolid: Centro de Creación y Estudios Jorge Guillén—Excelentísima Diputación Provincial de Valladolid, 1993.

Work about

Actas del Congreso en Homenaje a Rosa Chacel (1993: Logroño, Spain). Ed. María Pilar Martínez Latre. Logroño: Universidad de la Rioja, 1994.

Bellver, Catherine G. Absence and Presence. Spanish Women Poets of the Twenties and Thirties. Lewisburg, PA: Bucknell UP, 2001.

Cartas a Rosa Chacel. Ed., intro., and notes Ana Rodríguez Fischer. Madrid: Versal, 1992.

Cole, Gregory K. Spanish Women Poets of The Generation of 1927. Lewiston, NY: Edwin Mellen, 2000.

Foncea Hierro, Isabel. Barrio de Maravillas, de Rosa Chacel: Claves y símbolos. Málaga: Centro Cultural Generación 27, 1999.

———. Rosa Chacel: Memoria e imaginación de un tiempo enigmático. Málaga: Centro de Ediciones de Diputación Provincial de Málaga, 1999.

Mateo, María Asunción. Retrato de Rosa Chacel. Barcelona: Círculo de Lectores; Galaxia Gutenberg, 1993.

Scarlett, Elizabeth A. Under Construction: The Body in Spanish Novels. Charlottesville: UP of Virginia, 1994.

Eunice Myers

Champourcin, Ernestina de (1905–1999)

Despite advances in civil rights, literary circles of the 1930s did not receive Spanish women readily, even though several outstanding women poets were producing a considerable body of work. Ernestina de Champourcin, in particular, had published four collections of poetry by age 31. In spite of this unreceptive climate, Champourcin enjoyed a long, prolific life of creativity, remaining active into her eighty-eighth year as a poet with *Del vacío y sus dones* (1993; The Void and Its Gifts) and as a contributor to *Estudios juanramonianos ofrecidos a Francisco H. Pinzón en su LXXV cumpleaños* (1993).

Born to a noble family in Vitoria (Alava), her mother was Uruguayan and her father of French lineage. His heritage included not only his Provençal surname but also property dating from the Bourbon advent in Spain. Champourcin's parents raised her mostly in Madrid. Her father fostered education, especially literature, and in that environment, entrusted partly to French and English governesses, Champourcin learned three languages and grew into a young woman of universal culture. The poet herself remembers reading and writing French romantic poetry as a child. Much later in life she called her first efforts shameless plagiarism of Lamartine. After initial private tutorials at home and further education in a religious school, Champourcin took exams for her *bachillerato* (rough equivalent of a high school diploma) at the Instituto Cardenal Cisneros de Madrid. Her formal instruction ended when her father forbade her to attend the university unless chaperoned; Champourcin refused to follow that customary practice.

On her own, Champourcin chose Spanish to continue a literary vocation, fully understanding the choice might condemn her to obscurity. She entered actively in intellectual, cultural, and literary circles. In the late 1920s, her commitment to artistic innovation led her to the Lyceum Club where she presented some very early works and openly defended poets who introduced new ideas. In this milieu she met the poet Juan José Domenchina whom she would marry in 1936. She also was one of the founders and secretary of the *Lyceum Club Femenino, an organization concerned with women's culture and education. Even so, she consistently denied partisanship in organized feminism.

As her learning progressed, Champourcin discovered the poetry of *Juan de la Cruz (1542–1591) and Juan Ramón *Jiménez (1881–1958). Both left an indelible mark on the spiritual course of her writing. Jiménez, as poet and friend, became the greatest influence of her life; in 1981 she wrote a memoir on her recollections of him, *La ardilla y la rosa (Juan Ramón en mi memoria)* (The Squirrel and the Rose [My Memory of Juan Ramón]). Although literary histories have often classified her as one of very few female poets of the Generation of 1927, the consideration remains uncertain. Some recognition on the part of the *generación* came in 1934, when Gerardo Diego, in spite of the disapproval of his male contemporaries, included Champourcin and Josefina de la *Torre (1907–before 1989) in the second edition of his celebrated *Antología de poesía española*. Further recognition came in 1991, when the Centro Cultural de la Generación del '27 dedicated the eighth edition of its publication *La ola gratinada* to Champourcin.

While she has maintained a spiritual and aesthetic coherence, Champourcin's works can be divided by the phases and poetic inspirations of her life. The youthful period—the early poems up to 1928 and the more mature poetry up to 1939—ends with the Spanish Civil War. The years of exile in Mexico, 1940–1972, frame the poetry written on the theme of religion and divine love. Her return to Spain in 1972 marks the subsequent period of mature introspection and nostalgia.

In 1926, with her father's financial backing, Champourcin published her first book of poetry, *En silencio* (In Silence). Sonnets, *romances* (ballads), and *octavillas* (octets) are the principal metrics in which she exhibits a romanticism tempered with modernism and traces of Juan Ramón Jiménez as the poem dedicated to Platero bears witness. In her twenties Champourcin published two more books of poetry, *Ahora* (1928; Now) and *La voz en el viento* (1931; The Voice in the Wind), both stamped with the lyric influence of Jiménez as well as the insight she had gained from reading original French and English texts in her youth. In these two collections she assumes a poetic voice whose vision moves between the external "divine pleasure of all created" and the internal enjoyment born in the very beauty of the soul. This fluctuation does not mitigate the romantic orientation of her earlier poems but rather joins with them to announce the panoply of her future poetry. *Ahora* finds the poet opening "golden scars" on today's blank page, moving style and theme to the present as she experiments with meter and vanguard imagery. In *La voz en el viento*, the poetic voice signals a modern, independent woman. Through the automobile imagery in the section "Caminos" (Roads), Champourcin delineates a strong, feminine persona: "I am the terminus girl." She magnetizes stars with her hair and encircles the universe in the hollow of her lover's hands. In this position of strength Champourcin projects a self-conscious poetry of pleasure and satisfaction whose metaphors are female-oriented, willful, sexual, and often maternal. She also establishes here a major and constantly evolving theme: the road.

Just before the outbreak of the Spanish Civil War, Champourcin published her fourth book, *Cántico inútil* (1936; Useless Canticle). Critical opinions, among them Antonio Machado's (1875–1939), considered that she wrote this collection in a more refined and substantive language. In *Cántico inútil*, she renders love more complex by connecting the passionate extremes of "this poor love of ours" with the love for God. With the energy of her womanly experience she draws bodily images of physical love and links them to concepts of the eternal. At that same time Champourcin published the only novel she completed, *La casa de enfrente* (1936; The House across the Street).

In Madrid during the early months of the war Champourcin worked with abandoned children and orphans in a hospital run by Lola Azaña. Domenchina was secretary to Manuel Azaña, president of Spain's leftist Second Republic. Afraid that Franco would soon invade the city, Champourcin and Domenchina married in November 1936 and followed Azaña's Republican faction to Catalonia until they were forced into France. They later fled to Mexico, finding employment as teachers and translators. Domenchina felt ill-suited for the work and suffered continual depressions brought on by the imposed exile. Given her education in languages, however, Champourcin fared better and enjoyed extensive travels as a translator.

Despite the acclaim awarded Champourcin for her first four volumes of poetry, she found herself subsequently ignored by the canonizers of Spanish literature. Her marriage to a poet compounded her marginalization as a woman writer, and refuge in Mexico cloaked her in obscurity. Champourcin did not publish another book of poems until 1952; *Presencia a oscuras* (Presence in Darkness) begins several decades of a spiritual quest that deepens with the death of her husband in 1959. In this collection the poet identifies the divinity as a dark presence who communicates with the poetic voice through the contradictory quality of absence. Holding to that concept, Champourcin went on to write *El nombre que me diste* (1964; The Name You Gave Me), *Hai-Kais espirituales* (1967; Spiritual Hai-Kais), *Cartas cerradas* (1968; Closed Letters), and *Poemas del ser y estar* (Poems of Being and State) in 1972, the year of her definitive return to Spain. These five works are nearly unfindable whether published in Mexico or Spain, as are those published from 1926 to 1936. Fortunately, they have recently been reunited with her collections from 1972 to 1991, published as *Poesía a través del tiempo* (1991; Poetry over Time). Champourcin also edited and wrote the introduction to a selection of religious poetry of Spain and Spanish America in 1970, *Dios en la poesía actual*.

The predominantly religious outlook and mystic voice of her maturity countered the social poetry that was prevalent in Spain in the 1960s. The first poem of *Cartas cerradas* declares that she knows nothing of social or protest poetry; for her the life of a poet is a dialogue with God to whom she writes so that her works may light the road to faith. The dynamic of these aspirations remains deep-rooted in her poetry and will reemerge in the final section of Del vacío y sus dones. The symbols and images of Champourcin's earlier poetry later become the metaphorical expression of the poet's anguish and frustration. Her road imagery is transformed into obstacles such as the wall that blocks the way or the island that isolates the individual. These phenomena appear early; in Cántico inútil the poetic voice presents herself as an island without a sea. Later, her very titles reveal a spiritual evolution: Presencia a oscuras, Cartas cerradas, Cárcel de los sentidos (1964; Jail of the Senses). Diverging from the accepted poetics of her own and postwar generations, she focuses on a woman's struggle with life not only in spiritual but also in human terms. In Cartas cerradas she describes herself as a forgotten, blind cricket at the edge of the tabernacle, useless, athirst to share the love God has given her. In La pared transparente (1984; The Transparent Wall), blocked on all sides, an older woman contemplates the void, a reflection of the poet's own existence during the 1980s. The darkness in this stage of her writing will give way to brighter poetic concepts symbolic of the path toward the light of inner faith.

Champourcin shows her capacity for renewal in Huyeron todas las islas (1988; All the Islands Fled); she borrows the symbol of the individual as island and takes up the burning debate between flight and togetherness, solitude and solidarity. The poet counters the concept of groups of islands with the antithesis of flight or death. Yet her creative vitality now bursts with light, vegetation, creatures, and fragrances in the milieu of her second key symbol, the ivy. Like the individual, the ivy slowly climbs toward the sky and light. In Champourcin's subsequent collection Los encuentros frustrados (1991; Thwarted Encounters) and Del vacío y sus dones, the poet deals with the frustration of existential alienation evoked by her confrontation with the void and unanswered questions of faith. In Los encuentros frustrados Champourcin writes of wilting roses whose perfume crumbles in our hands; yet something moves and is born at the same time. In the debate on essence and existence in these collections, the road represents the fugitive nature of islands and flowers. What remains of these images haunts Champourcin: islands, flowers, and by extension, the human being do not perish without leaving a trace of what once was. We forget, she indicates, that nothing can ever come to an end. In this discovery Champourcin finds the triumph of the everlasting. Champourcin continues this art of reversal in Del vacío y sus dones. After extracting positive elements from previous frustrations, she affirms a strong belief in eternal values and the gifts the void can offer. She assumes life is flight and death, transformation. Thus the anguish of unanswered questions subsides as she portrays faith in simple terms: The road toward the light has become her true vision of God. She writes that even if we have perpetual mysteries to resolve, at the end we want absolute beauty because the "light is new."

While her mature works present a profoundly personal expression of faith, they are also a coherent affirmation of Champourcin's poetics. The power of her poetry has always resided in her will to create and is reconfirmed in the last poem of Los encuentros frustrados. She refuses mere dreams or knowledge of "that uncertain light." Always the individualist, she herself will invent everything with words.

Work by

Cántico inútil; Cartas cerradas; Primer exilio; Huyeron todas las islas. Ed. Milagros Arizmendi. Málaga: Centro Cultural de la Generación del 27, 1997.
Poesía a través del tiempo. Prol. and bio. J.A. Ascunce Arrieta. Barcelona: Anthropos, 1991.

Work about

Ascunce Arrieta, José Angel. "La poesía de exilio de Ernestina de Champourcin: Expresión límite de una depuración expresiva." *Poesía y exilio: Los poetas del exilio español en México*. Ed. Rose Corral, Arturo Souto Alabarce, and James Valender. Mexico City: Colegio de México, 1995.

Bellver, Catherine G. *Absence and Presence. Spanish Women Poets of the Twenties and Thirties*. Lewisburg, PA: Bucknell UP, 2001.

Pérez, Janet. *Modern and Contemporary Spanish Women Poets*. New York: Twayne, 1996.

Wilcox, John C. *Women Poets of Spain, 1860–1990*. Urbana and Chicago: U of Illinois P, 1997.

Glenn Morocco

Chivalry Literature
See *Caballerías, novelas de*: Their Treatment of Women

Chula
See *Cigarrera*

Cielo, Sor Violante del, or Sor Violante do Ceo (1601–1693)

Born in Lisbon on May 30, daughter of Manuel da Silveira Montesino and Elena Franco, Sor Violante del Cielo professed in the Dominican convent of Our Lady of the Rosary in Lisbon on August 29, 1630. Writing in both Portuguese and Spanish, she produced secular love poems, satirical and occasional poetry, and religious poems. She saw one volume of her poetry published in France during her lifetime: The *Rimas varias de la Madre Soror Violante del Cielo, religiosa en el monasterio de la Rosa de Lisboa* (Various Poems of Mother Sister Violante del Cielo, Nun in the Lisbon Monastery of the Rose) was published in Rouen in 1646. Vasco Luis da Gama, the Portuguese ambassador in Paris, was Sor Violante's patron in publication of this volume. A two-volume book of religious poetry, the *Parnaso Lusitano de Divinos e Humanos Versos* (Lusitanian Parnassus of Divine and Human Verse), also in Portuguese and Spanish, was published posthumously in 1733 in Lisbon.

Among her secular poems are several that refer to close friendships with other women: Notable are the sonnet "Belisa, el amistad es un tesoro" (Belisa, Friendship Is a Treasure) and the *romance* (ballad) "Si vivo en ti transformada" (If I Live Transformed in You). She wrote a number of satirical poems addressed to men, but Sor Violante's religious poetry represents her best work, exhibiting a distinctly feminine voice (as in the sonnet "Altísimo Señor, monarca trino" [Highest Lord, Threefold King]) and a predilection for Nativity themes ("A la Navidad del Niño Jesús en Belén," "A San Joseph," "Al Niño Jesús nacido," "Al Niño Jesús, buena dicha de una gitana que le canta" [To the Child Jesus, Good Fortune from a Gypsy Who Sings to Him]). One *villancico* (poem with eight-syllable lines), "Al Nacimiento en la Misa" (To the Nativity in Mass), exemplifies a motif with precedent among mystic nuns both of the seventeenth century and of some centuries earlier: the correlation between the incarnation motifs, the corporality of divinity, in both the Nativity and the Mass. Poems contrasting human and divine love are also common among Sor Violante's works. *See also* Nuns Who Wrote in Sixteenth- and Seventeenth-Century Spain

Work by

Olivares, Julián, and Elizabeth S. Boyce, eds. *Tras el espejo la musa escribe: Lírica femenina de los Siglos de Oro*. Madrid: Siglo Veintiuno de España, 1993.

Work about

Serrano y Sanz, Manuel. *Apuntes para una biblioteca de escritoras españolas desde el año 1401 al 1833*. 2 vols. Madrid, 1903. Rpt. Madrid: Atlas, 1975.

Elizabeth S. Boyce and Julián Olivares

Cienfuegos, Beatriz de (eighteenth century)

From Cádiz, Beatriz de Cienfuegos is author of the first journal for women to appear in Spain, *La *pensadora gaditana* (1763–1764; The Woman Thinker from Cádiz). Since no historical documents have been found, some critics have assumed that Cienfuegos is a male writer, most probably a priest, who used this name to better address a female reading public. Cienfuegos herself admitted to use of a pseudonym and bragged that no one would ever guess her true identity. All that is known about her comes from details she discloses in her own articles. She explains that since her parents wanted her to become a nun, they prepared her for this life by providing her with excellent teachers. This early education, plus the six years she spent in a convent, gave her the background necessary for writing her periodical. *La pensadora gaditana* was published weekly, starting in 1763, and it reached a total of 52 issues. Her *Pensamientos* (Thoughts) were written in the style of José Clavijo y Fajardo's *El pensador matritense*. Both journals comment and criticize all sorts of contemporary manners and customs.

Work by

La pensadora gaditana. 4 vols. Cádiz: Manuel Jiménez Carreño, 1786.

Work about

Serrano y Sanz, Manuel. *Apuntes para una biblioteca de escritoras españolas desde el año 1401 al 1833.* 2 vols. Madrid: Rivadeneyra, 1903. Rpt. Madrid: Atlas, 1975.

Sullivan, Constance. "Gender, Text, and Cross-Dressing: The Case of 'Beatriz Cienfuegos' and *La pensadora gaditana*." *Dieciocho* 18.1 (Spring 1995): 27–47.

María A. Salgado

Cigarrera

From the end of the eighteenth century when women replaced men in Spain's growing number of tobacco factories (there were 11 by 1900) the *cigarrera* (female worker in a tobacco factory) emerged as a picturesque type in art, literature, and the popular imagination. The *cigarrera* became familiar as a cultural type outside of Spain largely due to the success of Prosper Mérimée's (1803–1870) novella *Carmen* (1845) and the 1875 opera of the same name by Georges Bizet (1838–1875). The fictional Carmen did work briefly in the Seville tobacco factory and shared many traits attributed to *cigarreras*. Both in real life and as a literary and artistic type, the *cigarrera*'s lineage may be traced to the *maja* and *manola* of the eighteenth and early nineteenth centuries and to the *chula* of the late eighteenth and nineteenth century. These terms designated attractive young women from certain lower-class neighborhoods in Madrid whose distinctive speech, pert, assured manner, and style of dress set them apart. In the eighteenth century, Francisco de Goya portrayed the type in cartoons he painted for the Royal Tapestry Factory in Madrid. In the same period the *maja* or *manola* often appeared onstage in the short plays of Ramón de la Cruz, as in his *sainete* (one-act farce) *La maja majada* (1774; The Harrassed Coquette). In his 1886 study *Majas, manolas y chulas*, E. Rodríguez-Solís outlined the characteristics of the archetypal *maja*—applicable for the most part to the *manola* and the *chula* as well. The *maja* was often married to a ne'er-do-well and had children to support. She loved bullfights, dances, fiestas, and clothes. She disliked upper-class hypocrisy and everything foreign. And finally, everyone took for granted her superiority to the men around her.

The *cigarrera*, like the *maja*, *manola*, and *chula*, was a quintessential object of male desire. In Bizet's opera, men gathered in the evening to look at the *cigarreras* as they filed out of the tobacco factory. In real life, the women were often subjected to the indignity of strip searches before they left the building, but when they did emerge, those who were young, attractive, and able to do so rewarded oglers not only with the sight of their beauty but also with a glimpse of patent leather shoes, silk shawls, and stockings paid for with the women's own wages. Foreign travelers to Spain during the nineteenth century made a point of visiting the Seville factory, in particular to look at Carmen's latest incarnations at work in the stifling heat of the shops, often in titillating near undress. Like her counterparts, the *cigarrera* was famous for her generosity in providing companionship and comfort to poor students. Nineteenth-century *sainetes* and *zarzuelas* (vaudevillesque operettas) such as Alfonso Benito y Alfaro's *La chula* (1896) and Angel Munilla and Luis Ferreiro's *Las cigarreras* (1897) testify to the *cigarrera*'s goodwill and to the students' gratitude and readiness to back *cigarreras* when they needed support.

Like the *maja*, *manola*, and *chula*, the *cigarrera* worked at a time when women in Spain were restricted for the most part to agricultural and domestic service, to needlework carried out in the home, or in Catalonia, to work in textile factories. But in the course of the nineteenth century, the *cigarreras'* labor disputes and acts of Luddite violence—especially in Madrid—distinguished them from the *castiza* (traditional) *manola* and linked them increasingly with the Madrid working class. Employment gave *cigarreras* some degree of financial autonomy, especially if they were unmarried. This autonomy together with their monopoly of tobacco factory jobs fostered a labor militancy uncommon among other Spanish women workers. In effect, many observers noted that their large numbers—there were as many as 5,000 in Madrid in the 1880s and 1890s—when added to popular movements had a significant impact, while their militancy was unsettling to public authorities who found that the people always supported striking *cigarreras*.

Cigarreras saw themselves and were perceived as traditionally devout and monarchist. In her 1882 novel *La tribuna*, whose protagonist is a tobacco worker in Galicia, Emilia *Pardo Bazán represented the *cigarreras* as initially susceptible to partisan press propaganda in support of the 1868 revolution and republicanism. But the novelist eventually reveals the protagonist's (and the other women's) radicalism to have been short-lived and conditioned from the outset, in the author's view, by an essential femininity. Toward the end of the century, *cigarreras* supported conservative popular causes such as continued Spanish rule in Cuba. Madrid tobacco workers could always be counted on to give a rousing send-off to soldiers on their way to the colonial war. And *cigarreras* demonstrated vigorously in 1896 amid large crowds in Madrid against the Spanish general in Cuba, Martínez Campos (soon to be replaced by General Weyler), whom they believed to be an advocate of Cuban autonomy.

A strike of about 6,000 *cigarreras* in Seville in 1896 illustrated the often-observed phenomenon of public support referred to above. Widespread sympathy in this instance, as in many others, depended partly on the fact that relatives, spouses, and children of the women brought the number of people affected by the action to well over 8,000. More significantly, the 1896 strike demonstrated that the Seville *cigarreras* had achieved a higher level of sophistication in labor disputes by the late nineteenth century. It is apparent first in their deliberate use of the press to advance their cause. To the dismay of socialists, *cigarreras* were not unionized, but they knew how to make use of the telegraph to mobilize workers quickly in tobacco factories elsewhere in Spain. They were also successful in their calls for other kinds of workers in Seville to suspend work in a gesture of solidarity. In the end, the women strikers in Seville did not hesitate to make use of their reputation as seductive Carmen figures in contacts with men in authority judged useful to their purposes. The financial autonomy some *cigarreras* achieved could lead to sexual autonomy. And, like Carmen, the fact that they worked sometimes allowed them to keep a man rather than to be kept. Carmen was fiercely proud of being able to support the man she had chosen. Sexual freedom was explicit in Carmen's way of life; while it led to disaster in her case, it continued to be a component of the autonomy to which some working women aspired. It must be noted that women who applied for work in tobacco factories in order to be hired were obliged to demonstrate good moral character. It is also apparent, according to the authors of *La mala vida en Madrid* (1901), that *cigarreras* were generally assumed to be unchaste.

The most famous literary *chula* from the nineteenth century, rather exceptionally for one who lived in Madrid, was not a tobacco worker. Fortunata (from Benito Pérez Galdós's *Fortunata y Jacinta* [1886–1887]) worked as a prostitute and in a poultry shop before she became a mistress and sometime wife. Even though she conforms outwardly to the image of the classic lower-class object of desire, she is too vulnerable and passive to qualify as a genuine *chula*; she lacks the type's self-assertive drive. The reaction of Jacinta, her nouveau riche lover's wife, to Fortunata does suggest a final important aspect of the type's impact on Spanish culture. Jacinta almost unconsciously begins to model herself on the lower-class woman, aping her speech in particular. Other middle- and upper-class women imitated dress and manner as well in an homage to the *maja/manola/chula* type that made a signal contribution to the socalled plebeianization of Spanish culture that marks the nineteenth century. *See also* Nelken y Mausberger, Margarita (1896–1968); Women's Situation in Spain: 1786–1931: The Awakening of Female Consciousness

Work about

Bernaldo de Quirós, Constancio, and J.M. Llanas Aguilaniedo. *La mala vida en Madrid*. Ed. and notes, Justo Broto Salanova. Intro. Luis Maristany del Rayo. Zaragoza: Egido, 1998.

Morange, Claude. "De manola a obrera." *Estudios de Historia Social* 12–13 (1980): 307–321.

Rodríguez-Solís, Enrique. *Majas, manolas y chulas*. Madrid: F. Cao y D. de Val, 1886.

Vallejo Fernández Cela, Sergio. "Las cigarreras de la Fábrica de Tabacos de Madrid." *Madrid en la sociedad del siglo XIX*. Vol. 2. Madrid: Alfoz, 1986. 136–149.

D.J. O'Connor

Claramunt, Teresa (1862–1931)

In an obituary published by *La Revista Blanca* (May 1, 1931) feminist anarchist "Soledad Gustavo" (Teresa Mañé) characterized her dear friend Teresa Claramunt de Gurri as the personification of "50 years of revolutionary action and anarchist propaganda." Indeed, a staunch feminist and advocate of workers' rights, Claramunt's recognition of the double exploitation of working women in terms of class and gender earned her great prestige among the working class, especially women. Her efforts to raise the consciousness of the working class were not limited to soapbox speeches and the organization of picket lines and general strikes but also included education of the masses through the written word. Throughout her life Claramunt contributed numerous articles and essays to a wide variety of anarchist journals. She reestablished one of the most important anarchist newspapers in early-twentieth-century Spain, *El Productor* (out of print since 1893), and in 1905 she published the groundbreaking treatise *La mujer: Consideraciones generales sobre su estado ante la prerrogativa del hombre* (Woman, General Considerations on Her Status in View of Man's Prerogative).

Born in the textile city of Sabadell, Claramunt was a garment worker who became active in anarchist labor organizations at age 22 by organizing the workers in her factory into anarchist collectives that would later become part of the largest labor organization in nineteenth-century Spain, the Federación de Trabajadores. Claramunt's commitment to improving the life of the working class, especially women, would eventually result in numerous prison terms and periods of exile for her. As early as 1888 she immigrated to Portugal with her companion in order to avoid incarceration. Upon her return to Barcelona, Claramunt continued to support a nine-hour shift, fairer wages, an end to child labor, and unionization among factory workers. In 1893 she was taken into custody following her intervention in an anarchist meeting in the Teatro Gran Via of Barcelona. Throughout the 1890s Claramunt was repeatedly jailed in the notorious women's prison of El Raval slum in Barcelona and in the infamous Castle of Montjuich, as a result of her revolutionary activities in defense of workers' right to organize. Exiled to Great Britain and later to France in 1896, Claramunt survived by working in various garment factories. In 1898 she and her companion returned to Spain and continued their political activism in anarchist circles.

With "Leopold Bonafulla" (Juan Bautista Esteve), in 1901 Claramunt reissued *El Productor* in Barcelona. In 1902, she was incarcerated for instigating a strike among the garment workers. Released in 1903, she returned to her prior activities and embarked upon a propaganda tour throughout Andalusia. Following the events of the Tragic Week of 1909 where many anarchist labor leaders, workers, and intellectuals were imprisoned and executed (including the influential pedagogue Francisco Ferrer i Guardia), Claramunt moved to Zaragoza in hopes of avoiding yet another prison term. However, her involvement in the general strike of 1911 led to her detention and later sentencing to a four-year prison term. During this incarceration she developed a progressive paralysis that would eventually prove fatal. Released in 1915, she moved to Seville and cared for the children of famed anarchist photojournalist Antonio Ojeda. Ill and nostalgic for Catalonia, Claramunt returned to her sister's house in Barcelona in 1924. Considered the only "truly revolutionary woman in Spain" by her peers, Claramunt was frequently visited by young activists as well as by famed anarchist leaders Max Nettlau and Emma Goldman, among others. Her last public appearance took place in 1929. Teresa Claramunt died in the arms of anarchist leader Federica *Montseny (1905–1994) the night before municipal elections that prompted the fall of the monarchy on April 12, 1931. Fittingly, her funeral was held on April 14, the very same day of the proclamation of the Second Republic. *See also* Women's Situation in Spain: 1786–1931: The Awakening of Female Consciousness

Work by

La mujer: Consideraciones generales sobre su estado ante la prerrogativa del hombre. Mahon: n.p., 1905.

Work about

Alcalde, Carmen. *La mujer en la guerra civil española*. Madrid: Cambio 16, 1976.
Alvarez Junco, José. *La ideología política del anarquismo español: 1868–1910*. Madrid: Siglo Veintiuno de España, 1991.
Litvak, Lily. *El cuento anarquista*. Madrid: Taurus, 1982.
———. *Musa Libertaria*. Barcelona: n.p., 1981.
Montseny, Federica. *Mis primeros cuarenta años*. Barcelona: Plaza y Janés, 1987.
Scanlon, Geraldine. *La polémica feminista en la España contemporánea: 1868–1974*. Madrid: Akal, 1986.
Segura, Isabel. *Guia de dones de Barcelona: Recorreguts històrics*. Barcelona: Ajuntament de Barcelona, 1995.
Tuñón de Lara, Manuel. *El movimiento obrero en la historia de España*. 2 vols. Madrid: Taurus, 1972.

Patricia V. Greene

Clarín

See *Regenta, La* (1885): Female Enemies in the Novel; *Regenta, La* (1885): Protagonist Ana Ozores

Colmeiro Laforet, Carlos (1906–1986)

Carlos Colmeiro Laforet, count of Pardo Bazán, gynecologist and internationally renowned medical researcher, was able to bridge his commitment to the socially responsible practice of women's medicine, that is, his outreach work among gypsy and prostitute communities during the post–Civil War period, with his work as scientific researcher. This double commitment is reflected in more than a dozen books and many scholarly articles on sexuality and gynecology translated into English, German, and Dutch.

Orto y ocaso del feminismo (1956; The Sunrise and Sunset of Feminism) presents a comprehensive review of the different theories of feminism from the onset of the industrial revolution until the mid-twentieth century. Colmeiro's work is particularly relevant considering the time and place of its publication, given the scarcity of Spanish books on feminism published during the 1950s, especially in peripheral areas of the Peninsula like Galicia. This text appeared at a time when traditional notions of femininity sponsored by the Francoist state were beginning to be challenged by the reality of Spanish women progressively incorporating themselves in the workforce, and the influx of feminist ideas from outside Spain was beginning to be noticed. Most important, the work boasts a surprisingly tolerant and progressive attitude toward women's issues not characteristic of the times, if rather outdated by today's standards.

Orto y ocaso analyzes in great detail the historical development of the ideas and aspirations of the feminist movement, focusing with particular attention on Great Britain as an individual case study. With the unbiased attitude and scientific methodology of an objective medical researcher, Colmeiro sets the scientific parameters of the "sunrise" and "sunset" of feminism; following more closely the book title's etymology, Colmeiro explores with the attentive eye of an obstetrician the "birth" and "death" of feminism, as a phenomenon to be studied and understood in order to accurately predict its future development. Colmeiro traces the origins of the feminist movement to social changes caused by the industrial revolution in the eighteenth century and follows the gradual incorporation of women into the industrial workforce and the ensuing fight for equal rights, leading to the suffragist movement at the turn of the century. After the extraordinary momentum caused by the suffragettes' success and the experience of World War II where women were a central part of the workforce (all references to the Second Republic and the Spanish Civil War are carefully avoided in the book, in a typical elliptical discourse of omission), women were relegated to the more traditional roles of housewife and mother. In spite of the progress made, their aspirations for equality had not been fully met, and therefore feminist ideas had collapsed. For Colmeiro, the reason for this "decline" is based on the fundamental fallacy of the major arguments presented in support of the feminist movement; the sociological (Marxist) or psychological (Freudian) views of women's need for equality are necessarily limited; their collective or individual efforts for equality are bound to fail, since women are inherently different from men. Following other liberal physicians like Gregorio Marañón (1887–1960) in his understanding of women's nature, Colmeiro proposes that women's identity, although in part culturally constructed, is basically biologically determined and therefore by definition "different." There can never be full equality between the sexes. Colmeiro argues, however, "different" must not be understood as "inferior," although in reality that is exactly how it always is translated. For all practical purposes, a defense of difference, and therefore inequality, inevitably results in a defense of the status quo.

Orto y ocaso holds an ambivalent position vis-à-vis the feminist movement. On the one hand, Colmeiro recognizes the situation of the unjust inferiority women suffer in patriarchal society and advocates for due reform: deregulating their judicial inferiority, securing universal education and equal rights. On the other hand, he defends the "natural" division of labor arrived at through the ages, underlining the biological difference that makes women better suited for some jobs and men for others and ultimately claiming that the most important job of all for women is the biological task of being a mother, an unsurprising claim, coming from an obstetrician. Colmeiro's work represents a moment of transition and ambiguity, still based on some traditional concepts of woman but clearly announcing the more open attitudes of the 1960s studied by Geraldine Scanlon in *La polémica feminista en la España contemporánea (1896–1974)*. It is a symptomatic response to the development of the feminist movement and particularly the progressive incorporation of women in the workforce, in part celebrating it for the new possibilities opened to women and criticizing the relative backwardness of the situation of women in Spain in comparison with most other European nations, and in part glorifying the idea of "home" and lamenting the "loss" of women's traditional and most important role, that of mother, which he sees as somehow at odds with the new reality. The book devotes 260 pages to arguing its theoretical points and ends with an appendix where he summarizes in 10 pages "The Situation of the Spanish Woman," a very eloquent statement about the real situation of Spanish women under Franco. In an effort to circumvent censorship, another of his books, *La sexualidad de la mujer* (Woman's Sexuality), had to be published as *Nuevos problemas ginecológicos* (1955; New Gynecological Problems).

Colmeiro's work, while far from radical or revolutionary, is moderately progressive and insightful, well intentioned, and well researched. Each chapter includes a separate annotated bibliography in several languages. Often repetitive and digressive, but always clear and coherent, continually relying on scientific evidence, common sense, and rationality in his analysis, the results are at times engaging and at times infuriating. Although it is undoubtedly outdated, it illuminates superbly an important period in the development of feminist ideas in Spain. See also Feminism in Spain: 1900–2000

Work by

Nuevos problemas ginecológicos. N.p., 1955.
Orto y ocaso del feminismo. Vigo: Faro de Vigo, 1956.

José F. Colmeiro

Colombine
See Burgos, Carmen de (1867–1932)

Comadrona
A centuries-old secular reality, the *comadrona* (midwife) becomes a stock character or stereotype fairly early in Spanish literature, although the type proliferates with the advent of *costumbrismo* (depiction of local customs), regionalism, realism, and naturalism. The *comadrona* combines aspects of the Wise Woman and the witch and, while usually a minor figure, may be benevolent, ambiguous, or malevolent. Although she is often a hag, positive aspects tend to prevail, and in many small towns and villages the *comadrona* not only attends births but also provides neonatal care and may be called upon to assist in cases of death and other instances of sickness or injury. However, a traditional association between the *comadrona* and go-between often makes the character negative, associating her offices both with seduction and with the frequent outcome thereof. See also Celestina, La. Comedia o tragicomedia de Calisto y Melibea; Tercera

Janet Pérez

Comedia nueva, La
See Moratín, Leandro Fernández de (1760–1828): His Portrayal of Women

Conde, Carmen (1907–1996)
Poet, novelist, and critic Carmen Conde Abellán holds the unique position of having been the first woman admitted to the Royal Spanish Academy of the Language in nearly two centuries (from its foundation in 1784 to her admission in 1979). Chronologically, Conde is contemporaneous with poets of the "Generation of 1927" and had ongoing friendships with some, including Ernestina de *Champourcin and 1978 Nobel Prize winner Vicente Aleixandre; she also maintained an intimate friendship for many years with Gabriela Mistral, then a Chilean diplomat in Madrid. Canonical anthologies and literary histories do not usually include Conde or her husband, poet Antonio Oliver Belmás, among members of this prestigious "generation" (many of whose first works were published in 1927), despite the fact that Conde's

first book, *Brocal* (1929; Well Rim), appeared a year after the first volume of Aleixandre. Generation members lack identical esthetics, some being more associated with neo-gongorism than others; nuclear members participate in varying vanguard movements, including futurism, *ultraísmo*, and surrealism. Conde was fully involved in vanguard experimentation by 1931, and ultrast and surrealist echoes sound clearly in *Júbilos* (1934; Jubilation). Her omission in studies of the Generation of 1927 typifies neglect or rejection of women by the canon makers, for Conde with nearly 100 books to her credit is far more entitled to inclusion than oft-cited male poets such as Altolaguirre. Her social preoccupations have been cited to justify her exclusion, but this reasoning is specious: Rafael Alberti and Miguel Hernández evinced *engagement* before the Civil War, and critics now recognize the social content of *García Lorca's poetry and theater, to cite only three male poets whose abandonment of "pure poetry" did not exclude them from either the "Generation of 1927" or the canon.

Conde's works include some 40 collections of poetry, plus anthologies and editions of collected works, nine novels, several plays, some 20 volumes of children's literature, and 20-odd collections of criticism, memoirs, and miscellany, published under her own name and a pair of pseudonyms; she also published various translations under pseudonyms. Born August 15, 1907, in the Mediterranean port of Cartagena (Murcia), maritime motifs prove pervasive in her work; love of the sea prompted her adoption of the pseudonym Florentina del Mar. The only child of a doting father, born to a well-to-do goldsmith and his wife in the fourteenth year of marriage, she was especially close to her father, who believed unreservedly in her talent, while her mother—a profoundly religious, devout Catholic—encouraged repression of her daughter, having little faith in her abilities. The adult poet exhibits numerous Christian attributes, such as consistently chaste expression, enduring altruism, and idealism. Autobiographical writings depict her youthful self as uninterested in material possessions but fascinated by literature, rejecting typical gender stereotypes, restless, independent, studious, and imaginative. Following catastrophic business losses, Conde's father migrated to Melilla (another port) in Spanish Morocco, where Conde and her mother joined him in 1914, remaining until 1920. Her life there in the multiethnic atmosphere, between the sea and desert, is reflected in several works, including *Júbilos* and *Empezando la vida* (1955; Beginning Life).

Financial exigency led to Conde's seeking work, which few young ladies then did. Escaping her mother's implacable insistence on domestic skills, she worked sketching ship parts in a British firm in Cartagena (1923–1928), publishing stories and poems in the local press from 1925 onward. In 1927, she began certification in pedagogy, obtaining a degree in primary education (1930) and eventually passing government examinations for teachers in 1936. Also in 1927, she met Antonio Oliver, whom she married in 1931; he became her most trusted critic and introduced her to modernist poets, especially Juan Ramón *Jiménez, who became both an influence and future mentor. In the year of their marriage, the couple founded an extension school, the "Adult University of Cartagena," where both worked as teachers until war's outbreak (1936). In 1934, the poet's only daughter was stillborn due to inadequate obstetric care, precipitating an emotional crisis (aggravated by her father's death soon afterward); the deaths of children become thereafter an enduring symbol of pain, loss, and tragedy in Conde's work. Poetic references to motherhood and children, to empty cradles and young mothers in mourning, combine with images of grieving maternity turned to sterility in her lyric outpourings of horror at war's destruction; all mothers, including animals, suffer symbolic barrenness, and the poet calls upon women to "refuse to conceive children until men erase war from the earth."

No political activist, Conde nevertheless found herself in the Republican camp because of her social concerns and her husband's service in the Loyalist forces. Following the war (1939), Oliver was imprisoned for six years, and Conde—politically unable to obtain work—lived with friends and relatives in Madrid, chastised by decrees prohibiting Republican intellectuals' publication under their own names (they could not exploit prewar literary reputations or receive critical notice). She did translations, bibliographical work, and archival jobs, maintaining a low profile for fear of incarceration; most poetry written during the immediate postwar years remained unpublished until long afterward. Unemployable in Spanish-run educational institutions because of official refusal to recognize her degree, she taught contemporary Spanish novel and poetry to foreign students, publishing juvenile fiction, biographies, and historical works; two titles under the pseudonym "Magdalena Noguera" treat religious monuments.

Conde began with prose poems, often brief pieces whose distinguishing characteristics are original metaphors and humor. Passion for nature and life accompanies expressions of joyful, newfound love, exuberant vitalism, and sensuous dynamism (contrasting with immobility and petrification in early postwar works). The rhetoric of pieces composed during the hostilities abounds in violence and visceral imagery, succeeded after war's end by mystic impulses, resignation, aspirations to faith, and desires to realize her dreams. Apparently reassured by the permanence of things beyond war's destructive power, Conde also finds refuge in the structures of more traditional poetic format, abandoning her earlier prose poems and beginning to use free verse and other verse formats, employing unrhymed lines in traditional meters, as well as assonance and consonant rhymes, and experiments with blank verse. Major lyric devices are repetition, cadence, parallelistic structures, metaphors, condensation, and ellipses. Simple and quasi-conversational, compositions of the 1940s and 1950s wax more prosaic than earlier lyric prose. Physical aging becomes a major theme in Conde's middle years: She rejects old age, wishing to avoid shriveled breasts, swollen belly, inflexible waistline, and flaccid legs, reveling instead in colors, sounds, laughter and song, nature's beauty, and the pleasure of being. Senectitude is negative for Conde: Physical aging connotes the erosion of plenitude.

Hoping to strengthen her academic credentials, Conde produced scholarly anthologies and critical works: *Dios en la poesía española* (1944; God in Spanish Poetry) and *La poesía ante la eternidad* (1944; Poetry Faces Eternity). *La Amistad en la literatura española* (1944; Friendship in Spanish Literature) appeared under the pseudonym "Florentina del Mar." She did an introductory essay on the Brontë sisters for an edition of their selected works in translation and produced anthologies of women poets: *Poesía femenina viviente* (1955; Living Feminine Poetry), *Once grandes poetisas americohispanas* (1967; Eleven Great Spanish-American Women Poets), and *Poesía femenina española* (Spanish Women's Poetry) in two volumes (1939–1950 in 1967 and 1950–1960 in 1971). No comparably inclusive compilation exists for later years. *Poesía amorosa contemporánea* (1969; Contemporary Love Poetry) follows a specialized, esoteric anthology, *Viejo venís y florido* (1963; Medieval Spanish Ballads), collecting songs from the oral tradition of Sephardic Jews and Muslims learned from Moorish friends in Melilla.

Ansia de la gracia (1952; Longing for Grace), considered one of Conde's most significant works, portrays poetic fusion with the sea and the earth—the soil, but not the stones, which symbolize pain and anguish. Flora and fauna represent vitality and hope. *Ansia de la gracia* has been seen as an impassioned investigation into human destiny and the meaning of existence, as well as a search for plenitude prompted by her husband's release from prison. By contrast, *Sea la luz* (1947; Let There Be Light) evokes the seeds of death that each person carries. Conde rejects death vitally and aesthetically, viewing decomposition as degrading and disgusting, even as she faces existential limit situations. Humble things such as fresh thyme and Mediterranean sunlight symbolize life's values.

Mujer sin Edén (1947; *Woman without Eden*, 1986), Conde's most significant collection, has been deemed by Leopoldo de Luis's introduction to the 1985 Torremozas edition "the most significant book of poetry written by a woman in the Spanish language," a work in which woman—half of humanity—"investigates her stock and, without pathos, sings its praises." Protesting traditional Judeo-Christian treatment of women, *Mujer sin Edén* was both brave for Francoist Spain and unorthodox in its premises, employing biblical intertexts (seeming religious allegory includes motifs of expulsion from Paradise and God's wrath that accompany implicit equation of the Republic's fall with the fall from grace, the Civil War's horrors with divine retribution). The book's rebellious bent appears in subversion of traditional concepts of guilt and Original Sin, as the poet argues that if Eve's union with Adam in Eden was her destiny, she was innocent, together with all who followed. Conde polarizes Eve and Mary, converting the work to an allegorical discourse on woman's difficult condition throughout history. Five unequal cantos comprise *Mujer sin Edén*: Canto 1, the Garden, recounts expulsion from Eden; Woman wrestles with her conscience, arguing that Original Sin was predestined. Conde postulates the original notion that the Creator wanted Man for Himself; because of Woman, He lost Man, and hence His wrath against her. In Canto 2, portraying the early years after expulsion, the primal pair admires their earthly domain, savoring the first fruits. Woman addresses God, affirming that He doesn't love her, nor—because of her transgression—her son Cain. Intertextually complex biblical resonances camouflage intent, with Cain and Abel motifs and the myth of fraternal hate and murder suggesting Spain's Civil War. Woman suggests that divine preference for Abel creates injustice, arbitrary discrimination, and hatred among humankind: Divine favoritism causes war, exodice, genocide, pestilence, famine, and racial differences. In Canto 3, Woman contemplates the world newly emerged from the flood, daring not to affirm life but limiting herself to rhetorical questions. Canto 4 recreates major events of the four synoptic Gospels and alluding to the Apocalypse of John. Mary's role apotheosizes Woman as the mother of God, logically implying pardon for all women. This canto also presents Woman's struggle with the Beast and rejection of evil. In the brief final canto, Woman inquires whether God never pardons, implicitly questioning whether men will ever cease insisting on Woman's "guilt." Conde often described *Woman* as protest, proclaiming "that business of Adam's rib and all the rest is drivel. . . . It seems like God didn't care for woman; although He created her so that man would not be alone, the one He really loved was man." *Woman* suggests the divinity's anthropocentric narcissism, bitterly protesting society's millennial gender inequality.

Work by

Ansia de la gracia. Madrid: Adonais, 1952.
Brocal. Madrid: La Lectura, 1929.
Empezando la vida. Teguán (Morocco): Al-Motamid, 1955.
Iluminada tierra. Madrid: n.p., 1951.
Júbilos. Prol. Gabriela Mistral. Murcia: Sudeste, 1934.
Mientras los hombres mueren. Milan: Disalpino, 1953.
Mujer sin Edén. Madrid: Jura, 1947.
Obra poética 1929–1966. Madrid: Biblioteca Nueva, 1967.
Sea la luz. Madrid: Mensaje, 1947.
Woman without Eden—Mujer sin Edén. Trans. J.R. De Armas and A. Levitin. Miami: Universal, 1986.

Work about

Bellver, Catherine G. *Absence and Presence. Spanish Women Poets of the Twenties and Thirties*. Lewisburg, PA: Bucknell UP, 2001.

García de la Concha, Víctor. "Pasión de Carmen Conde"; "Dramáticamente arraigada." *La poesía española de 1935 a 1975*. 2 vols. Madrid: Cátedra, 1987– . 2: 517–527.

Gutiérrez-Vega, Zenaida, and Marie-Lise Gazarian-Gautier. *Carmen Conde, de viva voz*. Montclair, NJ: Senda Nueva de Ediciones, 1992.

Homenaje a Carmen Conde. Spain: Ayuntamiento de Majadahonda, 1996.

Inclán, Josefina. *Carmen Conde y el mar/Carmen Conde and the Sea*. Miami: Universal, 1980.

Martín, Pilar. "Carmen Conde." *The Dictionary of Literary Biography*. Vol. 108: *Twentieth-Century Spanish Poets: First Series*. Ed. Michael Perna. New York: Brucoli, Clark, Layman, 1991. 88–99.

Newton, Candelas. "El discurso heroico de Carmen Conde." *Monographic Review/Revista monográfica* 6 (1990): 61–70.

Pérez, Janet. "Carmen Conde." *Modern and Contemporary Spanish Women Poets*. New York: Twayne, 1996. 72–88.

Richards, Judith. "The World without End: Mythic and Linguistic Revision in Carmen Conde Abellán's *Mujer sin Edén*." *Monographic Review/Revista Monográfica* 6 (1990): 71–80.

Rubio Paredes, José María. *La obra juvenil de Carmen Conde*. Madrid: Torremozas, 1990.

Janet Pérez

Conde Lucanor, El (1335)

The *Libro de los enxiemplos del Conde Lucanor e de Patronio* (1335; *The Book of Count Lucanor and Patronio. A Translation of Don Juan Manuel's El Conde Lucanor*, 1977) by Don Juan Manuel is a masterpiece of Spanish medieval didactic narrative that establishes and formalizes Castilian prose. The 51 stories in this collection, entitled *ejemplos* (examples), reflect Spanish society with astonishing realism in characters ranging from noblemen, vassals, farmers, and peasants to Jews and Arabs. The stories include historical accounts, folktales, allegories, and fables. Female characters such as queens, noblewomen, and peasant girls are the protagonists in at least 9 stories (*ejemplos* VII, XXVII, XXX, XXXV, XXXVI, XLII, XLIV, XLVII, and L). Six other tales have wives, maids, and prostitutes in the background (*ejemplos* I, XI, XXV, XLIII, XLVI, LI). At first, such significant representation of both positive and negative female roles might seem to be another feature of Juan Manuel's realism in depicting fourteenth-century Castilian society. Yet after considering the purpose as clearly stated in the prologue and some of the frequent techniques of characterization used, the modern reader cannot help but recognize the subtle overtones of *misogyny in this medieval work.

Consistent with didactic literature of the fourteenth century, in the carefully drafted prologue to his work Juan Manuel repeatedly expresses his hope that, among the entertaining stories he has compiled, readers will find *cosas provechosas* (profitable things) that will advance their intellectual and spiritual understanding. Ten times he refers to his readers as *homes* (men), and only once does he use the more inclusive term *gentes* (people). Juan Manuel is very specific about his intended audience: men like him, that is, noblemen who read in Spanish and are careful, critical readers. In accordance with the Dominican order's belief in maintaining the status quo (Juan Manuel was a patron of the order), the didactic purpose of this collection further modifies how the stories are presented and interpreted at the end. Thus, when one reads about Doña Truhaña's greed (*ejemplo* VII), or the ill-tempered woman in a version of "The Taming of the Shrew" (*ejemplo* XXXV), or the Arab Queen Ramaiquía's capricious and ungrateful nature (*ejemplo* XXX), one recognizes that the stories are to be read not so much as warnings against such particular foibles as lessons to husbands on how to handle their wives and keep them in their place. By the same token, female protagonists who embody *honor and virtue (*ejemplos* XXVII, XXXVI, XLIV, L) are included not as models for female readers but as examples of the rewards men can obtain for their own honorable conduct. For example, the perversely contrary wife of Emperor Fradrique and the devoted Doña Vascuñana, loving spouse of Don Alvar Hañez, are introduced to warn men to select wives carefully (*ejemplo* XXVII). The emperor married his wife without knowing about *las maneras que avía* (her ways), while Don Alvar, on the other hand, carefully tested three girls and according to their answers selected the one most suitable for a wife.

Since these didactic examples are intended for noblemen like Don Juan Manuel who were constantly confronted by issues of managing estates, politics, family affairs, inheritance, and wars, the author frames the stories within the narrative structure of a fictitious count, Conde Lucanor, who poses problems to his loyal servant and adviser Patronio. Patronio answers each problem with a story that illustrates his advice or solution to the situation. Not only Lucanor approves of these stories; Juan Manuel himself, who seems to be secretly listening to them, also judges them worth recording. To each one, he adds concluding verses that summarize what he takes the moral of the story to be. The examples then are overlaid with three male voices that stifle and silence women's voices. Most of the female characters are denied direct speech. The omniscient narrator Patronio tells us what they are thinking and paraphrases what they say. In the few instances where female characters are permitted to speak, they only echo their husbands' words. Throughout the narrative of *ejemplo* XXXV, Patronio quotes directly the threats of the young man as he tries to tame his wife, while reporting indirectly the fears and thoughts of the ill-tempered woman. The only time she is allowed to speak is when she repeats her husband's warning of what will happen to her if he is awakened. On hearing these words from her, the townspeople nod in approval that she has finally learned her proper place. In *ejemplo* XXVII, Doña Vascuñana's words are also directly quoted when she settles some arguments between her husband and his nephew. The husband keeps pointing to animals along the road and insisting on calling them something else—that is, a cow becomes a mare, and so on. Doña Vascuñana, although perplexed at her husband's statements, affirms his identifications and thereby proves to the nephew that she is indeed a devoted wife, deserving her husband's love and attention. In the first part of the same example, the words of Emperor Fradrique's crude wife are quoted only to underline the garrulousness of her character. Of course, soon after speaking those words she is killed by "her own stubbornness."

Aside from characters' own words, adjectives used to describe them and their actions add to their characterization. Female characters slowly emerge through the few carefully selected adjectives used by male narrators. For the most part, only two adjectives are used to describe the positive female characters, "good" and "of good judgment" (*buen entendimiento*), while males are termed "good," "intelligent," "kind," "honorable," "righteous," "brave," and "strong," even though the male characters are generally allowed to speak loud and clear for themselves. When the last two adjectives, "brave" and "strong," are applied to a woman, they acquire a negative connotation. In *ejemplo* XXXV, the woman is constantly described as *muy fuerte et muy brava* (strong and ill-tempered) and called a *diablo* (devil), as if usurping the male role were an evil thing. Furthermore, Patronio constantly reduces the woman to a *cosa* (thing) and puts her at the same level as the other animals in the house when he recounts the moment the young man realizes that there is no other *cosa viva* (thing alive) except for his wife after he has killed the dog, cat, and horse.

Patronio consistently characterizes women who do evil as being the devil incarnate, for example, the girl of *ejemplo* XXXV and the false pious woman (*la beguina*) of *ejemplo* XLII. In the latter case, she achieves what the devil himself could not do, breaking and destroying the relationship of a happy couple. On the other hand, men's improper behavior is shown to be the result of external circumstances and not of their own evil nature. Thus, when the sultan Saladín falls in love with his vassal's wife and tries to seduce her, Patronio explains how the devil can disguise himself and lead astray even the most honorable man (*ejemplo* L). Throughout the stories, Patronio carefully introduces characters in the role of good and bad advisers to warn the count about the perils of following just anyone's advice. The false pious woman who becomes the adviser of the ill-fated couple in *ejemplo* XLII serves as a foil to Patronio, who only brings happiness and honor to his master. Of all the advisers in this collection, none proves to be as evil and destructive as the false pious woman, who brings about the death of the couple and the destruction of two families.

Clearly, the characteristics and motivations of characters are depicted differently according to their gender, and their actions are interpreted in a different light. In *ejemplo* L, for instance, the good wife diverts the sultan's advances by asking him a question: What is the best quality a man may have? The question sends Saladín on a long quest throughout the continent. Once the sultan has learned that *verguenza* (shame) is the answer, he cannot act against that which has taken him so long to comprehend. Yet according to Patronio's summary at the end, the moral of the story is not about the astute way in which the woman defends her honor but about the most precious virtue, which the sultan obviously exemplifies. In a similar manner, the loyal and brave actions of Count Rodrigo, Pero Núñez, and Roy González are described in detail in *ejemplo* XLIV, while their wives' actions are introduced as symbolic of the rewards granted to these honorable men.

Juan Manuel's unwillingness to name most of the female characters also betrays a misogynistic attitude. In spite of their prominent roles in the stories, Emperor Fradrique's wife (*ejemplo* XXII), the count of Provencia's wife and daughter (*ejemplo* XXV), the merchant's wife (*ejemplo* XXXVI), the false pious woman (*ejemplo* XLII), the loyal wives of Count Rodrigo, Pero Nuñez, and Roy González (*ejemplo* XLIV), and the good woman defending her honor from Saladín (*ejemplo* L) are all anonymous female characters defined according to their relation to men, as daughters, wives, sisters, and so on. In other stories, women are conspicuously absent. No queen, wife, or mother is mentioned in *ejemplo* XXIV when a king tries to test his sons to determine which one should be heir to the throne.

When one takes into account the role of women in Juan Manuel's life, the misogynistic overtones of his work become not only apparent but also ironic. For a man educated by his mother, who witnessed the power that María de Molina had as regent of Castile not only in educating her children but also in ruling the kingdom, to address his didactic stories only to noblemen is to deny the reality of his own life. On the other hand, for a man who manipulated his marriages as political negotiations where the young brides were merely pawns, it is not surprising that he objectifies female characters and reduces them to "things." All in all, *El Conde Lucanor* does reflect the complex and contradictory realities of women in Castilian society, a patriarchal system in which men were charged with maintaining law and order and ensuring that the women in their families kept their proper place. In spite of their anonymity, many of Juan Manuel's female characters influenced Spanish Golden Age dramatists such as Lope de *Vega and *Calderón de la Barca.

Work

The Book of Count Lucanor and Patronio. A Translation of Don Juan Manuel's El Conde Lucanor. Trans. John E. Keller and L. Clark Keating. Lexington: UP of Kentucky, 1977; New York: Peter Lang, 1993.

"El Conde Lucanor." *Obras completas*. Ed. José Manuel Blecua. Vol. 2. Madrid: Gredos, 1983.

"Libro de Patronio." *Escritores en prosa anteriores al siglo XV*. BAE 51. Ed. Pascual de Gayangos y Arce. Madrid: Real Academia Española, 1952.

Work about

Biglieri, Aníbal A. *Hacia una poética del relato didáctico: Ocho estudios sobre* El Conde Lucanor. Chapel Hill: UNCSRLL, 1989.

Dunn, Peter N. "Don Juan Manuel: The World as Text." *MLN* 106.2 (March 1991): 223–240.

Grabowska, James A. "The Rhetoric of Power in Juan Manuel's *El Conde Lucanor*." *South Central Review* 11.3 (Fall 1994): 45–61.

Jaffe, Catherine M. " 'Las vestias que van cargadas de oro': The Reader and 'Exemplo L' of Juan Manuel's *El Conde Lucanor*." *Revista de Estudios Hispánicos* 21.1 (January 1987): 1–12.

MacPherson, Ian, ed. *Juan Manuel Studies*. London: Tamesis, 1977.

Sturcken, H. Tracy. *Don Juan Manuel*. New York: Twayne, 1974.

Carmen S. Rivera

Contreras y Alba de Rodríguez, María del Pilar (1861–1930)

Born in Alcalá la Real, María del Pilar Contreras y Alba de Rodríguez started writing at a very young age in *La verdad* (Jaén). From 1890 on she lived in Madrid and published the newspaper *El amigo del hogar* (Home Companion). She was also a composer of waltzes (*Cástor y Polux*), zarzuela (*Entre castaños* [Among the Chestnuts]), opera (*La Virgen del Torrente* [The Virgen of the Torrent], with music by Pérez Giralde y Vázquez), and several hymns.

Her book *Muñecos y muñecas o Las niñas en el bazar* (1917; Puppets and Dolls or Little Girls at the Bazaar) is a verse *zarzuela* (vaudeville-style operetta) in one act. It deals with the dreams of two girls in a dolls' shop, contrasting their cleverness with the clumsiness of the shop's owner.

Work by

Domésticas . . . sin domesticar. Madrid: Vda. de A. Alvarez, 1917.

Impresiones del veraneo en El Escorial. Tipos, costumbres y pasajes. Madrid: Antonio Alvarez, 1920.

Mis distracciones (poesías). Madrid: Antonio Alvarez, 1910.

Muñecos y muñecas o Las niñas en el bazar. Madrid: Vda. de Antonio Alvarez, 1917.

Páginas sueltas. Madrid: Alvarez, 1903.

Pasado, presente y futuro. Madrid: Vda. de A. Alvarez, 1912.

Los pícaros intereses. Madrid: Vda. de Antonio Alvarez, 1914.

Work about

Simón-Palmer, María del Carmen. *Escritoras españolas del siglo XIX. Manual bio-bibliográfico*. Madrid: Castalia, 1991.

Carmen de Urioste

Converso Poets' View of Women

See Isabel I, Queen of Castile: The Vision of the Queen in *Converso* Poetry (c. 1474–c. 1480)

Corbacho, El (1438)

Also known as *El Arcipreste de Talavera* and *Reprobación del amor mundano*, the *Corbacho* (trans. as *Little Sermons on Sin*, 1959) is a four-part book written in 1438 by Alfonso Martínez de Toledo (1398?–1482?), a clergyman associated with Toledo Cathedral in the first half of the fifteenth century and onetime chaplain to King Juan II (1405–1454). Written in a mixed blend of imagined dialogues, discursive arguments, and didactic discourse, the *Corbacho* is in large part a misogynist work aimed at discouraging men from keeping the company of women.

The first part of the book contains observations on earthly love and the many disasters that can occur if man succumbs to love and desire for woman. These include the offense brought about against God and religion by loving woman, the risk of insanity, the likelihood of turning to crime, and the danger of losing one's virtues. In the second part Martínez de Toledo raises the topic of women, offering a panorama of the many areas in which women reveal their destructive traits. His attacks are based on the conviction that women are hypocritical, deceitful, lustful, and disobedient, among many other vices. In part three the author turns to medical facts and, having outlined the role of the four humors in determining the character of men, he discusses how certain humors cause men to lead useless lives. The third part includes also a brief categorization of undesirable and desirable marriages in terms of age differences between bride and groom. In the fourth part the clergyman makes a number of observations on astronomy and fortune.

The *Corbacho* holds a prominent place in the tradition of medieval *misogyny. The author's use of imagined, everyday scenarios and dialogues between men and women lends a dynamic quality to his discourse and allows him to represent the wiles of women with rigor. In the attacks on women he saturates the text with countless examples of women's defects, attributing direct and indirect speech to them to underscore their tactics of manipulation and deceit. His satirical edge and blatantly negative portrayal of women inscribe him fully in the long line of misogynist satirists and theologians from antiquity to the Middle Ages. These include Tertullian (155/160?–220?), Cyprian (200?–258), Ambrose (339?–397), Augustine (354–430), and Thomas Aquinas (1224/1225?–1274), among many others, whose main purpose for writing attacks on women and sexual love was to encourage chastity and divine love in men. This attitude stemmed from the example of Eve and how she had caused the downfall of man. While the promotion of chastity figures as the self-declared reason for writing misogynist literature, it is clear that Christian theologians and clergymen such as Martínez de Toledo employed the female sex as a trope for the expression of many other anxieties as well. The *Corbacho* was written at a time when medical theories on *sexuality were circulating in the West, often confronting learned men of the Church and other walks of the establishment with what seemed like the indecipherable realities of feminine sexuality, reproduction, and anatomy, all of which could potentially cause the downfall of man because of their enigmatic and all-consuming nature. As Solomon astutely observes, the writer of the *Corbacho* seems convinced that man's sexual well-being has to do with his knowledge of medicine and the ability to cure the illness of desire, staying well away from woman in the process.

Alongside the exoticization and rejection of the female body—and by extension of physical desire—the *Corbacho* employs a series of devices to make the misogynist content more accessible to readers. The most important tool employed by Martínez de Toledo is his relentless use of speech in ways that would strike the modern reader as stream-of-consciousness writing. In those sections of the book dealing with desire and with women, the author sets up a lively scenario in which he imagines the monologues or dialogues carried out by characters whose words underscore the defects of women, exploring the many variations that each vice can have. When spoken by women in particular, the barrage of complaints, deceits, or vanities contained in the monologues creates an all-encompassing effect that drives home not just the vice being denounced but also the conviction that women have an unnatural proclivity toward endless chatter. The blend of expository discourse and fictional situations fuels the author's didactic force and creates a wide range of stylistic registers for the work. Martínez de Toledo draws on high and low speech, popular tales, moral fables, and topics from courtly and noncourtly literature to convey his points. The ranges of linguistic register and the abundance of reported speech have led many critics to comment first and foremost on the dynamic and creative qualities of the clergyman's work in terms of language. Indeed, the text has proved useful for linguists studying particular aspects of fifteenth-century Spanish grammar and syntax. In addition, the *Corbacho* provides a valuable source for the further comprehension of rhetorical techniques used in sermons and didactic writing in the fifteenth century. The observation has also been made that the work paves the way for subsequent texts on the wiles of women (for example, *La *Celestina* [1499] of Fernando de Rojas). As regards the text's importance for feminist studies, there can be no doubt that the *Corbacho* is a prime example of the literary and religious stereotypes that commanded the discourse of Western medieval writers working in the tradition of misogyny. Not only does the work draw from the solid genealogy of antifeminist texts past and contemporary, but also, in its use of everyday speech and situations in particular, it offers readers a distinctly lively model of fifteenth-century attitudes to women. See also *Libro de las virtuosas y claras mujeres* (fifteenth century); *Tratado en defensa de las virtuosas mujeres* (before 1448); Women's Deceits: Medieval Approaches to the Topic

Work

Arcipreste de Talavera o Corbacho. Ed. E. Michael Gerli. Madrid: Cátedra, 1981.

Little Sermons on Sin. Trans. and ed. Lesley Bird Simpson. Berkeley and Los Angeles: U of California P, 1959.

Work about

DiFranco, Ralph. "Rhetoric and Some Narrative Techniques in the *Corbacho* of Alfonso Martínez de Toledo." *Romance Quarterly* 29.2 (1982): 135–142.

Sims, Edna N. "Towards a More Complete Portrayal of Womankind." *Círculo: Revista de Cultura* 19 (1990): 165–172.

Solomon, Michael. *The Literature of Misogyny in Medieval Spain: The "Arcipreste de Talavera" and the "Spill."* Cambridge: Cambridge Studies in Latin-American and Iberian Literature, 1997.

Leyla Rouhi

Córdoba, Martín de

See *Jardín de las nobles donzellas* (written c. 1468)

Coronado, Carolina (1823–1911)

One of eight children born to a family of wealthy landowners in the village of Almadrejo, Extremadura, Spain's most western region, Carolina Coronado was educated in accordance with contemporary social expectations regarding women; she was prepared to be a wife and mother. Reading was one of Coronado's favorite childhood pastimes, and before long she began to compose her own poetry. In 1848, Coronado's family moved to Madrid. There she met and married an American diplomat, Horace Perry, in 1852. Coronado's adult life spanned six decades of the nineteenth century, yet the bulk of her work appeared in print between 1843 and 1873. Encouraged by playwright Juan Eugenio Hartzenbush (1806–1880), she published her first volume of poetry, *Poesías* (1843; Poems), when she was only 23 years old. After 1873, the year her daughter Carolina died at age 16, Coronado wrote and published very little. Coronado is considered one of the more prominent poetic voices of Spain's Romantic period. She was also the author of short fiction and novels.

During her lifetime, Coronado published her poetry in three separate collections, all titled *Poesías* (1843, 1852, 1872). The 1852 edition included poems from her first collection. The 1872 edition was primarily an anthology of previous compositions and included only a few new poems. The poems in the first collection are lyrical compositions that focus primarily on themes related to nature. Among the most popular are those dedicated to flowers ("La rosa blanca" [The White Rose], "Al lirio" [To the Lily], "Al jazmín" [To the Jasmine]) that characteristically symbolize the romantic notion of personal solitude and melancholy. In other early compositions ("Mérida," "A Cádiz"), she uses landscape to evoke Spain's historical grandeur and compare it to the social and political unrest of the nineteenth century. The idea of the feminine in Coronado's early poetry centers on the conventional image of women as frail and submissive, yet one gets the sense that there is a female poetic voice striving to break free. This initial expression of the feminine in a lyrical context in time evolves in her later poetic compositions to coincide with present-day feminist notions of women's writing and the elaboration of a feminist consciousness.

The poems in the 1852 edition convey a more precise definition of the female experience within a social and historical context and are linked directly to other compositions that express her concern for Spanish society in general, such as "Un año más" (Another Year), "España" (Spain), and "A la juventud española del siglo XIX" (To Spanish Youth of the Nineteenth Century) in which she talks with anticipation of the nation's future as a time of change and progress. While the romantic tone persists in later compositions, her voice no longer masks itself behind the traditional guise of feminine subjectivity. Two aspects of Coronado's later poetry invite feminist analysis, the notion of feminine enclosure (*Encierro) and a general call to other women poets of the day to break with their artistic silence. Two poems in particular are representative of the latent feminism in her poetry from this period, "Flor del agua" (On the Water's Surface) and "El castillo de Salvatierra" (Salvatierra Castle). In "Flor del agua," Coronado builds on the image of the flower as a representation of the fragile and passive woman who, tossed and turned by the movement of the water, strives to stay above water and make its presence known. The delicate flower, determined to survive in its threatening environment, is equated with a woman poet who must strive to express herself and confront the centuries-old artistic oppression of the female voice. The image of water lilies grounding themselves firmly in the earth below in order to overcome their turbulent surroundings metaphorically calls for solidarity among women to root themselves firmly in a male-inscribed literary tradition. In "El castillo de Salvatierra," inspired by a visit Coronado made to the castle located in her native Extremadura, the poet addresses the historical oppression of women and their need to be liberated from their natural state of entrapment. Surrounded by the ruins of the castle, Coronado likens the medieval structure to feminine entrapment, while the pigeons in the castle's towers represent the image of women breaking with traditional enclosure. The context of the poem is personal. Coronado speaks of the eternal condition of female imprisonment and how society was not able to keep her wings from taking flight. The composition exemplifies Coronado's most explicit criticism of the social and historical oppression of women.

The call to women to bond together and express themselves through their creative work is echoed both in a series of critical articles about contemporary women poets and in poems dedicated to specific women poets. Female poets of her day that she encouraged to write and publish and for whom she sought to garner public recognition include Manuela Cambronero, Josefa Massans, María Verdejo, Victoria Mérida, and Amalia Fernollosa. In compositions such as "Cantad, hermosas" (Sing, Beauties), Coronado offers general words of support. In others, she directs herself to specific individuals, imploring them to overcome their typical melancholy poetry and address issues of greater social substance, such as Robustiana Armiño in "A la señorita Armiño" and Angela *Grassi in "A Angela." Other compositions, such as "A Elisa," "A Lidia," and "Yo no puedo seguirte con mi vuelo" (I Cannot Follow You with My Flight) have the same objective. Collectively, this poetry seeks to achieve a sense of sisterhood and solidarity among the women poets of the time much along the lines of present-day feminism.

In 1850, Coronado published two short pieces of fiction, *Adoración* (Adoration) and *Paquita*. In 1854, she published the first of three historical novels, *La Sigea*. The other two, *Jarilla* and *La Rueda de Desgracia* (The Wheel of Misfortune), appeared in print in 1873. Although not widely recognized for her prose works, Coronado's novelistic production is in many ways much more decisively feminist in theme than her poetic compositions. The female protagonists in these works are characteristically individuals trapped by age-old notions of womanhood. *Paquita* focuses on the traditional role of women and social expectations as regards the institution of marriage. In the case of *La Sigea* the idea of female oppression takes on an intellectual dimension. The novel uses two historical figures, Luisa Sigea de Toledo (c.1530?–1560?) and Princess María of Portugal. The work focuses on the princess's determination to educate herself as a means of freeing herself from patriarchal dominance. Coronado's prose fiction essentially promotes an alternative view of woman and calls to mind the historical revisionist perspective so prominent among today's women writers.

Coronado wrote very little during her final years. What she did write was directly related to the social and political unrest of turn-of-the-century Spain. Many of Coronado's final poems speak of a national reality of despair and a need to regenerate the country. In poems such as "Vates, la muerte que cercano vemos" (Prophets, We See Death Close By) and "El siglo va a partir" (The Century Is Departing) she talks of a fragmented nation unable to control its destiny. In others, such as "¡Oh mi España! ¡Oh, mi patria!" (Oh My Spain! Oh My Homeland!) she contrasts Spain's glorious past with its decadent present, and in "Arribo al siglo veinte" (I Arrive at the Twentieth Century) and "Pues hay en nuestra tierra quien me llama" (For Someone in Our Land Calls Me) she calls to future generations to save Spain from its squalid condition. The poetry Coronado writes at the end of her life is in many ways similar to ideological and social concerns espoused in the works of authors of the Generation of 1898.

The notion of woman projected in Coronado's work is not so revolutionary as to promote a feminist critique. Much of what she reveals about women through her poetry and prose is imbued with feminine subjectivity and subscribes to the traditional notion of gender during her lifetime. Nevertheless, there is a feminist orientation to Coronado's work. Specific works present issues relevant to the female experience that have become more defined with time and on which subsequent authors have elaborated, concepts such as feminine entrapment, the opposition of the public and the private, the notion of female silence, the idea of the female experience as one that transcends the individual to include all women, and above all, a consciousness that women have not been permitted to express themselves by means of a personal voice.

Work by

Jarilla. 1873. Barcelona: Montaner y Simón, 1943.
Paquita, Adoración. Madrid: San Fernando, 1850.
Poesías. Ed. and intro. Noël Valis. Madrid: Castalia, 1991.
La Rueda de la Desgracia. Madrid: M. Tello, 1873.
La Sigea. Madrid: Anselmo Santa Colomo, 1854.

Work about

Castilla, Alberto. *Carolina Coronado de Perry.* Madrid: Beramar, 1987.
Gutiérrez Macías, Valeriano. *Carolina Coronado. Crítica e interpretación.* Badajoz: Diputación Provincial de Badajoz, 1965.
Kaminsky, Amy. "The Construction of Immortality: Sappho, Saint Theresa and Carolina Coronado." *Letras Femeninas* 19.1–2 (Spring–Fall 1993): 1–13.
Kirkpatrick, Susan. "Irony in Carolina Coronado's *Paquita*: The Voice of the Female Subject in Spanish Romanticism." *Letras Peninsulares* 10.1 (Spring 1997): 169–183.
———. *Las Románticas: Women Writers and Subjectivity in Spain, 1835–1850.* Berkeley and Los Angeles: U of California P, 1989.
Manso Amarillo, Fernando. *Carolina Coronado: Su obra literaria.* Badajoz: Diputación de Badajoz, 1992.
Valis, Noël. "Autobiography as Insult." *Culture and Gender in Nineteenth-Century Spain.* Ed. Lou Charnon-Deutsch and Jo Labanyi. Oxford: Clarendon P, 1995.

John P. Gabriele

Correa, Isabel de (second half of seventeenth century)

Extremely little is known about this seventeenth-century poet, polyglot, and translator who played an active role in the lively cultural community of Sephardic Jews then living in Amsterdam. López Estrada bases his conjecture that Isabel de Correa was born in Portugal on her knowledge of Portuguese and the fact that her family surname is shared by several Portuguese families of the day. One clear biographical fact is Correa's marriage to Mallorcan Jew Nicolás de Oliver y Fullana, a soldier in several military campaigns in Cataluña and France who also collaborated on several literary works. The introduction to Miguel de Barrios's *Coro de las musas* (1672; Chorus of the Muses) indicates that Correa published a book of poems, but it has been lost.

The single extant work of Correa is an elegant translation of Battista Guarini's popular dramatic masterpiece *Il Pastor fido* (1590; The Faithful Shepherd), published in 1694. Her prologue to the translation accomplishes several personal goals. First, in anticipation of the inevitable negative reaction this work by a woman will provoke, Correa sets forth a spirited and cogent defense of women as writers, displaying her familiarity with classical literature and rhetoric and famous women writers of both past and present. Three personal desires conspired to awaken her *casi sepultado ingenio* (almost entombed talent): to grow in wisdom, to attain fame, and to provide healthy diversion from her other responsibilities. Correa then discusses the guiding principles used in her translation. Using both the original Italian and a French translation as sources, she states she will employ a variety of verse forms (unlike the original, written in *silvas*), to better capture the sense and spirit of the work, thereby demonstrating her knowledge of theoretical criteria involved in the art of translation. While she opts for freedom of form in her translation, she rigorously protects the integrity of the original text by refusing to add explanatory verses to the original work without indicating them as such. Instead, she clearly marks each of her additions/illustrations, which, as López Estrada remarks, is quite unlike what is seen in other translations of the day. Correa's defense of women and her rigorous approach to translation make her most deserving of inclusion in histories of poetics of the seventeenth century.

Work

López Estrada, Francisco. "Poética barroca. Edición y estudio de los preliminares de *El Pastor Fido* de Guarini, traducido por Isabel Correa (1694)." *Hommage a Robert Jammes*. Ed. Francis Cerdan. Vol. 2. Paris: Presses Universitaires du Mirail, 1994.

Work about

López Estrada, Francisco. "Isabel Correa, escritora sefardí del Amsterdam barroco." *La Torre* 7.26 (1993): 123–146.

Maureen Ihrie

Cosmetics in Medieval and Renaissance Spain

Applying makeup and coloring one's hair have been an integral part of Mediterranean civilization since prehistoric times. In early Spanish culture, use of cosmetics was prevalent in all sectors of society because it had been introduced by Moorish customs that overwhelmed the Peninsula in the early eighth century. Consequently, virtually all native-Spanish products have names derived from Arabic. By the sixteenth century, Spain had attained its most prestigious age in beauty products. The word *cosméticos* was not used during that period, however; the word *afeites* was employed instead for makeup women used on their face, teeth, hands, and neck as well as for everything to paint or dye the hair.

One of the main concerns of Renaissance women in Spain and elsewhere was to look as white as possible. To achieve this look they used *albayalde* and *solimán*. *Albayalde* was a white powder produced by melting lead and dissolving it in vinegar. After the vinegar solution evaporated, a white powder remained that was used as face powder and as a base for rouge. *Solimán* was produced in the same manner as *albayalde*, except with mercury instead of lead. *Solimán* was also white and was used as a base for other cosmetics and for whitening teeth. The equivalent of today's rouge was produced with the pits of pomegranate and vermilion. This product was called *arrebol* and was produced as a powder in order to put blush in the cheeks already whitened by *albayalde* or *solimán* and also in pencil form to paint lips, like today's lipstick. According to the fifteenth-century diatribe titled *El *Corbacho*, the most common *afeites* or cosmetics used by women were *albayalde* and *arrebol*.

In order to enhance the whiteness of the face and enlarge their eyes, women used a powder produced from a stone called *alcohol* (kohl), which was then made into a blueblack ointment used to darken eyelashes, eyelids, and eyebrows, much like today's mascara, eye shadow, and eyebrow pencil. It was put on with a little stem of fennel, perhaps to conceal the smell of the product.

Before the Renaissance, the fashion of ladies was to dye their hair black in order to enhance the whiteness of their skin and to cover gray hair. However, by the sixteenth century Spanish ladies were dyeing their hair blond or red in imitation of a fashion brought to Spain from Italy. To *enrubiarse* (make one's hair blond), they took walnut leaves and bark from pomegranate trees and boiled them in water until a dye was extracted. The final product was used to wet their hair for about 15 days until it turned blond or red.

Women of the Golden Age also enjoyed many colognes that during that period were identified with the generic name of *aguas*. Any liquid extracted from vegetables, flowers, or fruit for the purpose of producing scented water was called an *agua*, such as *agua de ángeles*, *agua de azahar*, *agua de jazmín*, *agua de rosas*, and *agua de trébol*. Most of the other face and hand lotions, astringents, and moisturizers were also called *aguas*. For example, *agua de almendra* and *agua de hiel* were used as moisturizers, while *agua rosada* was used as an astringent. *Agua de cebada* and *agua de calabaza* served as skin softeners. For aging, there was also *agua de alumbre* made from aluminum, potassium, and water, which was supposed to eliminate wrinkles. *Agua* then was what today we call *perfume* or cologne, while the Spanish word *perfume* was an incense in the form of a pill or something similar used to scent pieces of clothing, linen, or furniture. Such perfume pills were burned to release their fragrance.

The use of cosmetics was not always accepted or considered an acceptable practice for women, especially by the religious moralists. Face painting, hair dyeing, and wearing cosmetics in general were heavily criticized by humanists and clerics, who linked this use with sinful and sexually illicit professions. Several books appeared in the sixteenth century criticizing and forbidding the use of cosmetics, the most popular being *Instrucción de la mujer cristiana* (c. 1530; Instruction of a Christian Woman) by Juan Luis *Vives (1492–1540) and *La perfecta casada* (c. 1570; The Perfect Wife) by Fray Luis de *León (1527/1528–1591); then in the early seventeenth century Antonio Marqués published his influential *Afeite y mundo mujeril* (Cosmetics and Women's World). Nevertheless, cosmetics remained a huge and very profitable business. Curiously, by the end of the Golden Age, males were also dyeing their hair as well as using some makeup on their faces, as is comically denounced in Agustín *Moreto's (1618–1669) *El lindo don Diego* (c. 1660; Don Diego the Dandy). By that time, however, the use of cosmetics had become a European phenomenon, and the unique Spanish makeup inherited from the Arab world had been assimilated or displaced by trends from Italy and France. After 1700, in fact, the Gallic mode completely crushed the native styles and the terminology that described them. *See also* Misogyny in Medieval and Early Modern Spain; Women's Deceits: Medieval Approaches to the Topic

Work about

Arrelano Ayuso, Ignacio. "Sobre el léxico de los afeites del Siglo de Oro y las dificultades del contexto." RILCE 6 (1990): 179–199.

Howe, Elizabeth Teresa. "The Feminine Mistake:

Nature, Illusion, and Cosmetics in the *Siglo de Oro*." *Hispania* 68 (September 1985): 443–451.

Rubio, Fernando, ed. *Antonio Marqués: "Afeite y mundo mujeril."* Barcelona: Juan Flors, 1964.

Terrón González, Jesús. *Léxico de cosméticos y afeites en el Siglo de Oro.* Extremadura: Servicio de Publicaciones de la Universidad, 1990.

Eric V. Alvarez

Courtly Love

Webster's Third New International Dictionary defines courtly love as "a late medieval highly conventionalized code prescribing conduct and emotions of ladies and their lovers and providing the theme of an extensive medieval courtly literature." The ideology, codes, and conventions of this complex sociocultural phenomenon, practiced in European high culture and courts from the eleventh century through the Renaissance, thoroughly infused countless aspects of Western culture. In general terms, courtly love begins when the lover (usually a male) is instantly, deeply smitten by the *sight* of the beloved (usually a beautiful lady). Descriptions of her golden hair, clear forehead, slender brows, smiling face and lips, white hands, thin waist, elegant dress, and so on, are idealized visions rather than individualized portraits. The passion felt by the lover is a mixture of the carnal and the spiritual, for physical beauty provokes physical desire, on the one hand, but also inspires adoration, obedience, and a desire to ennoble oneself and thereby be worthy. The beloved is infinitely superior to the lover, who suffers, experiences jealousy, and even comes near death, so strong are the effects of this unrequited love. Yet he persists, and this fidelity in the face of indifference, danger, rejection, or inaccessibility improves the character, sensitivity, and strength of the lover. The beloved's indifference to the lover makes her his superior since she is not a slave to desire. Linguistic codes employed to express these circumstances include those of games, religion, and medicine, and antithesis and paradox often figure. There are infinite variations to this rough scheme, so that courtly love's basic glorification of sentimental love, of unions based on affective rather than political interests, has figured in countless artistic works over the centuries and clearly persists to this day.

The causes, specific characteristics, and development of courtly love, which first clearly manifested itself in the troubadour poetry of twelfth-century France, have been much debated. The diverse possible sources of courtly love help explain its polysemous nature. Boase identifies seven distinct "theories of origin" scholars have used in analyzing courtly love: (1) The "Hispano-Arabic" theory, which emphasizes the influence of culture and writing in southern Spain; (2) the "chivalric-matriarchal" origin, in which courtly love resulted from the combined influence of Christianity and a matriarchal tradition in Germanic, Celtic, and Pictish nobility; (3) the "crypto-Cathar" possibility, in which courtly love reflects the Albigensian heresy; (4) the "Neoplatonic" theory, which focuses on ideological rather than sociohistorical influences; (5) the "Bernardine-Marianist" inspiration, which argues for a spiritual, mystical beginning to the movement; (6) the "spring folk ritual" theory, which discerns popular and pagan roots, and (7) "feudal-sociological" causes, which focuses on class and economic conditions. Boase ends his analysis by arguing for multiple causation, concluding that the Hispano-Arabic and feudal-sociological theories are the strongest and mutually reinforcing. Menocal agrees with the idea of multiple causation but maintains that aspects of the other theories of causation contain relevant aspects and, more important, that ideological critical prejudice and ignorance have obstructed proper consideration of the Hispano-Arabic theory.

J.A. and Cosme Carpentier de Gourdon have traced parallel elements of Arabic/Oriental love poetry and the European courtly love tradition. Using as a point of departure the deep Platonist roots of Eastern thought, they observe that the two traditions share the following attributes: (1) Existing power roles in society are inverted—the (superior) male subjects himself to the authority of the (inferior) female; (2) fidelity and devotion to the beloved are practiced; (3) there are a variety of attitudes regarding physical versus spiritual love (some writings advocate or celebrate physical enjoyment in vibrant detail, while others sublimate the physical to the spiritual and seek joy through intellectual or spiritual contemplation of the beloved); (4) the woman does not reciprocate; she is chaste, or unreachable like the Virgin Mary, making the focus of the writing that of unfulfilled male desire; (5) love is glorified as an ennobling force; (6) such love does not exist or occur between spouses. The Carpentier de Gourdons also note that Ibn Hazm's *El collar de la paloma* (11th c.; The Dove's Ring) is considered a primary source for what has been identified as the first European treatise to codify the phenomenon, Andreas Capellanus's *De amore* (c. 1185).

Warner argues that courtly love initially was quite separate from *Marianism. Based on distinctions of class and social positions, courtly love at first pursued adulterous unions and celebrated sexual joy, while the cult of the Virgin Mary exalted chastity, and did not generalize into the adoration of women. By the thirteenth century, however, cross-pollination of the two movements began, with the encouragement of the Church, which saw an opportunity to counter the idealization of adultery with the model of chastity/disinterest in physical love as a required characteristic of desirable women. In his dedication to the *Cantigas de Santa María* (written 13th c.; Canticles to Holy Mary), King Alfonso X the Wise (1221–1284) addresses the Virgin as a courtier would his lady, clearly identifying with the *ennobling* influence of courtly love on the lover (stated also in Part 2 of the *Siete partidas*), as well as the beloved's perfect chastity. The subsequent commingling of the sacred and the profane is characteristic in later courtly love literature and affects the portrayal of and attitudes toward women in such literature. Gerli, for example, documents a systematic adaptation of religious forms, formulas, and concepts to exalt carnal love in sixteenth-century *cancionero* (verse anthology collection) poetry.

In considering how the cultural phenomenon of courtly love affected the lives of medieval women, Duby observes that the literary model of a married lady who inspires intense desire in a young knight of inferior social rank, causing him to discreetly adore her and serve her, in the hope that he will be rewarded with a smile, a kiss, and progressively more, served to influence (and improve) the attitude and behavior of certain men (initially, unmarried knights) toward certain women (initially, married women of some nobility). The social practice of courtly love soon generalized to become a popular diversion among married and unmarried nobility. In male noblemen, courtly love encouraged self-restraint and friendship as knights proffered gifts, courtesies, and obedience to their ladies, and in female nobility it provided a model of resistance, self-control, and temporary power. Duby concludes that courtly love was a men's game that, although it defined and improved codes of behavior for both men and women of the upper class, and proved the nobility of male and female participants, it stereotyped women as (initially) inaccessible objects of physical desire and pleasure, to be pursued and possessed.

Weiss also has observed that courtly love rituals are a game that affirms certain class- and gender-related values that ultimately serve to silence women and secure male domination, offering in support an analysis of Alvaro de Luna's defense of woman, the *Libro de las virtuosas y claras mujeres* (fourteenth c.; Book of Virtuous and Illustrious Women). Another example of how courtly love conventions serve to define the superior male is found in the *Abencerraje y la hermosa Jarifa* (1561–1565), where the hero offers as one proof of his illustrious lineage the fact that no male lacking a beloved to adore could ever call himself an Abencerraje. Certainly the life and the poetry of Garcilaso de la Vega (c. 1501–1536) attest dramatically to such courtly love conventions.

Bloch, among others, presents a strong case for equating antifeminism with courtly love. He considers the essence of "courtliness" to be a collective daydream of escape from the tedious reality of medieval marriages, which were entirely utilitarian. He also notes how the roots of courtly love are tightly intertwined with the early Christian church's promotion of asceticism and with the Church's paradoxical, simultaneous definition of woman as virgin bride of Christ/gateway to the Devil. As he states, the key paradoxes of courtly love include: (1) worship of a woman as goddess—vilification of woman as evil temptress; (2) idealization of virginity, chastity, and sublimation of the physical to the spiritual—goal of adultery, wooing to attain physical possession, to deflower illicitly, outside of marriage. Courtly love writings parallel antifeminist literature in that each depicts the woman as silent—in the latter because her tongue is wicked and in the former, because the exclusive focus is individuation of the male—the detailed description of his sufferings resulting from her cruelty or indifference. Eloquent expression of this essentially schizophrenic state of affairs is found in *Lope de Vega's sonnet number 191.

Thus works of literature that celebrate or emulate courtly love offer contradictory models and morals, not to mention the many other texts (*Celestina, *Libro de buen amor, *Corbacho, *Don Quijote de la Mancha) that parody, criticize or reject *amor cortés*. The starting point for all is the same: Sight of a beautiful lady ignites an intense passion. Troubadour love poems and much *cancionero* poetry celebrate erotic, physical love and emphasize the game aspect. Novels of chivalry (*caballerías) like *Amadís de Gaula* were criticized by moralists for their frank descriptions of the beloved's charms and depictions of adulterous carnal union only sometimes ameliorated by secret betrothals, and these tended to have happy endings. The psychological landscapes of the sentimental novel like Diego de *San Pedro's *Cárcel de amor* present extended consideration of the lover's frustration and suffering brought about by the rejection, forced separation, or death of the beloved. The complications of romantic love are also a staple of Golden Age theater. Rhodes finds that pastoral books, which exalt the blessed nature of suffering for love, do not belong to the courtly love tradition, because of the very different role women play in them. The shepherdesses possess experience and intellect equal to that of male shepherds; they play active roles equal to those of male characters, desiring as well as being desired, in a rural rather than urban setting. To sum up, despite the very mixed effects of courtly love for women, one must recognize it as an inexhaustible source of inspiration for some of the most significant and popular literature written. See also Hispano-Arabic Poetry by Women

Work about

Bloch, R. Howard. *Medieval Misogyny and the Invention of Western Romantic Love*. Chicago: Chicago UP, 1991.

Boase, Roger. "Courtly Love in Spanish Literature: A Continuing Debate." *Journal of Hispanic Philology* 9 (1984): 67–73.

———. *The Origin and Meaning of Courtly Love: A Critical Study of European Scholarship*. Manchester: Manchester UP, 1977.

Carpentier de Gourdon, J.A., and Cosme Carpentier de Gourdon. "El amor cortés de los juglares, sus fuentes y sus paralelos árabes, persas e indios." *La juglaresca*. Madrid: EDI, 1986. 73–87.

Carrillo, Elena. "La función de la enfermedad cortés de amor." *Bulletin of Hispanic Studies* 77 (2000): 201–224.

Duby, Georges. "The Courtly Model." *A History of Women in the West. II. Silences of the Middle Ages*. Ed. Christiane Klapische-Zuber. Cambridge and London: Belknap P of Harvard UP, 1992. 250–266.

Gerli, E. Michael. "La 'religión del amor' y el antifeminismo en las letras castellanas del siglo XV." *Hispanic Review* 49 (1981): 65–86.

González, Aurelio. "La imagen de la dama cortés." *Voces de la edad media.* Ed. Concepción Company, A. González, Lilian von der Walde, and Concepción Abellán. Mexico: UNAM, 1993. 139–155.

Green, Otis H. *Spain and the Western Tradition. The Castilian Mind in Literature from El Cid to Calderón.* Madison: Wisconsin UP, 1963.

Ibn Hazm de Córdoba. *El collar de la paloma.* Spanish trans. E. García Gómez. Madrid: Alianza, 1996.

Lazar, Moshe, and Norris J. Lacy. *Poetics of Love in the Middle Ages. Texts and Contexts.* Fairfax, VA: George Mason UP, 1989.

Menocal, María. "Close Encounters in Medieval Provence: Spain's Role in the Birth of Troubadour Poetry." *Hispanic Review* 49 (1981): 43–64.

Parker, Alexander A. *The Philosophy of Love in Spanish Literature 1480–1680.* Ed. Terence O'Reilly. Edinburgh: Edinburgh UP, 1985.

Rhodes, Elizabeth. "Skirting the Men: Gender Roles in Sixteenth-Century Pastoral Books." *Journal of Hispanic Philology* 11 (1987): 131–149.

Warner, Marina. *Alone of All Her Sex. The Myth and the Cult of the Virgin Mary.* New York: Knopf, 1976.

Weiss, Julian. "Alvaro de Luna, Juan de Mena and the Power of Courtly Love." *Modern Language Notes* 106.2 (1991): 241–256.

Maureen Ihrie

Criada

See Women's Professions in Early Spanish Literature: *Santas, Rameras, Casadas, Amas,* and *Criadas* (Saints, Whores, Wives, Governesses, and Servants)

Cruz, Juana de la (1481–1534)

This visionary nun was born to a humble farm family. When her relatives sought to marry her off at age 15, Juana de la Cruz donned male clothing and fled to a Franciscan convent located between Madrid and Toledo. She professed in 1497 and rose to become abbess in 1509. Church politics forced her to step down briefly, but she was later vindicated and reinstated, holding the position until her death. She enjoyed great renown during her life, receiving visits, support, and protection from Cardinal Cisneros and King Charles V. Her life story, which is more spiritual life than historical record, was first compiled by a fellow nun under the title *Vida y fin de la buenabenturada virgen sancta Juana de la Cruz* (Life of the Blessed Virgin Saint Juana de la Cruz). In the early seventeenth century, two biographies of her life were composed, and Tirso de Molina used her as inspiration for his dramatic trilogy *La Santa Juana* (1613–1614).

Her mystical experiences began when she was quite young. Healings are attributed to her, she worked with souls in purgatory, taking over their suffering, and Christ allowed her to experience the Passion. For 13 years, she received sermons from God, which were transcribed by the other nuns and collected in *El libro del conorte* (The Book of Consolation). Surtz and Giles have studied the strongly dramatic, representational nature of her sermons, which may be considered holy theater. Some sermons present radical interpretations, such as Juana's recounting of Creation, which explains the Fall as provoked by Eve's refusal to yield to Adam's lust. The daring, dangerous assumption of the male role of spiritual instructor, which her sermons represent, was resisted with much animosity by certain male clergy during her life and beyond. In 1568 all extant copies of *El libro del conorte* were ordered to be turned over to the Inquisition. Various attempts to have her canonized failed.

Surtz has also studied the strong concerns that emerge in Cruz's visions regarding gender, both as it relates to social and religious roles in society and as contrasted to God's indifference to male versus female identity. One vision recounted in her *Vida* revealed that she was originally conceived as male but that the Virgin Mary requested that she be changed to a female, and God did so, leaving her with a male Adam's apple to attest to the miracle. Surtz suggests that this consciousness of her own androgyny allowed Cruz to recognize the arbitrary nature of sexual difference and by extension to question the different power granted to males and females on the basis of gender. Her writings feature few figures of male authority, emphasize the feminine characteristics of males to increase her identification with them, and generally blur the line between male and female, thereby elevating the latter. They comprise a record of remarkable resistance to patriarchal domination of spirituality. *See also* Autobiographical Self-Representation of Women in the Early Modern Period; Nuns Who Wrote in Sixteenth- and Seventeenth-Century Spain

Work about

Giles, Mary. "The Discourse of Ecstasy: Late Medieval Spanish Women and Their Texts." *Gender and Text in the Later Middle Ages*. Ed. Jane Chance. Gainesville: UP of Florida, 1996. 306–330.

Surtz, Ronald E. *The Guitar of God. Gender, Power and Authority in the World of Mother Juana de la Cruz (1481–1534)*. Philadelphia: U of Pennsylvania P, 1990.

Maureen Ihrie

Cubiertas and *Tapadas*

These terms refer to women who cover most or all of their faces and bodies with sheets, veils, shawls, and the like. The practice of covering female faces and bodies is thousands of years old, and its interpretation has changed markedly a number of times. Women originally were covered up to control or distance their untrustworthy nature, but when early Christianity adopted the custom it was interpreted as an indication of modesty and desire to avoid arousing male passion.

A *cubierta* hung a sheet of cloth from the crown of her head, covering her entire face and body, down to her feet. The cloth was such that the woman could see out, but no one could see in. This practice was rarely criticized. The *tapada* was much more controversial. She used a veil or shawl of varying material, style, and quality, wrapping it around her head and shoulders but leaving one eye, and sometimes a shoulder and hand, revealed. By this time, the practice began to be equated with false modesty, coquetry, and deceit. The practice had been introduced to Spain by Moors during the Middle Ages but became quite popular among Christians also, especially in Madrid and Seville. Around 1563, at the urging of his attorneys, King Philip II imposed a penalty of 3,000 maravedis on any woman who covered her face; nonetheless, the custom continued. Poets and writers throughout the Golden Age depicted *tapadas* or referred to the practice, including Cervantes (1547–1616), *Quevedo (1580–1645), Lope de *Vega (1562–1635), Tirso de *Molina (1582–1648), to mention only a few. All presented the *tapada* as a deceptive, flirtatious, brazen woman who never fails to charm the men, then swindle and/or betray them.

Work about

Arizmendi Amiel, María Elena. "Las tapadas." *Revista de dialectología y tradiciones populares* 48 (1988): 53–59.

Maureen Ihrie

Cueva y Silva, Leonor de la (early seventeenth century–?)

Born to minor nobles in northwest Spain, there is no evidence that Leonor de la Cueva y Silva ever married. Author of poetry and a play, all of her extant poems form part of a seventeenth-century manuscript, perhaps her personal anthology, which also includes verse by Lope de *Vega, Góngora, and other luminaries of the day. In addition to several sonnets celebrating family members and two *romances* (ballads) about Alvaro de Luna, many of her poems examine the *courtly love tradition from a woman's perspective, be it that of a woman deceived, one aware of double standards, or one who resists love's (and a man's) duplicitous emotional bondage through intellectual resolve.

As Soufas observes, Cueva continues her analysis of women's responses to contemporary social and literary traditions in her play

La firmeza en la ausencia (written 1630s–1660s; Steadfastness in Absence). After a mutually agreeable courtship with Juan, the play's female protagonist, Armesinda, suddenly finds herself the object of the king's aggressive affection as well. Inverting the patriarchal concept of man as soul or guiding spirit ordained to rule over woman who, as physical body, is destined to obey, Armesinda maintains her spiritual virtue and fidelity to Juan and resists the king's numerous deceits contrived to possess her. Thus it is she who exemplifies the moral superiority that ultimately prevails over (the king's) physical desires and restores order at the play's conclusion.

Work by

Antología de poetisas líricas. Ed. and sel. M. Serrano y Sanz. Madrid: Real Academia, 1915. 364–392.

La firmeza en la ausencia. In *Women's Acts. Plays by Women Dramatists of Spain's Golden Age*. Ed. and intro. Teresa Scott Soufas. Lexington: UP of Kentucky, 1997.

Work about

Elman, Linda L. "Between a Rock and a Hard Place: Armesinda Sets Her Own Parameters in *La firmeza en la ausencia* by Leonor de la Cueva y Silva." *Engendering the Early Modern Stage*. Ed. Valerie Hegstrom and Amy R. Williamsen. New Orleans: UP of the South, 1999.

Soufas, Teresa Scott. *Dramas of Distinction. A Study of Plays by Golden Age Women*. Lexington: UP of Kentucky, 1997.

Maureen Ihrie

Dama de Elche, La

Spain's equivalent of the Venus de Milo in that she represents the eternal feminine there, *La Dama de Elche* is the most important example of Iberian statuary. It is a bust of a female, either an earth goddess or a priestess, carved from hard limestone and originally painted in bright colors. The expressionless head is adorned with a painted tiara and large wheels on each side of the face. The overall result is a mixture of Greek style, Carthagenian jewelry, and Iberian features. The date of its execution is still approximate but was probably in the fourth century B.C.E.

Because of a number of strange circumstances, *La Dama de Elche* is now a patriotic symbol of Spain and the idea of the Spanish female. It was discovered in 1897, precisely when Spaniards lost their last overseas colonies and began to examine the nature of "Spanishness," which many sought in the residues of the Celtic and Iberian cultures. Inexplicably, the statue was sold to France and placed in the Louvre, where it remained until 1941, when Francisco Franco convinced Marshal Pétain to return the icon to Spain. The statue immediately became the most visited item in the Prado Museum and is now the showpiece of the National Archeological Museum, where it has been in the central exhibition room since 1971. Recently, questions have been raised concerning the bust's authenticity, which the Spanish government has vigorously denounced.

Work about

MacKendrick, Paul. *The Iberian Stones Speak.* New York: Funk & Wagnalls, 1969.

Moffitt, John F. *Art Forgery: The Case of the "Lady of Elche."* Gainesville: UP of Florida, 1995.

David H. Darst

Defensa de las mujeres (1726)

Defensa de las mujeres (In Defense of Women) is the title of Fray Benito *Feijóo's (1676–1764) essay on women in society. Its publication provoked a polemic spearheaded by "Contradefensa crítica a favor de los hombres" (1726; Critical Counterdefense in Favor of Men), written by Laurencio Manco de Olivares, who became the leading eighteenth-century antifeminist. Feijóo's *Defensa* was reprinted 20 times by the 1780s, and it is credited with initiating "the feminist debates" among intellectuals of the latter part of the century.

The *Defensa* forms part of *Teatro Crítico Universal* (Universal Theater of Criticism), a larger project in which Feijóo uses inductive reason to combat outdated prejudices. His *Defensa* vigorously attacks prejudices long held against women by the Church and society at large, using biblical, classical, and historical sources to make its points. Feijóo's attacks on prejudice are exemplified in his rewriting of the biblical story of Adam and Eve. His version reverses the traditional reading to condemn the commonly held belief that Eve is to blame for the fall of humankind. He points out that while Eve was tempted by an angel, a creature of superior intelligence, Adam fell to the temptation of a mere human being—a fact that significantly diminishes her error, when compared to his.

Feijóo also opposed the *courtly love tradition that revered women's physical beauty to the detriment of their moral and spiritual worth. He maintains that women are morally superior to men, but arrogance and stubbornness blind men to their own faults. He defends women's intellect, explaining that women have been unable to develop their capabilities because they have been excluded from all educational and intellectual opportunities. As intelligent beings, they have the right to receive quality education. He asserted that the long-held view of women's physical and intellectual inferiority stemmed solely from their lack of instruction and that as intelligent beings they have the right to receive quality education. *See also* Feminism in Spain: 1700–1800

Work

Defensa de las mujeres. In *Obras (Selección)*. Ed. Ivy McClelland. Madrid: Taurus, 1985. 133–141.

Work about

Coughlin, Edward V. "The Polemic on Feijóo's 'Defensa de las mujeres.'" *Dieciocho* 9 (1986): 74–85.
Franklin, Elizabeth M. "Feijóo, Josefa Amar y Borbón and the Feminist Debate in Eighteenth-Century Spain." *Dieciocho* 12. 2 (1989): 188–203.
Llanos M., Bernardita. "Integración de la mujer al proyecto de la Ilustración en España." *Ideologies and Literature* 4.1 (Spring 1989): 199–223.
Oñate, María del Pilar. *El feminismo en la literatura española*. Madrid: Espasa-Calpe, 1938.

María A. Salgado

Delibes, Miguel (1920–): Women in His Novels

One of Spain's most distinguished and best-loved novelists, in addition to careers as publisher, professor, and journalist, Delibes holds a doctorate in business and taught mercantile law for many years, simultaneously serving as longtime editor and director of *El Norte de Castilla*, one of Spain's oldest and most prestigious daily newspapers. Elected to the Royal Spanish Academy of the Language in 1973, he has published at least 40 books, including some 20 novels, half a dozen collections of short stories and novelettes, and several volumes each of memoirs, travel books, works on hunting, fishing, and the environment, plus numerous journalistic articles and miscellaneous essays. Delibes holds Spain's most prestigious literary awards: the 1955 Premio Nacional de Literatura, the Critics' Prize (1962), Príncipe de Asturias (1982), Premio de Letras de Castilla y León (1985), the National Prize for Letters (1991), and the internationally acclaimed Cervantes Prize (1993), given by consensus of the Academies of the Spanish Language in the 23 countries where Spanish is the national language. An outspoken defender of the environment and spokesman for ecological causes, he is no reactionary; what he opposes is ill-conceived "development" sacrificing irretrievable natural resources and historical treasures. As an avid fisherman and small-game hunter, Delibes is intimately acquainted with the terrain portrayed in his fiction, populated by laconic, earthy peasants, untutored or semiliterate villagers, and numerous "backward" or primitive mentalities. His predominantly realistic works usually incorporate a lyric vision or symbolic intent. The style now inseparably associated with Delibes—colloquial, ironic, bristling with aphorisms and lapidary pronouncements in rural Castilian dialect, abounding in humorous tag-lines, folkloric toponymy, and nicknames—first appears in his third novel, *El camino* (1950; *The Path*). His themes and settings—closely tied to the soil, to relationships with nature, the out of doors, and round of seasons—belong to what has traditionally been termed "a man's world," especially in Spain during the 40 years of Franco's conservative dictatorship. Consequently, women are frequently minor or peripheral characters in his fiction, although clearly etched and memorable, ranging from quite negative to very positive.

In *La sombra del ciprés es alargada* (1948; Long Is the Cypress's Shadow), the narrator-protagonist is a middle-aged ship's captain; orphaned early in life, he has avoided emotional commitments to escape suffering additional loss. Women in his life are shadowy, distant figures, until he meets a young American and impulsively marries her, returning to Spain to prepare a home. As his ship is docking, he witnesses a fatal accident: The car driven by his pregnant bride collides with a truck and sinks beneath the waters of the port. Delibes's second novel, *Aun es de día* (1949; There's Still Daylight), presents several women in the life of the young hunchback Sebastian, via a protagonist-narrative perspective of a neo-naturalistic slice of life in the provincial town of Valladolid. Sebastian's little sister, Orencia, the only one with any real affection for him, is "a pale, awkward, poorly dressed creature, with an empty gaze . . . and glacial frigidity, inappropriate for her age," abused and exploited by their widowed mother, Aurelia. A former servant, Aurelia married Sebastian's father (also a hunchback) for economic reasons; she speaks with disgust of both father and son. Prematurely aged, filthy, drunken, and obese, she has red-streaked eyes and prominent varicose veins. The family lives on Sebastian's small salary as a delivery boy in the market, in a house overflowing with garbage, cockroaches, and despair; lacking any mythic stature, Aurelia nonetheless recalls the archetype of the Terrible Mother. She arranges with the grocer's wife to trick Sebastian into a fast marriage with Aurora, who is expecting an illegitimate child (the father has no intention of marrying Aurora): Short, myopic, unattractive, and cloyingly affectionate, with a bad reputation and disillusioning life experiences, Aurora accepts the plan by her mother and future mother-in-law to seduce Sebastian, concealing her pregnancy, but the plot is discovered by Orencia, who reveals the secret to her brother. Other than 12-year-old Orencia, whose privations have forced her to become "street smart," with insight beyond her years, there are no really sympathetic feminine characters: None are idealized (possibly excepting a beautiful, young upper-class woman whom Sebastian adores from a distance). The others reflect historical reality: Feminine independence is nonexistent, even as an aspiration. Women characters exhibit various strategies of adaptation to their patriarchal, *machista*, phallocentric world, from the marriage of convenience and subsequent alienation (Aurelia) to conformity and subterfuge (the grocer's wife) and acceptance of cynical ploys to conceal "dishonor" (Aurora).

Four feminine figures appear in *Mi idolatrado hijo Sisí* (1953; My Idolized Son, Cecil), a long novel of anti-Malthusian thesis. The protagonist is Cecilio Rubes (Sisí's father), son of a widow best described as a caricature of the stereotypical mother-in-law (she misses no chance to criticize her daughter-in-law's "defects"). Even as a grandmother, she remains hostile, stressing that the grandson is inferior to his father, due to traits inherited from the "inferior family" of her son's wife. Rubes, who married Adela for her youthful beauty, is a paunchy, balding, middle-aged "mama's boy," a wealthy businessman with no attractions but his money. Adela, whose beauty is fading with age, is slightly old-fashioned, fatigued, passive, "absolutely unfamiliar with techniques of seduction. . . . [S]he responds as though fulfilling her duty." As her mother died in childbirth, Adela wants no children and is terrified upon learning she is pregnant; subsequently, her husband forbids her to nurse the baby and "spoil" her figure. Prized exclusively for her body, a sex object whose status diminishes and limits her role as mother, she sees her value decline with middle age. Multiple contrasts are established between Adela and Gloria, a happily married neighbor with many children who presides over an idealized home (despite economic problems); Gloria—and her daughter, with whom Cecilio's son later falls in love—are somewhat idealized, positive feminine models. Practically from the beginning of the marriage, Cecilio has kept a mistress, red-haired Paulina, who aspires to become an actress, a "professional" sex object (she is emphatically objectified by other characters' emphasis on her body). As the spoiled, selfish, delinquent younger Rubes ("Sisí") reaches his late teens, he seduces his father's mistress. When Sisí is killed by a stray mortar shell in the Civil War, Rubes hysterically demands another son of Adela, only to learn that she is now too old; he makes the same demand of Paulina, learning that she is already pregnant—with Sisí's child, which provokes Rubes's suicide.

Among the numerous Delibes characters with primitive or abnormal perspectives are several who are illiterate or retarded—culturally deprived or disinherited, of various ages and both genders. In *La hoja roja* (1959; The Red Leaf), such a character is Desi, an illiterate orphan from a small village who serves as cook, laundress, and maid in the modest home of protagonist Don Eloy, a widowed, retired minor bureaucrat (himself an orphan who lacked love, companionship, and human warmth during his marriage to a frigid, domineering wife; his ambitious, egotistical, uncaring elder son has eliminated him from his life, while the younger son has died). Two lonely people with nothing in common but proximity and their human needs for communication, companionship, and warmth, one at the end of life and the other at the beginning, Desi and Don Eloy differ culturally: He has an average education; Desi does not even know how to write her name. During the long winter when Don Eloy's penury and inability to heat the whole apartment forces him into the kitchen for warmth—both physical and symbolic—he and Desi untiringly repeat stories of their respective worlds, his in the provincial capital of a former generation, hers a backward, remote village, with its superstitions, folklore, and traditions, blending the violent and picturesque. Don Eloy teaches Desi to read and expands her cultural horizons by taking her to movies on her day off. When her ruffian boyfriend "Picaza" attempts to rape her during one of his visits, she valiantly fights him off (despite being madly enamored); having internalized traditional moral values and standards for women's behavior, she aspires only to be a wife and mother. By contrast, her friend Marce (another maid) thinks only of exploiting her physical attractions to the maximum for a profitable marriage. Although no illusion of romance exists in the relationship between Eloy and Desi, there is affection, and she accepts his proposal of marriage—she will care for him in his few remaining years and inherit his home and sparse possessions, which for her seem a fortune. It should be noted that Delibes does not present this as exactly a "happy ending" but rather the conjunction of members of two marginalized groups (senior citizens and poor, uneducated women) making the best of a desperate, lonely situation.

The almost exclusively domestic ambient of *La hoja roja* (more typical of novels by women writers) recurs in *El príncipe destronado* (1973; The Dethroned Prince), written from the narrative perspective of a spoiled three-year-old boy who has just lost the privileged position of "baby of the family" following the birth of a younger sibling. Here as in several other novels, Delibes writes sympathetically and insightfully of the travails of women in so-called marriages of convenience, loveless but profitable or necessary unions undertaken because of the lack of viable alternatives in a society that systematically discouraged higher education, careers, and financial independence for women. The toddler's parents exemplify the "war of the sexes" insofar as mealtimes seem devoted to sniping, with the several children caught in the crossfire. A comparable situation is recreated in *Cinco horas con Mario* (1966; Five Hours with Mario) wherein the putative protagonist has died suddenly of a heart attack. Mario's widow Carmen, the primary narrative consciousness, spends the night beside his casket after other attendees at the wake have departed, engaging in silent monodialogue with her husband's corpse. They dated before the Civil War, and subsequently married, although the war divided them (their families were on opposite sides, and the couple personifies the opposing ideological extremes): Their marriage, another war of the sexes, differs in that the victim is not the wife but Mario—an idealistic professor with socialist convictions, caught in an emotionally abusive domestic situation. Carmen (who has interiorized the traditional, moralizing, conservative, materialistic values of her family) cannot forgive Mario for not making more money, for not abandoning his values for hers, for not being a hypocrite and conformist. Both very human and very unsympathetic, Carmen is not so much a real person as an incarnation of an ideology.

Delibes's late wife and ideal woman Angeles de Castro, who died some two decades ago, is the model for the portrait in *Señora de rojo sobre fondo gris* (1991; Lady in Red against a Gray Background). The protagonist-narrator, a famous painter whose wife has recently died, dialogues with his eldest daughter, recently released together with her husband from political incarceration (she is an almost completely mute interlocutor, recalling the situation in *Cinco horas con Mario*). The "confession" to his daughter of what he now sees as his shortcomings in the marriage serves both as a homage to the wife (taken too much for granted during her life) and a self-accusation of egotism in overlooking her constant help, companionship and understanding, support, and sacrifices. *Señora de rojo* maximizes Delibes's conscious preoccupation with gender relations and sexual politics, as seen when the painter remarks of Ana (his late wife) that "the formal aspects of the struggle for power in . . . matrimony seemed grotesque to her." *Cartas de amor de un sexagenario voluptuoso* (1984; Love-Letters from a Voluptuous Sexagenarian) offers a variation on the theme, again analyzing how the masculine consciousness interprets the woman correspondent's silences to suit his own fancy (or fantasy), making no allowances for his own painfully obvious limitations.

From more traditional beginnings, Delibes has traversed a long distance in his study of gender relations; he is arguably the most sensitive of Spain's contemporary male writers to the nuances of power and subordination, sexual politics, and individual autonomy within matrimony. While he clearly believes in marriage and the family as institutions, he also depicts the need for women to be educated, to have other options, to be capable of self-sufficiency and not forced to be housekeepers, concubines, or spouses because the alternative is starvation.

Work by

Aun es de día. Barcelona: Destino, 1949.
El camino. Barcelona: Destino, 1950.
Cartas de amor de un sexagenario voluptuoso. Barcelona: Destino, 1984.
Cinco horas con Mario. Barcelona: Destino, 1966.
Diario de un cazador. Barcelona: Destino, 1955.
Diario de un emigrante. Barcelona: Destino, 1958.
Diario de un jubilado. Barcelona: Destino, 1995.
El disputado voto del señor Cayo. Barcelona: Destino, 1979.
Las guerras de nuestros antepasados. Barcelona: Destino, 1975.
La hoja roja. Barcelona: Destino, 1959.
Mi idolatrado hijo Sisí. Barcelona: Destino, 1953.
Obra completa. Barcelona: Destino (Multiple volumes, years).
Parábola del náufrago. Barcelona: Destino, 1969.
El príncipe destronado. Barcelona: Destino, 1973.
Las ratas. Barcelona: Destino, 1962.
Los santos inocentes. Barcelona: Planeta, 1981.
Señora de rojo sobre fondo gris. Barcelona: Destino, 1991.
La sombra del ciprés es alargada. Barcelona: Destino, 1948.

El tesoro. Barcelona: Destino, 1985.

377A madera de héroe. Barcelona: Destino, 1987.

Work about

Agawu Kakraba, Yaw. "Miguel Delibes and the Politics of Two Women: *Cinco horas con Mario* and *Señora de rojo sobre fondo gris*." *Hispanófila* 117 (1996): 63–77.

Alvar, Manuel. *El mundo novelesco de Miguel Delibes*. Madrid: Gredos, 1987.

Boucher, Teresa. "The Widow's Peak/The Widow Speaks: Carmen's Idle Talk in Miguel Delibes's *Cinco horas con Mario*." *Cincinnati Romance Review* 15 (1996): 50–56.

Díaz, Janet. *Miguel Delibes*. New York: Twayne, 1971.

Estudios sobre Miguel Delibes. Madrid: Universidad Complutense, 1982.

García Domínguez, R. *Miguel Delibes: Un hombre, un paisaje y una pasión*. Barcelona: Destino, 1985.

Hickey, Leo. *Cinco horas con Miguel Delibes. El hombre y el novelista*. Madrid: Prensa Española, 1968.

Pauk, Edgar. *Miguel Delibes: Desarrollo de un escritor (1947–1974)*. Madrid: Gredos, 1975.

Pérez, Janet. "Miguel Delibes presenta la tercera salida de Don Lorenzo, cazador andante." *Confluencia* 13.1 (Fall 1997): 52–62.

Rey, Alfonso. *La originalidad novelística de Miguel Delibes*. Santiago de Compostela: Universidad, 1975.

Sánchez Pérez, F.J. *El hombre amenazado. Hombre, sociedad, educación en la novelística de Miguel Delibes*. Salamanca: Universidad, 1984.

Sobejano, Gonzalo. Introduction to *La mortaja*. Madrid: Cátedra, 1984. 11–75.

Umbral, Francisco. *Miguel Delibes*. Madrid: EPESA, 1970.

Valle Spinka, R. *La conciencia social de Miguel Delibes*. New York: n.p., 1975.

Janet Pérez

Delicado, Francisco

See *Lozana andaluza, La* (1528)

Detective Fiction by Spanish Women Writers

Detective fiction has traditionally been a male-dominated genre, where patriarchal values are conventionally upheld and reinforced and female presence—by authors and fictional characters—has been limited and/or unable to radically modify the patriarchal molds. The situation has only begun to change with the recent emergence of new generations of detective fiction women writers, due no doubt to the impact of the feminist movement. In Spain, where patriarchal domination has been especially severe and long-lasting, it is only after the end of Franco's regime that alternative/feminist modes of detective fiction have begun to emerge among Spanish woman writers. In new feminist detective fiction, the reversal of genre expectations and gender roles adjudicates a new and central place to women, amounting to a subversion of patriarchal values.

The history of detective fiction by Spanish women writers begins with Emilia *Pardo Bazán (1852–1921). Her interest in sociology, psychology, criminology, and new literary currents attracted her to the new imported form of detective fiction, increasingly popular in turn-of-the-century Spain. Her ambiguity toward the genre, criticizing its superficiality and underlying Victorian morality but realizing the literary possibilities of the new medium, was repeatedly expressed in her "La vida contemporánea" (Contemporary Life) columns of *La ilustración artística* between 1900 and 1916. Simultaneously, she wrote several stories and short novels in the detective fiction mode, particularly "La cana" (1911; The White Hair), *La gota de sangre* (1911; The Drop of Blood), and its still unpublished continuation *Selva* (c.1914; Forest). Her detective stories assumed a great familiarity with the genre on the part of the Spanish audience, with frequent parodies, reversals of readers' expectations, metafictional markers, and intertextual allusions creating excellent portraits of moral decadence. Although the investigators are invariably male and amateurs, Pardo Bazán's innovations in the genre include a central preoccupation with the subordinate situation of women, reflecting the author's reformist intentions and her nonconforming views of the official moral and social rules.

Another pioneer author of the genre in Spain was Mercè Rodoreda (1908–1983) with *Crim* (1936; Crime), the first detective novel written in Catalan and a parodic version of the British-style murder mystery. The author's ambivalence toward the genre is reflected in the excessive use of caricature, culminating in the absurd killing of a shoe. The novel is a parody of the imported form but also of the inadequacy of the native land, revealing the shortcomings of a native bourgeois class at odds with the needs of modernity and its dependency on foreign impositions. *Crim* was an original and highly reflexive experiment, although ultimately deemed unsatisfactory and rejected by the author. It was never reprinted or made part of her collected works and has been totally forgotten until recently.

During the post–Civil War period, a number of women writers published, generally in popular collections, mimetic detective novels following the molds of British and American popular mysteries, such as Laura de Cominges and Luisa Cases, often using foreign-sounding pseudonyms like Rocq Morris (Mercedes *Ballesteros), Mary Francis Colt (Fernanda Cano), Sean Saint Cyr (Laura García Corolla), and Glen Wyman (María de las Nieves Grajales). The only author during this period who stands out from the rest is Maria Aurèlia *Capmany (1918–1991), a pioneering author of the *novela negra* (detective story) in Spain directly following Dashiell Hammett (1894–1961) and Raymond Chandler (1888–1959), whom she translated into Catalan. *Vés-te'n ianqui! o, si voleu, traduït de l'americà* (Yankee Go Home, Or, If You Prefer, Translated from the American), originally published in Catalan in 1959 and later corrected and expanded in 1980, is a clever and ironic metafictional novel-within-a-novel. Marc is an investigator from New York writing his memoir of a case after a difficult mission in Albania where he was sent to investigate the disappearance of American Tomàs Compton Bates, a young rebellious heir to his huge family fortune. In Albania, Marc explores the dangerous territory between Tirana and Valona (an obvious transposition of Madrid and Barcelona), pursues, and is persecuted, finally uncovering the hidden links between police corruption, organized crime, and political dictatorship. His mission, nevertheless, proves to be a bittersweet failure. Capmany's second excursion in the genre, *El jaqué de la democràcia* (1972; Democracy Jacket), is a highly original experimental novel stretching the *novela negra* conventions to their limits. Its complex narrative has several different narrators and points of view and various metafictional layers and narrative threads, proposing alternative versions of the main plot. The novel presents the disordered fragments of an unfinished thriller written by American author Dennyson Heath (Di Eix); the interaction between Maria Aurélia and her friend Gregory Kenneth (G.K.), an American scholar who is obsessed to identify the fictional city in the text as Barcelona; the provisionally reorganized fragments, chronologically numbered; and finally the fictional reconstruction of the story, with all gaps filled. The novel is therefore a mystery-within-a-mystery. The protagonist of the story is the city, its landscape and the human conflicts in the streets. Like Hammett's Poisonville, what predominates is the violent, corrupt, and treacherous atmosphere or the urban underworld. The detective in the text, Malhaquias Ryt, investigates the mysterious deaths of Jeroni Corona, a wealthy industrialist, and Esteve Coris, a labor leader, and in the process he unmasks the underworld of political intrigue, anarchist movements, and counterrevolutionary paid killers. As in *Vés te'n ianqui*, here the names of places are again easily transposed to local realities—Salona is Barcelona, Balvacària is Catalonia. The novel offers a metaphor of Barcelona in the 1920s and is a clear precursor in both theme and literary technique of Eduardo Mendoza's *La verdad sobre el caso Savolta* (1975; The Truth about the Savolta Affair).

With the restoration of democracy in post-

Franco Spain and the boom of the *novela negra*, more women authors started writing detective novels. Lourdes *Ortiz's (1943–   ) *Picadura mortal* (1979; A Fatal Sting) was the first, a fast-paced, unpretentious novel with slight political undertones, hastily written at the request of Sedmay Editions for the newly established "Club del crimen" series. As a highly parodic work, its characters, situations, and settings are cardboard clichés reminiscent of television soap operas and follow the basic formulas of the hard-boiled *novela negra*. *Picadura mortal* stands as a landmark, for it includes the first female private detective in Spanish fiction. Ortiz's greatest innovation lies in the creation of the main character, Bárbara Arenas; her name has a dual significance: on the one hand, it marks her as a foreigner, a stranger out of place, one of the "godos," as the inhabitants of the Peninsula are referred to in the Canary Islands; but it also emphasizes the fact that she is a woman in a man's world and a brave one playing a traditional male role. Throughout the novel she underscores the lack of respect, chauvinism, aggressive machismo, and sexual harassment she must face on a daily basis. This is particularly obvious in the case of the macho police, but even her client in the Islands and her boss in Madrid (significantly named Juan Carlos), as well as the rest of the male characters, all suspect and mistrust Barbara as a woman. She responds with strength, anger, and determination; she can be tough but is willing to use her feminine charms and wiles when necessary. In spite of the political undertones of the novel, directly linking smuggling, drug dealing, and tobacco monopoly with Francoism, the novel lacks in characterization and development and is not well resolved. Ortiz's greatest merit is the creation of a believable female sleuth, the first in Spanish fiction. Bárbara Arenas made a second brief appearance in the highly metafictional detective short story "Moralejas del ciego con pistola" (1981; Lessons of the Blind Man with a Pistol), dealing with terrorist activities, extortion, and organized crime.

Rosa *Montero's (1951–   ) *Te trataré como a una reina* (1983; I Will Treat You Like a Queen), although not a detective novel per se, shares many of the elements typical of Spanish *novela negra*, revealing the darker side of reality against an urban landscape of crime, sex, violence, and the sordid atmosphere of decrepit night clubs and equally sordid passions. The fragmented narrative is interwoven with sensationalist newspaper clippings, personal letters, sentimental bolero songs, and incisive dialogues, creating a powerful, suggestive, and moving story. The novel offers a feminine perspective of crime fiction, showing a central preoccupation with women as the victims of male power, while unmasking the ultimate creation of Spanish patriarchy: the Don Juan myth.

Another author whose work has been associated with detective fiction is Marina *Mayoral (1942–   ), an avid reader of the genre in its American and British varieties. This attraction becomes particularly clear in her short story "El asesino y la víctima" (The Assassin and the Victim) and the novella *Cándida otra vez* (1992; Cándida Again), which explores Galician semifeudal class relations in an investigation of the murder of an illegitimate member of an old Galician family, mixing a classic murder mystery with the political exposé typical of the *novela negra*.

Of all contemporary Spanish women writers, Maria Antònia Oliver is perhaps the one who has most consistently and successfully managed to write convincing detective novels transposed to local milieu. Her stories, written in Catalan (Oliver was born in Manacor, in the Balearic Islands), are packed with action and emotion, simultaneously moving, witty, and ironic with a sad, bitter aftertaste. As a committed feminist writer, Oliver turns around genre and gender conventions in her detective novels. Her protagonist is Lònia Guiu, a detective from Majorca and owner of a small investigative agency in Barcelona. Her cases always involve women and are solved by a woman with the help of her gay assistant Quim and a network of "sisters." Women's issues are central to the story line, whether it be sexual harassment, rape, abortion, sexism, mother-daughter relations, or the questioning of patriarchal values. Her strong feminist beliefs also encompass ecological and nationalist concerns, such as the underlying accusation throughout her novels of the "rape" of the Balearic Islands' natural landscape for tourist development. Lònia first appeared in the short story "¿Dónde estás, Mónica?" (Where Are You, Monica?) in Ofèlia Dracs's *Negra y consentida* (a pun involving an old bolero song and the new *novela negra*) in 1984. Ofèlia Dracs is in fact the pseudonym used by a writers' collective, mostly male, which flourished in the 1980s. Although in embryonic form, the work showed promising signs: It was filled with action, irony, and a vibrant language and featured a congenial feminist detective (and lipstick collector). In her first appearance, Lònia skillfully solves the case of Mónica's disappearance, uncovering her lesbian relationship and discovering she was killed due to her opposition to her family's plan for tourist development. Lònia's first full-fledged appearance took place in *Estudi en lila* (1987; *Study in Lilac*, 1987), which was an immediate success and was translated to other languages. Here Oliver was able to develop more fully her feminist concerns; the two cases of the novel involve a runaway teenager in search of acceptance and a 40-year-old woman in search of revenge; what they have in common is that they both have been silent victims of rape. In both cases, the resolution has tragic consequences for everybody. The sequel was *Antípodes* (1988; *Antipodes*, 1989), which narrates the search for a young girl in Australia, revealing the hidden relationship between enforced prostitution and the desecration of the Balearic Islands by international developers and tour operators. Small and big island, Majorca and Australia are mirrors showing the interrelationship of the global village, also serving as metaphors of incommunication among humans and the failed attempts to bridge them. The most recent installment of Lònia's adventures, *El sol que fa l'ànec* (1994; The Adorning Sun), is another engaging episode, offering Lònia's clearest defense of her cultural identity and her mother tongue, Mallorquí, a distinct variant of Catalan, spoken by all characters in the novel except the Spanish police, characterized as aggressive bullies and contemptuous colonizers. Once again, Lònia is searching for a missing young girl, and the investigation takes her and Quim to a travel agency in Germany and eventually back to Mallorca, where they discover behind the façade of tourist plot developments an organized ring of child pornographers and pederasts. In the process, Lònia is physically attacked and almost raped and survives several murder attempts. Oliver forcefully presents a picture of moral degradation, equating the sexual exploitation of children with the exploitation of the environment.

Blanca Alvarez's *La soledad del monstruo* (1992; The Solitude of the Monstrous One) is the most unusual detective novel by a Spanish woman writer. It has as its main protagonist Bárbara Villalta (Baby), whose name immediately evokes Ortiz's Bárbara Arenas. Baby is the first (and until now the only) openly lesbian fictional investigator in Spain, and she is also one of the most disturbing portraits in Spanish detective fiction. Physically deformed and emotionally injured, Baby's "monstrous" characterization is a grotesque portrayal of *esperpento* (frightening/absurd) quality. She is a total outcast, her ultimate social marginality inscribed physically on her body as a woman and a lesbian, severely overweight, suffering from a severe case of body odor and a menstrual hemorrhage of monstrous proportions. Baby's self-hate is only equal to her hate for the world around her. Baby is both the enraged victim and the vengeful victimizer, the violent killer and the criminal investigator. The disheartening mix of sex, crime, and violence, the crudeness and sordid descriptions of the homosexual underground culture, foreshadow the inevitably shocking and distressing results of Alvarez's novel.

Assumpta Margenat (1953–) published *Escapa't d'Andorra* (1989; Wild Card, 1992), a contemporary thriller with a feminist twist. The protagonist-narrator Rossi, a temporary immigrant worker in Andorra from Barcelona, is a young "liberated" heroine, freely exploring romance and hallucinogenic mushrooms. Determined, free-spirited, and woman identified, she teams up with her assaulted neighbor Maite to take revenge on her male attacker. Tired of her alienating job as store clerk and of her male boss's harassment (Jaume Coll), Rossi enlists her sister Mari in her particular vendetta against his abuses. Rossi uncovers Coll's illegal tradings and outsmarts him at his own game with the help of a network of "sisters": Maite, Mari, and the cocktail waitress Chus. In the end, the tourist paradise of duty-free shopping and ski resorts reveals itself as a mafia-controlled enterprise from which she must escape.

Isabel-Clara Simó (1943–), a writer from Valencia, has published a number of works in Catalan related to detective fiction. In the short mystery novel *La veïna* (1990; The Neighbor), the narrator-protagonist, a bank teller named Leonard Bent, finds himself incriminated in the assassination of his neighbor's hated husband. Fired from his job and abandoned by almost all of his friends, Leonard must take charge of the investigation to prove his innocence against all odds. In the process, Leonard falls in love rather predictably with his neighbor Dalia. The novel is entertaining and has a solid narrative rhythm but is perhaps too formulaic and the outcome too predictable. Simó has also published *Una ombra fosca com un núvol de tempesta* (1991; A Corpse of One's Own, 1993), another fast-paced, engaging crime mystery but at the same time a female *Bildungsroman* and an exploration of a female fantasy. The protagonist, Sara Costa, is a middle-aged, middle-class, bored, submissive, and hopelessly empty housewife who one day sees her secret wish come true, when she discovers that her hated husband has been assassinated and has surprisingly left her a millionaire. The story follows the belated blossoming and liberation of Sara from crochet-knitting housewife to investigator of her newly acquired inheritance from her dead husband, as she unravels the complex operation of illegal export of weapons to ruthless dictatorships around the globe. In the process of investigation Sara enlists Eva, a former employee of her husband Oscar, who must overcome her emotional dependency on her boyfriend, a business associate of Oscar's illegal activities. Sara and Eva develop a sisterlike relationship, and together they overcome their grief and submissiveness to male authority, eventually solving the case. With this unlikely pair of detective heroines, the novel presents a reversal of traditional male-centered genre conventions and a good example of a female-centered *roman noir*. The novel, however, is not a mere utopian fiction of wish fulfillment, as the unhappy ending brings us back to reality. Other novels by Simó include *La Nati* (1991) and *El mas del diable* (1992; The Devil's Grange).

This general overview can only begin to explore the growing field of detective fiction written by woman authors in Spain today. The increasing number of women writing detective novels in Castilian, Catalan, and Galician also includes Núria Mínguez, Margarida Aritzeta, Assumció Maresma (*El complot dels anells* [1988; The Conspiracy of the Rings]), and Margarita Ledo Andión ("Ironpark Crime"), among others. With this in mind, one can imagine that this trend will continue and will encourage other Spanish women authors to seek new forms of rewriting the canon of detective fiction from feminist perspectives.

Work

Alvarez, Blanca. *La soledad del monstruo*. Madrid: Grupo Libro 88, 1992.

Capmany, Maria Aurèlia. *El chaqué de la democracia.* Spanish trans. Barcelona: Plaza y Janés, 1984.

———. *El jaqué de la democràcia.* Barcelona: La Magrana, 1987.

———. *Vés-te'n ianqui! o, si voleu, traduït de l'americà.* Barcelona: Laia, 1980.

———. *Vete, Yanki!* Spanish trans. Madrid: Sedmay, 1980.

Dracs, Ofèlia. *Negra y consentida.* Spanish trans. José Batlló. Barcelona: Alfa, 1984.

Margenat, Assumpta. *Escapa't d'Andorra.* Barcelona: La Magrana, 1989.

———. *Wild Card.* Trans. Sheila McIntosh. Seattle: Women in Translation, 1992.

Mayoral, Marina. "El asesino y la víctima." *Morir en sus brazos y otros cuentos.* Alicante: Aguaclara, 1989.

———. *Cándida otra vez.* Ed. Germán Gullón. Madrid: Castalia, 1992.

Montero, Rosa. *Te trataré como a una reina.* Barcelona: Seix Barral, 1983.

Oliver, Maria Antònia. *Antípodes.* Barcelona: La Magrana, 1988.

———. *Antipodes.* English trans. Kathleen McNerney. Seattle: Seal Press, 1989.

———. *Estudi en Lila.* Barcelona: La Magrana, 1987.

———. *Estudio en lila.* Spanish trans. Manuel Quinto. Barcelona: Vidorama, 1989.

———. *Study in Lilac.* English trans. Kathleen McNerney. Seattle: Seal Press, 1987.

Ortiz, Lourdes. *Picadura mortal.* Madrid: Sedmay, 1979.

Pardo Bazán, Emilia. *Obras completas.* Madrid: Aguilar, 1964.

Rodoreda, Mercè. *Crim.* Barcelona: La Rosa dels Vents, 1936.

Simó, Isabel-Clara. *A Corpse of One's Own.* English trans. Patricia Hart. New York: Peter Lang, 1993.

———. *Una ombra fosca com un núvol de tempesta.* Barcelona: Area, 1991.

———. *La veïna.* Barcelona: Area, 1990.

Work about

Clarke, Anthony. "Doña Emilia Pardo Bazán y la novela policíaca." *Boletín bibliográfico Menéndez Pelayo* 49 (1973): 375–391.

Colmeiro, José F. "Relectura de la novela policíaca: *La gota de sangre* de Emilia Pardo Bazán." *Hispanic Journal* 10.2 (1989): 33–48.

Hart, Patricia. "Catalan Culture and Identity through Popular Forms: The Collaborative Effort of the Ofèlia Dracs Group in *Negra i consentida* (Hardboiled and Spoiled)." *Imagination, Emblems and Expressions: Essays on Latin American, Caribbean, and Continental Culture and Identity.* Ed. Helen Ryan-Ranson. Bowling Green, OH: Bowling Green UP, 1993. 301–314.

———. *The Spanish Sleuth. The Detective in Spanish Fiction.* Rutherford, NJ: Fairleigh Dickinson UP, 1987. 172–181.

Mandrell, James. " 'Experiencing Technical Difficulties': Genre and Gender, Translation and Difference: Lourdes Ortiz, María Antònia Oliver, and Blanca Alvarez." *Journal of Narrative Technique* 27.1 (Winter 1997): 55–83.

McGovern, Lynn. "A 'Private I': The Birth of a Female Sleuth and the Role of Parody in Lourdes Ortiz's *Picadura mortal.*" *Journal of Literary Interdisciplinary Studies* 5.2 (1993): 251–279.

Paredes Núñez, Juan. "Doña Emilia y el cuento policíaco." *Los cuentos de Emilia Pardo Bazán.* Granada: Universidad de Granada, 1979. 262–274.

Resina, Joan Ramón. "Detective Formula and Parodic Reflexivity: *Crim.*" *The Garden across the Border: Mercè Rodoreda's Fiction.* Ed. Kathleen McNerney and Nancy Vosburg. Selinsgrove: Susquehanna UP, 1994.

Spires, Robert. "Lourdes Ortiz: Mapping the Course of Postfrancoist Fiction." *Women Writers of Contemporary Spain: Exiles in the Homeland.* Ed. Joan Lipman Brown. Newark: U of Delaware P, 1991. 198–216.

Zatlin, Phyllis. "Detective Fiction and the Novels of Mayoral." *Monographic Review/Revista monográfica* 3.1–2 (1987): 279–287.

José F. Colmeiro

Diálogo de mujeres (1544)

The author of this text, Cristóbal de Castillejo (1490?–1550), was a Cistercian monk who spent the majority of his life at court, first as a page and in service to Ferdinand and *Isabel's grandson, the Archduke Ferdinand. In 1525, he left the Spanish court to follow Ferdinand to Vienna, serving as his secretary there until his death in 1550. The cosmopolitan life at court and travel to Italy and England defined Cristóbal de Castillejo's life much more strongly than his earlier religious calling.

The *Diálogo de las condiciones de las mugeres* (Dialogue on the Qualities of Women) presents a discussion in 3,760 verses between two men who hold opposing profeminist and misogynist views on the nature of women. Fileno, whose name symbolizes "he who loves women," is in love and wishes to share his delight with Alethio, the etymology of whose name means "he who seeks or states the truth." Alethio immediately cautions secrecy regarding Fileno's love and warns against basing one's pleasure on such an unsure thing as woman, thereby opening the debate between the two. After a brief introduction to the topic of women in general as opposed to in particular, the text progresses methodically through seven subtopics: married women; maidens; nuns; widows; single women; procuresses; and (in a final summing up) women in general. The presentation of each side of the debate is unequal but consistent. As defender of woman, Fileno is also presented as less experienced than Alethio. Early on in the text, he describes women metaphorically as the source of joy and delight of the world, comparing a world without woman to a body without a heart, reason without understanding, trees without fruit or flower, or a soul lost in the wind. Alethio responds vigorously and at greater length by declaring women to be necessary in the same way as horses or other beasts of burden that address physical needs, or as possessions like houses and jewels. Alethio produces vividly concrete, dehumanizing descriptions and anecdotes of women throughout the text, while Fileno responds primarily as a rhetorician, questioning certain observations and terming Alethio's examples old wives' tales, exaggerations, one-sided observations, flawed reasoning, or expressions of "sour grapes" caused by a lack of personal success. He opposes Alethio's vilification with very few specific praises of his own, and thus, although his rebuttals are on point, they are much shorter than Alethio's responses, and they fail to effectively counter the much lengthier accumulation of invective that the latter produces.

Fileno also moves the discourse along from topic to topic. When he introduces the topic of single women (prostitutes), he begins somewhat humorously by stating that since Alethio has consistently attacked good women and characterized them as evil, perhaps with this topic he will characterize these admittedly bad women as good. Despite denying any personal experience to draw from when discussing this group, Alethio nonetheless holds single women entirely responsible for unfairly inflaming and corrupting men. The portrayal of nuns as wildly lustful, unreligious hypocrites constantly fighting among themselves was expunged in its entirety from the *Diálogo* by the Inquisition.

As the voice of experience, Alethio's general characterization of all women as vain, inferior, inconstant, lustful, scheming, and deceitful creatures whose very virtues provoke flaws (e.g., beauty inspires female arrogance), and as sources of evil more adept than the devil at corrupting and torturing men, falls solidly within the medieval European misogynist tradition. While it is not a particularly innovative text, its lively, vivid language is undeniably entertaining. Eight editions of the *Diálogo* as a single text were produced in the sixteenth century, as well as five editions in which it comprised part of Castillejo's Works, followed by four in the seventeenth century.

Work

Diálogo de mujeres. Ed., intro. and notes Rogelio Reyes Cano. Clásicos Castalia 150. Madrid: Castalia, 1986.

Maureen Ihrie

Diálogo en laude de las mugeres (1580)

Published in Milan, this little-studied profeminist tract dedicated to Empress María of Austria is the only surviving work of Juan de Espinosa (c. 1518–c. 1580) whose distinguished career as soldier and secretary to various nobles serving in the courts of Carlos V and Philip II took him to France, Germany, the Netherlands, and especially, Italy. Although it upholds conventional attitudes regarding the proper roles, behaviors, and strictures necessary for women, the *Diálogo en laude de las mugeres* (Dialogue in Praise of Women) also clearly defends women's worth and rejects the idea that they are inferior to men. Popular themes unrelated to women's worth that are also touched upon at some length include tyranny, parricide, and the relative value of water and wine.

Two speakers participate: Philolithes, the "friend of truth," functions as the learned instructor who presents the defense of women, and Philodoxo, the "friend of opinion," represents the opposing view. His disgust at having learned that his wife has just given birth to a daughter rather than a son precipitates the dialogue. Philolithes defines the parameters of the conversation early on, thereby defusing many possible objections to his pro-woman stance. First, he acknowledges that individual examples of both good and bad women exist (and does not hesitate to mention negative examples later in the discussion). He then observes that the same is equally true for men and argues that when one looks at the two groups in general, it becomes clear that the significant, even vast, majority of women are superior to the majority of men. Philolithes's ability to cite concrete example after example (taken from Antiquity, the Bible, Spanish and European history and even that of the New World) to support each point he makes is, at best, briefly and weakly countered by Philodoxo, who easily accedes to each point made by his mentor, offering virtually no counterarguments or resistance. Indeed, sometimes he even requests more examples of superior women from his teacher. Specific qualities or virtues that women possess or utilize to a greater degree than men include valor, industry, strength of spirit, moderation in eating and drinking, and control of concupiscence.

Despite this overarching superiority of women, the text does not challenge established ideas regarding women's vulnerability to temptation and their awesome ability to tempt others to sin. Part IV of the text explains the proper roles of (good) women in society. Using the traditional categories of virgins (and nuns), wives, and widows, Philolithes outlines the appropriate limitations and activities for each group. Virgins are to dress modestly, obey parents, keep only good company, eat and drink in moderation, not talk with men unless supervised, read only good books, and in general avert their eyes and ears from any sight or sound of *deshonesto amor* (carnal love). Parents should squelch any influence that might stimulate their vanity and not "spare the rod" in correcting them. Nuns too must be protected from evil influences that might unleash their innate ability to tempt even saintly men. Married women and widows likewise need to be kept in "safe" situations (*Encierro) and avoid spending time at the windows of their homes or walking outside when unaccompanied. Wives are to obey husbands, talk little, and only use *cosmetics to please a present or future husband. Widows are considered the most vulnerable group of all, because their "appetites" have been awakened and they are no longer subject to a husband, father, mother, or brother.

In Part V, after briefly condemning the behavior of a few concupiscent women and men, Philolithes offers an extended list of exemplary behavior models for each sex, including many contemporary historical figures. He concludes by exhorting Philodoxo to celebrate God's decision to give him a daughter and ponder the importance of obedience to God's will.

After its initial publication, the *Diálogo* was not reedited until 1875.

Work

Diálogo en laude de las mujeres. Ed. and intro. José López Romero. Granada: A. Ubago, 1990.

Maureen Ihrie

Diana, La (1559)

This pastoral romance is written in seven books or chapters of unequal lengths, interspersing prose and poetry, some parts of which are written in Portuguese. Its author, Jorge de *Montemayor, was born in Montemor-o-Velho, Portugal, but later joined the Spanish court of Charles V. Montemayor's claim that his work is written in the lowly pastoral style is a convention for this *roman a clef*, considered the first genuine modern pastoral romance. *La Diana* achieved a success outside Spain comparable only to Cervantes's *Don Quijote* (1605; 1615) in readership. *La Diana* was a bestseller in its day and was published in five editions in different cities within the author's lifetime. Its numerous versions and continuations by other Spanish authors became so popular that "Diana" became a generic term, describing any pastoral romance of its kind.

The author was a chorister, a musician who began his writing career penning biblical commentaries on the Psalms. In 1559, the publication date of *La Diana*, all of Montemayor's religious and devotional works were placed on the *Index of Forbidden Books*. *La Diana* was prohibited in Portugal from 1581 to 1624 but was widely read at the Spanish court and, according to critics, was omnipresent. It was one of the books Don Quijote rescues from the fire, and it is mentioned in Lope de *Vega's (1562–1635) prose masterpiece *La Dorotea* (1632). The popularity of the work became a matter of concern, especially since women were the main readers. One exasperated critic, Malón de Chaide (c. 1530–1589), despaired at what to do once a young lady, as soon as she was old enough to read, would carry *La Diana* wherever she went. Since *La Diana*'s main theme was love, it was deemed dangerous, profane, and likely to corrupt women. The Holy Office pronounced this and similar works trivial and lewd, adding that therein was the reason why women constantly read them.

The importance of the work lies in its transitional nature and its genre. *La Diana* is a romance that introduced the psychological analysis of love and in which female characters dominated both the conversation and the action. The pastoral setting leveled the field for women's participation. The purity and simplicity of shepherd life was contrasted with the corruption and artificiality of courtly and city life. The work blended poetry, fiction, and events from the author's life. This resulted in a genre in which the complexities of human love could be discussed against a background of simplicity. In the work, the conversation was opened for both sexes. Montemayor stands both outside the work as narrator and inside the romance as a lovelorn character. The action of *La Diana* supposedly takes place in Spain and Portugal, but Montemayor idealized the landscape.

The controlling themes of the work are love, fate, and time. The author's thesis seems to be that while love is ennobling, it is seldom a happy experience. Poetic exchanges revolve around the themes of unrequited love, melancholy, and misfortune. There are allusions to Orpheus, Pan, and Apollo, all disappointed lovers who turned to art and poetry. The first three books introduce a shepherdess caught in an unhappy relationship. She shares her personal story for catharsis, but this eventually leads to communal and mutual support as the characters journey to Felicia's palace to seek solace. The characters' growth is from self-absorption to sympathy for others. Much of the change takes place in the female characters, who are presented as archetypes: Felismena is the warrior maiden, both beautiful, braver than her lover, and selfless. Felicia is the white witch, the enchantress, wizard, wise woman, adviser, healer, and dispenser of happiness. Diana, the eponymous heroine, is a beautiful absence, evoked through song, poems, letters, and love-tokens, who does not appear until Book 5. She is the *malmaridada*, a woman not true to her first love, who married for convenience. Since her problem could not be solved in this work, Montemayor had planned a sequel in which Diana would be redeemed; unfortunately, Montemayor died in Piemonte, Italy (probably in a duel over a love affair), before composing it.

The nymphs who inhabit Felicia's palace are chaste maidens who provide a sounding board for the lover's laments and who help to echo Felicia's Neoplatonic doctrine on the nature of human love. Felicia's preaching borrows heavily from León Hebreo's (1460?–1521) *Dialoghi d'amore* (pub. 1535). Belisa is the provincial, small-town girl who goes into self-exile to atone for what she considers to be her sins. Courted by an older man, she falls in love with him, and later with his son, both of whom appear to be killed in an elaborate staged illusion. Selvagia is the most pastoral of the women characters, a flesh-and-blood creation whose story is told against a rustic, pagan world.

The two male characters, Sylvano and Sireno, are presented as simple shepherds, removed from the world of male heroic action to one where the contemplation of love is their sole preoccupation. Since Montemayor allows women the kind of action that was usually in the domain of male heroes, women advance to the foreground so that at times the men serve as foils or as objects for their affections or the cause of their torments.

In the telling of these love affairs gone awry, there are glimpses of latent sexual ambivalence: instances of lesbian love, in the Felismena/Felis episode, and later in the Armia/Duarda episode, and transvestism in the Ysmenia/Selvagia episode as well as in the Don Felis/Celia episode. The action begins *in medias res*. The climax occurs in Book IV at the sacred center of Felicia's palace, and the denouement occurs in Books V–VII. The visit to Felicia's palace also allows Montemayor to pay homage to virtuous and famous Spanish and Portuguese women, both living and dead, in the "Canto de Orfeo."

In blending pastoral and romance, it is the female characters who prevent *La Diana* from becoming a prolonged eclogue. It is the women who are on a quest, who often take matters into their own hands, and it is a woman who tries to solve the problems of the lovelorn shepherds. One of the novelties of the work is that it allows women to speak about love in a noncourtly setting. Several case histories of the varieties of love possible between men and women and two possibilities of women falling in love with other women are presented. The characters come together to form a temporary community so that their grief and self-absorption can give way to discussion, song, and music. *La Diana* set a precedent by providing a pastoral backdrop to the discussion of love outside the humanistic love treatise or the courtly dialogue form. The prose narrative allows the shepherds to ask questions on the nature of love, whose answers are framed in the Neoplatonic search for perfection of all possible human characteristics. The poetry is often about the purification of the lover through suffering. *See also* Lesbianism in Early Modern Spanish Literature: 1500–1700

Work

La Diana. Ed., prol., and notes Juan Montero. Study Juan Bautista de Avalle-Arce. Barcelona: Crítica, 1996.

The Diana. Trans. RoseAnna Mueller. Lewiston, NY: E. Mellen P, 1989.

Los siete Libros de la Diana. Ed. and intro. Julián Arribas. Rochester, NY: Tamesis, 1996.

Work about

Fosalba, Eugenia. *La Diana en Europa: Ediciones, traducciones e influencias.* Barcelona: Seminari de Filologia I d'Informatica Departament de Filologia Espanyola Universitat Autonoma de Barcelona, 1994.

Gillette, María. "Foolish Fancies? Maybe Not: Symptoms of Melancholy in *La Diana*." *Romance Notes* 39.1 (Fall 1998): 95–101.

Johnson, Carroll B. "Amor-Aliqua Vincit: Erotismo y amor en la *Diana*." *Erotismo en las letras hispánicas. Aspectos, modos y fronteras.* Ed. Luce López-Baralt and Francisco Márquez Villanueva. Mexico City: Colegio de México, 1995. 165–181.

Nepaulsingh, Colbert. *Apples of Gold in Filigrees of Silver: Jewish Writing in the Eye of the Spanish Inquisition.* New York: Holmes and Meier, 1995.

Rhodes, Elizabeth. *The Unrecognized Precursors of*

Montemayor's *Diana*. Columbia: U of Missouri P, 1992.

RoseAnna Mueller

Díaz-Mas, Paloma (1954–)

Born in Madrid, Paloma Díaz-Mas is a professor (Universidad del País Vasco) and scholar with publications in medieval and Golden Age language, literature, and culture. Her creative work echoes material from these research areas, but the translation from "fact" to fiction reveals a postmodern overlay that often includes a feminist perspective.

Biografías de genios, traidores, sabios y suicidas, según antiguos documentos (1973; Biographies of Geniuses, Traitors, Wise Men and Suicides, According to Ancient Documents) begins her literary career with an unusual treatment of a traditional genre: It contains 100 short "biographical" sketches of the most diverse types. However, the subjects are fictional; each piece concentrates on a single quirky, tragicomic, or (less commonly) tragic aspect of their lives; and a dominant note of irony underlies most of the presentations. Experimentation with narrative strategies (the confusion of fiction and reality; metafiction), the undermining of literary convention, the strategic use of irony, parody, and humor initiate a career in subversion that mocks custom and questions the status quo.

Díaz-Mas attempts a different genre and tone with *La informante* (1983; The [Female] Informer, Rojas Zorrilla Prize for Short Theater), a short piece that dramatizes an interview in which an old Sephardic woman describes her life and in so doing recovers a culture about to disappear. Public and private history overlap as she poignantly recreates scenes from her past. A final *endecha* (dirge) of mourning links the persecution and Diaspora of the Jews in fifteenth-century Spain with the twentieth century. The use of contrast (a consistent device in this writer's literature) is apparent here in the opposition between two ways of life—the old and the modern—with their conflicting values and generational concerns.

Tras las huellas de Artorius (1985; Following the Footsteps of Artorius, Cáceres Prize for Short Novel) describes the trials and tribulations of Ana's doctoral research on Artorius, a troubadour from the Middle Ages. The novel chronicles her activities during a single day but is enriched with additional stories, sketches, and myriad details about university life and Ana's research. Multiple voices, styles, and perspectives suggest the polyphony that becomes an increasingly important aspect of her work.

El rapto del Santo Grial o el Caballero de la Verde Oliva (The Sequestering of the Holy Grail) was a finalist for the Premio Herralde de Novela in 1983. Its unusual treatment of legendary material (the Arthurian cycle; the ballad of the *doncella guerrera* [warrior maiden]) confirms Díaz-Mas's inventive imagination in this story of the consequences of the discovery of the Grail. A mock-epic style, parody, plays on words, and double meanings (particularly in dialogue between the sexes) subvert and deconstruct the epic idealism of the original material. The many tongue-in-cheek examples of sexual innuendoes and phallic imagery suggest a jocose mode, but this is undermined in turn by serious considerations that impinge on contemporary values, particularly the consequences of attaining one's ideal, as King Arthur's unchivalresque motives and behavior show. The feminist slant that was only partially glimpsed in earlier works emerges full force. Female characters are clear examples of the destiny awaiting a woman in the patriarchal structure: The desire for equality and independence is doomed to failure, as illustrated by the unhappy end of the lone brave maiden disguised as a knight. The 100 women weavers typify the opposite point of view: By sheer force of numbers, they represent the majority of females who accept and enjoy their role as erotic object and are rewarded for it. Whether read as an allegory of human nature or as an example of feminist criticism, it is a sorry view of the human condition in any epoch. In the words of the author, "the cynics win and the idealists lose."

Nuestro milenio (1987; Our Millennium), a finalist for the prestigious Premio Nacional de Literatura, continues Díaz-Mas's interest in stretching literary boundaries by combining the personal essay and fiction. The 14 pieces in this collection include her favorite themes: famous people or literary characters considered from a new perspective; studies of unusual psychological types or unhappy people. She laces a serious subject with double meaning and subverts conventional, accepted themes and norms through irony, parody, and the rereading of texts, often with a tongue-in-cheek, irreverent tone. Also apparent is the emphasis on visual material (particularly medieval art), which fills her prose with rich, detailed descriptions.

In *El sueño de Venecia* (1992; The Dream of Venice), which received the Premio Herralde de Novela, the description of a painting serves as a device to link five different stories and time periods as it passes from owner to owner. The narrative style changes radically in each episode, using intertextuality to reflect the literary conventions of the period it describes. In the last chapter, an art historian pompously supplies a completely erroneous explanation of the provenance and subject matter of the painting. The shifts in tone, style, and perspective display the author's versatility and command of narrative form. More seriously, they suggest a certain instability of life, which in turn corroborates the fallacy of a monolithic truth.

The time Díaz-Mas spent as a visiting professor at the University of Oregon inspired the travel narrative *Una ciudad llamada Eugenio* (1992; A City Called Eugene). Her talent for creating skillful, pithy sketches with an economy of words, ironic overlay, and her interest in contrast and presenting reality from a fresh perspective are simply continuations of her literary techniques in another mode. She also continues to insinuate a serious note into these clever, often humorous, subjects—a caution to the reader that surface appearances can be deceiving.

"La dama del unicornio" (1988; The Lady of the Unicorn), based on the famous set of medieval tapestries, is a short exercise in rich description, laced with commentary about the "protagonists" that reveals life hidden behind artistic form. The description of a "seventh nonexistent tapestry" proposes a possible love story.

"La discreta pecadora, o ejemplo de doncellas recogidas" (1989; The Discreet Sinner, or Lesson for Cloistered Maidens) confirms Díaz-Mas's interest in cleverly subversive fiction with a feminist slant. Hagiography and resonances of *Don Quijote provide the inspiration for a tongue-in-cheek treatment of a young woman who sallies forth to seek her (mis)fortune and salvation: She wishes to emulate and even surpass the greatest female sinners so that her repentance will be proportionately greater. Unsuccessful in her quest, still a virgin, she meets a dashing Moorish pirate who initiates her into the joys of sex. The association of Muslim culture with eroticism and sexual fulfillment sharply contrasts with the rigid norms of the Christian world; this "happy" ending is similar to that of *El rapto del Santo Grial* ... in which the women weavers, happily pregnant by one of the knights, sail off with him to "tierra de moros," where polygamy is permitted.

In all her works, Díaz-Mas smashes monolithic, univocal discourse and, with good humor but critical intent, replaces it with a polyphonic text. Ambiguity, contrast, and contradiction mark these works, suggesting that deconstruction is one way to demythify ideals that have nothing to sustain them. *See also* Short Fiction by Women Writers: 1975–1998, Post-Franco

Work by

Biografías de genios, traidores, sabios y suicidas, según antiguos documentos. Madrid: Nacional, 1973.
Una ciudad llamada Eugenio. Barcelona: Anagrama, 1992.

"La dama del unicornio." *Revista de estudios hispánicos* 22 (January 1988): 93–98.
"La discreta pecadora, o ejemplo de doncellas recogidas." *Cuentos eróticos.* Ed. Carmen Estévez. Barcelona: Grijalbo, 1989. 11–15.
La informante. Toledo: Excmo. Ayuntamiento de Toledo, 1983.
Nuestro milenio. Barcelona: Anagrama, 1987.
El rapto del Santo Grial o el Caballero de la Verde Oliva. Barcelona: Anagrama, 1984.
Sephardim: The Jews from Spain. Trans. George K. Zucker. Chicago: U of Chicago P, 1992.
El sueño de Venecia. Barcelona: Anagrama, 1992.
Tras las huellas de Artorius. Cáceres: Institución cultural "El Brocense," 1985.

Work about

Hernández, Juana Amelia. "La postmodernidad en la ficción de Paloma Díaz-Mas." *Romance Languages Annual* 2 (1990): 450–454.
Jones, Margaret E.W. "La obra de Paloma Díaz-Mas." *Alaluz* 27 (Spring 1995): 73–86.
Levine, Linda Gould. "The Female Body as Palimpsest in the Works of Carmen Gómez-Ojea, Paloma Díaz-Mas, and Ana Rosetti." *Indiana Journal of Hispanic Literatures* 2 (Fall 1993): 181–205.
Myers, Eunice. "The Quixerotic Quest: Paloma Díaz-Mas's 'La discreta pecadora, o ejemplo de doncellas recogidas.'" *Monographic Review/Revista monográfica* 7 (1991): 146–156.

Margaret E.W. Jones

Diosdado, Ana
See Drama by Spanish Women Writers: 1970–2000

Disciplina clericalis (eleventh century)

Poet, astronomer, cosmographer, and physician, Pedro Alonso's (1064–1115?) knowledge of Eastern culture allowed him to introduce Arab topics to Spanish medieval literature and folklore via his *Disciplina clericalis* (Instruction on Life for the Educated). His work has not been well studied, probably because he wrote in Latin and also because of his personal condition as a convert to Christianity. Nonetheless, his mixing of Talmudic, Arabic, and Judeo-Christian biblical traditions in his artistic production accurately reflects the Romanic cultural mixture characteristic of twelfth-century Aragon. One of the topics these cultures treated and that Pedro Alonso included is women in *exempla* (examples).

Disciplina clericalis is a collection of short didactic stories, fables, and poems of oriental origin. Its purpose is to educate, mixing enjoyment with instruction. Framed by a dialogue between a man and his pupil, their conversation is enriched by the 34 *exempla* the teacher selects to illustrate his lessons about life. Topics include human virtues and faults, human relationships (with women, neighbors, the king), the temporality of worldly values, and the relationship of man and God. Friendship, fidelity, the goodness of the soul, and the love of God are the positive values that bring knowledge and peace to the soul, according to Pedro Alonso. Among human vices that endanger the soul are greed, lust, and deception.

Women are included in the *exempla* in section VIII, which is devoted to men deceived by their senses. This section is followed by five stories where women exhibit their proverbial "evilness." The leading reason for the malicious behavior of the women in these anecdotes is lust, which drives them to lie and commit adultery. The focal point of the stories is more the cleverness of women than the condemnation of their sins, since the narrator emphasizes their industry and resourcefulness in accomplishing their desires, using a humorous tone.

In the first story of this section (*exemplum* IX), a wife manages to blind her husband in order to hide her lover. In *exemplum* X a wife receives her mother's assistance in deceiving her spouse with a sheet. *Exemplum* XIII contains an antecedent of the future go-betweens Trotaconventos (see *Tercera*) and Celestina (**Celestina, La*), a persistent old woman who functions as emissary for a young lover and defeats the initial resistance of a virtuous woman. *Exemplum* XIII is used to demonstrate how women will always outsmart men, even if men try to study and understand women's ways; it narrates a tale in which a betrayed man ends by asking for forgiveness from his unfaithful wife. The collection closes with an attempt to credit women with some good deeds. In *exemplum* XV, a woman hermit helps a man recover his possessions from a neighbor. The conclusion drawn from this tale is that men try to learn by study that which women know by natural instinct.

Disciplina clericalis follows the traditional Judeo-Christian representation of women as clever but dangerous to men. Women are shown to be lustful, capricious, and willing to obtain carnal satisfaction by any means. Although the final story exemplifies a positive contribution by the eremite, it also sows the idea that woman can use her intelligence for any purpose she might desire, and because she is a woman, the situation is dangerous. This idea is reinforced by another story that, even though women do not figure directly, connotes their dangerous nature. In story V, a man liberates a snake only to have the snake turn against him. The man then asks a fox for help. After helping the man, the fox reminds him that men cannot alter the nature of things.

Work

Disciplina clericalis de Pedro Alonso. Ed. and Spanish trans. A. González Palencia. Madrid and Granada: Consejo Superior de Investigaciones Científicas, 1948.

Disciplina clericalis de Pedro Alonso. Ed. and intro. María Jesús Lacarra. Trans. Esperanza Ducay. Zaragoza: Guara, 1980.

The *Disciplina Clericalis* of *Petrus Alfonsi.* Ed. and trans. E. Hermes. English trans. P.R. Quarrie. Berkeley: U of California P, 1977.

Work about

David, Yonah. "Petrus Alfonsi and His *Disciplina clericalis.*" *Israel Levin Jubilee Volume: Studies in Hebrew Literature,* I. Ed. Reuven Tsur, Tova Rosen, and Hanna David. Tel Aviv: Katz Research Institute for Hebrew Literature, 1994. 63–68.

Taylor, Barry. "Wisdom Forms in the *Disciplina clericalis* of Petrus Alfonsi." *La Corónica* 22.1 (Fall 1993): 24–40.

María Luisa García-Verdugo

"Discurso en defensa del talento de las mujeres . . ." (1786)

The "Discurso en defensa de las mujeres y de su aptitud para el gobierno, y otros cargos en que se emplean los hombres" (Discourse in Defense of Women and Their Aptitude for Government and Other Positions Which Men Hold) was written by Josefa *Amar y Borbón (1753–1833). Published in 1786, six years before Mary Wollstonecraft's famous treatise on women's rights, Amar's *discurso* is part of the polemic initiated by publication of Francisco Cabarrús's (1752–1810) and Gaspar Melchor de Jovellanos's (1744–1811) essays opposing and defending the admission of women as regular members of the Madrid Economic Society. For some, this polemic is a direct result of *Feijóo's *Defensa*, written 60 years earlier.

The Economic Societies were started during the Enlightenment by a group of intellectual aristocrats interested in studying a series of subjects (such as agriculture, education, scientific advances, industry, economy, etc.) with the goal of modernizing Spanish society. By 1786, the Madrid Economic Society had admitted two women, María Isidra *Guzmán in 1784 and the Countess-Duchess of Benavente in 1786. It was precisely these two admissions that provoked the polemic, when the all-male membership confronted the possibility of a large number of women joining their ranks. Francisco Cabarrús spoke for those who opposed their admission. His "Memorial sobre la admisión y asistencia de las mujeres en la Sociedad Patriótica" (Memoir on the Admission and Attendance of Women to the Patriotic Society) argued that women would destroy the Society's intellectual atmosphere by introducing a frivolous attitude conducive to romantic liaisons. Gaspar Melchor de Jovellanos mildly favored the acceptance of women members in his "Memorias si se debían o no admitir a las señoras en la Sociedad Económica de Madrid" (Memoirs on Whether or Not to Admit Ladies into the Madrid Economic Society). His essay, written as a letter to the members of the Society, sought to grant full membership to women, to set fair rules of admittance, and to calm down the male members who feared a deluge of women's applications. He also favored women's entrance because they would offer new ideas and could serve as role models for other women.

Amar rejected Cabarrús's arguments and supported Jovellanos's in a most cogent, if somewhat sarcastic, style. Her essay reached beyond the controversy of acceptance into the Madrid Economic Society to address the larger concern of women's abilities. In this respect, her arguments paralleled those set up by Feijóo earlier in the century. Like him, Amar concluded that women's worst enemy was their lack of education. If educated, she argued, they would attain the same accomplishments as men. She believed that the acceptance of women as full members would encourage other women to study and pursue intellectual challenges, once convinced that their efforts would be publicly recognized.

Unfortunately, Amar's and Jovellanos's arguments in favor of full membership for women were unsuccessful. The Society voted to grant it, but the king rejected it, proposing instead the creation of a "sister" association. Thus, the Junta de Damas (Ladies' Assembly) was created under the presidency of the Countess-Duchess of Benavente. Amar became one of its first members as a Socia de Honor y Mérito. *See also* Feminism in Spain: 1700–1800

Work

Amar y Borbón, Josefa. "Discurso en defensa del talento de las mugeres, y de su aptitud para el gobierno, y otros cargos en que se emplean los hombres; Compuesto por Josefa Amar y Borbón, Socia de mérito de la Real Sociedad Aragonesa de Amigos del País." Ed. Carmen Chaves McClendon. *Dieciocho* 3.2 (1980): 144–161.

Work about

Feijóo, Benito Jerónimo. "Defensa de las mujeres." *Obras (Selección)*. Ed. Ivy McClelland. Madrid: Taurus, 1985. 133–141.
Franklin, Elizabeth M. "Feijóo, Josefa Amar y Borbón, and the Feminist Debate in Eighteenth-Century Spain." *Dieciocho* 12.2 (1989): 188–203.
Oñate, María del Pilar. *El feminismo en la literatura española*. Madrid: Espasa-Calpe, 1938.
Rudat, Eva M. Kahiluoto. "La mujer ilustrada." *Letras femeninas* 2.1 (1976): 20–32.
Sullivan, Constance A. "Josefa Amar y Borbón and the Royal Aragonese Economic Society (with Documents)." *Dieciocho* 15.1–2 (Spring–Fall 1992): 95–148.

María A. Salgado

Doña Jiménez, Juana (1919–)

The author of several prose works that denounced Francoism and defended communist positions, Doña Jiménez is often considered the second most influential woman of the Spanish communist movement. At age 14 (in 1933) she joined Las Juventudes Comunistas, the Communist Party youth group, and two years later she became a member of the Spanish Communist Party. The year 1936 marks the year of her marriage to Eugenio Besón; five years later, in July, he was executed by the Francoist justice.

In March 1939, when fascist troops rounded up and imprisoned all refugees trying to flee Spain from the port of Alicante, Doña Jiménez was among the group. Sent to the Almendros concentration camp, she was first sentenced to 12 years; then she was released, only to be detained again in 1947, this time sentenced to death because of her political activism. Although spared execution, she remained in prison for 15 more years. In 1963, a year after her liberation, she left the Communist Party and later joined the Trotskyite Revolutionary Worker's Organization (Organización Revolucionaria de Trabajadores).

Her first work is titled *La mujer* (1977; Woman). Published in the *Tribuna popular* collection, it is a brief study of women's condition in Spanish society. According to Doña Jiménez, the perennial problem of women in Spain is rooted in the class structure of capitalism. She proposes a Popular Democratic Republic as the solution to all social problems, including those of women. Her Marxist analysis reminds readers of the key role the Second Republic played in improving conditions for working women.

Desde la noche y la niebla (Mujeres en las cárceles franquistas) (1978; From the Darkness and Mist [Women in Francoist Prisons]) is labeled a "testimonial novel" by Doña Jiménez. It uses social realism to tell the story of Francoist prisons for women and the political resistance that took place behind these prison walls. The text denounces the torture, rapes, executions, and multiple types of human rights violations carried out during Franco's dictatorship and also bears witness to the inhumane treatment these women were subject to both from prison guards and nuns in charge of these institutions.

Gente de abajo (1992; The Underdog People) is a novel whose title clearly recalls Mariano Azuela's novel of the Mexican revolution, *Los de abajo*. It narrates the story of Irene, a poor woman from Lavapiés, a working-class neighborhood of Madrid. During the Second Republic, the protagonist learns her brother and sister are communists, and during the Civil War she helps the revolution by working in hospitals and with displaced children. After the war, Irene loses relatives and friends: her lover, brother, and sister are each executed by Franco's repressive troops. Irene decides to avenge her family and so adopts a respectable middle-class appearance to be able to conceal her participation in terrorist actions planned by the Spanish Communist Party. The novel ends at the beginning of Spain's transition to democracy, before the subsequent *desencanto* (disillusion).

Work by

Desde la noche y la niebla (Mujeres en las cárceles franquistas). Novela testimonio. Madrid: de la Torre, 1978.

Gente de abajo. Madrid: A-Z, 1992.
La mujer. Madrid: Emiliano Escolar, 1977.

Salvador A. Oropesa

Doña Perfecta (1876)

Set in the fictitious provincial town of Orbajosa in nineteenth-century Spain, *Doña Perfecta* is Benito Pérez Galdós's (1843–1920) examination of the dangers and evils of hypocrisy and oppression. According to a traditional reading, the plot presents a study in contrasts and explores the clash of opposing value systems. In what amounts to a life and death struggle—with the innocent Rosario as the final prize—Galdós pits Pepe Rey, the faithless scientist from cosmopolitan Madrid, against the seemingly pious Perfecta in provincial, ultratraditional Orbajosa. Along the way, a number of other polarizations come to light: male/female, good/evil, truth/hypocrisy.

More recently, feminist critics have argued against such oversimplification and demonstrated the inherent complexity of the work, especially with regard to the title character and female protagonist. Most probably modeled after Galdós's own austere mother, Perfecta is a powerful, prestigious female who, out of necessity, abandons her expected stereotypical femininity to co-opt a male role and embrace a masculinized social order. This is, at the same time, her greatest strength and her greatest weakness as she breaks with societal expectations in her roles as a woman and mother to her daughter Rosario, but not with the male-dominated power structure that originally dictated those roles. Gone is the nineteenth-century *ángel del hogar; gone is the stereotypical good mother. Instead, Perfecta is characterized as a cruelly manipulative, deceitful, devouring, perverted mother-figure.

In fact, Perfecta—an anomaly in her masculinization—is an interesting mixture of expected male traits and exaggerated female qualities. As seen especially in her relationship with her daughter, she is at the same time authoritarian, aggressive, controlling, and determined as well as fanatically pious and conformist. Even to the point of confinement (*Encierro), Perfecta forces such conformity upon Rosario so that the latter is a perfect example of the expected nineteenth-century *ángel del hogar*, exhibiting stereotypical female values of piety, submissiveness, and helplessness.

Ironically, to this end—in her effort at blind conformity to male-dominated societal expectations—Perfecta is even willing to compromise her own ethics, to order the death of the opposing force of modernity, Pepe Rey, and to see Rosario confined to an asylum. Far from a mere caricature or vehicle for simplistic contrast, then, Perfecta emerges as a complex woman in a surprisingly complex work, even—some may say—a tragic victim herself of nineteenth-century patriarchy.

Work

Doña Perfecta. Intro. Rodolfo Cardona. Madrid: Cátedra, 1984.

Work about

Buck, Donald C. "Geographical Places, Architectural Spaces, and Gender in Doña Perfecta." *Romance Languages Annual* 6 (1994): 417–421.
Fox, Linda C. "Power in the Family and Beyond: Doña Perfecta and Bernarda Alba as Manipulators of Their Destinies." *Hispanófila* 21 (1985): 57–65.
Higuero, Francisco Javier. "El discurso de lo silenciado en Doña Perfecta." *Monteariba* 22 (1996): 23–40.
Santana, Mario. "The Conflict of Narratives in Pérez Galdós' Doña Perfecta." *Modern Language Notes* 113.2 (1998): 283–304.
Varey, J.E. *Pérez Galdós: Doña Perfecta*. 2nd. ed. Critical Guides to Spanish Texts 1. London: Grant and Cutler, 1992.

Joan M. Hoffman

Donato, Magda

See Nelken, Carmen Eva, Pseudonym Magda Donato (1900–1966)

Don Juan

See Burlador de Sevilla, El (1627–1629): Its Women Characters; Sáenz-Alonso, Mercedes (1917–): Don Juan y el donjuanismo

Don Quijote de la Mancha (Part I, 1605; Part II, 1615): Its Representation of Women

Considered by many critics to be the first modern novel, Miguel de Cervantes Saavedra's *El ingenioso hidalgo don Quijote de la Mancha* (*The Adventures of Don Quixote*, 1986) relates the story of Alonso Quijana, a gentleman in his fifties who, driven insane by excessive reading of *novelas de *caballerías* (chivalric romances), declares himself a knight errant and sets out in search of adventure. Due to the novel's metafictional qualities, Cervantes's text affords scholars the opportunity to examine the confluence and parody of various literary genres upon which the author draws to tell his story. One aspect of this examination is an analysis of Cervantes's treatment of women, both as commentary on the typical roles in which females were cast in Golden Age Spanish literature and as characters in his own novel. Another element of the text significant for feminist readings and related to Cervantes's parodic irony is the problematizing of narrative and textual authority, which can be read as a subversion or denaturalizing of male-centered/male-created aesthetic and cultural norms.

A productive starting point in an examination of the feminine in *Don Quijote* is a study of the interpolated tales of Part I. These stories allow various female characters a voice in the narrative, inviting readers to examine critically the portrayal of women in the literary traditions novelized in *Don Quijote*. As a parody of pastoral romances, the Marcela/Grisóstomo episode reshapes the convention of the disdainful female, criticizing the scorning of women who choose not to be with men as simply illogical. Marcela the shepherdess speaks on her own behalf of her right to refuse Grisóstomo's advances. This speech is supported by Don Quijote, who also believes it is unfair to criticize a woman simply because she does not reciprocate her suitor's love. Dorotea is another character of these tales who is allowed to exhibit her rhetorical and acting skills in a metatheatrical adventure in which she disguises herself as Princess Micomicona and enlists the aid of Don Quijote to kill an evil giant. Dorotea's skills eventually bring Don Quijote home and result in the restoration of conjugal and social order for herself and Don Fernando, as well as for Luscinda and Cardenio and Clara and Luis. Dorotea's participation in and direction of the Princess Micomicona episode flaunt the artificiality of the role assigned to women in chivalric romances. The parodic quality of Cervantes's treatment of the passive, helpless female in need of a male savior is brought to the foreground through the control Dorotea wields over her situation and the ease with which Don Quijote is tricked into believing that the character is a princess in need of rescue. The final representation of women in the interpolated tales comes from "The Captive's Tale," which draws on historical fact, pastoral and *courtly love traditions, and tales of knight errantry to underscore the strength and intelligence of the Moorish princess Zoraida, confronting to some degree both gender and racial stereotypes. In these three examples, parody of existing genres and literary conventions posits alternatives to conventional interpretations that limit women's ability to determine and articulate their own selfhood, revealing the constructedness of the literary woman and, possibly, provoking scrutiny of the culturally defined and historically (de)formed woman.

Paradoxically, the ability to tell their stories may actually work against these female characters because in the end their tales implicitly or explicitly support conventional gender roles. The words put into the mouths of characters such as Dorotea or Marcela suggest complicity from the very individuals in a position to undermine societal constraints imposed upon women. For example, Marcela's refusal to reciprocate Grisóstomo's affection may also reflect male-constructed notions of the chaste woman; in this case, Marcela's assertions would simply reiterate one of the rather limited options women had in terms of their relationships with men and the control they were allowed over their own lives and bodies. Also worth mentioning is Marcela's disappearance, for after her poignant speech she scurries away, never to appear or speak again, leaving readers unsure of when and how her story really ends. In a less ambiguous fashion, Dorotea becomes a mechanism whereby the social status quo is maintained, given that her courage, strength, and ingenuity are ultimately exhibited in support of the Church and the institution of marriage. The tale of Zoraida stands out as a story in which the protagonist does not speak. Her only utterances are to deny her given name, her identity, insisting that she be called "María." Her captor/husband tells Zoraida's story of rejecting her faith and family in order to become a Christian and escape with him, emphasizing Zoraida's use of wits and courage to support the Church and the conventional social institution of marriage. Clearly, the world of metafiction affords these characters the opportunity to move beyond limitations imposed upon female activity and autonomy. They express and assert their own will and shape their own destinies in ways that can only occur in fiction. Nevertheless, as their stories close, all are rendered mute, either because of linguistic incompetence (Zoraida), self-imposed absence (Marcela), or a return to the world of social reality from the world of metafiction (Dorotea).

Though less significant as storytellers (but not, in some cases, as fiction-makers), female characters who do not narrate are also representative of the novel's somewhat ambivalent treatment of women. Practical, down-to-earth, and in some cases, utterly unremarkable figures such as the innkeeper's wife, Don Quijote's niece, his housekeeper, Don Diego de Miranda's wife, and Teresa Panza exhibit a degree of passivity that contrasts sharply with the activity of the novel's female *narrators*. Although Teresa does question Sancho's planned attempt at social climbing through the marriage of their daughter and her role becomes more active in Part II, the wife relents as she expresses explicitly her (woman's) obligation to obey Sancho (her husband). Such passivity points to the liberating nature of the novel's metafictional worlds and the stifling confines of its fictionalized images of real life.

In other cases, the characterization of non-narrating characters, though less passive, is also considerably more negative. Doña Rodríguez, Maritornes, the duchess, and Altisidora are cast in a less favorable light. And the generally hostile portrayal of these characters is inextricably bound to notions of female sexuality that posit a passive role for women in love relationships. The duchess, along with her husband the duke, is sadistically bent on tormenting and teasing Don Quijote. Although she never initiates physical contact with the knight, the duchess arranges for her maid Altisidora to feign romantic interest and pursue Don Quijote in a farce of seduction that suggests that when women take their sexuality into their own hands, it is with evil intent. This suggestion, as well as the generally odious portrayal of the figure of the maid in Don Quijote, parallels Leonela's role in Camila's and Lotario's downfall in the "Tale of Foolish Curiosity." Doña Rodríguez, whose exaggerated vanity ultimately becomes self-parody, represents the stereotypical aging lady-in-waiting desperately in search of a man. Maritornes's sexual appetite also has negative connotations, for in an attempted tryst with her lover, she mistakenly enters Don Quijote's room at the inn, which results in disaster for both her and the knight. Like many of the novel's aggressive women, the prostitute also delights in tormenting Don Quijote, using her sexuality to trick the protagonist and hang him from the barn door. Additionally, Maritornes's characterization as ugly, coarse, lascivious, and mean-spirited functions primarily as a contrast to, and perhaps subversion of, Don Quijote's ideal woman *Dulcinea, an observation underscored by the protagonist's initial belief that the prostitute is really a princess.

This sort of subversion is one aspect of a general weakening of textual authority throughout the work. As notions of genre and gender are destabilized, the novel undertakes an examination of the power of language (and especially the written word) to manipulate and impose authority. In fact, the novel's (pre)text, a warning against the dangers of reading chivalry romances, posits through Don Quijote's adherence to a literary model that literature not only reflects and comments on reality but also shapes it. The text suggests that struggles for power are often carried out through language, and one key aspect of this suggestion is the role that gender plays in these contexts.

Don Quijote's questioning of authority begins in the prologue when the author speaks directly to the reader, exposing the literary convention of citing classical texts as, perhaps, an unfounded faith in the word and in the authority of the great (male) thinkers of antiquity. The ease with which the reading public is fooled suggests the ability of texts to shape reality. Readers' expectations are met, the novel is successful, and the blind faith in convention is perpetuated. Although the prologue only refers to women in one sentence (the friend's advice to consult authors of classical antiquity as models for creating characters who are prostitutes, witches, and cruel women), the connections established between the text and the world, as well as the misreading of classical sources, are of significance to feminist readings of the novel.

The complex narrative structure of the *Quijote* may also relate to an examination of the feminine in the text. The multiple, at times contradictory, narrative voices resist the narrator's assertions that the stories told are entirely true. In fact, the novel is characterized as a translation of a document written by the Arab historian Cide Hamete, a figure who, according to the narrator, is of dubious honesty. As stories are told and retold, details may be forgotten or embellished, truth stretched and distorted. Temporal leaps, occasional omissions, and errors of fact all contribute to a deconstruction of the myth of objectivity, conflating fiction and history and problematizing essentialism. In this fashion, readers are invited to become more critical of texts in general and, significant for a feminist critique, of literary traditions that posit gender roles as natural rather than constructed.

Perhaps this invitation to scrutiny is one reason why the *Quijote* is so firmly placed within the canon of Spanish literature. The novel's openness to a variety of readings and theoretical perspectives offers successive generations of readers the opportunity to extract their own meanings from the text. For feminist scholars, Cervantes's treatment of female characters questions social and literary conventions but offers no easy answers. Why does Dorotea rigidly adhere to an *honor code that would force her to marry the man who deceived her? Why does Marcela exile herself to the wilds of Sierra Morena and the margins of textuality? How does Teresa Panza pass the time when Sancho accompanies Don Quijote on his adventures? Answers to these queries are pure speculation, but the questions themselves suggest a text receptive to such inquiry.

In addition to investigations of Cervantes's characterization of women, a feminist critique could also examine the way language and storytelling are treated in the novel. Problematizing narrative authority makes a general commentary on the relativity of truth and the importance of perspective and context in shaping meaning. Such assertions lend themselves to deconstructive textual practices; among these, feminist inquiry exposes the gender-inflicted biases inherent in any literary undertaking and exposes the ways in which language and textual authority have been used to control, shape, and suppress women's voices. *See also* Lesbianism in Early Modern Spanish Literature: 1500–1700

Work

The Adventures of Don Quixote. Trans. J.M. Cohen. Harmondsworth, Middlesex: Penguin, 1986.
Don Quijote de la Mancha. Ed. Martín de Riquer. 2 vols. Barcelona: Juventud, 1985.

Work about

Cameron, Edith. "Women in *Don Quijote*." *Hispania* 9 (1926): 137–157.
El Saffar, Ruth. *Beyond Fiction.* Berkeley: U of California P, 1984.
———. "In Praise of What Is Left Unsaid: Thoughts on Women and Lack in *Don Quijote*." *Modern Language Notes* 103.2 (1988): 205–222.
Jehensen, Yvonne. "The Pastoral Episode in Cervantes's *Don Quijote*: Marcela Once Again." *Cervantes* 10.2 (1990): 15–35.
Murillo, Luis. *A Critical Introduction to* Don Quijote. New York: Peter Lang, 1988.
Russell, P.E. *Cervantes.* New York: Oxford UP, 1985.
Williamson, Edwin. "Romance and Realism in the Interpolated Stories of the *Quixote*." *Cervantes* 2 (1982): 43–87.
Wiltrout, Ann. "Las mujeres del *Quijote*." *Anales Cervantinos* 12 (1973): 167–172.

Mindy Badía

Drama by Spanish Women Writers: 1500–1700

Western theater is generally characterized by women's relative absence as active, unmediated participants, but a particularly repressive moment occurred during the highly patriarchal society of sixteenth- and seventeenth-century Spain. An age when the standard of behavior for a "good" woman required silence, submission, chastity, and enclosure (*Encierro*) in private (as opposed to public) spaces, since theater requires *speech* in a *public* arena, women were excluded from participation on any level by the genre's very definition. As spectators, women were segregated to the *cazuela* (stewpot), which separated them farther than any other group from the stage; for the very few upper-class women who could afford it, seats behind the iron grillwork of second-floor, side balcony windows were available. As actresses, they were considered to be "public" women (prostitutes), for they occupied a public space. Thus it is remarkable that some women did break through such restrictions and compose secular plays. Full-length dramas by several women authors have survived; play titles are attributed to a number of other women, but the works have not been located. Relatively little is known about the women, and it is assumed that their works circulated in manuscript form among friends and peers and/or were performed in private. Teresa Soufas's recently published *Women's Acts* makes eight works by these women readily available to modern readers.

Angela de Acevedo was born in Lisbon to Juan de Acevedo Pereyra and Doña Isabel de Oliveira, probably in the early years of the seventeenth century. She was lady-in-waiting and favorite of Doña Isabel de Borbón, wife of Philip IV. When her husband died she retired to a Benedictine convent, where she died. She was famous as clever, discreet, and beautiful and wrote plays of which three are extant: *El muerto disimulado* (The Man Who Pretended to Be Dead), *La Margarita del Tajo que dió nombre a Santarem* (Margarita of Tajo Who Gave the Name to Santarem), and *Dicha y desdicha del juego y devoción de la Virgen* (Bliss and Misfortune in the Game and Devotion to the Virgin).

Ana *Caro Mallén de Soto (1565?/1660?–1652) was born in Seville, it is generally believed, or Granada, where her brother, Don Juan Caro de Mallén, was born. She resided in Seville and Madrid and belonged to the Literary Academy of the Count of la Torre. Vélez de Guevara (1579–1644) mentions her in his *Diablo cojuelo* as the Sevillian tenth muse. A friend of María de *Zayas, she wrote *El Conde Partinuplés* (The Count Partinuplés) and *Valor, agravio, y mujer* (Valor, Dishonor, and Woman).

Doña Leonor de la *Cueva y Silva, daughter of Don Agustín de la Rúa and Doña Leonor de Silva, was born in Medina del Campo at the beginning of the seventeenth century, and she remained there the greater part of her life. It is not known if she married or when she died. She wrote the play *La firmeza en la ausencia* (Unwavering Constancy in Absence).

Doña Feliciana *Enríquez de Guzmán, wife of Don Cristóbal Ponce de Solís y Farfán and, after his death, Don Francisco de León Garavito, was born in Seville in the last third of the sixteenth century. According to unattested legend she attended the University of Salamanca dressed as a man. She wrote *Tragicomedia los jardines y campos Sabeos. Primera y segunda parte, con diez coros, y quatro Entreactos* (Tragicomedy of the Sabean Gardens and Fields. First and Second Part, with Ten Choruses and Four Entreacts).

María de *Zayas y Sotomayor was born in Madrid on September 12, 1590, the daughter of Don Fernando de Zayas and Doña María de Barasa. Writers of the period document her presence and her literary relationships and activities in Madrid between 1621 and 1637. She was a friend of Pérez de Montalbán and Alonso del Castillo Solórzano, proof of which are her poems that appear in their books, and Lope de *Vega dedicated some verses to her in his *Laurel de Apolo* (Apollo's Laurel). Everything else about her life is a matter of conjecture. She wrote the play *Traición en la amistad* (written mid-1600s; Betrayal in Friendship) and several novellas published in 1637 as *Novelas amorosas y exemplares* (Romantic and Exemplary Novellas) and, in 1647, *Parte segunda del Sarao y entretenimiento honesto, Desengaños amorosos* (Second Part of the Sarao and Honest Entertainment, Romantic Deceptions).

Studies such as *Engendering the Early Modern Stage*, edited by Hegstrom and Williamsen, also document other ways in which women managed to participate and exert influence in the theatrical arena. From the beginning of the sixteenth century, noblewomen of the court, including some queens, were financial patrons, performers, and viewers of private performances at court and in private palaces. Several actresses managed to surpass the stigma attached to most women performers and become extremely famous; some also became managing directors of their own acting companies. *Engendering the Early Modern Stage* also comments on the important phenomenon of convent theater, produced and enjoyed entirely by women and sometimes composed by them. Convents used these performances to educate nuns, to commemorate religious events, and for enjoyment. There is also evidence that secular plays of the day were performed in convents for nuns' entertainment. *See also* Sexuality in the Golden Age: Fray Manuel de Guerra y Ribera (seventeenth century); Sexuality in the Golden Age: Fray Gaspar de Villarroel (?–after 1659); Women Writers in Spanish Literary History: 1500–1996

Work by

Arenal, Electa, and Georgina Sabat de Rivers, eds. *Literatura conventual femenina: Sor Marcela de San Félix, hija de Lope de Vega: Obra completa*. Barcelona: PPU, 1988.

Arenal, Electa, and Stacey Schlau, eds. *Untold Sisters: Hispanic Nuns in Their Own Words*. Trans. Amanda Powell. Albuquerque: U of New Mexico P, 1989. Contains original and English translations.

Caro Mallén de Soto, Doña Ana. *Amor, agravio, y mujer*. Ed. Lola Luna. Madrid: Castalia, 1993.

Enríquez de Guzmán, Feliciana. *The Dramatic Works of Feliciana Enríquez de Guzmán*. Ed. Louis C. Pérez. Madrid: Albatros Hispanófila, 1988.

Schlau, Stacey. *Viva al Siglo / Muerta al Mundo: Selected Works / Obras escogidas by / de María de San Alberto (1568–1640)*. New Orleans: UP of the South, 1998.

Serrano y Sanz, Manuel. *Biblioteca de autores españoles: Apuntes para una biblioteca de escritoras españolas*. 2 vols. Madrid: Atlas, 1975.

Soufas, Teresa Scott, ed. and intro. *Women's Acts. Plays by Women Dramatists of Spain's Golden Age*. Lexington: UP of Kentucky, 1997.

Zayas y Sotomayor, María de. *Novelas completas de María de Zayas*. Ed. María Martínez del Portal. Barcelona: Bruguera, 1973.

———. *La traición en la amistad / Friendship Betrayed*. Ed. Valerie Hegstrom. Trans. Catherine Larson. Lewisburg, PA: Bucknell UP, 1999.

Work about

Gascon, Christopher. "The Heretical and the Herethical in Angela de Azevedo's *Dicha y desdicha del juego y devoción de la Virgen*." *Bulletin of the Comediantes* 52. 1–2 (1999): 65–81.

Hegstrom, Valerie, and Amy R. Williamsen, eds. *Engendering the Early Modern Stage. Women Playwrights in the Spanish Empire*. New Orleans: UP of the South, 1999.

Soufas, Teresa S. "Ana Caro's Re-evaluation of the *Mujer varonil* and Her Theatrics in *Valor, agravio y mujer*." *The Perception of Women in Spanish Theater of the Golden Age*. Ed. Anita K. Stoll and Dawn L. Smith. Lewisburg, PA: Bucknell UP, 1991. 85–106.

———. *Dramas of Distinction. A Study of Plays by Golden Age Women*. Lexington: UP of Kentucky, 1997.

Wilkins, Constance. "Subversion through Comedy? Two Plays by Sor Juana Inés de la Cruz and María de Zayas." *The Perception of Women in Spanish Theater of the Golden Age*. Ed. Anita K. Stoll and Dawn L. Smith. Lewisburg, PA: Bucknell UP, 1991. 107–120.

Anita K. Stoll

Drama by Spanish Women Writers: 1770–1850

The Enlightenment and Romantic periods in Spain were no less important for women writers than for their more frequently studied male counterparts. From the 1770s through the 1850s, women began to make their mark not only in the more accepted genres of poetry and the novel but also in the very male-dominated Spanish drama. They were active participants of the literary movements of their day, writing neoclassic drama, *comedias lacrimosas* (tearful plays), *zarzuelas* (musical plays), *sainetes* (one-act farces), *tonadillas* (light popular songs), romantic tragedies, and *costumbrista*-style comedies that rivaled those of their male colleagues. Not only did the numbers of female playwrights increase during these some 80 years, but the numbers of plays by women published and produced for the stage also grew, paving the way for an explosion of female-authored dramas in the later post-Romantic period.

Most playwrights, of course, write for an intended audience. Plays by the earlier Enlightenment women dramatists were often meant for small, private audiences, reminiscent of the works of seventeenth-century authors like Sor Juan Inés de la Cruz (1651–1695). Sor Ana de San Gerónimo (1696–1771), for example, composed several *loas* (short dramatic panegyrics) to be performed for the sisters of her convent, such as the two published in her collection *Obras poéticas* (1773). Another venue for late-eighteenth-century women's drama was in the private gatherings of the numerous literary salons, which were also often hosted by women. The Marquise of Fuerte-Hijar, María *Lorenza de los Ríos wrote at least two plays to be performed at the turn-of-the-century literary gatherings in her home, *El Eugenio* and *La sabia indiscreta* (The Indiscreet Learned Woman), undated manuscripts of which can be found in the National Library in Madrid.

Yet many late Enlightenment and Romantic women dramatists wrote with the intention of sharing their creations with a larger audience. Margarita *Hickey (1753–after 1793), Isabel Morón (dates unknown), María Martínez Abello (dates unknown), and María Rosa *Gálvez (1768–1806) all published plays between 1789 and 1805, the latter producing seven of her works for the Madrid stage. Their works displayed the prevailing literary tastes of the times, and they attempted to contribute to the neoclassic renovation of the Spanish stage through translations of foreign (mostly French) works, such as Hickey's translations of Racine and Voltaire, or through their own original dramas.

Gálvez was undoubtedly the most remarkable of these late Enlightenment female dramatists. She composed 13 original plays and three translations, encompassing forms as diverse as opera, light comedy, and high tragedy. Most of her original plays were published in her three-volume *Obras poéticas* (1804), printed by the Royal Press. In her Moratín-style comedy *Los figurones literarios* (1804; The Literary Nobodies), the female protagonist Isabel ridicules the pedantry of her uncle and his friends. Gálvez utilizes in this, as in many of her works, the same Enlightenment themes found in male-authored plays, albeit through a female point of view. Thus, whereas in Moratín's *La comedia nueva* (1792; The New Comedy) it is Don Pedro who teaches the important lesson to Don Eleuterio and his friends, in Gálvez's *Figurones* it is the heroine Isabel who resolves the conflicts. Still other plays by Gálvez depart from established Enlightenment goals of instructing the masses, to express and even protest the female condition through themes of rape, incest, domestic abuse, slavery, free love, and feminine solidarity. Her tragedy *Florinda* (1804) attempts to vindicate the legendary Florinda, blamed for the loss of Spain to the Moors. Gálvez focuses on the act of King Rodrigo's uncontrollable passion, finding in the rape of the innocent Florinda an example of women's dual position as both victim and villainess. She sets further examples of this tragic female condition in her biblical drama *Amnón* (1804), which recounts the incestuous rape of Tamar by her brother Amnon. The play ends unresolved (atypical for neoclassic tragedy) as the dying Amnon curses his sister.

Gálvez's unsettling plays anticipated the great Romantic tragedies of Rivas (1791–1865), García Gutiérrez (1813–1884), and *Zorrilla (1817–1893), but they also provided an important link with women dramatists of the 1840s to 1850s. Women who composed plays during the period of Spanish romanticism followed in the footsteps of Gálvez, creating works for the public stage that rivaled those of their male colleagues. One of the earliest of these romantic women dramatists was Joaquina Vera (dates unknown), who published 14 plays between 1840 and 1858, the fifteenth being published posthumously in 1873. Most of Vera's plays were translations from French or English, and at least one, *El disfraz* (1844; The Disguise), was produced for the Madrid stage. While Vera (who was also an actress) only composed theater, other female dramatists of this period were widely known for their literary contributions in other genres as well, most notably Carolina *Coronado (1823–1911) and Gertrudis *Gómez de Avellaneda (1814–1873). Some, such as Angela *Grassi (1823–1883), got their start in drama but then continued in another literary form. Grassi, who was later known more as a novelist, began her career composing dramatic works. She was only 15 when she published and saw produced her first play, *Lealtad a un juramento o crimen y expiación* (1852; Loyalty to an Oath or Crime and Expiation). Some women who began to write for the theater during this period, such as Enriqueta Lozano de Vilchez (1830–1895), had careers that extended well beyond the Romantic age into the post-Romantic era of the 1860s and 1870s. Lozano, like Joaquina Vera, was also an actress and actually performed in her own play *Una actriz por amor* (1847; An Actress for Love) as the heroine.

Many dramas by these Romantic women writers had a religious or moralistic theme and tone, such as Avellaneda's famous *Baltasar* of 1858 or even Grassi's *Lealtad a un juramento*. Many also dwelled upon the complications of young love, although rarely did they display the same kind of rebellious love of male romantic drama. Despite their conservatism in comparison to the more libertine male romanticism of the 1830s and 1840s or the daring plays of María Rosa Gálvez at the beginning of the century, these female-composed works are nonetheless important and unique contributions to the Romantic movement in Spain as well as to the growing tradition of female-authored drama.

The most famous of Romantic women dramatists, and perhaps of all female dramatists of the nineteenth century, was Gertrudis Gómez de Avellaneda. Avellaneda, who was also widely regarded for her novels and lyric poetry, wrote 16 full-length original plays between 1840 and 1858, in addition to several shorter plays and a translation from French. Many of these plays were great hits at the box office and received the admiration of her most distinguished male colleagues. Some of her more widely studied plays, especially *Saúl* (1844) and *Baltasar*, perhaps seem less interesting from a feminist perspective because of their more conservative tone and their dominant male hero. Yet notably strong female characters stand out in many of Avellaneda's plays. The scheming Doña Juana of *El Príncipe de Viana* (1844; Prince of Viana) and her counterpart the faithful Isabel really direct the actions of this third drama by Avellaneda. Despite the more "masculine" elements of the play's title and the events of war that make up its setting, it is the two female protagonists who predominate and propel the action to its conclusion. Evidence of this can be observed in the very framing of the opening and closing scenes, beginning with Queen Juana's plans to ruin her stepson Carlos (the Prince of Viana) and ending with Isabel's suicide as she curses the queen for poisoning Carlos.

Others plays by Avellaneda directly highlight female characters as their main focus. *Egilona* (1845), like Gálvez's *Florinda* 41 years earlier, also turns to a legendary female figure of the famous Spanish defeat at the hands of the Moors in 711. This time the focus is King Rodrigo's widow, Egilona, who marries the ruling conqueror, Emir Abdelasis. In Avellaneda's version of this legend, Rodrigo is found still to be alive, and the heroine is torn between her duty to Rodrigo and her love for Abdelasis. In the end she chooses to stay with the doomed Abdelasis, defending him from his angry kinsman and taking her own life by his side. While some have criticized this play's overly complicated action, its presentation of women's expected obligations in marriage and of the problems surrounding cross-cultural relationships is interesting. Two other plays, one written at the beginning of Avellaneda's career and another toward the end, also portray women outside the limits of accepted social behavior. In *Leoncia* (1840) and *La hija de las flores* (1852; The Daughter of the Flowers), Avellaneda highlights the problems of an illegitimate birth. In both, the victims of a youthful seduction, believing their illegitimate children dead, later discover the true fate of their grown daughters. Also in both, the adult daughters have actually become their mothers' rivals for the love of a (notably younger) man. Yet while in *Leoncia* the play ends with the angry confrontation between seducer and victim and ultimately in the tragic death of the daughter, in *La hija de las flores* the young girl's (Flora) natural parents are finally married, clearing the way for the marriage between the younger, more suitable couple.

The Enlightenment and Romantic periods in Spain were both dominated by drama, and playwrights of both periods sought to equal the greatness of Spain's Golden Age through a renovation of the theater. This time of renewal was also a time of growth for women playwrights, who began to compete in this very male-dominated field in ever-increasing numbers. Women of both periods not only imitated the style and popular themes of plays written by men, but they also added their own unique contributions. They explored themes that especially affected women's lives and created memorable female heroines. As their numbers increased, and their works became familiar to the audiences of Madrid, Barcelona, Seville and other Spanish cities, they inspired other women to write for the stage, resulting in an explosion of female playwrights in the latter half of the nineteenth century. *See also* Women Writers in Spanish Literary History: 1500–1996

Work by

Gómez de Avellaneda, Gertrudis. *Obras de doña Gertrudis Gómez de Avellaneda*. Ed. José María Castro y Calvo. Biblioteca de Autores Españoles. Vols. 278–279. Madrid: Atlas, 1979.
Simón Palmer, María del Carmen. *La Biblioteca Nacional de Madrid: Escritoras españolas 1500–1900*. Madrid: Chadwick-Healey España, 1992. Microfiche.

Work about

Galerstein, Carolyn L., and Kathleen McNerney, eds. *Women Writers of Spain: An Annotated Bio-Bibliographical Guide*. Westport, CT: Greenwood P, 1986.
Gies, David Thatcher. *The Theatre in Nineteenth-Century Spain*. Cambridge: Cambridge UP, 1994.
Harter, Hugh A. *Gertrudis Gómez de Avellaneda*. Boston: Twayne, 1981.
Levine, Linda Gould, Ellen Engelson Marson, and Gloria Feiman Waldman, eds. *Spanish Women Writers: A Bio-Bibliographical Source Book*. Westport, CT: Greenwood P, 1993.
Serrano y Sanz, Manuel. *Apuntes para una biblioteca de escritoras españolas desde el año 1401 al 1833*. Biblioteca de Autores Españoles. Vols. 268–271. Madrid: Rivadeneyra, 1903. Rpt. Madrid: Atlas, 1975.
Simón Palmer, María del Carmen. *Escritoras españolas del siglo XIX: Manual bio-bibliográfico*. Madrid: Castalia, 1991.

Elizabeth Franklin Lewis

Drama by Spanish Women Writers: 1860–1900

From its beginnings through the eighteenth century, the Spanish stage was an almost exclusively male realm. It was not until the nineteenth century that women began truly to break into this male-dominated genre. Although their numbers were still small in the first half of the century, several women dramatists (most notably María Rosa *Gálvez [1768–1806] and Gertrudis *Gómez de Avellaneda [1814–1873]) did contribute significant numbers of plays for the stage and were applauded for their achievements. This small legion, barely more than a dozen strong, nonetheless paved the way for an explosion of women dramatists in the second half of the century. A comparison of the various bibliographies available, including those compiled by Simón Palmer and Gies, reveal more than five times as many women writing drama in the second part of the century as in the first. While many of these writers composed only one drama, others wrote a dozen or more and saw quite a few of them staged in the most popular theaters of Madrid, Barcelona, and Seville as well as other smaller cities. Although still much in the minority, by the 1860s women writers were no strangers to Spanish theater.

Women's drama of this period followed the same patterns as Spanish theater written by men. Women too wrote grand productions in the *comedia de magia* (magic play—with spectacular visual effects) style, light-hearted *juguetes cómicos* (comical short plays), as well as dramas that continued in the popular romantic vein or that explored issues of the new bourgeoisie through the *alta comedia* (high comedy). One form dominated by women dramatists was the *teatro infantil*, the theater for children that also became popular at this time. Yet despite the many similarities, dramatic works written by Spanish women were not mere imitations of male drama but rather were original contributions to this very important nineteenth-century genre.

While romantic-style drama persisted and even dominated through the end of the century, the 1860s and 1870s saw a new form especially suited to the growing strength of Spain's middle class. The problems, concerns, and vices of the bourgeoisie were dramatized for the stage in the *alta comedia* by such male writers as Tamayo y Baus (1829–1898) and López de Ayala (1829–1879). Joaquina *García Balmaseda's (1837–1883) contemporary comedies also ridiculed Madrid's high society, while they highlighted the problems of upper-middle-class woman. In Un pájaro en el garlito (1871; A Bird in the Snare), a young widow struggles against the pressures of society to maintain her independence. Rosario, who has decided to travel alone from Madrid to Salamanca by train, fights for her right to a hotel room with an innkeeper and another guest, Alberto, when they must unexpectedly pass the night in Avila. The impertinent Alberto teaches poor Rosario the perils of a woman traveling alone. The theme of the play is highlighted when in the second scene Rosario expresses with delight "me encuentro sola y libre como el pájaro en el aire" (I'm alone and free as a bird in the air). Her newfound freedom is contrasted later with the same bird image when Alberto states in scene eight that catching birds is his favorite pastime. Predictably the two decide to marry in the end, as Rosario gives in to forces stronger than she, exclaiming in the last scene "que por algo a la mujer la hizo esclava la experiencia" (there's a reason why woman is a slave to experience). This ironic ending leaves the play on a bittersweet note. While the nineteenth-century audience must have enjoyed seeing female independence comically beaten by the clever Alberto, the author does not let him do so without pointing out the unfairness in Rosario's situation. Balmaseda's message to women seems to be one of resignation—it's best not to fight a futile struggle.

While in Balmaseda's comedies woman reluctantly learns her place, dramatist Purificación Llobet (1852–1905?), known by her pseudonym Camila Calderón, teaches men a few lessons through her pieces for the theater. Her one-act comedy A media noche (1880; At Midnight) ridicules the new bourgeois "Don Juans" of the second part of the century. In the play, the heroine Isabel comes to Madrid from Cartagena to investigate rumors about her husband and a certain countess. She is surprised late one night by Luciano who sneaks in her open window with intentions of seducing her. Isabel embarrasses the overly confident Luciano and also catches her unfaithful husband Jacinto, who unknowingly had helped Luciano try to seduce his own wife. In one of many twists on José *Zorrilla's (1817–1893) Don Juan Tenorio (1844), Isabel puts the legendary seducer in his place as a middle-class husband.

Still, most women's drama of the second half of the nineteenth century, like that of men, continued the tradition of romantic drama that had been so wildly popular in the first half. This "neo romanticism" utilized many of the same themes, characters, settings, motifs, and language as the romantic dramas of the 1830s and 1840s, while often using them to emphasize contemporary issues. Rosario de *Acuña (1851–1923) returned to the historical settings of romanticism in her first play Rienzi el tribuno (1876; Tribune Rienzi). The political and social implications of this play about the last Roman patrician, Nicolás Rienzi, reflect Acuña's lifelong defense of the lower classes and her controversial librepensadora (freethinking) stance. Her play emphasizes the patriotic qualities of valor and honor—qualities she also highlights in her next drama, Amor a la Patria (1877; Love of Country). However, in this one-act drama trágico the models of true patriotism are not men but women. Set in Zaragoza during the Napoleonic invasions, the play tells the story of Inés, a 40-year-old mother and loyal citizen of Zaragoza, who is preparing with her daughter María and her neighbors to defend their city. When she discovers that her long-lost son has returned a soldier in the French army, Inés tries to inspire patriotism in him. In order to convince him to change, she sets before him the brave example of women by pointing out a mother who loads rifles with one hand while rocking her son's cradle with the other (scene six). Acuña's most controversial play was her drama El padre Juan (1891; Father John), which contrasts the corruption and backward behavior of a priest, Padre Juan, to the progressive ideas of a young couple, Isabel and Ramón. The play's anticlericalism shocked many, and further performance was banned after its first showing. While not all of Acuña's plays were so polemical, she did use the romantic style to spread her contemporary ideas of progress and rational freethinking.

Adelaida Muñiz y Mas (?–1906) also utilized elements of the romantic tradition to discuss her social and political ideas. She was one of the most prolific female playwrights of this period, writing 15 plays of varying styles and themes. Her first play, Mancha heredada (1892; Inherited Stain), touched upon topics explored earlier in the theater of Henrik Ibsen—questioning to what extent a child must suffer for sins of the father, and anticipates José Echegaray's similar Mancha que limpia (1895; The Stain That Cleanses) by three years. The play's heroine, Margarita, becomes the innocent victim of a social system that values family honor over personal virtue. The mancha on her family name caused by her murdering father eventually becomes the bloodstain of her own accidental death when a stray bullet between dueling lovers hits and kills her. Muñiz y Mas again exalts personal virtue over family heritage in El pilluelo de Madrid (1894; The Rascal from Madrid). Although less dramatic than the more romantic Mancha heredada, this play too displays hallmarks of romanticism. The play's hero, Gabriel (son of a gypsy), fights against the injustice with which high society treats him and his family. The persistence of Gabriel's adverse fate is only broken in the final scene (set in his jail cell, a typical romantic setting) when the pilluelo's innocence is revealed and the treachery of his rich rival, Miguel, is exposed. One of Muñiz y Mas's last plays, Roja y gualda (1898; Red and Gold [poetic allusion to the Spanish flag]), treated the war in Cuba, as Spain fought to keep its last remaining colonies. It presents a family divided over loyalty to Spain (the "fatherland" represented by the Spanish-born Don Carlos) and their home in Cuba (the madre patria [motherland] represented by his Cuban-born wife, Doña Dolores). This conflict is especially acute for Carlos's son by Dolores, Eduardo, who at first follows his mother's pleas to defend Cuba. Still, in the end patriotism and patriarchy triumph when Dolores leaves the family and Eduardo gives up attempts to fight for Cuba.

Muñiz y Mas was not the first female playwright to take interest in Cuba and its political and social issues. Faustina *Sáez de Melgar (1834?–1895), writer and abolitionist activist, set her La cadena rota (1879; Broken

Chain) in Cuba as well. Sáez de Melgar exposes the injustices of slavery in Cuba through the lives of two innocent slaves, *cuarterón* siblings (of mixed white and mulatto ancestry) Azella and Rudérico. The Spanish hero, Horacio, has fallen in love with Azella and sets out to free her and her brother. Shocked by the treatment his Cuban cousin/fiancée Rosa gives the young pair, Horacio risks his fortune and position to fight the cruelty of slavery. Thus a play that starts out as an *alta comedia* drama about an arranged marriage between upper-class cousins quickly becomes a passionate romantic work of impossible love and adverse fate, highlighted by Horacio's soliloquy in act two, scene three.

Eva Infanzón Canel (1857–1932) wrote another romantic-style drama highlighting the problems of race, *La mulata* (1893; The Mulatto Woman). Canel, who lived for periods in Bolivia, Argentina, Peru, and Cuba, is often described as a conservative writer who defended Spain's colonial rights in America. Yet in *La mulata*, it is the American mulatto Patria (Homeland) who triumphs over the injustice and greed of Spaniards. Patria fights for 20 years to find her son who was kidnapped as a toddler and taken back to Cataluña by his Spanish father Daniel. While Patria and her black father are hardworking and virtuous, the Spaniards—Daniel and his accomplice Captain Montagut, Montagut's wife, and his daughter—are greedy and dishonest. In the end, Patria exposes her husband and his cohorts' crimes and convinces her son to come back with her to America.

Women dramatists in the second part of the nineteenth century presented for the first time a formidable presence on the Spanish stage in both numbers and importance. They participated through their varied works in all the major trends of contemporary drama and addressed social and political themes important to men and women alike. While male dramatists continued to dominate into the twentieth century, no longer could it be said that drama was a genre reserved for men only. *See also* Women Writers in Spanish Literary History: 1500–1996.

Work by

Acuña, Rosario de. *Rienzi el tribuno. El padre Juan.* Ed. María del Carmen Simón Palmer. Madrid: Castalia, 1990.

Work about

Galerstein, Carolyn L., and Kathleen McNerney, eds. *Women Writers of Spain: An Annotated Bio-Bibliographical Guide.* New York: Greenwood P, 1986.

Gies, David Thatcher. "Dramaturgas decimonónicas: Preguntas sin contestar." Forthcoming in *Homenaje a Reinoldo Froldi*.

———. *The Theatre in Nineteenth-Century Spain.* Cambridge: Cambridge UP, 1994.

Levine, Linda Gould, Ellen Engelson Marson, and Gloria Feiman Waldman, eds. *Spanish Women Writers: A Bio-Bibliographical Source Book.* Westport, CT: Greenwood P, 1993.

Simón Palmer, María del Carmen, ed. *Escritoras españolas del siglo XIX: Manual bio-bibliográfico.* Madrid: Castalia, 1991.

———. *Escritoras españolas.* 2 vols. Madrid: Chadwick-Healey España, 1991–1992. Microfiche.

Elizabeth Franklin Lewis

Drama by Spanish Women Writers: 1970–2000

In the final years of the long Franco dictatorship (1939–1975), Ana Diosdado (1938–) was if not the only Spanish woman playwright of national stature, certainly the most famous. By the mid-1980s she was joined in the Madrid theatrical scene by several other women authors, most notably María Manuela Reina (1958–), Paloma *Pedrero (1957–), Carmen *Resino (1941–), Pilar Pombo (1953–1999), and Concha *Romero (1954–). At the end of the twentieth century, in response to the emergence of drama schools, theater workshops, festivals, new playwriting prizes (the Marqués de Bradomín for young authors and the María Teresa de León for women), and the development of numerous small, experimental playhouses (*salas alternativas*), the numbers of both men and women playwrights throughout Spain increased dramatically. Representative of this new wave of women authors are Yolanda García Serrano (1958–), Yolanda Pallín (1965–), Itziar Pascual (1967–), Lluïsa Cunillé (1961–), and Beth Escudé i Gallès (1963–). A total list of women playwrights who have won important prizes or had their works staged or published would include dozens of additional names. Collectively these authors encompass a wide range of themes and approaches to theater.

Diosdado's successful career dates back to the critical and box office triumph of her first play, *Olvida los tambores* (1972; Forget the Drums); this look at divergent lifestyles and lingering conservative/liberal conflicts ran for more than 450 performances, has been frequently revived in Spain and Latin America, and won her the Mayte theater prize. Another major hit, *Usted también podrá disfrutar de ella* (1973; Yours for the Asking, 1995), combines impeccable theatrical structure and sparkling dialogue with an underlying criticism of political divisiveness and materialism. Winner of the Fastenrath prize of the Spanish Royal Academy, it ran for more than 500 performances; its revivals include a New York staging (by Repertorio Español, 1987, directed by Joanne Pottlitzer). The technical brilliance of these early plays may be attributed to Diosdado's years of experience in the theater. The child of actors, she began her acting career in Argentina before the family returned to Spain in 1950.

In spite of these early successes and the visibility achieved through such television series as the highly acclaimed *Anillos de oro* (1983; Wedding Rings), in which Diosdado functioned as both author and actress, like many playwrights in the early years of democratic Spain, she had a difficult time being staged. After a 10-year absence from the stage, she formed her own company in 1986 to bring *Cuplé* (Ballad) to audiences. This tragicomic satire of economic problems in contemporary Spain introduced a series of box office hits, the most successful of which has been *Los ochenta son nuestros* (1988; The Eighties Are Ours). Focusing on young people and their search for self-identity, the play also continues Diosdado's typical deconstruction of binary oppositions by exploring prejudice based on ideology, class, and sexual orientation. Diosdado's most recent plays, *Decíamos ayer* (1997; As We Were Saying Yesterday) and *La última aventura* (1999; The Last Adventure), were also performed under her direction.

In general, Diosdado's 13 plays, staged between 1970 and 1999 in major theaters, have been well received by audiences, but even the prizewinning ones have not fared nearly as well with Spanish theater critics. Some histories of Spanish theater dismiss Diosdado with a mere sentence or two. Foreign scholars have paid far more attention to her works but at times have labeled them as nonfeminist, suggesting that they reflect the same values as traditional theater written by men. Such appraisals fail to consider Diosdado's theater in its historical context and overlook her consistent use of "feminine writing," that is, her tendency to subvert the binary oppositions imposed by the Francoist patriarchy. Her expressionistic historical drama *Los comuneros* (1974; The Commoners) uses spatial and temporal fluidity to speak against the political intransigence that led the youthful Emperor Charles V (Charles I of Spain) to order the execution of the leaders of the popular rebellion. Franco's censors correctly understood the play to be a pro-amnesty statement and initially forbade its performance.

In the *Anillos de oro* television series, which was aired shortly after Catholic Spain reluctantly instituted a divorce reform law, Diosdado portrayed a divorce lawyer. The 13 episodes took a softened approach, often suggesting reconciliation rather than divorce, but they also showed cases in which divorce was the only viable answer. Moreover, Diosdado portrayed a professional woman, struggling to combine career with marriage and motherhood and then coping with the sudden death of her husband. In the final episode, it is established that she will remarry. Her future husband, her former law partner, is 10 years her junior. Diosdado's character combines aspects of the conventional Spanish woman with emerging, and indeed radical, changes in Spanish society.

The old and the new were similarly blended in *Camino de plata* (1988; Silver Path), a three-character stage play in which Diosdado and her actor-husband Carlos Larrañaga played the lead roles. When an upper-middle-class, middle-aged woman discovers that her husband is leaving her for a younger woman, she turns to housecleaning and catering as a way to support herself—traditional women's work. In the end, however, she establishes her independence by rejecting both reconciliation with her former husband and marriage to her lover. Bourgeois audiences set aside their long-standing middle-class values to applaud Paula's double decision.

Among women authors born in the 1950s, the most commercially successful has unquestionably been María Manuela Reina, although Paloma Pedrero has achieved the greatest international recognition. Reina's *Lutero o la libertad esclava* (Luther, or Liberty Enslaved), winner of the Calderón de la Barca prize for 1984 and staged at Madrid's Central Cultural de la Villa in 1987, is an imaginary, philosophical dialogue between Luther and Erasmus. She quickly moved away from this kind of intellectual fare. Her first commercial staging was *El pasajero de la noche* (1987; Passenger in the Night). Her later works, such as *La cinta dorada* (1988; Gold Ribbon) and *Reflejos con cenizas* (1991; Reflections with Ashes), are conventional bourgeois dramas dealing with dysfunctional families and taboo sexual relationships. They enjoyed long runs in commercial playhouses and have been studied by American Hispanists, but by the late 1990s, Reina had disappeared from the stage.

Paloma Pedrero has not yet had a box office hit in Madrid on a par with those of Diosdado and Reina, but she has surpassed them in international stature, having had her works staged in England, France, other European countries, Latin America, and the United States. With the 1999 publication of nine of her short plays in *Juego de noches* (Night Games), she became the first twentieth-century Spanish woman playwright to be included in Cátedra publishing house's prestigious Letras Hispánicas series.

Pedrero won the 1987 Tirso de Molina prize for *Invierno de luna alegre* (Winter's Happy Moon), which she directed in 1989. That view of marginal members of society, including an ex-bullfighter who earns his living by staging street spectacles, calls for a cast of five. *Besos de lobo* (1986; Wolf Kisses, 1999) also has a cast of several characters, but thus far Pedrero's most-staged works are her intimate, intense, two-character plays that capture moments of crisis in self-identity or relationships. *La llamada de Lauren* (1985; Lauren's Call, 1998) reveals the problems of a young married couple resulting from the husband's ambivalence about his sexual identity; Pedrero herself played Rosa in the 1985 Madrid premiere at the Centro Cultural de la Villa. *El color de agosto* (1988; The Color of August, 1994) portrays the artistic and personal rivalries of two women artists who have been friends since childhood but are reunited after an eight-year separation. Other popular works from the 1980s include *Resguardo personal* (1985; The Voucher, 1994), which examines how a divorcing couple fight over their dog, and the one-act plays comprising *Noches de amor efímero* (1991; Nights of Passing Love, 1994).

Pedrero has been associated with a recent theater movement that wishes to explore, in realistic language, topics of concern to a younger generation of spectators. Nevertheless, she has extended her range of subjects to include older characters. *Una estrella*

(1998; *First Star*, 2001) is a psychodrama of a woman seeking to understand her dead father, an alcoholic gambler who neglected his family. *El pasamanos* (*The Railing*, 2001) continues in the vein of social satire while giving a tender view of the loving relationship of a poor, elderly couple. It received its world premiere in Costa Rica in 1999.

Other Pedrero plays of the 1990s explore a variety of theatrical structures and themes. *La isla amarilla* (The Yellow Island) is a fanciful, Brechtian satire of Western "civilization" from the perspective of "primitive" Samoans. It has been staged to acclaim in various theaters in the Madrid area by a unique acting group from a women's prison. *Locas de amar* (Love Crazy), a satire of what happens when a middle-aged wife is dumped by a husband in pursuit of younger women, was directed by the author at Madrid's municipal Centro Cultural de la Villa in 1996. In *Cachorros del negro mirar* (1999; Young Toughs), Pedrero examines skinhead violence as well as the construction of gender.

Pedrero's theater in general is characterized by overt metatheatricalism, frequent use of humor, and the constant questioning of traditional social norms, particularly gender roles. Increasingly she has focused on marginal members of society and serious social issues. Her skill at synthesizing dramatic elements allows her to create plays that may be staged with relatively small casts and limited sets.

Growing scholarly awareness in the 1980s of the group of women playwrights may be attributed in part to the efforts of Patricia O'Connor, founding editor of *Estreno*, an American journal dedicated to contemporary Spanish theater. A monographic issue in 1984 called attention to the work of women playwrights, and subsequent issues of the journal have featured plays by and articles about women authors. At O'Connor's suggestion, in 1987 women dramatists in Madrid created their own association as a support group, under the presidency of Resino.

Some, like Resino, Pombo, and Romero, have turned at times to writing dramatic monologues that can be produced inexpensively in cafés and other nontraditional playing spaces. Resino and Romero have also written larger-cast historical dramas, usually serving as a revindication of female figures, such as Resino's *Nueva historia de la princesa y el dragón* (1989; New Story about the Princess and the Dragon) and *Los eróticos sueños de Isabel Tudor* (1992; Isabel Tudor's Erotic Dreams), and Romero's *Las bodas de una princesa* (1988; The Princess's Wedding) and *Juego de reinas* (1991; A Game of Queens). Perhaps the most admired work in this category is Romero's *Un olor a ámbar* (1983; A Smell of Amber), an account of the conflict between the nuns from Saint *Teresa's order and the male hierarchy of the Catholic Church over the saint's miraculously preserved remains.

On occasion these authors have turned their talents to conventional comedy. Pombo's prizewinning *No nos escribas más canciones* (1990; Don't Write Us Any More Songs) satirizes a successful pop musician who tries to return, however briefly, to the neighborhood he left behind. Resino's wildly funny *Pop y patatas fritas* (Pop and French Fries) was staged in 1992 at the Reina Victoria, a large commercial theater in Madrid. On the other hand, Romero's *Un maldito beso* (*A Kiss for a Kiss*, 2000) was commissioned by a director in Spain but then not staged; it was published in 1989 by the American scholarly journal *Gestos*. A metatheatrical farce that uses the role of Lady Macbeth as an intertext, *Un maldito beso* deals with a middle-aged actress who apparently develops amnesia when she catches her director husband kissing a young woman. Romero's play cleverly parodies bourgeois comedies of marital infidelity as well as Pirandellian games of illusion/reality.

Many of the younger playwrights who have appeared on the Madrid theater scene in recent years have studied at the Royal School of Dramatic Art (RESAD). García Serrano is among the women who honed their skills there. She began writing and staging plays in the mid-1980s, but more recently she has dedicated herself to film and television. In 1998 she won the Hogar Sur theater prize for *Qué asco de amor* (Love Makes Me Sick), which subsequently enjoyed a successful run at Madrid's Infanta Isabel theater, under the author's direction. She wrote the comedy at the request of three actress-friends. At times devastatingly funny, the more or less feminist text presents women's complaints about men and confessions of their own sexual exploits. The episodic action centers on the wedding day of each of the women; as she dresses with the aid of her friends, she expresses her trepidations. The first marriage ends in divorce because of the husband's infidelity. The second likewise ends in divorce, this time because of domestic violence and problems with the man's ex-wife. Perhaps the third marriage will endure, but the bride's lament that the groom is less passionate than she suggests something less than marital bliss.

Itziar Pascual belongs to the first class of RESAD students to graduate, in 1996, specifically in the new curriculum of playwriting; she currently serves on the faculty of that school. *Nox Tenebris*, a text written collaboratively with six other women students, demonstrates eloquently the cooperative spirit developed at RESAD. Although Pascual's works have not yet received major stagings, they have been awarded a number of prizes. Her language tends to be poetic, the structure of her plays is generally fragmented, and she is as likely to be inspired by myth or movies as by contemporary reality.

Pascual's first play to be published, *Fuga* (1993; Flight), contains all three of her theater's typical characteristics. This poetic short work is structured on a series of monologues, delivered by characters reminiscent of Greek mythology. In a variation on the Ulysses story, Ariadna awaits the return from war of her father and self-consciously identifies herself with Penelope. Pascual's final project at RESAD, *Las voces de Penélope* (1996; Penelope's Voices), is clearly related. Its 20 sequences may be considered separate poems. The characters are Penelope and two contemporary women, who also find themselves waiting. Eventually the classic myth is debunked as the three women take down the blue cloth that Penelope has been weaving and exit, arm in arm.

Among Pascual's other plays are such varied works as *Holliday Aut* (1995; Holiday Out), a dramatic monologue that takes place in an airport and centers on a woman whose suitcase is lost; *Miauless* (1997; Meowless), a short play dealing with a homeless cat—played by a human actor—whose feelings are not well understood by the adolescent girl who takes him in but wishes to control him; and *Una noche de lluvia* (2000; Rainy Night), a series of episodes involving couples who are coming out into the rain after seeing Roberto Benigni's movie *Life Is Beautiful*. The couples are to resemble different pairs of Spanish movie actors, and the whimsical episodes are linked through the evocative use of theme music from American movies.

No doubt among playwrights born in the 1960s the women authors who have achieved the greatest visibility to date are Pallín in Madrid and Cunillé in Barcelona. Both have been recipients of various important awards, including the prestigious Calderón de la Barca prize: Cunillé in 1991 for *Rodeo* and Pallín in 1996 for *Los motivos de Anselmo Fuentes* (Anselmo Fuentes's Motives). Both have had multiple plays staged and tend to write small-cast, minimalist texts. Pallín has been closely associated with the *salas alternativas* in Madrid, small playhouses that might be compared to New York's Off-Off Broadway or the London fringe. Cunillé is a major player in the counterpart Sala Beckett in Barcelona.

Among Pallín's other notable works are *La mirada* (1995; The Gaze), which deals with the encounter between a middle-aged man and a young woman, and *Los restos de la noche* (1995; The Remainder of the Night), whose fragmentary structure and poetic prose revolve around a couple, Laura and Carlos, in counterpoint with other oneiric characters. The oneiric element is somewhat repeated in the humorous episodes of *Luna de miel* (2000; Honeymoon), which presents various scenarios of marital problems, perhaps played out in the imaginations of the unnamed newlyweds. *Los restos de la noche* ends in Laura's death. *Los motivos de Anselmo Fuentes*, a two-character drama involving a mysterious jazz musician who persuades a reluctant bartender to let him in at closing time, similarly ends in death.

Violence takes the foreground in Pallín's *Lista negra* (1997; Black List), an unnerving view of the gratuitous crimes of skinheads. Pallín's longest-running play to date, *Las manos* (1999; The Hands), is far different in tone and style. Written in collaboration with two male colleagues and the resident acting company of the Cuarta Pared theater, the play evokes the experiences of young people in rural communities in the 1940s and, through its imaginative staging, elicits a sense of audience participation in a nostalgic view of the past.

Since the mid-1980s, there has also been a resurgence of theater in Catalonia, most of it written and staged in the Catalan language. By 1999, Cunillé was the most-staged woman author, and her 14 staged plays placed her among the top four contemporary Catalan playwrights, regardless of age, in number of plays produced. Her prizewinning *Rodeo* was performed at one of Barcelona's major playhouses, the Mercat de les Flors. The play, which takes place in an office, incorporates the dominant characteristics of Cunillé's work. There is a simple, single set and few props. The characters do not have names. The dialogue is composed of everyday, natural language but yet remains ambiguous. Without an obvious plot, there is something menacing about the silences and emptiness in the text. The dramatic world of Cunillé is familiar and yet absurd.

Cunillé's *L'accident* (1995; The Accident), also staged at the Mercat de les Flors, deals with two men who meet in an automobile accident and develop a relationship of mutual dependence. *Aigua, foc, terra i aire* (1995; Water, Fire, Earth and Air) has two women characters whose daily routine is also broken by chance. *El empleo* (1999; The Job) revolves around a woman and a man with employment problems who find themselves in adjacent rooms in a boarding house; the play ends, but there is no conclusion.

In contrast to Cunillé, Escudé i Gallès has only begun to have her plays staged. However, her one major play to date, *El color del gos quan fuig* (1997; The Color of the Running Dog), has already been translated to Castilian Spanish, French, and Italian and is scheduled for publication in English in 2002. The two characters, a young woman and an old woman, discuss the related roles of Ruth and Naomi, Andromache and Hecuba, and other apparently mythical figures. As they resort to storytelling within their roles, the young woman massages the old woman with a poisonous lotion, thus precipitating a painless death. The haunting quality of Escudé i Gallès's poetic metaphor has launched her into the forefront of Catalan theater.

The 11 authors mentioned in this brief entry are only a few of the Spanish women playwrights whose presence on their national stage and abroad is becoming increasingly important. *See also* Feminist Theory and the Contemporary Spanish Stage

Work by

Cunillé, Lluïsa. *The Meeting.* Trans. John London. Ed. David Greig. *The Speculator.* London: Methuen, 1999. n.p.

———. *Rodeo.* Madrid: Sociedad General de Autores de España, 1996.

———. *Roundabout.* Trans. Oscar Ceballos and Mary Peate. *Spanish Plays.* London: Nick Hern Books, 1999. 187–238.

Diosdado, Ana. *Olvida los tambores.* 2nd ed. Madrid: Escelicer, 1972; *Teatro español, 1970–71.* Ed. F.C. Sainz de Robles. Madrid: Aguilar, 1972. 1–75.

———. *Usted también podrá disfrutar de ella.* Madrid: Ediciones MK, 1975; *Teatro español, 1973–74.* Ed.

F.C. Sainz de Robles. Madrid: Aguilar, 1975. 1–78.

———. *Yours for the Asking*. Trans. Patricia W. O'Connor. State College, PA: ESTRENO Plays, 1995; *Modern Women Playwrights of Europe*. Ed. Alan P. Barr. New York: Oxford UP, 2001. 226–273.

Dramaturges catalanes des années 1999. Paris: Les Éditions de l'Amandier/Théâtre, 1999.

Dramaturges espagnoles des années 1999. Paris: Les Éditions de l'Amandier/Théâtre, 1999.

Leonard, Candyce, and Iride Lamartina-Lens, eds. *Nuevos manantiales: Dramaturgas españolas en los noventa*. Ottawa: GIROL, in press.

O'Connor, Patricia W., ed. *Dramaturgas españolas de hoy. Una introducción*. Madrid: Espiral/Fundamentos, 1988.

———. *Mujeres sobre mujeres. Teatro breve español*. Madrid: Fundamentos, 1998. Spanish–English bilingual edition.

Pallín, Yolanda. *Los motivos de Anselmo Fuentes*. *Primer Acto* 270 (1997): 34–50.

Pedrero, Paloma. *First Star* and *The Railing*. Trans. Rick Hite. New Brunswick, NJ: Estreno Plays, 2001.

———. *Juego de noches. Nueve obras en un acto*. Ed. Virtudes Serrano. Madrid: Cátedra, 1999.

———. *Lauren's Call*. Trans. Patricia W. O'Connor. *Modern Women Playwrights of Europe*. Ed. Alan P. Barr. New York: Oxford UP, 2001. 274–303.

———. *Parting Gestures: Three Plays*. Trans. Phyllis Zatlin. State College, PA: Estreno Plays, 1994.

———. *Parting Gestures* with *A Night in the Subway*. Trans. Phyllis Zatlin. Rev. ed. New Brunswick, NJ: Estreno Plays, 1999.

———. *Wolf Kisses*. Trans. Roxana Silbert. *Spanish Plays*. London: Nick Hern Books, 1999.

Romero, Concha. *A Kiss for a Kiss*. Trans. John Zdziarski. Master's thesis. Rutgers State U, 2000.

———. *Un maldito beso*. *Gestos* 4.8 (1989): 109–144.

Solanas, Charo, ed. *Esencia de mujer. Ocho monólogos de mujeres para mujeres*. Madrid: J. García Verdugo, 1995.

———. *Femenino plural*. Madrid: La Avispa, in press.

Work about

Berardini, Susan P. "El metateatro en las obras de Paloma Pedrero." Diss. State U of New York at Buffalo, 1996.

Estreno. 10.2 (1984). Monographic issue devoted to Spanish women playwrights.

Estreno. 16.1 (1990). Monographic issue devoted to women as playwrights and as dramatic characters.

Estreno. 20.2 (1994). Special emphasis on Concha Romero.

Estreno. 21.1 (1995). Includes cluster on women playwrights.

Estreno. 26.1 (2000). Special emphasis on Itziar Pascual and Yolanda Pallín.

Halsey, Martha T., and Phyllis Zatlin, eds. *Entre actos: Diálogos sobre teatro español entre siglos*. University Park, PA: Estreno, 1999.

Lamartina-Lens, Iride. "Paloma Pedrero." *Spanish Women Writers. A Bio-Bibliographical Source Book*. Ed. Linda Gould Levine, Ellen Engelson Marson and Gloria Feiman Waldman. Westport, CT: Greenwood P, 1993. 389–396.

Nigro, Kirsten, and Phyllis Zatlin, eds. *Un escenario propio / A Stage of Their Own*. Vol. 1. Ottawa: GIROL, 1998.

O'Connor, Patricia W. "Women Playwrights in Contemporary Spain and the Male-Dominated Canon." *Signs* 15.2 (1990): 376–390.

Ragué-Arias, María-José. *El teatro de fin de milenio en España (De 1975 hasta hoy)*. Barcelona: Ariel, 1996.

Witte, Ann. *Guiding the Plot. Politics and Feminism in the Work of Women Playwrights from Spain and Argentina, 1960–1990*. Wor(l)ds of Change 20. New York: Peter Lang, 1996.

Zatlin, Phyllis. "Ana Diosdado." *Spanish Women Writers. A Bio-Bibliographical Source Book*. Ed. Linda Gould Levine, Ellen Engelson Marson, and Gloria Feiman Waldman. Westport, CT: Greenwood P, 1993. 158–166.

Phyllis Zatlin

Dueña

Initially, *dueña* was a title of some respect, used to refer either to a lady-in-waiting or a noblewoman in twelfth- and thirteenth-century society and literature and did not relate to the marital status or age of a woman. As Herdman Marianella observes, by the fourteenth century the *dueñas* of chivalric literature denoted either noblewomen or wives/widows as a group. As a literary type, they became more and more distinguished from *doncellas* (young virgin girls—one of the four legal classifications women fell into in *Alfonso X's *Siete partidas*), the romantically idealized young women who were featured much more prominently than *dueñas* in *novelas de *caballerías* (chivalry novels) and poems.

In her study *"Dueñas" and "Doncellas,"* Herdman Marianella finds that by the late sixteenth-century the meaning of *dueña* has changed markedly, referring exclusively to the (usually widowed) female servant who supervises all other female servants in a household and also watches over the young women in the family. In literature she was now a stock comic figure or a target of satire. Customarily dressed in black with a white headdress (the length of which bore an inverse relationship to her virtue) the stereotypical *dueña* was ugly, gossipy, hypocritically sanctimonious, venal, either sexually hungry or eager to serve as go-between for her young charges, a fertile source of inspiration, and target for the pens of Mateo Alemán, Cervantes (see *Don Quijote), *Quevedo, and other seventeenth-century writers.

Work about

Herdman Marianella, Conchita. *"Dueñas" and "Doncellas": A Study of the "Doña Rodríguez" Episode in "Don Quijote."* Chapel Hill: North Carolina Studies in the Romance Languages and Literatures, 1979.

Maureen Ihrie

Dulcinea del Toboso

Dulcinea del Toboso is a character in Miguel de Cervantes Saavedra's novel *Don Quijote de la Mancha* (Part I, 1605; Part II, 1615). Driven mad by his excessive reading of chivalry romances (*novelas de *caballerías*), Alonso Quijana, the novel's protagonist, determines to become a knight errant and renames himself Don Quijote. Based on the model of knights errant of the *novelas de caballerías*, Don Quijote recognizes the need for a lady to serve and, in a Neoplatonic imaginative frenzy, invents the character of Dulcinea, an ideal woman whose physical and spiritual beauty know no equal. Central to a feminist reading of the novel is the fact that, although quite significant within the context of *Don Quijote*, Dulcinea exists only as a figment of the protagonist's imagination. Therefore, her curious absence (in corporeal terms) denies Dulcinea's subjectivity, since she exists only as the object of Don Quijote's desire.

Despite Dulcinea's physical absence in the text, the character occupies a central role in development of the novel, both thematically and at the level of plot. Dulcinea represents Don Quijote's ideal, not only in terms of the idealized woman but also as a symbol of the virtues for which the protagonist struggles. She is his dream, his motivation, and his escape from the realities of a mundane existence. Dulcinea is spiritual, a sort of religious icon, and Don Quijote's misguided attempts to worship her result in many hilarious, pathetic, and physically destructive encounters with members of society unable (or unwilling) to join the knight errant in his quest for the restoration of the mythical "Age of Gold." It is for the sake of Dulcinea that Don Quijote battles windmills, aids Dorotea/Princess Micomicona, and does penance in Sierra Morena. And in the end, when the protagonist professes to have come to his senses and rejected his folly, it is really Dulcinea that he rejects.

Criticism dealing with Dulcinea tends to analyze the character in terms of her effect on other figures in the novel, often relating the protagonist's conception of his ideal princess to his development as a character. Don Quijote's quest to restore an ideal golden age, a quest symbolized by Dulcinea, has been read nationalistically as the glorification of the best values of Spanish culture and civilization, exemplified in the novel's protagonist. Other readings underscore Don Quijote's changing conception of Dulcinea as a parallel to his psychological development and his rejection of a purely idealistic philosophy. At first, Don Quijote conceives the perfect woman and, even when he is confronted with the reality of the village girl, explains her humble appearance as the work of enchanters. Some assert that gradually

Don Quijote realizes that Dulcinea only exists in his imagination. In an example in Part II, the protagonist insists to Sancho that he has never actually seen her (even though in Part I he asserts that he had seen Dulcinea a few times). Once Don Quijote realizes the incompatibility of his ideal world (represented by Dulcinea) and reality, he gives up his attempts at knight errantry in a sort of deathbed confession. Psychoanalytical approaches underscore Dulcinea as a clever excuse for Don Quijote, who has sworn eternal fidelity to his lady, to avoid contact with real women, such as Maritornes, a prostitute who appears at the inn in Part I, or Altisidora, a maid of the duchess, who appears in Part II. Although such situations are characteristic of chivalric romances, the parodic element of Don Quijote's exaggerated chastity and often mistaken perceptions of romantic pursuit are consistent with the novel's humorous, ironic treatment of literary conventions. From a feminist perspective, these readings clearly posit Dulcinea as a mechanism to expand on or explain Don Quijote's character. Further, her characterization as the literary woman moves her from the particular to the general, making an important commentary on the conventional roles of women in many literary traditions. Dulcinea exists because of and for the sake of Don Quijote, and once his mission is concluded, she disappears from the novel because she is no longer useful.

In similar fashion, Dulcinea's presence/absence also effects change in Sancho's character. Assuredly, the scenes in which Sancho must describe Dulcinea afford him the best opportunities to perfect his talents as a storyteller. In Part I Sancho enumerates the physical characteristics of the village girl Aldonza; his discourse is characteristic of genres traditionally contrasted with idealized fiction and differs considerably from his master's description of Dulcinea. Later, Sancho fails in his mission to deliver a letter to Dulcinea and, once again, must display his ability to manipulate language as he lies to Don Quijote. In Part II, Sancho becomes a key instrument in Dulcinea's disenchantment when, during "Dulcinea's" second apparition (which is really achieved by a male page who plays the role of Dulcinea as part of the duke and duchess's trick), he is instructed to give himself 3,000 lashes to break the spell. In this instance, Sancho's willingness to accept Don Quijote's worldview is underscored by his relationship to Dulcinea as he is symbolically "punished" for having lied to the protagonist.

Other characters also seize the Dulcinea myth in order to manipulate the novel's protagonist. Although without reference to the specific character of Dulcinea, the priest and barber (and later Dorotea) use the image of a beautiful princess in distress to trap Don Quijote into returning to his village. Don Quijote's release of the galley prisoners is due in part to their promise to pay homage to the peerless Dulcinea. In Part II, a page from the ducal palace exhibits his (rather poor) acting skills in a metatheatrical tour de force that underscores the mean-spirited natures of the duke and duchess and ultimately results in Don Quijote's recognition of the incompatibility of his worldview with the brutalities of reality.

A critical examination of Dulcinea would be incomplete without also studying her alter ego, the village girl Aldonza Lorenzo. The name Aldonza is archetypically rustic, as evidenced by popular sayings that characterize women with that name as morally loose and coarse. Exhibiting similar characteristics as the Marqués de *Santillana's (1398–1458) medieval *serranías* (pastoral poems often featuring lascivious country girls) or Juan Ruiz el Arcipreste de Hita's (1283–1350?) *cantigas de serranas* in the *Libro de buen amor*, Sancho describes Aldonza as physically large, hairy, completely unrefined, and quite aggressive. She pitches hay, cares for pigs, and has a voice like thunder. Sancho's description, with picaresque undertones, differs significantly from his master's highly artificial enumeration of Dulcinea's perfect features, each one compared to objects of natural beauty (gold, marble, roses, the sun). Faced with this obvious contradiction to his ideal of Dulcinea, Don Quijote concludes that the transformation must be the work of some evil enchanter and resolves to restore his princess to her former glory.

Additionally, the contrast between Dulcinea and Aldonza is highly gender-inflected. Dulcinea, in Don Quijote's mind, is the ideal of textual Renaissance womanhood: She is beautiful, chaste, and in desperate need of rescue. Aldonza, however, can never equal this princess in any respect: She is ugly, crude, and stronger than most men. In fact, because the village girl does not fit the stereotype, she is portrayed as obviously *unfem*inine, a characterization that suggests that women who cannot or will not conform to conventional gender norms are not really women at all. Nevertheless, the exaggerated characteristics of both Dulcinea and Aldonza may serve to question the binarity of the two poles, complicating extreme and limiting views of women's textual presence. Readers cannot imagine Dulcinea without the image of Aldonza, and Aldonza is always conceived in terms of her relationship as the spiritual, ideal Dulcinea's material Other.

Because of her absence and, paradoxically, her importance in the novel, Dulcinea is a character fraught with ambiguity. On the one hand, both characters' presence emerges through a doubly male-authored discourse. As seventeenth-century Eve figures, Dulcinea and Aldonza exist only as products of the language and imagination of male characters, themselves the creation of a male author. Nevertheless, Cervantes's ironic intertextuality may also have more positive connotations for feminist scholars. Dulcinea (and her double Aldonza) can be read as a parody of Renaissance literature's feminine ideal—as well as its binary opposite—an implicit articulation that women like them, physically and spiritually perfect or rustic to the extreme—simply did (and do) not exist. In order to appreciate the significance of this stance, one must recognize literature as not only reflective but also constitutive of cultural realities. Perhaps, then, Dulcinea as a subversion of the myth of the ideal woman can be understood as a necessary preliminary step toward the development of a healthier, less polarized image of real women.

Work

The Adventures of Don Quijote. Trans. J.M. Cohen. Harmondsworth, Middlesex: Penguin, 1986.
Don Quijote de la Mancha. Ed. Martín de Riquer. 2 vols. Barcelona: Juventud, 1985.

Work about

Efron, Arthur. *Don Quijote and the Dulcineated World.* Austin: U of Texas P, 1971.
El Saffar, Ruth. "In Praise of What Is Left Unsaid: Thoughts on Women and Lack in *Don Quijote*." *Modern Language Notes* 103.2 (1988): 205–222.
Goggio, Emilio. "The Role of Dulcinea in Cervantes's *Don Quijote de la Mancha*." *Modern Language Quarterly* 13 (1952): 285–291.
Herrero, Javier. "Dulcinea and Her Critics." *Cervantes* 2.1 (1982): 23–42.
———. *Who Was Dulcinea?* New Orleans: Graduate School of Tulane U, 1985.
Murillo, Luis. *A Critical Introduction to* Don Quijote. New York: Peter Lang, 1988.
Redondo, Agustín. "Del personaje de Aldonza Lorenzo al de Dulcinea del Toboso: Algunos aspectos de la invención cervantina." *Anales Cervantinos* 21 (1983): 9–22.
Torres, Federico. *Dulcinea del Toboso.* Barcelona: Selección, 1955.

Mindy Badía

Eboli, Princess of, Doña Ana de Mendoza y de la Cerda (1540–1592)

One of the most intriguing figures in the history of Spain is the princess of Eboli, an independent, well-educated woman whose story inspired many fascinating historical and literary works. The princess was born on June 29, 1540, in Cifuentes, a province of Guadalajara, and grew up in Cifuentes and Alcalá. As the only daughter of the prince of Eboli and Mélito, she received an excellent education that included the study of Latin and music. In 1553, at age 12, her parents gave her in marriage to Ruy Gómez de Silva, a Portuguese noble 24 years her senior who was secretary of state to King Philip II. Although she received the title of duchess of Pastrana in 1569, Doña Ana de Mendoza preferred to be called by her original title, princess of Eboli.

In several documents of the day she is described as a small but beautiful woman of pale complexion that contrasted with her dark hair. She seems to have possessed a strong personality, making her more willing to fight than to surrender. Her favorite activities included horseback riding and fencing, and she lost her right eye during a fencing match. In an anonymous print of the period she appears wearing a patch, and it is alleged she was called the one-eyed woman by her friends. Many accused her of being arrogant, domineering, and willful. She was, however, a favorite of Elizabeth of Valois, Philip II's wife. The 14 years spent with Ruy Gómez appear to have been happy ones. She bore him 10 children, 4 of whom died in infancy.

The first great literary work that mentions the princess of Eboli is Santa *Teresa de Avila's *Libro de las fundaciones*. In chapter XVII, Teresa refers to disagreements between the princess and herself regarding foundation of a Carmelite convent in Pastrana. This did not prevent Eboli from later requesting admission to the convent immediately after the death of Ruy Gómez on July 29, 1573. She became Sor Ana de la Madre de Dios. Her brief stay there disrupted the convent's religious life, causing the nuns to abandon Pastrana in 1574. Eboli then returned to her residential palace and remained in Pastrana for three years. In 1577 Philip II requested her presence at court so she could personally supervise her children's education and administer her affairs. In Madrid she met Antonio Pérez, secretary to Philip II and former protégé of Ruy Gómez and perhaps his illegitimate son. Documents of the day describe Pérez as brilliant, ambitious, elegant to a fault, and handsome. He became Eboli's lover. The court, and especially the king, refused to tolerate this relationship once it became overt. Eboli and Pérez lost favor with

Philip II and the consequences were dramatic for each, but more so for the princess. Pérez was a suspect in the murder of Juan de Escobedo, a former close friend of Ruy Gómez and secretary to Don Juan of Austria. It was known that Escobedo had bitterly opposed the liaison between the lovers and had himself brought it to the king's attention. For political and personal motives, Philip II was anxious to get rid of Escobedo, and he apparently used Pérez to achieve his own ends. Eboli vehemently defended herself and Pérez against their enemies and even dared to question the king about the Escobedo affair.

On the night of July 28, 1579, Antonio Pérez and the princess of Eboli were arrested. Eboli disappeared from public life, but Pérez continued to carry out some of his functions as secretary to the Spanish Crown. In 1584, a series of legal proceedings were brought against him. He was accused of corruption but was allowed to defend himself legally. Pérez also pleaded for Eboli's freedom, to no avail. On February 23, 1590, he was tortured, and on April 19 of the same year he managed to escape to Aragon and from there to France and England.

Whereas Pérez was afforded the opportunity to defend himself, from the first night of her arrest Eboli was condemned to life imprisonment without a trial. First she was taken to the Tower of the Pinto, near Madrid, and from there to Santorcaz, an ecclesiastic prison under jurisdiction of the archbishop of Toledo. Although the conditions of her imprisonment were extremely harsh, she continued to petition the king and the court on her own behalf. In 1581 she was taken to her palace in Pastrana, terribly debilitated by then from her long ordeal. Her condition improved. But in 1590, after Pérez made his escape, Philip II ordered that she be even more strictly confined to her quarters. Her imprisonment became unbearable. Loneliness and illness eventually killed her. She died on February 2, 1592, at age 52.

Gaspar Muro, in his *Vida de la princesa de Eboli* (1877), places her in the context of her political and social time and concludes that her haughty rather than submissive attitude toward Philip II made her punishment all the more severe. However, in an earlier depiction of the Spanish Court, *Relación del viaje de España* (1691), Madame d'Aulnoy comments that it was generally believed that Philip II was in love with Eboli and therefore all the more angry that she had taken Pérez as a lover.

Fantasy, legend, and fact all converge in the story of the princess of Eboli. Friedrich Schiller (1759–1805) gave prominent place to the princess in *Don Carlos*. Giuseppe Verdi (1813–1901) presented Eboli as an intriguer in his opera based on Schiller's work. In *La alcaidesa de Pastrana* (1911), Eduardo Marquina (1879–1946) portrays Eboli as an unscrupulous woman. The most positive image of Eboli appears in Kate O'Brien's novel *That Lady* (1985), published in Spanish as *Esa dama* (1986). In this book the character of Eboli is a unique, intelligent, passionate, and rebellious woman. In sum, Eboli's life has been interpreted in many different ways. What is clear is that she was a remarkable woman.

Work about

Aulnoy, Madame d'. *Relación del viaje de España*. Ed. J. García Mercadal. *Viajes de extranjeros por España y Portugal*. Vol. II. Madrid: Aguilar, 1959.

García Mercadal, José. *La princesa de Eboli*. Barcelona: Iberia-Joaquín Gil, 1944.

La princesa de Eboli y Pastrana. Ciclo de Conferencias celebrado en Pastrana en 1992 en el IV Centenario de su muerte. Guadalajara: AACHE Ediciones, 1993.

Marquina, Eduardo. *La alcaidesa de Pastrana. Obras completas*. Madrid: Aguilar, 1944. 1095–1140.

Muro, Gaspar. *Vida de la princesa de Eboli*. Madrid: Librería de D. Mariano Murillo, 1877.

O' Brien, Kate. *Esa dama*. Spanish trans. María José Roseller. Barcelona: Edhasa, 1986.

———. *That Lady*. New York: Penguin Books, 1985.

Pérez, Antonio. *A Spaniard in Elizabethan England. The Correspondence of Antonio Pérez*. Ed. Gustave Ungerer. London: Tamesis, 1974.

Schiller, Friedrich. *Don Carlos Infant von Spanien*.

Werke. München: Droemersche Verlagsanstalt, 1954. 1: 475–633.

Teresa, Santa. *Libro de las fundaciones. Obras completas de Santa Teresa*. Ed. Efrén de la Madre de Dios and Otger Steggink. Madrid: BAC, 1967. 516–628.

Verdi, Giuseppe. *Don Carlo*. Ed. Kurt Pahlen. München: Goldmann, 1985.

Carlota Caulfield

Ecín, María
See Salisachs, Mercedes (1916–)

Education
See Women's Education in Spain: (1860–1993)

Eiximenis, Francesc (1330?–1409): His Views on Women

A Franciscan theologian, born in Gerona and ordained in Barcelona, Francesc Eiximenis is known to have traveled and studied in Valencia, Cologne, Oxford, Toulouse, and Paris, among other cities, settling finally in Valencia in the 1380s at the convent of San Francisco. He was an influential theologian in his time, participating in the complex politics of the Great Western Schism (1378–1417, when up to three popes battled over religious and political power) and acting as adviser to King Juan I (1379–1390), as well as holding other prominent posts. Eiximenis produced many religious and didactic works in Catalan and Latin, writing in an accessible style and using much variety in delivery so as to secure the attention of a readership not ordinarily versed in matters of doctrine. His best-known work is the monumental *Crestiá* (Christian), a compendium initiated in the 1370s. In this unfinished encyclopedic work he proposed to explain and discuss many topics from a Christian standpoint. The first three volumes and the twelfth of the *Crestiá* were completed and offer valuable sources of study for the state and development of medieval Catalan religious and political thought. The *Dotzen Libre del Crestiá* (composed between 1385 and 1386; The Twelfth Book of the Christian) is a discussion of the political theory that would help create the ideal city based largely on St. Augustine (354–430). The *Llibre dels Angels* (1392; Book of the Angels), a simply written, didactic explanation of angels and their cult, is directed at the less learned members of the community. Eiximenis also wrote extensively in Latin, producing a manual for monks to aid them in delivering sermons (the *Ars Praedicandi Populo*, 1384?) and a *Summa Theologica* (1383?) in which he discussed ethical issues pertaining to Christianity.

The particular significance of Eiximenis regarding women has to do with the frequent mentions that he makes of their role for theology and society, principally in his treatise entitled *Llibre de les dones* (1396; The Book of Women), a didactic work whose focus on women centers upon their categorization into five groups: girls, maidens, married women, widows, and virgins devoted to God. The *Terç de Crestiá* (1384; The Third Book of the Christian), an impressive text dealing with a wide range of political, theological, and social issues, also contains a section on the family in which women are frequently mentioned, with references to the types of women deemed unworthy of marriage and family life. These include immoral and loose women as well as those who lead men astray with their irrational desires. In his *Vita Cristi* (composed between 1397 and 1399; Life of Christ), a text on doctrine again aimed at a readership not equipped with sophisticated reading strategies, he attacks the use of *cosmetics as well as the custom of some men to behave like women by adorning themselves excessively. In the *Crestiá* he states explicitly that men and women must dress in such a way as to only reveal their hands and faces. Eiximenis's prolific writings on social, political, and theological topics thus touch on numerous occasions on the question of woman's role in society. He laments in particular the existence of prostitution, procuring, and adultery as obstacles to creation of an ideal society.

The Catalan-language *Llibre de les Dones* is written in the tradition of didactic and theological writing of his time: In this text Eiximenis draws freely on a number of sources that inspired many medieval writers concerned with the issue of woman's place in doctrine and society. Such sources include the Bible, Church Fathers, St. Augustine, St. Thomas Aquinas (1224/1225?–1274), contemporary treatises on women, literary anecdotes on the wiles of women, and Marian literature, among others. The treatise abounds in the customary medieval display of women's vices: vanity, adultery, inferior intelligence, senseless chatter, and sexual immorality. These are exposed by Eiximenis using a variety of stylistic techniques. The author focuses especially on that which he considers excessive behavior in women, namely, their use of cosmetics, adornments, and other instruments that indulge vanity. In the tradition of medieval didacticism aimed at the largest possible readership, the Franciscan makes ample use of anecdotes, *exempla*, satirical images, and narrative fragments to convey moral and doctrinal concerns. In the meantime, he maintains a rigorous theological framework for the treatise and addresses questions of doctrine, virtue, and sin throughout. To ensure the salvation of men, he recommends the avoidance of woman altogether, as well as regular recourse to prayer and contemplation.

The only possibility of salvation that Eiximenis considers for woman exists in her strict adherence to domestic tasks, obedience to men, and the categorical retreat from vanity. Some scholars have argued that Eiximenis cannot be labeled a misogynist writer, for he shows in his plans for the ideal society a marked desire for the salvation of men as well as women. He is not against marriage, for example—as long as it takes place on the basis of strict religious beliefs. Critics have also remarked that the tone used by Eiximenis is by far less harsh than that of his contemporary theologians or subsequent didactic writers such as the archpriest of Talavera (1398?–1482?, author of *Corbacho*), or Juan Luis *Vives (1492–1540), especially in light of the fact that Eiximenis attacks the vanity of men as well. The instructive and educational thrust of his work, aimed at the masses and based on scholastic training, has also been underlined as an element that diminishes the antifeminist stance of his writings.

Rather than quantify the degree of the theologian's *misogyny or lack of it, it is perhaps more useful to contextualize his writings on women and to evaluate the extent to which they represent a characteristic pattern of religious and political thought in his lifetime. As regards his contribution to medieval Catalan didactic writing, there is no doubt that his simple and admirable prose, his management of diverse sources, and his ability to bring together stylistic registers to sustain his readers' interest offer a particularly fine example of medieval thought and the vehicles used to transmit it to the public. At the same time, Eiximenis maintains a strict attitude when discussing women, perceiving them as destructive elements in the creation of an ideal society and therefore in need of rigorous restriction and instruction. His ideas on women betray a strong desire to restrict the scope of their presence and activity as much as possible so that a perfect religious morality may be achieved in society. Eiximenis therefore represents a typical fourteenth-century Franciscan stance regarding the question of women, informed largely by the ideals inherited from past theologians, expressing his ideas in an exceptionally fluid and uncomplicated prose.

In his own lifetime, Eiximenis's writings enjoyed great circulation and fame. After his death, his ideas and style continued to influence those writing in the didactic and religious traditions in Spanish, Latin, and Catalan, as well as some of those hailing from France. *See also* Misogyny in Medieval and Early Modern Spain; Women's Deceits: Medieval Approaches to the Topic.

Work by

Llibre de les dones. Ed. Gracia Lozano López. Madison: Hispanic Seminary of Medieval Studies, 1992. Partial Spanish translation.

Lo libre de les dones. Ed. Frank Naccarato. Barcelona: Curial, 1981. In Catalan.

Work about

Cervera, Luis. *Francisco de Eiximenis y su sociedad urbana ideal*. Madrid: Grupo Editorial Swan, 1989.

Viera, David J. "Francesc Eiximenis, Courtly Love, and the De Amore (I-II)." *Romance Quarterly* 34.3 (1987): 311–316.

———. "The Structure and Division of the *Llibre de les dones* by Francesc Eiximenis." *Josep Maria Solá-Solé: Homage, Homenaje, Homenatge: Miscelánea de estudios de amigos y discípulos*. Ed. Victorio Aguera and Nathaniel B. Smith. Barcelona: Puvill, 1984.

Viera, David J., and Jordi Piqué. *La dona en Francesc Eiximenis*. Barcelona: Curial, 1987.

Leyla Rouhi

Encierro

The desire to delimit and control spaces and spheres of activity that subordinant cultural groups occupy has been a constant theme of human behavior. With respect to women, the discourse of *encierro* (enclosure) has determined women's roles in secular and religious realms, operating on physical, spatial, and spiritual levels. In medieval and Golden Age Spain, female enclosure translated to a locked house (convent, family home, harem or brothel), marriage, a sexually closed, chaste body (except for purposes of procreation with one's husband), and a closed mouth. In the religious context, where claustration is used to secure a spiritual space free of worldly distractions, it has always formed part of the monastic life for both men and women. Nonetheless, as Schulenberg shows, enclosure has been regulated much more strictly for women religious because the reasons used to recommend enclosure of women in general applied to nuns in convents as well. Three main justifications for claustration were given. The first, most vital motive was protection of a woman's virginity. This extended to include the preservation of untainted lineage and family honor or, in the case of a nun, protection of a Bride of Christ. A second stated benefit of enclosure was to protect women from worldly temptations or influences. Since woman, as the inferior sex, was understood to be dominated by emotions rather than the (superior) reason that guided male behavior, she easily could unwittingly succumb to carnal lust or even be tripped up by curiosity. A final reason for *encierro* was to keep women from tempting men, revealing an underlying fear of the (diabolical) power women might exert over men.

Church fathers and officials from the Middle Ages on defined enclosure as the appropriate condition for all women and warned of the dangers that ensued when women were let loose. Luis *Vives (1492–1540), Luis de *León (1527–1591), and other moralists admonished women, single and married, to be industrious, obedient, cheerful, and silent within the home. In general terms, *encierro* prevented women from attaining autonomy, keeping them legally and economically dependent on men. For women in convents, however, enclosure did afford nuns greater liberty, for they enjoyed freedom from childbirth, rearing a family, and managing household responsibilities and properties, and they possessed greater opportunity to read, study, and conduct their lives without the constant supervision of males, despite the control of male confessors. María de *Zayas's (1590–after 167?) "La fuerza del amor" (The Strength of Love) dramatizes the powerlessness of women in society as they are passed from the house and control of a father to that of a husband. At the conclusion of the work, protagonist Laura, a beautiful young noblewoman who has been brutally abused by her husband, opts to enter a convent rather than return to her contrite spouse, stating that Christ will surely be a more pleasing lover.

Perry has studied women's situation in

sixteenth-century Seville, where the exodus of men to the New World, a growing economy, and an expanding city population combined to create a need for more labor and consequently an unusual number of opportunities for women to work. She argues persuasively that as the city grew and changed, the Church and government perceived a growing lack of order in the city. Attributing it to a failure to adequately control the female populace, they then collaborated in using tactics and justifications of enclosure to curtail any growth of power for women as their participation in society became increasingly visible. Women were defined as "good" or "bad" on the basis of their sexual availability to men and then confined either in the convent, the home, or in municipally sponsored, male-administered brothels. As Perry concludes, these definitions of women's ordained spheres of activity endure to this day.

The discourse of enclosure that society maintained is reflected in many works of literature. Enclosure as a fact of life delimited locations of feasible chance encounters between male and female characters to churches (or streets traveled to and from mass), gardens in the woman's home, conversations from a window, public festivals, and so on. Appropriate and inappropriate physical venues for a "good" woman were also used to define female characters. In her study of Lope de *Vega's honor plays, Yarbro-Bejarano finds that some works uphold or idealize women characters who comply with enclosure, but others feature characters who resist or escape such confines, most notably by cross-dressing. The less-than-effective cloistering of some nuns is another recurring topic, seen in the miracle of the pregnant abbess in Berceo's (c.1196–c. 1260?) *Milagros de nuestra señora* (Miracles of Our Lady), mocked in Juan Ruiz's (1283?–1351?) *Libro de buen amor* (Book of Good Love), and ridiculed in *Quevedo's (1580–1645) *Buscón*. Probably the most memorable treatment of enclosure is found in Cervantes's (1547–1616) ironic, brilliant lampoon in "El celoso extremeño" (The Jealous Extremaduran), which narrates the outlandish, exaggerated attempts of an aging husband to enclose his ingenuous young bride. *See also Ángel del hogar*

Work about

Cervantes, Miguel de. "El celoso extremeño." *Novelas ejemplares II*. Ed. Juan Bautista Avalle-Arce. Madrid: Castalia, 1982.

Perry, Mary Elizabeth. *Gender and Disorder in Early Modern Seville*. Princeton, NJ: Princeton UP, 1990.

Quevedo, Francisco de. *Vida del buscón*. Ed. Domingo Induraín. Madrid: Cátedra, 1981.

Schulenberg, Jane Tibbens. "Strict Active Enclosure and Its Effects on the Female Monastic Experience (ca. 500–1100)." *Medieval Religious Women I. Distant Echoes*. Ed. John Nichols and Lillian Thomas Shank. Kalamazoo: Cistercian, 1984. 51–86.

Wright, Chad C. " 'Un millón de ojos': Visión, vigilancia y encierro en *Doña Perfecta*: Actas del Simposio Centenario de *Fortunata y Jacinta*." *Textos y contextos de Galdós*. Ed. John W. Kronik and Harriet S. Turner. Madrid: Castalia, 1994. 151–156.

Yarbro-Bejarano, Yvonne. *Feminism and the Honor Plays of Lope de Vega*. West Lafayette, IN: Purdue UP, 1994.

Maureen Ihrie

Enclosure
See Encierro

Enríquez de Guzmán, Feliciana (late sixteenth–early seventeenth centuries)

In her day, Feliciana Enríquez de Guzmán was a well-known poet and playwright. She married twice: Her first husband was Cristóbal Ponce de Solís, and her second one, Francisco de Leon Garavito. By 1630 she was widowed for the second time and administering a chaplaincy left to her by her first husband. Despite these details, Enríquez's identity has not been conclusively established. Critics refer to a legend, quoted in Lope de *Vega's (1562–1635) *Laurel de Apolo*, that suggests that Enríquez was a daring *aventurera* (adventuress) who attended the University of Salamanca and, dressed as a man, broke many a woman's heart. Eventually, she fell in love. Jealousy forced her to put aside her disguise and admit her real sex. Serrano questions whether this woman and the writer are the same person.

Enríquez's only surviving work is *Tragicomedia de los jardines y campos sabeos* (Tragicomedy of the Sabean Gardens and Fields), a text composed of a Prologue, two parts (with one *tragicomedia* in each), 10 *coros* (choruses), four *entreactos* (interludes), and a *carta ejecutoria* (letter patent of nobility). The first part is dedicated to her sisters Carlota and Magdalena, nuns in a Seville convent, and the second to her husband Garavito. Some critics consider Maya and Clarisel, the lovers of the second part, to be doubles of Enríquez and Garavito.

Certain sections of her verse "Prologue" have been published under the title "Censura las antiguas comedias españolas" (Censure the Traditional Spanish Plays). This text, as well as the *carta ejecutoria*, unequivocally establish Enríquez's esthetics as opposing Lope's *Arte nuevo* and favoring the classical tradition. She strongly defends Aristotelian rules and brags of the laurels won by her classical plays. Enríquez's open challenge to the male-dominated theatrical conventions of the *comedia* reveals a strong woman, one who may well have had the daring to dress as a man in order to gain access to a university education.

In addition to her plays, Enríquez wrote lyric poems. Critics single out her *madrigal* "El sueño de Gelita" (Gelita's Dream), her *décima* "Las doncellas de Simancas" (The Damsels of Simancas), and her sonnet "Las bodas de Maya y Clarisel" (Maya and Clarisel's Wedding).

Work by

Segunda parte de la Tragicomedia los jardines y campos sabeos. . . . In *Women's Acts*. Ed. Teresa S. Soufas. Lexington: UP of Kentucky, 1997.

Tragicomedia de los jardines y campos sabeos. 1st Part. Coimbra: Iacome Caruallo, 1624; 2nd Part. Lisbon: Pedro Crasbeeck, 1624.

Work about

Castro, Adolfo de. "Feliciana Enríquez de Guzmán." *El Conde-Duque de Olivares y el Rey Felipe IV*. Cádiz: Vicente Caruana, 1906. 14–20.

Serrano y Sanz, Manuel. *Apuntes para una biblioteca de escritoras españolas desde el año 1401 al 1833*. 2 vols. Madrid: Rivadeneyra, 1903.

Soufas, Teresa Scott. *Dramas of Distinction: A Study of Plays by Golden Age Women*. Lexington: UP of Kentucky, 1997. 147–168.

María A. Salgado

Epístolas familiares
See Guevara, Antonio de (1481?–1545): Women's Roles in the *Epístolas familiares*

Erauso, Catalina de (1578?/1585?/1592?–after 1630)

The reputed autobiography of this remarkable female transvestite, published as *Historia de la monja alférez, doña Catalina de Erauso, escrita por ella misma* (1829; Story of the Nun-Ensign, doña Catalina de Erauso, Written by Her), was in the nineteenth and early twentieth century judged to be pure fantasy. Numerous historical documents, however, prove solidly that Catalina de Erauso, the *monja alférez*, did accomplish the majority of feats recounted in her life story. Because the narrative also contains some unverifiable, fanciful incidents, a few anachronisms, and errors, earlier critics such as Serrano y Sanz and Menéndez y Pelayo rejected it out of hand as apocryphal. Vallbona suggests that the oldest surviving manuscript was composed either by someone who had read her original (lost) manuscript and refashioned it or by an amanuensis informed orally by Erauso about her life, who then embellished the tale.

The solid facts structuring the autobiography include the following: Born in the Basque village of San Sebastián, at age 4 she was placed in a Dominican convent to be reared. At age 15, shortly before taking final vows as a novitiate, she fled the convent, immediately cut up her convent garments, sewed male clothes out of them, sheared off her hair, and began presenting herself as a male. After three years of wandering in Spain, supporting herself in various servant capacities, in 1603 she sailed to the New World and for the next 17 years lived the life of an itinerant soldier in Peru. Using the pseudonym Alonso Díaz Ramírez de Guzmán, she received promotions and commendations for her bravery in battle against the Araucan Indians in Chile. Both the autobiography and independent secondary sources of the period attest to Erauso's aggressive, volatile nature, her penchant for gambling, fighting, killing without remorse, her numerous stays in jail, and also a few flirtatious, suggestive encounters with women. Finally, in 1620, in yet another desperate clash with the law in Peru, a local bishop suddenly appeared outside his palace, offering refuge, if she would lay down her arms. She did so, the bishop protected her, and the following day Erauso revealed herself as a woman and virgin to her protector. From there, she returned to Spain and in 1626 requested and was granted a yearly stipend from King Philip IV. Then she traveled to Rome, meeting with Pope Urban VIII and obtaining permission to wear male attire and change her name. Both in Madrid and Rome (where the autobiography ends), the novelty of her story and condition made her an overnight sensation. Adopting the name of Antonio de Erauso, she returned to Mexico, began working as a muleteer, and disappeared into history.

Garber notes that unlike England, where young male actors routinely played female roles in the theater, or Venice, where courtesans and prostitutes often wore male attire, in Counterreformation Spain female cross-dressing was repeatedly banned, in 1600, 1608, 1615, and 1642. Homosexual activity was punishable by the death penalty. Certainly Erauso's virgin state was a determining factor in her attainment of celebrity and permission to move freely. Her audacious rejection of established roles—of "female" dress, behavior, and occupation, of "gentlemanly" behavior for a male, and of the celebrity her notoriety provoked in urban environments of Seville, Madrid, and Naples, served as inspiration for a number of literary works, most notably the play *La Monja Alférez* (1626?), traditionally attributed to Juan Pérez de Montalbán but recently demonstrated to be by Luis Belmonte Bermúdez. *See also* Lesbianism in Early Modern Spanish Literature: 1500–1700

Work by

Lieutenant Nun. Memoir of a Basque Transvestite in the New World. Trans. Michele Stepto and Gabriel Stepto. Foreword M. Garber. Boston: Beacon, 1996.

Vida i sucesos de la monja alferes. Autobiografía atribuida a Doña Catalina de Erauso. Ed., intro., and notes Rima de Vallbona. Tempe, AZ: Center for Latin American Studies, Arizona State U, 1992.

Work about

Martin, Adrienne L. "Desnudo de una travestí: O, La 'Autobiografía' de Catalina de Erauso." *Actas Irvine-92.* Ed. Juan Villegas. Irvine: U of California P, 1994. vol. 2. 34–41.

Vélez, Irma. "Vida y sucesos de la Monja Alférez: Un caso de travestismo sexual y textual." *La seducción de la escritura: Los discursos de la cultura hoy, 1996.* Ed. Rosaura Hernández Monroy and Manuel F. Medina. Mexico: n.p., 1997. 391–401.

Maureen Ihrie

Eroticism in Contemporary Spanish Women Writers' Narrative

In the process of transition from the Francoist dictatorship to a system of democratic government, Spain experienced significant transformations in political, economic, social, and cultural areas. Relaxation of sexual moral codes provided the impetus for one of the most popular of these changes. Crucial factors that affected the modification of sexual attitudes include the influence of tourism in the 1960s and 1970s, the government's tendency toward greater openness after Franco died, and Catholicism's increasing loss of influence in Spanish society. *El destape* (the undressing) became the term that defines the inauguration of this new epoch in Spain's history. It refers to the profusion of images of naked bodies in the press, theater, cinema, and television from 1975 to 1976. All these circumstances contributed to an increased production of erotic literature, a genre that had been severely censored during the dictatorship.

In *La represión sexual en la España de Franco* (1977), Alonso Tejada divides this period into two main parts: "the epoch of autarchy" (1936–1956) and "the Spain of development" (1957–1975). During "the epoch of autarchy," the values of "national Catholicism" were strictly dictated and imposed on the population. The old Civil Code from 1889 was reinstated, with clearly *machista* (male-exalting) and misogynist laws. Civil marriage, divorce, and coeducation (all established during the Second Republic) were abolished. In 1938, the "40 Orden de la Junta de Burgos" was decreed. It prohibited "pornographic," "socialist," "communist," "libertarian," and in general, "corrupting" literature. Consequently, a strong apparatus of censorship was established to control the mass media, literature, cinema, and theater. Following Catholic morals, sex was proscribed as an "abominable infringement of the law of God." In the 1950s the Comisión Episcopal de Ortodoxia y Moralidad promulgated the *Normas de decencia cristiana* (Norms of Christian Decency), establishing austere codes of decency in dress, sexual conduct, courtship, and so on. Close dancing was condemned as a grievous mortal sin inspired by Satan. The norms and discourse of Francoist ideology concerning women attest to an extremely sexist concept of woman as slave. Females were raised to be submissive to males and to accept their lot in life with resignation. The primary goal of a woman was to marry, and her ideal purpose in life was to procreate, to be a mother, to raise her children according to the government's ideology, and to give comfort to her husband. Her place was the home. Concerning sexual morality and love relationships, a woman had to adopt a passive role. Virginity was her supreme virtue, even though she also was responsible for controlling her husband's extramarital affairs. Otherwise, men's concupiscence could threaten the institution of the family, the basis of the Francoist hierarchical system.

During the "Spain of development" epoch, censorship of sexual matters begins to ease somewhat, though in an arbitrary and haphazard manner, due to economic and political opportunism (i.e., to avoid irritating international public opinion). Tejada states that because greater sexual openness was provoked by economic and tourist pressure, it was a feigned openness, and there was in fact no deep transformation in ideas, education, or cultural and legislative structures from 1957 to 1975. Then, when Franco died, Spain experienced the famous "undressing." Sexual attitudes were liberalized, but great contradictions still existed as new codes were implemented. For instance, some magazines would still suddenly be banned by the government.

Spanish sexual liberation was therefore based on profit-oriented principles. What really mattered was the new market opportunity to sell (and exploit) images of the naked body. Even the concept of sexual liberation as mere spectacle (the exhibition of sexual parts) reflects its banal and typically folkloric character. Likewise, the fact that it was the image of naked *women* that was marketed demonstrates its sexist nature. Tejada concludes that in the *destape* of Spain there was no fundamental change in mentality, and it will take time for Spanish society to integrate sex in an enriching way, as a source of dynamism and personal liberation, without pejorative connotations. Behind the superficial image of *destape*, many taboos, prejudices, and much coercion remained hidden, and Spanish society must begin to deal with these attitudes before conquering new frontiers of tolerance and permissiveness. The problem, as Tejada understands it, resides in the fact that Spain went from an era of compulsory repression of sex to an era of compulsive sex, without any clarification that a personal and collective catharsis of old attitudes would provide.

Notwithstanding, one of the most important contributions in the sexual awakening in the field of literature was that of Beatriz de Moura, editor of Tusquets publishing house. In 1978 she created the erotic collection "La sonrisa vertical" (The Vertical Smile). The following year, an annual prize of the same name was established. This award has contributed to the dissemination of works of renowned figures in contemporary Spanish literature, among whom there are several women writers. As a result of more open sexual attitudes combined with advances of the women's movement in Spain, Spanish women writers have entered the field of erotic literature. Women writers have begun to examine their position of marginalization in the sexual arena and break with limiting stereotypes and sexist prejudices typical of traditional sexist ideology. In their writings, they are abolishing old taboos, questioning patriarchal myths about women's sexuality, and presenting women protagonists who do not respond to traditional precepts. It is instructive to contrast the previous, prohibitive national-Catholic axiom about women's sexual pleasure (that women who enjoy themselves or flirt are traitors to their country and their faith and despicable to all others) contrasts strikingly with the capacity for sexual enjoyment seen in Marta, protagonist of María Jaén's *Amorrada al piló* (the narrator explains that "she really loved to fuck"). Other ideas reflected through women protagonists that subvert sexist stereotypes include: Women take the initiative in sexual relationships, negating the idea of passivity; women have sexual fantasies; women are moved by physical attraction or pure sexual instinct rather than sentimentalism alone; the clitoris is an organ of pleasure, marking the self-sufficiency of women in the erotic arena (and the possibility of dispensing with the phallus); lesbian relationships are revealed as erotic; some protagonists in heterosexual relationships prefer sadistic and masochistic practices, breaking with the idea that women in love relationships only desire harmony. Finally, and most radically, men are sometimes presented as "sexual objects," and the taboo topic of male impotence is explored.

Women writers have incorporated the erotic in their works in several different ways. Among some of the first to introduce an important erotic element in their writings are Rosa *Chacel (1898–1994), Esther *Tusquets (1936–), Ana María *Moix (1947–), Carme Riera (1948–), and Rosa *Montero (1951–). In their works the erotic strain represents one more essential facet of the protagonists' lives. What makes their writing different from the erotic literary production of younger authors is that, in the latter, sex constitutes the central axis in the story.

Other writers such as Consuelo *García (1935–) and Marta *Portal (1930–) pursue an intellectual questioning of changes in sexual attitudes in democratic Spain and how they have affected women. *Un espacio erótico* (1983; An Erotic Space), by Portal, portrays the protagonist's search for identity and her wish to find a harmonious erotic space. The description of thoughts, remembrances, conversations, and numerous moral and philosophical considerations gives the work a serious intellectual tone. Elvira has lost her political and religious faith and faces existential disappointment due to her life experiences and her constant practice of self-analysis. Sexual instinct becomes the only force that can bring a sense of surprise to her life. In this novel, different types of love and sexual relationships are analyzed through the protagonist's ordeals. In Mexico, she divorces a Mexican man, and in her native Spain, she has an affair with a younger man, then with her female cousin. In presenting the relationship with her husband, the author explores the pattern of sexual degradation and humiliation to which an abusive *machista* (male-exalting) man subjects his wife. Because her husband is unfaithful and has almost destroyed her, Elvira questions the validity of marriage as a sacrament. As the protagonist analyzes her inability to act effectively in that past situation of oppression, she realizes that her liberation was impossible because she had assumed a fatalistic "it's my destiny" attitude and let herself succumb to a comfortable masochism. One day, however, after another violent attack by her husband (he kills her dog), she becomes acutely aware of her situation and decides to divorce him, breaking with the debasement, impotence, and absurdity of her life with him. In her new relationships in Spain she also feels hurt and disappointed. Thus, at the end of the novel she formulates her idea of avoiding the suffering brought about by human relationships. In a pessimistic, almost autistic tone, but also as a mechanism of survival, Elvira wishes that everyone and everything would cease to exist, leaving only herself.

A third group is formed by narrators such as Ana *Rossetti (1950–), Almudena *Grandes (1960–), Mercedes *Abad (1961–), and María Jaén (1962–). In their works eroticism has a priority above other preoccupations and stands as the central impulse in the protagonists' lives, around which everything else revolves. The erotic material is therefore much more explicit and the sexual practices are more unconventional, diverse, and eccentric. Abad, Grandes, and Rossetti each won the erotic literature prize, "The Vertical Smile," in 1986, 1989, and 1991, respectively.

An important aspect of these writers is that only Jaén describes celebratory aspects of eroticism. In *Amorrada al piló* (1986), a Catalan novel translated into Spanish as *El escote* (Low Neckline), the protagonist is a young woman with a fulfilling professional, emotional, and sexual life. She works as an announcer in her radio program *L'escot*, where she is in charge of the music and erotic scripts. This novel provides two levels of contention in relation to a woman's role in sexual relationships. On one level, the novel represents an obvious reply to "the official morality" established by the Catholic Church and the Francoist government in relation to sex. There is a questioning of precepts of the fascist national-Catholic ideology that affected Spanish society in general and women in particular. At a deeper level, the novel unmasks implicitly sexist ideas found in any patriarchal system, bringing to light prejudices and intolerant attitudes that limit women and reduce their possibilities of action and choice in the erotic field. This novel celebrates the effects of women's sexual liberation, understood as acquisition of a new capacity for autonomy, decision, and action in sexual relationships.

In the other three writers, sex is closely related to death; a disenchanted vision of eroticism is reflected in descriptions of the alienating effects of sex. The prevailing conception is that of an abyss toward which the protagonists are drawn, as violence, degradation, and dehumanization recur in these novels and short stories. The book of short stories *Alevosías* (1991; Treacheries) by Rossetti explores everyday sexual and love relationships. These are characterized by resentment, betrayals, and violence. Rossetti, who has also written several books of erotic poetry, uses a highly poetic language in her narrative, breaking with the commercial stereotype of an enthusiastic, successful sexuality. She presents pathological cases such as sexual complexes, impotence, dependence on prostitutes, and an inability to enjoy sex if it is not engaged in with surrogates (such as those found in sex shops). Another field of investigation that appears in these short stories is related to Catholicism and the effects of its teachings regarding sex. Catholic morality fosters deep tensions, frustrations, and traumas in the psychology of the protagonists, functioning as a repressive and inhibiting force that brings about pathological cases driven to tragic ends. Only an innocent child, in the story "El diablo y sus hazañas" (The Devil and His Feats), manages to escape the influence of religion, thanks to the fact that he interprets the religious symbols from his childish view, to his own advantage. In the heterosexual relationships portrayed, men are not up to the task. Instead, they have affairs with other people, suffer some kind of sexual impotence, or are unable to establish a deep and committed relationship within their partnership. Women, who consider themselves betrayed, hope then to establish a certain sense of justice through vengeance. In homosexual relationships, endings are also devastating and accompanied by an exploration of sadistic and masochistic tendencies.

Still another group of writers, including Paloma *Díaz–Mas (1954–), Marina *Mayoral (1942–) and Lourdes *Ortiz (1943–), experiments in the field of erotic literature with a ludicrous and parodied intention, typical of postmodernism. Some of Carme Riera and Mercedes Abad's writings can also be included in this category. In these short stories, thought of as an intellectual game, intertextuality is a main feature. Through varying techniques and narrative playfulness, the writers deconstruct different discourses related to women's sexuality in order to question and demystify oppressive stereotypes, codes, and categories of rhetoric. Several of these short stories can be found in the anthology of contemporary women writers, *Relatos eróticos* (1990) (Erotic Short Stories), edited by the "Instituto de la mujer."

In "La discreta pecadora, o ejemplo de doncellas recogidas" (The Discreet Sinner or a Model of Modest Maidens) by Díaz-Mas, written in the Golden Age style, a prudish young maiden whose parents are overly protective spends her days reading the stories of women saints. She decides then, in quixotic fashion, to imitate the life of such saints as María Magdalena and María Egipciaca, for she is amazed by their conversions to the true faith, after leading lives of fornication and sins against nature. So she chooses to go on a search of erotic debasement; unfortunately, the men she approaches react with incredulity to her sexual offerings and flee from her. In the end, as she lies on the beach, a pirate boat arrives and the captain falls in love with her. She then decides to abandon her previous exploits and converts to Islam, since her future husband belongs to this religion. As Pérez points out, this constitutes a parodied inversion of hagiography, of Golden Age *literatura ejemplar* (cautionary literature), the quixotic character, the Moorish novel, the *novela rosa* (romance), and even the erotic genre, because the author also subverts reader expectations in this field.

In "En los parques, al anochecer" (In the Parks, at Night) by Mayoral, the president of the women's Catholic Action Association asks the town teacher to write her autobiography as a lesson to their daughters, as an homage to her, for she is retiring. The protagonist, who narrates her story in the first person, thinks that it's better if she doesn't provide them with the story of her life. Dead of boredom and the routine of her life as a single woman, she anxiously awaits the holidays, which afford her the opportunity to practice a new language and be sexually harassed by virile, violent men with whom she makes love in the parks at night. Apart from the parody of the cautionary short story, this story subverts two important stereotypes about women's sexual nature. First, men become the "sexual objects" because the woman seeks them out and chooses them simply for sexual intercourse, and second, the notion that it is impossible for women to separate love from sex is refuted. The protagonist explains very clearly that she does not pursue men for emotional involvement, for understanding, or for spiritual or intellectual company. What she really craves is pure, mutual sexual satisfaction in its basic form of two bodies in "complete fight and total possession."

In her short story "Alicia," Ortiz describes a friendship and sexual relationship between a man and a girl, narrated from the perspective of the innocent child. She has fun with her friend, but she sometimes feels afraid, seeing how he transforms himself from Humpty Dumpty into the Cheshire Cat. The story illustrates how the man takes advantage of the girl's innocence and manipulates her to obtain sexual favors. The story's intertextual reference to Lewis Carroll's *Alice in Wonderland* provides an implicit accusation of Carroll's pederasty.

In Riera's *Epitelis tendríssims* (1981; Very Tender Epitheliums), humorously erotic, intranscendent, and amusingly absurd stories predominate. Riera plays with reader expectations to create an effect of surprise. Story endings often reflect the idea of a "deserved reward," which brings about ironic, humorous twists. The objects that can arouse sexual pleasure multiply. For instance, in "Mr. Flower, un savi botanic" (Mr. Flower, a Wise Botanist) the protagonist experiences passion and sexual intercourse with a cauliflower, and in "Estimat Thomas" (Dear Thomas) the protagonist feels sexually excited and writes love letters to a dog. The last story, "Josep Luis Jacotot agonitza," however, differs from all the others in tone and intention. This story denounces the sexual abuse of a little girl by her grandfather, with the approval of the girl's father, who does not want to lose the fortune in his own father's will.

A prevailing tendency in the foregoing stories by contemporary Spanish women writers is the impossibility of fulfilling experiences in sexual and love relationships between a man and a woman. The few relationships that work (and only for a short period of time) are between women, often described in highly poetic language. However, the lesbian relationships portrayed lack the possibility of a future. The plot pattern that recurs is one of a harmonious relationship between two women, which in the end is hindered by the influence of the social environment. The intervention of a masculine figure and the indecision of one protagonist in breaking with convention and dealing with society's marginalization constitute two key discouraging factors. The happiness that is found is intense but precarious because it is only temporary. Having said this, there are also cases that describe conflicting factors between the two women in the couple such as the drive for power and the wish to control the partner in the relationship. This parameter of conduct breaks with the concept of the lesbian relationship as a safe haven or panacea for women.

Spanish women writers thus have fully entered the field of erotic literature and begun to explore sexuality on their own terms. These works represent an undeniably significant achievement: They assert the validity of women's sexual will and imagination. By means of their literary works, women authors contribute to the continuing debate of the sexual dialectic in Spanish and Western culture.

Work by

Abad, Mercedes. *Ligeros libertinajes sabáticos*. Barcelona: Tusquets, "La Sonrisa Vertical," 1991.

Chacel, Rosa. *Acrópolis*. Barcelona: Seix Barral, 1984.

———. *Barrio de las maravillas*. Barcelona: Seix Barral, 1976.

———. *Ciencias naturales*. Barcelona: Seix Barral, 1988.

———. *Memorias de Leticia Valle*. Buenos Aires: Emecé, 1946.

———. *La sinrazón*. Buenos Aires: Losada, 1960.

García, Consuelo. *Luis en el país de las maravillas*. Barcelona: Lumen, 1984.

Grandes, Almudena. *Las edades de Lulú*. Barcelona: Tusquets, "La Sonrisa Vertical," 1992.

Jaén, María. *Amorrada al piló*. Barcelona: Columna, 1986.

Moix, Ana María. *Ese chico pelirrojo a quien veo cada día*. Barcelona: Lumen, 1971.

———. *Julia*. Barcelona: Seix Barral, 1970.

———. *Las virtudes peligrosas*. Barcelona: Plaza y Janés, 1985.

———. *Walter ¿por qué te fuiste?*. Barcelona: Barral, 1973.

Montero, Rosa. *Crónica del desamor.* Madrid: Debate, 1979.

———. *Te trataré como a una reina.* Barcelona: Seix Barral, 1983.

Portal, Marta. *Un espacio erótico.* Madrid: Ibérico Europea de Ediciones, 1983.

Relatos eróticos. Madrid: Castalia, Instituto de la mujer, 1990.

Riera, Carme. *Epitelis tendríssims.* Barcelona: Ed. 62, 1981.

———. *Jo pos per testimoni les gavines.* Barcelona: Laia, 1977.

———. *Te deix, amor, la mar com a penyora.* Barcelona: Laia, 1975.

Rossetti, Ana. *Alevosías.* Barcelona: Tusquets, "La Sonrisa Vertical," 1991.

Tusquets, Esther. *El amor es un juego solitario.* Barcelona: Lumen, 1982.

———. *El mismo mar de todos los veranos.* Barcelona: Lumen, 1979.

———. "Olivia." *Revista Litoral.* Madrid: Visor Libros, 1986.

———. *Varada trás el último naufragio.* Barcelona: Lumen, 1980.

Work about

Pérez, Janet and Genaro J. Pérez. "Hispanic Marginal Literatures: The Erotic, the Comics, Novela Rosa." *Monographic Review/Revista Monográfica* 7(1991): 9–22.

Tejada, Alonso. *La represión sexual en la España de Franco.* Barcelona: Luis de Caralt, 1977.

Valls, Fernando. "La literatura erótica en España entre 1975 y 1990." *Insula* (February 1991): 29–30.

Eva Legido-Quigley

Escolano, Mercedes (1964–)

Born in Cádiz in southernmost Spain on February 15, Mercedes Escolano belongs to the present generation of younger women poets. Although Cádiz, like Seville and Granada, has a long poetic tradition, Escolano has competed successfully, despite her youth, garnering several prizes. She received the master's degree in Spanish literature, then prepared to take the government examinations for professional librarians, as poets do not live by the pen.

Escolano described her first book, *Marejada* (1982; Undercurrent) as a "secret diary"; in fact, its underlying theme (as suggested by the title) appears to be the lure of the sea and the siren call of love. Both love and the sea, motifs of many Escolano works, acquire further importance in *Las bacantes* (1984; Women Worshippers of Bacchus). Death appears as a third major theme; Eros and Thanatos combine with the sea, a traditional thematic trio that becomes a constant in future collections, as seen in *Antinomia* (1987; Antinomy). In this third book, the poet invokes varied classical references, including the homosexual as a classical motif. Larger metaphysical issues and a transcendent quest motif in Escolano's poetry are characteristic of post-1970s poets, who reject their immediate predecessors, the "social poets" of the 1950s and 1960s, looking backward to the later poetry of Juan Ramón *Jiménez and his search for essence.

In *La almadraba* (1986; Tuna Trap) and *Felina calma y oleaje* (1986; Feline Calm and Surf), both of whose titles continue the maritime allusions, Escolano reiterates the association between love and death, symbolized by the sea, indulging her generation's predilection for classical tradition by playing the game of Eros, using maritime imagery (fishing in particular) to depict flirtation, courting, and the process of seduction and final disintegration of romance. The nontraditional element here is Escolano's feminine persona, an active erotic predator seeking a mate. Like Ana *Rossetti and other young women poets of her generation, Escolano is noteworthy for her innovative (sometimes explicit, sometimes playful, sometimes ironic) erotic discourse. The theme of death reasserts itself in *Paseo por el cementerio inglés* (1987; Stroll Through the English Cemetery); this graveyard in Cádiz is noteworthy as the first civil cemetery authorized in Spain, where Protestants and other "nonbelievers" (non-Catholics) could be buried rather than being dumped in the sea.

Escolano suppresses most punctuation, employs often difficult imagery, and invokes the reader's participation. Intertextual allusions abound, ranging from Homer through medieval balladry and Jorge Manrique to a host of modern and contemporary writers both Spanish (Antonio Machado, Luis Cernuda, Esther *Tusquets) and foreign (e.g., Marcel Proust, Robert Louis Stevenson, Herman Melville, and many more). She stresses style and seeks formal perfection, employing rhetorical devices carefully chosen to create rhythmic patterns reminiscent of the waves, fusing form and content to mimic the sea so much in evidence throughout her work. She has won the Poema Joven prize for young poets (Elche, 1981, for *Marejada*); and the same prize a second time (1984) for *Las bacantes*; the University of Cádiz prize (1985) for *La almadraba*; and the Luis de Góngora prize (Cordoba, 1986) for *Felina calma y oleaje*. Her work has been anthologized by Ramón Buenaventura in his anthology of young women poets, *Las Diosas Blancas: Antología de la joven poesía escrita por mujeres* (1985); and by Lorenzo Saval and J. García Gallego in *Litoral femenino: Literatura escrita por mujeres en la España contemporánea* (1986).

Work by

Las bacantes. Madrid: Catoblepas, 1984.
Felina calma y oleaje 1983–1985. Cordoba: Exma. Diputación Provincial, 1986.

Work about

Naharro Calderón, José María. "El cuerpo marino de la poesía de Mercedes Escolano." *Canción de Marcela: Mujer y cultura en el mundo hispánico*. Ed. David Valjalo. Madrid: Orígenes, 1989. 73–87.
———. "Tradición marina y modernidad erótica en la poesía de Mercedes Escolano..." *La escritora hispánica*. Ed. Nora Erro Orthmann and Juan Cruz Mendizábal. Miami: Universal, 1990. 131–143.

Janet Pérez

Espinosa, Juan de
See *Diálogo en laude de las mugeres* (1580)

Espronceda, José de (1808–1842): His Portrayal of Women

The most important poet of his generation, José de Espronceda's work epitomizes Spanish Romanticism with its extreme idealization and debasement of women. Espronceda develops an extensive network of metaphors relating to the natural world—flowers, the sun, the wind—that will dominate both contemporary and subsequent writers, male and female. His most famous works consist of lyrical poetry and two longer narrative poems, *El estudiante de Salamanca* (1840; *The Student of Salamanca*, 1953) and the unfinished *El diablo mundo* (1841; Devil World).

Espronceda's youthful involvement with a secret society, Los Numantinos, and subsequent emigration lend a political tone to his early works. Woman serves as a symbol of violated Spain; Rodrigo's rape of Florinda in *El Pelayo* (published 1840) draws an implicit comparison between the last Visigothic king and the newly restored Fernando VII. Likewise, the current sovereign appears as a tyrannical sun that blasts a virgin flower in "A la patria" (1836; To the Homeland). While Espronceda's later poetry focuses on other themes, this obsession with sexuality, guilt, and victimized women will endure. The identification between women and flowers continues in poetry written upon Espronceda's return to Spain. But now the poet focuses almost exclusively on woman as sentimental object, as seen with "A Matilde" (published 1841; To Matilda), which compares Matilde to a flower. Drawing on a long practice coupling flowers with maidenhood, every aspect of this flower evokes chastity: its white color, innocence, and virginal scent. Urged to imitate the personified flower, woman becomes in turn an object, a literary image akin to the flower.

Likewise, innocence lost finds expression through floral metaphors. Elvira, the heroine of *El estudiante de Salamanca*, spends her life in a perfumed, edenic garden. Abandoned by her lover, this delicate woman simply fades away, the ghastly destruction of her ideal beauty revealing a kinship with Shakespeare's Ophelia and Goethe's Margarite. This emphasis on the aftermath of seduction distinguishes Espronceda's version of the

Don Juan myth from those of Tirso de *Molina (1582–1648) and *Zorrilla (1817–1893). Yet, in spite of her seduction, Elvira acts as a surrogate for the poet; they are both victims of an unfeeling world. Further disillusionments find expression through another female intermediary, the prostitute Jarifa. In "A Jarifa en una orgía" (1840; To Jarifa in an Orgy), Espronceda describes the debasement of the feminine ideal through mud and desert dryness. The blasted landscape of the prostitute's virtue, or the poet's soul, offers no lingering trace of purity.

This romantic fascination with corruption comes to a head with the "Canto a Teresa" (1841; Song to Teresa), inspired by the death of Espronceda's lover and the mother of his daughter. In contrast with the fictional personae—the poet defends Elvira and shows some compassion even for Jarifa—Teresa is exposed and vilified. The extreme cruelty shown toward her discomfits many readers, both female and male. But readers should note Espronceda's attempts to contend with the issue of guilt. Although he ultimately insists on his blamelessness, in the "Canto a Teresa" the poet briefly identifies himself with the destructive power of the sun's heat, a perhaps subconscious reference to the rapists of his earliest poetry. Earlier, in *El estudiante de Salamanca*, Félix changes from a forceful, masculine blast into a plantlike victim of the wind; as he dies, Félix literally folds in upon himself, a leaf swept away by the spirits. Even more closely connected with flowers, the childlike Adán of *El diablo mundo* reverses Félix's trajectory. Adán's naive entry into the world and his blissful love for Salada find expression through flowers. But when Adán rejects his lover, he becomes the destructive, male wind. The conundrum created early on by identifying the feminine with innocence and the male with the destruction of virginity becomes increasingly problematic as Espronceda's career progresses, especially in light of the unfinished *El diablo mundo*. Yet Espronceda's willingness to experiment, to potentially reverse male and female roles, merits further study.

Finally, Espronceda's increasingly irreverent attitude toward his own work calls old ideas into question. In the first canto of *El diablo mundo*, the poet mocks his desire for literary immortality. In Canto III, the poet debunks the romantic view of love, revealing instead the vanity of both partners. As Polt has noted, these verses alter the larger framework of *El diablo mundo*. They enclose the most personal, heartfelt section—the "Canto a Teresa" (Canto II)—between a sarcastic assessment of Espronceda's merit as a poet and a sardonic denial of both love and his worth as a lover.

The parodic aspect of Espronceda's work has inspired similar efforts in other writers. Ramón del *Valle-Inclán (1866–1936) comments ironically on Espronceda's view of women and love in *Sonata de otoño* (1902) and *Tirano Banderas* (1926). A feminine response to—and perhaps even gentle mockery of—Espronceda appears in Rosalía de *Castro's (1837–1885) *En las orillas del Sar* (1884). Here the female voice adopts the male poet's imagery with all the ambiguity and contradictions that it entails.

Work by

El estudiante de Salamanca. El diablo mundo. Ed. Robert Marrast. Madrid: Castalia, 1982.

Poesías líricas y fragmentos épicos. Ed. Robert Marrast. Madrid: Castalia, 1970.

Work about

Goody, Jack. *The Culture of Flowers*. Cambridge: Cambridge UP, 1993.

Kirkpatrick, Susan. *Las Románticas: Women Writers and Subjectivity in Spain, 1835–1850*. Berkeley: U of California P, 1989.

Marrast, Robert. *José de Espronceda y su tiempo*. Barcelona: Crítica, 1989.

Polt, John H.R. "Espronceda's 'Canto a Teresa' in its Context." *Studies in Eighteenth-Century Spanish Literature in Honor of John Clarkson Dowling*. Ed. Douglas Barnette and Linda Jane Barnette. Newark, DE: Juan de la Cuesta, 1985. 167–176.

Jennifer Rae Krato

Estevarena y Gallardo, Concepción (1854–1876)

A native of Seville, the poet Concepción Estevarena y Gallardo exemplified in many respects the economic vulnerability of middle-class Spanish women in the nineteenth century. She was one of the most promising of Spain's nineteenth-century women poets but died young. Estevarena's mother died when she was only 17 months old, and most of her youth was dedicated to caring for her elderly and impoverished father. When he died in 1875, she was left penniless, tubercular, and with no close living relatives. She had no choice but to go to an uncle who was choir director in the cathedral of Jaca, despite the adverse effects the cold northern climate was likely to have on her health. Indeed, her health rapidly deteriorated, and she died at age 22, only months after her arrival in Jaca.

The pathos of Estevarena's life and death is heightened by the expressive power of her poetry. Linked to Seville literary circles that were influenced by the late Romantic poetry of Gustavo Adolfo *Bécquer (1836–1870), she developed an effective lyrical style using simple, evocative language, assonant rhyme, and image systems built around dual oppositions. Her poems poignantly express the existential anxiety of a woman poet whose social identity is secured neither by her vocation (regarded as idiosyncratic in a woman) nor by an economically sound male family member. In her poem "Vacilación" (Vacillation), for example, she seems to speak for many women of her period when she says that her "unknown story" is "to desire much, but to be nothing." Like Bécquer, she wrote of the struggle to achieve adequate verbal expression. In being more pessimistic than the male poet about the possibility of achieving "the desired hymn," she revealed her sense of marginality as a woman. Nevertheless, by fully acknowledging the difficulty of her position, she managed in her poetry to convert her marginality into aesthetic transcendence.

Several of Estevarena's poems were published in small Andalusian periodicals, but she achieved greater recognition in the last year of her life, when nine were published in as many issues of Madrid's widely circulated women's magazine, *El Correo de la Moda*. Several more were published posthumously. After her death, literary friends in Seville raised the money to publish a limited edition of her complete poetic works with a biographical prologue by José de Velilla. In 1979, Josefina *Romo Arregui (1913–) published a new edition of Estevarena's poetry, with a stylistic study by Diana Ramírez de Arellano.

Work by

Ultimas flores. Poesías. Prol. José de Velilla. Seville: Girones y Orduna, 1877.

Work about

Kirkpatrick, Susan, intro. *Antología poética de escritoras del siglo XIX*. Madrid: Castalia, 1992. 52–56.

Ramírez de Arellano, Diana, intro. *Poetas románticos desconocidos. Concepción Estevarena*. Ed. Josefina Romo Arregui. Madrid: Librería Internacional de Romo, 1979.

Susan Kirkpatrick

Fagundo, Ana María (1938–)

In "Cincuenta cumpleaños" (Fiftieth Birthday, found in *El sol, la sombra, en el instante*, 1994), Ana María Fagundo reflects on the significance of that day while offering a useful account for the understanding of her life and poetry. She describes her mixed state of jubilance and uneasiness, which impels a constant struggle to affirm her identity against time and nothingness. The self and its dissolution in time, writing, and the world are main concerns in Fagundo's 12 poetry collections. Fagundo shares the commitment to poetry as knowledge with poets such as José Angel Valente (1929–), Eladio Cabañero (1930–), Angel González (1925–), and Claudio Rodríguez (1956–), whose works appear mainly in the 1960–1970 decade.

A native of the Canary Islands, Fagundo traveled to the United States where, since 1967, she has taught Spanish literature and creative writing at the University of California, Riverside. An active poetry reader and lecturer, she also directs and edits *Alaluz*, a journal she founded in 1969. This journal has published the work of both well-known and experimental writers from Spain and Latin America and also gave women authors a voice long before feminism became popular.

The title of her first book of poems, *Brotes* (1965; Sprouts), prefigures the "burning uneasiness" of her fiftieth birthday poem. Writing and the identity it articulates are painful processes of continuous becoming. In *Isla adentro* (1969; Within the Island), Fagundo's search for ontological identity is associated with her native island of Tenerife, standing upright in the surrounding ocean. The same image of self-affirmation is reiterated in *Diario de una muerte* (1970; Diary of a Death). This book is offered to counteract her father's premature death. This traumatic experience also motivates her return to the Tenerife childhood in the following three collections: *Configurado tiempo* (1974; Configuration of Time), *Invención de la luz* (1978; Invention of Light), and *Desde Chanatel, el canto* (1982; Chant from Chanatel). The island landscape is the site of primordial language; by naming its elements, the speaker reenacts the original contact with the world's fullness. In *Como quien no dice voz alguna al viento* (1984; As One Who Says Nothing to the Wind), the landscape's physical elements (sea, vegetation, island, etc.) and those of the body (thigh, muscle, lip, etc.) give physical evidence to being. The striving to encapsulate matter in words is counteracted by the irreality of the section entitled "Visión," where ontological traces are diluted in the all-pervasive whiteness of nonbeing. *Retornos sobre la siempre ausencia* (1989; Returns to the

Absence Always) reiterates the need to continue "shaping" being through the word and the agency of memory. The initial poem, "Oración de la palabra" (Prayer of the Word), recounts the author's explorations into writing in the 10 poetry collections published to date. The budding word/identity in *Brotes* becomes the island circumscribed by natural boundaries in *Isla adentro* and the erasure by time and death in *Diario de una muerte*. In *Configurado tiempo*, the word regains its capacity to shape being, and in *Desde Chanatel*, it renews the link with the primordial or semiotic realm of being in order to recreate the original light of *Invención de la luz*. *Como quien no dice* articulates the nature of matter as concrete presence marked by absence, just as in *Retornos* the recovery of the past is an enterprise inscribed by its dissolution in time. In Fagundo's later book, *El sol, la sombra, en el instante* (1994; The Sun, the Shade, in the Instant), poems attempt to encapsulate the instant where light and shadow, presence and absence, fuse. Writing is thus a process more than a teleology. No poem purports to provide the full answer, and each leads to the next in a seduction that never discloses the full meaning.

The 26 short stories in *La miríada de los sonámbulos* (1994; The Myriad of Sleepwalkers) oppose social conventions and personal affirmation (History Lesson, Hideouts); consciousness and the unconscious (The Funeral Wake, The Nightmare); inside and outside (Vermins, The Representation; The Painting); lesbianism and homosexuality (The Odd Ones, Mrs. Innocence and Mrs. Generous).

Work by

Ana María Fagundo: Antología (1965–1989). Ed. Antonio Martínez-Herrarte. Islas Canarias: Publicaciones de la Viceconserjería de Cultura y Deportes del Gobierno Autónomo de Canarias, 1994.
Isla en sí: 1965–1989. Madrid: Rialp-Adonais, 1992.
La miríada de los sonámbulos. Miami: Universal, 1994.
Obra poética: 1965–1990. Madrid: Endymion, 1990.
Retornos sobre la siempre ausencia. Riverside, CA: Alaluz, 1989.
El sol, la sombra, en el instante. Madrid: Verbum, 1994.

Work about

Rolle, Silvia. La obra de Ana María Fagundo: Una poética femenina-feminista. Madrid: Fundamentos, 1997.

Candelas Gala

Fairy Tales in Novels by Spanish Women

Intertextuality is a common feature of almost all literary texts. Every author can point to early readings that most influenced him or her and that inevitably enter his or her own written creations later in life. Frequently in post–Civil War narrative by Spanish women, the authors compile, alongside (or at times in place of) a bibliography of canonized texts, another canon of required intertexts: fairy tales. Why do women with vast literary educations, like Ana María *Matute (1926–), Carmen *Martín Gaite (1925–2000), Ana María *Moix (1947–), and Esther *Tusquets (1936–), choose fairy tales such as "The Little Mermaid," "The Snow Queen," "Cinderella," and so on, as their most recognizable intertexts? This type of intertextuality productively points to elements that set off some female-authored writings as "feminine" texts.

Up until the middle of this century, female protagonists were mainly male creations. The same is true of the fairy tales, which are the earliest texts most readers enjoy. Yet many of the most famous fairy tales offer female audiences crippling images of themselves and their potential for literary creation. To achieve success, a fairy tale heroine must be beautiful and passive; the only other active option is the role of wicked witch. Another striking feature of fairy tales is that they are usually devoid of mother figures and wise, older females to guide the young protagonists. Fairy tales seldom portray women engaged in positive relationships with each other. The mothers are either dead or they are so evil that part of the pleasure of the text comes from destroying her.

Zipes points out that the fairy tales we all know today were born when writers who espoused the values of an emerging bourgeois class appropriated folktale motifs to create a genre that was amusing to adults and children and also didactic. Thus writers such as Charles Perrault (1628–1703), the Brothers Grimm (1785–1863 and 1786–1859), Hans Christian Andersen (1805–1875), and even Walt Disney Studios offered tales that socialized the young and helped them internalize the values of a male-dominated Christian civil order. Psychoanalyst Bruno Bettelheim assures parents that children need fairy tales because they offer examples of both temporary and permanent solutions to pressing difficulties associated with childhood. Thus when a child sees that Hansel and Gretel do find happiness after being left to starve in the woods, he or she is reassured of the ability to survive tragedy and consequently overcomes common fears of abandonment, death, rejection, and alienation. Long after readers have outgrown reading fairy tales, these stories continue to help internalize recurrent patterns of values and stable expectations about the roles and relationships that are part of their culture. There is a pretense of universality in fairy tales. Individuals may change, but the situations in which the male is dominant and the female must be subservient and beautiful to be worthy of love remain static. In sum, fairy tales are ruled by very rigid patterns that convey a common patriarchal cultural tradition.

After centuries of being represented mainly by male authors, how can the female writer break out of the patterns established for her gender by others? The role of fairy tales in the works of Spain's leading contemporary authors dramatizes this particular struggle. Thus, one cannot fully comprehend Ana María Matute's *Primera memoria* (1960; *Awakening*, 1963) without recognizing the importance of Hans Christian Andersen's "The Little Mermaid" and "The Snow Queen" and J.M. Barrie's *Peter Pan* as essential intertexts. In the beginning, the young protagonist of *Primera memoria*, Matia, relies on her cherished stories to teach her the meaning of life. Accordingly, the relationship between Kay and Gerda from "The Snow Queen" mirrors her relationship to her cousin Borja just as "The Little Mermaid" ultimately teaches her about the love affairs between men and women. Matia, however, gives a very negative reading of these tales by the end of her story. She believes the Little Mermaid to be a fool who lost her voice and must live in constant pain for a man who did not love her. On a more political level, direct quotes from *Peter Pan* describe war games that the boys play on the island, mirroring the atrocities of the Civil War raging on the mainland. As a female, Matia is excluded from her own intertexts since she refuses the passive role of Wendy. But at the end of *Primera memoria*, Matia (like the Little Mermaid, Wendy, and Gerda) is rendered passive and for a time speechless when she is incapable of escaping the preestablished textual patterns marked out for female protagonists in her favorite, defining stories, which she ultimately feels have betrayed her.

Likewise, the lonely protagonist of Esther Tusquets's *El mismo mar de todos los veranos* (1978; *The Same Sea as Every Summer*) counts fairy tale characters among her closest friends on whom she relies to teach her the meaning of her life and society. There is hardly a page in this novel that does not include at least one reference to a fairy tale or myth. One lesson the nameless protagonist has incorporated well is that as a homely child, and later woman, she will be unworthy of love. As in traditional fairy tales, the suffering heroine is mainly a victim of other women, namely, her beautiful and rejecting mother and daughter. The entire novel presents a struggle to escape these restrictive patterns, a struggle that the protagonist ultimately loses because the patterns she has incorporated are too firmly ensconced.

Many other novels and short stories by Spanish women concern a struggle against societal structures the protagonists internalized through reading fairy tales as a structuring or metaphorical element. Carmen *Laforet's *Nada* (1945; *Andrea*, 1964) incorporates the Cinderella motif. Ana María Moix in her short story "Erase una vez" (1985; Once Upon a Time) parodies the most famous females in fairy tales, while the narrator, condemned to repeating the beginning phrase that gives the story's title, goes insane from having to repeat the same tales she so hates. Tusquets continues the struggle against fairy tale restrictions begun in *El mismo mar de todos los veranos* in the remaining novels of her trilogy, *El amor es un juego solitario* (1979; *Love is a Solitary Game*, 1985) and *Varada tras el último naufragio* (1980; Beached after the Last Shipwreck).

Recently a few texts have appeared that present positive feminist reworkings of fairy tales. In Martín Gaite's *La Reina de las nieves* (1994; The Snow Queen), the Hans Christian Andersen tale of the same title structures the plot in which a mother's reunion with her illegitimate son brings about his (and to a lesser degree, her) emotional reawakening. The difference now is that in Martín Gaite's text the female characters are not forced to give up their voice and sexuality in order to be loved. Martín Gaite previously published a series of feminist rewritings of fairy tales for the children's market. In both *El Castillo de las tres murallas* (1986; The Castle with Three Walls) and *El pastel del diablo* (1985; Devil's Pastry) a young female character embarks on a dangerous but successful quest for knowledge of the type only undertaken by male characters in traditional fairy tales. Likewise, in *Caperucita en Manhattan* (1990; Little Red Riding Hood in Manhattan) a little girl in a red raincoat conquers the forest (in this case, Central Park) in which she meets the lonely millionaire Edgar Woolf, who turns out to be the perfect boyfriend for her grandmother.

Spanish women of earlier generations who wrote for children served as an inspiration for later writers such as Martín Gaite, who has publicly expressed her admiration for the work of Elena *Fortún (1886–1952) not only in print but also through her adaptations of Fortún's Celia series for Spanish television. Through their parodies of values that traditional Spanish society has long held sacred, Fortún's female characters question the system. The mischievous Matonkiki refuses to believe the fairy tales and all the values therein that her elders thrust upon her, just as Celia places sacred religious teachings of her convent education on a fictional level when she confuses descriptions of heaven with Aladdin's palace. In the midst of the Franco regime, Borita *Casas's (1911–?) heroine, Antoñita la Fantástica, offers her little sister a collection of feminist rewritings of fairy tales as a birthday gift. In *Antoñita en el país de la fantasía* (1952; Antoñita in Fantasy Land), traditional, passive fairy tale beauties such as Snow White and Cinderella are mocked, while a new generation of intelligent, active heroines conquers their world.

The Spanish woman writer's struggle with values taught through fairy tales is a particularly female trait, for while male characters are active and brave and forge their own destinies, female characters must rely on their passivity and beauty to attract a prince who will endow their lives with purpose. Only when the crippling effects of these texts aimed at keeping women silent are recognized and fought can women authors emerge and portray their own lives with greater accuracy.

Work about

Bettelheim, Bruno. *The Uses of Enchantment: The Meaning and Importance of Fairy Tales*. New York: Vantage Books, 1977.

Bottigheimer, Ruth B. *Grimm's Bad Girls and Bold Boys: The Moral and Social Vision of the Tales*. New Haven, CT: Yale UP, 1987.

Cronan Rose, Ellen. "Through the Looking Glass: When Women Tell Fairy Tales." *The Voyage In: Fictions of Female Development*. Ed. Elizabeth Abel,

Marianne Hirsch, and Elizabeth Langland. Hanover: UP of New England, 1983. 209–227.

Gross Reed, Suzanne. "Notes on Hans Christian Andersen Tales in Ana María Matute's *Primera memoria*." *Continental, Latin-American and Francophone Women Writers: Selected Papers from the Wichita State University Conference on Foreign Literature*. Eunice Myer, ed. and Ginette Adamson, ed. and intro. Lanham: UP of America, 1987. 177–182.

Lieberman, Marcia R. "Some Day My Prince Will Come: Female Acculturation through the Fairy Tale." *College English* 34 (1972): 383–395.

Tatar, Maria. *The Hard Facts of the Grimms' Fairy Tales*. Princeton, NJ: Princeton UP, 1987.

Zipes, Jack. *Breaking the Magic Spell: Radical Theories of Folk and Fairy Tales*. Austin: U of Texas P, 1979.

———. *Fairy Tales and the Art of Subversion: The Classical Genre for Children and the Process of Civilization*. London: Heinemann Educational Books, 1983.

María Elena Soliño

Falcón, Lidia (1935–)

The personal and professional life of Lidia Falcón epitomizes the feminist ideal. She grew up in a family of strong female figures: Her grandmother, Regina de Lamo, was an outspoken political activist; her mother, Enriqueta O'Neill, was a novelist and author of numerous articles dealing with women's issues; and her aunt, Carlota *O'Neill, was an accomplished playwright and editor of a Communist Party publication during the Spanish Civil War. As fate would have it, men were the exception in Falcón's immediate reality. Her grandfather was killed during the war. Following the Nationalist victory, her father left Spain and her uncle was executed shortly after the war ended. Falcón married Alfred Borrás in 1953, but three years later, Borrás abandoned Falcón and their young daughter. In many ways, her personal life served as a catalyst for her future endeavors.

A lawyer and journalist by profession, Falcón has spent more than three decades using her knowledge of law and journalism to defend women's rights and speak out against female oppression in an effort to integrate feminism into Spanish reality. During the Franco years, Falcón's written work was often censored and her political activity very closely scrutinized. As a political activist during the 1960s and 1970s, she worked tirelessly to found Spain's first feminist party, El Partido Feminista de España, which was finally legalized in 1981. In 1972 she was arrested for publishing and distributing antifascist literature and spent six months in Barcelona's La Trinidad prison. In 1974 she was accused of pro-ETA (Euskadi Ta Askatasuna, or Basque Homeland and Freedom) terrorist activity, which led to a second prison sentence of nine months in Madrid's infamous Yeserías prison. She has founded two journals, *Vindicación Feminista in 1976 and *Poder y Libertad* in 1979, and has authored numerous works of fiction and nonfiction, including articles, essays, novels, and plays.

The objective of Falcón's published work is political, and her radical point of view is the overarching principle of her writing. Straightforward and direct in approach, her work is intended to disrupt antiquated notions about gender. She has authored hundreds of articles and short essays in which she theorizes extensively about the physical, intellectual, and psychological oppression of women. What she espouses in her shorter texts is elaborated exhaustively in her longer works. *La razón feminista, 1. La mujer como clase social y económica. El modo de producción doméstico* (1981; Feminist Reason, 1. Woman as a Social and Economic Class. The Domestic Production Mode), *La razón feminista, 2. La reproducción humana* (1982; Feminist Reason, 2. Human Reproduction), and *Violencia contra la mujer* (1991; Violence against Women) expound on the notion of social class consciousness as it regards women. In these works, Falcón comments on the varying ways in which women have been oppressed and made to feel and act inferior to males throughout history. *Violencia contra la mujer* is particularly important because of its universal appeal. It is an in-depth study of the many forms of violence (physical, psychological, spiritual, etc.) that have been traditionally leveled against women with no other objective than to maintain the status quo of the patriarchy.

Other works of nonfiction, such as *Los derechos civiles de la mujer* (1963; Women's Civil Rights), *Los derechos laborales de la mujer* (1964; Women's Labor Rights), *El alboroto español* (1984; The Spanish Uproar), and *El varón español a la búsqueda de su identidad* (1986; The Spanish Male in Search of His Identity), further develop the radical idea that patriarchy represents all systems of male dominance and is the primary cause of the oppression of women that reduces them to a subhuman status. These works are biting exposés of the negative effect of male dominance on women's history. Through extensive documentation and theorizing, Falcón illustrates how women have been kept from developing their own sense of self while fueling the dominant, self-serving male culture. Still in other works, such as *Mujer y sociedad. Análisis de un fenómeno reaccionario* (1969; Woman and Society. Analysis of a Reactionary Phenomenon) and *Mujer y poder político. Fundamentos de la crisis de objetivos e ideología del Movimiento Feminista* (1992; Women and Political Power. Reasons for the Crisis in Objectives and Ideology of the Feminist Movement), Falcón promotes the feminist movement as the revolutionary means that can ultimately effect change in the social status of women. *Mujer y poder político* in particular has all the makings of a political manifesto for the Spanish feminist movement, yet what Falcón espouses in these works is not limited to Spain but bears universal significance for the feminist cause. In sum, the critical discourse of Falcón's nonfiction works is founded on the sharp criticism of the patriarchy and on revolutionary change.

Several of Falcón's works are testimonial in nature and borrow heavily from her personal experience. *Los hijos de los vencidos (1939-1949)* (1978; Children of the Defeated), for example, recounts Falcón's childhood in poverty-stricken post–Civil War Spain. *En el infierno. Ser mujer en las cárceles de España* (1977; In Hell. To Be a Woman in Spanish Jails) and *Viernes y 13 en la calle de Correo* (1981; Friday and Thirteen on Correo Street) dwell on her political activism and subsequent imprisonment under the Franco regime. Both texts depict in graphically disturbing terms the deplorable living conditions and hostile treatment of women prisoners in Spanish jails under the Franco dictatorship. *En el infierno. Ser mujer en las cárceles de España* is set exclusively within the prison and addresses in great detail the day-to-day effects of female institutional oppression under the penal system of Francoist Spain. The work documents firsthand how authoritarian social structures strip women of their personal sense of dignity and what they must comply with in order to survive in their dehumanized condition. Enclosure (*Encierro), both symbolic and concrete, permits Falcón to elaborate a consciousness of the universal entrapment of women in her prison texts.

Falcón is equally relentless in her condemnation of female exploitation and her intention to disenfranchise the male canon in her works of fiction. Women characters that populate her novels and plays strive in every way possible to claim a voice and identity of their own by challenging the edicts of institutional oppression. The works showcase the senseless and inexplicable objectification of women at the hands of the self-serving patriarchy and the insignificance historically accorded the personal dilemmas of women. In Falcón's novels and plays, as in her works of nonfiction, politics and gender ideology are intricately interwoven in such a way as to move woman from the position of object to that of subject of her critical discourse. A reading of Falcón's novels and theater suggests that fiction is a communicative process that serves both a personal and political objective.

In *Es largo esperar callado* (1975; The Long Silent Wait), *Camino sin retorno* (1992; Road with No Return), and *Postmodernos* (1993; Postmoderns), Falcón champions the courage of militant women and openly criticizes the ideologies of Spanish right-wing politics. In other novels, such as in *El juego de la piel* (1983; The Skin Game), *Rupturas* (1985; Ruptures), and *Clara* (1993), she skillfully combines historical facts about the feminist movement in Spain and feminist critique to underscore to what degree reality is imbued with sexist ideologies and skepticism about liberal thinking. The works are part social documentary, part historical novel, and part ideological treatise. Falcón's novels touch on a wide range of issues universally associated with radical feminist thought, themes such as feminine bonding or sisterhood, the notion of women as an oppressed class, the duplicitous image of men who are essentially weaker than women and resort to aggression to mask their innate fears and shortcomings, the dichotomy of the public and private as a paradigm by which gender distinction has been differentiated traditionally, and more.

Though less recognized for her dramatic production, Falcón's theater is equally direct in underscoring how certain institutions have succeeded in distancing women from any source of power. At the level of representation, Falcón's theater seeks to demonstrate the degree to which male-female relationships bespeak a power-structured arrangement that is informed by an essentialist notion of gender. Men and women in Falcón's theater, whether represented mimetically or diegetically, are always conceived as binary opposites. The image of woman is that of the perennial victim of patriarchal oppression both on a personal and on a social level. Yet Falcón's female characters are strong-willed and determined individuals. On the other hand, her male characters, despite their aggressive behavior, are shallow, hypocritical individuals who inevitably resort to subterfuge in order to exploit women and diminish their self-worth while fueling their own false sense of supremacy. Graphic scenes involving physically and psychologically abused and abandoned women and children and themes such as contraception, divorce, and abortion prove a useful means of communicating the immediacy and urgency of her message.

¡No moleste, calle y pague, Señora! (1984; Don't Disturb, Be Quiet and Pay, Ma'am), *Tu único amor* (1991; Your Only Love), and *¡Parid, parid, malditas!* (1994; Give Birth, Give Birth, Damned [Girls]) are indicative of how Falcón's dramatic technique appropriates the ideological concerns of radical feminist thought. *¡No moleste, calle y pague, Señora!* tells the story of three different women, Magda, Margarita, and María, who seek justice for the inhuman treatment they are subjected to by the dominant culture. The insignificance attributed to women's personal dilemmas by institutions such as the church, law, and medicine is epitomized by the total and blatant disregard displayed by the men in the play. The focus is on the need for a transcendental bonding among women as a community and for an acceptance of their oppression as a shared experience. *Tu único amor* deals with the socialization of gender roles and illustrates that gender is an imposed social construct. The play dramatizes Isabel's lifelong relationship with various men who evolve from reticent and timid young males to openly violent dictatorial figures in their treatment of her. Male characterization in the play suggests that maleness is a process of social indoctrination, the ultimate objective of which is to prevent women from achieving full self-expression. *¡Parid, parid, malditas!* focuses on a young woman's right to have an abortion. The female body is the symbolic and concrete site of feminine consciousness in the play, the image of genderized meanings that resembles from a theoretical perspective the notion of writing the body as proposed by *l'écriture féminine*. In the play, the female body serves at once as the primary site of feminine entrapment and a means of liberation.

Falcón displays the same determination in revealing how women have been effectively subordinated by institutions in *Las mujeres caminaron con el fuego del siglo* (1994; Women Walked with the Fire of the Century), which dramatizes how women's active role in historical events, in this case the Spanish Civil War, has been suppressed and marginalized. *Tres idiotas españolas* (1994; Three Spanish Idiots) focuses on the oppression of women in the workplace, the sexual liberation of women, and the myth of femininity. *Siempre busqué el amor* (1994; I Always Looked for Love) is based on a true story and recounts how the members of a family agree to commit murder in order to rid themselves of an abusive husband and father. The extreme to which Falcón goes in presenting the female experience on the stage functions rhetorically to carry a persuasive message intended to influence the convictions of the audience regarding the institutional oppression of women. In Falcón's plays, the action evolves in Brechtian-like episodic structure that permits Falcón to convey her message strikingly and bring her spectators to a critical perspective vis-à-vis otherwise familiar or ordinary facets of the female experience.

Falcón's life and work speak to the depth of her feminist convictions. Her work is polemical. It serves as a platform to posit a critical view of patriarchal social structures, of the authoritative political underpinnings of our society that have historically sought to strip women of self-worth and relegate them to a subordinate position. Falcón does not create positive images of women but instead provides vivid, graphically revealing portraits of female oppression in order to raise public consciousness. Much of Falcón's work has been misrepresented or sharply criticized due to the radical point of view she promotes. Yet she has not been deterred. She is persistent in her struggle to keep women's issues in the public eye and defend her feminist commitment. Her intention is to reject entrenched ideologies and bring about greater recognition of the female experience as a means toward change by encouraging women to find a coherent identity in her writing. See *also* Feminism in Spain: 1900–2000; Feminist Theory and the Contemporary Spanish Stage

Work by

El alboroto español. Barcelona: Fontanella, 1984.
Camino sin retorno. Barcelona: Anthropos, 1992.
Clara. Madrid: Vindicación Feminista, 1993.
Los derechos civiles de la mujer. Barcelona: Nereo, 1963.
Los derechos laborales de la mujer. Madrid: Montecorvo, 1964.
En el infierno. Ser mujer en las cárceles de España. Barcelona: Ediciones de Feminismo, 1977.
Es largo esperar callado. Barcelona: Pomaire, 1975.
Los hijos de los vencidos (1939–1949). Barcelona: Pomaire, 1978.
El juego de la piel. Barcelona: Argos Vergara, 1983.
Mujer y poder político. Fundamentos de la crisis de objetivos e ideología del Movimiento Feminista. Madrid: Vindicación Feminista, 1992.
Mujer y sociedad. Análisis de un fenómeno reaccionario. Barcelona: Fontanella, 1969.
Postmodernos. Madrid: Libertarias, 1993.
La razón feminista, 1. La mujer como clase social y económica. El modo de producción doméstico. Barcelona: Fontanella, 1981.
La razón feminista, 2. La reproducción humana. Barcelona: Fontanella, 1982.
Rupturas. Barcelona: Fontanella, 1985.
Teatro. Madrid: Vindicación Feminista, 1994.
Tu único amor. Art Teatral 3.3 (1991): 19–24.
El varón español a la búsqueda de su identidad. Barcelona: Plaza y Janés, 1986.
Viernes y 13 en la calle de Correo. Barcelona: Planeta, 1981.
Violencia contra la mujer. Barcelona: Círculo de Lectores, 1991.

Work about

Gabriele, John P. "Lidia Falcón y el feminismo: Una entrevista." *Hispania* 74.7 (1991): 947–950.
Gazarian, Marie-Lise Gautier. "Lidia Falcón." *Interviews with Spanish Writers*. Elmwood Park: Dalkey Archive P, 1991. 126–136.
Goodnough, Robin. "Voces femeninas y discursos patriarcales en *No moleste, calle y pague, señora*." *Estreno* 23.1 (1997): 39–42.
Levine, Linda Gould, and Gloria F. Waldman. "Lidia Falcón." *Feminismo ante el franquismo: Entrevistas con feministas de España*. Miami: Universal, 1980. 67–85.
Starcevic, Elizabeth. "*Rupturas*: A Feminist Novel."

Anales de la Literatura Española Contemporánea 12.1–2 (1987): 175–189.

Vosberg, Nancy. "On Post-Transition Politics, Picardía, and Power. Lidia Falcón's El alboroto español." Spanish Women Writers and the Essay: Gender, Politics and the Self. Ed., intro. Kathleen Glenn and Mercedes Mazquiarán de Rodríguez. Columbia: U of Missouri P, 1998.

Waldman, Gloria Feiman. "Lidia Falcón." Spanish Women Writers. A Bio-Bibliographical Source Book. Ed. Linda Gould Levine, Ellen Engelson Marson, and Gloria Feiman Waldman. Westport, CT: Greenwood P, 1993. 167–180.

John P. Gabriele

Feijóo y Montenegro, Fr. Benito Jerónimo (1676–1764)

Born in Casdemiro (Orense), not much is known about his private life. He studied at the Real Colegio de San Esteban de Ribas de Sil and entered the Benedictine Monastery of San Juliás de Samos at age 14. After completing his studies he taught theology at the Monastery of San Vicente in Oviedo. In this city he attended the university and received both the licenciado (licenciate) and the doctorate in Letters. After completing his degrees he taught at Oviedo University from 1710 until he retired due to ill health at age 63. Though deeply devout, Feijóo's curiosity and depth of knowledge made him known as the "Spanish Voltaire," and he was highly esteemed in European Enlightenment circles. The Mercure de France praised his works, which were translated to five different languages before the end of the century.

Feijóo did not begin to publish until well into his fifties. He used the inductive method to deal with all fields of knowledge competently and wrote in a simple, methodical, direct style. His first publication was the defense of a book in which a medical doctor had attacked contemporary medical practices and the scholastic method. Feijóo's defense pointed out that to attack scholasticism was not heretical and that the scholastic method, as taught and practiced in Spain, was useless. This defense set up the pattern of Feijóo's writings. He went on to combat ignorance and superstition in all walks of life, while promoting new methods and sound scientific and philosophical advances.

His two main works, Teatro Crítico universal (1726–1740; Universal Theater of Criticism) and Cartas eruditas (1742–1760; Erudite Letters), contain hundreds of essays. One of the most effective from the point of view of feminism is his *Defensa de las mujeres. Published in 1726, it defends women's intellectual capacity, explaining that women have not developed their intellect because man-made laws have prevented them from accessing education and its concomitant intellectual pursuits.

Work by

"Defensa de las mujeres." Obras (Selección). Ed. Ivy McClelland. Madrid: Taurus, 1985. 133–141.

Work about

Coughlin, Edward V. "The Polemic on Feijóo's 'Defensa de las mujeres.'" Dieciocho 9.1–2 (1986): 74–85.

Llanos M., Bernardita. "Integración de la mujer al progreso de la Ilustración en España." Ideologies and Literature 4.1 (Spring 1989): 199–223.

María A. Salgado

Feminism in Spain: 1700–1800

Though the term feminism does not strictly correspond to eighteenth-century thought, the question of women's abilities and rights was one of the main concerns of the Spanish Enlightenment. Women participated in various aspects of Spain's social and political changes, especially during the second half of the century. They were involved in educational and civic reforms, Economic Societies (Sociedades de Amigos del País), salons (academias), as well as in the growth of the printed press. Women shared their ideas with each other, debated important issues in their writings and through their participation in civic and social groups, and worked to educate and improve the lives of other women and people in general.

These "enlightened feminists," by and large educated members of the nobility and upper classes, were united by a strong belief in the spiritual and intellectual equality of men and women; education as an effective means of social change; the dignity of the individual; and the power of rational thought. Paradoxically, since they had to depend on men to accede to the public arena, their writing strategies often sought not to alienate male power structures that dominated thinking of the Church, the state, and the intellectual elite. Many managed to do so—some through subtle subversion and others through open confrontation—publishing their works while gaining the respect of their male peers. Most important, they effectively influenced ongoing debates. This fact is clearly exemplified by the 1786 polemic over admitting women to the Madrid Economic Society. The arguments were led by Jovellanos, who defended admission, and Cabarrús, who opposed it. Josefa *Amar y Borbón's (1749–1833) contribution to the polemic, "Defensa del talento de las mujeres," presented women's thinking not only on the subject of membership in the Madrid Society but also on women's talents and abilities in general.

The stage for these revolutionary changes had been set earlier in the century by Fr. Benito *Feijóo's (1676–1764) controversial essay of 1726, *Defensa de las mujeres* (reissued 20 times by 1787). Later in the century, Carlos III used a bright young noblewoman, María Isidra Quintina de *Guzmán, to exemplify enlightened womanhood. He appointed her to the Royal Spanish Academy, and to justify it, he ordered the prestigious University of Alcalá to grant her a Doctorate in Letters. She graduated in 1785—the first Spanish woman to do so. The faculty then elected her Honorary Professor of Modern Philosophy. The king also granted her membership in both the Basque and the Madrid Economic Societies.

Although things were not as easy for other women, many managed to exert a great deal of influence. Some did it through their literary salons. That of Josefa Zúñiga y Castro, countess of Lemos (later marchioness of Sarriá), called Academia del Buen Gusto (Academy of Good Taste), was one of the most influential; but those of the duchess of Alba and the countess-duchess of Benavente (later duchess of Osuna) were also famous. In these salons, artists, writers, musicians, and other intellectuals met to socialize and share their works and ideas. Women also met and debated at all-female gatherings. The Junta de Damas, the women's auxiliary of the Madrid Economic Society, was established by royal order in 1787. This group actively worked to better the situation of women through basic education, vocational training, and encouragement of cottage industries. It also reorganized the Inclusa (municipal orphanage). The Asociación de Mujeres worked toward a more humane treatment of prisoners.

Another avenue used by these enlightened feminists was the printing press. Despite censorship, publishers and writers enjoyed a high degree of freedom during the second half of the century. The number of periodicals increased dramatically, and the first newspaper for women appeared. *La *pensadora gaditana* was published (1763–1764) by a Beatriz de *Cienfuegos, whose historical identity has not been established. Many women and men freely published journal articles dealing with topics such as education for women and women's health. The Royal Press, founded in 1787, was another outlet effectively used by writers such as María Rosa *Gálvez (1768–1806) and Margarita *Hickey (1753–after 1793) to publish their works.

Women also availed themselves of the theater to spread their enlightened ideas. Although some, like Hickey, limited themselves to translating European plays, others wrote original works. One of the most successful was María Rosa Gálvez. Unfortunately, the death of Carlos III in 1788, and the horror spread among the sympathizers of the *ancien régime* by the French Revolution (1789), brought to an abrupt end Spain's enlightened incursion into the Age of Reason. *See also* Drama by Spanish Women Writers: 1770–1850; Women's Situation in Spain: 1700–1800; Women's Situation in Spain: 1786–1931: The Awakening of Female Consciousness

Work about

Coughlin, Edward V. "The Polemic on Feijóo's 'Defensa de las mujeres.'" *Dieciocho* 9 (1986): 74–85.

Fernández Quintanilla, Paloma. *La mujer ilustrada en la España del siglo XVIII*. Madrid: Ministerio de Cultura, 1981.

Franklin, Elizabeth M. "Feijóo, Josefa Amar y Borbón, and the Feminist Debate in Eighteenth-Century Spain." *Dieciocho* 12.2 (Fall 1989): 188–203.

Llanos M., Bernardita. "Integración de la mujer en el proyecto femenino de la Ilustración en España." *Ideologies and Literature* 4.1 (Spring 1989): 199–223.

Rudat, Eva E. Kahiluoto. "La mujer ilustrada." *Letras Femeninas* 2.1 (1976): 20–32.

María A. Salgado

Feminism in Spain: 1900–2000

Spain has never had a vigorous and organized feminist movement. Generally blamed for this lack have been Spain's slow and late development of capitalism, its unprogressive labor and educational systems, and an entrenched conservatism reinforced by the pervasive influence of the Catholic Church. During the nineteenth century, except for the writings of Concepción *Arenal (1820–1893) and Emilia *Pardo Bazán (1852 1921), little discussion was held on the improvement of social conditions for women until a group of male social reformers connected with the intellectual movement known as *krausismo* began to take concrete steps to develop education for women.

The surge in the feminist movement outside Spain after World War I helped promote interest in women's issues within the country. During the 1920s there was an intense debate on women's roles and needs. Traditionalists continued to depict women as the "angel of the hearth" (**ángel del hogar*) and as intellectually inferior beings. Equally misogynist were views like those of essayist Gregorio Marañón (1887–1960), who adhered to the notion of gender "complementarity." A few more moderate male intellectuals argued in favor of feminism, although even they defined women along reactionary lines, as essentially wives and mothers. The Church took measures, including the formation of several women's organizations, purportedly to defend women but actually in order to guarantee their loyalty to its conservative doctrine. Political parties of the Left—socialists and anarchists—despite their claims of support for working women, did little to advance women's civil rights.

The growing need for middle-class women to work outside the home brought demands for new job opportunities and better work conditions. Although none was a radical feminist, a number of women's associations were formed after 1918, the prime one being the Asociación Nacional de Mujeres Españolas. Other noteworthy groups designed to advance the status of women included Juventud Universitaria Femenina, and Unión de Mujeres Españolas. Also individual women, such as Carmen de *Burgos (1867–1932), Carmen Hildegarte, María de la O Lejárraga (1874–1974), María de *Maeztu (1882–1948), and Margarita *Nelken (1896–1968), began to speak out on the economic, educational, or political situation of Spanish women.

With the establishment of the Republic in 1931, the political and legal status of women changed radically. In that year women's *suffrage was approved by the Parliament to a large extent through the efforts of Clara *Campoamor (1888–1972). Under the Republic, women gained equality with men before the law, they were given the right to work in the occupation of their choice, and divorce was legalized.

The advances made by Spanish women before the Civil War were eradicated under the dictatorship of Francisco Franco. Married women were no longer allowed to work, prestigious and lucrative professions were closed to women, and coeducation was eliminated. Legislation was passed to encourage and protect the family. Marriage and motherhood were again the only roles acceptable for women; and self-sacrifice, domestic industriousness, and silent submission to male authority were exalted as feminine virtues. The Sección Femenina of the fascist Falange, under the leadership of the fervently antifeminist Pilar Diego de Rivera, was in charge of indoctrinating girls into this national social agenda. As industrialization, urbanization, and international tourism grew in Spain during the 1960s, a number of reforms were introduced, particularly with regard to work. Women's legal rights, however, continued to be highly restricted, and the Church continued to exert its strong antifeminist influence upon Spanish society.

Spanish feminism underwent notable changes in the 1970s and particularly after the death of Franco in 1975. The Constitution of 1978 prohibited discrimination on the basis of sex, and a series of laws instituted equality between the sexes. At the same time, a new women's movement was developing in response to the political changes reshaping Spain and to the women's liberation movement outside of the country. The women's movement flourished in Spain between 1975 and 1982, with the period 1975–1978 characterized by great expansion and the years 1979–1982 marked by polarization between differing attitudes and ideologies. In 1983 the Instituto de la Mujer was set up by the socialists to expand the antidiscrimination measures of the Constitution. Government support of women's issues institutionalized the feminist movement in Spain, and the proliferation of organizations dispersed it. Yet many women consolidated their efforts to secure, in 1985, a woman's right to abortion, under certain prescribed circumstances. Increasing numbers of professional women have formed organizations to promote women's rights, and a greater proportion of the general female population has developed an awareness of feminist concerns; but few groups clearly defined as feminist exist in Spain. *See also* Burgos, Carmen de (1867–1932); Campo Alange, Condesa de (1902–1986); Colmeiro Laforet, Carlos (1906–1986); Lyceum Club Femenino (1926–1936); *Mujeres libres* (1936–1938); *Mujer moderna y sus derechos, La* (1927); *Versos con Faldas* (1951)

Work about

Campo Alange, María Lafitte, Condesa de. *La mujer en España: Cien años de su historia. 1860–1960.* Madrid: Aguilar, 1964.

Capel Martínez, María Rosa. *El trabajo y la educación de la mujer en España (1900–1930).* Madrid: Ministerio de Cultura, 1986.

Capel Martínez, María Rosa, and Julio Iglesias de Ussel. *Mujer española y sociedad: Bibliografía (1900–1984).* Madrid: Instituto de la Mujer, 1984.

Capmany, Maria Aurèlia. *El feminismo ibérico.* Barcelona: Oikos-Tau, 1970.

Durán, María Angeles. *La mujer en el mundo contemporáneo.* Madrid: Universidad Autónoma de Madrid, 1981.

Durán, María Angeles, and María Teresa Gallego. "The Women's Movement in Spain and the New Spanish Democracy." *The New Women's Movement: Feminist and Political Power in Europe and the USA.* Ed. Drude Dahlerup. London: Sage, 1986. 200–216.

Durán, María Angeles, et al. *Mujer y sociedad en España 1700–1975.* Madrid: Dirección General de Juventud y Promoción Socio-Cultural, 1982.

Febo, Giuliana di. *Resistencia y movimiento en España. 1936–1976.* Madrid: Icaria, 1979.

Folguera, Pilar, ed. *El feminismo en España. Dos siglos de historia.* Madrid: Pablo Iglesias, 1988.

González, Anabel. *El feminismo en España, hoy.* Bilbao: Zero, 1979.

González, Anabel, et al. *Los orígenes del feminismo en España.* Bilbao: Zero, 1980.

Martín-Gamero, Amalia. *Antología del feminismo.* Madrid: Alianza, 1975.

Moreno, Amparo. *Mujeres en lucha. El movimiento feminista en España.* Barcelona: Anagrama, 1977.

Nash, Mary. *Mujer, familia y trabajo en España, 1875–1936.* Barcelona: Anthropos, 1983.

Scanlon, Geraldine. *La polémica feminista en la España contemporánea: 1868–1974.* Madrid: Akal, 1986.

Varia. *Mujer y sociedad en España. 1700–1975.* Madrid: Ministerio de Cultura, 1982.

Catherine G. Bellver

Feminist Theory and the Contemporary Spanish Stage

To speak of a feminist theory of the contemporary Spanish stage implies a consideration of Spanish women playwrights whose contribution to the theater from 1975 to the present is marked by an ever-increasing effort to appropriate in dramatic terms particular ideologies that are fundamental to feminist thought and criticism. On the whole, their work seeks to confront the absence of women from a conventional, male-inscribed literary tradition and to document women's realities from a female perspective. Their dramatic expression assumes a prevailing social condition that excludes women from the dominant discourse, presupposes a critique of male dominance, and calls for change. Collectively, the work of these women playwrights theorizes ways of exposing women's inferior social status.

The dramatic works of Carmen *Resino (1941–), Concha *Romero (1945–), Paloma *Pedrero (1957–), and Lidia *Falcón (1935–) are the most representative of Spain's contribution to the three principal categories of feminist playwrighting: materialist or socialist, liberal, and radical or cultural. Resino and Romero are exponents of the first of these three categories. This means that they maintain that the female experience cannot be understood outside a specific historical or political context. Beyond depicting woman as the victim of patriarchy, Resino and Romero are committed to revealing how the oppression and inferior status of women have evolved and persist within the existing social order. Their works do not showcase the female experience as separate from the male experience but in relationship to it and demonstrate that gender is hierarchically opposed. Both Resino and Romero employ a variety of techniques, such as irony, metatheater, and historical drama, to deconstruct woman as mythic subject in order to focus on woman as an oppressed class within a power-structured social order. Also characteristic of their affiliation with a materialist feminist perspective is the notion of female community that pervades their plays. Frequently in their works, female characters allude to bonding in order to confront their oppressors.

Women in Resino's and Romero's plays suffer from enclosure (*Encierro*). Resino, for example, underscores how both history and a socially codified notion of gender roles have effectively trapped women into acting prescriptively in accordance with traditional and antiquated ideas. She challenges the notion of woman as naturally submissive. Resino's female characters are individuals on a quest for self-determination in a male-oriented world. Her female protagonists pursue liberty regardless of the consequences, including death, and always strive to place the personal above the social, such as Penelope in *Ulises no vuelve* (1983; Ulysses Doesn't Return), princess Wu-Tso in *Nueva historia de la princesa y el dragón* (1989; New Story of the Princess and the Dragon), and Isabel in *Los eróticos sueños de Isabel Tudor* (1992; Isabel Tudor's Erotic Dreams). In other plays, she represents a general dehumanized condition founded on deception where nothing is as it seems and uses women to unmask the falsity of surface reality. Such is the case, for example, in *La sed* (1981; Thirst) and *La actriz* (1990; The Actress), where women as the objects of the male gaze desperately resist being pressed and stamped in the traditional mold of submissive and demure females, or in *La recepción* (1994; The Reception), where the female character Ella (She) provides the necessary answers for the crucial link between everyday reality and illusion. In *Ultimar detalles* (1984; To Finish the Details), the protagonist Lunarcitos is portrayed as the victim of her fiancé who attempts repeatedly to strip her of her personal identity prior to their wedding until she calls off the marriage in defiance. Reality and illusion are intricately interwoven in Resino's plays as they pertain to the female experience in order to illustrate to what extent women have been perceived from a predominantly male view.

Romero uses history in *Un olor a ámbar* (1983; A Smell Like Amber) and *Las bodas de una princesa* (1988; A Princess's Wedding), contemporary settings in *Un maldito beso* (1989; A Cursed Kiss), classical mythology in *Así aman los dioses* (1991; So Love the Gods), and metatheater in *Allá él* (1994; That's His Affair) to feminize the context of her drama and explore gender ideology in Spanish society. The conflictive interaction that takes place between her male and female characters serves as the basis for Romero's portrayal of women as victims of dominant social structure. The binary opposition of gender is fundamental to Romero's feminist discourse. Romero's male characters resort to subterfuge in order to exploit women. Power, and more specifically the abuse of it, and the different ways it manifests itself in male-female relationships are central to Romero's ideological premise. She employs a variety of feminist techniques, such as the notion of writing the body as espoused by *l'écriture feminine* and the concept of feminine silence, to depict women visually as objectified and promote the feminist idea that women must reclaim their bodies and a voice of their own in order to be independent and free from male dominance. Whether through historical female figures, such as Santa *Teresa de Jesús (1515–1582) in *Un olor a ámbar* and *Isabel la Católica (1451–1504) and *Juana *la Loca* (1479–1555) in *Las bodas de una princesa*, contemporary types, such as María in *Un maldito beso* and Pepa in *Allá él*, or mythological figures, such as Venus and Juno in *Así aman los dioses*, the exploration of female identity lies at the very center of Romero's critical discourse.

Pedrero subscribes to a liberal feminist perspective in her theater. Her intention is to minimize the difference between men and women by promoting change within the social order as presently constituted. Unlike Resino and Romero, Pedrero places more emphasis on the individual than the group to illustrate how the dialectics of power informs the dynamics of human relations to the detriment of women. Gender constructs in Pedrero's plays are also binarily opposed and bespeak a power-structured relationship. Feminine sexuality is a predominant theme in her plays. Through the curious doubling of her characters, whether male or female, who are at once protagonists and antagonists, such as in *La llamada de Lauren* (1984; Lauren's Call), *Invierno de luna alegre* (1987; Winter of Happy Moon), and *El color de agosto* (1987; The Color of August), Pedrero is able to broach ontological questions as they pertain to all individuals, but especially women. In *Besos de lobo* (1987; Wolf's Kisses), she uses homosexuality to that end. In more recent plays, such as *El pasamanos* (1995; The Handrail) and *De la noche al alba* (1995; From Night to Dawn), Pedrero has intensified her exploration of human sexuality as a means of a more androgynous understanding of human relationships. Pedrero's theater begs an understanding of feminine epistemology as a multifaceted concept that stands in direct opposition to the female image as canonically constructed by a patriarchal mind-set.

Of all the feminist dramatic expressions in post-Franco Spain, nowhere is a radical perspective more evident than in Falcón's work. Falcón's theater carries a personal and political message and promotes a female countercanon. Her theater serves as a speaking platform to posit a critical view of the authoritative political underpinnings of Spanish society that have historically sought to strip women of self-worth and relegate them to a subordinate position. In plays such as *¡No moleste, calle y pague, Señora!* (1984; Don't Disturb, Be Quiet, and Pay, Ma'am!), *Tres idiotas españolas* (1994; Three Spanish Idiots), and *¡Parid, parid, malditas!* (1994; Give Birth, Give Birth, Cursed [Girls]!), she concerns herself with achieving a transcendental bond among women in an effort to address them as a community and suggest that their oppression is a shared experience. She relies on the female body as a source of achieving a feminine consciousness, as the concrete image of genderized meanings, as in ¡Parid, parid, malditas! In *Tu único amor* (1991; Your Only Love) she deals with the socialization of gender roles and addresses both the personal and institutional oppression of women by pointing to the fundamental ideological separateness and difference of males and females. In other plays, Falcón turns to events of national history, such as the Civil War in *Las mujeres caminaron con el fuego del siglo* (1994; Women Walked in the Fire of the Century), to illustrate how history has minimized the active role of women in its evolution. *Siempre busqué el amor* (1994; I Always Looked for Love) recounts in vivid detail the true story of a family who, after long years of tyrannical oppression by the patriarch, resorts to murder in order to attain freedom and retribution for the unjust abuse they suffered.

Regardless of perspective, what is evident in the evolution of Spanish theater authored by women during the last decades is an evident progression in their works to focus on the feminine as the site of the dramatic text and critical discourse in an effort to represent the female gender. The procedure is ultimately liberating. It runs counter to the historical literary tradition of relegating the woman, as either author or character, to marginal roles. The objective is to legitimize the female voice, defend a feminist ideal, and elaborate a feminist consciousness. *See also* Drama by Spanish Women Writers: 1970–2000; Feminism in Spain: 1900–2000

Work by

Falcón, Lidia. *Teatro*. Madrid: Vindicación Feminista, 1994.

———. *Tu único amor*. Art Teatral 3.3 (1991): 19–24.

Pedrero, Paloma. *Besos de lobo*. Madrid: Fundamentos, 1987.

———. *El color de agosto*. Madrid: Antonio Machado, 1989.

———. *De la noche al alba*. Madrid: Sociedad General de Autores de España, 1995.

———. *Invierno de luna alegre*. Madrid: Fundamentos, 1987.

———. *La llamada de Lauren*. Valladolid: Caja de Ahorros Provincial, 1985.

———. *El pasamanos*. Primer Acto 258 (1995): 67–90.

Resino, Carmen. *Los eróticos sueños de Isabel Tudor*. Madrid: Fundamentos, 1992.

———. *Nueva historia de la princesa y el dragón*. Madrid: Lucerna, 1989.

———. *La recepción*. Alcorcón: Ayuntamiento de Alcorcón, 1994.

———. *Teatro breve. El oculto enemigo del profesor Schneider*. Madrid: Fundamentos, 1990.

———. *Ulises no vuelve*. Madrid: Instituto del Teatro Internacional, 1983.

Romero, Concha. *Allá él*. Estreno 20.2 (1994): 8–14.

———. *Así aman los dioses*. Madrid: Ediciones Clásicas, 1991.

———. *Las bodas de una princesa*. Madrid: Lucerna, 1988.

———. *Un maldito beso*. Gestos 8 (1989): 109–144.

———. *Un olor a ámbar*. Madrid: La Avispa, 1983.

Work about

"Dramaturgas españolas: Presencia y condición en la escena española contemporánea." *Estreno* 19.1 (1993): 117–120.

Gabriele, John P. "Concha Romero." *Spanish Women Writers. A Bio-Bibliographical Source Book*. Ed. Linda Gould Levine, Ellen Engelson Marson, and Gloria Fieman Waldman. Westport, CT: Greenwood P, 1993. 441–450.

Lamartina-Lens, Iride. "Paloma Pedrero." *Spanish Women Writers. A Bio-Bibliographical Source Book*. Ed. Linda Gould Levine, Ellen Engelson Marson, and Gloria Fieman Waldman. Westport, CT: Greenwood P, 1993. 389–396.

Leonard, Candyce. "Women Writers and Their Characters in Spanish Drama in the 1980s." *Anales de la Literatura Española Contemporánea* 17.1–3 (1992): 243–256.

O'Connor, Patricia W. *Dramaturgas españolas de hoy. Una introducción*. Madrid: Fundamentos, 1988.

Ragué, María-José. "La mujer como autora en el teatro español contemporáneo." *Estreno* 19.1 (1993): 13–16.

Serrano, Virtudes. "Hacia una dramaturgia femenina." *Anales de la Literatura Española Contemporánea* 19.3 (1992): 343–364.

John P. Gabriele

Fernán Caballero
See Böhl de Faber, Cecilia, Pseudonym Fernán Caballero (1796–1877)

Fernández Cubas, Cristina (1945–   )

Although she has a degree in law and has worked as a journalist, fiction is the first love of Cristina Fernández Cubas. As a child she listened, entranced, to the marvelous tales told by her nursemaid and her brother; as an adult she has invented her own narratives where fantasy and reality, the extraordinary and the quotidian, coexist. Doubles are a constant in her work, as is a preoccupation with the "unspeakable," a term that encompasses the unutterable, unreadable, and incomprehensible.

The four stories of *Mi hermana Elba* (1980; My Sister Elba) are an excellent introduction to the distinctive and remarkably coherent fictive world of Fernández Cubas. "Lúnula y Violeta" exemplifies what will be a continuing interest in split personalities. The titular characters are inverted images of one another. Violeta is timid, unsure of herself, and a struggling writer; Lúnula is uninhibited, self-assured, and a gifted teller of tales. There are repeated references in the story to mirrors and windows in which the characters see themselves reflected, and the ending dramatizes the paradox of doubling: simultaneous unity and duality, identity and difference. In "La ventana del jardín" (The Window on the Garden), unintelligible language and inexplicable behavior draw attention to problems of communication and decoding. The narrator's misreading of events and behavior dramatizes the difficulty, if not the impossibility, of deciphering what goes on around him. "Mi hermana Elba" recreates the magic and power of a child's imagination and her special way of looking at and being in the world. The ability to become invisible can be interpreted as an expression of the fantastic or as a commentary on the fact that children are often not "seen" by adults and what is real for the former is dismissed as imaginary by the latter. Elba's death coincides with her older sister's first kiss and entry into adolescence, thus raising the possibility that Elba is a manifestation of the self now left behind.

Los altillos de Brumal (1983; The Highlands of Brumal) also includes four narratives. The title story, which has been made into a film, exhibits the ambiguity and sense of mystery that have come to be associated with Fernández Cubas's fiction. The narrator, Adriana, returns to the village where she was born in order to recover her past and her younger self, known as Anairda. Earlier she had abandoned the study of history in favor of the art of cooking and the creation of dishes whose main ingredient is lacking, as in vegetable soup without vegetables and fish fillets that contain no fish. Confronted with a series of strange occurrences, Adriana ends by accepting illogicality and foregoing explanations. The story has been read as a celebration of the fantastic and as a validation of the semiotic and corresponding rejection of the symbolic world of order, logic, and rationality. Humor is important in "La noche de Jezabel" (The Night of Jezabel), which is both a ghost story and a parody of that form. The fluid relationship between the frame narrative and a series of embedded tales blurs the distinction between outside and inside. Conflicting versions of events undermine narrative authority and destabilize the fact/fiction dichotomy. The metafictional dimension of this story is accentuated in Fernández Cubas's first novel, *El año de Gracia* (1985; The Year of Grace), an ironic rereading of a series of texts that include *Robinson Crusoe* and the Bible. Books are the protagonist's constant point of reference, but his experience consistently undercuts his literary models and renders them invalid. In a subversion of the traditional rite of passage, Daniel is blighted rather than enriched by his stay on the desolate island where he is shipwrecked, and his attempt at (self-) understanding is frustrated. The roles of intertextuality, self-conscious referentiality, parody, and irony in the novel have been analyzed, as has the question of knowledge and its relation to gender considerations (see Bellver, Margenot, and Spires).

A third collection of short fiction, *El ángulo del horror* (The Angle of Horror), appeared in 1990. Indecipherability is foregrounded in "La Flor de España" (The Flower of Spain), where verbal and nonverbal messages abound. The narrator's decoding of signs is complicated by the fact that she is in a foreign country, and her interpretations of words and deeds are problematic. Fernández Cubas's interest in perception takes a somewhat different form in "El legado del abuelo" (Grandfather's Legacy), a study of the mind of a boy, his limited view of the world, and his fall into knowledge when he eventually realizes his responsibility for his grandfather's death. If vision, like knowledge, is ambiguous and elusive in Fernández Cubas's fiction, it is especially so when the seeing eye is that of a child. Vision is also an issue in the title piece, which involves seeing things from a different and horrifying angle. Such typically Gothic elements as monsters, demons, and sex-starved villains are absent from Fernández Cubas's tales, and horror is provoked instead by rhetoric. Uncertainty and an atmosphere of foreboding are created by the use of indefinites, circumlocutions, expressions of conjecture, contradictions, omissions, the undermining of narrators' credibility, and the proliferation of lexical items that inspire apprehension or revulsion. These techniques, identified by Pérez in her study of *El ángulo del horror*, are found throughout Fernández Cubas's work.

The tales of *Con Agatha en Estambul* (1994; With Agatha in Istanbul) confirm the author's predilection for first-person narration, concern with problems of identity and communication, and penchant for indeterminacy and enigmatic, open endings. The closing and titular narrative is an affectionate tribute to Agatha Christie. Its narrator, like her counterparts in "La ventana del jardín" and "La Flor de España," vainly tries to solve a mystery (her husband's possible infidelity), but it proves as impenetrable as the secrets of the Turkish language and the fog that envelops the city. The opening story, "Mundo" (Trunk, also World), is an intriguing exploration of female creativity and forms of storytelling. Zatlin has examined the five stories of this collection as woman-centered texts. Fernández Cubas's second novel, *El columpio* (1995; The Swing,) is set in an isolated valley in the Pyrenees and an old house where space is threatening and a sensation of vague menace lurks. Many of the elements of the book are familiar: a strained mother-daughter relationship, a journey in space and time, multiple instances of duplication and doubling, the narrator's struggle to make sense of peculiar incidents, and a blurring of distinctions between the natural and the supernatural, between waking moments and dreams. In addition, Fernández Cubas has published two narratives for children: *El vendedor de sombras* (1982; The Seller of Dreams) and *Cris y Cros* (1988; Cris and Cros). They present in simplified form concerns that are characteristic of her writing for adults and utilize many of the same strategies, devices, and symbols, thus affording a vision in miniature of her fictive world. *See also* Short Fiction by Women Writers: 1975–1998, Post-Franco

Work by

El ángulo del horror. Barcelona: Tusquets, 1990.
El año de Gracia. Barcelona: Tusquets, 1985.
"The Attics of Brumal." Trans. Phyllis Zatlin. *Short Story International* 14.80 (1990): 53–75.
El columpio. Barcelona: Tusquets, 1995.
Con Agatha en Estambul. Barcelona: Tusquets, 1994.
Cris y Cros, seguido de El vendedor de sombras. Madrid: Alfaguara, 1988.
Mi hermana Elba y Los altillos de Brumal. Barcelona: Tusquets, 1988.

Work about

Bellver, Catherine G. "*El año de Gracia* and the Displacement of the Word." *Studies in Twentieth Century Literature* 16 (1992): 221–232.

Bretz, Mary Lee. "Cristina Fernández Cubas and the Recuperation of the Semiotic in *Los altillos de Brumal*." *Anales de la Literatura Española Contemporánea* 13 (1988): 177–188.

Glenn, Kathleen M. "Gothic Indecipherability and Doubling in the Fiction of Cristina Fernández Cubas." *Monographic Review/Revista Monográfica* 8 (1992): 125–141.

Margenot, John B., III. "Parody and Self-Consciousness in Cristina Fernández Cubas' *El año de Gracia*." *Siglo XX/20th Century* 11 (1993): 71–87.

Pérez, Janet. "Cristina Fernández Cubas: Narrative Unreliability and the Flight from Clarity, or, The Quest for Knowledge in the Fog." *Hispanófila* 122 (1998): 29–39.

———. "Fernández Cubas, Abjection, and the 'retórica del horror.'" *Explicación de Textos Literarios* 24.1–2 (1995): 159–171.

Spires, Robert C. "Disempowerment and Knowledge: *El año de Gracia*." *Post-Totalitarian Spanish Fiction*. Columbia: U of Missouri P, 1996. 156–172.

Talbot, Lynn K. "Journey into the Fantastic: Cristina Fernández Cubas' 'Los altillos de Brumal.'" *Letras Femeninas* 15 (1989): 37–47.

Zatlin, Phyllis. "Amnesia, Strangulation, Hallucination and Other Mishaps: The Perils of Being Female in Tales of Cristina Fernández Cubas." *Hispania* 79 (1996): 36–44.

———. "Tales from Fernández Cubas: Adventure in the Fantastic." *Monographic Review/Revista Monográfica* 3 (1987): 107–118.

Kathleen M. Glenn

Fernández de Alarcón, Cristobalina (1576?–1646)

A celebrated poet in her own time, Doña Cristobalina Fernández de Alarcón was born in Antequera, the illegitimate daughter of Gonzalo Fernández Perdigón. Her father recognized her as his daughter in his will of May 6, 1597, leaving her one-fifth of his estate. Educated by Bartolomé Martínez and the renowned humanist Juan de Aguilar, in 1591 she married Agustín de Ríos, a merchant, who died 12 years later, leaving no children. In 1606 she married Juan Francisco Correa, a Portuguese student, with whom she had three daughters and a son. Her husband was graduated Bachelor of Canon Law in 1613. Fernández de Alarcón was a widow when she died in 1646.

Fernández de Alarcón's verse was praised by Lope de *Vega (1562–1635) in his *Laurel del Apolo* (Silva II). She won several poetry competitions, and Pedro Espinosa (1578–1650) published some of her poems in his *Primera parte de las flores de poetas ilustres de España* (1605). Rodríguez Marín suggests that Espinosa and Fernández de Alarcón were lovers while she was married to Agustín Ríos and that her marriage to Correa caused Espinosa to retire to a monastery.

Only 15 poems by Fernández de Alarcón remain today. One is a love poem, perhaps to Espinosa. Most of the others are entries in poetic competitions—commemorations of religious/civic events: the canonization of Saints Ignacio de Loyola (1491–1556) and Francisco Xavier (1506–1552), the beatification of Santa *Teresa de Jesús (1515–1582), and praises of authors. Given Fernández de Alarcón's considerable fame among her contemporaries, it seems likely that she wrote other works that have been lost.

Work by

Serrano y Sanz, Manuel. *Antología de poetisas líricas*. Vol. 1. Madrid: Revista de Archivos, Bibliotecas y Museos, 1915.

Work about

Olivares, Julián, and Elizabeth S. Boyce, eds. *Tras el espejo la musa escribe: Lírica femenina de los Siglos de Oro*. Madrid: Siglo Veintiuno de España, 1993.

Rodríguez Marín, Francisco. "Nuevos datos sobre Cristobalina Fernández de Alarcón." *Boletín de la Real Academia Española* 7 (1920): 368–423.

———. *Pedro Espinosa: Estudio biográfico, bibliográfico y crítico*. Madrid: Tipografía de la Revista de Archivos, 1907.

Serrano y Sanz, Manuel. *Apuntes para una biblioteca de escritoras españolas*. Madrid: Rivadeneyra, 1903. 1: 283–286.

Elizabeth S. Boyce and Julián Olivares

Figuera Aymerich, Angela (1902–1984)

Together with other Basque social realist poets, such as Blas de Otero and Gabriel Celaya, whose writings appear mainly in the 1950s, Angela Figuera Aymerich rejects the aesthetics of pure poetry of the 1927 generation to which she belonged by birth. While she joins her generation in denouncing social injustice and violence, and in defending the rights of the dispossessed, it is her female perspective on those issues that provides her poetry with its unique and distinctive character.

Her father's death provoked the family's move from Bilbao to Madrid in 1930. With a degree in philosophy and humanities from the University of Madrid, Figuera Aymerich passed the official exams and obtained a permanent teaching position. She married Julio Figuera Andú. The outbreak of the Spanish Civil War in 1936 surprised them in Madrid where they remained during the war and after. Their son, Juan Ramón, was born on December, 30 1936, while the father was at the front. From 1954 to 1962, Figuera Aymerich worked for the National Library and the "Bibliobús," bringing books to Madrid's depressed neighborhoods. In 1957, with a grant to pursue library-related studies, she traveled to Paris where she met Chilean Nobel Prize–winning poet Pablo Neruda. They spoke of the poet's struggle in the repressive atmosphere of postwar Franco's Spain, and these conversations inspired Neruda's "Letter to Spanish Poets," which Figuera Aymerich delivered to her fellow writers. Due to censorship, it was not published in Spain until 1973.

She began publishing at age 46. *Mujer de barro* (1948; Earthen Woman) consists of brief poems where a female voice sings of union with her sister the earth and with her lover. Her praise of a "natural" way of being contrasts with preconceived notions about woman's identity. "Mujer," for example, dispels the traditional male literary construction of "woman" as delicate and weak. Woman's identity is not fixed, nor is her body a hermetic container, but a transforming and transformative vessel, open to the outside. The sense of fusion with nature continues in *Soria pura* (1949; Pure Soria), a collection that pays tribute to nature symbolism in Antonio Machado's verse. However, a poem like "Cortad el árbol" (Cut the Tree) questions the relation of language to the world. The beauty of the real tree eclipses its linguistic rendition. Only by cutting it can the poet create the tree in the poem; thus language emerges in the absence of reality.

In *Vencida por el ángel* (1950; Defeated by the Angel, 1949 "Verbo" prize) and in following collections, the intimate and personal give way to more public concerns. "Mujeres del mercado," (Market Women) from *El grito inútil* (1952; The Useless Shout, "Ifach" prize) offers a stark portrait of women reduced by poverty to scavenging the market for the most meager foods. While culture praises them as creators of life, poverty dehumanizes them. The "Mundo concluso" (World Concluded) from *Víspera de la vida* (1953; The Evening before Life) is a "fabricated," "rigid" structure where everything is determined. Poems in *Los días duros* (1953; Harsh Days) expose the hypocrisy of cultural and religious systems that glorify woman as mother but exclude her from power. Women's traditional shields (motherhood, tenderness, the home) have become useless in view of more pressing social issues, such as hunger and violence.

In *Belleza cruel* (1958; Cruel Beauty, "Nueva España" prize), beauty is cruel because it is unreachable from reality. The prologue by León Felipe recognizes the struggle of Spanish poets to achieve freedom and justice. In "Rosa incómoda" (Uncomfortable Rose), the rose as image of beauty becomes an annoying inconvenience to carry around in the midst of poverty and injustice. High aesthetic ideals are confronted with concrete, poverty-stricken human beings. In *Toco la tierra. Letanías* (1962; I Touch the Earth.

Litanies), the speaker intones a litany of repetitions, apostrophes, and interrogations. These linguistic devices attempt to bring language closer to reality in order to affect social change. In the uncollected poem "Exhortación impertinente a mis hermanas poetisas" (Impertinent Exhortation to My Sister Poets), Aymerich urges a literary sisterhood to imitate Eve's example and asserts the life-affirming value of "biting the apple" in contrast to following the programs and models culture has assigned to women. *Cuentos tontos para niños listos* (1980; Stupid Stories for Bright Children), from stories she told her granddaughter, and *Canciones para todo el año* (1984; Songs for the Whole Year) reflect Aymerich's love for children and animals as the only remaining pure creatures in a world gone astray.

Figuera Aymerich does not postulate a program for feminine vindication. Her poetry, however, challenges the system of fixed cultural assumptions and emphasizes, instead, process and transformation. Other contemporary poets voiced the same polemic against societal values, but Figuera Aymerich offers a woman's vantage point, feminizing the generic masculinity of the poetry of protest and commitment.

Work by

Antología de Angela Figuera Aymerich. Ed. Alfredo Gracia Vicente. Monterrey: Sierra Madre, 1969.
Antología total. Ed. Julián Marcos. Madrid: Videosistemas, 1973.
Canciones para todo el año. Monterrey: Trillas, 1984.
Obras completas. Ed. Roberta Quance. Madrid: Hiperión, 1986.
Primera antología. Caracas: Lírica Hispana, 1961.

Work about

Evans, Jo. *Moving Reflections: Gender, Faith and Aesthetics in the Work of Angela Figuera Aymerich*. London: Tamesis, 1996.
Mandlove, Nancy. "Historia and Intra-historia: Two Spanish Women in Dialogue with History." *Third Woman* 2 (1984): 84–93.
Manrique de Lara, J.G. "Prosaísmo árido y ardiente humanidad en la poesía de Angela Figuera." *Poetas sociales españoles*. Madrid: Epesa, 1974. 49–56.
Robbins, Jill. "La mujer en el umbral. La simbología de la madre en la poesía de Angela Figuera." *Anales de la Literatura Española Contemporánea* 25.2 (2000): 557–585.
Wilcox, John. *Women Poets of Spain, 1860–1990*. Urbana and Chicago: U of Illinois P, 1997.
Wright, Eleanor. *The Poetry of Protest under Franco*. London: Tamesis, 1986. 154–157.

Candelas Gala

Flores, Juan de
See *Grisel y Mirabella* (published c. 1495)

Forest, Eva (1928–)

Born in Barcelona, Eva Forest is a Spanish psychiatrist, feminist, essayist, and storywriter. She studied medicine at the University of Madrid and then worked in the psychiatric clinic of a well-known psychiatrist, José López Ibor. Married to the controversial dramatist Alfonso Sastre, her writing most often deals with social justice, ranging from prison memoirs to revolutionary agitation to philosophical preoccupations. Her personal beliefs and commitments have often engaged her in solidarity movements and sedition. She has written that she supports all struggles for liberation and fellowship for all condemned people in Spain and elsewhere.

One of her most widely read works, *Diario y cartas desde la cárcel* (1975; *From a Spanish Prison*, 1975), was first published outside Spain in Paris as a bilingual (French and Spanish) edition in 1975 as well as in English that same year. This book was the direct result of her imprisonment in September 1974 after the bombing of the Café Rolando in Madrid, a coffeehouse frequented by police. At first suspected of hiding the perpetrators of the bombing, she was subsequently accused of complicity in ETA's (Euskadi Ta Askatasuna—Basque freedom fighters) December 20, 1973, terrorist assassination of Spain's then prime minister and Franco supporter Admiral Luis Carrero Blanco in Madrid. As her title indicates, the book is composed of a diary and letters; Forest claims her purpose was to write to her children. After being held at the Dirección General de Seguridad where she endured interrogations and torture, she was placed in solitary confinement and there managed to write. The letters were written in Yeserías, a women's prison in Madrid.

Her journal and letters deal only with family matters and her concern for her children's education. In one instance she expresses gratitude to her family for the inquiring attitude her children have adopted, for she feels that serious questions educate the entire family. Such practices have helped her family to eliminate to a high degree the authority principle that has ruled the bourgeois family. In Forest's opinion, the microcellular family, like hers, allows humankind to flower, develop, and advance in a favorable milieu.

Forest's imprisonment first became a cause célèbre in France due to publication of the diary by Editions des Femmes and to accounts of her treatment in prison that appeared in French publications such as *Elle* and *Les Temps Modernes*. In spite of her stated intent for writing the letters and diary, critical readers have recently indicated that one of Forest's major goals was to present a favorable image to offset the negative portrayal of her that came from the media.

Forest's involvement in insurgent activities prompted another book, *Operación Ogro: Cómo y por qué ejecutamos a Carrero Blanco* (1974; *Operation Ogro: The Execution of Admiral Luis Carrero Blanco*, 1975). This work, written under Forest's pseudonym Julien Agirre, presents the rationale and tactics of the Basque commandos responsible for assassinating Carrero Blanco, the "Ogre." Its authorship was one of the charges that provoked Forest's imprisonment from 1974 to 1977. Of historical value, the author presents testimony in the form of journalistic interviews and includes several appendices that present ETA manifestos and police documents. Under her pseudonym, Forest wrote in her preface that her militant solidarity with ETA created the bond that brought the organization to ask her to write about the so-called execution. Her complicity was finally made explicit with publication of *Operación Ogro, diez años después: Edición popular en la que se revela que "Julien Agirre" fue el seudónimo de Eva Forest* (1983; Ten Years after Operation Ogro: A Popular Edition in Which It Is Revealed That "Julien Agirre" Was the Pseudonym of Eva Forest); this edition recreates the episode carried out by the Basque commandos.

Another testimonial of her prison experience appears in *Testimonios de lucha y resistencia: Yeserías 75–77* (1977; Testimonies of Struggle and Resistance: Yeserías [Women's Prison] 1975–1977). Forest considers the major theme of the modern state's use of torture and introduces her own story and testimony of other prisoners, 30 women and one man. After putting their stories in the context of the situation of Basque political prisoners in Spain, Forest deals with theoretical aspects of marginal existence and the difficulties of seeking expression in the sociopolitical arena. For the 1979 edition of this book, Alfonso Sastre wrote a long introductory essay on the theme of institutionalized torture in the modern bourgeois state.

Onintze en el país de la democracia (1985; Onintze in the Land of Democracy) is Forest's first attempt at writing fictional narrative, but it depends heavily on her own history and the theme of torture. Onintze, a Basque schoolteacher, is arrested on suspicion of political subversion, although her detention is an apparent mistake. She is tortured and subsequently decides to throw in her lot with the revolutionaries. The message is that police brutality and institutionalized methods of interrogation do not change from dictatorial regime to the putative democracy. In this work Forest does not show that she has made the transition from transcription of testimony to literary authorship, but the force of her narrative is often powerful.

Work by

Diarios y cartas desde la cárcel. Paris: Femmes, 1975. French and Spanish.

From a Spanish Prison. Berkeley: Moon Books; New York: Random House, 1975.
Onintze en el país de la democracia. Madrid: Libertarias, 1985.
Operación Ogro: Cómo y por qué ejecutamos a Carrero Blanco. Hendaye: Mugalde, 1974.
Operation Ogro: The Execution of Admiral Luis Carrero Blanco. Trans. and intro. B. Probst Solomon. New York: Quadrangle/New York Times Book Co., 1975.
Testimonios de lucha y resistencia: Yeserías 75–77. Hendaye: Mugalde, 1977.

Work about

Glenn, Kathleen M. "Resistance and Survival: Eva Forest's *Diario y cartas desde la cárcel*." *Monographic Review / Revista Monográfica* 11 (1995): 110–120.

Glenn Morocco

Fórmica, Mercedes (1918–)

She was an active member of the Falange during the Spanish Civil War, but after receiving her law degree in 1948, Mercedes Fórmica became an ardent defender of women's rights. She was instrumental in a major legal campaign that changed the situation for Spanish women in 66 statutes in 1958. In 1966, she gave a series of lectures that affected women's civil rights. Fórmica has published nine books—four novels, three books of memoirs, and two historical biographies—but she has not received the critical attention she justly deserves. A new edition by Bravo (1991) of her novel *A instancia de parte* (1955; On Behalf of the Third Party) has in part remedied this situation.

Her two first novels, *Monte de Sancha* (1950; Sancha's Mount) and *La ciudad perdida* (1952; The Lost City), deal with the effects of the Civil War. Unlike many women writers of postwar Spain, Fórmica has written extensively about her activities during the war years. Although her political affiliation was not a secret, she defends no ideology in her writing; in fact, she has been unfairly labeled as one of the most important novelists of the Falange by Julio Rodríguez Puértolas. The value of these novels, aside from their artistic worth, is that they comprise a historical document seen through the eyes of a woman.

A instancia de parte shows Fórmica's interest in women's rights illustrated by the unfair treatment of women in cases of adultery in contrast with the situation of their male counterparts. Her last novel, *Collar de ámbar* (1989; Amber Necklace), which presents an unusual juxtaposition of history and fiction, continues to demonstrate the author's feminist concerns, this time with regard to Jewish women.

History is a constant theme in Fórmica's work. Her two historical biographies, *La hija de don Juan de Austria. Ana de Jesús en el proceso al pastelero de Madrigal* (1973; The Daughter of Don Juan of Austria. Ana de Jesús at the Trial of the Madrigal Pastry Cook) and *María de Mendoza. Solución a un enigma amoroso* (1979; María de Mendoza. Solution to an Amorous Enigma), show her at her best. The latter won the important Fastenrath Prize of the Royal Academy. The combination of strong female characters, suspenseful historical events, and a mastery of narrative techniques make for very compelling reading.

Fórmica has published two volumes of autobiographical memoirs, *Visto y vivido (1931–1937)* (1982; Seen and Lived) and *Escucho el silencio* (1984; I Listen to the Silence), and a short reminiscence of her childhood, *La infancia* (1987; Childhood). Interestingly, in a pattern typical for male writers, her autobiographical texts tend to be more a cultural description of her times than a personal account of her life. Her memoirs can be read as a historical document about the most important intellectual and political figures of Franco's Spain and also as a denunciation of social repression.

Fórmica is a complex writer who incorporates her diverse, seemingly contradictory concerns in all her works. A defender of the Falangist ideology, she points out the unfairness of repression and fights for women's rights. Her interest in history takes her from sixteenth-century Spain to the Civil War, and she is as adept at portraying Jewish women as she is writing about fascist leaders.

Work by

A instancia de parte. Ed. María Elena Bravo. Madrid: Castalia, 1991.
La ciudad perdida. Barcelona: Caralt, 1952.
Collar de ámbar. Madrid: Caro Raggio, 1989.
Escucho el silencio. Barcelona: Planeta, 1984.
La hija de don Juan de Austria. Ana de Jesús en el proceso al pastelero de Madrigal. Madrid: Revista de Occidente, 1973.
María de Mendoza. Solución a un enigma amoroso. Madrid: Caro Raggio, 1979.
Monte de Sancha. Barcelona: Caralt, 1950.
Visto y vivido (1931–1937). Barcelona: Planeta, 1982.

Work about

Alborg, Concha. Cinco figuras en torno a la novela de posguerra: Galvarriato, Soriano, Fórmica, Boixados y Aldecoa. Madrid: Libertarias, 1993.
Olazagasti Segovia, Elena. "'En busca del tiempo perdido': Tres novelistas cuentan su historia." Letras Femeninas 18 (1992): 64–73.
Pérez, Janet. Contemporary Women Writers of Spain. Boston: Twayne, 1988.

Concha Alborg

Fortún, Elena, Pseudonym of Encarnación Aragoneses Urquijo (1886–1952)

Before the Civil War (1936–1939), Encarnación Aragoneses Urquijo was one of the most influential Spanish writers for children, and she remained so after it, despite her political views. Even though she was a Republican and went into exile in 1938, her books were widely acclaimed. Her extremely popular character Celia Gálvez de Montalbán was a favorite among Spanish girls during the 1940s, 1950s, and 1960s. In 1957, only a few years after her death in Madrid, her friends María Martos de Baeza and Matilde Ras sponsored a fund-raising effort to erect a monument in her memory in the Parque del Oeste, Madrid, which stands with the dedication words "A Elena Fortún, los niños de España" (To Elena Fortún, from the Children of Spain). During the early 1980s a general new edition of her works was published, and in 1987 the first edition of Celia en la revolución (Celia in the Revolution) appeared. This last work provided an astonishing revelation of the author's mysterious identity for several generations of faithful readers who had followed her characters for decades. Most recently the television series (1993) based on Aragoneses's Celia lo que dice (What Celia Says), directed by José Luis Borau with script by Carmen *Martín Gaite (1925–2000), returned Celia to the limelight. Aragoneses's appeal and success as an author of children's literature have been evident during the three sharply defined periods of twentieth-century Spanish history: pre-Republican and Republican years, the long postwar period, and finally democracy. Yet very little has been published about her personal life.

In 1987 Marisol Dorao edited Aragoneses's surprise book Celia en la revolución in the classical collection "Celia y su mundo" (Celia and Her World) by Aguilar Publishers, where all her books have been published since 1935 when Cuchifritín el hermano de Celia (Cuchifritín Celia's Brother) appeared. According to the publishers, the book definitively completes Celia's family saga. It is a very different work, emotionally charged and almost autobiographical in character. It seems that events narrated in the text may have come from notes taken by Aragoneses as events unfolded during her Civil War experience on the Republican side and that they might have formed part of a diary that Aragoneses never made public. A draft of the book was finished in Argentina in 1943, during her exile years, and it is apparent that Aragoneses never went back to it. The possible existence of the manuscript was known by Aguilar Publishers and it was actually given to Professor Marisol Dorao to publish by Aragoneses's daughter-in-law, Ana María Link de Gorbea. For Dorao, the character Celia was created by the author in her own image. Even though Aragoneses began her literary career in the 1920s as a mature woman of about 40, it seems that Celia resembles her and expresses many aspects of the author's personality. *Celia en la revolución* allows the reader to understand Aragoneses's position vis-à-vis the Civil War. Dorao's prologue also gives brief information about Aragoneses's life and career.

Carmen *Martín Gaite's research widened this perspective in a series of lectures given at the time of the TV program's broadcast and partially published in her prologue to a new edition of *Celia lo que dice*. The writer was born in Madrid to a Castilian father, from Segovia, and a Basque mother, as was the case of Celia. In 1906, when Aragoneses was 20, she married her cousin Eusebio de Gorbea y Lemmi, a military man, intellectual, and writer. Two boys were born; one died at age 10, and the second eventually married a young Swiss student studying at the Residencia de Señoritas in Madrid, Ana María Link. As a member of the group of writers dubbed the "Generation of 1914," Gorbea introduced his wife to the company of writers and artists. Perhaps stimulated by this intensely intellectual atmosphere, Aragoneses began her own writing in the late 1920s. Dorao says that although Aragoneses took her pen name from one of her husband's characters, Elena Fortún, she began to write, encouraged by her friend María Lejárraga (1874–1974), wife of Gorbea's friend Gregorio Martínez Sierra. Lejárraga was a well-known feminist and a socialist militant as well as a playwright, coauthor with her husband of numerous pieces. Another good friend was Matilde Ras, also one of the nucleus of feminist writers during the 1920s and 1930s with whom Aragoneses collaborated.

According to Nieva de la Paz, Ras's diary gives some details about Aragoneses's life, particularly regarding her exile. These three writers—Lejárraga, Ras, and Aragoneses—belonged to the strong supporting group of middle-class women, many of them university educated, who advocated for women's advancement during Primo de Rivera's dictatorship. Their club, the *Lyceum, founded by María de *Maeztu in 1926, included well-known women such as Victoria *Kent (1898–1987), Zenobia Camprubí, Pura Maortúa de Ucelay, Margarita *Nelken and her sister Carmen *Nelken (1900–1966; pseud. Magda Donato), Rosa Spotorno, and María Martos de Baeza. After her exile in Argentina, Aragoneses returned to the Lyceum, which actually continued its activities in an unofficial and rather clandestine way into the 1980s.

Aragoneses's early works were short stories published from 1928 on in literary magazines such as *Cosmópolis*, *Crónica*, and *Gente Menuda*, the children's supplement for *Blanco y Negro*. Her main character Celia first appeared in 1928 in the short story "Celia dice a su madre" (Celia Tells Her Mother). Celia has proven to be constantly modern and fresh over the years. Aragoneses's gift as a writer springs as much from her fresh, dialogue-based prose (which her playwright husband may have taught her) as from her concise, perceptive re-creation of a child's world in which there is no place for adults—they appear in the background as illogical, remote, often hostile entities. This timeless juxtaposition between child and adult, where the adult figure loses stature and disappears before the beauty, logic, and truth that children possess, has made Aragoneses's characters irresistible to successive generations. As a gifted observer of life, Aragoneses, according to one critic, drew inspiration for Celia and her brother Cuchifritín from her friends' children, particularly the family of a military friend of her husband. Martín Gaite suggests other friends' children to be sources of inspiration as well. In any case, Celia and her world still stand as a re-creation of a child's perception of life, written for children.

While Celia as a character appeared faithfully in *Gente Menuda* of *Blanco y Negro* from January 1929 on, the first books of the noted postwar series "Celia y su mundo" were published by Aguilar in 1935; they were *Cuchifritín el hermano de Celia* and *Cuchifritín y sus primos* (Cuchifritín and His Cousins). The first Celia book to appear in Aguilar, *Celia en el colegio* (Celia at School), was published during the war, in 1938, but other publications preceded this debut. According to Nieva de la Paz, Aragoneses's first play for children, *Luna, lunera* (Moon, Moonlike?) was staged in Madrid in 1930, in 1932 *La merienda de Blas* (Blas's Afternoon Snack) premiered, and in 1936 the play *Celia Dice* was performed.

After July 1936, Aragoneses stayed in Madrid with her husband, who was loyal to the Republic. In the prologue to *Celia en la revolución*, Dorao equates the admiration, tenderness, and respect that Celia feels for her father with Aragoneses's feeling toward her husband and argues that Celia, in this last book, expresses the author's own thoughts and sufferings during the war. The text is a historically accurate portrayal of Republican Spain during the war, particularly of a Madrid besieged physically from without and wracked by revenge from within. Celia wonders who was right and expresses horror at having arrived at a point where "they shoot everyone, killing each other in the mountains."

Aragoneses was appointed Member of the Comisión del Teatro de los Niños in 1938, and in July of that same year, her play *Moñitos* (Baubles), written before the war, was staged. That same year, Aragoneses and her husband went into exile in Argentina, leaving from Paris with help from their daughter-in-law's family. It seems they hoped to return to Spain very soon, but their exile lasted 10 years. Unlike the experience of other writers who left the country as a consequence of the war, Aragoneses's "Celia" books continued to be published and read in Spain with even greater intensity, despite the fact that Celia was a convinced Republican, with no specific party affiliation, like Aragoneses and her husband. All the book-length stories that follow Celia's life from age 7 (*Celia lo que dice*) to her wedding (*Celia se casa* [Celia Marries]) were published in Madrid by Aguilar after the war's end in 1939.

According to the Biblioteca Nacional, the publishing history of first edition Aragoneses books is as follows: 1939: *Celia en el mundo, Celia lo que dice, Celia madrecita, Celia y sus amigos, Matonkiki y sus hermanas*; 1940: *Travesuras de Matonkiki, El bazar de todas las cosas, Celia novelista, Aventuras con los titiriteros, Las vacaciones de Lita y Lito*; 1942: *Cuchifritín en casa de su abuelo, Cuchifritín y Paquito, Las travesuras de Matonkiki, Teatro para niños* (several of these short plays had been staged before the war); 1944: *Celia institutriz en América*; 1947: *El cuaderno de Celia*; 1949: *La hermana de Celia Mila y Piolín*; 1950: *Mila, Piolín y el burro, Celia se casa. Cuenta Mila, Los cuentos que Celia cuenta a las niñas*; 1951: *Los cuentos que Celia cuenta a los niños, Patita y Mila, estudiantes*. It is abundantly evident that her copious production was published and read in Spain throughout three postwar decades, in spite of her personal circumstances.

It is a paradox that during the most repressive period of Franco's regime, an exiled Republican was widely published with great success. Of course, with the exception of *Celia en la revolución* and some clear hints in *Celia institutriz in América* (Celia, Governess in America), nothing in the works indicates this circumstance. Indeed, some ideological traits of the books, particularly in *Celia madrecita* (Celia a Little Mother), would fit in the Falange Sección Femenina's concept of women's duties to home, men, and motherhood surprisingly well. At the same time, certain stories written during these particular years (and not before), like Celia's character as a young child in the "Mila and Mila" and "Patita" books, easily reflect an exaltation of nationalism through cultural and historical references to the cities, villages, and provinces that Mila and Maimón or Mila and Doña Benita witness in their pilgrimage (*correr mundo*) through northern Spain.

In 1948, Aragoneses returned to Spain and to her old friends of the Lyceum Club who were still in Madrid. Her husband, still in Buenos Aires, committed suicide a few months after she left. María Baeza and Matilde Ras helped Aragoneses during these difficult years, and Aragoneses became part of the silent network maintained by some early Spanish feminists. Pío Caro Baroja remembers that his mother, Carmen Baroja, once visited Aragoneses as part of the silent network that early Spanish feminists continued to maintain. In the late 1940s Carmen Baroja was writing short stories and articles to earn a living, and she sought the advice and experience of the successful Aragoneses. Pío Caro, a very young boy at the time, remembers one streetcar trip to *La Ciudad Jardín*, the search for a small house, and the return to Madrid before dark.

After Aragoneses's death, María Baeza undertook the task of building the monument to her writer friend. Not far from the new site of Concepción *Arenal's restored statue, Aragoneses's monument stands in solitude; her other monument, the 21 volumes of the series "Celia y su mundo," is alive and well.

Work about

Bravo Villasante, Carmen. *Historia de la literatura infantil española*. Madrid: Revista de Occidente, 1959.

Cervera, Juan. *Historia crítica del teatro infantil español*. Madrid: Nacional, 1982.

Dorao, Marisol, prol. *Celia en la Revolución*. Madrid: Aguilar, 1987. 9–14.

———. *Los mil sueños de Elena Fortun*. Cádiz: Universidad de Cádiz, 1999.

Martín Gaite, Carmen. "Pesquisa tardía sobre Elena Fortún." *Celia, lo que dice*. Madrid: Alianza, 1992. 7–37.

Nieva, Francisco. "Elena Fortún y Richmal Crompton." *ABC* June 3, 1990: 1.

Nieva de la Paz, Pilar. "Las escritoras españolas y el teatro infantil de preguerra: Magda Donato, Elena Fortún y Concha Méndez." *Revista de Literatura* 55.109 (1993): 112–128.

Toral, Carolina. *Literatura infantil española II*. Madrid: Colcusa, 1956.

María Elena Bravo

Fuentes Blanco, María de los Reyes (1927–)

Born in Seville, Fuentes Blanco has spent most of her life in her native city, serving for many years as head of its social welfare agency. She began writing poetry in the late 1950s, garnering several regional and metropolitan prizes for her free-verse collections, plus special mention for the National Literary Prize of 1961. She founded the periodical *Ixbiliah*, and during four years she directed a regular poetry segment for Spain's National Radio.

Fuentes Blanco's predominant themes are Andalusia's past, especially Seville's classical (Roman) and Arabic periods, regional folklore, oral traditions, and love. She is not a major writer, although a somewhat independent one, neither following the literary fashions of the day nor adhering to preconceived "women's topics." Nor is she particularly experimental or innovative, tending instead to favor traditional and classical metrics. Fuentes Blanco's most productive period, from the late 1950s to the mid-1980s, saw publication of some 20 collections, including *Actitudes* (1957; Attitudes), *De mí hasta el hombre* (1958; From Me to Man), *Sonetos del corazón adelante* (1960; Sonnets from the Heart Forward), *Elegías del Uad-el-Kebir* (1961; Elegies of the Guadalquivir), *Romances de la miel en los labios* (1962; Ballads of Honey on My Lips), *Elegías Tartessias* (1964; Tartessian Elegies), *Oración de la verdad* (1965; Prayer for Truth), *Concierto para la Sierra de Ronda* (1966; Concert for the Ronda Mountains), *Acrópolis del testimonio* (1966; Acropolis of Testimony), *Pozo de Jacob* (1967; Jacob's Well), and *Aire de amor* (1977; Love Air). Also attributed to her (under the pseudonym "Reyes Fuentes") are *Fabulilla del diamante salvado* (1967; Fable of the Saved Diamond), *Motivos para un anfiteatro* (1970; Motifs for an Amphitheater), *Misión de la palabra* (1973; Mission of the Word), *Apuntes para la composición de un* drama (1975; Notes for Composing a Drama), *Elegie Andaluse* (1985; Andalusian Elegy), and *Jardín de las Revelaciones* (1985; Garden of Revelations). Hers are often not gendered themes, and Fuentes Blanco's work will be of more interest for gynocritics than those seeking feminist themes and personae; nevertheless, she is a prolific poet who achieved considerable visibility and as such has earned a place in women's literary history.

Work by

Acrópolis del testimonio. Seville: Ayuntamiento, 1966.
Aire de amor. Madrid: Rialp, 1977.
Elegías del Uad-el-Kebir. Sevilla: n.p., 1961.
Elegías Tartessias. Orense: Comercial, 1964.
Oración de la verdad. Jerez: Grupo Atalaya, 1965.
Pozo de Jacob. Sevilla: Ayuntamiento, 1967.
Romances de la miel en los labios. Sevilla: La Muestra, 1962.

Janet Pérez

Fuertes García, Gloria (1918–1998)

A contemporary of Blas de Otero and Gabriel Celaya, to name only two of the more important among Spain's first generation of post–Civil War poets, Gloria Fuertes occupies a unique position in twentieth-century Spanish letters. She shares Celaya's and Otero's attitude of protest and commitment regarding social concerns. Approximately a decade older than Angel González, the next oldest of those comprising the second wave of Spain's postwar period, she began to publish, as they did, during the 1950s. Her poetry is similar to that of the mid-century group, at least in her preference for everyday themes and in some of her attitudes and stylistic choices. She is the only woman associated with that group, making her work distinctive for its forthright expression of a woman's perceptions and feelings.

Although some sources note her date of birth as 1920 (an error that Fuertes herself attributed to a moment of vanity), the poet was born on July 28, 1918, in the working-class district of Lavapiés in Madrid. Her parents were both of modest origins. Her father was employed principally as a beadle and doorman but was the only member of Fuertes's family accustomed to reading books. As for her seamstress-mother, she was a person of strong character but difficult temperament whose relationship with her daughter was uneasy, in part due to the latter's propensity from the first for letters. The youngest daughter in a family of eight siblings, of whom only four survived, Fuertes was a solitary, imaginative child who felt keenly her isolation despite her natural affability and outgoing ways. She was sent to school at age three, a turn of events welcomed by the future author, since she longed not only for the companionship but for the knowledge and experiences she sensed reading and books would provide. Quick and clever, she learned soon to read and write, yet her early school experiences were marred by the severity of the nuns' disciplinary practices.

Fuertes's formal education continued when her mother enrolled her in a women's institute where she eventually received a diploma in cooking, sewing and design, child care, and similar subjects deemed proper for young women of the working class. Literature sparked her interest for the first time, but like the sports she also loved, it was considered an unsuitable outlet for women. She began to cultivate her interest in poetry and even to write it herself at age 14, perhaps initially as a distraction from and consolation for the hardships that plagued her adolescence and despite her understanding that at that time women in Spanish society were discouraged from writing. After the death of her mother in 1934, the teenager was sent to do bookkeeping in a factory that manufactured howitzers (ironic, in view of Fuertes's innate pacifism). Spain was also experiencing a period of intense turmoil that culminated in 1936 with the outbreak of the Civil War. Fuertes suffered another traumatic loss, that of her first love, as a result of that conflict. Like so many of her countrymen during those years, she endured bombings and severe hunger.

Despite these tragic circumstances, Fuertes dedicated a part of each day to writing poetry and stories. One of her first efforts in verse, entitled "Isla ignorada" (Ignored Island), was written at age 17, though it did not see print until some years later. Some of Fuertes's earliest writings were published in magazines for juveniles, and in fact, she joined the editorial board of *Maravillas*, heading their poetry section. She was also broadcast with some frequency reading her poems on Radio Madrid and Radio España. Her career as an accomplished children's author was thus launched.

In 1942 she met another young writer, Carlos Edmundo de Ory, who played a significant part in Fuertes's budding career. While not often given to acknowledging literary influences, preferring to focus on her own uniqueness as a writer, she readily recognizes Ory's influence. Under his guidance and in the company of Eduardo Chicharro and Silvano Sernesi, Fuertes participated (the only woman to do so) in the poetic movement called *postismo*. This collaboration, though little known and of relatively short duration, was considered heir to surrealism; as such, their poetics, rooted in the concept of language, rhyme, and poetry itself as play, valued imagination over reason. These writers' rebellious attitude toward traditional literary strictures resulted in poetry characterized by novel, surprising, and often humorous effects. These precise qualities most patently characterize Fuertes's writings as a whole.

Ever more committed to her literary vocation, during the late 1940s and early 1950s she contributed regularly to numerous poetry journals and was one of the founders of *Arquero*, a publication dedicated to verse and criticism. For two years she met with other women poets who, calling themselves *Versos con Faldas* (Verses with Skirts), initiated weekly readings of their works. These recitals in cafés and taverns became a way not only to participate actively in Madrid's literary scene but also to fulfill one of Fuertes's fondest ambitions: to bring poetry to ordinary people.

Even Fuertes's first published works offer evidence of the issues and themes she returns to repeatedly throughout her career. For example, in *Isla ignorada*, which included the poem of that title penned years earlier, loneliness and longing are expressed in an intimate voice that anticipates Fuertes's tendency to blur the distinctions between art and autobiography. The fanciful quality that some critics have called "magical realism" is likewise on display in this debut publication. Following the 1950 appearance of *Isla ignorada*, Fuertes collected her mounting body of verses into a volume that in 1954 appeared as *Antología y poemas del suburbio* (Anthology and Poems from the Suburbs). The tone underlying many pieces in this book is one often associated with Fuertes: a keenly felt compassion and sense of justice, and at times rage, regarding the plight of the needy, abused, and neglected. *Aconsejo beber hilo* (I Advise Drinking Thread), published later that same year, reveals another hallmark of Fuertes's poetry: a surrealistic playfulness and humor, especially in the face of what she perceives as life's essential absurdity, if not insanity.

Unable to earn a living from her literary activities, in 1955 Fuertes began to study English and library science at Madrid's International Institute on Miguel Angel Street. Still, she steadily persisted in her creative pursuits and in 1958 published *Todo asusta* (Everything Frightens), full of eerie scenes and phantasmagorical, irrational images. Eventually employed in one of the city's public libraries, she entered a period of great personal contentment, enhanced by her friendship with Phyllis Turnbull, who headed Smith College's program for American students at the International Institute. Through Turnbull's intervention, in 1961 Fuertes was awarded a Fulbright grant to teach Spanish poetry at Bucknell University in Pennsylvania. She remained in that position until 1964, earning a measure of financial independence as well as time to devote to poetry. Indeed, her sojourn in the United States proved fruitful, for during this time she authored two more volumes: *Que estás en la tierra* (1962; For You're on Land) and *Ni tiro, ni veneno ni navaja* (1968; Neither Gunshot, Nor Poison, Nor Knife).

Once back in Madrid, her income supplemented by classes taught at the International Institute, Fuertes penned one of her most important volumes. *Poeta de guardia* (1968; Poet on Guard) was the first of her collections to be given serious attention. Critics acknowledged the social commitment and rebellion, the irreverence and tenderness to which Fuertes's lyricism gave passionate voice. In each of the book's poems, the author assumes the perspective of a sentinel charged, by the grace of her poetry, with loving vigilance over the world's unfortunates. Employing intimate, forthright tones and the colloquial, often unpolished accents typical of the Spanish capital, in *Poeta de guardia* Fuertes emerged as heir to the Spanish oral tradition rather than to the rhetorical refinements and formal meticulousness of classical Spanish poetry. At the same time, her expression of solidarity with the humbler classes underscores her firm belief in the social responsibility, not to mention the healing capacity, of her art.

Cómo atar los bigotes al tigre (1969; How to Tie the Tiger's Moustache) was also successfully received, winning second place in the Premio Vizcaya poetry competition. The book is inhabited by many of Fuertes's most recognizable characters, including a mime, a tightrope walker, and her particular favorite, a clown. The animal world is likewise represented, albeit in a whimsical form that recalls Aesop's fables and Fuertes's own writings for children: There are harp-playing octopuses, a leaping platypus, and an especially musical centipede. Significantly, some poems utilize modes of discourse not generally viewed as poetic: namely, bureaucratic jargon, letters, prayers, and riddles, manifesting Fuertes's belief that poetry can be found in the most unlikely places. By the same token, poetry exalts the modest figures (criminals, the poor, sick, and orphaned) that continue to merit her compassionate attention.

Fuertes's growing stature during ensuing years was marked by a number of important additions to her body of work. *Antología poética, 1950–1969* (Poetic Anthology) appeared in print in 1970. While not the first to recognize Fuertes's singular gifts, Francisco Ynduráin's extensive prologue is significant for acknowledging the poet's importance as an author for children, especially insofar as her contributions to this field are inseparable from her other writings. *Obras incompletas* (Incomplete Works) was compiled in 1980 and has subsequently enjoyed numerous editions. Preceded by a lengthy exposition (by the poet) of her life and work, this anthology also includes in its entirety one of her most poignant collections, *Sola en la sala* (1973; Alone in the Living Room). Written during a period of illness, *Sola en la sala* is distinctive for poems that resemble haikus in their brevity and the intensity of emotion swiftly conveyed. The most salient themes of these very intimate poems are loneliness, death, joy, and above all, the author's need to communicate the essence of her own being.

This autobiographical impulse was perhaps Fuertes's most enduring source of inspiration, as subsequent writings demonstrate. The title *Historia de Gloria (Amor, humor y desamor)* (1980; Gloria's History [Love, Humor, Unlove]) demonstrates anew that poetry is inextricably interwoven with Fuertes's own life. The opening poem cites Walt Whitman's assertion that "Who touches this [book] touches a man" but pointedly changes the original words to underscore her own womanhood. Again, many of the poems are strikingly brief, mere glimpses into the poet's emotional core or penetrating insights into the nature of poetry. "Autobío" (Autobio[graphy]) and "Poética" (Poetics) are frequently repeated titles in the book, as they are in *Mujer de verso en pecho* (1995; Woman with Verse on [Her] Chest), which followed *Historia de Gloria*. The pieces in the former volume continue to mine the poet's innermost feelings. Still, Fuertes never lost sight of the suffering and tribulations of others, especially children, women, and those consigned to the fringes of social respectability. Her concerns were not limited to one nation, one religion, or one gender but rather were human and universal. A problem that commanded her attention in *Mujer de verso en pecho* is the decaying state of the planet, and human responsibility for this condition. The solution that, perhaps idealistically, she found for almost all afflictions is, ultimately, love. Hence, love provided the impetus and prevailing theme in *Pecábamos como ángeles (Gloripoemas de amor)* (1997; We Sinned Like Angels [Gloripoems of Love]), a compilation of previously published pieces.

To summarize Fuertes's long-standing career is to circle back to the issue of her own singularity. Much more learned than at first apparent, she was an appreciative reader of Spain's most esteemed writers: Berceo (c. 1196–c.1260), San *Juan de la Cruz (1542–1591), Santa *Teresa de Avila (1515–1582), *Unamuno (1864–1936), and many others. Yet she preferred to underplay her erudition and to remain more broadly accessible to those who do not form part of an intellectual elite. Her work abounds with appealing rhymes, repetitions, and rhythmic games. An inveterate punster, wordplay is a constant in Fuertes's poetry. These features are precisely the ones habitually associated with children's verses. Indeed, that she was a prolific author of children's books (who makes little distinction between that genre and her writings for "adults") might explain why she was not consistently given the same favorable reception accorded other poets of the mid-century generation. Yet Fuertes attained widespread popularity in Spain. She made frequent television appearances, did public readings of her poetry, and was honored by King Juan Carlos. She favored everyday themes expressed in direct yet subtle ways, and one of her proudest achievements was her ability to connect emotionally, even personally, with the common people who comprise her preferred readership.

Work by

Antología poética, 1950–1969. Prol. and sel. Francisco Induráin. Barcelona: Plaza & Janés, 1970.

Glorierías: (para que os enteréis). Madrid: Torremozas, 2001.

Historia de Gloria: amor, humor y desamor. Ed. Pablo González Rodas. Madrid: Cátedra, 1980.

Mujer de verso en pecho. Prol. Francisco Nieva. Madrid: Cátedra, 1995.

Off the Map: Selected Poems by Gloria Fuertes. Ed. and trans. Philip Levine and Ada Long. Middletown, CT: Wesleyan UP, 1984.

Pecábamos como ángeles: gloripoemas de amor. Madrid: Torremozas, 1997.

Work about

Benson, Douglas K. "La voz inconfundible de Gloria Fuertes, 1918–1998: Poesía temprana." *Hispania* 83 (May 2000): 210–221.

Cano, José Luis. *Vida y poesía de Gloria Fuertes*. Madrid: Torremozas, 1991.

Cooks, Maria L. "The Humanization of Poetry: An Appraisal of Gloria Fuertes." *Hispania* 83.3 (September 2000): 428–436.

Debicki, Andrew P. "Gloria Fuertes: Intertextuality and Reversal of Expectations." *Poetry of Discovery: The Spanish Generation of 1956–1971*. Lexington: UP of Kentucky, 1982. 81–101.

Mandlove, Nancy. "Oral Texts: The Play of Orality and Literacy in the Poetry of Gloria Fuertes." *Siglo XX* 5.1–2 (1987–1988): 11–16.

Persin, Margaret H. "Humor as Semiosis in the Poetry of Gloria Fuertes." *Recent Spanish Poetry and the Role of the Reader*. Lewisburg: Bucknell UP, 1987. 119–136.

Sherno, Sylvia R. "Weaving the World: The Poetry of Gloria Fuertes." *Hispania* 72. 2 (May 1989): 247–255.

Wilcox, John. *Women Poets of Spain 1860–1990*. Chicago and Urbana: U of Illinois P, 1997. 197–230.

Sylvia R. Sherno

Gala, Antonio (1936–)

Playwright, essayist, poet, and novelist, Gala at times centers his creative work on male characters, but more frequently he develops female protagonists. With respect to both theater and life, he maintains that women express themselves better than men: They are more direct, and because they are more likely to explain how they feel rather than rely on cold logic, they are also more interesting. In his theater, Gala often uses an eloquent and witty female spokesperson who, in opposing the dominant ideology, champions the cause of individual freedom. That freedom includes the right to love the person of one's choice and tolerance with respect to marginalized members of society. Key plays such as *Anillos para una dama* (1973; Rings for a Lady) and *Petra Regalada* (1980) thus readily lend themselves to feminist interpretations. Recent works have also openly advocated the rights of homosexuals.

Gala first introduced a feminist deconstruction of official history in his commemorative television scripts. In *Eterno Tuy* (Eternal Tuy) and *Oratorio de Fuenterrabía* (1968; Fuenterrabia Oratory), he revealed with pathos the situation of daughters in royal families who were reduced to objects of exchange, to be bartered by the patriarchy. In *Anillos para una dama*, he elaborates this theme in an anachronistic vindication of *Jimena, widow of the Cid, Spain's epic hero. Jimena's efforts to live her own life and achieve love on her own terms are doomed, but she forcefully speaks for personal freedom and against war.

Gala's female characters generally preach love, not war; they equate the latter with exploitation of the individual for the materialistic gain of those in power. The theme recurs in *¿Por qué corres, Ulises?* (1975; Why Are You Running, Ulysses?) and *La vieja señorita del Paraíso* (1980; The Old Maid from Paradise), as well as other works. The favoring of what might be considered feminine values over traditionally masculine ones is elaborated further in the musical *Carmen Carmen* (written 1975; staged 1988). In separate stories, the irrepressible Carmen, symbol of happiness, is killed by her lovers: a soldier, a politician, a seminarian, and a bullfighter. On occasion, however, the forces of repression or exploitation may be represented by female characters. In *Los buenos días perdidos* (1972; The Bells of Orleans, 1993), the manipulative Hortensia coerces her son into stealing and mistreats her daughter-in-law; in *El cementerio de los pájaros* (1982; Bird Cemetery), the abuser of power is Emilia, a domineering figure in the mold of *García Lorca's (1898–1936) Bernarda Alba.

Generally, the search for paradise in Gala's theater ends in failure, although sometimes with the hope that others may carry on the cause of the defeated idealists. Exceptions to this pattern are *Petra Regalada*, an allegory of the end of the Franco era, and *La Truhana* (1992; The Lady Trickster), a metaplay that borrows farcical devices from Golden Age theater and is set in that period. Petra Regalada is an archetypal character who fulfills simultaneously the stereotypes of virgin and whore. Victimized by Don Moncho, she is just one in a series of Petras who are worshipped by the people and used by the men in power; Don Moncho, in turn, is just one in a seemingly eternal series of Big Brothers. The cycle is broken when Petra and her allies—the humblest of the humble—rebel against all exploiters and escape their enclosure to start a new life. The end of *La Truhana* is strikingly similar. Having outwitted the lecherous king who pursues her and won the heart of the man she loves, the irrepressible comedienne and her company set sail for a brave New World.

In *La Truhana*, the clever title character is able to achieve both love and freedom. More typically in Gala's works, love leads to despair, not happiness. Petra Regalada becomes the leader of repressed people only after she rejects a false savior with whom she had fallen in love. The childlike, fanciful Consuelo in *Los buenos días perdidos* cannot overcome a similar disillusionment and commits suicide instead.

Although quite different in genre and tone, Gala's second novel, *La pasión turca* (1993; Turkish Passion), repeats the underlying story of *Los buenos días perdidos*: An unhappily married woman falls in love with an exploitative but virile rogue; her passion leads to her death. While Gala portrays these women victims with sympathy, their willingness to be treated as objects distances them from such feminist characters as Jimena and Petra.

The protagonist of Gala's 1995 novel *Más allá del jardín* (Beyond the Garden), on the other hand, is reminiscent of Jimena. Like Jimena, Palmira is challenged to start a new life, without her husband, and must accept the loss of a son and her alienation from her grown daughter. Like Desideria in *La pasión turca*, Palmira succumbs to passion, but she eventually breaks from her destructive path, learns nursing skills, and becomes a medical missionary in Africa. The novel's disastrous end reflects Gala's habitual pessimism about earthly paradises, but Palmira proves her strength of character and, at least temporarily, finds both self-fulfillment and love.

Work by

The Bells of Orleans. Trans. Edward Borsoi. University Park, PA: Estreno, 1993.
Carmen Carmen. Madrid: Espasa Calpe, 1988.
El cementerio de los pájaros. Madrid: Espasa Calpe, 1982.
The Green Fields of Eden. Trans. Patricia W. O'Connor. *The Contemporary Spanish Theater: The Social Comedies of the Sixties*. Ed. Patricia W. O'Connor. Madrid: SGEL, 1983. 189–254.
Más allá del jardín. Barcelona: Planeta, 1995.
Obras escogidas. Madrid: Aguilar, 1981.
La pasión turca. Barcelona: Planeta, 1993.
La Truhana. Madrid: Espasa Calpe, 1992.

Work about

Lamartina-Lens, Iride. "*Petra Regalada*: Madonna or Whore?" *Estreno* 11.1 (1985): 13–15.
Newberry, Wilma. "Antonio Gala's *El cementerio de los pájaros* and the Problem of Freedom." *Hispania* 70.3 (1987): 431–436.
Sheehan, Robert Louis. "Antonio Gala and the New Catholicism." *The Contemporary Spanish Theater: A Collection of Critical Essays*. Ed. Martha T. Halsey and Phyllis Zatlin. Lanham, MD; UP of America, 1988. 113–129.
Zatlin-Boring, Phyllis. "Atacando al patriarcado: Los ejemplos de Gala y Nieva." *Boletín de la Fundación Federico García Lorca* 19–20 (December 1996): 301–316.
———. Introduction to *Noviembre y un poco de yerba*. *Petra Regalada*. Madrid: Cátedra, 1981. 9–109.

Phyllis Zatlin

Galician Women Writers: A Brief History

In names, numbers, and titles of works, the history of women writers in Galicia is rather straightforward because, until about the 1980s, virtually all Galician women writers, regardless of the genre practiced, were known by name, creative techniques, and titles of their publications. This does not mean that these writers were respected, read, or included on an equal basis with male counterparts. Even recently, anthologies include few women authors. Complex factors also surround the double set of *Contos eróticos* (Erotic Stories) published by Xerais—a volume by "Elas" (The Women) and one by "Eles" (The Men). The "Elas" were integrated by an "El," as if not to be allowed out on their own. Indeed, far more women's books carry introductory remarks by men than men's books have prologues by women. For some years, it was even an oddity to see them as prologuists for other women.

Thus the familiarity of female participants in an area containing roughly 2.5 million speakers, with a reading public limited to an inner circle of Galician readers, kept these minority-language writers in obscurity to readers and critics in other areas of the Spanish state as well as internationally. A few years after Franco's death in 1975, however, Galician women's writing began to take on a different appearance, showing greater variation in content. This was enabled and furthered by the changing status of the nation and the gradual assimilation of gender theory and feminist literary criticism by Galicians— a process that is still ongoing. It is both ironic and natural that Rosalía de *Castro, whose work had given birth to the *Rexurdimento* or Renaissance of Galician literature, also became the first, or nearly the first, Galician woman whose writing attracted a large number of feminist interpretations. Carmen Blanco (1991) cites Isabel de Castro e Andrade as author of a poem in the sixteenth century and also notes the appearance of a poem by Francisca de Isla e Losada in the eighteenth century. These would be the only precedents of her sex for Rosalía de Castro. In the nineteenth century, only three books would be published by women, all of the poetry genre. Two were by Castro, and the third was the work of Filomena Dato Muruais.

The 1985 conference Rosalía de Castro e o seu tempo (Rosalía de Castro and Her Time), held on the hundredth anniversary of her death, attracted over 400 intellectuals who contributed both traditional and new analytical approaches, attesting to the initial post-Franco feeling of immense optimism. The stage was set for revisioning the past and looking forward to the future of Galician literature and women's literature in particular. Castro's two-part legacy was affirmed, reaffirmed, and used in theoretical and visionary discussions of the cultural diversity that the transition to democracy was expected to promote.

A periodization of women's writing in Galicia, then, must begin with Castro. *Cantares Gallegos* (Galician Songs) was published on May 17, 1863. A century later, this was designated O Día das Letras Galegas (Day of Galician Letters). *Cantares Gallegos* was less important for its female authorship than for its role as the first book published in Galician in four centuries. It surprises no one that there were few works of female authorship, given the higher level of illiteracy in this rural geographical region. The imbalance persists to a lesser degree today, in part because during the period of regeneration and liberalism, the first priority was to give voice to an entire people.

In an agile yet politically ambiguous gesture, readers embraced Castro's use of the "vernacular." Criticism of the time both relegated the author of the *Cantares* to the sensitive, romantic, "feminine" perspective and recognized her as representative of Galician (as opposed to Spanish) ideals. Critics associated the region with feminine characteristics, a relationship that reveals their self-identification with the stereotypically "softer" (biologically and topographically) nature. The image of the region is linked to the concept of the ideologically and economically less-developed (Galicia as a poor, rural, victimized, abandoned part of Spain). Castro's feminist *Lieders* (written in Spanish), with its theme of women writers as a monstrously shackled breed, could thus be a symbol of rebelliousness in a cultural context in need of outspoken individuals to erase the weight of four centuries of literary silence, centuries still oft recalled in popular conversation. The critic who is conscious of Galician cultural identity knows the stifling effect of the long silence. Even during its own time, *Cantares Gallegos* was seen primarily as a Galician work and less as a woman-identified text. Its strength resided in its emphasis on national origins, even for readers who were far from separatist thinkers. It was also a woman's book, weaving a comforting blanket of pain, poverty, and intimacy. The woman became the nation, as critics (all male for many years, although female critics were not in dissonance) bound Castro and Galicia together inextricably. Although originating in the concept of regeneration, for Galicia the union resulted in the shackling of both in their condition of inequality. Neither element was thought capable of overcoming these limitations, geographical, economic, climatic, or biological. Castro's lucid protest against the oppression of both nation and woman was simply ignored.

Castro vacillated between two languages, using Galician for two books of poetry, a short story, and little else. Her published works also include five novels and three other volumes of poetry in Spanish. The sum of her writing in that language may never be known, since she ordered some works destroyed. The term "Galician literature" now includes only those works written in that language and not those written in Spanish, a criterion that also eliminates the work of Virginia Felisa Auber (1825–1897), who wrote in Spanish and spent years in Cuba. Her first novel, *Un aria de Bellini* (1843; An Aria by Bellini), was followed by six more books, and other works of hers are extant. Also omitted is Emilia Calé (1837–1908), despite her considerable list of publications (short novels, poetry, theater) and the fact that the Galicia Literaria society met in her home. Calé was one of several women named as correspondents to the Real Academia Gallega (Royal Galician Academy)—her nomination came in 1906—but not admitted as a member. Librarian Olga Gallego (Ourense), more than a decade after Franco's death, would be the first woman to actually occupy a seat in the Real Academia Gallega. This would ironically eliminate a goodly portion of the work of the very promoter of the *Rexurdimento*, although linguistic politics provide a logical explanation for the criterion.

The question has yet to be resolved for the earliest writers, but those from post-1975 are unambiguous: Writing in Spanish represents a clear choice, a distancing from the concerns inherent to Galicia. The bilingual work of 1936–1975 is either mostly unevaluated or silently marginalized (cf. Luz Pozo Garza, María do Carme Kruckenberg, Anxeles Penas), while those women who never wrote in Galician (Emilia *Pardo Bazán, Concepción *Arenal, Elena *Quiroga) do not hold a position in Galician literature despite their acceptance as Galician writers. Blanco provides more interesting figures for poetry books published by women: 8 between 1900 and 1939; 23 between 1939 and Franco's death in 1975; and 54 between 1975 and approximately 1992. Since 1992, although the figure is not readily available, production in all genres by women has obviously risen. Their short, scarce pieces were sandwiched in among essays and discourses of nationalistic sentiment in publications such as *Nós* (Us) and *A Nosa Terra* (Our Land). Again, Blanco compares the number of titles as to genre: 33 books of poetry, as compared to 17 in other genres, were published by women between 1863 and 1975. This number, if accurate, indicates how much the presence of women in literary circles depended on periodical publications and unpublished, public performance.

Some of the earliest foremothers have been forgotten, such as Clara Corral Aller of

Coruña, author of a small number of poems at the end of the nineteenth century, some of them compiled by a relative years later (Dimas Romero Vázquez, *Poemas en gallego y en castellano* [1980; Poems in Galician and Castilian]); Filomena Dato Muruais, author of *Follatos* (1891; Twigs); and Carmen Prieto Rouco, whose published works include *Horas de frebe* (1926, 1928; Feverish Moments), *A virxe viuda: Hestorea d'un amor* (1964; The Virgin Widow: A Love Story), *Lluvia menuda* (1956; Light Rain), with portions in Galician, and *O derradeiro. Versos galegos* (1977; The Last One. Verses in Galician). Years later María Mariño Carou received but a modicum of attention, mostly from authors of the same interior mountain region of O Courel, from relatives or those who had a personal relationship with them.

Gender rather than geography is the stronger muzzle for these writers, but it is coupled with ideology when the political aperture allowed for more demanding, committed attitudes on the part of its intellectuals. Thus Francisca Herrera Garrido (1869–1950) was momentarily the object of attention when she was honored by Festa da Palabra Silenciada and the Día das Letras Galegas in 1986, but criticism has not sustained interest in her work. Herrera Garrido published three books of poetry, *Sorrisas e bágoas* (1913; Smiles and Tears), *Almas de muller . . . ¡volallas na luz!* (1915; Women's Souls . . . Sparks in the Light!), and *Frores do noso paxareco* (1919; Flowers from Our Garden); the first novel in Galician by a woman, *Néveda* (1920); and two novellas, *A y-alma de Mingos* (1922; Mingus's Soul) and *Martes d'Antroido* (1925; Carnival Tuesday). Nominated for the Real Academia Gallega near the end of her life, ill health and the resisting male literati intervened, and she died before she could enter the "hallowed halls" of official culture.

Other women writers of the early twentieth century, such as Herminia Fariña Cobián (1904–1966), Dolores Parga Serrano (dates unavailable), and Mercedes Viso Troncoso ("Mechitas de Vigo," dates unavailable), are still little known and studied. Another, Teresa Juega (1885–1979), was shot several times, but not killed, by her military fiancé (who then committed suicide), because she insisted on trying to publish her book *Alma que llora* (1908; Crying Soul). Literary analyses will have to take into account not only the texts but their contexts. Resources are slowly becoming available. The nineteenth century and the early twentieth century are still much less familiar to scholars of Galician culture than for those of Spain during the corresponding periods. Adding to the complexity of the research is the fact that whatever the ideology, much of the earlier publication was in Spanish.

Writing by women between the end of the Civil War and 1975, but especially after the 1950s, is represented by a few names, the total number for poetry being around a dozen. In narrative, there is only a handful of books and authors, including María Xosé Queizán (1939–), Xohana Torres (1940–), Dora Vázquez (1913–), and Maruxa Fernández Fernández. Later additions include Pura Vázquez (1918–), Margarita Ledo Andión (1951–), Susana Antón, and Teresa Otero Sande.

Narrative as a woman's genre does not gain strength until the 1990s. Some of these writers have been prolific and to the public eye constitute an interlocking community of *literatas* (women of letters) who recognize their heritage as coming from Rosalía de Castro and know one another's work. Journals such as *A Saia, Andaina, Festa da Palabra Silenciada, Dorna, Nordés,* and others (some chiefly for women, others not) provide ample publishing space for women of all ages during the late 1970s and 1980s. In some cases the editors were women who encouraged the younger writers, through direct mentoring, friendship, or simply a sense of solidarity and the desire to create safe spaces in which to exhibit work. Blanco notes that three generations of Galician women writers actually meet during this time: that of 1936, that of the 1950s, and that of the 1970s.

Gender, then, is an important factor in the formation of literary groups in Galicia as the dictatorship wanes and the so-called transition begins. After 1975, didactic, journalistic, and children's literature increase, with the first and third categories actually outnumbering poetry. While this may appear anachronistic in the development of gynoliterature, it reflects the strong upsurge in numbers of women who for the first time find easy access to the world of publication. Their public voice may feel more secure in the "traditionally female" world of schoolteachers and children's literature, but we cannot forget that creating a nation of speakers, readers, and consumers for the Galician language was fundamental to the (re)building of national identity, which had been so actively persecuted from 1936 to 1975.

Marilar Aleixandre (1947–) is representative of the multifaceted woman writer in Galicia. Trained in science and currently in the College of Education at the Universidade de Santiago de Compostela, Aleixandre has written short stories and novels for young readers (most recently, *A banda sen futuro* [1999; The Band with No Future]) and novels for adults (*Tránsito dos gramáticos* [1993; Grammarians' Way], *A compañía clandestina de contrapublicidade* [Premio Alvaro Cunqueiro, 1997; The Clandestine Counterpublicity Campaign]), has received the Premio Esquío for poetry for her book *Catálago de velenos* (1998; Poison List), and has published translations from English (*A caza do Carbairán*, trans. of Lewis Carroll's *The Hunting of the Snark*; *Muller Ceiba*, trans. of Sandra Cisneros's *Loose Woman*). Since her arrival in Galicia in the 1970s, Aleixandre has become an important member of the literary environment.

The grand-dames, all of whom are still writing, editing, and performing at this time, include Pura Vázquez—whose sister Dora is also her occasional collaborator; Luz Pozo Garza (1922–) who won the first Miguel González Garcés prize for poetry; and María do Carme Kruckenberg Sanjurjo (1928–). They are followed by Xohana Torres and María Xosé Queizán. Other names from this period include Emilia Estévez Villaverde, Aurea Lorenzo Abeijón, Xaquina Trillo, Cristina Amenedo, Anxeles Penas, Pilar Cibreiro, Luisa Castro, María Xosé Canitrot, Luisa Villalta, Margot Chamorro, and Marica Campo. Queizán, however, is the forerunner and agglutinator of Galician feminism as it is today. She is the author of *Unha orella no buraco* (1965; An Ear to the Wall), the first *nouveau roman* in Galician, and the first author of self-proclaimed feminist writing (other than Rosalía de Castro's short prose pieces in Spanish, "Lieders" and "Las Literatas") and her first novels, including the landmark essays *A muller en Galicia* (1977; Woman in Galicia), *Recuperemos as mans* (1980; Take Back Our Hands), and *Evidencias* (1989; It Goes without Saying). Queizán led the charge for feminist criticism through organizations such as FIGA (Feministas Independientes Galegas [Independent Galician Feminists]); her entire career has been devoted to women's rights and writing. She was the first "out" lesbian writer and still is one of only a handful who overtly address woman-woman sexuality, as in her novel *Amantia* (1984), her poetry books *Metáfora da metáfora* (1991; Metaphor of the Metaphor) and *Despertar das Amantes* (1993; The Lovers' Awakening), and her novel *Amor de tango* (1992; Tango Love). Her novel *A semellanza* (1988; The Resemblance) reflects on gender in general. In addition to novels and essays, Queizán has published literary criticism, short stories, plays, and translations. Her most recent novel is *Ten o seu punto a fresca rosa* (2000; The Cool Rose Has Its Spot).

The work of Helena Villar Janeiro (1940–) has evolved from a close collaboration with her writer husband (Xesús Rábade Paredes) to a more feminist perspective, particularly in poetry such as *Rosalía no espello* (1985; Rosalía in the Mirror). She maintains this stance to some extent in short stories (cf. the collection *O enterro da Galiña de Domitila Rois* [1991; The Burial of Domitila Rois's Chicken]). Recently she has been writing journalistic prose, but she is also well known as the author of children's literature. Among the hefty list of children's literature authors are, in addition to Villar Janeiro, Marilar Aleixandre, Palmira Boullosa, Silvia Gaspar, Carme López Taboada, and María Victoria Morena Márquez.

Ursula Heinze de Lorenzo (1941–), whose first language is German, cultivates several genres, including children's literature and documentary/journalistic texts such as *Arredor da muller en 18 mundos* (1985; Around Woman in 18 Worlds), *Xente coma min* (1989; People Like Me), and *Mulleres* (1991; Women). However, she would not be, nor want to be, classified as a feminist. Former president of the PEN (poets, playwrights, essayists, editors and novelists) Club of Galicia, she has recently focused on translation from German to Galician and has ventured into the area of poetry. In addition, she has published short stories (*Remuíños en coiro* [1984; Surprise and Confusion]) and novels (*O soño perdido de Elvira M.* [1982; Elvira M.'s Lost Dream], *Anaiansi* [1989]). Other writers in Galician as a second language include Kristina Berg and Anne Marie Morris. Their work, and that of others, is classified as Galician literature because of the language. Interestingly, the Galician PEN Club includes as members, among others, a Galician-born citizen of Brazil, Nélida Piñón, and a U.S. citizen, Kathleen March. Membership, which is by invitation, is based on work published in Galician in the area of literature and creative writing, rather than on nationality or place of residence, underlining the fundamental criterion of language for the literary canon.

A number of poets could be mentioned, including María Manuela Couto, Elsa Fernández, and others, but two names are representative of the transition between generations from the immediate post-Franco era that is so important to Galician literary culture and the decade of the 1990s, Luisa Castro (1966–) and Marina *Mayoral (1942–). Castro initiated her publication in Galician in 1988 with the book of verse *Baleas e baleas* (Whales upon Whales) but would not continue her creative writing in that language. While residing in Madrid, her verse and narrative have been in Spanish and thus not considered part of the Galician canon. Through selection by the Spanish government, Castro has represented Galicia in literary gatherings, but she is not considered a participant in its cultural production. Again, this is because of the linguistic medium rather than her place of residence. Note that any creative works written or published originally in Galician are included in the canon, despite the author's origin. Thus Anne Marie Morris (United States), Ursula Heinze, and several other writers are classified among the group of "Galician authors." This does not mean the doors are permanently closed to her or to any writer who consciously chooses a cultural identity. Comparison can be made with Mayoral, who resides in Madrid and frequently publishes in Spanish but whose linguistic and cultural ties are more evident, either through past research (her thesis was on Rosalía de Castro), translation to Galician, participation in cultural events, symposia, or original texts in that language. However, Hispanists do approach Mayoral's work only from the perspective of Spanish, just as they mistakenly approached Rosalía de Castro only as a Spanish writer.

No longer the "precocious" young poets of several years ago, writers such as Pilar Pallarés, author of *Entre lusco e fusco* (1980; Dusk) and winner of the Esquío Award for her second book *Sétima soidade* (1984; Seventh Solitude) and Ana Romaní (*Palabra de mar* [1987; Sea Word], *Mareas* [1996; Tides]) have proven to be capable contributors to Galician women's writing as well as practitioners of literary criticism and other cultural media. Neither is especially prolific as regards poetic production, but their presence at cultural and political events is an important aspect of the Galician literary fabric. It is particularly with Queizán and Pallarés that gender is linked to nationalism.

The last decade of the twentieth century saw the definitive establishment of Galician women writers and literary/cultural criticism in accepted proportions. As has been noted, the 1985 centennial of Castro's death was a turning point for gynocriticism. Castro was vindicated as a feminist and nationalist, and the revisioning of her work opened up possibilities for others. At times a simple article of gynocriticism has been a feminist gesture. Other times translation has fulfilled this role, as has Queizán's translation of feminist stories from English. Although the quality of translation is to be lamented, E. Souto's version of Zora Neale Hurston's *Their Eyes Were Watching God* (1993) shares this same goal of promoting women's and minority views. Recent anthologies of women writers are further testimony to the growth in acceptance. The first anthology of Galician women poets, *Festa da palabra* (1989; Word Festival), was followed by *Palabra de muller* (1992; Woman's Word). However, the collective works originating in Madrid and in Spanish present thorny questions as to the promotion of Galician women writers as opposed to promoting women writers living in Spain.

New writers appear constantly. Rapidly established as a woman's poet is Chus Pato (1955–), author of *Urania* (1991), *Heloísa* (1994), *Fascinio* (1995; Fascination), *Ponte das poldras* (1996; Stepping Stones), *Nínive* (1996), and *m-Talá* (2000). Yolanda Castaño (1977–) has published *Elevar as pálpebras* (1995; Lift Your Eyelids), *Vivimos no ciclo das erofanías* (1998; We Live in the Era of Erophanies), and *Delicia* (1998; Delight). Other younger poets are Inma Antonio Souto, María do Cebreiro Rábade Villar (1973–), and Cristal Méndez Queizán (1964–). Xela Arias (1962–), who as of this writing works for the publisher Xerais, was once more prolific, with titles such as *Denuncia do equilibrio* (1986; Proclamation against; Equilibrium) and the photo-poetic-erotic *Tigres coma cabalos* (1990; Tigers Like Horses), but she has published less in recent years. One of her latest works, *Darío a diario* (1996; Darío Every Day), is a poetic view of motherhood. Arias has received awards for her translations from English and Portuguese, including works by James Joyce, James Fenimore Cooper, Jorge Amado, and Camilo Castelo Branco. Castaño has collaborated with Olga Novo on such cultural projects as the AELG (Asociación de Escritoras en Lingua Galega [Association of Writers in the Galician Language], Letras de Cal (publishing house for new poetry), and Valdeleite. One of the youngest members of the current generation, Emma Couceiro (1977–) attracted attention in 1997 with her book of verse *Humidosas* (Moist), awarded the Premio Espiral Maior literary prize. *As entrañas horas* (Intimate Hours) appeared the following year. Couceiro also is a member of the group Letras de Cal and is one of the younger poets included in collective volumes such as *Mulher a facer vento* (1998; Woman on the Wind).

Theater, the genre least popular among women writers in Galicia, is influenced by the fact that dramatic works in general are subject to funding for staging and thus are less often selected by writers. Some of the first dramatic texts were produced by Prieto Rouco in her *Horas de febre*. The first entire book may be Edelmira Cacheda Otero's *Contos que van pra feira* (1961; Stories That Go to Market). It was followed by Xohana Torres's *A outra banda do Iberr* (1965; On the Other Side of the Iberr) and *Un hotel de primeira sobre o río* (1968; A First-Class Hotel by the River). Dora Vázquez is the author of *Tres cadros de teatro galego* (1973; Three Scenes of Galician Theater), while the talented Queizán has also written *Antígona, ou a forza do sangue* (1989; Antigone or the Blood's Power), in which she once again melds feminism with nationalism and a historical-mythical-legendary perspective. Queizán seems devoted to creating a literary-cultural space for women of all ages and in all ages. This tactic has not been overlooked by writers coming after her; in the future Queizán will surely be seen as the writer who almost single-handedly opened doors and widened horizons for an entire generation of authors. Also not to be overlooked are Inma Souto, the author of *Era nova e sabia a malvaísco* (1991; She Was Young and Tasted Like Marshmallow), and Fina Casalderrey (1951–), dramatist and theater director. Recognized with several awards for her children's literature, Casalderrey also received the Premio Cidade de Pontevedra in 1996 for her literary accomplishments.

By no means can it be said that an adequate level of respect and inclusion of women writers in Galicia has been achieved. Old traditions and a dearth of theoretical orientation in the language still influence anthological and round-table participation, so vital to the promotion and development of the Galician identity. Feminist criticism from within is accepted to some extent but not widespread nor always broad in scope or of sufficient depth. It has enjoyed external contributions and will continue to develop as theories of gender, nationalism, and diversity are spread through Galicia, through translation and research. Already the names of Carmen Blanco, Camiño Noia, Pilar García Negro, Marga Romero, and Helena González (all born after 1970) are associated with gender criticism. Writers like Pilar Pallarés and Luz Pozo Garza are recognized critics, although their objects of study are not always, nor often, women. Other contemporary literary critics may show no particular interest in gender concerns, yet maintain a visible presence in academic publishing. With the establishment of a chair of women's studies in Vigo and a degree in translation at the university in this same city, the situation has changed already from the early 1990s, when there was a monographic course neither on Rosalía de Castro nor on Galician women writers in all of Galicia.

Work about

Blanco, Carmen. *El contradiscurso de las mulleres*. Vigo: Nigra, 1997.

———. *Historia da literatura galega de muller*. Vigo: Xerais, 1991.

———. *Mulleres e independencia*. Sada: Ediciós do Castro, 1995.

Freire Lestón, Xosé Vicenzo. *A Prensa de mulleres en Galicia 1841–1994*. Lisbon: Edições Lusófonas, 1996.

González Fernández, Helena. "Las poetas y las poéticas desde la posguerra hasta hoy: '¡Yo también navegar!'" *Breve historia feminista de la literatura española (en lengua catalana, callega y vasca)*. Coord. Iris M. Zavala. Barcelona: Anthropos, 2000. 4:196–218.

March, Kathleen. *De musa a literata: Feminismo en la narrativa de Rosalía de Castro*. Sada: Ediciós do Castro, 1994.

———. "Rosalía de Castro como punto de referencia ideolóxico-literario nas escritoras galegas." *Actas do Congreso internacional sobre Rosalía de Castro e o seu tempo*. Santiago de Compostela: Consello da Cultura Galega-Universidade de Santiago de Compostela, 1986. 1:283–292.

Marco, Aurora. *As precursoras*. A Coruña: La Voz de Galicia, 1993.

Noia Campos, Camino. *Palabra de muller*. Vigo: Xerais, 1992.

Rodríguez Sanchez, Francisco. *Análise sociolóxica da obra de Rosalía de Castro*. Vigo: AS-PG, 1988.

Kathleen March

Galindo, Beatriz (1475–1534)

Known as *la Latina* because of her humanist learning, Beatriz Galindo was the most famous teacher and tutor in the early Renaissance. She entered the service of *Isabel la Católica (1451–1504) at an early age as a lady-in-waiting but soon began to teach Latin to Isabel and the four royal daughters (*Catalina [de Aragón], *Juana [la Loca], Isabel, and María). Over time, she became the queen's personal counselor. Galindo wrote a number of commentaries on ancient authors and some Latin poetry, none of which has survived, but her true fame lies in her role as a teacher and promoter of classical studies at the Spanish court.

Galindo married King Ferdinand's secretary, Francisco Ramírez de Madrid, bearing two sons. When her husband died in 1501, Galindo retired from her duties as royal tutor but stayed with the queen until the latter's death in 1504. Then, she dedicated the rest of her life to charity. Following her husband's last will, she oversaw construction of the Conceptionist hospital for the poor in Madrid (known today as La Latina), with a convent alongside it. She also founded another convent. Galindo worked actively at the hospital until her death there.

Work about

Arteaga, Cristina de. *Beatriz Galindo, "La Latina."* Madrid: Espasa Calpe, 1975.

Llanos y Torriglia, Félix. *Una consejera de estado. Doña Beatriz Galindo, la Latina.* Madrid: Reus, 1920.

Ximénez de Sandoval, Felipe. *Varia historia de ilustres mujeres.* Madrid: Ediciones y Publicaciones Españolas, 1949.

Nereida Segura-Rico and David H. Darst

Galvarriato, Eulalia (1905–)

Eulalia Galvarriato's literary career has been eclipsed by the eminent figure of her husband, Dámaso Alonso (1898–1990), a president of the Spanish Royal Academy, poet, and literary critic. Most of her life she was his faithful collaborator, secretary, his right hand, even though she has not been properly credited with the contribution she made to his illustrious work. Since his death, she has continued to catalog and revise his writings, although she does not consider it a sacrifice.

Galvarriato's only novel, *Cinco sombras [en torno a un costurero]* (1947; Five Shadows [Around a Sewing Table]), was a finalist for the Nadal Prize and has been praised by literary critics despite its traditional, nineteenth-century structure. Unlike her contemporaries Ana María *Matute (1926–) and Carmen *Laforet (1921–), Galvarriato describes an antiquated society where five young women are oppressed by the strict rules of their father. A feminist interpretation would conclude that the author was trying to denounce said situation, but this was not her intention. In the novel there are many images of closeness and entrapment that reflect the limited confines of the women's lives. The image of the sewing table where the five sisters sit serves to unite them to the memory of their deceased mother. This is a trait that Galvarriato's novel shares with her contemporaries; mothers are mostly absent in the postwar novels written by women.

Galvarriato's other book is *Raíces bajo el tiempo* (1985; Roots under Time) where she has collected her short stories, poems, recollections, dreams, and travel notes, some of which she published during the postwar years in literary magazines. Time in its different manifestations (personal, existential, oneiric) is the true protagonist of her short stories. Diverse themes, characters, and situations give them uniqueness, while a general lyric quality unifies them. Some female characters are reminiscent of the oppressed women in *Cinco sombras*, but in fact children and older people alike all seem to have a hopeless view of life.

The poems, recollections of her past, and dreams are all autobiographical. Their obvious personal nature lends itself to a psychological interpretation that would confirm Galvarriato's modesty and her feelings of inadequacy in comparison with her husband. The paternal figure is the dominant one in her life as well as in her fiction. *See also* Short Fiction by Women Writers: 1900–1975

Work by

Cinco sombras. 4th ed. Barcelona: Destino, 1967.
Raíces bajo el tiempo. Barcelona: Destino, 1985.
"Una amistad: Pedro Salinas y Dámaso Alonso." *Revista de Occidente* 126 (1991): 45–54.

Work about

Alborg, Concha. *Cinco figuras en torno a la novela de posguerra: Galvarriato, Soriano, Fórmica, Boixadós y Aldecoa.* Madrid: Ediciones libertarias, 1993.

Irizarry, Estelle. "*Cinco sombras* de Eulalia Galvarriato: Una novela singular de la postguerra." *Novelistas femeninas de la postguerra española.* Ed. Janet Pérez. Madrid: José Porrua, 1983. 47–56.

López, Ignacio Javier. "Eulalia Galvarriato, Azorín and the Reaction against 'tremendismo' in Post-War Spanish Literature." *Hispanic Journal* 12.2 (1991): 341–347.

Pérez, Janet. "Portraits of the 'Femme Seule' by Laforet, Matute, Soriano, Martín Gaite, Galvarriato, Quiroga, and Medio." *Feminine Concerns in Contemporary Spanish Fiction by Women*. Ed. Robert C. Manteiga, Carolyn Galerstein, and Kathleen McNerney. Potomac, MD: Scripta Humanistica, 1988. 54–77.

Concha Alborg

Gálvez de Cabrera, María Rosa (1768–1806)

A distinguished poet and playwright, María Rosa Gálvez was the adopted daughter of Colonel Antonio Gálvez and María Ana Ramírez de Velasco. She married Captain José Cabrera y Ramírez, but the marriage did not last long. They separated shortly after moving to Madrid. Tradition has attributed this separation to her rumored love affair with Manuel Godoy, the prime minister and court favorite. It is alleged that the captain requested a divorce from his wife and the post of attaché in the Spanish embassy in the United States. More recent scholarship presents a different interpretation of the marital rift. The estrangement seems to have been precipitated by Captain Cabrera's gambling habits. It was the Gálvez family who used its considerable influence to send him as far away as possible from his wife. Be that as it may, Gálvez's poor health, the gossip around her marriage, her difficulties with the censors, and her early death paint a rather sad picture of this talented woman's life.

Gálvez was an admirer of the neoclassic poet José Quintana, who considered her the best woman writer of the time. Her poetry possesses a clear and elegant style and easy-flowing versification. These are the most admired traits in her lyrical odes: the eloquent "Oda en elogio de la Marina Española" (Ode in Praise of the Spanish Navy), the fiery "Oda al Combate de Trafalgar" (Ode to the Battle of Trafalgar), and the inspired "Viaje al Teyde" (Journey to Teyde). Despite the value of her poetry, Gálvez is better known as a dramatist. In this genre she availed herself of patriarchal theatrical conventions to legitimize her own, very different, plays. In Madrid, Gálvez was known both for her translations from French and for her own works, written in the new neoclassic style. She wrote tragedies, *Amnón*, *Blanca de Rossi*, *Florinda*, *Zinda*, and *Ali Beck* (criticized for its excessive violence and defended by Gálvez in a letter to *Memorial Literario*); *comedias*, *La delirante* (The Delirious One), *El egoísta* (The Egotist), *La familia a la moda* (The Fashionable Family), *Las esclavas amazonas* (The Amazon Slave Women), and *Los figurones literarios* (Pretentious Writers); a *zarzuela*, *El Califa de Bagdad* (The Caliph of Baghdad); and one-act plays like *Saúl*, *Safo*, and *Un loco hace ciento* (One Fool Is One Too Many). See also Drama by Spanish Women Writers: 1770–1850.

Work by

Ali Beck [Tragedy]. Madrid: n.p., 1801.
Obras poéticas [Teatro y poesía]. 3 vols. Madrid: Imprenta Real, 1804.
Safo. Ed. Daniel S. Whitaker. *Dieciocho* 18.2 (Fall 1995): 189–210.

Work about

Jones, Joseph R. "María Rosa de Gálvez: Notes for a Biography." *Dieciocho* 18.2 (Fall 1995): 173–186.
Lewis, Elizabeth Franklin. "Breaking the Chains: Language and the Bonds of Slavery in María Rosa Gálvez's *Zinda*." *Dieciocho* 20.2 (1997): 263–275.
———. "The Tearful Reunion of Femininity in María Rosa Gálvez's Neoclassic Theater." *Letras Peninsulares* 9.2–3 (1996–1997): 205–216.
Serrano y Sanz, Manuel. *Apuntes para una biblioteca de escritoras españolas desde el año 1401 al 1833*. 2 vols. Madrid: Rivadeneyra, 1903.
Whitaker, Daniel S. "Absent Mother, Mad Daughter, and the Therapy of Love in *La delirante* of María Rosa de Gálvez." *Dieciocho* 16.1–2 (1993): 167–176.

María A. Salgado

García, Antona (?–1476)

This brave, energetic woman led an insurrection against Portuguese invaders of Toro in July 1476. The city had been seized in 1474 by Castilian and Portuguese troops fighting for Juana la *Beltraneja, the purportedly illegitimate daughter of Enrique IV *el Impotente* (the Impotent) and wife of King Alfonso of Portugal. Antona García and two other citizens of Toro led a general uprising to oust the Portuguese and were captured and executed. When Fernando and *Isabel finally freed the city in September, they granted Antona's descendants perpetual exemption from taxation in recognition of her valor. In the 1620s, Tirso de *Molina immortalized her actions in his famous play *Antona García*.

Work about

Wilson, Margaret, ed. *Tirso de Molina: "Antona García."* Manchester: UP, 1957.

David H. Darst

García, Consuelo (1935–)

Author of novels, short stories, and articles, Consuelo García was born in Murcia, a province in southeastern Spain. She studied philology in Murcia, Madrid, and Berlin. García's contribution to Spanish narrative resides in her thorough analysis of subjects related to Spanish society. Her great accomplishment as a novelist and philosopher derives from her ability to capture and elucidate all sides of any topic she addresses. In her novels, she does not aim to establish truth but rather to problematize accepted conventional precepts. Her ironic, comic, and occasionally sarcastic tone is aimed above all at complacent characters who, out of ignorance, selfishness, or stupidity, act mechanically without realizing the effects of or assuming responsibility for their conduct. Penetrating and incisive criticism is a main feature of her narrative.

Luis en el país de las maravillas (1982; Luis in Wonderland) is the story of the breakup of a marriage in 1970s Spain, when the country was experiencing significant changes. The couple's personal story (the numerous affairs that the husband has outside the marriage and the sense of frustration and humiliation that the wife experiences) provides the basis for a sociological analysis of the period. There is an exploration of topics related to *feminism such as *machismo* (male exaltation) and the sexual liberation of women after the time of the dictatorship. García shows great critical and ironic understanding of that reality through her protagonist Clara, who is also a writer. She makes fun of men's obsessions with their penises (and their unawareness of the existence of the clitoris in women as an organ of pleasure), of the enthronement of coitus in sexual relations, and of the role of victim that men often enact when confronted with women's liberation. All of this has the effect of demystifying patriarchal ideology. In a serious tone, she also warns about the dangers of women who practice a superficial form of feminism, which can lead to men manipulating feminism to their own advantage to counteract the gains of the women's movement. García criticizes a type of bogus feminism that is manifested in fashionable attitudes but has nothing to do with the liberation of women. She combats the dichotomy of "woman victim, guilty man" by pointing out the degree of responsibility that women must assume when they find themselves in situations of injustice. She is also critical of so-called sexual liberation. Clara explains how women left behind the "popedom" (as backed by Franco and the Church) of the town priest only to fall into the "popedom" of psychologists (i.e., Freud, etc.) and how both ideologies aim at controlling women's lives and orgasms (the first by censoring and repressing, and the second by inciting and establishing the models of "bad orgasm" and "frigid woman"). She also laments the entire nation's obsession with sex once democracy was reestablished in Spain (the prevailing criterion of "hagotodoloquemeproporcionaplacer" [Idoeverythingthatgivesmepleasure]), and of the generally frivolous and consumerist atmosphere of sexual practices wherein sex is converted into mere gymnastics.

Las cárceles de Soledad Real (1982; The Jails of Soledad Real) constitutes a documentary type of novel concerning the protagonist's life from the period of the Republic up to the postwar period. García narrates the different stages in her life: an unhappy childhood, adolescence and political militancy in the Communist Party, and her youth when the Civil War breaks out (her defense of Republicans' flight to the refugee camps in France and subsequent escape when the war is lost, the Communist Party's clandestine resistance organization in opposition to fascism, fear of the police, the anguish of detention, torture, and prison). Soledad spends 16 years in eight Francoist prisons, but she does not give up because she has a vital character imbued with solidarity and because she had already experienced cold, hunger, filth, and illness in her marginal neighborhood "la Barceloneta." There is also a place in this novel for criticism of the Communist Party's intransigency and dogmatism (i.e., the nonacceptance of homosexuals and lesbians). This novel constitutes a historical document of great value principally because the topic of repression suffered by communist women during Franco's dictatorship has not been widely explored in Spanish literature. *See also* Eroticism in Contemporary Spanish Women Writers' Narrative; Short Fiction by Women Writers: 1975–1998, Post-Franco

Work by

Las cárceles de Soledad Real. Madrid: Alfaguara, 1982.
Luis en el país de las maravillas. Barcelona: Lumen, Palabra Menor, 1982.

Work about

Suñén, Luis. "Consuelo García: Dos libros y dos mujeres." *Ínsula* 437 (1983): 5.

Eva Legido-Quigley

García Balmaseda, Joaquina (1837–1883)

The literary artistry of Joaquina García de Balmaseda displays itself primarily in the genre of theater through female protagonists who claim a will of their own. They stand out among independent literary characters in contrast to the traditional role of woman as complement of man and are unyielding to the secondary role of submissiveness in the dramatic works. García Balmaseda does, however, revert to these traditional descriptions of women in several articles and in the novel *La mujer laboriosa* (1876, The Industrious Woman) as testimony to the conventional classification of female domesticity. She employed nine different pseudonyms when writing: J.G.B., Ketty, Lady, Baronesa de Olivares, Pérez Mirón, Aurora, Samb, Adela, and Zahara.

Her three major contributions to theater, *Genio y figura*... (1860; Temperament and Image...), *Donde las dan*... (1868; If One Sows Evil...), and *Un pájaro en el garlito* (1871; A Bird in the Snare), consider antagonism between the sexes in which woman fights to affirm her independence even though in the end she is persuaded to accept the love offered by her male antagonist, as Caldera has noted. The three dramatic pieces treat similar situations: a couple at the point of separation due to their mutual hostility, a separation that is thwarted by the couple's ability to solve their problems, thereby allowing sentiments of love to prevail. The woman plays the role of protagonist opposite the man, the antagonist. These works are written from the feminine perspective, and in *Genio y figura*, the feminine conflict is associated with contemporary customs. As protagonist of *Genio y figura*, Carlota illustrates the strength of a spoiled daughter who successfully manipulates others for her own benefit. For this reason, she is able to avoid a failed relationship with Rafael, determined that he will regain interest in her through her affections and kindness. The theme of the dominant woman appears in Victoria, protagonist of *Donde las dan*. Dressed as another woman, Victoria receives the attentions of her boyfriend, Luis, who flirts with what he thinks is the other woman while speaking ill of Victoria. The strength of Victoria's will, implied in her name, demands apologies of Luis.

In *Un pájaro en el garlito*, Rosario plays the role of an independent woman who travels without a male escort, thereby incurring the disapproval of Alberto Sandoval, her (unbeknownst to her) fiancé.

In addition to 18 novels and seven translations, a thorough listing of about 50 of García de Balmaseda's journalistic contributions to *Educación Pintoresca*, *La Floresta*, *La Aurora de la vida*, *La América*, and *La Educanda* from 1857 to 1864 has been compiled by her biographer, María del Carmen Simón Palmer. As with other nineteenth-century female writers, García Balmaseda voices concerns of the contemporary woman, both as independent controller of her environment and as traditional performer within the patriarchal framework. *See also* Drama by Spanish Women Writers: 1860–1900

Work by

Donde las dan . . . Proverbio en un acto en verso. Madrid: Eduardo Cuesta, 1868.
Genio y figura: Proverbio en un acto. Madrid: J. Rodríguez, 1860.
La madre de familia: Diálogos instructivos sobre la religión, la moral y las maravillas de la naturaleza. Madrid: Santa Coloma, 1860.
La mujer laboriosa: Novísimo manual de labores que comprende desde los primeros rudimentos de costura, hasta las más frívolas labores de adorno: Obra utilísima para las señoras profesoras y la mujer en general. Barcelona: J. y A. Bastinos, 1884.
Un pajarito en el garlito: Comedia en un acto y en prosa. Madrid: J. Rodríguez, 1871.

Work about

Caldera, Ermanno. "La perspectiva femenina en el teatro de Joaquina García Balmaseda y Enriqueta Lozano." *Escritoras románticas españolas*. Ed. Marina Mayoral. Madrid: Fundación Banco Exterior, 1990. 207–216.
Galerstein, Carolyn and Kathleen McNerney, eds. *Women Writers of Spain: An Annotated Biobibliographical Guide*. Westport, CT: Greenwood P, 1986.
Simón Palmer, María del Carmen. *Escritoras españolas del siglo XIX: Manual bio-bibliográfico*. Madrid: Castalia, 1991.

Lisa Nalbone

García de la Torre, Ana (nineteenth century)

Very little is known of this interesting nineteenth-century writer, not even the dates of her birth and death or the places in which she lived. An alternate name found in some bibliographical listings (possibly a pseudonym) is "Ana García del Espinar" (or perhaps "de la Torre" is the pseudonym and "del Espinar" her birth name). Given the ideologies that underlie her works (including an interest in utopian socialism and workers' movements), it seems probable that she came from an intellectual and politically involved family, some of whom must have had leftist contacts, even if not close ones. Apparently a contemporary of Benito Pérez Galdós and Emilia *Pardo Bazán (given similar aesthetics and thematics in her writing), she was quite progressive for her day in her presentation of problems of gender, class, and the proletariat. García de la Torre is among the first Spanish writers to portray the "working girl" in Spain, and she stands out for her objective examination of the institution of marriage from a variety of perspectives. Unlike writers speaking for the patriarchy, she presented alternatives for women other than marriage and the convent, painting "decent" independent lifestyles.

Several novels of García de la Torre, coeval with those of Galdós and other leading realists of the 1870s and 1880s, have survived. Despite a sometimes moralizing tone and occasional echoes of idealistic perspectives such as those of predecessors including "Fernán Caballero" (Cecilia *Böhl de Faber) and Carolina *Coronado (or her more conservative contemporaries including Angela *Grassi and María del Pilar *Sinués), García de la Torre's works are more original in their subject matter and usually superior in structure and expression. She combines *costum-*

brismo (local color) and realism, reflecting a multiplicity of contemporary topics and social problems. Her first novel, *Cosas del mundo. Novela de costumbres* (1877; Things of the World. Novel of Customs) examines the institution of marriage, earning high marks for (relative) objectivity. Neither apology nor idealization, the novel reflects a thoroughly believable reality, with characters illustrating a wide range of marital relationships (some are prisoners of unhappy mismatches, others are mildly bored, and still others are happily married). García de la Torre utilizes contrasting pairs to present her implied thesis that altruism contributes significantly to happiness in the married state.

Later novels contain similar motifs, as in *Por una lágrima* (1878; For a Tear), recreating the life of a virtuous working girl in Barcelona during the second half of the nineteenth century. Painting a broad gamut of male-female relationships, ranging from exploitative and abusive concubinage to happy marriage, the novelist avoids the "happily ever after" trap: By no means are all marriages she presents felicitous. Nevertheless, the women who do find happiness play fairly traditional roles. *Los esclavos del trabajo* and *La asociación* (1878; Slaves of Work [and] The Association), a two-part novel and sequel form a unit whose two halves coincide in rejecting international socialist movements (then recently arrived in Spain). The author suggests that their promises of security often failed to materialize. The first part presents the workers' plight and response to organizers, while the second portrays their disillusionment when the hoped-for benefits are not forthcoming. García obviously had knowledge of syndicalism and adequately grasped the principles of utopian socialism, indicating that she moved in very different circles than most other women writers of the day. Her attitude toward the proletariat, socialism, freedom, and other contemporary issues stands in stark contrast to Coronado's stance on the same questions (as set forth in *La rueda de la desgracia*). Although García de la Torre's work has received little attention, her superior narrative achievements, pioneering thematics, and atypical grasp of politicoeconomic developments render her novels especially deserving of study.

Work by

La asociación. Barcelona: P. Casanovas, 1878.
Cosas del mundo. Novela de costumbres. Barcelona: P. Casanovas, 1877.
Los esclavos del trabajo. Barcelona: P. Casanovas, 1878.
Por una lágrima. Barcelona: P. Casanovas, 1878.

Work about

Criado y Domínguez, Juan Pedro. *Literatas españolas del siglo XIX: Apuntes bibliográficos*. Madrid: Pérez Dubrull, 1889.
Ferreras, Juan Ignacio. *Catálogo de novelas y novelistas españoles del siglo XIX*. Madrid: Cátedra, 1979.

Janet Pérez

García Diego, Begoña (1926–)

A member of the early postwar generation, a time when it was not easy to become a career journalist, Begoña García Diego entered this professional field and contributed to the modernization of Spanish middle-class women through her writings in popular magazines and newspapers. The daughter of a well-known art critic, García Diego received a traditional Catholic education and was not allowed to pursue university studies. After graduation from high school she became a Red Cross nurse and volunteer. As she puts it, in the 1950s and 1960s women did not work unless they needed to, and those who did work either relinquished their position or were fired once they married. García Diego began writing in 1953 for the society pages of short-lived newspapers. She next became a reporter for *Don José*, a humor magazine directed by Antonio Mingote, working at the same time for the magazine *Semana*, where she actually learned journalism. She also published short stories in the Falange newspaper *El Español* (1954 to 1957). In 1957, García Diego won the Café Gijón short novel prize for *Bodas de plata* (Silver Wedding Anniversary) and began work as a reporter and columnist for *Blanco y Negro*, writing the section "Cuarto de estar" (Living Room). In 1965 she worked in New York for the Cuban magazine *Vanidades* but then returned to Spain to marry an aristocrat from Extremadura. In 1979 she moved back to Madrid, attended the Universidad a Distancia, and graduated with a degree in literature.

Bodas de plata is an original, well-crafted piece, particularly in its narration of different time levels, which are arranged around the death of a young woman, in the style of Faulkner's *As I Lay Dying*. García Diego also has two unpublished novels, but her best work to date is found in her short stories and journalistic writing. Her articles reflect changing societies of the 1950s and 1960s and represent a lively facet of the postwar, a document that must be taken into account in order to understand the full spectrum of middle-class women's mentality during that time. Some of her best columns for *Blanco y Negro* and *ABC* are collected in two early volumes, *Chicas solas* (1962; Girls on Their Own) and *Los años locos* (1972; The Crazy Years). In 1991 she added to them under the title *Del mal de amor y otras calamidades. Guía para desenamorar* (On the Sea of Love and Other Calamities. Guide for Falling Out of Love). Her earlier books deal with original feminine situations that show a new type of woman, one who has many male and female friends, who travels abroad in her own car, earns her own living, and lives independently. She is a role model for the times as she contests a world full of selfishness, conventions, and blindness in which she was raised. Her writings denounce, accuse, correct, and advise readers. She promotes work, independence, self-confidence, and humorous self-criticism. We are allowed to see the bourgeois *niñas de Serrano* (privileged girls from the Serrano neighborhood in Madrid) but also young students and budding professionals.

Noted for her sense of humor and an ability to capture essential details that depict the pulse of the moment, García Diego participated in the same trend of feminine perspective, ironic journalism, cultivated by Mercedes *Ballesteros ("Baronesa Alberta") and continued in the late 1980s and 1990s in the writings of Carmen *Rico Godoy and Maruja Torres. She wrote about work, independence, woman-man relationships, and family. While she kept away from active feminists such as Lidia *Falcón (1935–), she did not quite belong in the circle of professional writers like Carmen *Laforet (1921–) or Dolores *Medio (1911–1996) and did not come in contact with the gender studies group of María *Campo Alange (1902–1986). She did form part of the group of Mercedes *Fórmica (1918–) and other young professional women of the Madrid postwar intellectual bourgeoisie and must be considered an influential woman of the postwar period.

Her recent work, *Del mal de amor* (On Lovesickness), continues the social portrait and satire of the now dramatically changed society of the end of the century. There is a certain retrospective quality to this work. Her perspective as a writer has appropriately changed from the young reporter struggling for liberation; she is now an aging woman thrown in the middle of divorce. Empty nest and loose ethics are problems she still tackles with vigor and humor. Her aim in this series of vignettes is to give advice for reconstructing one's life, mending past errors, falling out of love, and surviving. Most of the persons undergoing these crises are her own age, so there is truly a link between the *niñas de Serrano* of her youth and these mature ladies. She describes some of what she calls the most rewarding therapeutic methods, while at the same time denouncing the difference in expectations of each gender. García Diego's works provide a quintessential example, full of humor and nuances, of the evolution of middle-of-the-road Spanish women from the 1950s to the 1990s.

Works by

Los años locos. Madrid: Prensa Española, 1972.
Bodas de plata. Madrid: Café Gijón, 1957.
Chicas solas. Madrid: Prensa Española, 1962.
Guía para desenamorar. Madrid: Biblioteca Nueva, 1991.

María Elena Bravo

García Lorca, Federico (1898–1936): Women in His Rural Trilogy

Federico García Lorca dramatizes the stultifying and sexually repressive life of women in provincial Spain in a rural trilogy formed by his three most famous plays, *Bodas de sangre* (1934; Blood Wedding), *Yerma* (1934; Barren), and *La casa de Bernarda Alba* (1935; The House of Bernarda Alba). The leading poet and playwright of his generation in Spain, Lorca unifies the dramas both thematically and stylistically, though each play also functions independently.

Bodas de sangre begins with the apprehensions of an old mother who has lost her husband and all but her last son to a bitter blood feud with a clan ironically named the Felixes (Happy Ones). Her last son, called only *Novio* (bridegroom), is about to marry the former fiancée of a member of that rival clan, a man named Leonardo, who is now married to a cousin of his former sweetheart in this ever-widening family tragedy. Leonardo, who is associated with a lion, or stud figure, is the only major character named in the drama. The rest, including the young bride-to-be, *la Novia*, are mere abstractions as Lorca shows the young woman being forced to marry a man she does not love. By not naming the characters, or by clearly giving them symbolic import, here and in the other two plays Lorca universalizes his themes.

On the wedding day the passion-filled Leonardo seizes the all-too-willing *Novia*. The two flee, but before they can sexually consummate their relationship, the *Novio* and Leonardo kill each other in a brutal knife fight. Shedding of the bride's blood when the hymen is broken during intercourse never occurs. She remains a virgin, though her reputation is destroyed. It is the blood of the two would-be lovers, Leonardo and the *Novio*, that flows.

The central figure in the second play of the trilogy is Yerma, whose name means barrenness or desert. Through this name, which also titles the play, her destiny is made known to the audience from the very first, and a sense of implacable fate emerges as society and gender stereotyping precipitate destiny. In a village where the only legitimate role for a woman is that of a wife and mother, Yerma longs obsessively for a child, yet her materialistic husband, Juan, given the very common name John, is unable to satisfy her and prefers to work in his fields rather than to fill her with child. There is the further suggestion that Juan is onanistic; like the biblical figure Onan, he prefers to spill his seed on the ground rather than impregnate his wife. Images of swelling, bursting, and filling permeate the play as Yerma yearns for a child. Since Lorca sublimates the theme of sexual desire to suggest the need for creative fulfillment in general, Juan implies the philistine nature of Spanish society. A possible paramour for Yerma is a local shepherd, ironically named Víctor, but he, like the sheep he tends, is too shy or cowardly to defy convention and break from the herd. Always lurking in the shadows are Juan's withered, black-clad sisters, spying on Yerma's every move. These menacing, self-righteous women unite with Juan to represent all that is stultifying in Spanish society. By the end of the play, Yerma is so distraught and desperate for a child that she is visiting sorceresses and others who suggest that much of the problem is in her and her inability to enjoy her own sexuality. In the very last scene of the play, Yerma strangles her husband to death in a parody of lovemaking—killing both him and any potential child they might have had.

The climax of the rural trilogy is *La casa de Bernarda Alba*. Here all the many images and themes that Lorca presents in the two earlier plays culminate. The sense of claustration in Spanish society, particularly in its treatment of women, overwhelms the action. Water, seen as a strong sexual principle, surges through all three productions, yet in *Bernarda Alba* it is the overwhelming sexual thirst that Lorca emphasizes. Sensations of sweltering heat to simulate sexual passion, experienced in the earlier plays, recur in *La casa de Bernarda Alba*, as do castration images of knives, serpents, and dismemberment as violence and sexual passion are continually yoked.

The dominant image in *La casa de Bernarda Alba* is the white-walled house of the widow, Bernarda Alba, who keeps her five daughters imprisoned within their own home in order to maintain their reputation. In all three plays there is strong but usually implicit criticism of the Roman Catholic Church. Bernarda, for instance, is associated through verbal clues with the Spanish Inquisition. *Bernarda Alba* opens with the wake for Bernarda's second husband. She enters, accompanied by women, dressed in black. Silhouetted against the sterile, impenetrable walls of the house, this cold woman, who bore her own children only out of a sense of necessity and duty, wants to impose a stern eight-year mourning period on her daughters. She also seeks to stifle her own mother, María Josefa, a parodic white-haired figure, lusting for a man and personifying the madness of repression that awaits the entire household. Bernarda Alba's first and last words on stage are calls for silence. Like Juan in *Yerma* and like society in general in *Bodas de sangre*, Bernarda wishes to stifle true expression or to distort it into rigid, socially accepted patterns.

As in the earlier plays, characters in *La casa de Bernarda Alba* tend to carry symbolic names. This is particularly true in the case of the daughters, named Magdalena (who recalls the prostitute Mary Magdalene), Angustias (the oldest, whose life is anguish and humiliation, as she is palmed off on a much younger man eager only for her dowry), Martirio (the martyr, whose name in Spanish can be a synonym for virgin), Amelia, and Adela. Only the youngest, Adela, whose name echoes the verb to advance (*adelantarse*, or *adelante*, to go forward) escapes the vise of her mother's authority. Adela has been sneaking to the stable at night where she meets her lover, opportunistic young Pepe el Romano, who is the man betrothed to 39-year-old Angustias. Lorca further heightens the sexual frustration of all characters by allowing no male figure to appear on stage. Men are spoken of; they are lusted after, but they are never seen.

In a momentary victory in Act 3, Adela, whose affair with Pepe has been exposed, taunts her mother and breaks her cane, symbol of Bernarda's authority. Enraged, Bernarda seizes a gun and rushes to the stable to destroy Pepe. A shot is fired, and Bernarda allows her distraught daughter to believe that Pepe has been killed, though he has in fact escaped. Adela then hangs herself. The tyrannical, soul-denying Bernarda Alba is in control and screaming for silence, maintaining that her daughter died a virgin and, therefore, with *honor. However, Adela now is free, and she, unlike her conforming sisters, has at least been able to express her inner feelings.

That Lorca, who is said to have been a homosexual, identified strongly with the repressive plight of women in Spain, is obvious. His rural trilogy is a powerful presentation of the status of women in the first half of the twentieth century in Spain and an eloquent plea for greater self-expression, both sexual and artistic, in all human beings. *See also Zapatera prodigiosa, La* (written 1926): The Representation of Honor

Work by

Obras completas. Ed. Arturo del Hoyo. 22nd ed. Madrid: Aguilar, 1986.

Three Tragedies of Federico García Lorca. Trans. James Graham-Luján and Richard O'Connell. New York: New Directions, 1955.

Work about

Cobb, Carl W. *Federico García Lorca*. New York: Twayne, 1967. Also available on *DiscLit: World Authors*. (Twayne's World Authors Series and OCLC World Authors Catalogue on CD-Rom.) Dublin: G.K. Hall and OCLC, 1994.

Colecchia, Francesca, ed. *García Lorca: An Annotated Primary Bibliography*. New York: Garland, 1982.

———. *García Lorca: A Selectively Annotated Bibliography of Criticism*. New York: Garland, 1979.

Durán, Manuel, ed. *Lorca: A Collection of Critical Essays*. Englewood Cliffs, NJ: Prentice-Hall, 1962.

Klein, Dennis A. *Blood Wedding, Yerma and The House of Bernarda Alba: García Lorca's Tragic Trilogy*. Boston: Twayne, 1991.

Newton, Candelas. *Understanding Federico García Lorca*. Columbia: U of South Carolina P, 1995.

Smith, Paul Julian. *The Theatre of García Lorca: Text, Performance, Psychoanalysis*. Cambridge: Cambridge UP, 1998.

Stainton, Leslie. *Lorca, a Dream of Life*. New York: Farrar, Straus, Giroux, 1999.

Jeanne J. Smoot

García Morales, Adelaida (194?–)

Born in Badajoz but raised in Seville, Adelaida García Morales has used the region of Andalusia as the setting for almost all her works. She lived in seclusion for five years in a village of La Alpujarra and currently resides in Madrid. García Morales received her *licenciatura* (master's degree) in philosophy in 1970 from the University of Madrid and later studied script writing in the Escuela Oficial de Cinematografía. Besides her career as a writer, she has taught Spanish language, literature, and philosophy in secondary schools and was a translator in Argel for OPEC (Organization of Petroleum Exporting Countries). She has also worked as a model and actress. García Morales has published five novels, two novelettes, and a collection of short stories. Her first full-length novel, *El silencio de las sirenas* (1985; The Silence of the Sirens), was widely celebrated by Spanish critics and was awarded the Herralde Prize for the Novel in 1985, as well as the Icaro Prize, given by the Spanish newspaper *Diario 16* to the outstanding new literary talent of the year. In addition, she has written poetry and two novels, still unpublished, one of which, "Archipiélago" (Archipelago), was a finalist for the Sésamo Prize in 1981.

Although her first narrative, *El sur* (1985; The South), was in its final form by 1981, it appeared as a film by Víctor Erice in 1983, before its publication. The film version is a free adaptation of the work in which the first-person narrator's voice is rendered via voice-over. *El sur* was finally published with another short novel, *Bene*, under the title *El sur seguido de Bene* (1985; The South Followed by Bene). In this work, as well as in all her novels—with the exception of *Las mujeres de Héctor* (1994; Hector's Women)—García Morales uses a first-person narrator. In both *El sur* and *Bene* the narrator's monologue creates the illusion of an implied listener within the narrative by invoking her dead father and her dead brother, respectively. The setting of *El sur* is an abandoned, dilapidated house, which creates an uncanny mood for the adult protagonist's confrontation with her family's past. As her monologue unravels, she delivers a poignant farewell to her dead father, finally coming to terms with his suicide when she was still a child. In *Bene*, the narrator/protagonist Angela addresses her dead brother Santiago and recounts a dream in which she revisited their childhood. She recalls the arrival of Bene—the young gypsy maid—into their household, the adolescent Santiago's love for Bene, which led to his death, Bene's mysterious ways, and the ensuing supernatural events. She ultimately searches for an explanation to the circumstances surrounding her brother's death and in her dream pleads with him to take her with him. Both *El sur* and *Bene* are set in isolated places where the real and the surreal seem to blend, and in both the taboo theme of incest is present.

García Morales began work on *El silencio de las sirenas* in 1979. The novel, dedicated to Víctor Erice, evokes the same haunting eerieness of *El sur* and *Bene*. Its site is a remote village in La Alpujarra, where the rarefied mountain air creates an appropriate scenario for protagonist Elsa's love fantasy—in which she pursues the feeling of love rather than a lover—while her friend and alter ego María prompts and records Elsa's dreams and fantasies. This very lyrical rendition of Elsa's pursuit of romantic love presents an ironic reversal of roles in that a man is presented as the object of a woman's desire. The limits between fantasy and reality are blurred, past and present are one, the supernatural is natural, and the central focus is the female creation of a male muse by Elsa and María, the storyteller. In *La lógica del vampiro* (1990; The Vampire's Logic), García Morales again creates a misty, shadowy setting for characters. The protagonist Elvira is summoned to Seville when her brother dies mysteriously, and as she probes the circumstances of her brother's death, she is drawn into his strange circle of friends at whose center is Alfonso, "the vampire." This "vampire" symbolizes anachronistic patriarchal forces within Spanish society as "the living-dead"; he thrives not on the blood of others but on exercising control over them. As in *El sur seguido de Bene* and *El silencio de las sirenas*, the author uses Gothic devices and conventions in *La lógica del vampiro*, which is preceded by an epigraph from Bram Stoker's *Dracula*.

García Morales's next novel, *Las mujeres de Héctor* (1994), has an omniscient narrator and in a way revolves around the police investigation of a crime. The suspects are Laura, Hector's estranged wife, who caused the accidental death of a woman at the very beginning of the novel but denies any involvement in the case; Hector, who found the dead woman's purse in his wife's house; Margarita, Hector's lover (and the dead woman's best friend); and Irina, a young woman whose infatuation with Hector leads her to lie and incriminate Margarita. The novel is really about each woman's analysis of her own circumstances and feelings toward Hector, the self-absorbed character who wants something from each of them but refuses to accept any responsibility in their relationship. Ironically, Hector's women are not really so—he is just the common denominator in their lives—and at the end they reject his companionship. This work was followed by *La tía Agueda* (1995; Aunt Agueda). In this novel, which García Morales dedicated to her children Galo and Pablo, once again a child protagonist narrates her story many years later, and the Gothic surroundings and cast of characters are reminiscent of *El sur* and *Bene*. Young Marta has just lost her mother and is taken by her father to live with his sister in a small town in Huelva. Marta's aunt Agueda lives with her husband Martín and a housekeeper in a big, dimly lit house. She sets rigid rules of conduct for Marta and is totally undemonstrative. During the year Marta spends at Agueda's house she twice comes face to face with death, first Martín's and later Agueda's; she learns about vengeance and cruelty and has her first brush with sexuality. When she returns to Seville with her father after Agueda's death, she feels that she has grown up way beyond her years.

García Morales's latest novel, *Nasmiya* (1996), is a long, slow-paced narrative. The story takes place in Madrid, and the characters are all members of a closely knit community of Spaniards who converted to Islam, adopted Muslim names and customs, worship together, and attend weekly social gatherings. The protagonist/narrator's Islamic name is Nadra, which means *única* (the only one); it was chosen by her husband Khaled, who (ironically) after many years of marriage, decides to take up a second wife. The couple was originally from Madrid, where both attended the university, but met in Granada, there converted to the Islamic faith, and after marrying, returned to Madrid. Although at the time of their conversion Khaled had pledged not to abandon monogamy, 15 years later, he decides to take a second wife, Nasmiya, a young woman whose parents were also Spanish converts to Islam. Unlike Nadra, Nasmiya gleefully agrees to share the man and house with Khaled's first wife and children. Through Nadra's perspective, the novel explores love relations and ponders whether it is possible for someone—in this case, a man—to love two women at the same time and whether monogamy is the only acceptable system. While Nadra and Khaled belong to the generation of the early post-Franco years, Nasmiya, with her free ways and detachment, clearly belongs to the generation that followed theirs. The clever juxtaposition of Nadra and Nasmiya serves to underscore and question women's changing attitudes and values in post-Franco Spain. Despite the bonding that finally develops between the two women, a gnawing doubt persists on the part of Nadra about the feasibility of an amiable love triangle in which two women share life with a man or, rather, are shared by him.

A later work published by García Morales is a collection of seven short stories, *Mujeres solas* (1996; Women Alone), in which all stories are related by a third-person narrator. In each narrative, the protagonist is a middle-aged woman in her forties, divorced or separated from her lover. As the title foretells, the unifying theme of the work is solitude, a pervading theme in García Morales's narrative. She examines aloneness from a woman's perspective, presenting a gamut of feelings and reactions to life without a male companion. She seems to purport that solitude can be an enjoyable state of being. In some of these stories, as in most of her narratives, the supernatural intrudes, and the limits between reality and fantasy blur.

García Morales's fictive world is a woman's world; male characters are few and occupy a secondary, distant position. *La lógica del vampiro* and *Nasmiya* possess a certain degree of interaction between male and female characters but are dominated by the female narrator.

Work by

La lógica del vampiro. Barcelona: Anagrama, 1990.
Las mujeres de Héctor. Barcelona: Anagrama, 1994.
Mujeres solas. Barcelona: Plaza y Janés, 1996.
Nasmiya. Barcelona: Plaza y Janés, 1996.
The Silence of the Sirens. Trans. Concilia Hayter. London: Collins, 1988.
El silencio de las sirenas. Barcelona: Anagrama, 1985.
El sur seguido de Bene. Barcelona: Anagrama, 1985.
La tía Agueda. Barcelona: Anagrama, 1995.

Work about

Alborg, Concha. "*El sur*, novela y película: Dos versiones de un mismo conflicto." *Anuario de Cine y Literatura en Español: An International Journal on Film and Literature* 3 (1997): 15–24.
Ciplijauskaité, Biruté. "Intertextualidad y subversión en 'El silencio de las sirenas' de Adelaida García Morales." *Revista Hispánica Moderna* 41.2 (December 1988): 167–174.
Glenn, Kathleen M. "Gothic Vision in García Morales and Erice's *El Sur*." *Letras Peninsulares* 7.1 (Spring 1994): 239–250.
Malaxecheverría, Coro. "Mito y realidad en la narrativa de Adelaida García Morales." *Letras Femeninas* 17.1–2 (1991): 43–49.
Martin Marquez, Susan. "Desire and Narrative Agency in *El sur*." *Cine-Lit II: Essays on Hispanic Film and Fiction*. Portland, OR: Portland State U, Oregon State U, Reed College, 1995. 130–136.
Nimmo, Clare. "García Morales's and Erice's 'El sur': Viewpoint and Closure." *Romance Studies* 26 (Fall 1995): 41–49.
Ordóñez, Elizabeth J. "Beyond the Father: Desire, Ambiguity, and Transgression in the Narrative of Adelaida García Morales." *Voices of Their Own. Contemporary Spanish Narrative by Women.* Lewisburg: Bucknell UP, 1991. 174–192.
———. "Writing Ambiguity and Desire: The Works of Adelaida García Morales." *Women Writers of Contemporary Spain: Exiles in the Homeland.* Ed. Joan L. Brown. Newark: U of Delaware P, 1990. 258–277.
Rodríguez, Mercedes Mazquiarán de. "Gothic Imagery, Dreams, and Vampirism: The Haunting Narrative of Adelaida García Morales." *Monographic Review/Revista Monográfica* 7 (1991): 124–134.
———. "The Metafictional Quest for Self-Realization and Authorial Voice in 'El silencio de las sirenas.'" *Romance Language Annual* (1990): 477–481.
Sánchez Arnosi, Milagros. "Adelaida García Morales: La soledad gozosa." *Insula* 472 (March 1986): 4.
Suñén, Luis. "En pos de la quimera: Una nueva de

Adelaida García Morales." *El País*. February 6, 1986: 8.

Thompson, Currie K. "Adelaida García Morales' 'Bene' and That Not-So-Obscure Object of Desire." *Revista de Estudios Hispánicos* 22.1 (January 1988): 99–106.

Mercedes Mazquiarán de Rodríguez

Gatell, Angelina (1926–)

A poet and pacifist born in Barcelona, Gatell moved to Valencia as an adolescent, completing her *bachillerato* (high school equivalency) there. Active in noncommercial theater, she scored several successes as an actress, funding one of Spain's first chamber theaters in collaboration with her future husband. In Valencia, she published her first book of poems and bore her first child, later moving to Madrid in 1959. Gatell's activism in peace movements (a courageous stance under the Franco regime) resulted in poetry of outspoken testimonials, including her dramatic monologue *El poema del soldado* (1954; The Soldier's Poem) commemorating the death of Miguel Hernández, Republican poet and soldier, who died in a Franco prison. Gatell's soliloquy denounces war, violence, and injustice.

Although the regional language of both Valencia and Barcelona is Catalan (legal during Gatell's childhood, outlawed by the dictatorship following the end of the Spanish Civil War, 1936–1939), Gatell apparently wrote entirely in Castilian. Like Ana María *Matute and others of the generation who were children during the Civil War, she was scarred by the civil conflict; this experience imparts a somber preoccupation and denunciatory tone to her work. She identifies with opponents of the Franco regime, artists and intellectuals whose largely neorealist writings are works of protest, denouncing the absence of political freedom, injustice, and inequality. Later, Gatell cofounded several independent literary groups, became well known as a lecturer, and produced scholarly essays on other poets, including Latin Americans Delmira Agustini and Alfonsina Storni. She gave poetry recitals and became literary critic for the periodical *Poesía española*. In addition to her poetry and essays, she published a number of children's books, including *Mis primeras lecturas poéticas* (n.d.; My First Poetry Readings), *Mis primeros héroes* (n.d., My First Heroes), and *El hombre del acordeón* (1984; The Accordion Man), plus short stories for juvenile audiences.

Gatell's is a committed art, daringly frank in its criticism and defiance of censorial constraints, as seen in *Las claudicaciones* (1969; Surrenders), which observers consider her most moving and forceful denunciation of the regime's injustice and repressiveness. It typifies the tone and content of most of her work of the 1950s and 1960s, opposing not only Francoist oppression and abuse but also the patriarchal establishment supporting the dictator. Often employing feminist perspectives, Gatell speaks openly in favor of liberation, painting her generation's hopes and dreams, protesting the Vietnam War, meditating upon discouragement, humanity's futures, a daughter's accidental death. Although not a writer of the first rank, she was significant as a proponent of feminist values and perspectives during years when it was neither comfortable nor entirely safe to defend women's liberation. *See also* Feminism in Spain: 1900–2000.

Work by

Las claudicaciones. Madrid: Biblioteca Nueva, 1969.
Esa oscura palabra. Santander: Isla de los Ratones, 1963.
El poema del soldado. Valencia: Diputación, 1954.

Work about

Fagundo, Ana María. "Testimonio y poesía en Angelina Gatell." *Cultura 70* (San Salvador) (July–December 1980): 63–68.

———. "Testimonio y poesía en Angelina Gatell." *Alaluz* 13–14.1–2 (Fall 1981–Spring 1982): 20–36.

Flores, Angel, and Kate Flores. *Poesía feminista del mundo hispánico*. Mexico: Siglo Veintiuno, 1984.

Galerstein, Carolyn L., and Kathleen McNerney, eds. *Women Writers of Spain. An Annotated Bio-*

Bibliographical Guide. Westport, CT: Greenwood P, 1986.

Manrique de Lara, J.G. *Poetas sociales españoles*. Madrid: E.P.E.S.A., 1974.

Janet Pérez

Gimeno de Flaquer, Concepción (1860–1919)

This Spanish novelist, editor, and feminist was born in the small town of Alcañiz in the mountainous northeast province of Teruel. Despite being raised in a Catholic, conservative environment, and notwithstanding the difficulties for girls in gaining an education at that time—especially in the small provincial towns—she persevered with a largely autodidactic formation and began at quite an early age to write and to edit a number of women's magazines, including *La Ilustración de la Mujer*, in Madrid. She traveled extensively later in life and lived several years in Mexico, where she also edited various women's magazines. Gimeno de Flaquer was the author of more than a dozen volumes on women and consistently defended women's right to education. Given her religious conservatism, however, she did not espouse women's right to vote, believing that "women's place is in the home," and most of her works for women were in the exemplary vein, attempting to provide appropriate models and moral encouragement.

She is best remembered in the cultural arena for her four postromantic novels: *Victorina, o heroísmo del corazón* (2nd ed. 1873; Victorina, or Heroism of the Heart); *El doctor alemán* (1880; The German Doctor); *Suplicio de una coqueta* (1885; Suffering of a Coquette), and an amplified version or sequel of this latter work with the addition resembling a debate: *¿Culpa o expiación?* (1890; Guilt or Expiation?). It is these paired, interrelated narratives (with a tinge of the thesis novel) that most clearly reveal the degree to which Gimeno de Flaquer, putative feminism notwithstanding, acceded in the question of patriarchal constraints circumscribing women's behavior. The first part questions the extent to which a flirtatious woman is responsible for the impact of her coquetry upon "vulnerable" males: Using the worst-case scenario, the novelist presents an extreme situation wherein one impressionable suitor is driven to suicide. Subsequently, the "guilty" woman dies an early death, leading to debate in the extended version or sequel as to whether she is thereby expiating her destructiveness and whether or not she repented and will obtain salvation. Clearly, then, Gimeno de Flaquer stopped short of advocacy of "emancipation," with her feminist activities directed principally to the defense of women's right to education and her own efforts to contribute to their enlightenment. She died in Madrid. *See also Ángel del hogar*

Work by

Culpa o expiación? 4th ed. Mexico: Secretaria de Fomento, 1890.
El doctor alemán. Zaragoza: Ariño, 1880.
Madres de hombres célebres. Madrid: Alfredo Alonso, 1895.
La mujer ante el hombre. Zaragoza: Ariño, 1882.
La mujer española. Madrid: n.p., 1877.
La mujer intelectual. Madrid: Asilo de Huérfanos del Sagrado Corazón de Jesús, 1901.

Work about

Ferreras, J. Ignacio. *Catálogo de novelas y novelistas españolas del siglo XIX*. Madrid: Cátedra, 1979.
Galerstein, Carolyn L., and Kathleen McNerney, eds. *Women Writers of Spain. An Annotated Bio-Bibliographical Guide*. Westport, CT: Greenwood P, 1986.

Janet Pérez

Gómez de Avellaneda, Gertrudis (1814–1873)

Both Cuba and Spain claim the genius of romantic female author Gertrudis Gómez de Avellaneda for their respective literary traditions—Cuba, because it was the place of her birth and formative years as well as the subject of much of her writings, and Spain, because it was where she sought her career as an artist and established herself as an influential part of the Spanish Romantic movement. Born in Puerto Príncipe (Camagüey province), Cuba, on March 23, 1814, her mother, Francisca de Arteaga y Betancourt, was a *criolla* (Cuban born but of Spanish parents) and her father, Manuel Gómez de Avellaneda, a Spanish naval officer stationed at the island colony. Avellaneda's father died in 1823, and her mother soon remarried another Spaniard, Isidro Escalada, who eventually brought the family back to Spain in 1836. Avellaneda lived and worked in Spain for the next 23 years, returning to Cuba from 1859 to 1864. She died in Spain in 1873.

Avellaneda's writing was in many ways similar to that of her male peers, employing typical forms and themes of Spanish Romanticism. Yet throughout her long career and in every genre she attempted—poetry, novel, theater, and essay—Avellaneda made her own unique contributions to romantic writings, as a woman and as a colonial. Many of her works contain elements from Cuba—characters, settings, images from nature—which appealed to the romantic hunger for the exotic but also had very personal meaning for Avellaneda. Other typical romantic topics, such as the ever-present theme of love, took on new significance for Avellaneda in a world where writing was really the only arena in which women could express their desire.

Avellaneda began her life as a writer at a very early age. Her parents employed Cuban intellectual and poet José María Heredia as one of her tutors, and perhaps his influence moved her to write poems while only a young girl. The earliest of her published works was the poem "Al partir" (On Leaving), written upon departure from her beloved Cuba in 1836 at age 22 and printed five years later in her first book of poems. This poem, both a farewell to her native island home and a symbolic launching of her artistic career, remained important to Avellaneda; she used it to open all three of her poetry collections—the first in 1841, the second in 1850, and the third as volume one of her five-volume *Obras literarias* in 1869.

Avellaneda's poetry was well received by her peers and gained her the attention and respect of contemporary poets like *Zorrilla (1817–1893), Quintana (1772–1857), Lista (1775–1848) and *Espronceda (1808–1842). Avellaneda purposefully tried to prove her talents to these important male readers, especially in her numerous translations (really more adaptations, or "imitations," as she often entitled them) of poetry of such famous writers as Petrarch, Lamartine, Byron, and Hugo. These translations simultaneously demonstrated her knowledge of great European works and her skill in Spanish versification. In her original poems, Avellaneda chose themes and structures similar to those in poetry written by her Spanish male colleagues with strong romantic qualities.

Still, many important elements distinguish her talent and unique position as a woman and one born in the Americas. As in "Al partir," many poems refer to Cuba; many also treat the theme of love (especially love disappointed) from the female subject's point of view. Such is the case in the two poems entitled "A él" (To Him), written to her lover Ignacio de Cepeda. In "A la poesía" (To Poetry), a poem about artistic creation itself, Avellaneda seeks artistic achievement through the "feminine" muse of nature. Although she was most recognized for her poetry, it was really not her form of choice after the 1850 collection, when she began to concentrate her artistic efforts more on prose and drama.

Avellaneda's novels have been of particular interest to recent scholars, especially for their relation to important issues of feminism. She wrote novels throughout her career, in addition to shorter fictional prose in the form of *leyendas* (legends). Her first novel, *Sab* (1841; *Sab*, 1993), is commonly acknowledged as the first antislavery novel in Hispanic letters. *Sab* is particularly interesting for its comparison of the institution of slavery to the institution of marriage. In this novel Avellaneda creates the first of what will be a series of complementary heroines who represent different yet connected sides of oppressed nineteenth-century femininity. The same type of heroines in *Sab*—the angelic and innocent Carlota versus the darker and more "experienced" Teresa, both of whom are abused by male society—are found in later novels such as *Dos mujeres* (1842; Two Women) and *El artista barquero* (1861; The Artist Boatman). Three other novels treat historical themes ranging from a very romantic account of an Italian bandit's life in *Espatolino* (1844) to the story of Montezuma's successor in *Guatimozín, último emperador de México* (1846; *Cuauhtemoc, The Last Aztec Emperor*, 1898) and finally to the history of a medieval female ancestor of Avellaneda, *Dolores, páginas de una crónica de familia* (1851; Dolores, Pages from a Family Chronicle). All these novels, with the exception of *El artista barquero*, end in tragedy for the heroes and heroines, and true love proves impossible for each.

Avellaneda's participation in nineteenth-century theater is extremely important. While poetry and the novel were becoming accepted territory for women, the theater was still a world that most women writers avoided. Yet drama was an interest of Avellaneda's from early childhood, as she described in her *Autobiografía* (1839; *Autobiography*, 1993), and it was a genre at which she excelled during the heights of her literary career. She wrote 16 full-length original plays between 1840 and 1858. Several, such as *Munio Alfonso* (1844), *El príncipe de Viana* (1844; The Prince of Viana), *La hija de las flores* (1852; The Daughter of the Flowers), and *Baltasar* (1858), were huge box office successes. Romantic tragedy, especially historical drama, was Avellaneda's form of choice, although a few plays, such as *La hija de las flores*, were comedies that reflected the ideals of the bourgeois drama that was becoming popular in the second half of the century. As in her novels, some of these plays contained strong female characters that challenged the image of stereotypically passive romantic heroines. The tragedy *Egilona*, for example, portrays a woman's (Egilona) conflict between loyalty to her husband (Visigoth king Don Rodrigo) and her true love for another (Moor Abdelasis). In the end she sacrifices her life to die with her lover.

An often ignored but very important part of Avellaneda's work was her journalistic writing. Avellaneda was a frequent collaborator in numerous periodical publications of her day, especially in the fast-growing area of journals for women. In 1845 she took over editorship of the Madrid journal, *Gaceta de Mujeres*, changing its name to *Ilustración. Album de las Damas*. Unfortunately, this publication was interrupted by the death of her infant daughter after just one issue. But Avellaneda returned to journalism in 1860 when she began to publish *Album Cubano de lo Bueno y lo Bello*. This journal for women was also short-lived, lasting less than a year. Both *Ilustración* and *Album Cubano* attempted to educate the female reading public and contained interesting essays on famous women entitled "Galería de mujeres célebres" (Gallery of Famous Women) highlighting female leaders and intellectuals such as Sappho, Saint *Teresa de Jesús (1515–1582), and Queen *Isabel the Catholic (1451–1504), among others. It is in these periodical writings that Avellaneda's feminism—her interest in the education and the welfare of her sisters—is most evident.

Although Avellaneda achieved much recognition and success during her lifetime, her supreme professional disappointment was being denied entry into the Spanish Royal Academy in 1853. Despite this rejection, which haunted her until her death in 1873, Avellaneda clearly made an impact on Spanish romanticism, adding to it her very unique female perspective. *See also* Drama by Spanish Women Writers: 1770–1850; Poetry by

Spanish Women Writers: 1800–1900; Short Fiction by Women Writers: 1800–1900

Work by

The Love Letters. Trans. Dorrey Malcom. Intro. José Antonio Portuondo. Havana: Juan Fernández Burgos, 1956.

Obras de doña Gertrudis Gómez de Avellaneda. Vols. 277–279. Biblioteca de Autores Españoles. Madrid: Atlas, 1979.

Obras literarias, dramáticas y poéticas. 5 vols. Madrid: Rivadeneyra, 1869–1871. In *La Biblioteca Nacional de Madrid: Escritoras españolas.* Ed. María del Carmen Simón Palmer. Libros 213–217. Madrid: Chadwick-Healey, España. 1992. Microfiche.

Sab and Autobiography. Ed. Nina M. Scott. Austin: U of Texas P, 1993.

Work about

Alzaga, Florinda. *La Avellaneda: Intensidad y vanguardia.* Miami: Universal, 1997.

González Ascorra, Martha Irene. *La evolución de la conciencia femenina a través de las novelas de Gertrudis Gómez de Avellaneda, Soledad Acosta de Samper y Mercedes Cabello de Carbonera.* New York: Peter Lang, 1997.

Harter, Hugh A. *Gertrudis Gómez de Avellaneda.* Boston: Twayne, 1981.

Kirkpatrick, Susan. *Las Románticas: Women Writers and Subjectivity in Spain, 1835–1850.* Berkeley and Los Angeles: U of California P, 1989.

Miller, Beth. "Gertrude the Great: Avellaneda, Nineteenth-Century Feminist." *Women in Hispanic Literature: Icons and Fallen Idols.* Ed. Beth Miller. Berkeley and Los Angeles: U of California P, 1983. 201–214.

Picón Garfield, Evelyn. *Poder y sexualidad: El discurso de Gertrudis Gómez de Avellaneda.* Amsterdam: Rodopi, 1993.

Elizabeth Franklin Lewis

Gómez Ojea, Carmen (1945–)

Born in Gijón, Asturias, and educated at the Universidad de Oviedo, where she took a degree in Romance philology, Carmen Gómez Ojea came to the Spanish literary scene as one of the post-1970s generation of women writers influenced by North American and French feminist theory. Four of her novels have come to the attention of American scholars, but other novels, short stories, and poetry remain unpublished. Gómez Ojea deals with the issues of women's writing, self-definition, domesticity, and desire. Her work also reveals an interest in language and self-conscious writing, in particular the means of capturing the spoken word.

The complex family saga *Cantiga de agüero* (1982; Canticle of Omens) is set in Galicia. The novelistic technique is reminiscent of the Latin American "Boom" narratives in flow of language, magical drifts, and historical allusions. Protagonist Constanza lives in an environment of witches with all attendant evils and malevolence. Reality is dual and ambivalent, as the imaginative tales of characters contrast with the more prosaic interpretations of the narrator. Constanza's arranged marriage, her indifferent husband, her despair, and her isolation are offset by her love affairs with her uncle's administrator and husband's brother. Her daughter runs away at age 15, becomes a gypsy, and later organizes a religious cult, only to die at the hands of her followers. Constanza dies as a blind saint in a Mexican village shortly after the Revolution. Her body is allegedly cut into bits as relics and sold to her followers, who later learn that they bought only chicken parts. From such "miraculous" events and other matters of dispute, Constanza becomes the subject of a book by a foreign professor, suggesting the need for a revision of history. Gómez Ojea employs a feminist perspective to indicate the need for a rereading of Spanish history from a feminist viewpoint.

Gómez Ojea's second novel, *Otras mujeres y Fabia* (1982; Other Women and Fabia), revisits the problem of woman's relation to history. The protagonist Fabia, an unmarried 36-year-old literature teacher, wins the lottery. Tired of her job, she stops teaching, and after her mother's death, she takes an apartment in a poor city district. She then spends her time scrutinizing the local housewives through her window, and by means of the pictures in her apartment, she communicates with female ancestors and women authors of the past. From her solitary perspective, Fabia identifies with what she sees in both local and past representations as the basis of her myths and history. She struggles to comprehend what it means to be a woman, looking for what has remained hidden from her. Her quest of self evokes fabulous scenes of women's history that function as a verbal umbilical cord passed from mother to children. A sweeping vision of feminine history ensues as Fabia's invocations of her own female forebears and famous women in history intermingle with her conversations with her cousin Señora Efe and the sights, odors, and sounds emanating from the domestic neighborhood grind. From the window she sees the oppressive, never-ending cycle of a woman's life as mothers teach their daughters day after day to assume the role they have endured. Fabia turns to the pictures inside and contemplates the literary and genealogical past in an effort to understand how they affect her present existence. After examining portraits of literary foremothers and finding them unsettling, Fabia turns to the frames that hold the portraits of her mother, grandmother, and great-grandmother. In sleepless nights, she clasps hands with a line of female ancestors back to the imposing Mother of mothers, a linkage cast in the image of her daytime lookout. Fabia's obsessive visions voice inescapable recriminations of her childless state that undermine her quest for self-identity. Fabia's story ends with the final image of *Gone with the Wind* when Scarlett O'Hara offsets painful reality with an indefinite dream of tomorrow. With that echo from Margaret Mitchell's novel, Fabia is left at the end of the novel with voices from the wall and window in her confined apartment.

As its title suggests, *Los perros de Hecate* (1985; Hecate's Hounds) deals with the ancient mythological goddess of the moon, the underworld, and sorcery. It has a timeless atmosphere, in spite of an almost contemporary time frame. The protagonist, Tarsiana, a former prostitute and cynical libertine, renounces conventional religious authority and declares herself an idolater. She reveres Hecate the enigmatic, three-headed Greek goddess who emerges recurrently in this novel: This presence upsets the patriarchal Trinity and prevails as Tarsiana's narrative celebrates the desacralization of the major texts of Judeo-Christian tradition. Willful and forthright, Tarsiana clearly states her desire to learn sorcery and to be the enchantress Circe. The reverberation of the mythical female triumph over men reaches hyperbole when Tarsiana imagines that the book of Genesis will burn in every home. With such intertextual sources as the backbone of this novel, Gómez Ojea utilizes strategies that displace preconceived notions of the nature of narrative writing. As in *Otras mujeres y Fabia*, Tarsiana is a marginal person who chooses to inhabit an enclosed space, a den where Tarsiana listens to female voices telling stories, some whimsical or frightening and others often bloody. Regalina, her servant, is one of several characters who voice the blood motif with personal stories of getting pregnant during her menstrual cycle, her many abortions; she thus assumes a power that diminishes the commonplace representation that links blood to male valor. Other scrapes with "normal" order provide both fanciful and deviant humor to the narration. In one case, pots and pans talk dirty and even seduce each other in the kitchen. In another, a predatory woman relates to Tarsiana how she revels in the perverted sexual humiliation she imposes on older men.

Tarsiana will not tolerate conventional domestic or "women's" stories; she feels that she would be bored writing with order and precision. Furthermore, the kind of writing expected of a woman lacks imagination and humor. Yet *Los perros de Hecate* does not destroy all. Tarsiana and her cohorts rewrite and challenge not only the god of the patriarchy but also the great texts of literature. Thus, Tarsiana enacts a nonviolent rewrite of the *Poema de mío Cid in which she asks the hero not to go to war and to burn the text of his epic. Likewise, Regalina, who distrusts anything in print, whimsically recasts Holy Scripture as oral history passed on to her by her foremothers. Ultimately, the desacralization in this work marks the art and act of writing as suspect. Gómez Ojea once again negotiates adeptly the strategies of reflexive literature, for what she creates implies both destruction and a new life. Exemplary of this paradox is the ending of *Los perros de Hecate*: Aided by her beloved goddesses, Tarsiana transcends carrying an apple.

The title character of *La novela que Marien no terminó* (1988; The Novel Marien Did Not Finish) is a feminist, self-styled eccentric who composes her work in longhand. Her conversational and literary exchanges with the narrator, Celia, underscore the principle of dialogue, doubling, and opposites that orchestrates this novel. The two women have been friends since girlhood, and Marien once inspired in Celia the creative energy to write and improvise a diary. Celia is a middle-aged housewife and mother of one daughter, Majencia. One day while out shopping for Majencia's first bra, Celia falls and injures her leg. Consequently confined at home with her leg in a cast, she looks for something to fill her time and rediscovers some notebooks she had intended for her daughter. Since Marien had previously introduced her to keeping a journal, Celia starts to write again. At first she jots things down with what she calls unpardonable disorder but addresses a direct promise to her readers to improve her style and grammar. Invariably self-conscious, Celia comments on herself as a writer, reflecting the contradictory dilemma of female identity in writing women's experience. Celia writes her diaries in emulation of Marien, who advocates literature passed by word of mouth and matrilineal histories. Celia's desire is to be Marien, and so she writes a subversive admixture of fantasy and reality, without regard for literary convention or propriety. However, Celia writes herself as a typical wife and mother; and as she continues her dialogue with her friend, she finds similar contradictions in Marien. Celia notes several times over that Marien is a classicist and awfully traditional. What is more, the real characters (Celia and Marien) and those they write mirror each other so intelligibly that their dialogue turns to complicity. Marien too had once injured her leg and wrote a piece about a nasty crippled woman who considered her crutches as weapons. Marien identifies with this, yet Celia recognizes herself in the same story because of the personality defects Marien had incorporated in her tale. Celia then remarks that receiver and sender of the narrative have become indistinguishable. The symbolic leg cast is redoubled when Celia, doubtful of her journal and about to shelve it, cannot stop thinking of Margaret Mitchell who wrote *Gone with the Wind* after a similar accident. She does register envy but not downright ambition, so her writing remains unfinished, as does Marien's. At the end of this novel, at the time of the removal of Celia's cast, Marien dies inexplicably and mysteriously. An impression of emptiness then prevails, but the vacant ending insinuates another narrative, one that wonders what discourse can aptly portray woman's experience. Marien's death and unfinished novel reflect Celia's ambivalence to her notebooks, leaving the reader in the shadows of the unorthodox plot.

Work by

Cantiga de agüero. Barcelona: Destino, 1982.
La novela que Marien no terminó. Barcelona: laSal edicions de les dones, 1988.
Otras mujeres y Fabia. Barcelona: Argos Vergara, 1982.
Los perros de Hecate. Barcelona: Grijalbo, 1985.

Work about

Castillo, Debra A. "Frame Tale: Carmen Gómez Ojea's *Otras mujeres y Fabia*." *In the Feminine Mode*. Ed. Noël Valis and Carol Maier. Lewisburg: Bucknell UP; London and Toronto: Associated UP, 1990.
Ordóñez, Elizabeth. *Voices of Their Own*. Lewisburg: Bucknell UP; London and Toronto: Associated UP, 1991.

Glenn Morocco

Goyri y Goyri, María (1873–1954)

Erudite literary critic and educator, María Goyri y Goyri was born in Madrid to a Basque family. She lived briefly in Algorta (Bilbao), but when she was only five the family returned to Madrid, and Goyri resided there the rest of her life. Due to her delicate health as a child, she was educated at home by her mother, who organized a rigorous plan of studies and frequently taught her in the outdoors, in secluded areas of Retiro Park. That early contact with nature would later develop into a taste for long walks and excursions to the countryside that were instrumental in uncovering material for her study on the *Romancero* (the vast Spanish ballad tradition). Goyri's mother observed an aptitude for mathematics in her daughter and encouraged Goyri to begin official studies of Commerce at the Association for the Education of Women (1885–1888). There Goyri herself discovered that she enjoyed even more the study of grammar, an inclination that would later lead to her research on literary texts. She subsequently enrolled in the School for Governesses (1887–1891) to become a teacher, which then was one of the few ways a woman could acquire a professional education. But by 1890 she had abandoned the Normal School to attend classes as an auditor at the University of Madrid, in the School of Philosophy and Letters.

By 1892 Goyri had received permission from the General Secretary of Public Instruction to register officially as a female student and as such to attend classes at the university, though subjected to a certain protocol. She would need to have the approval of each professor stating that her presence in class did not distract male students. A commitment had to be made that this female student—the only one there—would not wait in the corridor but in an office adjacent to the classroom until the professor's arrival; that she would enter the classroom escorted by the professor or his beadle to a seat at an individual desk located near the professor; and that she would exit from class in the same manner as she entered. This pioneer female student opened the doors to subsequent women candidates who later on sought a university education.

Ever since she was very young, Goyri was drawn to the problems faced by women. In 1892, her first year at the university, she attended an international Congress on Pedagogy at the Madrid Ateneo. There Goyri heard the presentation of Emilia *Pardo Bazán (1852–1921) on "The Education of Men and Women" attacking Rousseau and Fenelon as antifeminist and defending Stuart Mill and especially Leibnitz for their progressive advocacy of educational reforms for women. Concepción *Arenal's (1820–1893) presentation of her views on women's duties and rights provoked violent attacks against her in response, prompting the 19-year-old Goyri to stand up and vehemently defend the person and ideas of the elderly Arenal. This courageous gesture of the young Goyri profoundly moved Pardo Bazán, who publicly embraced her. In their speeches, Pardo Bazán had advocated coeducation at all levels of education, and Arenal had proposed the right of women to receive academic and physical education. Goyri was an ardent believer of the principles advocated by the two speakers. At the insistence of her mother, she herself had attended a small public gymnasium and had benefited from coeducation when she took drawing lessons in classes where all the other pupils were male. Goyri attributed her successful acceptance by male university classmates to her early experience in coeducation.

Goyri's concerns with feminist matters became the subject of articles she penned for *Revista Popular*, a publication whose collaborators included Francisco Giner, Joaquín Costa, and Julián Besteiro. Beginning in 1898, she regularly published articles in the section *Crónicas femeninas* (Feminine Chronicles), where she would detail the accomplishments of other women, incorporating their valuable contributions into society. Of similar nature was her article "Los centros de cultura femenina" (1905; Feminine Cultural Centers).

Goyri completed a doctorate at the University of Madrid, having Menéndez y Pelayo, the foremost academic of the day, as one of her professors. Her dissertation on Lope de *Vega's drama *La difunta pleiteada*, which was later published, marks the beginning of her work in literary criticism. In 1900 Goyri married Ramón Menéndez Pidal, a young professor who had just attained a chair at the University of Madrid. The enthusiasm of the young couple for long walks and hikes in the countryside, very much attuned to the excursionist practices of the Institución Libre de Enseñanza, took them on their honeymoon to retrace geographic places of the *Poema de mío Cid* through the discovery of natural accidents in the terrain (rivers, hills, groves) that could be identified in the medieval text. Goyri's research interests included Lope de Vega and the presence of the *romance* (ballad) in his work, dramatist Vélez de Guevara, and the *Romancero* (Spanish ballad tradition), incessantly collecting materials. Some of her studies were published individually by her, but at her death many remained classified, annotated, and analyzed but unpublished. They later were included in the *Romancero hispánico* prepared by Ramón Menéndez Pidal. Goyri was a constant collaborator in the work of her husband, and her meticulous, rigorous research enriched the investigations and the lifetime work of Menéndez Pidal.

In 1890, two years before officially entering the university, Goyri came into contact with the Institución Libre de Enseñanza, an organization whose aim was a pedagogical renovation in Spain on a lay and liberal basis. The Institución invited Goyri to teach there when she finished her university studies. She collaborated with the Protectorado del Niño Delincuente (Child Delinquent Protectorate), an organization founded in 1916 by the Institución to avoid the incarceration of juveniles under age 16. When the Instituto Escuela was founded (1918) with a very progressive pedagogic system, intended at first for primary and middle education as a previous level of instruction to the Institución, once more Goyri provided an important contribution, teaching language and literature at the Preparatory level. In 1933, she was elected board member of the Patronato del Centro para Ampliación de Estudios. Goyri also prepared several volumes of literary texts for the collection Biblioteca Literaria del Estudiante, published by the Instituto Escuela and used in the instruction of their students. *See also* Feminism in Spain: 1900–2000

Work by

De Lope de Vega y del Romancero. Zaragoza: Librería General, 1953.
Romancero tradicional de las lenguas hispánicas. Colección de textos y notas, de María Goyri y Ramón Menéndez Pidal. 7 vols. Madrid: Gredos, 1957–1970.

Work about

Gaibrois de Ballesteros, Mercedes. *Homenaje a la memoria de Doña María Goyri de Menéndez Pidal*. Madrid: Ministerio de Asuntos Exteriores, 1956.

Pilar Sáenz

Grandes, Almudena (1960–)

Born in Madrid, she studied geography and history at Madrid's Universidad Complutense and now resides there. Almudena Grandes constitutes a phenomenon in Spanish culture; her bestselling novels, her youth, and her honest, frank personality have made her a renowned public figure of striking success. Her literary career has been stunning: She went from anonymity to sudden fame and extreme popularity with the huge success of her first novel, *Las edades de Lulú* (1989; *The Ages of Lulú*, 1995), which won the prestigious erotic literature award "La Sonrisa Vertical" prize for that year. It has been translated into 18 languages, and by 1997 it had sold a million and a half copies. All her subsequent novels have consistently made the top 10 sales list in Spain, and two works have been made into films. Bigas Luna produced a film version of *Las edades de Lulú* with Italian actress Francesca Neri in the leading role. *Malena es un nombre de tango* (1994; Malena Is a Tango Name) likewise was converted to film by director Gerardo Herrero with actress Ariadna Gil as Malena.

Las edades de Lulú explores the sexual and psychological development of María Luisa Aurora Eugenia Ruiz-Poveda y García de la Casa from her childhood and adolescence to her adult life. The sexually precocious protagonist initiates herself with Pablo, a famous older poet who calls her by the diminutive "Lulú." Throughout the novel (from her first sexual experience to those in her marriage with Pablo and the last one where she almost dies) Lulú shows an obsessive dependency on Pablo's desires, whims, tenderness, and cruelties. This fixation combines perfectly with Pablo's wish for Lulú to not grow up and always be his "dirty girl." Significantly enough, a cute baby's shirt is the garment that he most likes her to wear. Pablo and Lulú try out all kinds of sexual practices. In one that represents a turning point in the novel, Pablo ties Lulú to the bed, blindfolds her, and then he instructs her brother Marcelo to come in and penetrate her. After that, Lulú decides she must try to grow up and become self-sufficient and thus leaves Pablo. During this period of time she brings home homosexual prostitutes and becomes involved in sadomasochistic practices. She puts her life in danger (she is almost beaten to death) and Pablo comes to her "rescue." At the novel's end, Lulú again delays the decision to confront herself with her constant escapist refrain that she "will think about all this tomorrow."

This novel has provoked much controversy among feminist critics with respect to Lulú's attitudes toward life, sex, and love relationships. The debate is about women's sexual liberation, for while it is true that Lulú is a sexually active woman with a capacity for taking the initiative, she does not become an adult capable of independent, reliable behavior. She remains unable to take responsibility for her acts in sexual and other arenas of her life (i.e., her daughter). Two of Lulú's main problems are the priority of sex in her life to the exclusion of all else and her inability to break with the degrading, infantile role of "dirty girl." *Las edades de Lulú* is a rich, ambivalent novel whose interpretation depends very much upon which character (Pablo-Lulú) the reader identifies himself or herself with. Grandes explores both the satisfaction obtained from a common self-serving male sexual fantasy (having women act as slaves) and the anxiety that it provokes in women.

In her short story "Malena, una vida hervida" (Malena, a Boiled Life), included in the anthology *Los pecados capitales* (1990; The Deadly Sins), Grandes chooses the vice of gluttony and examines the ties between the pleasures of food and those of sex.

Te llamaré Viernes (1991; I Will Call You Friday), her second novel, has three main protagonists that represent modern antiheroes of urban Madrid. Benito is a man that defines himself as ugly and fearful. Manuela is an amateur actress in experimental theater and costume-jewelry street vendor. Polibio, owner of the bar Lo Inexorable (Inexorable), is a brilliant talker who likes "princesses" but only goes out with prostitutes. The novel explores the relationship between Benito and Manuela, two weak, gray characters. Benito despises and threatens Manuela but at the same time is bound to her by strange ties. Whereas Benito is an insensitive man unable to live fully, Manuela is a passionate woman who dares to live without thinking about life. Regarding her as a slave and savage, he gives her the name "Viernes." This novel establishes a tension between loneliness and the search for a love to redeem sordid reality. Other topics explored include lack of communication, fear, cowardice, passions, death, domination, and power in human relationships.

Malena es un nombre de tango (1994) narrates a girl's search for her own and her family's identity. The protagonist, Malena Montero Fernández de Alcántara, belongs to an upper-class family from Madrid. Two types of women have existed in this household for generations: white sheep and black sheep. The former are accepted by the rest of the family because they follow approved established roles—sweet girl; seductive adolescent; young industrious woman; perfect housewife. The latter, among whom Malena figures, are scorned because they act in "strange" ways that do not conform to the archetypal model of woman. Disoriented and perplexed as a child, Malena prays to become a boy because she knows that she will never be able to be like her twin sister, Reina (Queen), the "perfect" woman. The process of growing up and the recovery of her past allow Malena to recognize and understand her own fears and anxieties through knowledge of the other "imperfect" women relatives who preceded her. When she realizes she has not been the only "black sheep," she learns to accept herself and understands how social conventions can create dangerous complexes and frustrations within individuals.

This novel has been acclaimed by critics as a new "tour de force" in her novelistic career. The magnitude of the work (552 pages encompassing almost 100 characters and half a century of Spanish history from the Republican period until the 1980s), the exemplary Cervantine aim to establish a series of models of behavior, the oral basis that represents the memory and voice of women in the family, and the *costumbrista* (folkloric) traits and configuration of the novel as a family saga help make this novel an original, audacious work that was a finalist for the Premio de la Crítica in 1994.

Modelos de mujer (1996; Models of Woman) presents seven stories that deal with the life of women and share the wish to alleviate a sad, alienating present by recreating the past through memory. The subject of womanhood is explored in all of Grandes's novels. She analyzes the contradictions of contemporary women; on the one hand, women are liberating themselves, and on the other, they feel a strong emotional dependency on men. Passion is a conflicting factor in their lives as it creates an irreconcilable dichotomy between the independence women have achieved and their need to be with the man they love. Grandes has affirmed that in *Malena es un nombre de tango* she wanted to break with the stereotype of the eternal feminine and explore the difficult relationship of a woman with her own gender. Several of her most controversial opinions relate to this topic. Grandes questions the results of the feminist revolution, for women now must demonstrate they are more capable than men in their jobs and at the same time still be experienced housewives. She also argues that feminist postulates cannot be applied in the same way to all women because culturally and personally women live in very different circumstances. Finally, she worries about men being left aside in the feminist worldview. Her ideal would be a place wherein men and women are considered equally valuable, and no one is discriminated against. *See also* Eroticism in Contemporary Spanish Women Writers' Narrative; Short Fiction by Women Writers: 1975–1998, Post-Franco

Work by

The Ages of Lulú. New York: Grove/Atlantic, 1995.
Las edades de Lulú. Barcelona: Tusquets, 1989.
Malena es un nombre de tango. Barcelona: Tusquets, 1994.
Modelos de mujer. Barcelona: Tusquets, 1996.
Te llamaré Viernes. Barcelona: Tusquets, 1991.

Work about

Charnon-Deutsch, Lou, and Barbara Morris. "Regarding the Pornographic Subject in *Las edades de Lulú*." *Letras Peninsulares* (Fall 1993–Winter 1993–1994): 301–319.
Duchesne Winter, Juan. "Sorprenderla mirando." *La cuestión del género literario y la expresión femenina actual*. Ed. Carmen Cazurro García de la Quintana. N.p., 1998. 157–169.
Navajas, Gonzalo. "Duplicidad narrativa en *Las edades de Lulú* de Almudena Grandes." *Studies in*

Honor of Gilbert Paolini. Ed. Mercedes Vidal Tibbitts. Newark: Juan de la Cuesta, 1996. 385–392.

Eva Legido-Quigley

Grassi, Angela (1826–1883)

Born in Crema, Italy, on August 2, in the midst of the romantic period, little is known of her early life other than the fact that at age 5 she went to Barcelona, presumably with her family. Grassi must have been of a moderately well-to-do family, given the fact that she began her literary career at the precocious age of 16, publishing a historical romance with strong romantic overtones, *El juramento de la amistad o los Condes de Rocaberti* (1842; The Pledge of Friendship or the Counts of Rocaberti), a collection of poetry, and a drama, *Lealtad de un juramento o Crimen y expiación* (1842; Loyalty of a Vow or Crime and Expiation), with many of the melodramatic, Gothic elements typifying theater of the period as well as a number of historical ingredients. Her bent for the historical appears again in *Un episodio de la Guerra de Siete Años* (1849; An Episode in the Seven Years War). Also during the 1840s, she collaborated with Carolina *Coronado in the periodical *El Pensamiento* and became briefly involved with the midcentury protofeminists, although by the end of the decade, she distanced herself from the group (never strong enough to be termed a "movement") and abandoned her youthful "progressive" attitudes.

In 1850, Grassi moved to Madrid, apparently to concentrate on her writing, and another collection of her poetry, *Poesías de la señorita doña Angela Grassi*, appeared in 1851. She subsequently abandoned both drama and poetry and devoted her energies to the novel, beginning with *El bálsamo de las penas* (1864; The Balm of Sorrows), *El lujo* (1865; Luxury), *El hijo* (1865; The Son), and *Las riquezas del alma* (1866; Riches of the Soul), subtitled *novela de costumbres* (quite probably following the lead of "Fernán Caballero" [Cecilia *Böhl de Faber] who pioneered the "novel of customs"). *Las riquezas del alma* was especially well received and awarded an honorable mention from the Royal Spanish Academy (one of two of her novels to win prizes). In the same year, she published *El camino de la dicha* (1866; The Road to Happiness). Grassi succeeded both as a writer and in becoming director of *El Correo de la Moda*, a magazine catering primarily to women. She held this position from 1867 to 1883, publishing several of her own essays and serializing many of her novels in *El Correo de la Moda*.

Grassi wrote primarily, if not exclusively, for women and often stated that the purpose of her novels (as well as of *El Correo de la Moda*) was to improve the moral and intellectual condition of her readership. Most of her fiction upholds conventional values, extolling the traditional feminine virtues of domesticity, abnegation, obedience, faith, resignation, and chaste love. Woman's role is to uphold and defend all that is good and true, meaning especially the values of the past, and thereby contribute to the regeneration of a society that has become corrupted by the nineteenth century's materialism and progress. Following the lead of the patriarchal establishment in which she was socialized, she portrayed women who practiced the traditional virtues as being rewarded by happiness. Whether for these reasons or because she was an entertaining narrator, her novels were widely acclaimed, and Grassi produced at least a score of them between the mid-1860s and 1880s, thereby becoming one of the more prolific women writers of the period.

Most of Grassi's novels bear the subtitles "novel of customs" or "historical novel," and most of them advocate abandoning the decadent immorality of the late nineteenth century in favor of a return to past values. Much like María del Pilar *Sinués de Marco, another conservative contemporary who made women her primary and almost exclusive subjects, she treated marriage, motherhood, feminine role models, and other topics supposedly of special (or exclusive) feminine interest. Both successfully utilized the periodical press to reach women, and both ardently espoused patriarchal attitudes, writing manuals of behavior and feminine comportment as well as other didactic works, in addition to their fiction. Grassi's other novels include *Los que no siembran, no cogen* (1868; Those Who Don't Sow, Don't Reap), *La dicha de la tierra. Novela histórica* (1868; Happiness of the Land. Historical Novel), *La gota de agua* (1875; The Drop of Water), *El copo de nieve. Novela de costumbres* (1876; The Snowflake. Novel of Customs), *El capital de la virtud. Novela de costumbres* (1877; The Wealth of Virtue. Novel of Customs), *Marina. Narración histórica* (1877; Marina. Historical Narrative), *El primer año de matrimonio. Cartas a Julia* (published in the collection Biblioteca Ilustrada de las Familias, 1877; The First Year of Marriage. Letters to Julia), *Los juicios del mundo. Novela de costumbres* (serialized 1884–1887 in *El Correo de la moda*; Judgments of the World. Novel of Customs), *Palmas y laureles. Lecturas instructivas* (1884; Applause and Honors. Instructive Readings), *El favorito de Carlos III. Novela histórica* (also in *El Correo de la Moda*, 1884–1887; Carlos III's Favorite. Historical Novel). Near the end of her career, Grassi published a short story collection, *Cuentos pintorescos* (1886; Picturesque Stories). See also Ángel del hogar

Work about

Aldaraca, Bridget. "El ángel del hogar: The Cult of Domesticity in Nineteenth-Century Spain." *Theory and Practice of Feminist Literary Criticism*. Ed. Gabriela Mora and Karen S. Van Hooft. Ann Arbor: U of Michigan P, 1982. 62–87.

Andreu, Alicia G. *Galdós y la literatura popular*. Madrid: Sociedad General Española de Librería, 1982.

Simón Palmer, María del Carmen. "Escritoras españolas del siglo XIX o el miedo a la marginalización." *Anales de la literatura española* 2 (1983): 477–490.

Janet Pérez

Grisel y Mirabella (published c. 1495)

Traditionally considered a sentimental novel, this highly stylized prose narrative by Juan de Flores (fl. 1500) opens with a typical *courtly love situation: The impossible beauty of Princess Mirabella has so dazzled the knights of the realm that many have died of unrequited love. Her father the king, deeming no knight worthy of her, decides to staunch this costly loss of his warriors by imprisoning Mirabella (*Encierro*) in a secret place. Predictably, one knight, Grisel, succeeds in finding and wooing her, Mirabella returns his love, and the two immediately consummate the relationship. The illicit affair is shortly discovered, and the two lovers become subject to the Scottish law of the land, which requires that the party most responsible for the affair must die. In testimony to the altruistic purity of their love, Grisel and Mirabella each attempt to save the life of the other by claiming responsibility, and each is unswayed by physical torture.

At this point, the plot and focus of the novel shift from private to public arena; Grisel and Mirabella cease to occupy center stage, and a trial situation with clear contemporary resonances ensues. Since the question of greater guilt cannot be decided for these two lovers, the question is redefined to become: Are women or men generally more culpable in amatory indiscretions? The answer to this question will now determine which of the two will die. Two experts are brought in to present the case of each side. Women are represented by Bracayda, who recalls the feminist literary heroine Briseida of the *Trojan Chronicle*, while the male advocate, Torrellas, is taken from contemporary Spanish society. A prolific poet, courtier, politician, and notorious misogynist, Torrellas was and is most famous for authorship of a lengthy, much circulated diatribe in verse censuring women. The extended "battle of the sexes" debate that ensues comprises the major portion of the text. After listening to various attacks and rebuttals on each side, a panel of judges finds women to be the guiltier of the two parties in the arena of illicit love affairs. But the plot reverses directions again when, just as Mirabella is to be burned to death, Grisel throws himself on the flames, rendering her death unnecessary. The inconsolable Mirabella, again incarcerated in the castle, soon throws herself from an upper-story window to a patio where lions are kept and is eaten alive. The story, however, does not end with the sequential suicide of the two lovers. After the debate, the triumphant Torrellas finds himself obsessed by Bracayda, the quintessential *mujer esquiva* (aloof woman), and writes her a letter of love. Bracayda immediately shares the correspondence with the queen who, still outraged by the injustice done her daughter, plots a way to exact penance. With the queen's complicity, Bracayda answers Torrellas's missive and invites him to her rooms. When Torrellas, now blinded by lust and his mistaken belief that he has triumphed, comes to her private apartments, he finds that all the ladies of the court await him. They tie him up, torture him at length, and then, breaking for dinner, shower him with more invective as he slowly expires before them.

As may be gleaned from this abbreviated summary, the work's structure is surprisingly complex with multiple shifts of focus (private/public, individual/societal, feudal/courtly, male/female), symbolic elements, and many direct and inverse parallels. These multiple layers have led recent critics to discern quite contradictory interpretations of the work. Matulka, one of the first scholars to examine the work closely, interprets the "literary" assassination of the historical Torrellas for his libel of women to be conclusive evidence of the work's feminist bent. More recently, Rolfé has argued that despite the sentimental novel situation of idealized love and suicide the medieval debate tradition dominates the discourse and that although the vicious punishment of Torrellas that concludes the work represents a clear literary chastisement of Torrellas's antifeminist diatribe, the pro- and antiwoman arguments presented by Bracayda and Torrellas draw equally from the same, misogynist ideological tradition. This tradition fuses the Old Testament conception of women as cause of the Fall with the Aristotelian definition of woman as physical matter/uncontrolled appetite (versus the definition of man as spirit/intellect and reason) and the Ovidian tradition of love as a game or conquest. Just as Mirabella's death by lion's teeth and claws suggests symbolic punishment by hand of the king in the male power space she has violated, Torrellas's murder in Bracayda's (female space) apartments, where noblewomen torture him with pliers, nails, and even teeth, illustrates the consequences for violation of the traditional social order. John Cull, who finds the work more properly aligned with the romance novel tradition, concurs with Rolfé in finding the work clearly misogynist and antifeminist in its arguments.

Although the novel was first published around 1595, critics generally concur that it was probably composed sometime around 1480 to 1485. Via a 1521 Italian translation that was less than faithful to the original, the work became extremely popular, spreading throughout Europe in over 50 editions in Italian, French, English, Spanish, and numerous bilingual editions used for language instruction. *See also* Misogyny in Medieval and Early Modern Spain

Work

Grisel y Mirabella. The Novels of Juan de Flores and Their European Diffusion. Ed. and study Barbara Matulka. New York: Institute of French Studies, 1931. 331–371.

La historia de Grisel y Mirabella. Edición facsímil sobre la de Juan de Cromberger de 1529. Ed. Pablo Alcázar López and José A. González Núñez. Granada: Don Quijote, 1983.

Work about

Cull, John T. "Irony, Romance Conventions, and Misogyny in *Grisel y Mirabella* by Juan de Flores."

Revista Canadiense de Estudios Hispánicos 22.3 (Spring 1998): 415–430.

Gwara, Joseph J. "The Identity of Juan de Flores: The Evidence of the *Crónica incompleta de los Reyes Católicos.*" *Journal of Hispanic Philology* 112.3 (1987): 103–113; 205–222.

Rolfé, Mercedes. *La cuestión del género en Grisel y Mirabella de Juan de Flores.* Newark, DE: Juan de la Cuesta, 1996.

Maureen Ihrie

Guerra y Ribera, Fray Manuel

See Sexuality in the Golden Age: Fray Manuel de Guerra y Ribera (seventeenth century)

Guevara, Antonio de (1481?–1545): Women's Roles in the *Epístolas familiares*

A prolific writer who served both at court (as a commissioner for the inquisitor general and later as royal chaplain and chronicler of Charles V) and in church (as bishop of Guadix, subsequently bishop of Mondoñedo), Antonio de Guevara typifies the new sixteenth-century individual who aspires to greater nobility through service and letters rather than lineage and money. His writings, which address a broad range of typical humanist issues of the day, have been alternately condemned for their contradictory statements, fictionalization of history, and invention/falsification of sources and conversely highly praised for their stylistic innovation and creativity. Like other humanists, he addressed a wide variety of social themes and practices, most often from a satirical, moralizing stance, and thus the nature of women and their appropriate role in society figures directly or indirectly in much of his prose. Guevara's most influential texts, the fictional biography *Reloj de príncipes y Libro de Marco Aurelio* (1529; Dial of Princes and Book of Marcus Aurelius), the *Menosprecio de corte y alabanza de aldea* (1539; Criticism of the City and Praise of the Village), and his *Epístolas familiares* (1539 and 1541; Familiar Letters, referred to as I and II), were much read in Spain and throughout Europe.

The *Epístolas familiares* are more a collection of essays rather than a record of personal correspondence. The first collection contains 69 letters, and the second, 43. Undated, their subject matter is wide ranging, as is their style. Some are sermons, others discourse on medical, historical, or archaeological topics, on ethics, morals, and contemporary political events. Guevara discusses women and their roles in letters to both sexes. Each of his letters is directed to a specific individual/receptor, which at times contributes in determining the content and point of view expressed. All these factors help make the occasionally self-contradictory nature of his ideas as a whole more comprehensible. Following Erasmus, Guevara recognizes the absolute equality of male and female souls and at times also affirms the equal intellectual potential of men and women. Generally, the institution of marriage is highly praised (though it is satirized in letter I, 55), in part because it channels male sexual desires appropriately, limiting intramale competition and consequently promoting harmony. Marriage is considered the foundation of an ordered society. Within that order, women's area of movement and influence is strictly delimited to the private, domestic arena and subject to male control, but as Martínez-Góngora observes, her responsibilities there are highly valued, much more than seen in the writing of Luis *Vives, for example. In a much-quoted passage (I, 41), Guevara celebrates the enormous attraction the sight of an industrious wife represents as, with sleeves rolled up, she tends to children, directs servants, makes bread, and generally bustles about tending to household duties. Guevara states that women should be able to read and write, so they can discharge well the vital responsibilities of raising children and administering the household wisely. In this same regard, pregnant women merit special treatment, and nursing is extolled as essential. Friendship can exist between wives and husbands, and marriage is seen as a partnership in that both partners have responsibilities to meet. Monogamy is insisted on for both parties; Guevara criticizes one husband who persists in keeping a mistress, despite the excellence of his wife and her desire to serve him in every way possible (II, 24). Other male failings such as an excessive use of perfumes and *cosmetics, the exaggerated courtly deification of women, and the pursuit of young women by male geezers, are sharply rebuked.

Guevara departs from Renaissance Platonist ideas in rejecting physical beauty as a desirable attribute for a wife or an indication of superior moral virtue. A woman's beauty only provokes lust, jealousy, and discord. Following Aristotle, women (apart from their souls) are considered inferior in nature to men, in need of male control and guidance. Yet as he describes female shortcomings, the tremendous will women bring to bear in inciting and influencing men or resisting male control also attests to his recognition of their strength of will. A woman's weapon is her tongue, which must be controlled and limited to use in the privacy of the home, in service of her domestic responsibilities, and she must remain quiet in all other arenas.

Martínez-Góngora attributes the self-contradictory nature of Guevara's thought regarding women to the alternating influence of the two contradictory behavior codes under which he operated: that of courtier and of Franciscan monk. In each sphere woman is seen as subservient to male control, thereby affirming the definition of masculinity in the church and at court. Nonetheless, Guevara's portrayal of the value of women's activities within their delimited spheres is more sympathetic than that of other humanists of his day, and there is some recognition of men's responsibilities and failings as well. *See also* Encierro

Work by

The diall of princes. Trans. Sir Thomas North. Intro. and biblio. K.N. Colvile. London: P. Allan, 1919.

Epístolas familiares. Ed. J. Cossío. 2 vols. Madrid: RAE, 1952.

Menosprecio de corte y alabanza de aldea. Ed. Asunción Rallo Grauss. Madrid: Cátedra, 1984.

Relox de príncipes. Ed. Emilio Blanco. Madrid: CONFRES, 1994.

Work about

Jones, J.R. *Antonio de Guevara.* TWAS 360. Boston: Twayne, 1975.

Márquez Villanueva, Francisco. "Crítica guevariana." *Nueva Revista de Filología Hispánica* 28 (1979): 334–352.

Martínez-Góngora, Mar. *Discursos sobre la mujer en el Humanismo renacentista español.* Los casos de Antonio de Guevara, Alfonso y Juan de Valdés y Luis de León. York, SC: Spanish Literature Publications, 1999.

Orejudo, Antonio. *Las* Epístolas familiares *de Antonio de Guevara en el contexto epistolar del Renacimiento.* Madison, WI: Hispanic Seminary of Medieval Studies, 1994.

Maureen Ihrie

Guilló Fontanills, Magdalena (194?–)

A writer of Catalan and Spanish novels, Magdalena Guilló Fontanills was trained as a mathematician at the University of Barcelona. Since 1972 she has lived and taught in Salamanca. While not a prolific writer, Guilló has produced consistently well-acclaimed novels since she began writing in 1977. That year the first of her three novels, *En una vall florida al peu de les espases* (In a Flowery Valley at Sword Point), was a finalist for the Josep Pla prize. Set during Franco's final days in power, the book tells of the frustrations of Diego de Arjona, an ex-minister of the regime. Using a technique that reappears in her later work, Guilló alternates narrative point of view; a first-person narrative of Arjona's confused memories serves as counterpoint to third-person scenes of Franco's delirium. In addition, Arjona dreams of a future democratic Spain and hallucinates about Spain's past failures in his attempt to come to terms with his past complicity with the dictatorship. The novel closes with the announcement of Franco's death.

Guilló's next work, *Entre el ayer y la mañana* (1984; Between Yesterday and Tomorrow), treats the subject of Theodore Herzl and his efforts to establish a national homeland for the Jews. A Catholic herself, Guilló uses her enormous knowledge of political Zionism and religious Judaism to create a text rich in allusions to the Hebrew Bible, the Haggadah, the Talmud, and numerous rabbinic commentators. The novel also uses sketches of historical figures such as Moses Maimonedes and the Vilna Gaon to problematize nineteenth-century Zionism; this approach provides an unusual multidimensional view of a highly controversial subject.

Guilló's sympathetic portrayal of Herzl's frustrated attempts to unite the Jews and create a plan for the establishment of a Jewish state is offset by a romantic subplot. An adulterous love between Winifred Schöring, a Gentile woman, and a Jewish mystic named Shlomo Montaña-de-Estrellas reinforces one of the book's themes: the impossibility of peaceful coexistence between Gentiles and Jews. Guilló goes to great lengths to underline the brutal treatment of Jews at the hands of the Gentile majority that surrounds them; in the case of the two lovers, however, the situation is reversed. Montaña-de-Estrellas misuses his powers to dominate and eventually destroy the woman he loves.

Guilló's third book appears to moderate the negativity that pervaded *Entre el ayer y la mañana*. Although *Un sambenito para el señor Santiago* (1986; A Sanbenito for Mr. Santiago) maintains the sense of melancholy that marks Guilló's first two novels, this book makes explicit a plea for tolerance and understanding that was earlier left unsaid. Once again, the book's cultural theme centers around Judaism, this time during the Spanish Inquisition.

Benito Arias Montano, a *converso* who has embraced Christianity without rejecting his Jewish heritage, serves as chaplain to the king and is a well-known biblical scholar. Deeply in love with Anne Herents, a Protestant woman, Montano lives outwardly devoted to his king and Christianity but inwardly insecure about his successes as a Catholic. Montano's efforts to bring together the seemingly disparate elements of his beliefs lead to self-doubt and an imaginary trial before Torquemada. In this nightmarish hallucination, the scholar is called upon to defend himself from charges (which he refuses to deny) that he lacks *limpieza de sangre* (an ancestry untainted by Jewish blood). He also refuses to deny that he has encouraged discussion of dangerous issues and translated the Bible into Spanish. These scenes of the trial and numerous other chapters refer to the stifling repression of free thought and creativity under the intolerance of the Inquisition's censors.

Guilló's technique of mingling the "unreal" with the "real" is even further refined in this novel: Montano carries on numerous conversations with *el señor de las tentaciones* (the master of temptations), a figure representing his desire to reveal his heritage and heterodox beliefs without fear of recrimination. Another feature of Guilló's technique in this novel is the painterly descriptions she uses to evoke both the richness of interior settings as well as the lush beauty of gardens and landscape.

While none of these novels takes as its starting point the condition of women, they do indirectly raise issues of women's education and roles. For example, Winifred Schöring of *Entre el ayer y la mañana* refuses to marry Shlomo Montaña-de-Estrellas at least partly because she refuses to be bound by Orthodox Jewish strictures regulating a woman's sexual contact with her husband. In *Un sambenito para el señor Santiago*, Anne, due to her unusually high level of education, participates in Montano's scholarly work. Although academic interest in Guilló's work has not been great, these three novels provide ample thematic and technical material for both literary scholars and the general reading public.

Work by

Entre el ayer y la mañana. Barcelona: Muchnik, 1984.
En una vall florida al peu de les espases. Barcelona: Destino, 1978.
Un sambenito para el señor Santiago. Barcelona: Muchnik, 1986.

Work about

Martin-Maestro, Abraham. "La novela española en 1984." *Anales de la literatura española contemporánea* 101 (1985): 123–141.
Obiol, María José. "Madurez en el oficio de contar." *El País* (Libros) July 28, 1985: 1–2.
Pérez, Janet. *Contemporary Women Writers of Spain.* Boston: Twayne, 1988.

Deborah Hirsch

Gutiérrez Torrero, Concepción
See Lagos, Concha (1913–   )

Guzmán y de la Cerda, María Isidra Quintina (1768–1803)

Daughter of Diego Guzmán, count of Oñate, and his wife María Isidra de la Cerda, countess of Paredes, María Isidra Quintina Guzmán y de la Cerda showed a rare aptitude for learning in early childhood. Carefully educated, she received instruction in modern foreign languages, Greek, and Latin and was used by the reform-minded King Carlos III as an example of enlightened womanhood; he appointed her to the Spanish Royal Academy, making her the only woman admitted until the late twentieth century. To justify this action, the king asked the University of Alcalá to grant her a Doctorate in Letters. Despite the ensuing controversy, the degree was granted in 1785, just two months after the king's request. Guzmán was also made a member of the Basque Economic Society (the oldest in the country) and the Madrid Economic Society. She died at 35, shortly after marrying Rafael Alonso de Sousa, marquis of Guadalcázar. *See also* Feminism in Spain: 1700–1800.

Work by

Oración eucarística. [Reception speech to the Royal Academy.] In *Memorial Literario* 7 (March 1786): 357–361.

Work about

Serrano y Sanz, Manuel. *Apuntes para una biblioteca de escritoras españolas desde el año 1401 al 1833.* 2 vols. Madrid: Rivadeneyra, 1903.
Vázquez Madrugada, María Jesús. *María Isidra Quintina de Guzmán y la Cerda.* Alcalá de Henares: Centro Asesor de la Mujer, 1999.

María A. Salgado

Helguero y Alvarado, María Nicolasa de (?–1805)

Born in San Cebrián de Valbuena (Palencia), María Nicolasa Helguero y Alvarado was married to the marquis of San Isidro and entered the Convent of Las Huelgas (Burgos) upon his death. She wrote several biographies of religious personages and a large number of poems. Her poetry contains both religious and lay topics; some of the latter comment on women's accomplishments. At times she exalts them, such as in "A Santa Teresa de Jesús" (To St. *Teresa) or "Las heroínas de la Ley Antigua" (The Heroines of the Law of Moses), but at other times, for example, the "Décimas a las damas del Siglo Ilustrado" (Decimas to the Ladies of the Enlightened Age), she criticizes what she percieves as her contemporaries' arrogance and lack of true education.

Work by

Poesías sagradas y profanas. Burgos: Joseph de Navas, 1794.
Rasgo de la vida del Gran Patriarca San José. Burgos: n.p., 1794.
Vida de Clemente XIV. Burgos: n.p., 1794.
Vida de Santa Mafalda, reina de Castilla y monja cisterciense. Burgos: n.p., 1793.

Work about

Serrano y Sanz, Manuel. Apuntes para una biblioteca de escritoras españolas desde el año 1401 al 1833. 2 vols. Madrid: Rivadeneyra, 1903. Rpt. Madrid: Atlas, 1975.

María A. Salgado

Hernández de la Oliva, Antonia

See Hickey y Pellizzone, Margarita (1753–after 1793)

Hickey y Pellizzone, Margarita (1753–after 1793)

This talented poet and erudite was born in Barcelona to Domingo Hickey, an Irish lieutenant colonel in the Edinburgh Dragoons, and Ana Pellizzone, member of an Italian family. When she was a child, her parents moved to Madrid, where she lived the rest of her life. While very young, Margarita Hickey y Pellizzone married Juan Antonio de Aguirre, a wealthy septuagenarian who became a valet in the Royal Household. Aguirre died before 1779. Contrary to expectations, his young, wealthy, educated wife did not remarry but instead spent the rest of her life studying geography, writing poetry, and translating plays of some of the best-known French neoclassic writers.

One of Hickey's longest, most controversial texts is "Descripción geográfica e histórica de todo el orbe conocido hasta ahora" (Geographic and Historical Description of the Entire Known World), written in octosyllabic verse. Upon completion, she solicited the customary licenses for publication. Examined by Antonio de Capmany of the History Academy, permission was denied on the grounds that it was plagued with factual errors and that her style was too prosaic. The manuscript remains in the National Historical Archives. Not shortly after the rejection, Hickey's work was defended from the pages of the prestigious *Memorial Literario* (18: 341–342). The writer accused Capmany of judging the work harshly simply because it was written by a woman, then argued that male critics never gave women credit for the vast knowledge they acquired on their own, without any help from a system that denied them access to education. To vindicate the manuscript, the writer referred the readers to the polished texts of Hickey's *Poesías varias* (1789; Diverse Poems).

The severity with which women's writings were judged can be deduced from the many petitions written by Hickey, and published by Serrano y Sanz, in which she requests permission time and time again—even from the king himself—to be allowed to publish her works. Given these harsh circumstances it is not surprising that she avoided publishing under her own name. In one petition, she explains that the reason she wants to publish *Poesías* under the cover of "A Lady of This Court" is due to her "natural modesty." In fact, Hickey was so successful at disguising her name that her identity remained a mystery for many years. Her writings were listed under Antonia Hernández de la Oliva or M.H.—the pseudonym and the initials that masked her historical persona.

In addition to her original works, Hickey translated a number of French plays, including Voltaire's *Zayra* and Racine's *Andromaque*. She states that her translations, which toned down the liberal ideology of the originals to better suit Spanish taste, were intended to educate the public in the new French style. Some of her manuscripts can be found at the National Library. *See also* Feminism in Spain: 1700–1800

Work by

Poesías varias sagradas, morales y profanas o amorosas . . . Written by a Lady of This Court. Madrid: Imprenta Real, 1789. Also includes a translation, *Andrómaca*, and a pastoral novel in verse.

Work about

Deacon, Philip. "Vicente García de la Huerta y el círculo de Montiano: La amistad entre Huerta y Margarita Hickey." *Revista de Estudios Extremeños* (Badajoz, Spain) 44. 2 (1988): 395–421.

Salgado, María A. "El autorretrato clandestino de Margarita Hickey, escritora ilustrada." *L'Autoportrait en Espagne*. Actes du IVe Colloque International D'Aix-En-Provence. (December 1990). Aix-En-Provence: Publications de L'Université de Provence, 1992. 133–147.

———. "Reescribiendo el Canon: Góngora y Margarita Hickey." *Dieciocho* 17. 1 (Spring 1994): 17–31.

Serrano y Sanz, Manuel. *Apuntes para una biblioteca de autoras españolas desde el año 1401 al 1833*. 2 vols. Madrid: Rivadeneyra, 1903.

Sullivan, Constance A. "A Biographical Note on Margarita Hickey." *Dieciocho* 20.2 (1997): 219–229.

María A. Salgado

Hija de Celestina, La ingeniosa Elena, La (1612–1614)

This text is the second Spanish picaresque novel that focuses on the life of a female rogue (*pícaras). It was written by Alonso Jerónimo de Salas Barbadillo (1581–1635), who first published it in 1612 but then reworked the novel and published it again two years later with the title *La ingeniosa Elena*. Like other works of the picaresque genre, *La hija de Celestina, La ingeniosa Elena* (*The Daughter of Celestina*, 1912) presents the adventures and misfortunes of a *pícara*. Contrary to its predecessor *La *Pícara Justina* (1605), Elena's life story is not presented to the reader as if she had written it herself. In this way, Elena's tale breaks with the tradition of picaresque pseudo-autobiographical accounts by using a mixture of third- and first-person narratives and thus presenting her life from two different points of view. The narrator controls the majority of the story, recounting the most recent events in Elena's life. The task of representing her remote past (her genealogy and childhood) is undertaken by the pícara herself in a brief oral intervention. There is a simple reason for this peculiar division of labor: Elena is a dead pícara. And as is the case with all picaresque novels with a female protagonist, her life account has been framed by a male moral voice, that of the narrator.

The novel starts in medias res with the description of Elena's arrival in Toledo. The pícara is portrayed as a dangerously beautiful young woman who travels in the company of her pimp and an old prostitute. Elena's sole intent is to deceive rich men. Her beauty, her manners, and her ability to imitate courtly behavior allow her to pass for a true lady. Immediately after her arrival in Toledo, Elena accuses a gentleman of seducing and disgracing her. In exchange for her silence the pícara demands a sum of money from his family. Once she obtains the money she escapes for Madrid with her associates. Meanwhile, the accused gentleman has fallen madly in love with the pícara and, ignoring the advice of family and friends, abandons his new wife and goes in search of Elena, who by then has left Madrid and is on her way to Burgos. During her trip to Burgos she decides to abandon her abusive, controlling male companion and seek a husband who can protect her. Failing to liberate herself, she travels with him and the old procuress to Seville, where they are discovered by the police. The old prostitute is killed, but Elena and her pimp manage to escape to Madrid, where they marry, and again she is forced to work as a prostitute. Her miserable life continues until one day when she falls in love with a client. In her second attempt to free herself, Elena poisons her pimp-husband but is then apprehended by the police and publicly executed.

Both in form and content, this work represents a complex reelaboration of the figure of the pícara. The contrast between the female rogue and the lady provides a new incentive: the introduction of a gentleman as the main victim of the pícara. This urban, elegant female rogue manages to manipulate one of the main ideological structures of her time, the code of *honor. She does so by cunningly imitating to perfection the social behavior of the elite, which was based on linguistic mannerisms and codes of appearance. It is well known that the ladies and gentlemen of Imperial Spain were supposed to adhere to a rigid set of social rules that, combined with their noble blood, set them apart from the populace. Many of the male picaresque rogues who populated the Spanish novel at the turn of the seventeenth century were masters in the art of deceiving the system by intelligently using noble manners for their own social advancement. Elena is the first female rogue to use this strategy.

Salas Barbadillo was well known in Golden Age Spain for the critical, moralizing tone of his novels. One of the most important features of this text is its study of the social behavior of men and women. *La Hija de Celestina, La Ingeniosa Elena* reveals the fragile basis of patriarchal relations cemented in the seventeenth-century code of honor and the social practices associated with it. The gentleman of this novel violates the honor code when he abandons his true wife to follow a false lady. The code is broken further when his family agrees to buy the silence of the supposedly disgraced lady. Additionally, the author carefully explores a crucial aspect of the pícara's life: the practice of prostitution as a means of survival for poor women.

With this novel Salas Barbadillo offers a key element to the production as well as the interpretation of the novels of pícaras. The figure of Elena, her motives, and her actions are indicative of those practices of survival employed by the poor women of Imperial Spain and call attention to the dangers that those practices implied for maintenance of the patriarchal order. This work expands the social critique of the picaresque novel to include the underworld inhabited by women in early modern Spain. Building on previous picaresque themes such as poverty, robbery, deceit, and hypocrisy, the story of Elena goes one step further, bringing to the forefront the issues of prostitution and rebellion against male control. *See also* Celestina, La. Comedia o Tragicomedia de Calisto y Melibea

Work by

The Daughter of Celestina. Trans. F. Holle. Strasbourg: Heizt; New York: Steckert, 1912.

La hija de Celestina, La ingeniosa Elena. Ed. José Fradejas. Madrid: Instituto de Estudios Madrileños, 1983.

Work about

Dunn, Peter. *Spanish Picaresque Fiction. A New Literary History.* Ithaca: Cornell UP, 1993.

Hanrahan, Thomas. *La mujer en la novela picaresca española.* Madrid: Porrúa, 1967.

Peyton, M.A. *Alonso Jerónimo de Salas Barbadillo.* TWAS 212. New York: Twayne, 1973.

Rey Hazas, Antonio, ed. *Picaresca femenina.* Barcelona: Plaza & Janés, 1986.

Ronquillo, Pablo. *Retrato de la Pícara. La protagonista de la picaresca española en el siglo XVII.* Madrid: Playor, 1980.

Reyes Coll-Tellechea

Hispano-Arabic Poetry by Women

The descriptor *Hispano-Arabic* is given to the poetry produced in Arabic in medieval Spain—mostly Andalusia—during the period between the eighth and the fifteenth centuries. Several Andalusian women are known to have excelled as poets in this tradition.

Critics have debated the place of this poetry within Spanish and Arabic contexts: While some scholars argue that it represents an essentially Spanish artistic form written in Arabic, others point out that it belongs to the literary tradition of classical Arabic, given that it is produced in the Arabic language by Muslims fully aware of their Eastern heritage. It is perhaps more productive, however, to reformulate the question of the poetry's national or cultural identity in terms of the unique character of medieval Andalusian society, which permitted the simultaneous existence of the two spirits—Arabic and Romance—sometimes within the same form. In other words, Hispano-Arabic poetry represents Andalusia's capacity for nurturing a non-Western artistic form on Western soil and allowing the occasional entry of elements of bilingualism and Romance culture into a classical Arabic genre. At the same time, no doubt can remain as to the poetry's firm inscription within classical Arabic literature.

The trajectory of this poetry, which spans the period ranging from the beginning of the Moorish conquest until a short time after the downfall of Islam in Spain, mirrors the many changes of the Andalusian artistic, political, and social climates, best described by critic James T. Monroe. In addition to poetic discourse and aesthetic developments, Hispano-Arabic poetry offers the reader an artistic account of Islamic history in Spain, starting with the reign of the Ummayyads (711–1009), followed by the period known as the rule of the Party Kings—known as Muluk at-Tawa'if in Arabic—(1031–1091), the Almoravids (1091–1145), the Almohads (1145–1230), and the Nasrids (1230–1492). Each period brings with it some development in imagery, language, and structure and the Muslim poets of Andalusia work using the many molds available to them from the extraordinary wealth of classical Arabic poetry. Themes include love, war, praise of the patron, glorification of wine, and advocacy of religious belief, and forms range from neoclassical to modern, with the expected share of decadence known to all literary forms, depending on the political and artistic climate surrounding each poet as well as the literary inspiration serving as his or her model. Of special interest is the treatment, by Hispano-Arabs, of the *moaxaja* (muwashshahat), strophic poems written in classical Arabic on love (and from a courtly standpoint), which allowed for creation of a hybrid form that included the *jarcha (kharja), a fragment often uttered in *romance* (Romance, the medieval Spanish language) within the poem but from a less learned and refined point of view. The Romance kharja was subsequently to become a topic for consideration in the context of Spanish—and not Arabic—literature, as it became a component of early lyrical poetry in the vernacular in Spain. However, its close links with classical Arabic poetry point to the peninsula's facilitation of the meeting of the two cultures and call attention to certain artists' experimentation in forms that derived inspiration from Romance and Arabic.

The Andalusians who treated poetic themes with particular skill are many, and much is known about men poets in this regard: Ibn Quzman of Córdoba (1078?–1160) explored the *zéjel* form—another type of strophic poetry, using colloquial Arabic as well as several expressions and words in Spanish—to its fullest, leaving behind some of the most dynamic, lively, and ironic poems of the Middle Ages, poking fun at authorities or celebrating carnal love with an amusing dose of humor and frankness. Ibn Khafaja of Valencia (1058–1139) wrote accomplished poetry on nature. Al-Abyad of Granada (?–1130) composed numerous muwashshahat and outspoken satirical poems reflecting the discontents of his age. Ibn al-'Arabi (1165–1240), born in Murcia, wrote superior mystical poetry. The list is long, and the accomplishments of the poets are equally impressive: it must be remembered that the learned poets of medieval Islam often had political or scientific pursuits in addition to composing poetry and enjoyed a refined, well-rounded educational background that allowed them to boast a legitimate authority in many fields such as philosophy, medicine, religious law, and poetry.

The history of medieval Islam, of which Al-Andalus is an integral part, derives much material from a wealth of biographies available on the prominent politicians, poets, scientists, artists, and philosophers of the community. Medieval biographies, as well as anthologies of works, are an invaluable source for the study of Islamic sciences and arts in the Middle Ages. In the case of the most famous and accomplished members of society, it is often possible to turn to several biographies available on the subject and gather information on the person's life and times, their works, and their impact on others. On the whole, however, women occupy a relatively limited space in biographies and anthologies; while some have received substantial attention in historical sources and documents, in many cases the historian and critic must contend with a dearth of material when considering the life and works of women artists. Such is the case with most women poets of Al-Andalus, many of whose names are known but few of whom appear in a substantial manner in medieval biographies or anthologies.

From available sources—in medieval compilations as well as modern studies—most completely studied by Teresa Garulo, it can be seen that, by and large, those women who composed poetry in Andalusia were freeborn and upper-class (although slave women also composed poetry), living in families where education was extended to the daughter by a parent or a schoolmaster, rendering the women well versed in topics mastered by their male counterparts: for example, grammar, reading the Koran, and classical literature. Most women poets were from Córdoba, Seville, and Granada, although a few hailed from Toledo or Málaga, as well as other cities. Unlike their male counterparts, however, few, if any, of these women held important political or educational posts; yet the poetic styles and themes outlined above were explored by women poets also, since they were familiar with the literary traditions that informed their artistic work. Like their fellow male poets, they composed panegyrics, love poetry, satirical pieces, and poems addressed to specific parties for the exchange of compliments or insults. Very few religious poems and compositions on nature survive. Those slave women who composed verses focused on the entertaining and amusing quality of their work, given that their poetry had to fulfill a specific function, that of pleasing their masters. All in all, as Andalusian poetry developed, the 30 or so women of whom something is known contributed to the genre mostly by way of refined and sophisticated love poems, in addition to forays into topics mentioned above. The eleventh and twelfth centuries constitute a particularly fruitful period for women poets, given the wealth of great artistic activity in all of Andalusia at that time. Again, this reveals the extent to which women inscribed themselves in their contemporary traditions and did not allow—consciously or otherwise—the evolution of an overwhelmingly isolated category for women's poetry. It is important to bear in mind the adherence of women poets to the paradigms of artistic creation and to realize at the same time that Arabic poetry lends itself to a wide range of creative freedom: Thus, the rigorous awareness of tradition does not necessarily imply lack of creativity and originality.

Among the women poets who show much talent in both areas, that is, attentiveness to literary tradition as well as originality of spirit, and of whom some details are known, are Wallada (10??–1077?), Hafsa ar-Rakuniyya (1135?–11??), and Nazhun Bint al-Qala'i (fl. twelfth century ?). Wallada, a princess from Córdoba, appears in anthologies and biographies as a learned and refined poet; one of her greatest claims to fame is her relationship with the poet Ibn Zaidun (1003–1071), which inspired the composition of love poetry by both parties. She received an excellent education in spite of the fragility of the Caliphate of Córdoba at the time and the frequent vicissitudes brought about by wars with rival factions. Labeled an independent spirit and a beautiful woman, she generated praise and gossip by her contemporaries; while today the mention of a woman artist's physical beauty would appear irrelevant or even misguided, this attribute was considered quite significant by medieval biographers and used in a double-edged capacity, since it could be interpreted as ennobling or unsettling, according to the standpoint of the critic and biographer. Wallada wrote complex love poetry exploring the themes of physical desire and jealousy. She also produced some satirical verse, always revealing her mastery of traditional techniques, a flair for originality, and outspokenness.

Hafsa ar-Rakuniyya, a native of Granada, is also mentioned in biographies and anthologies as a beautiful, talented woman. Medieval sources indicate that she taught classes to Almohad princesses and that she was highly cultured: She was obviously privileged enough to have received some advanced education. She is known for her love affair with the poet Ibn Sa'id (fl. twelfth century); some of the verses she exchanged with him survive to this day. Biographers have written of her prominence as a poet in the Almohad Court. She composed panegyrics as well as love poetry; the latter are characterized by an elegant discourse that is nonetheless somewhat outspoken, with vivid images of physical desire and intimacy.

Nazhun al-Qala'i, probably a native of Granada, is referred to in Arabic sources as a shameless and blunt poet but skillful at her art nonetheless. Anecdotes found in anthologies and biographies speak of her sharp wit and great presence of mind, with a particular talent for debate and improvisation. She is known for composing outspoken poems on her talents as a woman poet, the ugliness of fellow poets such as Ibn Quzman, or the presumptuous demands of suitors.

Slave-poets appear in anthologies in terms of their talent for entertaining: Thus, Qamar (fl. eleventh century), a slave brought to Seville from Baghdad, is praised for her musical talents and panegyrics to her master, while Hind (fl. twelfth century), of whom so far only one poem has been found, appears to have impressed biographers as a skilled musician and singer. The poetry composed by slave women attests, above all, to the characteristics of a social structure that placed emphasis on a woman's ability to couple physical beauty with artistic talent, thereby providing a wide range of entertainment for her master.

On the whole, the place of women poets in Hispano-Arabic poetry is difficult to determine due to the scarcity of adequate and detailed sources on the life and times of all those poets whose names have survived. Those of whom some detail is known confirm that women played a significant part in the cultural life of Andalusia and that, once they had gained access to advanced education, they were able to make themselves known and form a legitimate part of the circle of poets in their time. As for those about whom little is known, or whose extant verses amount to a few lines only, one can hope either that some hitherto unedited biography or anthology will yield more concrete information or that intelligent speculation and further investigations of context will better trace the place of women within the rich and multifaceted tradition of Hispano-Arabic poetry. See also Alba; Cantiga de amigo; Courtly Love

Work by

Arberry, A.J. *Arabic Poetry: A Primer for Students.* Cambridge: Cambridge UP, 1965.

García Gómez, Emilio. *Antología de poemas arábigoanadaluces.* Barcelona: Seix Barral, 1978.

Garulo, Teresa. *Diwan de las poetisas de al-Andalus.* Madrid: Poesía Hiperión, 1986.

Jones, Alan. *The 'Uddat al-jalis of 'Ali ibn Bishri: An Anthology of Andalusian Arabic Muwashshahat.* Oxford: E.W.J. Gibb Memorial, 1992.

Middleton, Christopher, and Leticia Garza-Falcón, trans. *Andalusian Poems.* Boston: David R. Godine, 1993.

Monroe, James T. *Hispano-Arabic Poetry: A Student Anthology.* Berkeley: U of California P, 1974.

Work about

Brann, Ross. "Constructions of Exile in Hispano-Hebrew and Hispano-Arabic Elegies." *Israel Levin Jubilee Volume: Studies in Hebrew Literature*, I. Ed. Reuven Tsur, Rosen Tova, and David Hanna. Tel Aviv: Katz Research Institute for Hebrew Literature, 1994.

Garulo, Teresa. "Imágenes sensoriales en la poesía de andalusí." *Mélanges María Soledad Carrasco Urgoiti/Tahiyyat taqdir li'l-dukturah María Soledad Carrasco Urgoiti, I-II.* Ed. and intro. Abd Al Jellil al Tamimi. Zaghhouan, Tunisia: Fondation Temimi pour la Recherche Scientifique et l'Information, 1999. 45–62.

———. "La poesía femenina en árabe clásico y la expresión de los sentimientos." *Medievalia* (June 1998): 26–37.

Monroe, James T. "The Muwashshahat." *Collected Studies in Honor of Américo Castro's Eightieth Year.* Oxford: Oxford UP, 1965. 335–371.

Nykl, A.R. *Hispano-Arabic Poetry and Its Relations with the Old Provençal Troubadours.* Baltimore: J.H. Furst, 1946.

Pérès, Henri. *La poésie andalouse en arabe classique au XIème: Ses aspects généraux, ses principaux thèmes, et sa valeur documentaire.* 2nd ed. Paris: Adrien-Maisonneuve, 1953.

Rubiera Mata, María Jesús. *Literatura hispanoárabe.* Madrid: MAPFRE, 1992.

Leyla Rouhi

Honor *and* honra

During the Middle Ages through the Baroque period in Spain, the code of *honor* governed all aspects of life from personal to social relations. Broadly speaking, an honorable man was brave, obedient, loyal, and faithful to his word. Men who did not exhibit these qualities, who were rumored not to possess them, or who did not avenge a physical assault or verbal insult might lose their *honor*. Losing one's *honor* was considered worse than losing one's life. The code of *honor* had particularly serious ramifications for women because they were seen as receptacles of their male relatives' *honor*, and this belief influenced every facet of their lives.

The term *honra* refers to one's personal code of ethics and morals and how this code governs one's actions. *Honra* is an internal force dictated by a superior entity and can only be tainted by one's own actions—not the actions of others. *Honor*, on the other hand, is external. It is a code of actions imposed and interpreted by society. A person's *honor* can, therefore, be injured by the actions or words of another, and it must be publicly defended. Typically, a stain on one's *honor* could only be cleansed by a public apology, by spilling blood in duel, or by marriage.

A nobleman considered *honor* to be his birthright, whereas many writers believed that the lower classes could not possess *honor*. Maravall has demonstrated that by the mid-sixteenth and seventeenth centuries the noble class, fighting to maintain their privileges and power base in decades of social changes, successfully insisted that noble blood (which is different than pure blood) was the only way to possess *honor*, and that all virtues and talents *flowed from* this biological fact. Thus, the idea of *honra* derived from personal virtues or pure blood (lineage untainted by Jewish or Moorish ancestors) functioned in fact as a compensatory myth, as Yarbro-Bejarano's notes, as seen in the theater of the day. Despite the strong ideological influence of the myth, it did not, however, alter the nature or membership of the established power structure in society.

A nobleman's sense of *honor* governed all his social interactions. For the nobility, *honor* first dictated that one owed loyalty and obedience to one's superiors and, above all, to the king. The king, a ruler by divine right, was "God on Earth" and, as such, could not err or offend one's *honor* except by seducing a female relation. One's possession of *honor* determined how one dressed, how one spoke, what one ate, what games one played, and so forth. In dealing with inferiors, *honor* demanded that a nobleman protect his subordinates and do nothing to harm them. Since women were seen as man's inferior, and the weaker sex, a nobleman was obligated to aid any damsel in distress. An inferior, by virtue of the fact that he is an inferior, can do nothing to injure his superior's *honor*. Again, since women are man's inferiors, they cannot offend a man's *honor* through words or physical attacks. If a woman insulted or slapped a man in front of another man, the man insulted could not avenge himself against her, but he might duel with the witness at a later time, since dueling in the presence of women was also dishonorable. Only an equal capable of drawing a sword and defending himself could be made to answer to questions of *honor*.

Finally, *honor* also controlled a man's domestic relations, binding a nobleman to act with respect for his family name and to obey his father. Inside the family, male relatives jealously guarded the sexual purity of their women as the repository of family honor. A maiden's *honor* lay in her virginity, which was guarded by her father, brothers, or other male relatives. To protect their virginity, unmarried women were secluded within their homes (*Encierro) and permitted to leave only to attend Mass or fulfill other religious duties. When they left their homes they were carefully chaperoned and wore cloaks that covered them from head to foot (*C*ubiertas* and *Tapadas*). They were not to glance at men, speak to them, or do anything else that might attract attention, such as walking too quickly or slowly.

A man who seduced a maiden under the pretense of marriage was expected to keep his word, as *honor* dictated, and marry her. In fact, during the Middle Ages and Renaissance, to constitute a legal marriage, a couple only needed to promise to marry one another, even without benefit of witnesses, and consummate the marriage. If a man seduced a woman of equal rank without promising to marry her, he was still obligated to do so or to pay damages to her father. However, if a man seduced a woman of lesser rank, even under the promise of marriage, it could be assumed that she "allowed" herself to be deceived, and the man was only required to compensate her father or help to arrange a suitable marriage in her own class.

A wife's *honor* resided in her fidelity to her husband. Again, wives were secluded to safeguard their faithfulness. The concept of conjugal *honor* argued that through marriage a man and his wife's flesh are united into one body. Any blemish on that body offends the head—the husband. Christ said that an offending member should be cut off. Many husbands in Golden Age drama, such as Gutierre in *Calderón de la Barca's *El médico de su honra* (1635; Physician to His Honor), murder their wives solely on the *suspicion* that their wife has been unfaithful.

Women of the Middle Ages through the Baroque period were at the same time victims and, to a limited extent, beneficiaries of the *honor* code. Women in literature of the period are seen to exploit the male obligation to protect them as well as be exploited by the patriarchal belief that men must cleanse their blemished *honor* with female blood.

Work about

Castro, Américo. "Algunas observaciones acerca del concepto del honor en los siglos XVI y XVII." *Semblanzas y estudios españoles*. Madrid: Insula, 1956. 319–382.

Gutiérrez-Nieto, Juan Ignacio. "Honra y utilidad social: En torno a los conceptos de honor y honra." *Calderón: Actas del congreso internacional sobre Calderón y el teatro español del Siglo de Oro*. Ed. García Lorenzo Luciano. Madrid: Consejo Superior de Investigaciones Científicas, 1983. 881–895.

Maravall, José Antonio. *Poder, honor y élites en el siglo XVII*. Madrid: Siglo XXI de España, 1979.

Menéndez Pidal, Ramón. "Del honor en el teatro español." *De Cervantes y Lope de Vega*. Madrid: Colección Austral, 1963.

Salazar Rincón, Javier. "Honra horizontal y vertical en Cervantes." *Anales Cervantinos* 24 (1986): 9–26.

Yarbro-Bejarano, Yvonne. *Feminism and the Honor Plays of Lope de Vega*. West Lafayette, IN: Purdue UP, 1994.

Karoline J. Manny

Hore y Ley, María Gertrudis (1742–1801)

Born in Cádiz to Miguel Hore and María Ley, a couple of Irish background, her idiosyncratic personality and poetic prowess won her acclaim and the nickname "La Hija del Sol" (Daughter of the Sun), to indicate how her charm, sweet verses, and luxurious lifestyle made her sparkle among other women. In 1762, at age 19, María Gertrudis Hore y Ley married Esteban Fleming, a member of an English family from Puerto de Santa María. Unexpectedly, after a few years of marriage, she entered the Convent of la Purísima Concepción (Cádiz) with her husband's consent. She became a nun in 1780. The exact cause for this curious incident is not known. It became the object of much speculation after the nineteenth-century writer Cecilia *Böhl de Faber (Fernán Caballero) published a novelized account entitled "La Hija del Sol." Caballero depicted an affair between Hore and a lover, asserting that it took place while her husband was on a diplomatic mission in America.

The real reason for Hore's entrance in the convent remains a mystery, but prior to it, she was famous in Enlightened circles of Madrid and Cádiz for her beauty, talent, and sharp wit. However, these reports of her elegant, ostentatious lifestyle may have been unduly influenced by Caballero's tale.

Hore is said to have burned her best poems prior to entering the convent. After her confessor forbade her to do so, she continued to write, publishing in *Correo de Madrid*, *Diario de Madrid*, *Diario de Barcelona*, and other journals of the day. Her poetry, mostly self-centered and self-referential, underlines the seriousness of her poetic calling. Though her poems have been heavily edited by those who reprinted them, her manuscripts reflect the trends of secular, fashionable salon poetry favored by other European women poets of her day. Some critics associate her with the trends and style of José Cadalso, another *gaditano* (native of Cádiz) romantic writer.

Hore explored a variety of topics and meters (*romances*, silvas, sonnets), using her subjective feelings to study philosophical and personal concerns. Some poems are discretely erotic idylls; others such as the anacreontic "¡Hasta cuándo Gerarda?" (Until When Gerarda?) are considered autobiographical; others such as "A un pajarillo" (To a Little Bird) and "El nido" (The Nest) are philosophical reflections. Hore also wrote religious poems and exchanges with friends and relatives, such as "Amado primo mío..." (My Beloved Cousin...), "Oh, qué desventurada..." (Oh, How Unlucky...), and "El amor caduco" (Fleeting Love). Upon her death, she left her manuscripts to her father confessor, Pedro Chaves de la Rosa.

Work about

Lewis, Elizabeth F. "Mythical Mystic or 'Monja romántica'? The Poetry of María Gertrudis Hore." *Dieciocho* 16.1–2 (Spring–Fall 1993): 95–109.

Sebold, Russell P. "La pena de la hija del sol: Realidad, leyenda y romanticismo." *Estudios en honor de Ricardo Gullón.* Ed. Luis González del Valle et al. Lincoln, NE: Society of Spanish & Spanish-American Studies, 1984. 295–308.

Sullivan, Constance A. " 'Dinos, dinos quien eres': The Poetic Identity of María Gertrudis Hore." *Michigan Romance Studies* 12 (1992): 153–183.

María A. Salgado

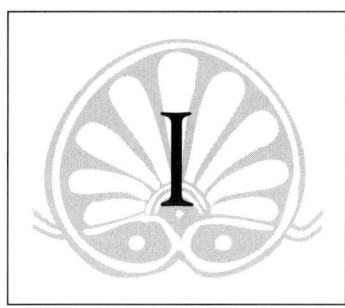

Ibarruri Gómez, Dolores (1895–1989)

Born near Bilbao, Dolores Ibarruri Gómez was one of 11 children of a Viscayan miner. At 15 she left school in order to go to work, first as a seamstress, then as a cook. The circumstances of her youth aroused her interest in politics, and in 1918 she published an article in a Basque newspaper under the pseudonym *La Pasionaria* (The Passionflower). Soon after, she helped to found the Spanish Communist Party and quickly emerged as one of its leaders. In 1915 she married Julián Ruiz. After bearing six children, one of whom died at Stalingrad while serving in the Red Army, she separated from Ruiz in order to dedicate herself to her political agenda.

A passionate, sometimes violent orator who almost always wore black in public, Ibarruri became the leading spokesperson for the Republic when the Spanish Civil War broke out in 1936. In one of her speeches she coined the phrase "¡No pasarán!" (They shall not pass!), which became the slogan of the Loyalist forces. Typical of her rhetoric is the admonishment of a speech she delivered in July 1936 at the outbreak of the Civil War: "It is better to die on your feet than to live on your knees." With the defeat of the Republic in 1939, she fled by plane to the Soviet Republic, remaining there until after Francisco Franco's (1892–1975) death and the legalization of the Spanish Communist Party. She represented her party in the Soviet Union until 1960, when Santiago Carrillo replaced her as secretary-general. After her return to Spain in 1977, Ibarruri apparently remained a fervent Stalinist. She was elected as a deputy to the Spanish Cortes, a post that she was forced to resign due to poor health. She continued as honorary president of the Spanish Communist Party until she died. Her body was displayed in Madrid at the headquarters of the Communist Party.

Most of Ibarruri's published works are articles and speeches of a political nature. Even her autobiography, *El único camino* (1962; *They Shall Not Pass*, 1976), deals principally with the development of her political ideology from her youth through the period of the Civil War. Additional information about her role in Spanish politics can be found in the various histories of the war and of the Spanish Communist Party. Many of Ibarruri's speeches and papers can be found on microfiche in the Blodgett collection of Spanish Civil War pamphlets at the Harvard College Library.

Work by

Guerra y revolución en España. 4 vols. Moscow: El Progreso, 1966–1971.

Liberate Spain from Franco. London: Communist Party, 1945.

Pasionaria: People's Tribune of Spain. New York: Workers Library Publishers, 1938.

Speeches and Articles. New York: International Publishers, 1938.

They Shall Not Pass: The Autobiography of La Pasionaria. New York: International Publications, 1976.

El único camino. Moscow: El Progreso, 1976.

Union of All Spaniards. Madrid: Communist Party of Spain, 1938. (Complete text of the report to the plenary session of the Central Committee of the Communist Party of Spain at Madrid on May 23, 1938).

Work about

Larsen, Kevin S. "The Literary Background of Dolores Ibarruri's *Memorias*." *Revista de Estudios Iberoamericanos* 10 (1993): 129–140.

Mangini, Shirley. *Memories of Resistance. Women's Voices from the Spanish Civil War.* New Haven: Yale UP, 1995. 38–47.

Pàmies, Teresa. Una española llamada Dolores Ibarruri (La Pasionaria). Barcelona: Roca, 1977.

Jean S. Chittenden

Icaza, Carmen de (1899–1979)

Considered the main exponent of the *novela rosa* (romances) in the early postwar years, Carmen de Icaza's novels deal primarily with upper-class women who struggle to find their identity amidst the social codes that dictate their behavior. Born in Madrid, Icaza was the daughter of Mexican poet and writer Francisco A. de Icaza. As a young girl of 15, Icaza started writing short stories and chronicles, many of which appeared in the so-called right-wing journals. She published her first novel, *La boda* (1916; The Wedding), at age 17. Her first commercial victory came with publication of *Cristina Guzmán, profesora de idiomas* (1936; Christina Guzmán, Foreign Language Teacher) in the popular Madrid journal *Blanco y negro*. The success of this work led to publication of her following novels: *¿Quién sabe?* (1940; Who Knows?), *Vestida de tul* (1942; Dressed in Tulle), *Soñar la vida* (1944; To Dream Life)—all of which deal with social themes related to the well-do-to classes. In subsequent novels, which are also described as *novelas rosas*, Icaza shows a shift in style that reflects themes of transcendental nature and a more literary focus. These novels include *El tiempo vuelve* (1945; Time Returns), *La fuente enterrada* (1947; The Buried Fountain), *Las horas contadas* (1951; Counted Hours), *Yo, la reina* (1955; I the Queen), *Irene* (1958), and *La casa de enfrente* (1960; The House across the Street). In general, however, her novels are treated as popular fiction and not considered part of the mainstream literature because of their focus on topics like love, emotionalism, and sentimentalism.

In *Las horas contadas* Icaza presents three different types of female characters that represent all the women that abound in the novel and, at the same time, exemplify the women of the time. Doña Jerónima and Berta's friends Doña Gertrudis and Doña Luisa all pórtray the self-abnegating mother. Doña Jerónima exemplifies the cold, hard female who considers her child to be the center of her universe and is blind to his repulsive deformity. As the product of a repressive, superficial society in which maintaining the appearance of decency means everything, she has never attained sexual or emotional happiness and consequently has turned bitter and demanding. Doña Jerónima expects any woman who considers herself decent to conform to her own ideas of decency even if it means leading an unfulfilling and empty life. For this reason, she despises Berta and refuses to speak to her daughter-in-law Catalina when the latter decides to take charge of her own life.

Berta is in a sense the antithesis of Doña Jerónima. An attractive woman very much aware of her sexuality, she thrives on passion. However, just as Doña Jerónima, she also finds frustration and emptiness in her life. When compared to the kind Margarita, her lover's wife, Berta appears immature, selfish, and ambitious, willing to go to any measure to obtain what she wants, since, as she herself admits, in life "el dinero era lo importante" (the important thing was money). Once her plan to marry Gabriel fails, she adopts the role of perfect wife and mother. When she is widowed she faithfully mourns her husband and concentrates all her efforts on realizing her ambitions through her daughter. Berta also enters a second marriage to a man who can give her a longed-for social and financial stability, but she keeps confusing the name of her current husband, Ernesto, with that of Eugenio, her former spouse. Both marriages are simply means to an end, and the figure of the amorphous husbands is directed to the same goals of financial stability and social respect.

Finally, the character of Catalina presents the struggle between the world of her mother's liberal ideas and that of Doña Jerónima's repressive regime. Catalina's life has been constructed by her mother, who pushes her into an unwanted marriage with a man she finds repulsive, solely to secure a social position. This marriage produces a child just as deformed as the groom and the marriage itself. However, Catalina renounces her own happiness and refuses to leave her miserable life when she has the opportunity to run away with the true love of her life, Biel. Upon returning from Madrid and facing a potentially life-threatening condition, Catalina defends her *derecho a vivir* (right to live) and her willingness to fight for it. Her physical transformation reflects her newly attained spiritual strength. She is, as other characters call her, the *hermosa momia* (beautiful mummy) that has come back from her deadlike life with the intention of reliving it.

In *La fuente enterrada* female characters also represent the author's conceptualization of women of her generation. The character of the aunt, Doña Estefanía, closely resembles that of Doña Jerónima; each is an old woman for whom appearances and decency are the most treasured aspects of life. Upon her brother's death, Estefanía is forced to raise her niece Irene. Affection is not a part of this upbringing, and the only interest the aunt shows in the niece is a desire to marry her well.

Like Catalina, Irene remembers a lonely childhood, deprived of love or tenderness. She also finds solace in a man who finds her shy, demure innocence captivating. She is portrayed as a naive woman who marries a successful man and loses her identity in his shadow. Initially charmed by Irene's refreshing approach to life, he quickly becomes bored and redirects his attention to Dolores, his former lover. Dolores is a sensual woman who uses her sexuality to captivate men. Nonetheless, she also fails to hold on to that love and is left with misery and loneliness. As the years pass, Dolores longs for her lost beauty since in her eyes her beauty is her identity, and without it, there is nothing left. The only way to obtain reassurance is to compete against other women for the affection of a man.

These novels present women who are constantly suffering because they have lost a man's love or are incapable of attaining it. For some characters struggling to overcome the pain, death is viewed as a liberating force. As a girl, Irene would lie flat on the floor and play that she had died; this "pretend death" would provide her with a sense of peace and detachment from the pain of the world. As an adult, years spent in the asylum made her confront death straight in the face. Her former self had died, and it was up to her to consume herself in that death or go through a rebirth that would make her stronger to fight life. For Catalina, her potential death also serves a liberating purpose. The possibility of having her "horas contadas" enables her to change the direction of her life. Religion is also viewed as a means of escaping. Irene envisions herself wearing a white habit that permits her to withstand her aunt's cruelty and fervently reads biographies of saints' lives, identifying her suffering with that of the martyrs.

Some of Icaza's novels also show a radical change in some protagonists' lives that partially allows them to recapture their lost sense of identity. In *Las horas contadas* and *La fuente enterrada*, Catalina and Irene metamorphose from obedient, submissive, beautiful young girls into gray, obscure creatures. This change enables them to acquire a level of maturity and understanding that takes them through a third transformation, where they are again beautiful, but now also confident, women able to pursue their own desires and take control of their lives. Still, it is a partial control since even at the end both Catalina and Irene are unable to blindly pursue the men they really want. Societal pressures still play an important role in their lives, and they are unwilling to break off completely with their social world.

Most of Icaza's novels present love as the only means for a woman to become truly fulfilled. Failing in love is equated with bitterness, resentment, and sadness. Happiness is only acquired through a man. However, for the protagonists of Las horas contadas and La fuente enterrada, attaining that love contradicts all the established mores of conduct. Faced with this conflict, these characters instead opt for saving their names and their virtue.

Work by

Obras selectas. Barcelona: AHR, 1957.
¿Quién sabe?. Madrid: Afrodisio Aguado, 1951.
El tiempo vuelve. Madrid: Afrodisio Aguado, 1945.

Work about

Andreu, Alicia G. "La obra de Carmen de Icaza en la difusión de un 'nuevo' concepto de nación española." Revista Hispánica Moderna (New York) 51.1 (June 1998): 64–71.
López, Francisca. "Mito y discurso en la novela femenina de posguerra en España." Diss. U of Connecticut, 1992.
Montojo, Paloma. Introducción. Cristina Guzmán, profesora de idiomas. Madrid: Castalia, 1991. n.p.
Roller, Marta A. "La obra periodística y narrativa de Carmen de Icaza." Diss. U of Kentucky, 1997.
Sainz de Robles, Federico Carlos. Introducción. Obras selectas de Carmen de Icaza. Barcelona: AHR, 1973.

Delmarie Martínez

Imab, Ticiano
See Biedma y la Moneda de Rodríguez, Patrocinio de (1848–1927)

Invisible Mistress
The plot pattern of the "Invisible Mistress" (Amante invisible) gained unprecedented popularity in the literature of the Spanish Golden Age, being used to foreground the imaginative power of women. The plays and novelas (novellas) that utilize the plot generally include most of its salient elements. A messenger comes to a young man and invites him to partake of an adventure: He is to follow the stranger in the dark (blindfolded, in some cases) and be led to an unknown site where a beautiful woman awaits him, promising him. Although moved by her "angelic" voice or soft touch, he is not allowed to see her. The lady remains in darkness or is veiled or masked. Although the young man is provided with sumptuous banquets, delightful music, and exquisite intimacies, he becomes obsessed with the identity of his mysterious jailer. Is she a phantom, a goddess, a magician, or a witch? Is she truly beautiful, or does she conceal her monstrous nature in the dark? This plot, which develops the angel/monster dichotomy in its representation of the female protagonist, is often a vehicle for more than a facile depiction of women as objects for male wish-fulfillment dreams. Writers who deal with the plot often attempt to provide women characters with a certain agency and autonomy. The richness and versatility of the plot depend on its venerable ancestry. It is both a reversal of the Cupid and Psyche myth and a displacement of the twelfth-century romance Partonopeus de Blois. The subject of Renaissance novellas by Masuccio Salernitano and Matteo Bandello, this plot pattern was assiduously utilized by playwrights of the Spanish Golden Age, including Lope de *Vega (1562–1635), Tirso de *Molina (1582?–1648), and *Calderón de la Barca (1600–1681).

Lope de Vega's La viuda valenciana (1595–1599; The Valencian Widow) is modeled after Bandello's novella on the subject but was probably revised immediately before publication in 1620 in order to establish a link between Lope de Vega's beloved, Marta de

Nevares, and Leonarda, the protagonist of the play. Through a series of role reversals the play both praises and counsels Marta. Even though the text elicits wonder at woman's imaginative powers, it also associates these wonders with witchcraft. The play ends with the humbling of the woman, with her acceptance of male superiority and her acquiescence to the marriage bond. But the spectator is also left with images of her creative powers and imagination. Though "invisible" in the end, Leonarda's "enchantments" may move the spectators to transform their vision of woman's character and of her role in society.

Tirso de Molina used the Invisible Mistress pattern for a series of plays including *Amar por señas* (1615?; To Love via Sign Language), *Quien calla, otorga* (1615; She Who Is Silent, Rewards), *La celosa de sí misma* (1621; Her Own Keeper), and *En Madrid y en una casa* (1635–1637?; In Madrid, in a House). These works exalt woman's power and imagination much more than Lope's theater. They counter men's weakness, using as remedy woman's powers of enchantment. Lope's dichotomies are assuaged in these plays. Veering away from didacticism, they delve into the human psyche and reveal the humanity and dignity of both male and female protagonists.

Calderón de la Barca's *La dama duende* (1629; Lady Goblin) develops the Invisible Mistress plot from an episode in the Gonzalo de Céspedes y Meneses novel *El soldado Píndaro* (1626; Pindar the Soldier). The Spanish novel, which imitates both the form and content of Apuleius's *Golden Ass*, includes a tale that recalls the Cupid and Psyche myth, which was interpolated within the classical novel. But Céspedes y Meneses reverses the roles of god and woman in the myth, thus questioning woman's inherent curiosity and ascribing this quality to the male. From Céspedes's episode, Calderón develops his play but reverts to the mythological tale in his emphasis on female rather than male curiosity. In spite of this return to the original myth, the play deals reflectively with woman's role in society, portraying Angela as moving from virtual incarceration to relative freedom with the aid of her imaginative powers. Like all previous heroines in this plot pattern, she is aware of woman's invisibility in society and uses this situation to her own advantage. Calderón exhibits his own satisfaction with this play by alluding to it in nine of his other plays.

A little-known version of the Invisible Mistress plot, the novella "Los efectos que hace amor" (The Effects of Love), included in Alonso de Castillo Solórzano's collection of tales entitled *Los alivios de Casandra* (1640), was one of the most influential works on this plot in other European countries. Together with Calderón's *La dama duende* it was the subject of novellas and plays in France by Boisrobert, d'Ouville, Scarron, Hauteroche, Vanel, and others. The French versions were the first to give a name to the plot, since these writers entitled their fictions *La belle invisible* or *L'amante invisible*. Castillo Solórzano's novellas, much more than the plays discussed above, create an atmosphere of wonder and enchantment, recalling the ambiance of the romances of chivalry. Here, the woman seems to stand above social norms, exercising her powers in order to test male faithfulness.

Two women writers of the seventeenth century also utilized the plot: Ana *Caro Mallén de Soto (1565?/1600?–1652?) and María de *Zayas y Sotomayor (1590–after 1647?). Surprisingly, both texts seem to have been composed once the popularity of the plot started to decline. Zayas's *Desengaños amorosos* (1647; Disillusion in Love), a collection of 10 novellas, includes the plot within the fourth tale "Tarde llega el desengaño" (Disillusion Comes Late). The Invisible Mistress plot occupies a small portion of the narrative and can be considered as an "interpolated" tale within the novella. The amorous "cruelty" of the Invisible Mistress may serve as contrast to the sadistic cruelty of the husband in the main narrative. Jaime has his cousin burned alive, suspecting him of having an affair with his wife. He then gives the cousin's skull to his wife to use as a glass. Imprisoning Elena, the husband allows her to emerge from her confinement (*Encierro*) only during dinner hours, when she is permitted to crawl on the floor and beg for leftovers. She eventually dies of starvation. Clearly, the cruelty of the Invisible Mistress pales in comparison with Jaime's murderous intentions. His behavior toward his wife serves as a metaphor for male confinement and victimization of women in a patriarchal society. The interpolated tale of the Invisible Mistress, on the other hand, shows woman attempting to use her social invisibility to surmount her condition.

In the prefatory material to this fourth novella, Zayas praises the poetry of Caro and proudly points to her theatrical successes. Caro, like Castillo Solórzano, stresses the wonder and enchantment of the plot through its link to chivalric romances. Indeed, she takes the plot directly from a Spanish translation of the *Partinopeus de Blois*. In her *El conde Partinuplés* (probably written in the 1630s and published in 1653; Count Partinuplés), she portrays a woman ruler in order to deal with the problematics of female power and succession in a patriarchal society. By representing the humanity of woman's power, Caro invites spectators to move away from the male bellicose spirit and toward a more balanced view of life.

Work about

Buchanan, Milton A. "*Partinuplés de Bles*. An Episode in Tirso's *Amar por señas* and Lope's *La viuda valenciana*." *Modern Language Notes* 21 (1906): 3–8.

De Armas, Frederick A. *The Invisible Mistress: Aspects of Feminism and Fantasy in the Golden Age*. Charlottesville: Biblioteca Siglo de Oro, 1976.

———. "Mujer y mito en el teatro clásico español." *Lenguaje y Textos* 3 (1991): 57–72.

Fernández, Jaime. "Honor y moralidad en *La viuda valenciana* de Lope de Vega: 'Un tan indigno ejemplo.'" *Hispania* 69 (1986): 821–829.

Larson, Catherine. "*La dama duende* and the Shifting Characterization of Calderón's Diabolical Angel." *The Perception of Women in Spanish Theater of the Golden Age*. Ed. Anita K. Stoll and Dawn L. Smith. Lewisburg, PA: Bucknell UP, 1991. 33–50.

Monti, S. "Il mito di Psiche e il suo rovesciamento: tre testi barocchi." *La metamorfosi e il testo. Studio tematico e teatro aureo*. Milan: Franco Angeli, 1990. 17–46.

Ordóñez, Elizabeth. "The Woman and Her Text in the Works of María de Zayas and Ana Caro." *Revista de Estudios Hispánicos* 19 (1985): 3–15.

Seidenspinner-Núñez, Dayle. "Symmetry of Form and Emblematic Design in *El conde Partinuplés*." *Romance Quarterly* 30 (1983): 62–76.

Frederick A. de Armas

Isabel I, Queen of Castile: The Vision of the Queen in *Converso* Poetry (c. 1474–c. 1480)

Upon her ascension to the throne in 1474, Queen Isabel I of Castile, who had married King Fernando II of Aragón (1452–1516) in 1469, was immediately faced with the task of dealing with a social crisis that had been plaguing the kingdom for over two decades: the legal and physical persecution of the New Christian minority, that is, the *conversos* (Jews who had converted to Christianity, or descendants of those who had converted, in order to escape mounting anti-Semitism), by an Old Christian (those who were not of Jewish lineage) community that refused to treat *conversos* as equal Christians. At first, Isabel seemed to side with the *conversos* in their struggle to assimilate into Spanish Christian society, a posture that was celebrated by several *converso* poets who praised Isabel's apparent desire to remedy the *converso* plight by ending social tensions. While this literary focus on the character of an individual woman represented a departure from the type of generic pro-feminism found in other late-medieval Spanish texts, the portrayal of Isabel by *converso* poets was ultimately premature, as Isabel's policies eventually contributed to establishment of the Spanish Inquisition and an enduring division between Old Christians and *conversos*.

During the 1460s and early 1470s, *conversos* were consistently threatened by both legal restrictions and violent attacks by Old Christians. When the reign of Isabel's predecessor, Enrique IV of Castile (1425–1474), came to an end in 1474, many *conversos* looked toward a new monarchy with great anticipation, in hopes that the shift of power would signify the beginning of a new period of stability and an end to discrimination. Indeed, Isabel, unlike Enrique, at first appeared to support the interests of the *conversos* when she attempted to improve relations between Old and New Christians. This attitude, coupled with her hesitancy for two years (from 1478 until 1480) toward enforcing the papal bull authorizing a Spanish Inquisition, provided *converso* poets with the ideological foundation for the distinct manner in which they depicted Isabel from the beginning of her reign until the official establishment of the Inquisition. There is a marked tendency for *conversos* writing during this time to express their confidence in the young queen by instilling her with divine attributes. Examples of this technique are found in poems by Antón de Montoro (c. 1404–c. 1480), Juan Alvarez (c. 1445–c. 1510), Pedro de Cartagena (1456–1486), and Fray Íñigo de Mendoza (c. 1424–c. 1508). Montoro virtually transforms Isabel into a divine being in his "Canción de Antón de Montoro en loor de la Reyna doña Ysabel de Castilla" (Song of Antón de Montoro in Praise of Queen Isabel of Castile) by asserting that she would have been just as capable as the Virgin of being the mother of Jesus Christ. In Alvarez Gato's "Coplas de Juan Alvarez Gato a la Reyna nuestra Señora" (Verses of Juan Alvarez to Our Lady the Queen) a *converso* poet again depicts Isabel as a being who is more divine than human, this time by writing that she was created more in God's image than in that of a mortal. Cartagena also portrays Isabel in a divine light in "Otras suyas a la reyna doña Ysabel" (Other Verses... to Queen Isabel) by declaring that she is different from other queens because she has been especially adorned by God. Mendoza speaks of Isabel in divine terms in two poems. In his "Dechado a la muy escelente reina doña Isabel, nuestra soberana señora" (Example to the Very Excellent Queen Isabel, Our Sovereign Lady) he professes that her arrival is due to the grace of God, and in his "Coplas al muy alto y muy poderoso príncipe, rey y señor... E a la muy esclarescida reyna doña Isabel..." (Verses to the Very High and Powerful Prince, King and Lord... and to the Very Illustrious Queen Isabel), a panegyric dedicated to both Isabel and Fernando, he avows that Isabel's beauty is "más divina que mortal" (v. 395; more divine than human).

All the poems heretofore considered were most likely composed between 1474 and 1480. The existence of such a corpus of *converso* poetry deifying Isabel, and the lack of contemporary Old Christian examples, suggests that the *converso* poems share a common motivation. Knowing the brighter future that Isabel represented during her early years as queen, it is reasonable to conclude that the *conversos* who deified her were utilizing poetry as a vehicle for communicating their aspirations felt during this time, that is, until 1480, the year that the establishment of the Spanish Inquisition tragically sealed the fate of the *conversos*. In fact, this underlying social foundation comes into clear focus when it is revealed that the tendency to deify Isabel is employed by the same *converso* poets who had either reflected on the precarious nature of their social situation during Enrique's reign or who were among those personally affected by the intensification of anti-*converso* sentiment. After having personally witnessed some of the worst anti-*converso* violence during the early 1470s, Montoro composed a poem to Enrique, "Montoro al rey nuestro señor sobre el robo que se hizo en Carmona" (1474; [From] Montoro to Our Lord the King on the Robbery Committed in Carmona), in which he embodies the frustration of a *converso* who had all but lost hope that the persecution would end and that he would be able to assimilate into Old Christian society. In contrast, his poem dedicated to Isabel illustrates that the presence of the new monarch had restored in him some degree of optimism for the future; while Montoro invokes the notion of death in connection with Enrique, Isabel is associated with life. In similar opposition to the bleak perspective he portrays in two poems dedicated to Enrique, Alvarez Gato also expresses the optimism felt by *conversos* during the early years of Isabel's reign in his poetic depiction of Isabel. Cartagena, whose uncle had been hung during the riots of 1467 in Toledo, indirectly refers to Isabel's ability to eradicate anti-*converso* violence by restoring social order—which Enrique had been unwilling and unable to accomplish—in a passage within "Otras suyas a la reyna doña Ysabel" in which, during the course of ascribing a different attribute to each of the letters in her name, he specifically underscores her sovereignty over everything within her kingdom. Finally, in his deification of Isabel, Mendoza, who undoubtedly felt some inquietude that his religious order (Franciscan) was one that persecuted the Jews, and who became a strong supporter of Isabel in part due to her advocation of reform of the religious orders, voices the sentiment felt by *conversos* who anticipated an end to discrimination and persecution and the beginning of an era of greater tolerance, symbolized in his panegyric by the use of the pronoun "nuestro" (v. 392; our) to emphasize that he is referring to the plight of his social class.

The sociopolitical nature of the *converso* poems sets them apart from the majority of contemporary Spanish pro-feminist compositions. While many other pro-feminist works praise women in general terms—by extolling feminine attributes such as beauty and chastity, advocating respect and admiration of women in general, enumerating the biographies of virtuous women of the past in order to underscore feminine virtue—the *converso* works center on one individual woman. The pro-feminist attitude of the *converso* works dedicated to the queen is therefore better understood as pro-Isabelian, due to the specific motivation of those works in the urgent need for an appeal that Isabel act on behalf of the New Christians.

When she became queen of Castile in 1474, Isabel I achieved true authority over her kingdom, something that few other contemporary women were able to accomplish. While she actively participated in the cultural development of the early Spanish Renaissance, she was much more than a patron and vigorously pursued objectives that would shape the course of Spanish history. One of these, the religious unification of Spain (which led to the institution of the Inquisition), was to bring to a close the brief period during which Isabel, who appeared to be working toward resolving the social conflicts that had relegated many *conversos* to second-class status, was portrayed in an optimistic light in *converso* poetry. In the end, the presence of Isabel on the Castilian throne did not ensure that the *conversos* would be able to assimilate into Old Christian society. On the contrary, the figure once depicted almost as if she were a divine savior ultimately served to further ostracize the New Christians and make them frequent targets of discrimination for many years to come. *See also* Isabel I de Castilla (1451–1504)

Work by

Alvarez Gato, Juan. "Coplas de Juan . . ." *Obras completas*. Ed. Jenaro Artiles Rodríguez. Madrid: Compaña iberoamericana de publicaciones, 1928. 126–131.

Cartagena, Pedro de. "Otras suyas a la reyna . . ." *Cancionero general*. Comp. Hernando del Castillo. Facs. ed. and intro. Antonio Rodríguez Moñino. Madrid: Real Academia Española, 1958. lxxxvii–lxxxviii.

Mendoza, Fray Iñigo de. *Fray Iñigo de Mendoza: Cancionero*. Ed. and intro. Julio Rodríguez Puértolas. Madrid: Espasa Calpe, 1968. 281–299, 318–346.

Montoro, Antón de. *Cancionero*. Ed. Marcella Ciceri and Julio Rodríguez Puértolas. Salamanca: U of Salamanca, 1991. 219–220, 296–301.

Work about

Jones, R.O. "Isabel la Católica y el amor cortés." *Revista de literatura* 21 (1962): 55–64.

King, Margaret L. *Women of the Renaissance*. Chicago: U of Chicago P, 1991.

Lida de Malkiel, María Rosa. *Estudios sobre la literatura española del siglo XV*. Madrid: Porrúa Turranzas, 1977.

Liss, Peggy K. *Isabel the Queen: Life and Times*. New York: Oxford UP, 1992.

Ornstein, Jacob, ed. and intro. *Luis de Lucena: Repetición de amores*. Chapel Hill: U of North Carolina P, 1954.

Rubin, Nancy. *Isabella of Castile: The First Renaissance Queen*. New York: St. Martin's P, 1991.

Gregory B. Kaplan

Isabel I de Castilla (1451–1504)

The daughter of Juan II and Isabel de Portugal, Isabel *la Católica* (the Catholic) was queen of Castile from 1474, when her half brother Enrique IV *el Impotente* (the Impotent) died, to 1504. She first lived with her deranged mother (Juan II had died in 1454) in a convent in Arévalo but was taken to her half brother's court in 1462 to serve Princess Juana, known as *la *Beltraneja* (1462–1530) because of her disputed parentage. Isabel came to detest the princess. When her younger brother Alfonso died in 1468, Isabel found herself in direct competition for the throne with the purportedly illegitimate Juana, and she left the court. Shortly thereafter, she signed an agreement with Enrique concerning her succession to the throne, then secretly contracted matrimony with Fernando de Aragón (1452–1516), who traveled to Valladolid for the wedding disguised as a muleteer.

As queen, Isabel insisted on complete equality with her husband in matters of state, an equality recognized in Castile and Aragón with the motto *Tanto Monta Monta Tanto*. She resolutely pursued her own agenda of activities in Castilla and single-handedly transformed the medieval kingdom into a modern rational state. Among many other centralizing innovations, she established a uniform and organized Inquisition in Castilla; she insisted upon naming her own bishops; she personally promoted the careers of the humanist priests Hernando de Talavera (1428–1507) and Francisco Ximénez de Cisneros (1436–1517); she made a lasting peace with Portugal after the civil war (1474–1479) with Juana *la Beltraneja* and the Portuguese monarchy; she personally supervised and participated in the war against Granada and was the first to enter the Alhambra on January 2, 1492; and she intervened to assure that Christopher Columbus (1451?–1506) had the ships and men necessary to initiate his trip of discovery and conquest to the Indies. She bore her husband five children, including **Catalina de Aragón (1485–1536) and the mad *Juana la Loca (1479–1555). See also Isabel I, Queen of Castile: The Vision of the Queen in *Converso* Poetry (c. 1474–c. 1480)

Work about

Liss, Peggy K. *Isabel the Queen: Life and Times*. New York: Oxford UP, 1992.

Suárez Fernández, Luis. *Isabel, mujer y reina*. Madrid: RIALP, 1992.

David H. Darst

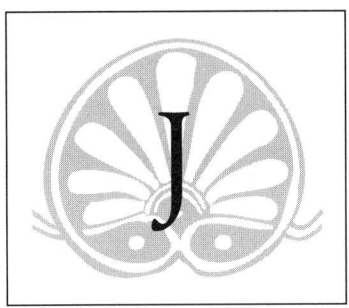

Janés, Clara (1940–)

Another of Spain's more prolific women poets who has received little consistent critical attention, Clara Janés was born in Barcelona, daughter of poet and editor Josep Janés. Janés has devoted her life almost entirely to a literary career, first as a student of philosophy and letters at the Universities of Barcelona and Pamplona and then of comparative literature and the Czech language at Oxford, the Sorbonne, and in Perugia, Italy. She has published an impressive number of literary works, mostly poetry, but also several novels, short stories, a travelogue, biographies, and translations, especially of the major Czech poets Vladimir Holan and Jaroslav Siefert. Janés is also a literary critic and has published editions of works of Pureza *Canelo (1946–), Juan Eduardo Cirlot (1916–1973) and Rosa *Chacel (1898–1994), one of her closest friends. Also included among her literary achievements is an anthology of early Spanish women poets, *Las primeras poetisas en lengua castellana* (1986; The First Women Poets in the Castilian Language).

As a poet, Janés offers an extensive selection of works, beginning in 1964 with *Las estrellas vencidas* (Defeated Stars) and followed by *Límite humano* (Human Limit), written between 1963 and 1965 but not actually published until 1975. Both books reflect the poet's metaphysical, existential anguish over the temporal and spatial limits of human existence. After a period of reflection, travel, and residence abroad, including stays in Rumania and Czechoslovakia, Janés is inspired especially by her interest in the life and work of Holan, resulting in her return to poetry and the publication of three successive works: *En busca de Cordelia y Poemas rumanos* (1975; In Search of Cordelia and Rumanian Poems), *Antología personal* (1979; Personal Anthology), and *Libro de alienaciones* (1980; Book of Alienation). *Antología personal* includes, along with selections from all of her previous works, poems from *Kampa*, not to be published in its entirety until 1986. For many, *Kampa*, whose inspiration stems from Janés's affinity with Holan, represents a transitional book in the evolution of her poetic trajectory. Her intellectual attraction to his poetry results in a kind of emotional fusion and synthesis with the "other" while at the same time provoking heightened awareness of the self—especially the feminine one.

With the genesis of *Kampa*, Janés seems to overcome her characteristic existential anguish in favor of a more positive, life-affirming approach, which in the two books to follow, *Eros* (1983) and *Vivir* (1986; To Live), takes on a specifically female form and expression. Two subsequent works, *Fósiles* (1987; Fossils) and *Lapidario* (1988; Lapidary), focus on the permanence of natural objects as a reflection/expression of the internal human self. In *Creciente fértil* (1989; Fertile Crescent), Janés returns again to erotic themes, presented this time from a mythical female perspective, and further enhances elements and images introduced in *Eros* and *Vivir*.

Since *Creciente fértil*, Janés has sustained her intense poetic activity into the 1990s, with publication of *Emblemas* (1991; Emblems), *Ver el fuego* (1993; To See the Fire), and *Paisajes y figuras* (1994; Landscapes and Figures). *Ver el fuego* is the most metapoetic of Janés's works thus far, for it alludes throughout to the creative process, represented in symbolic female terms. *Emblemas* and *Paisajes*, like *Lapidario*, for instance, are composed of brief, densely woven, tightly knit autonomous poems conceived in praise of a concrete entity (person, place, drawing, sculpture) but that then give way to more general poetic-philosophic musings in a life-affirming vein. This positive, outward-looking approach is projected further in a yet-unpublished manuscript, "In Paradisum," whose focus, as described by the poet herself, is a constant seeking of light and continuous progression toward it.

In her two major works of prose, quite distinct and distant in time and space, Janés reveals the scope of her personal and creative development: The first novel, *Desintegración* (1969; Disintegration), corresponds to the strident, repressive period under the Franco regime in the 1960s and portrays the *desengaño* (disillusion) of many young people, while the second, *Los caballos del sueño* (1989; The Horses of Sleep), although still depicting that same despair and frustration, holds open the possibility of a positive and more hopeful resolution to the tension of the times.

Janés's other varied interests are reflected in her diverse prose writings: her studies and travel in Rumania in *Sendas de Rumanía* (1981; Trails of Rumania), a literary travelogue; her close relationship with her daughter in a series of intimate letters addressed to her in *Cartas a Adriana* (1976; Letters to Adriana); and her interest in and fondness for the Rumanian culture in her biography of the classical musician, *La vida callada de Federico Mompou* (1975; The Silent Life of Federico Mompou).

Numerous prose and poetry translations from a variety of languages, including Czech, Rumanian, French, and Turkish, complete the extensive panorama of Janés's active literary career. Her importance as a literary figure is due primarily to her poetry, but her contributions in prose, criticism, and translation also help establish Janés as one of the more significant Spanish women writing today. See also Short Fiction by Women Writers: 1975–1998, Post-Franco

Work by

Antología personal (1959–1979). Madrid: Rialp, 1979.
Los caballos del sueño. Barcelona: Anagrama, 1989.
Creciente fértil. Madrid: Hiperión, 1989.
Eros. Madrid: Hiperión, 1983.
Federico Mompou: Vida, textos y documentos. Madrid: Fundación Banco Exterior, 1987.
El hombre de Adén. Barcelona: Anagrama, 1991.
Jardín y laberinto. Madrid: Debate, 1990.
Kampa. Madrid: Hiperión, 1986.
Lapidario. Madrid: Hiperión, 1988.
Libro de alienaciones. Madrid: Ayuso, 1980.
Las primeras poetisas en lengua castellana. Ed., and intro. Clara Janés. Madrid: Ayuso, 1986.
Rosas de fuego. Madrid: Cátedra, 1996.
Sendas de Rumanía. Barcelona: Plaza & Janés, 1981.
Vivir. Madrid: Hiperión, 1986.

Work about

Ciplijauskaité, Biruté. "De Medusa a Melusina: Recuperación de lo mágico." *La Chispa 97: Selected Proceedings*. Ed. Claire Paolini. New Orleans: Tulane U, 1997. 91–100.
Francis, Natalia. "El amor y el ser en la poesía de Clara Janés." *Romance Languages Annual* 6 (1994): 460–464.
Marson, Ellen Engelson. "Clara Janés: Mysticism and the Search for the Female Poetic Voice." *Revista de Estudios Hispánicos* 29.2 (1995): 245–257.
Newton, Candelas. "Mitopoesis, revisión y delirio en

Creciente fértil, de Clara Janés." *Revista Canadiense de Estudios Hispánicos* 19.1 (Fall 1994): 109–120.

Ugalde, Sharon K. *Conversaciones y poemas: La nueva poesía femenina española*. Madrid: Siglo XXI, 1991.

Wilcox, John. *Women Poets of Spain, 1860–1990: Toward a Gynocentric Vision*. Champaign: U of Illinois P, 1997.

Anne M. Pasero

Jarcha

The term *jarcha* (kharja) refers to a brief two-, three-, or four-line refrain attached to the medieval Arabic or Hebrew poetic form known as the *muguasaja*, but in Mozarabic Spanish. These short endings to the poems were not discovered until 1948 because they are transcribed in the same Arabic or Hebrew characters as the body of the poem.

Over two-thirds of the *jarchas* have a female voice, wherein the lover expresses her desire for an absent beloved or her pain at his leaving her bedside at dawn. The voice is always frank and often openly erotic, urging the lover, who is addressed as *al-habib* (beloved) or *señor* (master), to come quickly to her side or to stay longer with her in her bed chamber. In the songs not spoken directly to the beloved, the woman calls on her *madre* (mother), her friends, or even her town or the river that flows through it to witness her desire for the man.

These early poems are related in many ways to other European forms such as the German *Frauenlieder*, the French *chansons de femme*, and the Galician-Portuguese *cantiga de amigo; and all probably have a common pre-Roman source. The *jarchas* stand out, however, in the urban setting, their sexual bluntness, and the brevity with which they express the urgent desire to love. *See also* Alba; Hispano-Arabic Poetry by Women

Work

Solá-Solé, Josep María. *Las jarchas romances y sus moaxajas*. Madrid: Taurus, 1990.

Work about

Compton, Linda Fish. *Andalusian Lyrical Poetry and the Old Spanish Love Songs*. New York: New York UP, 1976.

David H. Darst

Jardín de las nobles donzellas (written c. 1468)

One of several fifteenth-century pro-feminist treatises, the *Jardín de las nobles donzellas* (Garden of Noble Maidens) enjoyed two editions, in 1500 and 1542, well after the author's death in 1476, an indication of the work's influence or popularity. It was composed by Martín de Córdoba, a theologian known to have taught at the University of Salamanca, and dedicated to *Isabel I at the moment she was to inherit the throne of Castile. The first part of the work discusses who and what women are via rather elaborate allegory; part two describes how women should behave, using many similes and references to the Bible and antiquity; part three reiterates the points made earlier with numerous examples from history that support the observations made. The author affirms that Christianity proclaims woman to be a person, with dignity, and the fact that she was made of a rib, rather than part of Adam's head or foot, illustrates that she is to be man's equal, not his ruler nor his slave. Woman's primary role is found in marriage, to beget children, and also to ensure peace through unions between different kingdoms. He rejects the idea of women as the devil's snare, arguing that they are morally superior to men in terms of chastity, virtue, clemency, religious devotion, and generosity.

Goldberg argues persuasively that this well-organized didactic-moral tract was directed both to the general reader and to Princess Isabel. For the general reader, it reflects current pro-feminist opinion regarding the appropriate virtues and role of women and uses references and examples that were readily recognized by the public; for Isabel, it indicates the benefits to be derived from feminine rule and also outlines a course of action for Isabel, in terms of what specific weaknesses (intemperance, loquacity, inconstancy, fearfulness) she should guard against in the role of queen.

Work

Jardín de nobles donzellas, Fray Martín de Córdoba. Ed. and study Harriet Goldberg. University of North Carolina Studies in Romance Languages and Literatures #137. Chapel Hill: University of North Carolina Department of Romance Languages, 1974.

Work about

See Goldberg edition, above.

Maureen Ihrie

Jesús, Isabel de (1611–1682)

Born Isabel de Sosa in Toledo, this visionary nun of the Carmelite order was directed by her confessor to spend one hour daily recording her ecstatic experiences; she did so for 10 years. The resulting text, monitored and edited by her confessor, and published three years after her death with the title *Tesoro del Carmelo* (1685; Treasure of [Mt.] Carmel), is a 758-page combination of diary, autobiography, poetry, political commentary, confession, religious doctrine, and record of visions. Many pages recount her violent struggles with the devil who, in his efforts to block the writing that God inspires from within her soul, assaults her physically and with horrific visions—such as that of him devouring dead holy people in front of her. Isabel also describes how such confrontations, which are sprinkled throughout the text, provoke violent nausea, pain, and vomiting in her. Velasco sees clear parallels between the rhetoric and physical abuse used by the (male) Church power structure and the verbal and physical attacks used by the devil against Sor Isabel; her response of nausea and vomiting can thereby also be seen as a rejection of the negative ecclesiastical authorities who monitored and attempted to restrict her written discourse. *See also* Autobiographical Self-Representation of Women in the Early Modern Period; Nuns Who Wrote in sixteenth- and seventeenth-Century Spain

Work about

Velasco, Sherry M. *Demons, Nausea and Resistance in the Autobiography of Isabel de Jesús, 1611–1682.* Albuquerque: U of New Mexico P, 1996.

Maureen Ihrie

Jimena (1056?/1058?–1104?/1122?)

Legendary and historical figure, Jimena is the wife of the Spanish national hero Rodrigo Díaz de Vivar (1040?/1043?–1099), better known as the Cid. She is equal to him in all respects. Proud, defiant, unwilling to bend in adversity, she appears as a key figure in the various epics, ballads, and dramas treating the exploits of the medieval warrior. The principal sources of the legend are a twelfth-century Latin chronicle, *Historia Roderici* (Story of Rodrigo); the *Cantar de Mio Cid* (Song of the Cid), dating from 1140; numerous ballads from around the 1500s; and *Las mocedades del Cid* (1618; Youthful Deeds of the Cid) by Spanish Golden Age playwright Guillén de Castro (1569–1630), though virtually all great Spanish writers have written about the theme or been moved by the grandeur of its characters. One of the most powerful presentations of the Jimena figure is by Pierre Corneille (1606–1684) in the form of the heroic Chimène from his *Le Cid*, a brilliant imitation of Castro's *Las mocedades*. In addition to the many literary adaptations of the theme, there are renderings such as the opera *Le Cid* (1885) by Jules Massenet (1842–1912).

Jimena and the Cid lived during a turbulent time of transition in Spain when Moorish lords were beginning to lose their grip on Spain and Christian warlords were eager to fill the resulting vacuum. Loyalties shifted often and rapidly. Another difficulty in studying the Jimena figure or the Cid himself is that they are multiple figures: There are, of course, the legendary and historical figures, who sometimes coalesce but often exist independently of one another; there are also sharp contrasts—particularly in the case of the Cid—in the artistic treatments by various authors who shape the legends. The Cid who is the Spanish national hero is a mature, exemplary man, loyal to God, homeland, and family. The Cid of the *Crónica de 1344*, or even at times of the *Cantar de Rodrigo* (a work written at some point after the *Cantar de mio Cid*), is often brash, impudent, and even petulant. In the case of Jimena, history also sometimes supplies conflicting evidence. While historical documentation exists for a marriage between Jimena Díaz and Rodrigo in 1074, there is also reference to a Jimena Gómez, who lived until 1122, prompting some scholars to believe the historical Rodrigo may have been forced to marry Jimena Gómez against his will after killing her father in a duel and that the couple subsequently divorced, which would still have been possible in eleventh-century Castile.

A more fruitful way to understand what Jimena represents in Spanish society is to concentrate on those elements of her character that set her apart as a superlative individual. The first author to distinguish her in this way is Guillén de Castro. He recalls earlier myths in which the Cid killed Jimena's father to avenge an insult to his own father's honor, but he interjects a strong element of love between the two. Far from being forced into matrimony, the two genuinely love each other and struggle between feelings of *honor, filial piety, and their own longings for one another. It is this theme that Corneille so brilliantly exploits in his rendering. But even in earlier epics and ballads, Jimena is a formidable individual. In the various stories of the Cid, she is often alone, while her husband is at war or suffering unjust banishment at the hands of corrupt leaders. Jimena protects hearth and home with valor; regardless of which historic Jimena one picks—Jimena Díaz, whom he is said to have married in 1074, or Jimena Gómez, whose father he is said to have insulted—she outlives her husband and protects their lands. After the historic Cid died in 1099, Valencia, which he had conquered, withstood a siege of more than two years under Jimena's stewardship.

Stories of the Cid are often stark in their realism. In one account, the Cid's daughters are brutally dishonored by their husbands, decadent aristocrats united by blood to the royal household. Both Jimena and the Cid endure that tragedy and live to avenge their daughters, who eventually remarry. Ultimately great-grandchildren of the Cid and Jimena sit on Spanish thrones, Blanca, queen of Sancho III of Castile, and her brother, Sancho VI of Navarre.

While loyalties to royal households remain strong in stories of the Cid, these legends fit into the strong antifeudal and prodemocratic strain in Spanish literature and culture. Though both the Cid and Jimena are of noble background, they are not clearly linked to the highest ruling households. This individualistic pair makes its way in the world through courage and valor, not by reliance on blood ties; and it is evident in the stories of the Cid that he loves and admires his wife and relies on her to protect the family's well-being and livelihood while he is away. Indeed, Jimena is one of the most formidable female figures in Western medieval literature. *See also Poema de Mio Cid*

Work about

Castro y Belvis, Guillén de. *Las mocedades del Cid*. Madrid: Espasa-Calpe, 1971.

Chicote, Gloria Beatriz. "Jimena, de la épica al romancero: Definición del personaje y convenciones genéricas." *Caballeros, monjas y maestros en la Edad Media*. Ed. Lillian von der Walde, Concepción Capmany, and Aurelio González. Mexico City: Colegio de México/UNAM, 1996. 75–86.

Deyermond, A.D., ed. *Mio Cid Studies*. London: Tamesis, 1977.

Evans, Carol Anne. "A Woman's Plea for Justice: Las quejas de Jimena." *Romance Notes* 38.1 (Fall 1997): 61–70.

Ferrante, J. *Women as Image in the Middle Ages.* New York: Columbia UP, 1975.

Harney, Michael. *Kinship and Polity in the Poema de Mio Cid.* West Lafayette, IN: Purdue UP, 1993.

McKendrick, Melveena M. *Woman and Society in the Spanish Drama of the Golden Age. A Study of the Mujer Varonil.* London: Cambridge UP, 1974.

Merwin, W.S., trans. *The Poem of the Cid.* New York: New American Library, 1962.

Ratcliffe, Marjorie. *Jimena: A Woman in Spanish Literature.* Potomac, MD: Scripta Humanistica, 1992.

Sponsler, Lucy. *Women in the Medieval Spanish Epic and Lyric Traditions.* Lexington: U of Kentucky P, 1975.

Jeanne J. Smoot

Jiménez, Juan Ramón (1881–1958): Women in His Works

The poetry of Juan Ramón Jiménez, winner of the Nobel Prize for Literature in 1956, can be summarized as a search for beauty. In all the evolutionary stages of his poetry beauty will assume different forms, and the most common form will be that of a woman. Very similar to the Platonic idea of love, love for Jiménez is both the desire to possess the universal ideal of beauty and the willingness to produce it. Woman will be the entity to exert the most powerful attraction over the poet's spirit and therefore is the one that constitutes the main stimulus in his creative process. By equating beauty with woman, all aspects of reality attractive to the poet will assume female features. Because of the amplitude of meaning that the female symbol has in the work of Jiménez, the poet's beloved can be either a real woman, an incarnation of natural beauty, or the symbolization of absolute truth.

If we concentrate on the theme of the search for the beloved, we can establish three evolutionary stages in the poetry of Jiménez. The first stage covers the early poetry of Jiménez, the poems written between 1898 and 1912. In this period the search for beauty coincides with the search for the human beloved. Beauty assumes all the characteristics of a real woman, known or imagined, whose physical attributes fully coincide with the representation of women in symbolist and decadent aesthetics at the turn of the century. The ideal woman for Jiménez will initially be an innocent young lady, pure and ethereal, the "novia blanca" (white bride) of his first love experiences in Moguer. In general terms, the poems of *Ninfeas* (1900; Water Lilies), *Almas de violeta* (1900; Souls of Violet), *Rimas* (1900–1902; Rhymes), and *Arias tristes* (1902–1903; Sad Airs), where Jiménez embraces the poetic tradition initiated by Petrarch (1304–1374), equate whiteness with inner spiritual beauty. White is the color Jiménez uses to describe the beloved's body and her clothes. The female ideal of the *novia blanca* of Jiménez's first poems will evolve and change by mixing itself with a strong necrophiliac tendency very common in turn-of-the-century art and literature. The tendency of decadent and symbolist writers and artists to fuse woman, beauty, and death in the personification of a beautiful dead virgin or in the representation of terminally ill young girls is reflected in the poems of *Ninfeas, Almas de violeta, Rimas, Jardines lejanos* (1904; Distant Gardens), and *Pastorales* (1905; Pastorals). The equation of women with flowers, so typical in all turn-of-the-century artistic manifestations, is also frequently found in many of these poems. A very specific group of flowers—madonna lilies, calla lilies, jasmines, and white roses—are used to evoke all the desirable characteristics the poet expects to find in a woman: fragility, purity, and virginal beauty.

With time, this pure, angelic female archetype encounters her counterpart: the sensual and dangerous woman-snake. The latter symbolizes the death of spiritual love by the desires of the flesh. The voluptuous love the woman-snake generates in the poet is equated with the loss of his possibility for eternal life. These two archetypes conflict with each other, but at the end, the woman-angel triumphs. If white is used to evoke purity and innocence, red is used to evoke just the opposite. Erotic pleasures are always associated with red and the range of colors related to it. The red rose is the emblem for the erotic love that simultaneously attracts and frightens the poet. The poems of *Ninfeas*, *Jardines galantes* (Gallant Gardens), and *Jardines lejanos* offer multiple examples of this erotic representation of women.

The second stage in his poetry constitutes an intermediate step between the process of amorous search and the attainability of stability, achieved through found love. This period is marked by the encounter between the poet and Zenobia Camprubí, his future wife. In the poems of *Monumento de amor. Epistolario y lira* (1913–1916; Monument of Love. Epistolary and Lyre), *Sonetos espirituales* (1914–1915; Spiritual Sonnets), *Estío* (1915; Summer), and *Diario de un poeta recién casado* (1916; Diary of a Newly Married Poet) we find a new attitude of the poet toward reality: His melancholic stance gives way to a sound determination to reach the love of the woman that for him incarnates the ideal. The love that Jiménez feels for Zenobia is so deep and radical that the poet equates it with his love for Beauty. For this reason it is very difficult to determine who is the beloved that Jiménez refers to, since both Zenobia and Beauty constitute the other reality the poet needs to know and possess.

In the poems of *Monumento de amor* we witness both the process of deification of Zenobia and the humanization of beauty. Beauty is now represented with all the attributes of a seductive and desirable woman. The ideal woman again is depicted as a white, celestial, and luminous being, paralleling the light of the sun and its power to give life. The sonnets of *Sonetos espirituales* are addressed to an ideal beloved that comprises all the physical traits and enchantment of woman and the attributes of divinity. The poet equates this ideal woman with all the most beautiful visible and invisible realities he perceives in the universe. The equation of woman with spring or with water, very common in these poems, clearly suggests the image of woman and beauty as a principle of life.

The third and last stage is composed of the poems written after his marriage with Zenobia in 1916. These poems irradiate the achievement of stability and peace through true love that the poet found in his young wife. Now that inner peace has been achieved, the poet throws himself toward the conquest of the supernatural beloved, of woman as the absolute Beauty, in an attempt to overcome and to transcend spiritually throughout his poetic art. For woman to become the end of his poetic horizon, Jiménez must trespass human boundaries and consider her as a symbol of the mystery of the universe. This feminine symbol will comprise all the beauty of the universe, all the mysterious and captivating visible and invisible realities. Beauty in itself as well as its representations, the mystery of the infinite, and death are conceived as a woman, as a "She." From his union with Beauty the poet derives his happiness, the realization of his longings for love, immanence, and eternity.

In the poems of *Eternidades* (1916–1917, pub. 1918; Eternities) and *Piedra y cielo* (1919; Stone and Sky), Jiménez has discovered that true love is the perfect antidote to temporality because it has the power to turn an instant into an eternal moment. Through love the poet reaches eternity and defeats death. Once again, in these series of poems the images of water, always female, reappear to suggest purity, freshness, transparency, female attraction, and the preserving power of life. Because of its richness and multiple meanings, the symbol of Beauty has multiple representations: the naked woman, the eternal water, and beauty as pure luminosity. They represent purity and essence, symbolizing the female properties in the universe.

Ríos que se van (1951–1954; Rivers That Leave) is the last homage that Jiménez renders to Zenobia. In these poems Zenobia's beauty parallels the image of Beauty that Jiménez has always pursued in women: a naked beauty, concentrated, internal. A beauty that is all spirituality, all soul. In this last stage, human love evolves into spiritual life. The search for a specific woman gives way to the search for absolute values: Beauty, Eternity, Truth. These absolute values are all present in his ideal of the supernatural beloved. The union with this supernatural woman, "the eternal naked woman," helps the poet to discover the unique, universal and fair conscience of Beauty.

Work by

God Desired and Desiring. Trans. A. de Nicolás. Intro. L. Simpson. New York: Paragon, 1987. English and Spanish.
Invisible Reality: 1917–1920, 1924. Trans. A. de Nicolás. Intro. L. Simpson. New York: Paragon, 1987. English and Spanish.
Three Hundred Poems: 1903–1953. Trans. E. Roach. Austin: U of Texas P, 1962.
Time and Space: A Poetic Autobiography. Ed. and trans. A. de Nicolás. Pref. L. Simpson. New York: Paragon, 1988. English and Spanish.

Work about

Cardwell, Richard. *Juan Ramón Jiménez and the Modernist Apprenticeship (1895–1900).* Berlin: Colloquium, 1977.
Del Rey da Rosa, Evangelina. *La mujer, símbolo y realidad, en la poesía de Juan Ramón Jiménez.* Mexico: Talleres Bedemex, 1983.
Ferreres, Rafael. "La mujer y la melancolía en los modernistas." *Cuadernos Hispanoamericanos* 53 (1963): 456–467.
Herrero, Angel. "El adamor y la voz femenina en el 'Cántico espiritual.'" *Hispanic Review* 66.1 (Winter 1998): 21–34.
Jaffe, Catherine. "Lyric Reading: Woman and Juan Ramón Jiménez." *Hispania* 73.3 (1990): 593–605.
Litvak, Lily. *Erotismo fin de siglo.* Barcelona: Antoni Bosch, 1979.
Palau de Nemes, Graciela. "Juan Ramón Jiménez." *Premio Nobel: Once grandes escritores del mundo hispánico.* Ed. B. Mujica. Washington, DC: Georgetown UP, 1997. 83–93.
Ullman, Pierre. "Juan Ramón Jiménez and Onanism: An Ironic Typical Interpretation." *Studies in Honor of Gilberto Paolini.* Ed. Mercedes Vidal Tibbitts. Newark, DE: Juan de la Cuesta, 1996. 301–307.

María Alejandra Zanetta

Jiménez Faro, Luzmaría (1937–)

Born in Madrid, where she has lived most of her life, this prolific poet is perhaps more important as editor-publisher, primarily of women's poetry. She and her husband, poet Antonio Porpetta, not only produce their own poems but assist many other poets, especially women and beginners, in finding outlets. Via their critical and editorial endeavors, they also save past texts from oblivion, and as founder and director of Ediciones Torremozas, Luzmaría Jiménez Faro has become Spain's unquestioned leader in identifying and promoting new women's voices.

Jiménez Faro began modestly as a publisher some two decades ago, printing her own poems, *Por un cálido sendero* (1978; Along a Warm Path) and *Cuarto de estar* (1980; Sitting Room), followed by *Sé que vivo* (1984; I Know That I Live). An early and significant critical work in collaboration with her husband was *Carolina Coronado: Apunte biográfico y antología* (1983; Carolina Coronado: Biographical Notes and Anthology), contributing to scholarly reevaluation of this nineteenth-century woman poet. Likewise in 1983, Jiménez Faro published a selection of works by new women poets entitled *Poemas*, and a year later, *Veinte poetisas* (1984; Twenty Women Poets), a second anthological selection of new or unknown women lyricists.

Subsequently, Jiménez Faro has brought out a series of similar, specialized anthologies, not quite annually but steadily. Significant collections include her *Panorama antológico de poetisas españolas (siglos XV al XX)* (1987; Panoramic Anthology of Spanish Women Poets from the fifteenth to the twentieth Centuries), *Ernestina de Champourcin: Antología poética* (1988; Anthology of Poems by Ernestina de *Champourcin), *Breviario del deseo (Poesía erótica escrita por mujeres)* (1989; Prayer Book of Desire [Erotic Poetry by Women]), and *Delmira Agustini, manantial de la brasa* (1990; Delmira Agustini, Fountain of Fire). Jiménez Faro herself has also published erotic poetry, specifically *Letanía doméstica* *para mujeres enamoradas* (1986; Domestic Litany for Women in Love), typifying her intimate, passionate discourse, structured as a dialogue with a beloved interlocutor. Hers is poetry of unfailingly feminine tone and sentiment, sometimes evoking the biblical Song of Songs and reviving or borrowing erotic metaphors of spiritual union from the mystics.

A more recent collection of prose poems or vignettes of lyric prose entitled *Bolero* (1993) comprises meditations on favorite songs of love and tributes to famous singers of boleros and to other women poets. *Mujeres y café* (1993; Women and Coffee) begins with a rapid overview of coffee in language and culture, a glance at coffeehouses, and women writers' preferences concerning coffee, introducing an anthology of poems (primarily but not entirely by women) with coffee as a common theme. Another specialized anthology, *Y vamos haciendo camino* (1993; And We Keep Walking), commemorates a major milestone for the Torremozas publishing enterprise, which during the 1990s has moved away from publishing only women and only poetry, opening its collections to a few selected men poets and beginning a new fiction series for novice women writers. Jiménez Faro would undoubtedly be better known as a poet in her own right if her contributions as discoverer, editor, and publisher of other women poets had not made her something of a feminist cultural icon, responsible almost single-handedly for making known the existence of a surprisingly large and varied group of female lyricists.

Work by

Bolero. Madrid: Torremozas, 1993.
Cuarto de estar. Alicante: n.p., 1980.
Letanía doméstica para mujeres enamoradas. Madrid: Torremozas, 1986.
Por un cálido sendero. Madrid: Torremozas, 1978.
Sé que vivo. Madrid: Torremozas, 1984.

Janet Pérez

Juana *la* Beltraneja

See Beltraneja, Juana *la*

Juana *la Loca* (the Mad One; 1479–1555)

The second daughter of Fernando (1452–1516) and *Isabel (1451–1504), *los Reyes Católicos* (the Catholic Monarchs), Juana de Castilla was born and raised in Toledo, where she was married in 1495 to Felipe *el Hermoso* (the Handsome), archduke of Austria and king of the Low Countries (Flanders). By way of a series of fortuitous deaths (her siblings Juan and Isabel and her nephew Miguel of Portugal), Juana and Felipe became the heirs to the Spanish crown, and they traveled to the Peninsula in 1501 to be recognized as such by the councils of Castile and Aragón. Felipe returned almost immediately to the Low Countries, but Juana, who had been suffering for some time from paranoia manifested in manic bouts of jealousy, remained in Castile. Shortly thereafter, she was declared totally mad, and Queen Isabel intervened to assure that her husband would be regent of Castile until Juana's son Carlos should come of age. Nevertheless, when Isabel died (1504), Felipe returned to Spain and was declared king with his mad wife. Their reign lasted less than a year because the 29-year-old king died under mysterious circumstances in 1506, and the regency reverted immediately to Fernando. Juana spent the next three years in the Burgos area guarding the coffin of her husband, who, some claim, she believed would one day come back to life. Finally, in 1509 Fernando enclosed her in Tordesillas, where she lived under supervisory care for 46 years, always addressed as the queen of Castile and visited often by children and relatives she no longer recognized.

Work about

Altayó, Isabel, and Paloma Nogués. *Juana I: La reina cautiva*. N.p.: Silex, 1985.
Pfandl, Ludwig. *Juana la Loca*. Madrid: Espasa-Calpe, 1937.
Walters, D. Gareth. "The Queen of Castile and the Andalusian Spinster: Lorca's Elegies for Two Women; Essays in Honour of J.M. Aguirre."

Lorca: Poet and Playwright. Ed. Robert Havard. Cardiff: U of Wales, 1992. 9–30.

David H. Darst

Juan de la Cruz, San (1542–1591)

Universally acclaimed as the finest love poems in the Spanish language, the *liras* (Italianate verse form) of San Juan de la Cruz (St. John of the Cross) were composed during his imprisonment for nine months by the regular Carmelites in Toledo in 1577. According to tradition he committed them to paper only after his escape. In 1578 he wrote two book-length commentaries on the first two stanzas of "Noche oscura del alma" (Dark Night of the Soul), *Subida del monte Carmelo* (Ascent of Mount Carmel) and *Noche oscura*, as well as beginning his commentary on the "Canciones entre el alma y el Esposo" (Songs between the Soul and Her Bridegroom), the *Cántico espiritual* (Spiritual Canticle), to which he returned in 1584. In 1582 he began the *Llama de amor viva* (The Living Flame of Love), an explication of "Canciones que hace el alma en la íntima unión en Dios" (Songs of the Soul in Its Intimate Communion of Union with God's Love). The *Subida*, the *Noche*, and the *Llama* were published in 1618 in Alcalá de Henares. The *Cánctico espiritual*, more dangerous, because it is more directly based on Scripture as a retelling of the Song of Songs, was published in the French translation of M. René Gaultier in 1622; it was published in Spanish in Brussels in 1627. The first collection of Juan's *Obras* (Works) appeared in 1630 in Madrid. Juan was beatified in 1675, canonized in 1726, and declared a doctor of the Church in 1926; his Feast Day is December 14.

While his passionate verses celebrate the consummated love of the Bride and the Bridegroom, symbols of the Soul and Christ, his prose treatises explain the mystical ascent to God through the "negative way" of rejecting all sensory communications from God whether in the form of imaginary or intellectual visions, touches, and the like, for direct, substantial union with God. Schematizing the mystic ascent, Juan harmonized his mystic theology with the rational theology of St. Thomas Aquinas (1225–1274). Juan portrays the Bride in three moments: search and pursuit of the beloved in the first stanzas of "Noche oscura" and "Canciones entre el alma y el esposo," erotic union with the beloved in the last stanzas of the first poem, in the center of the "Canciones," and throughout the *heptasílabos* (seven-syllable lines) and *endecasílabos* (eleven-syllable lines) of the orgasmic "Llama de amor viva," and finally quiescence and enjoyment of each other's companionship in the last stanzas of the "Noche" and the "Cántico." The Bride is characterized by the single-mindedness of her search, by her freedom to move within her world, by her need of the other and her adoration of him, and by her jealous insistence upon the privacy of the two lovers. At the same time she exults in her ability to capture him through her beauty—her eyes and the single hair playing on her neck. The male beloved shares certain characteristics of the Bride—that is, exclusivity, freedom, need—but he appears superior to the Bride in the knowledge he promises to share with her at the end of the "Cántico." In the "Llama" the beloved plays the active penetrative role, while the Bride is the passive recipient of his touches. The conjunction of biblical imagery (lilies, wine cellars, nymphs of Judea, doves, pomegranates, the wedding bed, the wounded deer) as well as the titles of the poems indicate the divine identity of the Beloved. Nevertheless, Juan seldom allows the religious level to obtrude into his love poems except perhaps in the delicate allusion to Original Sin and the fallen Eve in "Cántico" stanza 28 (Sanlúcar manuscript) / stanza 23 (Jaén manuscript): Here Juan expresses his orthodox belief in the doctrine of the redemption of the soul through Christ's crucifixion on a cross that, according to tradition, was crafted from an apple tree. The final note of the poems is the transforming union of the Bride into the

Bridegroom in solitude. Christ assumes feminine characteristics after union as in his "giving his breast" to the Bride ("Cántico espiritual" stanza 18 Sanlúcar/ stanza 27 Jaén) and in possessing "interior wine cellars" into which he thrusts the Bride. The "high, hidden caves" of the "Cántico" where the Bridegroom enjoys with the Bride the "must of pomegranates" exemplifies the union of masculine and feminine symbols of prominence and interiority. The desired state is the union of Bride and Bridegroom, of female and male.

Juan's identification of the Bride as the soul and the Bridegroom as Christ is in harmony with the Judaic/Christian interpretation of the Bride both as creation and the community of believers (Israel or the Church) and the Bridegroom as God. Swietlicki traces Juan's theology to the Jewish mystical tradition of the Cabala. In this tradition the Shekhinah or emanations of the Godhead, which resulted in the created upper and lower worlds, are viewed as feminine; God separates the feminine from himself in order that he might be reunited with it. The marriage of masculine and feminine within the Godhead is mirrored in the marriage of male and female on the human scale; thus human marriage too is sacred. Pepin points out that Henri Bergson (1859–1941) and Edith Stein (1891–1942) follow Juan in holding that human marriage is merely a dim reflection of the divine marriage; the latter is primary, the former secondary. Aranguren points out that the sexual act is in itself a striving for the absolute, a position that Giles endorses. It should be pointed out that psychoanalysts of the rationalist school from Freud to Lacan to Kristeva relate mystic desire for union with God to unresolved oedipal desire, that is, to the lower world of instinct rather than to the higher plane of moral spirituality. For all three, mysticism is a return to a narcissistic infantile need that fantasizes a beneficent relation to God and adopts the neurotic societal belief in the virgin birth (*Marianism) and the union of son and father in Christ/God.

Most of Juan's commentators affirm the value of religion and, specifically, mysticism. Dombrowski argues the relevance of Juan's mystic marriage for the modern reader by attempting to demonstrate that Juan is a bipolar theist who equally values characteristics traditionally viewed as male and female attributes of the divine: reason and emotion, justice and mercy, power and love, strength and delicacy, immutability and receptivity. In the centrifugal movement of his poetry he sought a transcendent God; in its centripetal movement, he sought an immanent/personal God within the soul, occupying its very center. Dombrowski further argues that the mutual surrender of God and the soul indicates a bipolarism not present in traditional systematic mono-polar theology. Refusing Platonic mind/body dualism, Juan believed that as the soul informs the body, so the divine informs creation; God is other, but not an absolute other from the soul. Dombrowski labels Juan not a pantheist but a panentheist (all is *in* God). In Dombrowski's view Juan, by postulating both male and female characteristics of the divine, avoided masculine bias ultimately traceable to the Aristotelian precept that the male engenders while the female merely provides the nurturing womb for the seed.

Women played an important role in the life of Juan de Yepes y Álvarez: His mother, as an impoverished widow, had to raise her youngest son without help after his fifth year; St. *Teresa de Jesús (1515–1582) recruited him to found the male branch of the Discalced Carmelites in 1567; and many other women testified to his saintliness and served as transmitters of his writings. Today Carmelite nuns and numerous women within and outside the Catholic Church continue to practice his doctrine and to analyze his writings. Ismael Bengoechea has catalogued the many women San Juan knew as confessor in the Discalced convents of Encarnación de Avila (September 1572 to December 1577), Beas (October 1578 to March 1581), Granada (April 1581 to April 1588), and

Segovia (August 1588 to June 1591). Bengoechea also points out that the saint's two works that carry individual dedications were directed to women: Ana de Jesús (the *Cántico Espiritual*) and Ana de Peñalosa (*Llama de amor viva*). Eighty percent of San Juan's extant letters were directed to women. While he encountered hostility from many men, especially those within the regular Carmelites, the saint followed Christ's example in being universally acclaimed by women for his spiritual leadership. Isabel de Jesús was the recipient of what is believed to be the only copy of the *Cántico* in Juan's own hand. Juan fought against the jurisdictional separation of the Discalced nuns from the Carmelite order. Despite his proximity to women, all evidence indicates that he maintained an inviolate chastity of body and spirit, gently reprimanding women seeking physical favors from him or supernatural touches from God.

The perennial question of who led whom in the elucidation of Carmelite mysticism is answered in favor of San Juan de la Cruz by Bengoechea, following Crisógono and Efrén de la Madre de Dios and opposing Donázar, who affirmed St. Teresa's guidance. Most modern commentators admit their mutual influence. Bengoechea concedes that Juan did not question the subordinate position of women in the Church. He points out that although the Carmelite seldom used the word *mujer* (woman), preferring the generic use of *hombre* (man) to signify the human being, he held woman's soul equal in value to man's. In his writings he used biblical women including Sarah, Rachel, Ruth, Esther, Judith, Delilah, Sarah of Tobías, the women of Adonis and of Solomon, the daughters of Sion, Mary Magdalen, the Samaritan, and the Virgin Mary to exemplify positive aspects of the soul; Eve, the Babylonian woman and the daughters of Jerusalem are used to personify the soul's enslavement to the senses. Bengoechea rejects interpretations of Juan's traditional use of spousal imagery that would suggest feminization of his own psyche or of his idea of God or of the "manly" valor necessary for the ascetic life except to concede with Gertrudis von Le Fort that religious values tend to be feminine values. Juan liberates both men and women from worldly concerns to divine; he leads both to transform themselves into the beauty of God.

Bengoechea betrays an annoying priestly bias in his book. He consistently refers to women as "the weaker sex." He smugly points out that Juan named only two women as sources for his doctrine and that modern women usually confine themselves to practicing his doctrine or commenting on his literary skill without analyzing his theology. The Basque priest insists that Juan kept women in their place by guiding them without being guided by them. Bengoechea fails to explain that until very recently women were barred from the theological study that would permit them to criticize Juan's doctrine. Nevertheless, Bengoechea provides a useful account of the women in Juan's life, of the female mystics who have been influenced by him, and of the more conservative modern women who have written about him—that is, Edith Stein but not Gertrude Stein.

Work by

Asún, Raquel. *San Juan de la Cruz: Poesía completa y comentarios en prosa*. Barcelona: Planeta, 1989.

Kavanaugh, Kieran, and Otilio Rodríguez, trans. *The Collected Works of St. John of the Cross*. Washington, DC: Institute of Carmelite Studies, 1973.

Peers, E. Allison, trans. *The Complete Works of Saint John of the Cross*. 3 vols. Westminster, MD: Newman P, 1949.

Work about

Aranguren, José Luis L. *San Juan de la Cruz*. Madrid: Júcar, 1973.

Baruzi, Jean. *Saint Jean de la Croix et le problème de l'expérience mystique*. Paris: Libraire Félix Alcan, 1924.

Bengoechea, Ismael, OCD. *San Juan de la Cruz y la mujer*. Burgos: Monte Carmelo; Cádiz: Carmelitas Descalzos, 1986.

Crisógono de Jesús Sacramentado. *San Juan de la*

Cruz, su obra científica y su obra literaria. Avila: n.p., 1929.

Dombrowski, Daniel A. *St. John of the Cross: An Appreciation.* Albany: State U of New York P, 1992.

Duvivier, Roger. *Le Dynamisme existentiel dans la poésie de Jean de la Croix: Lecture du "Cántico espiritual."* Paris: Didier, 1973.

Efrén de la Madre de Dios, Padre. *Dos maestros y una misma doctrina.* Ubeda: Carmelo Teresiano, 1984.

Giles, Mary E. *The Poetics of Love: Meditations with John of the Cross.* New York: Peter Lang, 1986.

Kristeva, Julia. *In the Beginning Was Love: Psychoanalysis and Faith.* Trans. Arthur Goldhammer. New York: Columbia UP, 1987.

Mallory, Marilyn May. *Christian Mysticism: Transcending Techniques.* Amsterdam: Van Gorcum, 1977.

McInnis, Judy B. "Eucharistic and Conjugal Symbolism in *The Spiritual Canticle* of Saint John of the Cross." *Renascence: Essays on Values in Literature* 36.3 (Spring 1984): 118–138.

Pepin, F. *Noces de Feu: Le Symbolisme nuptial du "Cántico espiritual" de saint Jean de la Crois à la lumière du Canticum Canticorum.* Paris: Desclée de Brouwer, 1972.

Sanson, Henri. *El espíritu humano según San Juan de la Cruz.* Madrid: Rialp, 1962.

Swietlicki, Catherine. *Spanish Christian Cabala: The Works of Luis de León, Santa Teresa de Jesús, and San Juan de la Cruz.* Columbia: U of Missouri P, 1986.

Thompson, Colin. *El poeta y el místico.* Madrid: Swan, 1985.

Judy B. McInnis

Kent Siano, Victoria (1898–1987)

The first woman lawyer in Spain (April 30, 1925), as a jurist, Victoria Kent Siano was a disciple of Luis Jiménez de Asúa and became famous during the defense of participants of the 1930 Republican Jaca revolt against the monarchy. Before attending Madrid's Universidad Central, she studied at the Normal School in Málaga, earning a degree in education in 1916. In Madrid, she lived in the women's branch of the Residencia de Estudiantes and met the famous pedagogue María de *Maeztu (1882–1948), director of the institution. The two later collaborated on various projects.

Appointed General Deputy of Prisons during the Second Republic in 1931, Kent instituted reforms to humanize the prison system. She was elected to a seat in Parliament in 1931 and 1936 as a member of the Radical Socialist Party. During the Constitutional Courts she debated women's *suffrage with the Radical Party Member of Parliament Clara *Campoamor. Kent opposed immediate women's suffrage, reasoning that the lengthy oppression of women would prompt them to vote for conservative parties. Kent argued that a period of education was needed before granting women the right to vote. During Spain's Civil War she worked with refugees at the Spanish embassy in Paris and stayed there after the war. In 1940, when the Nazis occupied Paris, she took refuge in the Mexican embassy, escaping with the help of the Red Cross. Under the alias Mme. Duval she wrote Cuatro años en París (1947; Four Years in Paris). From France she moved to Mexico in 1948, then to New York in 1950, where she directed the magazine Ibérica (1954–1987). During her exile she worked as professor of penal law and also worked for the United Nations as a member of its social defense section (1951–1952). Kent remained a symbol of democratic Spain during her exile in the United States. She was a militant of ARDE (B.U.R.N.), short for the Acción Republicana Democrática de Lucha (Republican-Democratic Action for Struggle). She returned to Spain in 1977 for a visit and died in New York 10 years later.

Cuatro años en París narrates the life of a Spanish refugee, Plácido, in Nazi Paris. During the time he spends hiding from the police, constantly moving to avoid capture, he reflects on the concept of freedom, its meanings, and consequences. It is a very beautiful book, full of life and hope in spite of the protagonist's position, surrounded by a police state. *See also* Feminism in Spain: 1900–2000

Work by

Cuatro años de mi vida 1940–44. Barcelona: Bruguera, 1978. Also published as Cuatro años en París (1940–1944). Buenos Aires: Sur, 1947.

Work about

González Calbet, María Teresa. "Victoria Kent: Vida y obra." *Homenaje a Victoria Kent.* Ed. María Dolores Ramos. Málaga: U de Málaga, 1989. 17–29.

Rodrigo, Antonina. "Victoria Kent." *Mujeres para la historia. La España silenciada del siglo XX.* Madrid: Compañía Literaria, 1966. 215–239.

Telo Nuñez, María. *Concepción Arenal y Victoria Kent.* Madrid: Instituto de la Mujer, 1995.

Salvador A. Oropesa

Kharja

See Jarcha

Kurtz, Carmen, Pseudonym of Carmen de Rafael Marés de Kurz (1911–)

This novelist and short story writer for adults and children experienced an unusual upbringing for her time. Both of Carmen Kurtz's grandfathers immigrated to the United States, married Anglo-Saxon women, and eventually returned to Spain. The cosmopolitan nature of her family contributed to a broad intellectual base that is manifested in the heroines of her novels. In addition, because she was sickly as a child, she was forced to leave school and be educated at home by her father, who introduced her to the great treasures of children's literature. This experience played a significant role in her eventual decision to become a writer.

At age 15, Kurtz met her future husband, Pierre Kurz Klein, of French nationality. They married in July 1933 and left immediately for France, where she would remain until 1943. Because Kurtz did not experience firsthand the horrors of the Spanish Civil War, she has never devoted a major portion of her writing to this theme. Instead, her work focuses on Spain during the 1920s and early 1930s, then on the period following the war. Although she often writes about the impact of war, she does so from a social rather than a political point of view. She received the Premio Ciudad de Barcelona for her first novel, *Duermen bajo las aguas* (1954; They Sleep Beneath the Waters), a *Bildungsroman* that chronicles her personal experiences in France during World War II and concentrates on the heroine's loss of love and subsequent search for intimacy.

While Kurtz's focus is social realism, she does not identify with a particular style of writing. Her work reflects her independence as she experiments with varying novelistic structures and approaches. Many of her themes remain constant—criticism of society's hypocrisy and concern for the individual and the human condition. She often describes the typical activities of young women of her social class in the postwar period. Although sexuality was not discussed openly in Spain during this time, it nevertheless played an important part in the culture. Frequently veiled to avoid censorship, female sexuality figures prominently in all Kurtz's literary production.

In 1956, Kurtz received the coveted Premio Planeta award for *El desconocido* (The Stranger), the story of isolation and estrangement between husband and wife separated by his incarceration in Russia for 12 years. *La vieja ley* (1956; The Old Law) uses the fascinating technique of multiple narrators to depict the loneliness and misery of a young woman in Spain from the 1920s to the 1940s. *Detrás de la piedra* (1956; Behind the Rock) is a Kafkaesque tale of unjust imprisonment, based upon an actual event.

After the success of her early novels, Kurtz continued to write prodigiously during the 1960s, producing six novels and two collections of short stories. In *Al lado del hombre* (1961; Beside the Man), a girl experiences a coming of age through a train trip with a mysterious stranger. *En la oscuridad* (1963; In the Darkness) was a finalist for the Café Gijón prize, although it was never published. *El becerro de oro* (1964; The Golden Calf) deals with hypocrisy and society's extreme desire for money. Interestingly, *Las algas* (1966; Seaweed), which contrasts urban hypocrisy with the purity of the country, was written with two different endings. *En la punta de los dedos* (1968; At Your Fingertips) has an outspoken female nonagenarian as its protagonist and is sharply critical of provincial mores. *Entre dos oscuridades* (1969; Between Two Darknesses) again uses the technique of multiple points of view to discuss the meaning of life. Her short story collections are *El último camino* (1961; The Last Road), tales related to aging and death, and *Siete tiempos* (1964; Seven Times), dealing with war, love, and death.

Kurtz's major literary achievement of the 1970s was publication of her trilogy *Sic transit* (Thus Goes Glory), comprised of *Al otro lado del mar* (1973; Beyond the Sea), *El viaje* (1975; The Voyage), and *El regreso* (1976; The Return), which recounts the peregrinations of her ancestors. Additionally, she produced the prizewinning *Cándidas palomas* (1975; Innocent Doves), which contrasts life through the eyes of a budding adolescent and her summer companion, a middle-aged schoolteacher. She also translated several French novels during this period.

In addition, her children's stories began to be recognized; they have won numerous prizes, and several have become popular films. Prizewinning stories include *Oscar cosmonauta* (1963; Oscar the Cosmonaut), finalist for the Lazarillo prize and honorable mention for the Hans Christian Anderson prize; *Oscar espía atómica* (1964; Oscar the Atomic Spy), CCEI prize for children's literature; *Color de fuego* (1964; The Color of Fire), Lazarillo prize; *Oscar y corazón de púrpura* (1966; Oscar and the Purple Heart), CCEI prize finalist; *Oscar espeleólogo* (1967; Oscar the Spelunker), CCEI prize; *Oscar en Africa* (1978; Oscar in Africa), CCEI prize and Ministry of Culture prize for children's literature; *Oscar en las islas* (1978; Oscar in the Islands), CCEI prize finalist and Ministry of Culture prize for children's literature; and *Veva* (1981), CCEI prize. Stories made into films include *Violeta en el Oeste* (1971; Violet in the West), gold medal winner in the Gijón Children's Film Festival; *Violeta y los piratas* (Violet and the Pirates); *Violeta y el cuco* (Violet and the Bogeyman); *Violeta y los buscadores de oro* (Violet and the Gold Seekers); *Violeta y el vagabundo* (Violet and the Vagabond); and *Oscar, Kina y El Lasar* (1978; Oscar, Kina and the Lasar), gold medal winner in the Gijón Children's Film Festival. *See also* Short Fiction by Women Writers: 1900–1975

Work by

Las algas. Barcelona: Planeta, 1966.
Al otro lado del mar. (Sic transit I). Barcelona: Planeta, 1973.
El autor enjuicia su obra. Madrid: Nacional, 1966. 111–122.
El becerro de oro. Barcelona: Planeta, 1964.
Cándidas palomas. Barcelona: Brugera, 1975.
El desconocido. Barcelona: Planeta, 1956.
En la punta de los dedos. Barcelona: Planeta, 1968.
Entre dos oscuridades. Barcelona: Planeta, 1969.
El regreso. (Sic transit III). Barcelona: Planeta, 1976.
El viaje. (Sic transit II). Barcelona: Planeta, 1975.

Work about

Gordenstein, Roberta. "Carmen Kurtz's *El viaje* as Quest Narrative." *Monographic Review/Revista Monográfica* 12 (1996): 201–210.
———. "From Social Realism to Proto-Feminism: Carmen Kurtz's *El desconocido* as a Challenge to the Mores of Francoist Spain." *Monographic Review/Revista Monográfica* 13 (1997): 245–251.
———. "Interview with Carmen Kurtz." *Belles Lettres* 10.1 (October 1994): 42–46.
Iglesias Laguna, Antonio. *Treinta años de novela española (1938–1968)*. 2nd ed. Madrid: Prensa española, 1970. 1:241–246, 347–351.
Martínez Mena, Alfonso. "Carmen Kurtz: El viaje." *La Estafeta Literaria* 568, (July 22, 1975): n.p.
Myers, Eunice D. "Autotextuality and Intertextuality in *El desconocido* by Carmen Kurtz." *Hispania* 71.1 (March 1988): 43–49.
———. "Carmen Kurtz's Trilogy, *Sic transit*, as Fictional/Historical Record." *Confluencia* 13.2 (Spring 1998): 48–54.
———. "Four Female Novelists and Spanish Children's Fiction." *Letras femeninas* 10.2 (Fall 1984): 40–49.

Roberta Gordenstein

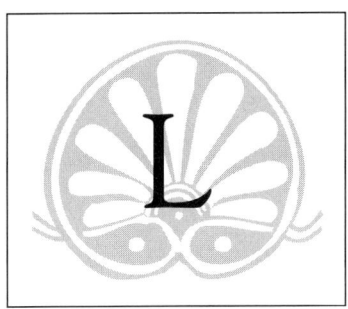

Laborda Medir, Clemencia (1908–1980)

Born in the Catalan city Lérida of a Cuban mother, Clemencia Laborda spent her childhood in Avila. Her father, a government lawyer, moved the family to Madrid during Clemencia's adolescence, and she lived there for the rest of her life. Somewhat isolated in the parental home, she read avidly from the Spanish classics to the Generations of 1898 and 1927, wrote poetry, plays, and some prose, and hosted literary *tertulias* (social gatherings). Her poetry appeared in the Madrid newspaper *ABC*, in poetry journals such as *Alma*, *Yedra*, *Piedralaves*, and *Poesía Hispánica*, and in Carmen *Conde's (1907–1996) anthology *Poesía femenina española viviente* (1954). The few books Laborda published are out of print and found only in select libraries.

Laborda's first book of poetry, *Jardines bajo la lluvia* (1943; Gardens under the Rain), earned her the praise of such critics as Joaquín de Entrambasaguas (1904–) and Dámaso Alonso (1898–1990). Noting her skill in the sonnet and her profound knowledge of sixteenth- and seventeenth-century Spanish classics, they found her poetry original yet within the classic equilibrium. The poems devoted to the lyricism of the garden are sonnets and *décimas* (stanzas of 10 eight-syllable lines) with specific reference to Gerardo Diego's poetry and to Debussy's music. In the central section, "Versos bobos" (Silly Verses), she moves in free verse toward the familiar ground of everyday events, objects, and people. With an innocent vision of her world she reveals postmen, street sweepers, toys, schoolgirls, and embroidery.

In Laborda's second book of poetry, *Ciudad de soledades* (1948; City of Solitudes), the poet creates a personal city of solitude in which she unveils her heart and releases her fantasy. The first poem, "Soledad en la estancia" (Solitude in the Sitting Room), expresses a desire to reveal the hidden soul of things. Then, at the center, furthering the spiritual intention of this work, she meditates on the advent of light in 10 *décimas* inspired by Gerardo Diego. Finally, speaking explicitly of her craft, Laborda remains the poet who "sees," even if her visions fade in the fog. Thus, she returns to the theme of embroidery as she stitches dreams to the urban mist so that others may see just as she did.

Laborda's next book of poetry, *Retorno a la provincia* (Return to the Province), based on memories and dreams of her childhood in Avila, was published in 1961 by the directors of Lírica Hispana of Caracas, Venezuela. Her recollections spring from nostalgia for her childhood and are constructed on the principle that the purity of things is seen through the filter of the age-old province of Avila.

The emblem of the centuries is a beggar woman, María Medalla, covered with aluminum medals "stabbed by the sun," forever in a corner of the poet's memory. Then in the poem "Desdoblamiento romántico" (Romantic Unfolding), Laborda's nostalgia becomes longing; she is caught in the conflict between soul and body. The split of the title, expressed in a series of antitheses, represents the struggle between the two forces driven by the dream of unifying them in resurrection.

In 1972 Laborda published *Tiempo del hombre, tiempo de Dios* (Time of Man, Time of God), whose title comprises the first two sections of this collection, complemented by two more sections on time to breathe and to remember. It is Laborda's most accomplished book in theme and conception as well as in the expression of her faith. Her purpose is to give her readers reasons to believe and hope. In this work she speaks with a new sense of proportion coupled with the abandonment of previous poetic art. A "resplendent humanity" rises up in rebellion, eager to change the world, quite unlike, Laborda says, the deified "I" in the poetry of Juan Ramón *Jiménez (1881–1958). Alternating classical forms and free verse, she has modernized her themes here—from preoccupation with metaphysical and spiritual concerns to interplanetary travel, the family, as well as the wave of physical and moral corruption that surrounded life as she saw it. Beginning with the theme of time as denominator of all, Laborda deals with anguish, hope, reality, and oppressive conformity in terms of the present day. At the same time she shows sensitivity to the changes occurring in the twentieth century, such as the "weightless ascension" of the first astronaut to reach the moon.

In 1943, Dámaso Alonso wrote of his hopes for Laborda's future; he wondered if, with such accomplished technical skill, fantasy, and passion, she would really face poetry as one must face God. In *Tiempo del hombre, tiempo de Dios*, she surpassed her earlier work and confronted new poetical themes and forms. In the final section, "Tiempo para recordar" (Time to Remember), she contemplates the figure of the God on several levels. He is a force who is always with us even in dreams, and when we awaken, we feel a "living absence, hearts beating." Laborda closes this book on a note of universal dignity, synthesis and return. In a sonnet titled "Tiempo último" (Last Time) she presents God the father, approaching to receive us all as brothers and sisters, when pain can no longer destroy us.

The only other work Laborda published was a play, *La sacristía* (The Sacristy), staged in Madrid's Teatro María Guerrero in April 1953. Before her death she had announced publication of several poetry collections such as "Caudal" (Wealth) and "Niños y jardines" (Children and Gardens), but these and other books of poetry as well as plays and novels remain unpublished in her parental home now occupied by Laborda's only surviving sister.

Work by

Ciudad de soledades. Madrid: J. Romo Arregui, 1948.
Jardines bajo la lluvia. Madrid: Afrodisio Aguado, 1943.
Retorno a la provincia. Caracas: Lírica Hispana, 1961.
La sacristía. Madrid: ALFIL, 1957.
Tiempo del hombre, tiempo de Dios. Madrid: n.p., 1972.

Work about

Galerstein, Carolyn L., and Kathleen McNerney, eds. *Women Writers of Spain: An Annotated Bio-Bibliographic Sourcebook*. Westport, CT: Greenwood, 1986.
Pérez, Janet. *Modern and Contemporary Spanish Women Poets*. New York: Twayne, 1996.

Glenn Morocco

Lacaci, María Elvira (1928–1997)

Born in El Ferrol, Galicia, María Elvira Lacaci moved to Madrid in 1952. Wife of the surrealist filmmaker and novelist Luis Buñuel, she published four collections of poetry, most in the 1960s, winning the Adonais

Prize for her first collection, *Humana voz* (1957; Human Voice).

Lacaci is most often considered a minor member of the social realist movement of postwar Spain. Her poems focus as sharply on the problems of poverty, homelessness, and despair as any of the time. However, she writes from a deeply spiritual viewpoint that separates her from the existential searching and vehement criticism of her contemporaries. Her chosen audience is the entire population of Spain, rich and poor, educated and illiterate, and she uses colloquial language and free verse over stylistic metaphors and structures, favoring accessibility over a high literary style.

In ordinary settings, in everyday situations, Lacaci converses with God about experiences near to her and common to all: birth and death, separation and reunion, joy and suffering. She asks why pain and sorrow must exist but never doubts the guiding presence of God, leading humanity to something better. In her later collections a separation evolves, with poems that are more exclusively critical of social ills next to more focused explorations of her relationship with God on a personal level, as a woman in a ravaged and recovering land and as a representative of humanity.

Work by

Al este de la ciudad. Barcelona: Juan Flors, 1963.
Humana voz. Madrid: Rialp, 1957.
Molinillo de papel. Madrid: Nacional, 1968.
Sonido de Dios. Madrid: Rialp, 1962.

Shannon W. Sudderth

Lacasa, Cristina (1929–)

A University of Barcelona graduate with a degree in psychology, Cristina Lacasa has published poetry collections and short stories, collaborated in journals and magazines, and been awarded several literary prizes. In "Mapa natal" (1964; Natal Map, from *Con el sudor alzado* [With Raised Sweat]) we learn that Lacasa was born under the sign of Taurus. Like the bull, Lacasa approaches life with pride and, like the bull, loses the battle against time and death. The allusion to immolation in the Taurus sign (as in the myth of Mithras and in the Spanish bullfight) is also suggested by the poet's own name, Cristina (feminine form of Cristo or Christ), who as a woman wonders if her destiny may be to exchange Eve's apple of the Fall for the rainbow of redemption. This early attention to the meaning of her name marks Lacasa's poetry with a sense of mission.

Her early works such as *La voz oculta* (1953; The Hidden Voice) echo the Platonic view of romantic poets like Gustavo Adolfo *Bécquer (1836–1870). For the young poet, the world, particularly as it encompasses modern technology and urbanization, is a space of confusion where she seeks the light of salvation in the sun, her "Platonic lover," but is constantly disappointed because it is unreachable. When she looks into water for answers, its reflections frustrate her attempt to reach the light. As the seven stanzas of "Soy" (I Exist) indicate, the speaker perceives herself as a minute, insignificant being with no control over her life. The four sections of *Los brazos en estela* (1958; Arms in Wake) trace the speaker's personal and artistic journey, beginning with "The Lily," symbolizing the purity of childhood, "The Quest," "The Wound," and "The Cross." As her name Cristina signals, she models her womanly and poetic quest on Christ's passion on the cross, where the lily joins the thorns of cruelty and Christ's healing hands are punctured by nails. Lacasa's poetic speaker views life and writing as balancing acts between life and death. The sense of Christian mission takes a social direction in *Con el sudor alzado*. Due to oppressive working conditions, the Eucharistic meaning of *bread* is lost because earning it implies the exploitation of human lives. While she champions social justice, the poet feels imprisoned within "the hermetic capsule of the letters." However, she persists in her social denunciation. In the much denser and longer poems of *Encender los olivos como lámparas* (1969; Lighting Olive Trees Like Lamps), she opposes greedy capitalism and war while trying to establish what she calls "the structures for Harmony."

In a later poetry collection, *En un plural designio* (1983; In a Plural Design), the speaker's mission for peace and justice fuses with a call to respect the world's diversity. This book is dedicated to all the children who do not enjoy the most essential human rights. The poems in *Ramas de la esperanza (Poemas ecológicos)* (1984; Branches of Hope [Ecological Poems]) focus on ecology in a language that mixes baroque elements with terms from the sciences, astrology, and a sort of new-wave thinking. In *Opalos del instante* (1982; Opals of the Instant), the speaker readdresses her concerns to the cosmic level, as was characteristic of her earlier poetry. Faced with temporal destruction, she concentrates on the instant as an "opal," an iridescent, rainbowlike gem in which all life-filled connotations of the sun are represented. In her search for wholeness, she revisits her childhood, the paradisiacal moment when the eyes/lips open to the purity of all colors. The sea is perhaps the major presence in the speaker's life, for the water's constant movement replicates her tenacious hope that things will return, that nothing ends completely. The sensorial dialogue with the surrounding world filtered through the speaker's heart finds a balance in her blood and tongue, that is, in her word. However, in this search for wholeness, the speaker, a middle-aged woman, realizes that her possibilities are limited. If in her earlier experience social repression reduced her voice to a "whisper," her words now lie protected among leaves of a book that almost no one will ever read. As she explains in "The Poet," she is "the" generic poet merely surviving in the Third World. While she would like to alleviate the suffering of the oppressed and open human horizons to other levels of existence, her voice is not heard because her paradigms do not conform to the rigid rules of the world. The poet lacks status in the socioeconomic world.

Pleamar del silencio (1990; Hightide of Silence) is dedicated to her parents. Vicente, the father, appears as the ultimate provider of safety and love, while María, the mother, is an all-sensorial creature in communion with surrounding nature. Identified mostly by her singing, the mother is the voice of nature, which the speaker wants to recapture. The meeting of both parents is seen as an epiphany, a confluence of two stars in the cosmos. Being TWO, her parents lived as ONE; hence, they represent the unity and wholeness that Lacasa has sought throughout her writings. *See also* Short Fiction by Women Writers: 1900–1975

Work by

Antología poética 1953–1976. Lérida: Instituto de Estudios Ilerdenses, 1977.
Los caballos sin brida. Lérida: Dilagro, 1981.
En el centro del arco iris. Relatos. Lleida: Larrosa, 1986.
En un plural designio. Cuenca: Col. El toro de barro, 1983.
Jinetes sin caballo. Barcelona: Ambito literario, 1979.
Mientras crecen las aguas (Antología poética 1953–1976). Lérida: Instituto de Estudios Ilerdenses, 1977.
Opalos del instante. Madrid: Adonais, 1982.
Pleamar del silencio. Madrid: Torremozas, 1990.
Ramas de la esperanza (Poemas ecológicos). Lérida: Dilagro, 1984.
Sin lastre en la cascada (Tres laderas de un pálpito). Lérida: Dilagro, 1995.
El viaje. Málaga: Col. Corona del Sur, 1981.

Candelas Gala

Lafitte y Pérez del Pulgar, María de los Reyes

See Campo Alange, Condesa de (1902–1986)

Laforet, Carmen (1921–)

Best known for her internationally acclaimed novel *Nada* (1945; Nothing, trans. as *Andrea*, 1964), Carmen Laforet was the first Spanish woman novelist to achieve wide public recognition after the Spanish Civil War. Author of four novels, numerous novellas and short stories, a collection of travel notes, and collaborations in various Spanish newspapers and magazines, this more productive than generally recognized writer was born in Barcelona on September 6, 1921, to a middle-class, professional, and artistically inclined family.

Laforet's tranquil childhood and adolescent years were quite different from those of many of her contemporaries. When Laforet was still a child her father, an architect, and her mother, a trained schoolteacher, moved to Las Palmas, in the Canary Islands; thus Laforet did not directly experience the tumultuous years of the de Rivera dictatorship, the Second Republic, and the Civil War (1923–1939). However, a somber event of these formative years that was to deeply mark Laforet both personally and creatively was the untimely death of her mother in 1934. This is evidenced in the author's work by a recurrent figure, that of the orphaned adolescent. Also of capital importance is Laforet's return to Barcelona in 1939 to pursue university studies. It was not until then that she observed firsthand the disastrous effects of the war. Due to this, Laforet's unique perspective on the national conflict was one of both outsider and insider, a position that is crucial to understanding her narrative.

During her three-year stay in Barcelona, Laforet began her literary career with several short stories published in local journals. These publications, however, have been lost; her first novel, *Nada*, written shortly after Laforet's move to Madrid, is the first extant record of her work. Laforet finished the novel at age 22, and at the urging of the man whom she would later marry in 1946, journalist and literary critic Manuel Cerezales, she sent the manuscript to a newly announced literary competition, the Nadal Prize, sponsored by Destino Publishing. Not only did Destino publish the novel; in 1945 *Nada* was named the first winner of the now-coveted Nadal Prize as well as the prestigious Fastenrath Prize awarded by the Real Academia Española.

Nada, one of the key novels initiating the resurgence of Spanish literature after the Civil War, is a first-person narration in which the older, more mature narrator-protagonist recounts her experiences and search for identity as an orphaned and convent-educated 18-year-old who arrives for a year's stay in war-ravaged Barcelona to pursue university studies while living with her emotionally disturbed relatives. Many of the principal thematic elements of this novel, such as the study of adolescent psychology, the rites of passage to self-identity, the fulfillment of artistic vocation, the limitations of women's roles, and the harsh realities of civil war and Francoist Spain, form the base of Laforet's future narrative.

Laforet's second novel did not appear until seven years later. Unaccustomed to the fame generated by *Nada*'s positive critical and public reception, Laforet did not write for the first three of these years. During the ensuing years she broke her writer's block by composing articles and short stories, the latter of which were published in a collection entitled *La muerta* (1952; The Dead Woman). However, the fact that Laforet was able to create at all, considering the responsibilities of a traditional marriage and the birth of four of her five children by 1952, is a testament to her struggle to fulfill her artistic vocation.

The theme of the growth of artistic vocation is in fact one of the central elements of the second novel, *La isla y los demonios* (1952; The Island and the Devils). Set in the Canary Islands during the Civil War, this novel is similar in many respects to *Nada*. Laforet again explores the maturation and experiences of an orphaned adolescent girl, Marta, living in isolation with an odd assortment of relatives who contribute to her disillusionment. Unlike Andrea in *Nada*, however, Marta is aware of her literary vocation and consciously strives to develop it in her journal, poems, and legends of Canary folklore. Ultimately, this third-person narration links maturation to the sacrifice of artistic vocation as Marta burns her manuscripts before leaving for the mainland at the novel's end.

In 1951 Laforet experienced a religious crisis that led to an intensive seven-year spiritual search. One of the fruits of this journey was her third novel, *La mujer nueva* (1955; The New Woman), winner of the Menorca Prize. The work focuses on the mystical experience of an adult, married woman, Paulina (whose name echoes that of Saint Paul), who must confront the moral choices resulting from her religious conversion. Set during the decades framing the Civil War, the protagonist's search for self-fulfillment leads her from the relative freedom of her youth during the Second Republic (the early 1930s) to the social, political, and religious limitations imposed on women during the Franco regime.

Laforet's last published novel, *La insolación* (1963; Sunstroke), was originally to form part of a trilogy entitled "Tres pasos fuera del tiempo" (Three Steps out of Time), the second volume of which, *Jaque mate* (Checkmate), remains in galley proofs. Set in the 1940s, *La insolación* is the only long novel by Laforet to feature a male protagonist, Martín. Yet the primary themes that spring from young Martín's relationships with his father, stepmother, and two adolescent neighbors during the three successive summers spent at a resort town are constants of Laforet's narrative: personal and artistic maturation amid the desolate social and political realities of postwar Spain.

Laforet's collections of short fiction employ a variety of themes, many of which appear in her novels, such as unfulfilled artistic vocation ("Rosamundo" [Rosamond], "La llamada" [The Call]), the desire for independence ("El piano" [The Piano]), Christian charity ("El aguinaldo" [The Christmas Bonus], "El último veraneo" [The Last Summer Vacation]), and the horrors of the Spanish Civil War ("El viaje divertido" [The Entertaining Trip], "Los emplazados" [The Summoned]). Although Laforet often focuses on feminine psychology and the limitations of women's roles ("Un noviazgo" [An Engagement]), she is rarely overtly feminist in her approach. Despite the fact that Laforet has not published in several decades, her work remains nonetheless an important component of postwar Spanish literature. *See also* Fairy Tales in Novels by Spanish Women; Short Fiction by Women Writers: 1900–1975

Work by

Andrea. Trans. Charles Payne. New York: Vantage, 1964.
La insolación. Barcelona: Planeta, 1963.
Mis artículos literarios. Eastbourne: Stuart-Spencer, 1977.
La niña y otros relatos. Madrid: Magisterio Español, 1970.
Novelas I. Barcelona: Planeta, 1957.
Paralelo 35. Barcelona: Planeta, 1967.

Work about

Dolgin Casado, Stacey. "Structure as Meaning in Carmen Laforet's *Nada*: A Case of Self-Censorship." *Studies in Honor of Gilberto Paolini.* Newark, DE: Juan de la Cuesta, 1996. 351–358.
Johnson, Roberta. *Carmen Laforet.* Boston: Twayne, 1981.
Jones, Margaret. "Dialectical Movement as Feminist Technique in the Works of Carmen Laforet." *Studies in Honor of Gerald E. Wade.* Madrid: José Porrúa Turanzas, 1979. 109–120.
McGibbony, Donna Janine. "Paternal Absence and Maternal Repression: The Search for Narrative Authority in Carmen Laforet's *Nada*." *Romance Languages Annual* 6 (1994): 519–524.
Nichols, Geraldine. *Escribir, espacio propio: Laforet, Matute, Moix, Tusquets, Riera y Roig por sí mismas.* Minneapolis: Institute for the Study of Ideologies and Literature, 1989.
Pérez, Janet. "Carmen Laforet." *Contemporary Women Writers of Spain.* Boston: Twayne, 1988.
Pérez Firmat, Gustavo. "Carmen Laforet: The Dilemma of Artistic Vocation." *Women Writers of Contemporary Spain.* Ed. Joan L. Brown. Newark: U of Delaware P, 1991. 26–41.

Kathleen Thompson-Casado

Lagos, Concha (1913–)

Although she has also written theater, prose, and short stories that have been translated into most major foreign languages, Concha Lagos is best known for her poetry. She has written for newspapers and founded and directed the literary journal *Cuadernos de Agora* (1956–1964), the "Agora" poetry collection, and the literary gathering "Fridays at Agora." She is a member of the Royal Academy of her native Córdoba in southern Spain. Her experiences in France and Galicia during the Spanish Civil War are collected in her novel *El pantano* (1954; The Swamp). Also from 1954 is her poetry collection *Balcón* (Balcony). Placed at the balcony window between the outside and the inside, Lagos's speaker rejects society's falsity and turns toward her inner being, following the mystical path of Arabic Sufism (from her native Córdoba) and of Santa *Teresa (1515–1582) and San *Juan de la Cruz (1542–1591), two of her favorite authors. In *Los obstáculos* (1955; The Obstacles), the inner/outer disparity reveals language's failure to coincide with experience. In *El corazón cansado* (1957; The Tired Heart), she admits that as a poet she can "unfold" words in order to make them mean something unexpected, only to find that they have already been used. Popular songs alone recover emotional truth in words. *Arroyo claro* (1958; Clear Stream), *Canciones desde la barca* (1962; Songs from the Boat), *La paloma* (1982; The Dove), and *En la rueda del viento* (1985; In the Wheel of the Wind) are collections of songs/poems whose philosophical tone about life, death, and love recalls the Deep Song compositions (the most authentic form of flamenco). *Agua de Dios* (1958; The Water of God) and *Para empezar* (1963; In Order to Begin) seek to recapture childhood through a language devoid of the false trappings of modern civilization. This world of greed is for Lagos another *Gótico florido* (Ornate Gothic, unpublished collection), the Renaissance style with which it shares an excessive surface decoration. In *La soledad de siempre* (1958; The Usual Loneliness), falsity and emptiness mark history and language since time devours their life/meaning. The speaker seeks a way out of her loneliness in love, as in *Luna de enero* (1960; January Moon). She appears to accept male expectations about women's passivity and submission, although she actively portrays it in her writings.

Golpeando el silencio (1961; Knocking on Silence) contains a series of elegies to childhood while the poet is surrounded by an unjust world. She feels impotent to do anything because, as she asserts sarcastically, the men in charge know so much more. Writing socially committed poetry is not the solution, as it was for most Spanish poets in the 1950s and 1960s, for reporting on reality does not assure the sincerity of the poem. To counteract social evils, Lagos offers the rose as the purest symbol of poetry and beauty. *Los anales* (1976; The Annals) and *Diario de un hombre* (1970; Diary of a Man) seek to retain time by recording it in language. However, language proves elusive because it is not owned, just temporarily loaned. The sense of being outside the enclosing experience of modern life becomes in *El cerco* (1971; The Fence) a question of identity. The poet seeks a language of ontological affirmation, as exemplified by Don Quijote whom, in *La aventura* (1973; The Adventure), she joins against the modern giants of fraud. In *Fragmentos en espiral desde el pozo* (1974; Spiraling Fragments from the Well), the speaker leaves the world to find truth in her inner being. But as "spiraling fragments," these poems move from mystery to revelation to mystery again. *Teoría de la inseguridad* (1981; Theory of Insecurity) refers to the elusiveness of meaning. Uncertainty is already lodged in words because their material nature distances them from experience. Lagos is openly critical of some misogynistic authors, of St. Paul, Baltasar Gracián, and Fray Luis de *León's (1527–1591) *The Perfect Wife*, an ideal Lagos unashamedly confesses she is not and never will be. Lagos moves away from her earlier acceptance of female passivity and asserts her dissension with the social order.

In *Elegías para un album* (1982; Elegies for an Album) and *Con el arco a punto* (1984; With the Bow Ready), although the speaker wants to return to childhood through the pictures in the album and the words on the page, they prove to be useless reproductions of the reality they purport to re-create. *Más allá de la soledad* (1984; Beyond Loneliness) pursues themes of loneliness and the quest toward the light of understanding, as does *Segunda trilogía* (1986; Second Trilogy). In these poetic monologues, writing is a pilgrimage of suffering that echoes San *Juan de la Cruz's mystical quest. The poem is the poet's cross of agony between faith and doubt, hope and despair. The 10-line stanzas and sonnets of *El telar* (1988; The Loom) weave words toward the elucidation of existential mystery.

Lagos's prose works *Cuando llegue el silencio* (1988; When Silence Arrives) and *Monólogo a contratiempo* (1994; Monologue in Syncopated Time) are "offbeat" monologues that dismantle conventional beliefs, such as the romantic notions fed to women throughout history. For the poet, love is an enchantment, and history and life are theatrical masquerades. Lagos's Platonic perspective views life as a process of increasing distancing from original perfection. Time masks truth and turns life into a labyrinthine series of Dantean circles of pain and ignorance.

Work by

Al Sur del recuerdo. Madrid: Agora, 1955.
Antología 1954–1976. Ed. Emilio Miró. Barcelona: Plaza & Janés, 1976.
Carta para después. Málaga: Cuadernos de María Victoria, 1957.
Con el arco a punto. Madrid: Colección de poesía Ibn Zaydún No. 1, 1984.
Cuando llegue el silencio (Prosas con música de fondo y un solo de laúd cada vez más lejano). Alicante: Sinaya, 1988.
Elegías para un album. Madrid: Gráficas orbe, 1982.
En la rueda del viento. Madrid: Susaeta, 1985.
Más allá de la soledad. Alicante: Sinhaya, 1984.
Monólogo a contratiempo. Córdoba: Albaida, 1994.
La paloma. Sinhaya: Alicante, 1982.
Por las ramas. Barcelona: Resurgimiento, 1980.
Segunda trilogía. Alicante: Sinhaya, 1986.
El telar. Alicante: Gráficas Díaz, 1988.
Teoría de la inseguridad. Madrid: Gran, Vía 43, 1981.

Candelas Gala

Larra, Mariano José de (1809–1837): Women in His Works

A Spanish writer best known for his *artículos de costumbres*, short sketches that ridicule contemporary types and expose social problems, as a satirist, Mariano José de Larra's works have from the beginning a strong misogynistic bent. This tendency is further enhanced by the author's gradual adoption of a romantic perspective endowing the feminine with either absolute value or blame. These views, taken with Larra's suicide, have at times confused the boundaries between life and art, creating a legend in which women play a pivotal role: the mother who ignored him, the grandmother who fostered his early education, his first love—an older woman who was his father's mistress, Pepita, the wife he married at too early an age, and the young daughter who found her father's body. Ironically, most of these notions owe their popular acceptance to a woman, Carmen de *Burgos (1867–1932). Her *"Fígaro" (Revelaciones, "Ella" descubierta, epistolario inédito)* (1919), relying on doubtful evidence and a vivid imagination, especially blames Dolores Armijo's rejection of Larra for the writer's untimely death, a perspective since embraced by many critics. In fairness to de Burgos, as a woman struggling on her own in early-twentieth-century Madrid, she was forced to publish much and quickly merely to survive.

Of course, Larra, too, wrote to survive, producing, besides his more creative essays, reviews that proffer observations on the actresses and opera singers of the day: Judith Grissi, Concepción Rodríguez, Matilde Díez, and others. Larra also had a female public; the implied reader in some of his articles is feminine, while the pieces published in *El correo de las damas* (1833), though few and superficial, reveal nascent consciousness of a growing body of women readers. Finally, during this period of civil strife, Larra's political articles defend the rights of two specific women—Queen Regent María Cristina and the young Isabel II—against claims made by Don Carlos.

As for women in Larra's literary works, they are almost entirely absent from his first periodical, *El Duende Satírico del Día* (1828; The Satirical Goblin of the Day). But his second publication, *El Pobrecito Hablador* (1832–1833; The Poor Chatterer) offers an abundance of female characters, almost all of them negative. This attitude reveals Larra's debt to the previous century. As *Martín Gaite explains in her *Usos amorosos del dieciocho en España*, whereas previously there existed a strict separation between the sexes, a lady of the upper and, more and more, the middle classes was now expected to take an active part in society. She was supposed to dress elegantly, know how to sing and dance, and carry on polite conversation. Instead of fleeing contact with men for fear of harming her reputation, a woman would lose prestige if she did not have a *cortejo*, a male companion other than her husband.

This freedom concerned both conservative moralists and enlightened thinkers as they questioned woman's ability to fulfill her duties as daughter, wife, and mother. In the first third of the nineteenth century, Larra still grappled with these issues. Braulio's wife, from "El castellano viejo" (The Old Castilian Man), attempts an elegant dinner party but completely lacks social graces. In "El casarse pronto y mal" (An Early, Bad Marriage), the narrator's "modern" sister rejects Spanish tradition for French innovations, giving her son such a poor upbringing that disaster must follow. Elena, the unfaithful wife of the same article, has received an elegant education—she can sing and flirt quite nicely and will in the end escape with her *cortejo*—but she cannot run a house or, by implication, raise her children. The lascivious women of "El mundo todo es máscaras" (The World Is All Masks) flock to masked balls, first popularized during the eighteenth century, because they afford an easy escape for wives and daughters. Throughout *El Pobrecito Hablador*, even the minor female characters show a lack of morals reminiscent of Goya's *Caprichos* (1799).

But, like Goya, Larra decries male faults as well. In "El casarse pronto y mal," Augusto's gambling contributes to the family's misfortunes, the nephew in "Empeños y desempeños" (Pawning and Redeeming) cheats a friend, and Braulio, whilst proclaiming himself a simple man, places unfair demands on his wife. In *El Pobrecito Hablador*, both men and women appear corrupt, as Larra maintains the balanced perspective advocated by the Enlightenment.

In Larra's later works, woman becomes increasingly culpable; the previous discussion of her new social freedom evolves into a Romantic topos of betrayal as Larra uses a lover's infidelity to express disillusionment. Larra's emotions often cloud the articles written toward the end of his life. The review of Dumas's *Antony* (1836) reveals some of the hypocrisies in his private affairs, while his passionate admiration for *Los amantes de Teruel* (1837; The Lovers from Teruel) could lend credence to the belief that Larra did indeed kill himself for love.

But in "La Nochebuena de 1836" (1836; Christmas Eve 1836), a work often read as a kind of suicide note, Larra does confront the question of blame. Ultimately, Larra uncovers another sort of "romantic fallacy"; the male "I" created this feminine ideal, and he, not "she," must bear whatever disappointments may ensue.

Work by

Obras. Ed. Carlos Seco Serrano. 4 vols. BAE 127. Madrid: Atlas, 1960.

Work about

Burgos, Carmen de. *"Fígaro" (Revelaciones, "Ella" descubierta, epistolario inédito)*. Madrid: "Alrededor del Mundo," 1919.

Kirkpatrick, Susan. "Liberal Romanticism and the

Female Protagonist in *Macías*." *Romance Quarterly* 35.1 (February 1988): 51–58.

——— "La retórica de la familia en el discurso liberal: Larra ante *Anthony*." *Texto y sociedad: Problemas de la historia literaria.* Ed. Bridget Aldaraca, Edward Baker, and John Beverly. Amsterdam: Rodopi, 1990. 193–201.

——— *Las Románticas: Women Writers and Subjectivity in Spain, 1835–1850.* Berkeley: U of California P, 1989.

Lorenzo Rivero, Luis. "La mujer en los artículos y cartas de Larra" and "Tipos femininos satirizados por Larra." *Estudios literarios sobre Mariano José de Larra.* Madrid: Porrúa, 1986.

Martín Gaite, Carmen. *Usos amorosos del dieciocho en España.* Barcelona: Anagrama, 1987.

Jennifer Rae Krato

Lebrija, Francisca de
See Nebrija, Francisca de (sixteenth century)

León, Fray Luis de (1527–1591)
Around 1571, Fray Luis de León translated the Song of Songs to Spanish for Madre Isabel Osorio of the Salamancan convent of Sancti Spiritus. His translation and commentary recognized the Songs' highly charged eroticism and emphasized their literal as much as their allegorical level; the work led to a five-year stint in the Inquisition's prisons. He dedicated La *perfecta casada* (1583; The Perfect Wife) to his niece, María Varela Osorio. In 1583 he also undertook publication of *Teresa de Jesus's (1515–1582) complete works except for her *Commentary* on the Song of Songs. In his prologue to that privately circulated commentary, León recognizes that the Holy Spirit might speak even through an uneducated woman, but he reminds his readers that women are not to teach but to be taught. In a carefully argued *Apología* and in a "Carta Dedicatoria" to the Prioress Ana de Jesús he defends publication of Teresa's other mystical works; both documents recognize Teresa as a teacher and assume the nun's literacy. Nevertheless, critics from Oñate to Acereda concur with Cruz's and Yamuri's view that the friar, despite his obvious empathy for women, regarded them as physically, morally, and intellectually inferior to men.

La perfecta casada, based on Proverbs XXXI, combines Ptolemaic astronomy, Platonic harmony, Aristotelian psychology, and biblical authority to place woman below man in the hierarchy of being. Responsible for Original Sin, she must work twice as hard as man to achieve outstanding virtue, for woman, unlike man, cannot be of "average virtue." León divides women into the good and the bad, then praises the former and condemns the latter. He defines not merely her virtue but her very essence by her chastity in accordance with the view of woman as receptacle of male *honor.

León perceives woman as ruled by coldness and wetness, hence less capable of thought and action than man. She may attain perfection by following the biblical precepts for virtuous conduct, which include obeying her husband and overcoming her endemic jealousy, pride, and disloyalty. León dispenses the praise of *mujer varonil* (honorary man) to the wife who fulfills his precepts. His complementary spheres of activity make man responsible for gaining the estate that woman guards and preserves. She operates within the private sphere, he within the public. León attacks the use of *cosmetics and luxurious dress as inappropriate means of women's attracting attention.

León advises the wife to have few children so that she can personally nurse and educate them. Critic Foulché-Delbosc points out that León mirrored Luis *Vives's (1492–1540) amazement that a woman would want children because they only bring work and anxiety. Oñate contrasts Vives's recommendations for women's education with León's silence on the subject. León's "perfect wife" accords more with modern ideas of maternity than does Vives's spartan wife/mother. Vives urged the woman to suppress all tender feelings toward her child to instill stoic independence. León emphasizes the gentle, loving character of the wife/mother who brings peace, harmony, and material well-being to her home.

A few critics in recent years have sought to revise feminists' negative view of *La perfecta casada*. Sánchez Zamarreño argues that the work, organized more as an aesthetic than as a moral *discurso panegírico* (panegyric discourse), shows the perfect wife's unusual accomplishment. Jones, following Errazuriz, points out that the harmony of León's universe depends upon woman assuming her place in the hierarchy of being. Jones argues that León upholds the perfection of the divine image in man, woman, and marriage, a blessed state established in Eden. These critics overlook León's consistent association of women and Original Sin in the treatise and throughout his works. Guy observes that in the *Commentary on Job* (finished in 1591 and published in 1779) a somewhat ambivalent León holds constitutionally weak woman responsible for the Fall while praising the beauty of Job's daughters. Nevertheless, Diez Borque's comparison of *La perfecta casada* with such handbooks as Fray Miguel Agustín's *Libro de los secretos de la agricultura, casa de campo y pastoril* (Zaragoza: Pascual Bueno, 1625) confirms León's greater liberalism. The puritanical and prescriptive Agustín prohibits diversions from dancing to plays and instructs the woman on the posture she should assume even while sleeping.

In his exegesis of the Song of Songs (not published until 1798) León privileges the married state: The literal level recounts Solomon's love for his bride, while the allegorical levels figure Christ's love for the Church and the Soul. Solomon's bride searches for the beloved in the countryside and in the city; she unites with him in an erotic abandonment seldom described in sixteenth-century Spain. Identifying with the female, Fray Luis advocates a submission of the wife/soul to the husband/Christ more radical than that of the *perfecta casada*. He posits a virtual obliteration of the feminine by the masculine, as the soul is transformed into God. The eroticism that León struggled to extirpate in his original poetry where the persona was more closely tied to his own personality could be released in the explanation of verses that not he but the Holy Spirit had dictated. León translated the Song of Songs not once but twice, into both *octavas reales* (stanzas of 8 hendecasyllables) and *liras* (7- and 11-syllable lines), then supplied a verse-by-verse exegesis noted for its sensitivity to the earthly beloved's passion. The priest's puritanism occasionally interfered with his explanation. Cuevas points out that León objected to the Vulgate's rendering of Hebrew *zama* as female pudenda rather than as hair (the Hebrew word admits both meanings) because of the subjective criterion that the Holy Spirit would not inspire a writer to use "dishonest" phrases. León's exegesis exacerbates the tension between the vibrant image of the acting present female on the literal level with her absorption into the male on the allegorical levels in Judaic-Christian interpretation.

The sections "Amado" (Beloved) and "Esposo" (Husband) of *De los nombres de Cristo* (1583; On the Names of Christ) depict Christ's marriage to the flesh (in communion) and to the spirit that he transforms into himself, implanting his image on the believer's soul. Divine spiritual union is superior to earthy physical union and raises the body to the endurance of mystical transports and/or persecution where the person desires to imitate Christ even to being eaten as the "wheat of God." Complete transformation of the soul obliterates the *flaqueza femenil* (feminine weakness) of body and spirit. Parker shows the basis of León's imagery in the idea that the male God is the possessor of the female soul, the possessed.

Chorpenning elucidates the maternal attributes of León's deity in the poem "En la Ascensión" (On the Ascension). The priest associates Christ with the nursing mother and believers (including the apostles and Mary) with the infant. Creel points out that

León's attitude toward Christ in this poem parallels Garcilaso's reproachful attitude toward the lady who absents herself: Both attitudes can be related to Ficino's concept that love is based on consciousness of affinity. Chorpenning observes that León continued this traditional mystical imagery in the discussion of "Pastor" (Shepherd) in *De los nombres de Cristo*. The nourishment Christ provides is both the Gospel and his flesh and blood. The medieval belief that mother's milk is processed blood facilitated León's association of the Eucharist with Christ's milk.

León perceived the Virgin Mary (*Marianism) as the highest example of womanhood, offering prophetic proofs of her virginity in *De los nombres de Cristo* from the Book of Isaiah (4:5, 8; 4:2) and from Psalms 109:3. Mary remained a virgin during Christ's birth (Proverbs 30:18–19) which occurred painlessly under the action of the Holy Spirit. León stressed Mary's being simultaneously a virgin and a mother. God was Father and Mother to Christ, while Mary was the receptacle, comparable to the tomb Christ left after the Crucifixion. León's biographers report that he requested a picture of the Virgin shortly after his imprisonment. In "Poema XXI, a Nuestra Señora" (Poem 21, To Our Lady), which begins "Virgen q'el Sol más pura" (1572; Virgin more pure than the sun), León presents the Virgin as a sun purer than the material sun and requests her help for freedom. Virgin, wife to the Father, mother of the Son, she is man's shield and the saintly temple of love. Soriani identifies the source of the poem in Petrarch's "Vergine bella, che di sol vestita," which closes the *Canzoniere*.

León's repressed sexuality and his equation of the female with the sinful flesh found an objective correlative in the popular Baroque figure of Mary Magdalene. In "Poema XX: De la Magdalena" he contrasts the worldly Elisa with the repentant and sanctified Mary Magdalene. He also discusses Magdalene in the section on "Jesús" in *De los nombres de Cristo*, referring to her as the *infame* (infamous one) who bathed Christ's feet with her tears. The Virgin Mary and Mary Magdalene, best and worst of women, superior to all other saints, are the only women, except for Santa Catalina de Alejandría, to be mentioned in the list of "Poema XIX: A todos los santos" (Poem 19: To All the Saints). Morreale endorses León's view of Mary Magdalene as a woman of *verdadera feminidad* (true femininity) in her uncalculating offer of service, her self-forgetfulness, and her consciousness of *mal ajeno* (neighboring evil).

In his poetry, published by *Quevedo (1580–1645) in 1631, Fray Luis spoke in different voices according to the rhetorical requirements of his theme. In "Poema VI: Canción al nacimiento de la hija del Marqués de Alcañices" (Poem 6: Song for the Birth of the Marquis of Alcañices's Daughter), the priest regards the child as heaven's blessing, comparing her to the sun, the highest model of beauty. In "Poema XI: Profecía del Tajo" (Poem 11: Prophecy of the Tajo River), León urges Rodrigo to flee the flames, pains, wars, deaths, destruction, and evil beasts of La Cava's arms. Woman as the source of evil informs this poem. Attraction/repulsion toward female flesh also permeates "Poema XIII: Las serenas" (Poem 13: The Sirens). León urges Querinto to flee the *sierpe mortal* (deadly serpent), the deceitful sirens who would transform him into a wild boar. The *femenil mano* (feminine hand), *la blanda Serena* (the tender Siren) with her *cantar divino* (divine song), will divert Querinto from his high tasks as Circe sought to divert Ulysses. In his "Oda IX: A Felipe Ruiz," León deplores the purchase of a thousand griefs for an hour with a pair of clear eyes and golden hair.

In his youthful imitations León adopted a conventional Petrarchan voice in several poems. "Poema XXIV: Vuestra tirana exención" (Poem 24: Your Tyrannous Exemption) develops the *carpe diem* theme. In "Poema XXV" the narrator loses his heart to a beautiful girl whom he sees in a *locus amoenus*. "Poema XXVI," an imitation of

Horace, describes the poet's love for the beautiful but coldhearted Nise; the poet presents himself as the handiwork of the lady before whom he humbles himself. "Poema XXVIII" continues the theme of his heart shattered by Nise's absence. The cold mistress figures again in "Poema XXIX." The ecstatic praise of the lady in "Poema XXX" equals that accorded to the Virgin Mary in León's religious poetry. In "Poema XXXI" León depicts a lover whose warring emotions leave him in despair over the lady's broken promises.

León's translations also reveal his attraction to love themes. His highly erotic translation of Joan de la Cossa develops the theme of a man who has grown old in service to his lady. León's translation of Euripedes's lament of Andromache reveals the modern poet's sympathy for the widow who became Hermione's captive slave. Ode XIX "Mater Saeva" contains the poet's complaint to Venus who has made him fall in love again. "Oda IX, Lib III: Donec gratus" presents a dialogue about the love of girls.

Several poems attributed to León develop themes consonant with those discussed above. His 10-year convalescence in Christ after repeated falls to worldly love in "Del conocimiento de sí mismo" (On Knowing Oneself) recalls Petrarch's anniversary songs, except for the vilifying of the lady's "corrupt and rotten cisterns." In "A la vida religiosa" (On the Religious Life) the narrator equates mortals' blind love with "mundo, demonio, carne pegajosa" (world, devil, contagious flesh). "Otra lira sobre la conversión" (Another Lira on Conversion) praises God for having turned the narrator from a sinful life, while "Selva rústica" (Country Woods) contrasts the joy of country life with corrupt urban riches. "Lira a la Magdalena" presents the fallen woman at Christ's feet as a happy soul who has exchanged carnal for divine love and now deserves to be the wife of the sacred master. Four poems to the Virgin Mary ("A la Asunción de Nuestra Señora" [On Our Lady's Ascension], "A Nuestra Señora" [To Our Lady], "Otra a Nuestra Señora" [Another to Our Lady], and "Canción a Nuestra Señora" [Song to Our Lady]) celebrate an intimate relationship between the repentant narrator and the Virgin. Although León developed Petrarchan topoi of the superior lady and worshipped the Virgin, he associated ordinary women with the flesh and considered them inferior to men. Even the worst woman could, like Mary Magdalene, earn salvation through conversion in a religious system imposing obedience to husband on the secular level and to Christ on the religious level.

Work by

Obras completas castellanas. Ed. Félix García. Madrid: BAC, 1959.

The Unknown Light: The Poems of Fray Luis de León. Trans. Willis Barnstone. Albany: State U of New York P, 1979.

Work about

Acereda, Alberto. "El prototipo femenino en la poesía de Fray Luis de León." *Cuadernos de Aldeeu* 9. 2 (November 1993): 171–182.

Chorpenning, Joseph F. "Christ the Nursing Mother in Fray Luis de León's 'En la Ascensión.'" *Journal of Hispanic Philology* 1.1 (Fall 1986): 199–204.

Creel, Bryant L. "Love's Protest against Sovereignty: Anguish and Reproach in Fray Luis de León's 'En la Ascensión' and in Garcilaso." *Journal of Hispanic Philology* 12.1 (Fall 1987): 37–50.

Cruz, Anne J. "Los estudios feministas en la literatura del Siglo de Oro." *Estado actual de los estudios sobre el Siglo de Oro: Actas del II Congreso Internacional de Hispanistas del Siglo de Oro.* Ed. Manuel García Martín, Ignacio Arellano, Javier Blasco, and Marc Vitse. Salamanca: Universidad, 1993. Vol. 1: 255–260.

Cuevas, Cristóbal. "'Estilo del espíritu santo': Crítica textual y polémica a propósito de un pasaje del *Cantar de los Cantares.*" *Insula* 539 (November 1991): 16–18.

Diez Borque, José María. "Acerca de la mujer campesina en el siglo XVII." *Estudios sobre literatura y arte dedicados al profesor Emilio Orozco Díaz.* Ed. Gallego Morell, Andrés Soria, and Nicolás Marín. Granada: U of Granada, 1979. 419–435.

Errazuriz, Helena. "La mujer en tiempos de Fray Luis de León." *Cuadernos americanos* 205 (1976): 153–160.

Guy, Alain. "La femme, selon Luis de León." *La femme dans la pensée espagnole*. Ed. Jean Guillon. Paris: CNRS, 1984. 63–77.

Jones, John A. "The Sweet Harmony of Luis de León's *La perfecta casada*." *Bulletin of Hispanic Studies* 62.3 (July 1985): 259–269.

———. "Verdad, armonía y vocación: El sentido de plenitud en *La perfecta casada*." *Insula* 539 (November 1991): 21–23.

Morreale, Margherita. "La oda VI de Fray Luis de León: 'De la Magdalena': Entre poesía humanística y tradición medieval." *Revista de Filología Española* 565.3-4 (July–December 1985): 181–271.

Oñate, María del Pilar. *El feminismo en la literatura española*. Madrid: Espasa-Calpe, 1938.

Parker, A. A. *The Philosophy of Love in Spanish Literature 1480–1680*. Edinburgh: Edinburgh UP, 1985.

Sánchez Zamarreño, Antonio. "*La perfecta casada* ¿sólo un vademécum para ánimos flacos?" *Insula* 539 (November 1991): 19–20.

Soriani, Rosanna. "Dos composiciones a la Virgen: Fray Luis de León y Francesco Petrarca (Una muestra de sorprendente analogía)." *Revista chilena de literatura* 43 (November 1993): 31–65.

Yamuri, Vera. "La mujer en el pensamiento filosófico y literario." *Anuario de letras* (1966–1967): 179–200.

Judy B. McInnis

León, Fray Luis de (1527–1591): Admiration and Misogyny in *La perfecta casada*

León has been traditionally a major proponent of feminine *encierro (enclosure) in sixteenth-century Spain. His prose work *La perfecta casada* (1583; *The Perfect Wife*, 1943) offers clear examples of Fray Luis de León's *misogyny but had a decisive impact on women's situation. Fray Luis wrote *La perfecta casada* for his just-married niece, María Varela Osorio, and by extension to all women in sixteenth-century Spain, constituting Fray Luis's exposition on the ideal Christian wife.

Fray Luis took into consideration several religious sources: the Fathers of the Church, as well as Spanish authors (*Vives [1492–1540], *Guevara [c. 1481?–1545], Gutiérrez de la Vera Cruz, Martín de Córdoba [c. 1398–c. 1468/1476]). His main inspiration was Chapter XXXI of Proverbs. Fray Luis made in *La perfecta casada* almost a literal commentary of each verse of that biblical chapter, praising the virtues of a good wife and, by contrast, condemning women who move away from the ideal Christian model. A peculiar form of feminist *costumbrismo* (depiction of local customs) accompanies Fray Luis's intention to convince, and he elaborates his ideas in a friendly manner with natural and direct language, contrasting different types of women (the hardworking woman and the idle one, the honest woman and the liar, etc.) and censoring luxurious fashions and vanity, above all in the use of *cosmetics.

Several details, and the general idea of *La perfecta casada*, have led critics to view it as evidence of Fray Luis's misogyny or the continuation of antifeminist thought in sixteenth-century Spain. Others (e.g., Félix García) have judged *La perfecta casada* as an apology for women. In spite of their differences, these two positions agree about one thing: Fray Luis's permanent concern for women, especially as wife and mother. If one considers Fray Luis's complete literary production, in prose as well as in poetry, one suspects Fray Luis could hide his passion for women under the veil of misogyny, common and accepted in his time and, in his case, self-imposed. Perhaps Fray Luis feared the power of women, in whom he found temptation and sin. Significantly, of all the biblical books, Fray Luis was interested in translating the Song of Songs (translated between 1570 and 1572), the most erotic book of the Bible, and the book of Proverbs, a chapter directly related to women. Perhaps, in spite of an aversion for the feminine, Fray Luis deeply admired women. Perhaps his self-imposed attitude concealed fear and weakness toward women. *See also* León, Fray Luis de (1527–1591); León, Fray Luis de (1527–1591): Women in His Poetry

Work by

García, Félix P., ed. *Fray Luis de León. Obras completas castellanas.* Madrid: Biblioteca de Autores Cristianos, 1951.

La perfecta casada. Study, sel., and notes Mercedes Etreros. Madrid: Taurus, 1987.

The Perfect Wife. Trans. William Carlos Williams. Denton, TX: College Press T.S.C.W., 1943.

Work about

Jones, John A. "The Sweet Harmony of Luis de León's *La perfecta casada.*" *Bulletin of Hispanic Studies* 62 (1985): 259–269.

———. "Verdad, armonía y vocación: El sentido de plenitud en *La perfecta casada.*" *Insula* 539 (1991): 21–23.

Sánchez Zamarreno, Antonio. "*La perfecta casada,* ¿sólo un vademécum para ánimos flacos?" *Insula* 539 (1991): 19–20.

Alberto Acereda

León, Fray Luis de (1527–1591): Women in His Poetry

Fray Luis de León (1527–1591) has sparked various opinions citing his *misogyny as evinced by *La perfecta casada* (1583; *The Perfect Wife,* 1943). However, feminine topics also appear in his original poetry, with its alternation of a positive and a negative vision of women. In some poems Fray Luis offers a sublime image of women. In the "Canción al nacimiento de la hija del Marqués de Alcañices" (Song for the New-Born Daughter of the Marquis of Alcañices), written in 1569, Fray Luis praises a baby girl as well as her noble lineage. Fray Luis exemplifies a chaste canon in these didactic verses, seeing the baby Tomasita as a future model for women according to his religious beliefs. Fray Luis dedicated poems to the Virgin Mary, model and guidance for the perfect woman and supreme archetype of femininity. Poem XXI, "A Nuestra Señora" (To Our Lady), expresses his personal *Marianism and admiration for the Virgin. This poem, written in 1572, follows both medieval Spanish tradition (Berceo, el Arcipreste de Hita Juan Ruiz) and Italian Renaissance tradition (Petrarch, Policiano). Fray Luis contemplates Mary simultaneously as the Mother of God and a virgin. In her chastity Fray Luis finds an absence of temptation. Mary provides a positive feminine archetype and divine example. Another poem attributed to Fray Luis, also entitled "A Nuestra Señora," reiterates his insistence on the immaculate and virgin condition of Mary.

In contrast to these poems offering a positive vision of women, others depict women as the incarnation of evil. The poem "De la Magdalena" (On the Magdalene) reunites two leitmotifs: the arrival of old age in a worldly woman, Elisa, negatively presented by Fray Luis, and the description of Mary Magdalene, the sinner, repentant and later sainted. Mary Magdalene also appears in two poems attributed to Fray Luis: the sonnet "Las manos que la muerte a tantos dieron" (The hands that gave death to so many) and a "Lira a la Magdalena" (Lira to the Magdalene). This topic connects to the *Libro de la conversión de la Magdalena* (1588; Book on the Conversion of the Magdalene) by Malón de Chaide, a contemporary and disciple of Fray Luis de León. In "Profecía del Tajo" (The Prophecy of the Tagus), written between 1551 and 1552, Fray Luis negatively portrays women via the historical legend of Don Rodrigo and la Cava. The young woman (Cava) represents temptation, sin, and lust and suffers blame for the loss of Spain to the Arabs. Morbid rejection of the feminine sex, exemplified by "A las serenas" (To the Mermaids), employs the classical figure of Ulysses, to advise one of his friends to avoid lust for women. Thus the poet attacks women indirectly, for these mermaids represent temptation and sin. Fray Luis also wrote love sonnets (acceptable in his time). One beginning "Agora con la aurora se levanta..." (Now with the Dawn She Arises ...) imitates Petrarch's poetry. This sonnet describes a woman's awakening in detail, and this feminine figure becomes a source of the poet's sadness, loneliness, and even anguish.

Despite his repeated misogyny, we should reevaluate Fray Luis de León's vision of women. In the poetry of Fray Luis de León we find a curious detail: He usually attacks women, while only a noble baby girl, the Virgin Mary, and (partially) the repentant Mary Magdalene escape censure. Poems in which the feminine is positively treated become didactic, moral examples, as in the case of *La perfecta casada*. Fray Luis's apparent misogyny perhaps had its source in a deep, secret admiration for women held throughout his life. His misogyny, then, would be personally imposed to accord with his religious status and misogynist traditions of his time. *See also* León, Fray Luis de (1527–1591); León, Fray Luis de (1527–1591): Admiration and Misogyny in *La perfecta casada*

Work by

Macrí, Oreste, ed. *Fray Luis de León. Poesías*. Barcelona: Crítica, 1982.

Work about

Acereda, Alberto. "El prototipo femenino en la poesía de Fray Luis de León." *Cuadernos de Aldeeu* 9 (1993): 171–182.

Guy, Alain. "La femme, selon Fray Luis de León." *La femme dans la pensée espagnole*. Paris: CNRS, 1984. 63–77.

Alberto Acereda

León, María Teresa (1903–1988)

Born in Logroño to a financially comfortable, conservative, socially prominent family, the multifaceted writer and political activist María Teresa León y Goyri showed a liberal spirit at an early age. When she later wrote of her Catholic education, she remembered how the forbidden novels she read scandalized her classmates and caused her dismissal from the school. But León's family encouraged literary pursuits; on the day of her first communion, they took her to meet Emilia *Pardo Bazán, who gave León a novel autographed with wishes for a literary career.

Moreover, her aunt and uncle, the distinguished philologists María *Goyri and Ramón Menéndez Pidal, became decisive components of León's intellectual formation and literary education. Their influence is reflected in León's extensive publications, especially in her affinity for the *Romancero* (Ballads), the Cid, and other classics of Spanish literature. Around 1920, León married Gonzalo de Sebastián, with whom she had two sons. The marriage failed despite attempts at reconciliation, and in 1929 it ended in a final separation. Marital difficulties and the Spanish Civil War kept mother and sons apart for many years. However, León had already begun her literary career. Between 1921 and 1928 she contributed stories and articles to the newspaper *El Diario de Burgos* under the pseudonym of Isabel Inghirami. In Burgos, her mother's birthplace and the city in which she felt more at home, she wrote one of her first controversial articles in defense of a young woman who had drowned her illegitimate child rather than face the shame imposed by society and also published her first book, *Cuentos para soñar* (1929; Stories for Dreaming). León also traveled frequently to Madrid and in 1929 met the poet Rafael Alberti, a member of the Generation of 1927. With him, León shared her life, her work, her concerns, and the long exile that was to come. After the Second Spanish Republic acknowledged divorce, they were married in 1933.

In the next decade, León and Alberti led a life of intense activity. They traveled as emissaries of the new Spanish Republic to the Soviet Union and to parts of Europe to study developments in theater. After their return in 1933, inspired by the trip to Russia, they founded the journal *Octubre*, publishing works of influential writers such as Antonio Machado. In 1934, after attending the First Congress of Soviet Writers in Moscow and the International Peace Congress in Amsterdam, León and Alberti traveled to the United States to raise money for the Asturian mine workers whose revolution in October 1934 had been severely repressed. León joined the Spanish Communist Party, and in 1935 she and Alberti became active in the development of the Alliance of Antifascist Intellectuals. During the Civil War, León assumed great responsibilities of cultural and political dimensions and became prominent in war efforts. The Board for the Defense and Protection of National Artistic Treasure entrusted her with rescuing and safeguarding invaluable collections of major museums. This experience forms the basis for her book *La historia tiene la palabra* (1944; History Has the Floor) and Alberti's play *Noche de guerra en el Museo de Prado* (1956; Wartime Night in the Prado Museum).

In 1937, after a trip to the Second International Congress of Writers in Russia, she collaborated in the formation of theater troupes for the antifascist Alliance, promoting the Theater of Art and Propaganda, housed in Madrid's Zarzuela Theater. Bombing during the siege of Madrid closed that operation, so she formed Guerrillas del Teatro (Theater Guerrillas), a voluntary, itinerant theater group giving performances in small towns and at front lines to entertain the troops. As writer, director, and actress she organized plays, poetry readings, song sessions, and other cultural activities on the front.

In 1939, at war's end, León and Alberti began an exile that lasted 38 years. After a flight to Algeria, they went to Paris, working in the Spanish-language broadcasting for Radio Paris Mondial. They found safety in Pablo Neruda's home, but with the approaching Nazi invasion and the Spanish dictator Franco asking the Vichy government for their extradition, they left Paris in 1940, moving to Argentina, where León immersed herself in literary production, coping with her sense of loss by writing novels, stories, biographies, screenplays, radio scripts, and memoirs. In 1941 her daughter Aitana was born. León and family traveled to the People's Republic of China in 1957. The product of this trip, *Sonríe China* (1958; China Smiles), including poetry by Alberti, reflects her political beliefs in social solidarity, respect for the people, and concern for women's issues in China. After 23 years, León and Alberti left Argentina, relocating in Italy, in the Roman quarter Trastevere, hosting gatherings for Spanish friends. León's emotions from years of expatriation welled up, and she began *Memoria* (Memory). In 1977 they returned to Spain, but León's memory had already begun to fade, and she remembered little of Madrid. She died there on December 14, 1988.

León's literary works are extensive and varied and show her constant evolution. Her first books are collections of stories for children: *Cuentos para soñar* (Stories for Dreaming), *Rosa-Fría, patinadora de la luna* (1934; Rosa Fría, Moon Skater), and *La bella del mal amor: Cuentos castellanos* (1930; The Beauty Wrongly Loved: Castilian Stories). The latter was inspired by traditional literature, featuring rural and urban elements, female protagonists, and one of León's distinctive characteristics, the lyrical aspect of her prose. She continued to write stories but with a profound change in content, as seen in *Cuentos de la España actual* (1936; Tales of Present-Day Spain). The consequences of the war and her resolute political outlook introduce national strife, loss, and defeat motifs in her writing. *Cuentos de la España actual*, the most ideologically propagandistic of León's fiction, exposes and denounces social injustice and oppression. *Morirás lejos* (1942; You Will Die Far Away) and *Fábulas del tiempo amargo* (1962; Fables of the Bitter Time) contain less political bias and greater attention to literary aesthetics. *Fábulas* reflects earlier literary influences, especially tenuous surrealism, emphasis on dreams, and the subconscious combined with Native American myths. León aspires to recapture the past through memory as everyday reality moves to the background; life in exile or social injustice still appear intermittently. These three story collections were later republished as the anthology *Una estrella roja* (1979; A Red Star), the name of one of the *Fábulas*. The title story recounts the death of the small daughter of an anarchist, killed while running daily missions carrying bombs for her father. The father requests a red star to bury with the child from the communist organizers who had befriended her. One of León's story collections most interesting for feminist critics is *Las peregrinaciones de Teresa* (1950; Teresa's Pilgrimages), which examines women's issues such as feminine psychology, resignation, desire, and submission to fate. Teresa appears in each of the nine stories as a symbolic personage.

León wrote three novels. *Contra viento y marea* (1941; Against Wind and High Seas), a two-part novel, attempts to connect Spain's Civil War to a greater historical context through the solidarity experienced when the International Brigades fought for the Spanish Republic. Part I traces the struggle of the poor in Cuba after the War of 1898 through the unrest prior to the Batista dictatorship. When news of Spain's Civil War reaches Havana, volunteer forces sail to the aid of the Republic. The second part portrays the siege and surrender of Madrid (the Cuban volunteers achieve little of consequence in historical terms). *Juego limpio* (1959; Fair Play) comes directly from León's war experiences, transposed as the episodic memoir entries of Camilo, a fictional character. An Augustinian monk fleeing his monastery and the war, after he is wounded at the front he joins the Guerrillas del Teatro. Camilo's memoir comprises most of the novel, but León also wanted to reflect upon the fatal undoing of the Republic; these considerations are often expressed through another important character, Claudio. Equally important is the leitmotif of "play"; the title alludes not only to the life-giving plays of the theatrical group but also to the foul war games of the fifth column, a name attributed to Nationalist General Mola. León's characters must resist fascist elements circulating inside Madrid. Camilo stands firm against a traitorous character and learns to play fair by not giving in to the enemy. The novel again re-creates the fall of Madrid as the Republican government moves on to Valencia as well as the departure of the International Brigades. In her third novel, León's fixation on Spain and her separation from it find poetic expression through a little-known mythological sailor of the *Iliad*. *Menesteos, marinero de abril* (1965; Menesteus, April Sailor) explores many of León's favorite themes: exile, loss, memory, travels, and the concept of paradise. Myth allows her greater artistic range in her version of the daring seaman's pursuit of lost love and his arrival on the Iberian coast. He wanders in search of Hades and dies near the ancient seaport of Cádiz, birthplace of León's husband Alberti.

León showed continuing interest in the medieval period, especially Spain's national hero and his wife, the Cid and *Jimena, and wrote fictionalized biographies about them for young readers: *Don Rodrigo Díaz de Vivar, el Cid Campeador* (1958) and *Doña Jimena Díaz de Vivar, gran señora de todos los deberes* (1960; Princess Jimena Díaz de Vivar, Great Lady of All Duties). Admired writers are also the subject of biographies: *El soldado que nos enseñó a hablar, Cervantes* (1978; The Soldier Who Taught Us to Speak, Cervantes) and *El gran amor de Gustavo Adolfo *Bécquer* (1946; The Great Love of Gustavo Adolfo Bécquer), portraying the popular nineteenth-century Spanish poet. Other works nearly defy classification of genre: León gathers her life, memories, and travels in *Crónica general de la Guerra Civil* (1937; Chronicle of the Civil War), *La historia tiene la palabra*, and *Sonríe China*. *Memoria de la melancolía* (1970; Memory of Melancholy), perhaps the most distinguished of all her writing, captures the feeling of a whole epoch. Here León sums up the struggle she had lived in forced exile as she evokes a constant, nostalgic remembrance of the past. Its form and language have been compared to Proust and other innovators of twentieth-century narrative. This work employs argumentation based on contradiction: the promise of a new life that depends on death of a former life, to her a lost paradise. As an exile, León wondered if she would ever enjoy the right to live out her history, a right she treasured. From her query came the often-cited and poignant phrase she used to express her weariness of not knowing where to die. *See also* Short Fiction by Women Writers: 1900–1975

Work by

La bella del mal amor. Madrid: Cairel, 1992.
Una estrella roja. Madrid: Espasa-Calpe, 1979.
Juego limpio. Barcelona: Seix Barral, 1987.
Rosa-Fría, la patinadora de la luna. Madrid: de la Torre, 1990.

Work about

Mangini, Shirley. *Memories of Resistance: Women's Voices from the Spanish Civil War*. New Haven: Yale UP, 1995.
Marco, Joaquín. Prologue. *Una estrella roja*. By María Teresa León. Madrid: Espasa-Calpe, 1979. 7–22.
María Teresa Leon. Valladolid: Junta de Castilla y León, 1987.
Rodrigo, Antonina. *Mujeres de España. Las silenciadas*. Barcelona: Círculo de Lectores, 1989.
Stewart, Melissa A. "Poet Wives María Teresa León and Anna Murià Tell Their Stories in Alternative Texts." *Letras Peninsulares 1988–1998*. Tenth Anniversary Issue (Spring 1998): 223–238.
Torres Nebrera, Gregorio. *Los espacios de la memoria: La obra de María Teresa León*. Madrid: La Torre, 1996.
Ugarte, Michael. "Women and Exile. The Civil War Autobiographies of Constancia de la Mora and María Teresa León." *Letras Peninsulares 1988–1998*. Tenth Anniversary Issue (Spring 1998): 207–222.

Glenn Morocco

Leonor de Navarra (1350–1415), Queen of Navarre

Daughter of Henry II of Castile, she became queen of Navarre after marrying Charles III of Navarre in 1375. Defined as a strong-willed, intelligent woman, she held strong political opinions and took action assertively in the Castilian government.

After her father died, Leonor inherited lands and an important estate that gave her great power. Although she was engaged to Ferdinand I of Portugal, this engagement was broken. Instead, as a result of a peace treaty between Navarre and Castile, she married Charles III of Navarre in 1375. She left her husband shortly after the marriage to travel to Castile, pretending she was ill and homesick. Apparently, her real reasons for leaving were related to personal conflicts with her husband, who had a lover. Additionally, Leonor appeared to feel much more comfortable in Castile where she could still participate in plots regarding her nephew's succession to the throne. Once in Castile, she became actively involved in the internal political affairs of the kingdom, especially during her nephew's minority. Her husband's efforts to bring her home were rather unsuccessful, but once the young king took full control of the Castilian government, he arranged a deal with Charles to take his aunt back home. Leonor refused and was besieged by her nephew in Roa, where she had retreated. She had to yield and was forced to return home in 1395. Back in Navarre, her relationship with Charles seemed to have improved. During her husband's trips to France, Leonor even ruled the kingdom. She died in Olite in 1415 and was buried in the cathedral of Pamplona.

Work about

Bleiberg, Germán. *Diccionario de historia de España*. 2nd ed. Vol. 2. Madrid: Revista de Occidente, 1968.

David H. Darst

Lesbianism in Early Modern Spanish Literature: 1500–1700

There is consensus among contemporary social scientists that *lesbianism*, as currently understood, is a modern term developed in the post-Victorian era. Physicians and Freudian psychiatrists first coined the term and medicalized the phenomenon of love and genital contact between women. Later, as part of the women's liberation movement, gay women proclaimed their right to love, live together, and make love to other women. Nonetheless, it is naive to think that sexual desire, love, and carnal contact among women did not occur before scientific and religious communities labeled and classified the phenomenon. Homosexuality has long been silenced by others and subject to a strong autocensorship. The sexual practice of lesbianism is further characterized by the facts that it does not lead to pregnancy and does not necessarily produce the loss of virginity; because she remained intact, a woman could keep her *honor despite a lesbian relationship. It must be added that lesbianism is not an exclusive practice; many instances occur in a bisexual context or under heterosexual guise, as in cross-dressing. This entry documents some moments of lesbian desire embedded in a variety of Golden Age texts, in roughly chronological order.

Lesbian desire figures explicitly in act 7 of the *Celestina (1499), which presents a classic male fantasy scenario. To induce his cooperation, Celestina has promised Pármeno the favors of Areúsa, and to achieve her goal, she enters the harlot's bedroom and starts touching the young woman's beautiful body while describing it to Pármeno, who listens with progressive arousal. The scene achieves a high degree of sexual ambiguity because Celestina takes heterosexuality to a point of crisis where it is impossible to discern between her own immediate desire and Pármeno's deferred need.

The *Papeles de Barbieri*, Ms. 14070 of the Biblioteca Nacional (Spain's National Library), contains a *villancico* (eight-syllable verse form) with music by Juan de la Encina (1469?–1529) in which three women are making *baldrés* (dildos) of sheep skin. This same product is described in Cristóbal de Chaves's *Relación de la cárcel de Sevilla* (c. 1600; Report on the Seville Prison), mentioned at the conclusion of this entry.

Book Two of Jorge de Montemayor's La *Diana (1559) retells the story of Filosmena and Felis as written by Matteo Bandello (1485–1561). Filosmena is madly in love with Don Felis, so when he is summoned to Court, she disguises herself as a man, assumes the male name Valeriano, and manages to fool Felis and convince him to take her along as his page. Her main function is to serve as messenger between Felis and his new love, Celia. Celia, however, falls in love with Valerio/Felismena, and they begin a relationship in which Don Felis now serves as the excuse for the two women to be together. Celia never learns that Valerio/Felismena is a woman, but when convinced of the impossibility of their love, she dies.

Cristóbal de Virués's *Atila furioso* (1580–1585; Attila Enraged) is a brief tragedy composed of a rapid succession of fascinating scenes filled with homoerotic encounters. The key character is the page Flaminia, a teenage female who combines ambition, aggression, coldbloodedness, and ambiguous beauty to achieve her criminal goal. Alternately appearing as a male (Flaminio) and female (Flaminia) page, she first seduces the king and then, cross-dressed, the queen of Hungary. Her intent is to persuade the king to kill his wife and allow her to become queen. At the play's conclusion, Flaminia is killed by Attila.

Perhaps the clearest example of lesbian lovemaking in Golden Age literature is contained in poem 30 of the erotic collection *Jardín de Venus* (1589; Venus's Garden). The first quatrain presents two women *tratando del amor* (dealing with love, talking about love). However, as Covarrubias indicates in his seventeenth-century dictionary, *tratar* also means "palpar alguna cosa con la mano o manosearla [to touch something with the hand or caress it]," indicating that they were fondling each other before disrobing. Line five is the most explicit, for it portrays the two women closely embraced, and then Cupid sends them an arrow. Alzieu et al. interpret this to mean that the second woman perfects the *agujeta*, a lace with metallic tips, making a dildo (*bragueta*) after putting clothes on it. My reading is that one of the two women had a dildo tied to her waist (which explains why she has the lace), and after the other woman reaches orgasm (*la una se apartó muy consolada* [the one moved away, very comforted]), she realizes she has the dildo on (given to her by Cupid) and decides to cover it with a masculine *brageta*, the Renaissance man's phallic cup. This poem constitutes an early example of pornographic male portrayal of a lesbian relationship.

Catalina de *Erauso (1578?/1585?/1592?–after 1630) recalls in her "memoirs" several instances replete with sexual innuendo. Catalina, a transvestite passing as a man, is first caressed by Doña Beatriz de Cárdenas. Later, Diego de Salazar's wife, who has taken a fancy to disguised Catalina and is accustomed to teasing and frolicking with her, lets Catalina run her hand up and down between her legs, while Catalina, who has her hair in the folds of the other woman's skirt, allows the woman to comb her (Catalina's) hair. In another episode, Catalina spends at least three years visiting the house of her brother's mistress. Catalina acknowledges a taste for pretty faces, and in the intriguing end of the text, she tells some harlots she is going to deliver 100 strokes to their pretty necks. The dramatic play version of Erausa's life, Juan Pérez de Montalbán's *La monja alférez* (1626; The Nun Ensign), preserves homosexual overtones, but they are feeble. Catalina's love for Doña Ana is weak, and the entire situation is quickly dismissed by Don Diego de Erausa. A historically documented incident involving the real Catalina has survived: In 1630, she became so infatuated with a young woman she was escorting from Veracruz to Mexico City that she challenged the lady's husband to a duel. Fortunately, friends persuaded her not to kill the husband.

Lesbian implications also figure in the theater of Lope de *Vega. In *La pérdida honrosa o los caballeros de San Juan* (1610–1615; The Honorable Loss or the Knights of San Juan [attributed to Lope]), Isabel, dressed as a man, meets Ana, also dressed as a man. Isabel falls in love with Ana, thinking she is a man, and asks him/her to marry. At this point, each is forced to confess their true identity. Lope's *El robo de Dina* (The Abduction of Dinah) has been seen by Yarbro-Bejarano as one of many Golden Age plays that reveal seventeenth-century Spanish society's efforts to control the female gaze, the desire of women to enjoy looking at and admiring other women.

In Cervantes's masterpiece *Don Quijote de la Mancha* (1605 and 1615), Aldonza (*Dulcinea's grotesque physical counterpart) has traditionally been considered a *serrana*, a shepherdess. Gossy ("Aldonza as Butch"), however, argues that Cervantes consciously created a female who refused to be an object of male desire and declined as well to participate in a desire for the male. Don Quijote's squire Sancho Panza observed that Aldonza knew how to *tirar la barra*—to pitch the bar, which in seventeenth-century Spain could also mean *futuere*, to have sexual intercourse with a woman.

Tirso de *Molina's *El vergonzoso en palacio* (1621; The Bashful Man at Court) has one of the most intriguing characters of Golden Age theater, Serafina, daughter of the duke of Avero. Serafina's inclination is to dress as a man (II, 737–739), and she acts out the role of a man in a play within the play so well that she causes Doña Juana to fall in love with her. In another twist to the plot, when she comes across a picture of herself, drawn when she was cross-dressed for the play, she falls in love with her cross-dressed image. At the work's end, Serafina marries Antonio, because he looks like her in drag. Antonio fulfills narcissistic Serafina's fantasies and fetish; if she cannot live like a man and dress like one, she can at least marry a man who looks like a woman dressed like a man. And not just any woman dressed like a man but Serafina herself.

María de *Zayas's *Desengaños amorosos* (1649; Disillusions of Love) also broaches the subject of love between two women. During the Sixth Night, Matilde narrates the story of Estefanía and Laurela. Estefanía in reality is Don Esteban, who has disguised himself as a woman in order to be a chambermaid for Laurela. Esteban/Estefanía declares openly her love for Laurela, and the other women of the house find amusement in the concept of a woman loving another woman. Estefanía uses witty remarks to justify this form of love, explaining that true love has no gender because souls have no sex and, in an ironic invocation of the conventions of *courtly love, reminding the other women how fine is the kind of love that cannot find reward.

Two other plays by secondary playwrights revolve around lesbian desire. In *La dama capitán* (1661; The Lady Captain), by the Figueroa y Córdoba brothers, the noble Basque lady Elvira flees her house and joins the Spanish army in Flanders, adopting the name Lope. Elvira, a blonde beauty, is characterized by her maid Lucía as *marimacho* (butch). Both women cross-dress as males when they join the military. The innkeeper Juana promptly falls in love with Elvira, and the two embrace on stage. Once in battle, Elvira soon earns the rank of captain and is further awarded acceptance to the prestigious (male) military Order of Santiago. At that moment, Elvira falls in love with the Baroness Madama Blanca. Blanca recognizes she is strongly attracted to a man she describes as *raro* (strange, queer); this key word illustrates her lack of comprehension of whom she loves. Only in the last minute of the play does Elvira/Lope reveal her true female identity, declare that she cannot marry Blanca, and concede Blanca's hand to her brother Fernando. Even so, Elvira's final speech includes the words "como ello pudiera ser / sí lo hiciera [casarme]," revealing her still present desire to marry Blanca. In Cubillo de Aragón's (1596?–1661) *Añasco el de Talavera* (n.d.; The Añasco from Talavera), Dionisia declares she is in love with her cousin Leonor. Dionisia is not taken seriously by her relatives, and she marries Don Juan at the play's conclusion, but, like Zayas's Estefanía, Dionisia declares that the merit of her love is validated by its lack of reciprocity. Further, during the play she repeatedly attempts to convince Leonor to respond. In one poem she sends Leonor, Dionisia concludes with a paradox: "siendo en la amorosa llaga / luz que sin soplo se apaga, / vela que en tinieblas arde" (living in the loving wound/light that dies without a breath/candle burning in the dark). The play itself contextualizes the queer situation, calling it a sign of the times because some women are fighting (*dando cuchilladas*) and others are writing poems (*otras escribiendo versos*). These are termed wonders (*prodigios*) of the new baroque times. One male character, the Conde, describes Dionisia's beauty as a marriage of beauty and courage. The conventional ending in marriage between Dionisia and Don Juan follows a moment of anagnorisis: Juan and Dionisia are fighting while Dionisia is dressed as a man, and Juan falls in love, thanks to the fetish of seeing her dressed as a man, while she falls in love with the man who is capable of understanding her "manhood."

Legal opinions concerning lesbianism were harsh in sixteenth- and seventeenth-century Spain. Crimes of sodomy were adjudicated by the state rather than the Inquisition. During the Golden Age, the main corpus of law in Castile was *Alfonso X's *Las siete partidas*. Gregorio López, a famous jurist of the day, commented on Part 7, Chapter 21, law 1, under "omes" (men), observing that women also should be included when considering the crime of sodomy, "cuando una con otra haga contra natura" (when one woman goes against nature with another). He acknowledges the pragmatic sanction of Ferdinand and *Isabel regarding sodomy (Medina del Campo, July 22, 1497), which states that this coitus is not punished under divine or human law, but cites as the basis of his condemnation Paul's letter to the Romans. He further observes that although this sin is grave, it is less important than sodomy between men because the violation of natural law is less critical, since women are more prone to passion, and semen is not wasted. López declares that women should only be punished with the death penalty if they use a dildo. Another Golden Age jurist who wrote about lesbian love is Antonio Gómez. In *Ad Leges Tauri commentarium absolutissium*, he states his support for death by fire as the penalty for lesbianism, especially if a dildo is involved, and declares his involvement in a case where the women were burned. Holding that when a dildo is not used, the sentence should be arbitrary, he cites a case in Granada where the women were whipped and sent to prison.

Regarding prisons, Cristóbal de Chaves states in his earlier-cited *Relación de la cárcel de Sevilla* that many women inmates there, wanting to be differently endowed by nature, had been making cocks out of sheepskin, then tying them to their waists. The punishment they received, when discovered, was 200 lashes. The fact that lesbian relationships were subject to harsh punishments attests to their existence. Lesbianism entered the literature of the Golden Age timidly, mainly as part of male sexual fantasy but also as acceptance of reality.

Work about

Alzieu, Pierre, Robert Jammes, and Yvan Lissorgues. *Poesía erótica del Siglo de Oro*. Barcelona: Crítica, 1984.

Blackmore, Josiah, and Gregory S. Hutcheson, eds. *Queer Iberia: Sexualities, Cultures, and Crossings from the Middle Ages to the Renaissance*. Durham, NC: Duke UP, 1999.

Delgado, María José, and Alain Saint-Saëns, eds. *Lesbianism and Homosexuality in Early Modern Spain*. Mississippi: UP of the South, 2000.

Gossy, Mary S. "Aldonza as Butch: Narrative and the Play of Gender in *Don Quijote*." *¿Entiendes? Queer Readings, Hispanic Writings*. Ed. Emilie L. Bergmann and Paul Julian Smith. Durham, NC: Duke UP, 1995. 17–28.

———. "Skirting the Questions: Lesbians and María de Zayas." *Hispanisms and Homosexualities*. Ed. Silvia Molloy and Robert McKee Irwin. Durham, NC: Duke UP, 1998. 19–28.

McKendrick, Melveena M. *Women and Society in the Spanish Drama of the Golden Age. A Study of the Mujer Varonil*. Cambridge: Cambridge UP, 1974.

Tomás y Valiente, Francisco. "El crimen y pecado contra natura." *Sexo barroco y otras transgresiones premodernas*. Ed. F. Tomás y Valiente et al. Madrid: Alianza, 1990. 33–55.

Yarbro-Bejarano, Yvonne. *Feminism and the Honor Plays of Lope de Vega*. West Lafayette, IN: Purdue UP, 1994.

Salvador A. Oropesa

Liaño, Isabel de (1570–after 1604)

Isabel (also Ysabel) de Liaño, author of a late-sixteenth-century epic poem on the life of St. Catherine of Siena (1347–1380), figures among the first women authors to publish poetry in Castile. Based on Antonio de la Peña's popular Castilian prose translation of Raymond of Capua's *Life of Saint Catherine* from the original Latin, Liaño's religious epic, *Historia de la vida, muerte, y milagros de santa Catalina de Sena* (1604; History of the Life, Death, and Miracles of St. Catherine of Siena) comprises 328 folios and includes 27 "cantos," all written in *octava rima*. Of particular importance are Liaño's "Prologue," her "Dedication to Queen Marguerite," and her "First Canto," announcing a particularly feminine writing style, defended by telling the men who might not like her verses: "For women only them I concocted, / Who with better devotion receive them do, / And though deserving less, are esteemed more, / Because of the feminine rhyming score." Liaño's "Prologue" mirrors the concerns of Teresa de *Cartagena (c.1420–after 1460?) before her, offering another instance of female defense against the literary double standard of Renaissance Spain that accused women (Olivia *Sabuco de Nantes [1562–1622?], for example) of male plagiarism and yet overlooked the same behavior in men. Obviously (from the "Prologue"), Liaño was accused of just such a crime.

The poem's dedication to Queen Marguerite of Austria (1584–1611) is but one instance of Liaño's constant subversion of male-dominant society. Whereas many books of the same period were dedicated to Philip III, the duke of Lerma, or the count of Lemos, by dedicating her poem to the queen, Liaño keeps her discourse among women. Her book, written by a woman, dedicated to a woman of prominence, concerned with the relationships between women in and outside of convents, features a female hero as principal protagonist. Furthermore, evidence suggests that the book was printed by a female printer (Margarita Sánchez) and probably funded by nuns, or at least sold to them. Hence the *Historia* represents the most thorough rejection of male patronage Spain had ever known.

Very little is known of Liaño's life; the few facts we can be confident about are: Liaño's poem was allegedly published by the well-known, established printer Luis Sánchez (the king's printer and one of few who ran printing presses in both Valladolid and Madrid during 1604); it is dedicated to the new queen; the men who wrote preliminary poems to the book were of high social standing; and finally, the poem enjoyed a timely release (after the death of Philip II and just after the court had moved from Madrid to Valladolid). All these facts point to Liaño as having powerful connections within the highest circles of Castilian society. Liaño was well educated, a widow, and probably a noble. The picture reveals a strong-willed individual disposed to stretch political conventions in order to publish her poetry.

Liaño had received the Dominican habit by the time she wrote the *Historia*; an engraving at the beginning of the poem depicts Liaño in her habit, with her right hand pointing to a book. Thus, the publication of the poem might have received financial backing from her religious order, which desired to promote, once again, the life of its most famous female saint, perhaps bargaining to purchase a certain amount of the copies printed.

Isabel de Liaño represents a defiant component of the Hispanic female poet's struggle to be read within a feminine code of justice, void of male harassment. From the very start, her *cantos* reject the notion that poetry need be steeped in the traditional secular meanderings of her male counterparts. Thus, Liaño's success does not rest in the hands of her male readers; she has rejected them entirely as unworthy of the fare and will now address herself only to women. She is the first woman to publish a complete epic poem in Castile. In terms of feminist posturing, her *cantos* deserve, at least, a consideration equal to that received by Cartagena's *Admiracion operum Dey*, Sor Juana's (1651–1695) *Respuesta a Sor Filotea*, or María de *Zayas's (1590–after 1647?) prologues to the *Novelas ejemplares y amorosas*. Liaño successfully broke through many of the boundaries that caused "unnatural silences" during the Spanish Renaissance. Unfortunately, publication was no guarantee against silencing. Today, the causes that continue to silence her poetry are being challenged, allowing a reemergence after nearly 400 years.

Robert Taylor

Libro de Apolonio (late 1200s): Its Portrayal of Women

Libro de Apolonio (Book of Apolonio), an anonymous poem in *cuaderna vía* (stanzas of four monorhymed Alexandrines) composed in the late thirteenth century, is a translation and Christian adaptation of a pagan Latin story, with an original and authentic Spanish flavor to it. The poem introduces two uniquely strong female characters in Spanish medieval literature: Luciana, Apolonio's wife, and Tarsiana, his daughter. Half of the poem narrates the adventures of these two women.

Both these characters reflect with acute realism the reality of women in Spanish society at the time. According to historians, parents were expected to seek their daughters' approval of chosen husbands, and wives assumed responsibility for the management of house, estates, and even business. Thus, the better educated a wife became, the more valuable she was to husband, family, and above all, to the estate. As the only heir of King Architrastes, Luciana has completed the trivium (grammar, logic, and rhetoric), so she can entertain court guests at her father's request, and she is also allowed to decide on a husband. Similarly, Apolonio leaves his only child, Tarsiana, in custody of a couple, to be raised and educated according to the expectations of her high birth. Not only does she finish the trivium, like her mother; she has also begun the quadrivium (arithmetic, music, geometry, and astronomy). Tarsiana's education saves both her life and her *honor. When sold to a brothel, she convinces the owner that she can make as much money or more by becoming a *juglaresa* (female jongleur) and entertaining men with her music, songs, and stories. Tarsiana's disclaimer that she is a *juglaresa* by force and not by choice reflects the reality of the period when jongleurs were the lowest level of poets and troubadours.

Family is a main theme in a poem that introduces a bookish hero as a model of how to rule in a learned and civilized manner. The poet describes the lives of five different families (King Antioch's, King Architrastes's, Apolonio's, and to a lesser degree, those of Estrangilo and Antinágoras) in order to emphasize Apolonio's qualities as a ruler and as head of his own family. The poem starts with a negative image of this social institution by recounting the destructive impact of King Antioch's incestuous relation with his daughter. Then King Architrastes and his obedient, well-educated daughter Luciana are introduced in direct contrast. Contrary to Antioch, who poses a riddle to all of his daughter's suitors with the threat of death if they fail, Architrastes welcomes the proposals of various young men and invites them to write to Luciana, allowing her to choose. It should be noted that in both families mothers are prominently absent.

These two examples are followed by Apolonio's family when he marries Luciana, who later supposedly dies while giving birth to Tarsiana. The hero, terrified of committing the same sin as Antioch, leaves Tarsiana with Estrangilo and his wife, Dionisa, to be raised and educated properly. In direct contrast to the parental devotion of Apolonio and Luciana, Dionisa is driven by jealousy and greed to hire an assassin to kill the beautiful child. Kidnapped and sold to a brothel, Tarsiana meets Antinágoras, who just paid to be the first to enjoy her. Thoughts about his own daughter together with Tarsiana's words stop him from such dishonorable action. In the end, Apolonio is reunited with his wife and daughter. He marries Tarsiana to Antinágoras, and he also has a son that would be heir to all his kingdom. Apolonio has indeed the perfect family. The hero has restored order as a ruler and as a father.

In spite of their vocal and active roles throughout the poem, Luciana and Tarsiana, together with other female characters, are defined by their relationship to male characters. As the poet indicates in his introduction, the poem treats Apolonio and how *he* lost his daughter and wife and how *he* found them again (stanza 2). Thus, Luciana's and Tarsiana's prominent roles are not because their adventures are significant per se but because they are, after all, the hero's wife and daughter, respectively. They help to reinforce the thematic focus on the family as the poet describes Luciana's obedience to her father, Architrastes, and her loyalty and devotion to her husband Apolonio. Tarsiana follows her mother's footsteps. On the other hand, Antioch's daughter, who even remains nameless, is introduced briefly only because of her blood relation to the sinful king.

Within their submissive domestic roles, women are allowed to negotiate some power, however limited. In *Libro de Apolonio*, Luciana and Tarsiana are empowered by language and their education. Luciana gains control over her future by choosing her own husband, while Tarsiana is able to protect her body from men seeking sexual favors. Tarsiana's words and stories become so powerful that they have a medicinal effect on those who hear her (stanzas 431 and 488). Moreover, when she is entertaining her father, each remains ignorant of the other's real identity; Tarsiana reclaims her own identity by telling the story of her life and *naming* the wetnurse who took care of her. Only after these pronouncements does Apolonio recognize and admit her as his daughter.

Yet Luciana and Tarsiana's access to language is limited and temporary. Once they find themselves under the protective arms of Apolonio, these characters are silenced forever since they now have a husband and/or father who will speak for them and protect their honor. The rest of the poem depicts Apolonio restoring order throughout the different kingdoms he has inherited. Even when female characters are allowed self-expression, it is only orally. Despite Luciana's musical talents, everyone concedes that her "natural" technique pales by comparison to the cultivated talents of Apolonio, who is envied even by Orpheus and Apollo! Apolonio recognizes Tarsiana's skills in telling stories and riddles, yet cannot help being bored and tired by them. For the most part, women in the poem lack access to written expression. When Luciana does write, she imitates masculine discourse by composing a riddle that would identify her choice for a husband. Such a recourse echoes the riddle composed for the potential suitors by Antioch at the beginning of the poem.

Notwithstanding the strong heroines in this poem, the story continually reminds readers of women's enormous capacity for evil. Antioch is not alone to blame for his incestuous relation. According to the poet, his daughter is also responsible because of her passive complicity (stanza 248). Thus, lightning kills both father and daughter in punishment. Dionisa is the most evil and cruelest character in the poem. Advised by the devil, she plots Tarsiana's death, builds a fake mausoleum to show to the grief-stricken Apolonio, and obstinately lies at the end. Estrangilo, her husband, is depicted as a weak man afraid of contradicting his wife. Teófilo, the reluctant assassin, is not only moved by Tarsiana's words to spare her but is remorseful enough to receive a pardon for his life, contrary to Dionisa, who is burned at the stake.

According to Brownlee, the act of writing is an important thematic motif in *Libro de Apolonio*, constituting one of the first of such instances in Spanish medieval literature. The poem epitomizes the tension of a society in transition between orality and literacy. Male characters are empowered by the permanence of writing: The young suitors are allowed to write letters to Luciana; Apolonio writes the identification and instructions on Luciana's casket; statues erected in Apolonio's honor bear inscriptions recording his achievements; and it was presumably a male poet that translated the story of the male hero and who insisted on a title that negates the two female protagonists. Luciana and Tarsiana are briefly empowered by the ephemeral spoken word, but their characters have left an indelible imprint on Spanish literature.

Work

"Libro de Apolonio." *Poetas castellanos anteriores al siglo XV*. Vol. 57, *Biblioteca de autores españoles desde la formación del lenguaje hasta nuestros días*. Ed. Tomás Antonio Sánchez et al. Madrid: Real Academia Española, 1952.

Libro de Apolonio. Ed. Manual Alvar. 3 vols. Valencia: Castalia, 1976.

Work about

Alvar, Manuel. "Apolonio, clérigo entendido." *Symposium In Honororem Professor M. de Riquer*. Ed. Margarita Badia and M. Antoni. Barcelona: Quaderns Crema, 1986. 51–73.

Brownlee, Marina Scordilis. "Writing and Scripture in the *Libro de Apolonio*: The Conflation of Hagiography and Romance." *Hispanic Review* 51.2 (Spring 1983): 159–174.

Dillard, Heath. *Daughters of the Reconquest. Women in Castilian Town Society, 1100–1300*. Cambridge: Cambridge UP, 1984.

Ferrante, Joan M. "The Education of Women in the Middle Ages in Theory, Fact, and Fantasy." *Beyond Their Sex. Learned Women of the European Past. Ed. Patricia H. Labalme. New York: New York UP, 1980. 9–42.

Lasry, Anita Benaim. "The Ideal Heroine in Medieval Romances: A Quest for a Paradigm." *Romance Quarterly* 32.3 (1985): 227–243.

Maier, John R. "The *Libro de Apolonio* and the Imposition of Culture." *La Chispa '87. Selected Proceedings*. Ed. Gilbert Paolini. New Orleans: Tulane UP, 1987. 169–176.

Musgrave, J.C. "Tarsiana and Juglaría in the *Libro de Apolonio*." *Medieval Hispanic Studies Presented to Rita Hamilton*. Ed. A.D. Deyermond. London: Tamesis, 1976. 129–138.

Rivera, Carmen S. "Defending Their Honor: Women's Voices in the *Libro de Apolonio*." *Cincinnati Romance Review* 13 (1994): 24–30.

Carmen S. Rivera

Libro de buen amor (1330, 1343): Its Portrayal of Women

A brilliant, very funny, much-debated work, the *Libro de buen amor* (1330, 1343; Book of Good Love, trans. as *The Book of the Archpriest*, 1975), presents a lengthy, complex compendium of Spanish medieval society and culture. Variously called burlesque erotic entertainment, an *ars amandi*, a didactic cautionary lesson, a guide for conduct, a retelling of the prodigal son tale, and so on, it draws on *courtly love conventions, religious texts, church liturgy, popular fables, Ovid's *Art of Loving*, goliardic poetry, proverbs, classical literature, the debate tradition, and carnivalesque discourse. Primarily written in *cuaderna vía* (monorhymed quatrains of 14 syllables), irony, parody, and ambiguity are also hallmarks of the work. Although certain double meanings, puns, and other extratextual references could only be understood by learned clerics, critics agree that author Juan Ruiz, archpriest of Hita's book, generally addressed a middle-class urban population of men and women. In such a complex work, the portrayal of women can be perceived in numerous ways.

Cohesion within the text of the *Libro de buen amor* is supported in several ways. The first-person narrative voice of the archpriest-protagonist provides fundamental unity, addressing God, the Virgin Mary, the reader, and other characters as he narrates, editorializes, moralizes, and prays. His quest—to secure for himself the "loving attentions" of a responsive woman—motivates all action in the text. The love-quest theme leads to frequent discussion in the text of what *buen amor* is and what distinguishes it from *loco amor* (wild, inappropriate love); *buen amor* connotes love of the soul for God but also is the favorite personal nickname of the work's infamous procuress, as Vasvari has noted, and it also can mean prostitute. The text offers itself to the reader as a "how to" guide: Humans perforce must contend with ambiguous, conflicting information and desires and must learn to separate "what seems to be versus what is" and employ Christian reason to "read" reality and secure salvation of their souls. This purpose is stated at the work's outset and dramatized throughout the story as the archpriest and other characters work through the process of judging, rightly and wrongly, situations they encounter and experience the appropriate consequences. Several didactic passages further reinforce the perils of evaluating situations inappropriately.

The narrator's quest, to secure for himself the sexual company of a woman, immediately classifies woman as object, satisfier of male appetite. He goes after many types of women characters, with the significant exception of married women. The mortal sin of adultery—defined in that time exclusively as a sexual encounter between a wife and a man other than her husband—is *not* endorsed in the work. Not all women accept the archpriest's advances; some correctly "read" him, perceive his real intentions correctly, and reject his advances; they disappear quickly from the narrative. Women characters who fail, who fall and succumb (such as the bakery-girl Cruz, or Doña Endrina), are described in more detailed fashion; the clearer depiction of women who succumb helps foster a dominant, misogynistic impression of woman as a weak, carnal object, as she is seen through the archpriest's eyes. Vasvari argues that Doña Endrina, featured in the longest episode of the text, reflects the accepted medieval stereotype of widows as sexually voracious and faithless.

The archpriest is rather a poor reader of signs himself and an often-unsuccessful Lothario. After being betrayed by a male go-between, he seeks counsel and assistance from three important characters—Sir Love, his wife Lady Venus, and the go-between Trotaconventos (convent-trotter; the memorable precursor to *Celestina)—to aid and abet him. As each figure offers advice, he/she discusses woman's nature, honing in on personality traits, possible weaknesses or defects of character, and other factors to be exploited or manipulated when trying to trip up women. Often the tone is playful, but woman is conceived here in Aristotelian terms—as matter to be exploited—and the focus is on identifying useful flaws. Language is the primary weapon of seduction, and Trotaconventos's linguistic prowess is her most outstanding trait. She in particular characterizes women in dehumanizing, misogynist terms—women as wax to be molded, horses to be mounted, dry tinder waiting to be lit. Francomani feels that the *Libro de buen amor* uses the legend of the Fall—Adam and Eve's disobedience (inspired by the duplicitous language of the serpent) and the catastrophic consequences—as an organizing principle for the entire narrative.

To go beyond this negative, traditional medieval portrayal of woman, it is useful to set aside what is said *about* women (and how it is said) by characters in the text and examine instead *which types* of women characters are included in the text and what they do. Gimeno has lucidly quantified the presence and function of women in the text, comparing it also with the presence and function of male characters therein. Much of the balance of this entry summarizes her observations.

At the outset of the *Libro de buen amor*, the archpriest does not define men and women in terms of gender but rather as beings with body and soul. Memory, understanding, and will, the three components of the soul, have the responsibility of directing, and controlling, the physical appetites of the body so that eternal life, available to the soul, can be attained. The body, particularly the male human, is besieged with a constant appetite for sexual consummation with a female, which must be controlled. The archpriest clearly states here that his book's purpose is to awaken the *memory* of good versus evil doings, so that readers will use the examples given to understand the world better and exercise their will in a Christian fashion, to secure salvation. The archpriest's equal presentation of male and female, as bodies with souls equally equipped to resist carnal urges, rejects the prevailing Aristotelian thought according to which woman is an imperfect or defective male, a putatively weaker vessel, or animal, in need of the superior soul or intellect of males. There does tend to be a male-female pairing up among characters, suggesting that arrangement as the natural order of things: The Virgin Mary is accompanied by Christ; Sir Love's counterpart is Lady Venus, Don Carnal accompanies his partner Lady Lent, and the archpriest represents the constant attempts of all men to secure a female partner.

There are 13 women in the work, with a balance between positive and negative, urban and rural, young and old. They may be divided into three categories. First, there are divine or supernatural authority figures: the Virgin Mary—the perfection of good; Lady Lent—also the perfection of good but only during her season; and Lady Venus—the evil temptress, betrayer of her sex, counterpart to Mary. The second category is composed of 9 unmarried mortal women who range from spiritually wise to utterly blind: young women, rural and urban, a widow, a nun, *serranas* (mountain girls), a Moorish woman, the lower-class baking girl. There are ultimately 5 spiritually wise women in this group. Although not spiritually wise, the *serranas* exercise a noteworthy function by shattering the idea of woman as pursued object that the archpriest has used throughout the text; here the tables are turned as *he* becomes the object of their aggressive carnal exploitation. The final category of women is composed of 1, the go-between Trotaconventos, who represents the sin and evil of the underworld, trying to blind women through words and clever reasoning, just as Lady Venus did. Recalling the mediating role of the Virgin Mary, but much more closely resembling Venus, she is a go-between.

Mortal males in the work are represented primarily by the archpriest, who portrays his sex as materialistic, imperfect, plagued with constant sexual hunger. Repeatedly, the archpriest recognizes his errors, sees the danger his soul is in, and would seem chastened. Several times he addresses women readers of the text and exhorts them to exercise their judgment and beware of male treachery and reject men who attempt to use them as objects. Inevitably, though, he backslides, succumbing to carnal desire. Unlike the group of human women, there are no spiritually wise mortal males. Lord Carnal is a carnivalesque, obscene caricature of all sorts of gluttony and lechery. Venus's husband, Sir Love, functions as Satan's representative, manipulating language in his attempts to promote lust and its satisfaction.

Given the equal value accorded to male and female souls, the balanced way in which women characters are portrayed, and the fact that women characters as a group are spiritually superior to male characters, Gimeno concludes that the *Libro de buen amor* does not conform to the *misogyny prevalent in other urban texts directed at the middle class and is best understood as a "how to" guide for discerning correctly, for male and female reader alike. Parker concurs, stating that there is good evidence for reading the text as an exploration of the role of learning and individual responsibility. Thus, despite many passages that present or comment on women in derogatory fashion, women are presented more favorably than men in terms of obtaining a soul in right relationship with God.

Work

Libro de buen amor. Ed. Jacques Joset. Madrid: Taurus, 1990.

Libro de Buen Amor. Ed., intro. and English paraphrase R.S. Willis. Princeton, NJ: Princeton UP, 1972.

Work about

Eisenberg, Daniel. "Juan Ruiz's Heterosexual 'Good Love.'" *Queer Iberia: Sexualities, Cultures and Crossings from the Middle Ages to the Renaissance*. Ed. and intro. Josiah Blackmore and Gregory S. Hutcheson. Durham, NC: Duke UP, 1999. 250–274.

Ferreras Savoy, Jacqueline. "El *Buen amor, La Celestina*: La Sociedad Patriarcal en Crisis." *Breve historia feminista de la literatura española (en lengua Castellana). II La mujer en la literatura española. Modos de representación desde la Edad Media hasta el siglo XVII*. Coord. Myriam Díaz-Ducaretz and Iris M. Zavala. Madrid: Dirección General de la Mujer; Barcelona: Anthropos, 1993. 69–100.

Francomano, Emily. "'Saber bien e mal': The Fall and the Fruits of Reading the *Libro de buen amor*." *La corónica* 26.2 (1998): 211–226.

Gimeno, Rosalie. "Women in the *Book of Good Love*." *Women in Hispanic Literature. Icons and Fallen Idols*. Ed. Beth Miller. Berkeley: U of California P, 1983. 84–96.

Jayne, Cynthia Powell. "Tales Told by Women in the *Libro de buen amor*." *Tennessee Philological Bulletin* 36 (1999): 49–55.

Miaja de la Peña, María Teresa. "'Donosas' y 'plazenteras': Las mujeres en el *Libro de buen amor*." *Actas de las VI Jornadas Medievales*. Ed. and intro. Concepción Company, Aurelio González, and Lillian von der Walde Mohens. Mexico: Universidad Nacional Autónoma de México, 1999. 439–449.

Parker, Margaret. "'Pensat qué fagades': Individual Responsibility in the *Libro de buen amor*." *Romance Quarterly* 35.1 (February 1988): 39–50.

Ramírez Pimienta, Juan Carlos. "La aventura de Doña Endrina y Don Melón de la Uerta: El matrimonio de la viuda como control social." *Hispanic Journal* 19.1 (Spring 1998): 169–181.

Reynal, Vicente. *Las mujeres del Arcipreste de Hita: Arquetipos femeninos medievales*. Barcelona: Puvill, 1991.

Vasvari, Louise O. "Múltiple transparencia semántica de los nombres de la alcahueta en el *Libro del Arcipreste*." *Medioevo y literatura. Actas del V Congreso de la Asociación Hispánica de Literatura Medieval*. Ed. Juan Paredes. Granada: U of Granada, 1995. 4:453–463.

———. "Why Is Doña Endrina a Widow? Traditional Culture and Textuality in the *Libro de buen amor*." *Upon My Husband's Death: Widows in the Literature and Histories of Medieval Europe*. Ed. Louise Mirrer. Ann Arbor: U of Michigan P, 1992. 259–283.

Maureen Ihrie

Libro de las virtuosas y claras mujeres (fifteenth century)

Penned by Constable Alvaro de Luna (1390?–1453), the powerful favorite of John II of Castile, the *Libro de las virtuosas y claras mujeres* (Book of Virtuous and Illustrious Women) takes the pro-feminist side of the fifteenth-century debate over women's worth. Although it is modeled somewhat on Boccaccio's *De claris mulieribus* (1361–1376?), Luna pursued an ethical and moral agenda rather than a literary one and thus includes only positive models of conduct in his catalog. Eschewing also Boccaccio's chronological arrangement, Luna groups his examples into three categories: (1) biblical examples of virtue, beginning with the Virgin Mary, followed by Eve, Sara, Esther, Susana, and others; (2) exemplary women like Lucrecia, Portia, Minerva, the goddess Diana, and Penelope, from pre-Christian, classical works; and finally (3) Christian saints, including Ana (the Virgin Mary's mother), Santa María Egipciaca, Paula, Mary Magdalene, and others. The main body of the text is introduced first by a preface from Juan de Mena, followed by Luna's preface, in which he argues that women's vices and flaws are caused by custom rather than being inherent and that women and men are equal in their propensity for evil; that men and women participate equally in the opportunity to attain God's blessing; that in the Original Sin of the Fall, women and men share equal responsibility; that the observations of Bible books like Proverbs and Ecclesiastes do not address all women but rather just the sinful minority; and finally, that his compilation will start with the Virgin Mary, since she is the most glorious example of and for all women. Throughout the text, the most prized virtues are chastity, virginity, and fidelity.

Work

Libro de las virtuosas e claras mujeres por el condestable don Alvaro de Luna. Ed. Marcelino Menéndez y Pelayo. Madrid: Sociedad de Bibliófilos Españoles, 1891.

Work about

Montoya Ramírez, María Isabel. "Observaciones sobre la defensa de las mujeres en algunos textos medievales." *Medioevo y literatura. Actas del V Congreso de la Asociación Hispánica de Literatura Medieval*. Ed. Juan Paredes. Granada: U of Granada, 1995. 3:397–406.

Maureen Ihrie

Linares, Luisa-María (1915–)

As a young writer, Luisa-María Linares drew from her experiences traveling with her father. As an adult, she has become extremely popular as the author of some 50 "racy" popular novels featuring romantic plots and exotic settings. Many of her romances have been translated into foreign languages, including English.

Linares began her publishing career in 1939 with *En poder de Barba Azul* (In the Power of Bluebeard). This novel, which she also assisted in adapting for theater and film, is typical of many of her later works in its adventurous, fast-paced plot, relating the adventures of the young heiress Miriam, pressured by her industrialist father into marrying the distasteful and graceless but wealthy Archibald Canfield. On the eve of her wedding, Miriam stows away on a yacht belonging to a handsome nobleman bound for Europe. Miriam reveals her presence to him, only to discover that he possesses a strong streak of *misogyny. In order to remain on board, the young woman must agree to serve as one of the sailors and dress in men's clothing; thus, Miriam transforms herself into Jacobo. Although she completes her duties admirably, the count's hostility toward her frustrates and finally attracts her. After arriving in Santiago de Compostela, she takes a job in a hotel, befriends the count's family, and finally succeeds in winning his heart away from her rival, a beautiful, haughty ballerina. Throughout this series of misunderstandings and mishaps, the lesson that the count invariably tries to teach Miriam is not to flirt.

Another novel that Linares adapted for the screen is *Un marido a precio fijo* (1940; A Husband for a Set Price). Heiress Estrella Vilar rejects the suitor her uncle has selected for her and impetuously marries a man she has known only briefly in a civil ceremony. When her new husband steals her money and abandons her before she has a chance to introduce him to her family, Estrella hires another man to impersonate her husband. Miguel Rivera teaches the snobbish young woman a lesson by forcing her to obey him during their "honeymoon" in the mountains. She learns to cook and keep house as the *reina del hogar* (queen of the hearth). When their agreement comes to an end, the two realize they have fallen in love. The novel ends when Estrella and Miguel are reunited in a domestic scene that previews their future together as husband and wife.

Linares's novels feature women protagonists who are either tamed of their independence by men or seek out men for protection. One text that falls into the latter category is *Juan a las ocho, Pablo a las diez* (1964; John at Eight, Paul at Ten, trans. as *Web of Fear*, 1979). Danielle Villiers, a recent bride, finds herself in financial straits when her husband, a famous photographer, abandons her in Paris for four months while he is on an expedition. She takes a part-time job as an illustrator of children's books and accepts a boarder, Dr. Juan Romano de Santiago. When her tenant apparently commits suicide, Danielle finds herself in the middle of a mystery involving huge sums of money and an international treasure-hunting scheme. Another Dr. Romano introduces himself to her, wins her confidence, and saves her life. The last chapter of the book sketches their idyllic life together in Paradise Valley, the doctor's estate in Africa.

In addition to writing novels, Linares has written for such magazines as *Elle*, *Marie Claire*, *Grazia*, and *Woman's Own*.

Work by

De noche soy indiscreta. Barcelona: Juventud, 1965.
En poder de Barba Azul. Barcelona: Juventud, 1943.
Juan a las ocho, Pablo a las diez. Barcelona: Juventud, 1964.
Un marido a precio fijo. Barcelona: Juventud, 1940.
Mis cien últimos amores. Barcelona: Juventud, 1963.
No digas lo que hice ayer. Barcelona: Juventud, 1969.

Deborah Hirsch

Literary History
See Women Writers in Spanish Literary History (1500–1996)

Llibre de les Dones
See Eiximenis, Francesc (1330?–1409): His Views on Women

López de Córdoba, Leonor (late fourteenth–early fifteenth century)

Daughter of the Master of Calatrava and Alcantara military orders, this Spanish noblewoman is the first person of Castile to record her life history, doing so at the end of her life in a short *Testamento* (Testament) destined for family members. This personal account of tumultuous events during the violent political struggles between Pedro I of Castile and his brother Enrique of Trastámara, who murdered Pedro in 1369, narrates the dramatic reversals of fortune she and her powerful family (supporters of Pedro) endured after Enrique's triumph. In a mix of public (male) legalese and private (female) concerns, she recounts being imprisoned, living under siege, surviving the plague, and witnessing the first mass destruction of Jewish lives and properties. Kaminsky and Johnson note in their modern edition of the text that it is organized around three deaths in the family: those of her father, her younger brother, and a 12-year-old son (at which point the narrative ends). Mirrer observes that López de Córdoba's generous use of legal terminology could either indicate the assistance of a notary or a conscious imitation of male language; in either case, she clearly is conscious of the power that writing holds and insists that it is she who writes. Her reactions to censure; her faith; her ability to survive amidst deceptions and intrigue, apart from her husband for years at a time; her pride, which remained unsullied by indignities suffered—all create a memorable personal portrait of an unusually strong woman.

López de Córdoba's life continued its dramatic course for many years after the death of her son. Eventually, she rose again, becoming a highly influential adviser to Queen Catalina of Lancaster, only to fall from grace once more and barely miss death by burning. *See also* Autobiographical Self-Representation of Women in the Early Modern Period

Work by

Ayerbe-Chaux, Reinaldo. "Las memorias de doña López de Córdova." *Journal of Hispanic Philology* 2 (1977): 11–33.

"To Restore Honor and Fortune: 'The Autobiography of Leonor López de Córdoba.'" Trans. Amy Katz Kaminsky and Elaine Dorough Johnson. *The Female Autograph*. Ed. Domna C. Stanton. Chicago: U of Chicago P, 1984. 70–80.

Work about

Mirrer, Louise. *Women, Jews and Muslims in the Texts of Reconquest Castile*. Ann Arbor: U of Michigan P, 1996. 139–150.

Sears, Theresa Ann. "Leonor López de Córdova (Late Fourteenth–Early Fifteenth Century)." *Spanish Women Writers: A Bio-Bibliographical Source Book*. Ed. Linda Gould Levine, Ellen Engelson Marson and Gloria Feiman Waldman.

Westport, CT: Greenwood P, 1993. 264–269.

Maureen Ihrie

Lorenza de los Ríos, María, Marchioness of Fuerte Híjar (c. 1768–after 1817)

The bio-bibliographical data on María Lorenza de los Ríos, marchioness of Fuerte Híjar, is very limited. Born possibly in Cádiz, she lived in Valladolid and in Madrid where she died after 1817, a year in which she was still president of the Junta de Damas de Honor y Mérito (Society of Ladies of Honor and Merit) of Madrid's Royal Economic Society. She married the marquis of Fuerte Híjar, Germano de Salcedo y Somodevilla (1748–1810), a little known but important figure of the Spanish Enlightenment as Subdelegado General de Teatros (an official in charge of theaters) during one of Manuel Godoy's terms.

As of this writing, there has been no specific or general study of the life and works of the marchioness of Fuerte Híjar. She left two unpublished comedies, "La sabia indiscreta" (The Indiscreet Wise Woman) and "El Eugenio," both kept in manuscript at the Biblioteca Nacional in Madrid, with no date, although the handwriting style dates to around 1800. In "La sabia indiscreta" the marchioness of Fuerte Híjar censures women's indiscretion in the tradition of Spanish comedy of the Enlightenment.

Work about

Herrera Navarro, Jerónimo. *Catálogo de autores teatrales del siglo XVIII*. Madrid: Fundación Universitaria Española, 1993.

Alberto Acereda

Lozana andaluza, La (1528)

Francisco Delicado (1480?–1534) published his *Retrato de la Lozana andaluza en lengua española muy clarissima, compuesto en Roma, el qual retrato demuestra lo que en Roma pas-*

sava, y contiene muchas mas cosas que la Celestina (Portrait of the Lusty Andalusian Woman in Very Clear Spanish, Composed in Rome, Which Portrait Shows What Occurred in Rome, and Has Many More Things Than the *Celestina*) in Venice. The book narrates the life and adventures of Lozana, an Andalusian woman who lived through the years that preceded the Sack of Rome, from 1513 to 1527. Written in dialogued prose, there is an emphasis on creating a realistic picture of the city, the inhabitants of the Roman underworld, and the adventures and personality of Lozana.

Delicado wanted to represent action, and his narration is dominated by the dynamics of conversations, walks, and characters in movement. Every scene is presented by an "author-narrator" who later in the text himself becomes friends with the protagonist. The development of action depends on the dialogue between characters. Since characters belong to the underclass, the language they use is a reproduction of colloquial Spanish mixed with "lingua franca," the mixed jargon acquired by Spanish expatriates, that included expressions and words in Latin, French, Portuguese, and especially Italian. Swear words, blasphemies, and obscene language also abound.

The book's structure is determined by the evolution of the main character. The first part deals with Lozana's childhood in Andalusia. In Seville she meets Diomedes, her first lover. He takes the young Aldonza, who later becomes Lozana, with him on his travels around the Mediterranean coast. After being kidnapped by her father-in-law and thrown into the sea, the young woman travels to Genoa and later to Rome, the stage of her adventures. In Rome, Lozana takes a young man, Rampín, as a servant/lover/pimp. Her adventures finish when Rome is invaded and destroyed by the soldiers of the Spanish and German emperor Charles V in 1527. Then she leaves Rome with Rampín and retires to live out the rest of her days in peace. There are 66 chapters, or *mamotretos*, 23 in the first part and 43 in the second, a Prólogo, and an Argumento. At the end of the narrative body Delicado added an Apología in "defense of women," in which he presents women's situation as one of being driven into the streets by the cruelty of men and excuses women from the guilt of being the origin of pain or sickness.

There are 125 characters in the novel, all connected to the protagonist by her business or through friendships. Lozana's businesses include making *cosmetics for prostitutes, prescribing remedies for *syphilis victims, and serving as go-between for the sexual needs of merchants and ecclesiastics. All characters are introduced either by the narrator-author or by their own intervention, specifying national origins, profession, and relationship with Lozana. There are references to well-known historical personalities including Pope Leo X and famous courtesans such as Imperia and Garza Montesina. (Montesina was also the object of poetic creation in Juan de la Encina's *Cancionero*.) Francisco Delicado intended to make a realistic portrait of Roman street life; thus he incorporates descriptions of daily routines, such as different methods for washing linen or how to cook a Spanish dish. Characters are described performing bodily functions, as when Lozana interrupts a conversation with another character to run inside her house and urinate. Characters' emotions range from erotic excitement to anger, fear, affection, humor, and sadness. The city of Rome is a living entity, its streets swarming with noisy crowds, and the protagonist guides the reader to different locations: the public baths, the banker's streets, the jail tower. Delicado paints a dynamic and colorful Renaissance portrait of Rome, a mixture of action, colors, and noise.

Published in Venice in 1528, there is no evidence that the *Retrato de la Lozana* was published in Spain until the nineteenth century when Pascual Gayangos included it in his editions of "Libros raros y curiosos." It has been rejected by traditional criticism; Menéndez Pelayo considered it "ugly and disgusting," and it has not been yet fully accepted in the canon of Spanish Renaissance literature. Sources that did or might have influenced the *Lozana* include *Libro de buen amor*, La *Celestina*, El *Corbacho*, *Tirant lo Blanc*, *Cuestión de Amor*, *Dechado de Amor*, and the *Cancionero de Burlas*. There are analogies in style and technique between the *Lozana* and Aretino's *Ragginamenti* (1533–1539) and in Cervantes's exemplary novel *Casamiento engañoso* (1613), although neither Aretino nor Cervantes mentioned Delicado in their writings.

The *Retrato de la Lozana* cannot be considered a picaresque novel because it is narrated by an exterior observer rather than the protagonist. It has been connected to the Celestinian saga because it deals with women and with prostitution and is written in dialogue, but the didactic intention of the author is not as clear as it is in *Celestina*. Delicado's attitude toward women characters in his novel is far less misogynist than that of Rojas in *Celestina*. Delicado attributes the origin of prostitution to poverty and lack of a supporting family (young Lozana becomes an orphan as a young child). During her evolution from childhood to maturity, the naive girl Lozana matures into a wise, worldly woman capable of surviving in a hostile environment by means of her physical gifts but more importantly by her intelligence. Rome in the *Lozana* is a corrupt city, and the protagonist uses her professional skills to survive. Although she is not an ideal of feminine virtue of the day, Lozana does possess many positive qualities; independence, intelligence, hospitality toward friends, kindness, and *gracia* (charm) separate her from feminine characters such as Justina or Celestina, who were conceived with a moralistic or didactic intention. Additionally, the relationship established between the narrator-author-turned-character and Lozana is a mutually sympathetic one.

Lozana herself is aware that her life is being written by her friend the narrator-author. Both protagonist and "author" are victims of a venereal disease common in Europe at the time: syphilis. This sickness played an important role in the genesis of the novel. Delicado declares in the prologue that his own suffering as a victim of syphilis led him to write his *Retrato de la Lozana andaluza* to forget his pain. Whether this statement is true or a literary device to justify creation of a libertine novel is difficult to demonstrate. Nevertheless, Delicado was the author of other writings that dealt with syphilis: *De consolationem infirmorum* (1525; On the Consolation of Illness) and *El modo de adoperare il legno de India* (1529; The Way to Use Lignum Vitae from the Indies), and this stigmatized illness was a very important component of sixteenth-century life in the Roman social underworld.

The Spanish poet Rafael Alberti (1902–) did a contemporary reading of Lozana. As a result of Alberti's interest, *Lozana* became the inspiration for a contemporary theater play and a topic in Alberti's book of poems *Roma, peligro para caminantes* (1967). See also Pícara Justina, La (1605); Pícaras and Pícaros: Female and Male Rogues in the Spanish Picaresque Canon

Work by

Portrait of Lozana: The Lusty Andalusian Woman. Tr., intro., and notes Bruno Damiani. Potomac, MD: Scripta Humanistica, 1987.

Retrato de la Lozana andaluza. Ed. Claude Allaigre. Madrid: Cátedra, 1985.

Work about

Beltrán, Luis. "The Author's Author, Typography, and Sex: The Fourteenth Century Mamotreto of La Lozana andaluza." *The Picaresque: Tradition and Displacement*. Ed. and intro. Giancarlo Maiorino. Minneapolis: U of Minnesota P, 1996. 86–136.

Bubnova, Tatiana. *Francisco Delicado puesto en diálogo*. México City: UNAM, 1987.

Damiani, Bruno. "Sentido y forma de la *Lozana andaluza*." *Moralidad y didactismo en el Siglo de Oro*. Madrid: Orígenes, 1977. 31–79.

García-Verdugo, M. Luisa. *La Lozana andaluza y la literatura del siglo XVI*. Madrid: Pliegos, 1994.

———. "Roma, peligro para caminantes y las Lozanas de Delicado y Alberti: Obras en el exilio." *Homenaje a don Luis Monguío*. Ed. Jordi Aladro Font and David Dabuco. Newark, DE: Juan de la Cuesta, 1997. 209–216.

Goytisolo, Juan de. "Notas sobre la *Lozana andaluza*." *Disidencias*. Barcelona: Seix Barral, 1978. 37–71.

Imperiale, Louis. *El contexto dramático de* La Lozana andaluza. Potomac: Scripta Humanística, 1991.

———. *La Roma clandestina de Francisco Delicado y Pietro Aretino*. New York: Peter Lang, 1997.

María Luisa García-Verdugo

Luca, Andrea (1957–)

Born in Madrid, after obtaining her bachelor's degree in philosophy, poet Andrea Luca spent a short period of time in Italy, where she collaborated with a radio station, worked as a translator, and started her career as a binder and curator of books. In 1983, Luca returned to Madrid where she opened a bindery, book restoration, and graphics documents business, dedicated also to teaching restoration techniques. Currently, she is director of the Sirena de los Vientos publishing house and writes for Spanish newspapers and literary journals.

After the Franco regime (1939–1975), Spaniards began to explore and question cultural, historical, and sexual identity. Luca's poetic corpus, published during the democratic period, registers the search for identity and modernity that characterizes the development of Spanish history fraught with massive sociopolitical change. The manner in which Luca creates and manipulates poetic space represents a search for liminality, a place beyond the gendered limitations imposed by ideology and discourse. In this space, a liminal speaking voice emerges, presenting a plurality of identities that undermine the classical sexual dichotomy, blurring its Manichean binarism. Gender marks are diluted, inverted, transgressed, and questioned. Specifically, Luca introduces a lesbian marginal discourse that decenters the speaking voice vis-à-vis patriarchal ideology.

Luca's publications are: *A golpes de sino* (1979; With Blows of Destiny), *En el banquete* (1987; At the Banquet, First Prize, Erotic Poetry, Ateneo of Guipúzcoa), *El Don de Lilith* (1990; Lilith's Talent), *Canción del Samurai* (1992; Song of the Samurai), and *Tinta de noche* (1994; Ink of Night). The poetic voice in these poems, independent of biological associations, presents both feminine and masculine traits in the same entity, which thus is able to function on both sides of the dyad.

A golpes de sino presents aspects typical of any first poetic work. The speaking voice has not yet found a comfortable space but is beginning to explore the revisioning use of mythology that will become characteristic of Luca's poetry. In *En el banquete*, the speaking voice begins searching the most hidden aspects of the human soul to find, little by little, her own particular space. Here, she faces her androgyny and looks for a historical mythical model of women outside of patriarchy. She chooses Lilith, the demon woman of the Bible and (sometimes) first wife of Adam. This biblical figure prefigures multiple historical identities who challenge the limitation of women by the patriarchy. All the poems distill a transformative spirit articulated through fluidity and gender multiplicity to arrive at liminal identities.

El Don de Lilith presents the evolution of the poetic figure of Lilith, creator of a new woman within a liminal space. The poetic discourse is in an interstitial space characterized by movements between center and margins. An oppositional relation is produced toward patriarchal feminine and masculine models and values, by decentering the experience of sexual desire from heterosexual to lesbian desire. Hence, this poetry acquires mobility, showing different forms of desire: woman to man, man to woman, and especially, woman to woman. The last form of desire evolves to project itself as a liminal desire. "Abrázame desde tu vaporoso estado" (Embrace Me from Your Vaporous State) presents an entity able to act sexually as man or woman, according to the kind of desire perceived. There is no fusion of desires—feminine or masculine desire is used, depending on the specific need in a particular moment. A third gender and sex is envisioned.

In *Canción del Samurai* and *Tinta de noche* gender makes room for seeking the pure incarnation of the word. The image of mobility persists, but the poetic space becomes dark and mysterious, seeking the moment of division of the word into signified and signifier. The general theme of searching for the origins of, on one hand, gender division and, on the other, sign division situates Luca's poetry discourse in liminal positions. The dichotomous and Manichean system is challenged, appealing to a reader open to a transformative reality in continuous movement.

Work by

A golpes del sino. Madrid: Vox, 1979.
Canción del Samurai. Madrid: Endymion, 1992.
El Don de Lilith. Madrid: Endymion, 1990.
En el banquete. Madrid: Endymion, 1987.
Tinta de noche. Madrid: Libertarias, 1994.

Work about

Buenaventura, Ramón. *Las diosas blancas. Antología de la joven poesía española escrita por mujeres.* Madrid: Hiperión, 1986. 164–170.

Ugalde, Sharon Keefe. *Conversaciones y poemas. La nueva poesía femenina española en castellano.* Madrid: Siglo XXI, 1991. 233–244.

———. "Subversión y revisionismo en la poesía de Ana Rossetti, Concha García, Juana Castro y Andrea Luca." *Novísimos, postnovísimos, clásicos: La poesía de los ochenta en España.* Ed. Biruté Ciplijauskaité. Madrid: Orígenes, 1991. 117–140.

Marina A. Llorente

Luna, Alvaro de

See *Libro de las virtuosas y claras mujeres* (fifteenth century)

Lyceum Club Femenino (1926–1936)

The Lyceum Club Femenino was formed in 1926 by María de *Maeztu (1882–1948) on the model of comparable women's clubs in England, France, and the United States. Intended as a meeting place where women could exchange ideas and promote their social and cultural concerns, the club was divided into six subsections devoted to social issues, music, the arts, science, literature, and international affairs. The organization sponsored lectures, concerts, exhibitions, and a variety of literary tributes. It advocated such measures as reformation of women's legal status and creation of day-care centers for working women, and it campaigned for such things as a statute in Madrid in honor of Concepción *Arenal (1820–1893). Its 150 founding members represented the feminine cultural elite of the day, a well-educated group of professional women, writers, or wives of well-known male writers. Its membership, which rose to 500 by 1930, included notable names such as Zenobia Camprubí, Ernestina de *Champourcin, María *Goyri, Victoria *Kent, María de la O Lejárraga, Concha *Méndez, Isabel Oyarzábal de Palencia, and Amalia de Salaverría. Religious groups and publications condemned the club for its liberal political ideas, its library collection, and for what they regarded as its threat to marriage, the family, and the Church. The Lyceum Club Femenino effectively united a variety of ideological perspectives in a collective attempt to advance the feminist movement in Spain. Although efforts of the group to create a collective consciousness were an isolated endeavor, they were sufficient to forge a common sensitivity to women's issues among its members and to nurture development of the works of many female writers of the period. The club symbolically declared woman's right in Spain to expand her intellectual and cultural horizons. *See also* Feminism in Spain: 1900–2000

Work about

Basauri, Mercedes G. "La mujer en el reinado de Alfonso XIII." *Tiempo de Historia* 46 (September 1978): 36–38.

Campo Alange, María Lafitte, Condesa de. *La mujer*

en España: Cien años de su historia. 1860–1960. Madrid: Aguilar, 1964. 208–210.

Fagoaga, Concha. *La voz y el voto de la mujeres. El sufragismo en España 1877–1931*. Barcelona: Icaria, 1985. 178–192.

Nieva de la Paz, Pilar. *Autoras dramáticas españolas entre 1918 y 1936*. Madrid: Consejo Superior de Investigaciones Científicas, 1993. 66–68.

Rodrigo, Antonina. *Mujeres en España. Las silenciadas*. 2nd ed. Barcelona: Plaza y Janés, 1979. 134–136.

Zulueta, Carmen de, and Alicia Moreno. *Ni convento ni college La Residencia de Señoritas*. Madrid: Consejo Superior de Investigaciones Científicas, 1993. 37–58.

Catherine G. Bellver

Madera, Asunción ("Chona") (1901–after 1980)

Long a dean of the Canary Islands school of twentieth-century women poets (together with Pino *Ojeda and Pino Betancourt), Madera was born in Las Palmas of Gran Canaria in 1901 and wrote under her nickname, "Chona." Madera began writing as a journalist and turned to composing poetry during the 1940s, including as prominent themes the inescapable sea and island geography, poetry and poetics, aspects of language, and love. Generally excluded from the canon and from poetic anthologies as well as literary histories, women writers in the Canaries were usually ignored or obliged to become their own chroniclers. Given her date of birth, Madera would belong chronologically to the "Generation of 1927," but women's writing in the Islands (as frequently is the case elsewhere) transcends traditional schemes of literary "generations," in part because most women writers have worked in isolation, publishing their compositions in private editions or as periodical collaborations. Occasionally, they have founded periodicals and literary reviews, often of considerable testimonial value, as is the case of Mujeres en la isla (Island Women), whose collaborators were all women, writing on diverse topics ranging from politics to plastic arts to the dramatic isolation of the woman writer. This review first saw the light in 1954, with Chona Madera and Pino Ojeda as its most significant collaborators; both wrote repeatedly of their dramatic solitude and that of other women, with Ojeda embracing her isolation, while Chona Madera often found it a source of sadness and desolation, expressed in her verses.

The anguish of solitude on the island, surrounded by an ocean seen as imprisoning and drowning the soul, echoes in Madera's lyrics. Her first book, El volcado silencio (1944; Emptied Silence), embodies a search for identity but finds only nostalgia for times past that will never return. Hers is a silence that speaks, that shouts in rebellion, and from that silence she seeks a space wherein she constructs her voice, her own personal and concrete being. Further works of Madera are Mi presencia más clara (1956; My Clearest Presence), Las estancias vacías (1961; Empty Rooms), La voz que me desvela (1965; The Voice That Keeps Me from Sleeping), Los contados instantes (1967; Counted Seconds), Continuada señal (1970; Continuing Signal), and Mi otra palabra (1977; My Other Word). Madera, who continued writing until nearly 80, lived to an advanced age, but little fundamental change is visible in her lyric production. For Madera, poetic creation is something totally personal and solitary, and one aspect of her singular poetics consisted in composing testimonies in place of those that might have been written by numerous other women who, for many different reasons, never wrote.

Work by

Los contados instantes. Las Palmas de Gran Canaria: n.p., 1967.
Continuada señal. Málaga: n.p., 1970.
Las estancias vacías. Las Palmas de Gran Canaria: n.p., 1961.
Mi otra palabra. Málaga: Guadalhorce, 1977.
Mi presencia más clara. Madrid: n.p., 1956.
El volcado silencio. Las Palmas de Gran Canaria: n.p., 1944.
La voz que me desvela. Las Palmas de Gran Canaria: n.p., 1965.

Janet Pérez

Madera, Chona

See Madera, Asunción ("Chona") (1901–after 1980)

Maeztu y Whitney, María de (1881–1948)

This important Spanish feminist devoted her life to teaching, to improving education for women, and to elevating women's status in her country. Born in Vitoria, María de Maeztu y Whitney began teaching in Bilbao in 1901, but after studying at the University of Salamanca from 1907 to 1909, she moved to Madrid in 1911. There, she concurrently pursued a liberal arts degree at the university and a second degree in education from the newly formed Escuela de Estudios Superiores del Magisterio. In 1908 she participated in a pedagogical commission in England, and she received a grant to study the schools of Europe in 1909 and to attend the University of Marburg in 1912. Upon her return, Maeztu worked with her former teacher José Ortega y Gasset (1883–1955) at the Centro de Estudios Históricos. Her work and ideas on education won her national recognition, especially among liberal reformers. In 1915 she was appointed the first director of the Residencia de Señoritas. Using American colleges like Smith and Vassar as her model, Maeztu fashioned a center that served as a residence hall for women attending the university or preparing for entrance exams and also as a non-degree-granting college offering lectures, scholarships, laboratories, field trips, sport events, and other social and intellectual activities. With close ties to both the Institución Libre de Enseñanza and the Instituto Internacional (founded by Boston missionaries and later associated with Smith College), the Residencia de Señoritas fostered development of the total woman—intellectually, physically, and ethically.

In 1918 Maeztu was also put in charge of the Instituto Escuela de Segunda Enseñanza, an exemplary secondary school that employed progressive pedagogical methodology, and in 1920 she organized university women into a group called Juventud Universitaria Femenina. In 1926, she became one of the few women chosen to sit on the national assembly created by dictator Primo de Rivera, and in that same year, she helped form and became president of the *Lyceum Club Femenino, Spain's first women's club. Her international reputation grew as a result of her many visits abroad to study foreign educational systems, give lectures, or participate in international conferences. During the Spanish Civil War, Maeztu left Spain to settle in Argentina, where she continued to lecture and assumed a university post in Buenos Aires. The horrors of war and particularly the murder of her brother (essayist Ramiro de Maeztu) led her to support conservative ideas in her years of exile. Maeztu also authored translations and an anthology of prose writers and published a number of books on culture, education, and child psychology, but she is primarily remembered for her advocacy of women's education. *See also* Feminism in Spain: 1900–2000; Women's Education in Spain: 1860–1993; Women's Situation in Spain: 1786–1931: The Awakening of Female Consciousness

Work about

Capel Martínez, Rosa María. *El trabajo y la educación de la mujer en España (1900–1930)*. Madrid: Ministerio de Cultura, 1986. 515–518.

Maillard, Maria Luisa. *Asociación Española de Mujeres Universitarias (1920–1990)*. Madrid: Instituto de la Mujer, 1990. 11–21.

Ocampo, Victoria. "Notas. María de Maeztu." *Sur* 160 (January 1948): 58–62.

Ortega, Soledad. "Evocación de una tarea educadora." *Cuadernos Hispanoamericanos* 193 (January 1966): 1–10.

Pérez-Villanueva Tovar, Isabel. *María de Maeztu: Una mujer en el reformismo educativo español*. Madrid: Universidad Nacional de Educación a Distancia, 1989.

Rodrigo, Antonina. *Mujeres de España. Las silenciadas*. 2nd ed. Barcelona: Plaza y Janés, 1979. 127–138.

Zulueta, Carmen de. *Cien años de educación de la mujer española. Historia del Instituto Internacional*. Madrid: Castalia, 1992. 201–213.

Zulueta, Carmen de, and Alicia Moreno. *Ni convento ni college. La Residencia de Señoritas*. Madrid: Consejo Superior de Investigaciones Científicas, 1993. 39–58.

Catherine G. Bellver

Maja
See *Cigarrera*

Malquerida, La
See Benavente, Jacinto (1866–1954): His Portrayal of Women in *La noche del sábado* and *La malquerida*

Manola
See *Cigarrera*

Manzanares, Teresa de
See *Niña de los embustes, Teresa de Manzanares, La* (1632)

March Alcalá, Susana (1918–1993)

This novelist and poet was born in Barcelona, of a middle-class family. Often beset by illness, she studied music, painting, and foreign languages during several enforced absences from schooling. Susana March Alcalá began writing poetry at an early age, publishing in periodicals by the time she was 15, and at 20 she published her first collection, *Rutas* (1938; Routes, Itineraries), privately printed during the Civil War (1936–1939). In 1940, she married novelist Ricardo Fernández de la Reguera, with whom she had one son and collaborated on 11 historical novels, resembling the *Episodios nacionales* of Pérez Galdós but set in the early twentieth century rather than the nineteenth. March continued writing poetry, publishing several collections: *Ardiente voz* (1948; Fervent Voice); *El viento* (1951; Wind); *La tristeza* (1953; Sadness), for which she was awarded honorable mention in the Adonais Prize competition; and *Esta mujer que soy* (1959; The Woman I Am). An anthology of her first two decades of poetry was published in 1966 and titled *Poemas: Antología (1938–1959)*, followed by *Los poemas del hijo* (1970; Poems for My Son). In addition to historical fiction in collaboration, March's prose writings include a collection of short stories, *Narraciones* (1945; Narrations), and five novels, of which the best received were *Nina* (1949), which focuses on a woman's passionate, undying love for a man (which long outlives the weak lover and survives his death), and *Algo muere cada día* (1955; Each Day Something Dies [Inside Us]), offering a broader portrayal of a woman's life against the background of the Civil War in Barcelona and portraying not so much the survival as the erosion of love. Employing the first person and an autobiographical point of view, the novel emphasizes the principal stages in the development of the central character, María, following her from childhood to youth and maturity, with old age presented via her relationship with her mother (their especially close mother-daughter relationship also appears repeatedly in March's poems). María may represent women of March's generation, as a clear chronological correspondence exists between the author and her protagonist who grows up in Barcelona in the years preceding the war, marries, becomes a poet and successful writer, and eventually supports her three children.

The autobiographical substrata are considerable in March's fiction, as well as her poetry, and both privilege "women's concerns," love, motherhood, feminine identity, and mother-daughter bonds. She also spoke out in interviews and in her writing against the inferior education accorded women under the Franco regime, the relegation of women to domestic space, and the regime's discriminatory work laws, effectively cloistering most women and condemning them to continuing inequality. March's poetry includes poems denouncing class and gender restrictions, the repression of feminine individuality, and prejudices that destroyed relationships or stifled emotions. Other poems indict conventional norms that impede communication in the name of "good taste" and victimize both sexes, but especially women, some of whom suffer violence as a result. This contemporary of Gloria *Fuertes is more restrained and less comedic in her language but also occasionally incorporates colloquial registers and, like other "social poets," portrays daily life. Her lyrics also frequently express frustration, disappointment, sorrow, and bitterness (with pessimism engendered by both the war and difficult postwar experiences). Loss, melancholy, rebellion, and idealism inspire other poems, usually featuring feminine speakers, but not all of her poetry belongs to the protest category, as shown by numerous poems poignantly treating her son, and a mother's love. *Poemas de la Plaza Real* (1987; Poems of Royal Square) remained unpublished for over four decades. These intimate, lyrical, introspective pages recall March's beloved childhood home, her youthful explorations in the forest, dreams, encounters with nature, and romanticized love of liberty. In *La pasión desvelada* (1946; Passion Unveiled), composed two years after the collection just described, but published four decades sooner, March celebrates the discovery of love, exalting life's beauty and extolling the lover's perfection. Strong erotic undercurrents lead to her viewing even eternity as erotic. Yet amid erotic plenitude and maternal stirrings are poems foreseeing the poet's death, a theme more fully developed in *Ardiente voz* (1951; Burning Voice), which also treats fraternity and collective concerns, incorporating aspects of "social poetry." *El viento* and *La tristeza* blend social concerns and pastoral visions with strong personal motifs (broken dreams, mortality, remembrances). *Esta mujer que soy*, a self-portrait emphasizing melancholy, unfulfilled longings, and fading youth, contains numerous motifs of aging: grave eyes, sorrow, graying hair, presentiments of death. Religious motifs become more prominent, with prayers to the Virgin and a dialogue with God, as well as prayers of supplication. *Los poemas del hijo* comprises not only poems written to her son in infancy celebrating his childhood discoveries and consciousness but his growth, his adolescence, his transition to manhood and fatherhood.

A prolific writer and a moderately successful poet (her poems were translated to French, English, Italian, Portuguese, Dutch, Swedish, and Russian), March defies facile classification. She coincided with many concerns of "social poetry," without being quite so leftist in her ideology, nor so prosaic and pedestrian in her poetics, and she expressed many concerns for women's condition without being militant. She was especially critical of the limited, circumscribed place assigned to women by Spanish society, the numerous conventions delimiting large areas where women could not go, the many things they could not do, blocks of things that "a lady" may not say. Less unmistakably nonconformist than some social poets, March couched her protest in metaphor, paradoxical language, and ambiguity, suggesting at once the complexities she faced as a writer and the fact that a woman's right to her own voice was disputed. *See also* Short Fiction by Women Writers: 1900–1975

Work by

Algo muere cada día. Barcelona: Bruguera, 1973.
Nina. Barcelona: Planeta, 1955.
Poemas: Antología (1938–59). Santander: La Isla de los Ratones, 1966.
Los poemas del hijo. Santander: Bedia, 1970.
La tristeza. Madrid: Rialp, 1953.

Work about

Cavallo, Susana. " 'Aquí estoy': Autonominación y autorretrato en la poesía de Susana March." *A Ricardo Gullón: Sus discípulos.* Ed. Adelaida López de Martínez. Erie, PA: Asociación de Licenciados y Doctores Españoles en Estados Unidos, 1995. 51–60.
M., A. "Poemas de Susana March." *Papeles de Son Armadans* (Mallorca) 44 (1967): 125–128.
Pérez, Janet. *Modern and Contemporary Spanish Women Poets.* New York: Twayne, 1996. 126–129.

Janet Pérez

Marco, Concha de (1916–)

Born in Soria, poet Concha de Marco spent part of her early years in Figueras, near the Mediterranean Sea. She graduated with a natural sciences degree, has traveled extensively, and was a visiting professor at the University of Puerto Rico. As a poet, Marco explores time as a dimension that shapes human lives. Due to her concern with time and history from a sociological perspective and her focus on women's issues, Marco has been considered one of Spain's social poets. Married to art critic José Antonio Gaya Nuño (1913–1976), she collaborated with him on several projects, including a travel guide. Besides poetry, Marco has worked as a translator and has written several short stories.

Marco's poetry, published later in her life, focuses on the passing of time and on historical events related to normal people and their daily lives and problems. The past usually serves as a means to understand the present. Marco's first book, *Hora 0.5* (1966; Hour 0.5), presents the reader with poems whose titles run for each quarter hour between 6:00 and 12:00 P.M. Within this time frame, there is an interruption called "intermedio" between 9:15 and 9:30. This work shows classical features both in form and tone. *Diario de la mañana* (1967; Morning Newspaper) describes daily events as they may appear in the newspaper. By using this technique, Marco tries to display how language is manipulated through commonplaces and the use of rhetoric to a point where words lose their meaning. Other books by Marco are *Acta de identificación* (1969; Certificate of Identification), where the author returns to her Mediterranean heritage and culture; *Congreso en Maldoror* (1970; Congress in Maldoror), which uses vocabulary taken from professional conferences; *Tarot* (1972); *Las hilanderas* (1973; The [Women] Spinners); *Cantos del compañero muerto* (undated; Songs of the Dead Comrade); and *Una noche de invierno* (1974; A Winter Night). Marco has explored other genres besides poetry. *La mujer española del romanticismo* (1969; The Spanish Woman of Romanticism) discusses women's issues from a sociological and historical perspective.

Work by

Hora 0.5. Santander: La Isla de los Ratones, 1966.
La mujer española del romanticismo. 2 vols. León, Spain: Everest, 1969.
Una noche de invierno. Madrid: Rialp, 1974.
Tarot. Madrid: Mediterráneo, 1972.

Work about

Galerstein, Carolyn L., and Kathleen McNerney, eds. *Women Writers of Spain: An Annotated Bio-Bibliographical Guide.* Westport, CT: Greenwood P, 1986.
Pérez, Janet. *Modern and Contemporary Spanish Women Poets.* New York: Twayne, 1996.

Violeta Padrón

María Fontán (novela rosa) (1944)

Impressionism in the visual arts came late to Spain, and when it did, it was rejected just as vituperatively by the Spanish art establishment as it had been in France some 25 to 30 years earlier (i.e., the 1870s). Given the reform-minded and antibourgeois attitude adopted by writers who belonged to the so-called Spanish Generation of 1898 in their youth, it is not surprising they would have been eager to incorporate impressionist stylistics learned from the French painters as well as Zola, the brothers Goncourt, and Flaubert to their own writing against the grain. While many of the '98 writers—Miguel de *Unamuno, Pío *Baroja, Antonio Machado—joined José Martínez Ruiz (1873–1967), better known by the pseudonym *Azorín, in creating impressionist verbal landscapes in their early work, impressionist techniques as well as references to impressionist painters and paintings continued to enjoy a position of privilege in Azorín's writing throughout his very long life and literary career.

Of his prolix literary oeuvre Azorín produced only one novel—*María Fontán (novela rosa)* (María Fontán [Romance])—which lends itself somewhat to a feminist reading in which the eponymous heroine happens to be a living art object, a "commodity," as it were, "bought" by a wealthy French duke for his extensive personal art collection, before she comes into her own as a knowledgeable collector of impressionist art after the duke's death. María is also the only feminine *contrafigura* (counterpart) in Azorín's literary corpus who voices the author's personal preferences for impressionist painters. The orphaned daughter of Sephardic parents from Toledo, Edit Maqueda, as she was first known, is sent abroad by her wealthy uncle-guardian to London and Paris where she is to shed her Jewish identity, acquire polish, and reinvent herself as "María Fontán," woman of the world and cultured heiress. After an unspecified period of time in Europe, María surfaces in Paris with a new name and image identity, and in the interim she has also acquired her uncle's estate and the attentions of the elderly, lonely, and very wealthy French duke, Lucien de Launoy. The two meet quite by accident in the Luxembourg Gardens where, in a few days, the duke extends a curious proposition to María. The tired aristocrat feels that having a lively, beautiful young woman living in his empty palace would be of great comfort to him, and he suggests María come live in his mansion on the fashionable rue de Monceau with no strings attached other than dining together twice a week. María accepts the offer, and although she and the duke see each other only at Thursday and Sunday dinner, the arrangement satisfies the aesthete in Lucien who finds personal satisfaction in sharing these short periods of time with an *obra de arte viviente* (a living work of art), as he calls María, the most recent addition to his collection of precious objets d'art.

Lucien de Launoy's fetishization of María as a work of art corresponds to the masculine voyeurism that sustains the patriarchal symbolic order. This artificial, objectified existence that María willingly allows to be superimposed upon her earthy Toledan roots undoubtedly leads her to feel decontextualized from the everyday world of contingency and causality with which ordinary human beings have to cope on a daily basis. María, nevertheless, also displays another, more individual side of her personality that is difficult to reconcile with the young woman who accedes to the controlling fiats of the duke's companionship. As part of her legacy, María inherited a spectacular diamond from her uncle. In a provocative departure from traditional Spanish gender norms, even before she met Lucien de Launoy, María would occasionally shed her mask of wealthy heiress, dress herself as a naive shop girl from the provinces, and in the company of her friends Denis Pravier and his fiancée Odette—authentic provincials whom she "adopts" precisely because they serve as her links to the real world—engage in masquerades designed to undermine the myth of the proleterian as ignorant of exchange value and exploitation by pretending to sell the gem she'd "found on the street" to society jewelers, maîtres d'hotel, and couturiers.

From time to time Denis and Odette join María and Lucien at dinner where the conversation usually revolves around art and artists: The masses of green trees at the Parc Monceau, near her home, remind María of those painted by Claude Lorrain or the Barbizon artist Jean-Baptiste-Camille Corot; she finds a bust that she likes very much of Second Empire sculptor Jean-Baptiste Carpeaux in a square on the rue de Marcadet. María herself is also quite adept at producing verbally generated impressionist landscapes. Returning from a visit to Odette's mother in Brittany, María attributes her inability to convince the elderly woman to come to Paris to the mother's refusal to give up the visual beauty of her farm, where she'd shared a life for 50 years. As the impressionists had intended, the scattering of white spots (*manchas blancas*) in the grass and heather that María observes at a distance are recomposed by her eyes into the geese that Odette's mother pastures on her farm.

Perhaps because María herself is a physically beautiful, human female specimen, she responds well to the visual stimuli around her and also has a sensitive eye for color. On a shopping expedition to a Paris fabric emporium she remarks that her favorite colors are the faded tones a painter from her native Toledo had told her were masterfully employed by *otro pintor toledano o de adoptiva tierra toledana* (another Toledan or adoptive Toledan painter). Examining bolts of silk, María comes upon a dusty yellow that reminds her of a very special hue with which she has been obsessed ever since running across the color in the *Manual del colorista* Denis Pravier had given her. The yellow she looks for is called *jaune de Naples*, a color that is barely yellow, more a "vague remembrance of yellow," as María describes it; a delicate tone that would make a lovely spring suit. The color manual to which María refers exists in its original French edition in Azorín's personal library, and in the book there is, indeed, a yellow called *jaune de Naples*, described as a pale yellow, the preparation of which the author describes in great detail since it is extremely difficult to produce commercially. It is not at all surprising, then, that of all the colors in the spectrum, María would prefer an exquisite yellow hue that is quite difficult to mass-produce.

María's existence as the Duc de Launoy's living, breathing work of art does not last long: The aged duke falls gravely ill, and after a hastily arranged bedside marriage designed so that she would have no difficulties with inheritance legalities, María acquires yet another identity as the *duquesa viuda de Launoy* (widowed Duchess of Launoy). Now free of the sublimated psychological baggage with which she had been burdened while playing a role for the duke's benefit, upon inheriting her husband's estate, María steps into the duke's empty shoes and herself becomes a formidable collector of art. In the process, she also acquires "the phallus," which, as Carole-Anne Tyler has noted, is unlike a penis, because of its frequent metaphoric or metonymic association with all the signs of power and privilege recognized by Western culture. The first dinner party she gives as the duchess of Launoy is also the occasion María chooses to unveil her recent purchase of an unknown painting by Edouard Manet. One of the dinner guests is the Spanish painter Anastasio Arlegui, a great connoisseur of Manet, whom María plans to surprise with her recent acquisition (it is said that Azorín modeled Arlegui on his friend the Spanish painter Ignacio Zuloaga). The duchess's instructions to her maître d'hotel are that the meal be exquisite, that the palace be filled with yellow roses, and that the Manet canvas be mounted in a new frame. At dinner María leads the conversation around to impressionist painting. Intending to corner Arlegui, she asks the artist whether he is familiar with the entire Manet oeuvre. Arlegui responds positively, observing that the paintings he has not seen firsthand he knows from photographs. María then reveals that after dinner she will show her guest a Manet he surely has never seen before, with a Spanish theme, worthy of hanging beside *The Dead Torero*.

This is not the first time Azorín cited Manet's painting *Le Torero mort*. Now at the National Gallery of Art in Washington, D.C., the painting once formed part of a much larger canvas titled *Episode d'un combat de taureaux* (1864). Because the painting was negatively received, Manet decided at some point to cut the canvas into pieces, retaining only the sections he found most satisfactory: the canvas now in the National Gallery of Art and another painting titled *Episode in a Bullfight*, now at the Frick Collection in New York City. Undoubtedly Azorín was aware of the painting's vicissitudes: In his copy of Louis Hourticq's *Manet* there is a piece of paper marking the page where the author observes that the painting known as *Le Torero mort* had at one time been part of a larger picture depicting a bull and the entourage of assistants that traditionally accompany a bullfighter. Hourticq, however, states incorrectly that of the original picture the only known piece to have survived was the fragment titled *Le Torero mort*. Thus Azorín seems to insinuate that María Fontán's important new acquisition may be one of the missing pieces from the dismembered *Episode d'un combat de taureaux*.

It is well known that Manet's early work was inspired by the great collection of seventeenth-century Spanish masters housed in the Louvre, a preference further reinforced by Manet's brief trip to Spain in late August–early September 1865. Nevertheless, the French artist's paintings of bullfighters, Spanish dancers, and itinerant musicians are terribly romantic interpretations of Spanish themes. Although Ignacio Zuloaga did not care for Velázquez, one of Manet's favorite sources, he did admire Manet, and in his own country Zuloaga, like Manet, was accused of creating an excessively stereotypical vision of Spain. In the lively debate Zuloaga's work generated among Spaniards, Azorín often sided with the painter's critics, although during the three years he spent in Paris during the Spanish Civil War (1936–1939), Azorín developed a close friendship with Zuloaga, and he later wrote in *Memorias inmemoriales* that he was able to appreciate the authenticity of Zuloaga's vision only after being exiled from his beloved country.

Like Zuloaga and Manet, Azorín himself created a "poetic" vision of Spain and things Spanish. In an article he wrote shortly after Zuloaga died late in 1945, Azorín remarked that whenever he saw Manet's painting of the Spanish dancer *Lola de Valence* (1862), his thoughts invariably turned to Zuloaga, and he attributed the association to the fact that Zuloaga's realism undoubtedly derived from the same formula as Manet's. The evolution of Azorín's personal response to Zuloaga's work is, perhaps, encoded in the cryptic remarks María Fontán directs to Arlegui when she observes that while she has been able to unravel the secrets of other painters, she cannot decipher the enigma of her guest's manner because the key to appreciating his work is the secret of Spain, which no one can divine because Spain is so diverse and complex.

Possibly because the subject matter of her newly acquired painting stirs childhood memories, María decides to reacquaint herself with her Spanish roots. Returning to Madrid she lodges at the Hotel Ritz, just a short walk from the Prado Museum, where she spends a great deal of time. At the museum she meets Roberto Cisneros, a talented but impoverished *copista* (copier) who specializes in the still lifes of a certain painter "Menéndez" (Azorín was surely thinking of the prominent eighteenth-century still-life painter Luis Meléndez [1716–1780]). Shortly thereafter, and in yet another reversal of the role she had earlier allowed a patriarchal culture to impose upon her, María becomes the benefactress of Roberto and his family. Her metamorphosis from commodity to full-fledged "commodities dealer" is completely realized in the novel's penultimate chapter titled "Tenía que ser así" (It Couldn't Be Otherwise), which recounts her marriage to

Roberto. The wedding festivities include a tour of the Prado Museum arranged by Arlegui, who shows off Spanish art treasures to María's French friends. María and Roberto, in the meantime, board ship in Barcelona and sail for the Bosphorus where they set up house in an old mansion with an abandoned garden whose stairway of worn stone leads down to the sea. María, a living work of art, formerly belonging to the personal art collection of Lucien de Launoy, of late friend to painters and collector of art in her own right, more recently benefactress and wife of an *artiste manqué*, has brought her life to a completed, perfect circle as she exchanges her status as an acquiescent object whose destiny was largely determined first by her uncle and then by her husband for that of self-determining subject, in full control of her own life. For Roberto, however, marriage does not signify any change whatever in ontological status; rather, he exchanges one form of financial dependence for another, thereby prolonging his objectification, represented first by the role he is obliged to play as a copyist rather than creator of original canvases and then by the contract of marriage he incurs with María Fontán.

In appropriating Roberto, María not only duplicates Lucien de Launoy's proprietary role, but she also adds a penis to "the phallus" she already has; and again like the duke, in ostensibly "freeing" her husband's family from financial worry and Roberto himself from the drudgery of duplicating another's pictures in the Prado, María also ironically perpetuates the fetishism of which she herself had been a victim—a fetishism that characterizes the imaginary relations between different races, social classes, or genders in which, as Tyler observes, signs of difference also signify phallic lack or wholeness. Furthermore, in returning to the Byzantine milieu of Constantinople, María likewise repossesses her Sephardic origins by settling in what had been one of the most important centers of the Jewish exodus from Spain in 1492, a unit of the world that was part of the same milieu into which El Greco, "*el pintor toledano o de adoptiva tierra toledana*" who utilized María's favorite color palette, was born and where he lived before leaving his native Crete to study art in Italy, finally settling permanently in the Semitic and Arabic climate of late-sixteenth-century Spanish Toledo.

Work by

"Ignacio Zuloaga." *La Prensa* (Buenos Aires), January 13, 1946, n.p.

Obras completas. Ed. Angel Cruz Rueda. 9 vols. Madrid: Aguilar, 1947–1951.

Work about

Isaacson, Joel. "Manet and Spain." *Manet and Spain. Prints and Drawings*. Ann Arbor: U of Michigan P, 1969. 9–16.

Jurkevich, Gayana. "Azorín's Magic Circle: The Subversion of Time and Space in *Doña Inés*." *Bulletin of Hispanic Studies* (Glasgow) 73 (1996): 29–44.

Steiner, Wendy. "The Causes of Effect: Edith Wharton and the Economics of Ekphrasis." *Poetics Today* (1989): 279–297.

Tyler, Carole-Anne. "The Feminine Look." *Theory between the Disciplines. Authority/Vision/Politics*. Ed. Martin Kreiswirth and Mark A. Cheetham. Ann Arbor: U of Michigan P, 1990. 191–212.

Wilson-Bareau, Juliet. *Edouard Manet: Voyage en Espagne*. Caen: L'Echoppe, 1988.

Gayana Jurkevich

Marianism in Spain

The cult of devotion to the Blessed Virgin Mary dates to the beginnings of Christianity. As she is mentioned only four times in the Gospels, her doctrinal history depends primarily on a few apocryphal writings, biblical exegesis that identifies presages and her symbolic presence in Old and New Testament writings, and later accounts of her apparitions and miracles. Benko and Warner, among others, have demonstrated how pagan traditions were also assimilated into early Christianity. The concept of virgin birth was commonly ascribed to Greek and Roman heroes and wise men, and reverence for motherhood is found in the Egyptian goddess Isis, who was often depicted nursing her son Horus. Perhaps most important, numerous pagan religions understood clearly that divinity was not exclusively male or female.

Marianism has traditionally been seen as a fundamentally grassroots movement, reflected in and inspired by countless works of art, music, and literature that depict her life and her miracles and celebrate her various roles. Nonetheless, representations of Mary, and definition of her character, as Warner, Diz, and others have demonstrated, have also been strategically used by the Catholic Church to secure political goals and consolidate power. The cult of the Blessed Virgin Mary, like that of the saints, remains a point of clear division between Catholic and Protestant beliefs.

Four articles of faith comprise Mariology: divine motherhood—first declared in 431 at the Council of Ephesus; perpetual virginity, for she both conceived and gave birth without pleasure or pain—accepted in 431; the immaculate conception, whereby Mary is the only human free of Original Sin inherited from Adam and additionally is incapable of sinning herself despite her unimpaired free will—proclaimed in 1854; and the assumption of her body and soul to heaven, whereby she avoided death and putrefaction of the body—accepted in 1950. Warner identifies five roles generally ascribed to her: virgin, queen of heaven, bride of Christ, mother, and intercessor. She has also been seen as the co-redemptrix of humans, although this is not accepted by Catholic dogma; the issue, however, is sufficiently alive to have appeared as cover article of the August 25, 1997, *Newsweek* magazine. In general terms, the first seven centuries of Christianity are characterized by reverent admiration of Mary's holiness as mother of God, and from the eighth through the fifteenth centuries, more emphasis is given to her roles as heavenly queen, spiritual mother, and intercessor.

Two key historical figures stimulated early diffusion of Marian devotion in Europe, St. Bernard (1090–1174) in France, and in Spain, St. Hildephonse (607–667). A leading churchman of his day, St. Bernard wrote the Mariological treatise "Praises of the Virgin Mary" and became a major champion of the Virgin. St. Hildephonse, who rose to become archbishop of Toledo, composed the *Libellus de virginitate beatae Mariae* in which he passionately defends Mary's virginity and her roles as co-redeemer and mediator. Of even greater influence is the much-diffused miracle legend that his devoted life provoked. In it, the Virgin appears to Hildephonse to thank him for having composed the defense and for felicitously rescheduling the Feast of the Annunciation from Lent to shortly before Christmas and presents him with a miraculous chasuble, to be worn only by him. When Hildephonse dies, the next archbishop, Siagrus, feeling himself equally worthy, ignores the Virgin's command, dons the vestment, and is strangled by it. One of the most popular, widely diffused legends, it is typical of hundreds of miracles that circulated in collections written in Latin and vernacular languages.

The greatest flowering of Marian devotion in Western Christianity reached its peak around 1150 and maintained this level for some 200 years. Cathedrals were dedicated to Mary, pilgrimages devoted to her, and numerous apparitions and miracles collected and recounted in song and literature. The iconography of her life and roles at this moment played a decisive part in her definition and popularization. It was a time of renewal, conversion, liturgical consolidation, and re-emphasis of the cult of images throughout Europe. As W. Christian documents, Spain quickly became a stronghold of the cult of the Virgin Mary, in part because of the new cult of images. Prior to the eleventh century, lay devotion to saints was always based on relics, along with martyrdom and miracles. Since popular belief held that Mary was lifted to heaven, leaving no body relics, growth of her influence had been hampered, although some articles of clothing, strands of hair, nail parings, and her milk were "discovered" and used to promote devotion. However, once images were introduced as objects of veneration, establishment of Marian shrines was greatly facilitated. In the Iberian peninsula, this "rechristianization" and new devotion to the Virgin Mary coincided with the reconquest of Spain—which between 1035 and 1250 recuperated 80 percent of the peninsula from Muslim hands. Many new shrines and chapels were dedicated to her as the reconquest progressed, and she gradually supplanted local saints of many existing shrines, and some of their miracles were ascribed to her also. Various important religious orders were consecrated to the Virgin, including the Cistercians, Carmelites, Dominicans, Franciscans, and later, the Jesuits.

The most enduring aspects of the flowering of Marianism are the artistic and literary products. Two of thirteenth-century Spain's finest literary pieces celebrate her life and miracles: Gonzalo de Berceo's (c. 1196–c. 1260) *Milagros de Nuestra Señora* (Miracles of Our Lady), which, after an allegorical introduction celebrating the Virgin, recounts 25 Marian miracles in 911 *cuaderna vía* quatrains, and King *Alfonso X el Sabio's (1221–1284) *Cantigas de Santa María* (Canticles of Holy Mary), a collection of 427 songs, accompanied by music and exquisite miniature pictures, compiled between 1257 and 1279. Despite the common subject matter, the style, tone, language, and intended audience of each are quite different. Berceo's elegant opening allegory compares the Virgin to a perfect, supernatural *locus amoenus*, emphasizing, as Ackerman notes, her virginity but everlasting fecundity and her independent power to console, refresh, sustain, and save sinners. After this abstract discussion of qualities and abilities, the miracles present her as concrete protagonist traveling about on earth, arguing, chastising, praising, persuading, dealing directly with humans and devils, and mediating with Christ. Uniquely approachable and lively, she expresses a wide range of emotions as she advocates for all who profess devotion to her, regardless of their past sins. At the conclusion of the *Milagros*, Berceo offers his efforts to the Virgin as a gift, but he clearly intended his work to inspire Marian devotion in the general populace, teaching that Mary's grace and compassion as mediator and supreme advocate were endlessly available to all. King Alfonso compiled the *Cantigas de Santa María* for an entirely personal reason—as a gift of singular devotion, offered in the hopes that the Virgin help save his soul. Using the Galician-Portuguese language preferred for lyric poetry by cultured nobility of the day, he sings as a troubadour to his beautiful lady, promises her his exclusive devotion, and terms his request for salvation a *galardón* (reward) she would grant, all of which clearly reflect a *courtly love tradition and underscore her role as Queen of Heaven. Using a wide variety of meter and music, some 356 miracles are recounted, including 28 that involve Alfonso or his close relatives. Every tenth poem is a song of praise to Mary. Despite the influence of the courtly love tradition, characters in the miracles come from all strata of society. Both Alphonse's *Cantigas* and Berceo's *Milagros* attest to and inspire personal devotion to Mary, they celebrate her ability to advocate for human souls, as she lends a feminine, maternal character to divine judgment.

How did the cult of Mary, and the concept of the Virgin, affect the position of women in Europe? As Warner and others have proven, from the beginnings of Christianity the Virgin Mary was opposed to Eve—as the Church Father Jerome (died 419) stated, "Death through Eve, life through Mary." Mary's feminizing, mediating presence initially made the divine more approachable for humans, and over time this function was partially appropriated by male figures. The increasing feminization of Christ, pictured as nurturer or even mother, encouraged a more personal devotion to the Son. Likewise, the use of feminized language is seen from the twelfth century on, as in St. Bernard's characterization of bishops and abbots who nurse and nurture congregations. This appropriation of female qualities, as Diz comments, fostered increasingly personal devotion among the populace but did not contribute to a more favorable view of women.

Mary's function as a role model that women could emulate in daily life yielded a number of negative consequences for women. Using the example of the Virgin Mary, Christianity defined women by their virginity or lack thereof. Consistent with the Aristotelian belief that woman was but an imperfect man, virginity was felt to confer special strength, to partially reverse the effects of Eve's fall, and to raise the (carnal) female closer to the level of the (spiritual) male. The virgin state, which denies women their sexual and reproductive roles, paradoxically was deemed superior to one that recognized these functions. Virginity equaled the integral wholeness of the female body, its purity and holiness; loss of chastity validated woman's innate sinful nature.

Mary's body did not follow the basic rules of the female body. As Diz points out, she did not menstruate, lose her virginity, experience emotion during sex, feel pain in childbirth, or decay bodily upon dying. Mary's distance from women who did so (i.e., all women) was equal to her distance from Eve. In Spain, like the rest of Europe, Mary thus served to emphasize the proximity of Eve's sinful nature to that of all women, and as a role model she taught women that the path to a holier self was one that distanced each woman from her own body, denying basic body functions of her sex—rejection of reproduction, abstinence from sexual activity, extreme fasting to provoke amenorrhea and suppress body secretions in general. Not even the role of nursing mother—so tenderly portrayed in sixteenth- and seventeenth-century paintings—carried over to daily life; any family able to afford to do so hired a peasant wet nurse to suckle newborn children, despite the example of Mary and the exhortations of moralists such as Luis *Vives, Luis de *León, and others. In sum, part of the Virgin Mary's influence as a role model has roots in contempt for and rejection of the female body and confirms the degradation or inferiority of woman as sexual beings.

Although the courtly love tradition might seem to offer evidence of respect and even worship of women, Warner has shown that it began as a separate movement that meshed somewhat with Marianism only in the thirteenth century. Courtly love was an aristocratic phenomenon that initially celebrated sexual pleasure rather than the denial of physical yearnings for a beloved. Andreas Capellanus's *De arte honeste Amandi* (c. 1180) codified the symptoms, procedures, and etiquette of this upper-class cult of adultery, in which women were worshipped illicitly by other men but remained servants of their husbands. For complex sociopolitical reasons (various heretical movements, the question of matriliny versus patriliny, the Church's debate over marriage), the image of the Virgin as Queen—inviolate, supremely beautiful, inspirer of ascetic denial and self-sacrifice—did, with the Church's blessing, fuse with the courtly love tradition in the thirteenth century. Chastity and spiritual, psychological love (as opposed to glorification of carnal appetite) were then introduced to the movement, and this is the tradition reflected in Alfonso's *Cantigas*. The paradoxical fusing of adultery and chastity may be seen as another example of the contradictory virgin-whore paradigm used to define women.

How was a woman who did not opt for virginity to overcome her condition? In the thirteenth and fourteenth centuries, Franciscan thought provided the accepted answer. St. Francis's (1181–1226) message of total, self-effacing humility, charity, gentleness, poverty, and obedience to authority profoundly affected the cult of the Virgin by recommending to sinners these and similar "feminine" virtues as the pathway to forgiveness. Submission to authority and joyful acceptance of suffering were Mary's new lessons for the populace. The Franciscans, who were very instrumental in promulgating devotion to Mary, began to depict her now as a docile younger woman, unpretentiously clothed, whose supreme moment occurred when she tenderly cradled her Son after giving birth, even kneeling to him. What began as recommended virtues for all then gradually became "female" virtues that, in Catholic countries, were for that reason scorned by males. This new Franciscan-inspired focus of the cult that idealized Mary's contented, caring obedience to authority, as opposed to her role as queenly co-redeemer and advocate, was deemed by Simone de *Beauvoir a supreme masculine victory, for it rehabilitated woman through the accomplishment of her defeat, as the mother kneels before her son, acknowledging her inferiority. Maternal sovereignty has been vanquished.

Luis de *León's La perfecta casada (1583; The Perfect Wife) communicates these messages of innate female evil and necessary submission and obedience to male authority in his book of advice on how to be the perfect Christian wife. Although the book is overtly based on the Old Testament book of Proverbs, the underlying ideology is that of the cult of the Virgin Mary. León defines women in terms of their chastity, holds them explicitly responsible for Original Sin, and requires them to have more virtues than men to compensate for their more defective nature. Women are to cheerfully obey their husbands/fathers/male caretakers—long-suffering compliance is a virtue. Through the institutional promotion of these messages, Catholic doctrine consolidated control of the female populace.

As was mentioned earlier, the flowering of Mary's cult during the Christian reconquest of the Iberian peninsula allowed religion to play a much greater role in Spain in forging national characters and policies. By the sixteenth century, Spain was the center of Catholic thought, and most of the active shrines there were Marian. One of the charges made against Erasmus, brought against the alumbrados (a sixteenth-century Spanish mystical sect), and held against Protestants, was their rejection of the cult of the Virgin Mary. By the mid-sixteenth century, all women in Spain lived within the physical confines (*Encierro) of three male-controlled institutions: the family, the convent, or the brothel. (Unlike the rest of Europe, Spanish houses of prostitution had male administrators until the seventeenth century.) In 1555 the Council of Trent confirmed the perpetual virginity of Mary, and in the seventeenth century the doctrine of Immaculate Conception was taken up as a national cause in Spain. The issue was fiercely debated; the Jesuits (founded in 1534) vehemently supported the Immaculate Conception; the Dominicans did not. The entire populace took part in the dispute, works by Lope de Vega and *Calderón de la Barca brought the issue to the theater, and Velázquez, Murillo, Zurbarán, and Ribera celebrated the event in their paintings. Finally, in 1644, the feast of the Immaculate Conception was declared a national event, to be celebrated everywhere each December 8.

Even among nuns, a population one might expect to consider the Virgin Mary as a particularly suitable role model, there is no evidence of a particular tendency to do so. Bynum has noted that female mystics tend to identify more with the suffering Christ, through fasting and self-flagellation, consistent with the cult's rejection of the female body. Neither Teresa de *Cartagena (c. 1420–after 1460?) nor the Mexican Sor Juana (1651–1695) cited the Virgin Mary as a model when they defended the dignity of women, although male writers such as Alvaro de *Luna (1390?–1453) did use the Virgin Mary repeatedly in their defense of females. María de *Agreda's relation to the Virgin merits special mention. Her Mística ciudad de Dios (Mystical City of God) is a detailed story of the life of the Virgin, based not on the few paltry facts of doctrinal material but on information revealed to her personally by the Virgin. In it, Agreda explicitly defends the Virgin as Immaculate, Mother of God, Co-Redeemer, Mistress of the Church, Queen of Heaven, and future co-judge of humanity, alongside her Son. Published five years after her death, it provoked strong reactions both for and against the text and was widely read in Europe (89 complete editions, and 68 partial ones, appeared).

The basic antithesis between Eve—carnal root of human temptation, Original Sin, and death—and the Virgin Mary—spiritual offerer of salvation, forgiveness, and life—continued to inform doctrinal and secular writings through the seventeenth century and beyond and to delimit basic role choices for women. Certainly no one would deny the consolation, inspiration, and guidance that the Virgin Mary has offered to millions of faithful over the centuries and the inspiration she has provided for countless artistic and literary works of exquisite beauty and power. Nonetheless, the underlying messages the Virgin Mary carries as a role model for women, that the ideal woman must be estranged from her own body and sexuality, that women are inferior to men, that woman's proper role is compliance to (male) authority, must be recognized in all their negativity, and the underlying agenda of Church doctrine must be acknowledged.

The usefulness of this misogynist agenda for the Catholic Church is apparent today. Its position on contraception and abortion is consistent with Marian tenets. As Diz concluded in her study, the Virgin Mary's continuing role in consolidating Church power is perhaps best demonstrated by a quote from Josemaría Escrivá de Balaguer, founder of the Roman Catholic Church's secular organization Opus Dei (established 1928): "Mary continually builds the church and keeps it together. It is difficult to have devotion to Our Lady and not to feel closer to the other members of the mystical body and more united to its visible head, the Pope. That's why I like to repeat: All with Peter to Jesus through Mary." *See also* Misogyny in Medieval and Early Modern Spain

Work about

Ackerman, Jane. "The Theme of Mary's Power in the *Milagros de Nuestra Señora.*" *Journal of Hispanic Philology* 8 (1983): 17–31.

Alfonso el Sabio. *Las cantigas.* Ed. W. Mettman. Madrid: Clásicos Castalia, 1986.

Benko, Stephen. *The Virgin Goddess. Studies in the Pagan and Christian Roots of Mariology.* New York: Brill, 1993.

Berceo, Gonzalo de. *Obras completas.* Ed. Brian Dutton. 5 vols. London: Tamesis, 1967–1981.

Bynum, Caroline Walker. *Fragmentation and Redemption. Essays on Gender and the Human Body in Medieval Religion.* New York: Zone Books, 1991.

Christian, William A., Jr. *Local Religion in Sixteenth-Century Spain.* Princeton, NJ: Princeton UP, 1981.

Diz, M. Ana. *Historias de certidumbre: Los Milagros de Berceo.* Newark, DE: Juan de la Cuesta, 1995.

El Saffar, Ruth. *Rapture Encaged. The Suppression of the Feminine in Western Culture.* London: Routledge, 1994.

Flory, David A. *Marian Representations in the Miracle Tales of Thirteenth-Century Spain and France.* Washington, DC: Catholic U of America P, 2000.

Gold, Penny Schine. *The Lady and the Virgin.* Chicago: U of Chicago P, 1985.

Graef, Hilda. *Mary: A History of Doctrine and Devotion.* New York: Sheed and Ward, 1964.

Howe, Elizabeth Teresa. "Heavenly Defense: Dramatic Development of the Virgin Mary as Advocate." *Journal of Hispanic Philology* 4 (1980): 189–202.

———. "Lope de Vega and the Immaculate Conception." *Bulletin of the Comediantes* 38.1 (Summer 1986): 39–53.

Ibáñez Rodríguez, Miguel. *Gonzalo de Berceo y las literaturas transpirenaicas.* Logroño: Consejería de Cultura, Deportes y Juventud, 1995.

Kelly, Mary Jane. "Spinning Virgin Yarns: Narrative, Miracles, and Salvation in Gonzalo de Berceo's *Milagros de Nuestra Señora.*" *Hispania* 74 (1991): 814–823.

León, Luis de. *La perfecta casada.* Study, Sel. and notes Mercedes Etreros. Madrid: Taurus, 1987.

Marchand, James W., and Spurgeon Baldwin. "Singers of the Virgin in Thirteenth-century Spain." *BHS* 81 (1994): 169–184.

McNamara, Jo Ann. "Sexual Equality and the Cult of Virginity in Early Christian Thought." *Feminist Studies* 3 (1975–1976): 145–158.

Warner, Marina. *Alone of All Her Sex: The Myth and*

the *Cult of the Virgin Mary*. New York: Knopf, 1976.

Maureen Ihrie

Marías Aguilera, Julián (1914–): On Female Human Condition in Spain, 1965–1992

An eminent Spanish philosopher and essayist, Julián Marías Aguilera was the José Ortega y Gasset Professor of Spanish Philosophy at the Universidad Complutense in Madrid from 1980 to 1984. A disciple of Ortega, Marías graduated in 1936 from the same university where he later taught. He was a senator by royal appointment from 1977 to 1978. Until his death, he held a seat as member of the Royal Spanish Academy of Letters and at the Academy of Fine Arts.

During his extended life, Marías made important contributions to Spanish philosophical thought. His work is composed of a variety of topics that deal with existence, values, and the meaning of individual and collective human life within Spain's own historical reality. In his over 100 books, numerous articles, and lectures, the author aims to shed new light on the centuries-old interpretations of the country and its people, perceived by foreigners as unintelligible and conflicted. In the 10 volumes of his *Obras completas* (1941–1970), Marías undertakes the task of revisiting many controversial aspects of Spain and the Spaniards, as well as the male and female human condition. His analyses are rooted in the historical past, although his main concern is the significance of the human being in the contemporary world, freed from past misconceptions. The author avoids the use of critical methods and interpretations that misconstrue Spanish reality throughout time by constantly comparing it to that of other European countries.

Within the framework of his studies, Marías carefully reflected on the significance of men's and women's lives, historical existence, and the meaning of their relationship in various circumstances, crises, and cultural changes. In *Antropología metafísica; la estructura empírica de la vida humana* (1970; Metaphysical Anthropology; The Empirical Structure of Human Life), which he worked on for two decades, Marías established the philosophical path that points equally to both sexes, male and female, as the undeniable and unequivocal two shapes of the human condition. Further investigation led Marías to consider the forces that emanate from this powerful source of strength, possibilities, and effectiveness, as they interplay in the projection of a person's life. In this line of thought, it becomes a relevant consideration given the reality of the female when contrasted with the controvertible stereotype purveyed in interpretations of the feminine.

In a book reprinted several times with the title *La mujer del siglo XX* (1980; Twentieth-Century Woman), Marías considers several steps in a serious attempt to dissipate the fallacy surrounding women's portrayals. By analyzing the attributes that motivate female behavior, he proceeds to investigate the pattern fixed in the minds of many. Reason is sought in the argument that provokes the conceptualization of a woman's fault finding as the criterion that fails to project her singularity. For the Spanish philosopher, in order to grasp the female's real sense of being, one must understand her dimension as a "person." He insists that reality for both sexes must be understood in terms of their male or female condition as "person," not personality, in order to avoid becoming an "abstraction," or an "object." Marías reflects on the male-female polarity, within the reality of their own condition that is "mundane" and therefore circumstantial, following Ortega's principle. Marías's elucidation substantiates the importance of the relationship between sexes with the world and within themselves due to the intrinsic mutual relation that defines their condition. Thus, the complexity of the female being must be understood in terms of being a person, the historical time in which she lives, her life, her psyche, her womanhood not intellectually apprehensible without reference to manhood, and her femininity.

Marías investigates further the fluctuations that have defined the female condition from the Victorian era to the time of Spain's democratization, noting trends that depersonify the female's life by destroying old myths in favor of innovative ideas and new ways of life. The implications of drastic changes to the "persona" in the pursuit of freedom affect the essence of the female being, establishing that the search of her definition, within the political, legal, labor, and civil rights, will undermine the meaning of her condition. The possibility of a twist that affects her reality is seen at the junction of her historical projection and her actual transformation in a time of cultural changes, crises, and transitions when, in general, women are under pressure to suppress the "person," at the risk of becoming impersonal instead. In *La mujer y su sombra* (1986; Woman and Her Shadow), the female condition is again considered in the totality of the human being, and her dimension is further perceived in the uniqueness of the body-soul duality. Hence, the female person is defined by her physiological and biological dimension, her sex, "the feminine factor," as well as the emotional and psychological scope revealed in her attitudes and reason of being. In that sense only is it possible to comprehend the significance of the word *woman*.

Upon considering the relevant aspects of the female person, Marías reflects on her need to move forward with history and her actual transformation, pointing to the intrinsic danger involved in new definitions of femininity and womanhood. This trend is noticed in the social ramifications of her emancipation and the redefinition of her role in society. When carried to extremes, the interpretation of freedom often leads to a lack of interest in human relationship, a loss of enthusiasm for personal attractiveness, and the risk of losing insight into one's own reality.

Several other works written by Marías focus on alternatives to the hazards of depersonification. Very significant are *Breve tratado de la ilusión* (1984; Brief Treatise on Illusion), *La libertad en juego* (1986; Liberty at Stake), *La felicidad humana* (1987; Human Happiness), and *La educación sentimental* (1992; Sentimental Education). In addition to examining the real meaning of spontaneity, authenticity, affection, friendship, and love as elements of freedom, he addresses the uniqueness of imagination, which must become part of the dynamics for women to find themselves in the real world. These reflections are directed to protecting a woman's essence from being reduced to the shadow of her real representation.

Work by

España inteligible: Razón histórica de las Españas. Madrid: Alianza, 1985.
Los españoles. 2nd ed. Madrid: Revista de Occidente, 1963.
La experiencia de la vida. Madrid: Alianza, 1966.
Generaciones y constelaciones. Madrid: Alianza, 1989.
La justicia social y otras justicias. Madrid: Espasa Calpe, 1979.
Tres visiones de la vida humana. Madrid: Salvat, 1972.

Work about

Castro, María Rosario. *Una visión de España de Julián Marías*. New York: Peter Lang, 1991.
Raley, Harold C. *A Watch over Mortality: The Philosophical Story of Julián Marías*. Albany: State U of New York, 1997.

María Jesús Mayans Natal

Marimacho

Marimacho is a despective reference to a woman whose appearance or actions are identified as masculine. Applied to women who are unusually tall or ungraceful, especially large, corpulent, or masculine in dress and mannerisms, it connotes both a lack of femininity and a mixture of traits of both genders (the term, of popular origin, is considered vulgar and has long been an epithet for lesbians). While the first half of the word—*mari*—may be derived from María, and hence in some sense is a quintessentially feminine woman, the latter half—*macho*—nullifies the former, placing emphasis on the male of the species, sexuality, the reproductive organs. The combination connotes not harmonious union but instead suggests to the popular mind something abnormal, for which reason it is almost always used as an insult. *See also* Lesbianism in Early Modern Spanish Literature: 1500–1700

Janet Pérez

Martel, Carmen (1915–)

Born in Cádiz, over the span of some three decades Carmen Martel has written more than 60 novels for children. A nurse who worked in several hospitals during the Civil War (1936–1939), she later traveled throughout Europe and organized several artistic exhibitions for the Departamento de Artesanía de la Organización Sindical.

Work by

Al rasgar el velo del pasado. Madrid: Pueyo, 1950.
Una aventura extraña. Barcelona: Brugera, 1963.
Cambié por tu amor. Barcelona: Brugera, 1967.
Concurso para novios. Madrid: Pueyo, 1948.
Gardenias en el ojal. Madrid: Pueyo, 1938.
La guerra a través de las tocas. Cádiz: Establecimiento Cerón, 1938.
Isabel de Valderas. Córdoba: Oficinas y Almacenes, 1943.
Pierrot Rojo. Madrid: Pueyo, 1943.
San José de Calasanz. Barcelona: Vilamala, 1963.
Yo quiero ser futbolista. Bilbao: Paulinas, 1965.

Delmarie Martínez

Martínez de Toledo, Alfonso

See Corbacho, El (1438)

Martínez Mediero, Manuel (1939–): Women in His Theater

Feminist issues play an integral role in the evolution of Manuel Martínez Mediero's socially committed theater. The female experience serves Martínez Mediero as an effective means of elaborating his social critique. Three distinct periods mark his use of female characters. During the final years of the Franco regime, he focused on the female's degraded social status as a means of conveying his general concern with the theme of social and political oppression. Such is the case of *Jacinta se marchó a la guerra* (1967; Jacinta Went Off to War) and *Las planchadoras* (1971; The Ironers). The themes of freedom and control are intimately linked to the roles of the female protagonists in both plays and underscore the pivotal role of women in the Spanish playwright's dramatic stage rhetoric.

Jacinta se marchó a la guerra is a realistic, deeply moving portrait of an impoverished and lonely woman abandoned by her family and friends. Despite her humiliating and ruinous social condition, Jacinta strives to maintain her human dignity in a society deeply rooted in the opportunistic exploitation of unfortunate individuals. Her actions transcend the immediacy of her situation to expose a world that has overextended itself in its dehumanizing dimension and to illustrate that oppression, whether physical or psychological, is not cause enough to compromise one's personal integrity. In *Las planchadoras*, cruelty is elevated to a level of spectacle and takes on definite cathartic dimensions. Human interaction is reduced to a ludicrous but conscious game of control in which everyone participates as either oppressor or oppressed and where violence has become a prerequisite for survival. The play centers on the lives of three sisters, Libertad, Clavelina, and Dionisíaca, who engage in a fascinating power struggle as the action evolves. The dynamics of their relationship are such that it is never clear who is the undisputed victim and who the uncontested victimizer. The three sisters both exert control and feel the effects of control. Thus the struggle to survive is intensified. The play illustrates that oppression takes place in ways that are not always visible and that freedom is as much a social responsibility as a personal one.

In plays such as *Las hermanas de Búfalo Bill* (1974; Buffalo Bill's Sisters) and *La novia* (1978; The Fiancée) during the period of Spain's transition to democracy, Martínez Mediero intensifies his portrayal of women. Although both plays make use of gender to carry a strong political message, *Las hermanas de Búfalo Bill* is the more compelling of the two in demonstrating the playwright's concern for feminist issues. Characters in *Las hermanas de Búfalo Bill* exist in a world that is essentially disconnected and dysfunctional. They are alienated individuals who lack the necessary means to communicate effectively. Curiosity about the forbidden pleasures of sex is the play's central metaphor. The male protagonist, Amadeo (the proverbial dictator figure), tyrannizes his sisters Cleo and Semíramis. Cloistered (*encierro) within the four walls of their home, Amadeo chains his two sisters in order to prevent them from being seduced by the outside world. Following Amadeo's death, Cleo and Semíramis attempt to exercise their newfound freedom. They kidnap the neighborhood baker, lock him up in the basement, and decide to take advantage of him sexually at will. They fail in their objective because their task involves developing faculties heretofore repressed in them as a result of years of oppression. Gender and repression are linked metaphorically and theoretically in *Las hermanas de Búfalo Bill* to demystify and promote a more liberating view of woman as a source for change.

Martínez Mediero's most sustained defense of women's issues comes in the works written after 1980. In *Lisístrata* (1980), *Juana del amor hermoso* (1982; Juana of the Beautiful Love), *Madrecita del alma querida* (1986; Dearest Darling Mother), *Las hermanas de Búfalo Bill cabalgan de nuevo* (1989; Buffalo Bill's Sisters Ride Again), and *Lola, la divina* (1989; Lola, the Divine), the Spanish playwright assumes a definite feminist stance, promoting an image of woman that breaks with the conventional notion of the female as a submissive and passive individual. Octavia, protagonist of *Madrecita del alma querida*, like Jacinta before her, is determined to forge an identity and voice of her own amidst her squalid surroundings. In *Las hermanas de Búfalo Bill cabalgan de nuevo*, the themes of freedom and national identity are once again linked to its female protagonists. *Lola, la divina* portrays woman as an objectified being, object of the male gaze, and victim of institutional and prescriptive notions of gender. *Lisístrata* and *Juana del amor hermoso* display Martínez Mediero's most effective use of female characters as a dramatic premise for his ideological concerns regarding women. *Lisístrata* is based on the classical Greek play of the same title by Aristophanes. The second is a revisionist look at the life of *Juana la Loca (1479–1555). Martínez Mediero draws on feminist theory in representing his image of the Spanish female in both plays in order to destroy universal myths about gender and move toward cultural change. Typical of the playwright's indomitable characters, both Lisístrata and Juana challenge authoritarian ideals and struggle to become integrated into society and overcome their marginality. As strong, independent individuals who never hesitate to speak their mind, regardless of the consequences, they challenge and question appearances in society in an effort to unmask the ills hidden below the surface. They are rebellious women determined to affirm their individual identities in both social and political terms. Both Lisístrata and Juana are driven by a need to investigate gender stereotypes. The opposition of patriarchal discourse and feminist ideals provides the dramatic tension in both plays. Lisístrata and Juana metaphorically espouse egalitarian principles and personify liberal ideals with regard to the social condition of women.

Martínez Mediero's theater functions at once on a political and aesthetic level to destroy pervasive myths in Spanish society. One facet of that society is the physical and emotional oppression of Spanish women by patriarchal social structure. Martínez Mediero's feminism is a part of his ongoing crusade against society's paradoxical nature, showing how intransigent traditions persist when individuals seek to legitimize themselves. His dramatization of the Spanish female experience serves the cause of liberation as it regards society in general and women in particular. In celebrating liberal-minded and irrepressible women characters, Martínez Mediero is able to adopt a feminist perspective that further authenticates his overall concern for Spanish society. *See also* Feminist Theory and the Contemporary Spanish Stage

Work by

Las hermanas del Búfalo Bill. Madrid: Fundamentos, 1980.
Las hermanas de Búfalo Bill cabalgan de nuevo. Madrid: Fundamentos, 1989.
Jacinta se marchó a la guerra. Mérida: Editora Regional de Extremadura, 1988.
Juana del amor hermoso. Madrid: Fundamentos, 1982.
Lisístrata. Madrid: Fundamentos, 1980.
Lola, la divina. Madrid: Fundamentos, 1989.
Madrecita del alma querida. Mérida: Editora Regional de Extremadura, 1988.
La novia. Madrid: Fundamentos, 1980.
Las planchadoras. In Teatro antropofágico. Madrid: Fundamentos, 1978. 116–77.

Work about

DiPuccio, Denise M. "Juana del amor hermoso. A Struggle for Identity." Estreno 13.1(1987): 8–11.
Gabriele, John P. "Gender and Patriarchy in Juana del amor hermoso." Selected Proceedings of the Pennsylvania Foreign Language Conference 1991. Ed. Gregorio C. Martín. Pittsburgh: Duquesne U, 1995. 4–90.
———. "Lisístrata, de Manuel Martínez Mediero: En busca de una identidad femenina en la España de transición." Anales de la Literatura Española Contemporánea 17.1–3 (1992): 229–241.
———. "Performing Feminisms in Manuel Martínez Mediero's Lisístrata and Juana del amor hermoso: A View from the Masculine." Revista de Estudios Hispánicos 27 (1993): 257–274.

John P. Gabriele

Martínez Ruiz, José
See Azorín (1873–1967): Feminism in His Novel Doña Inés (1925)

Martín Gaite, Carmen (1925–2000)

She is Spain's most studied contemporary novelist, according to records compiled by the Modern Language Association of America in its annual *Bibliography* (from 1981 through August 1995). Scholars and readers alike recognize the rare combination of qualities that characterize Carmen Martín Gaite's literature: astute observation of the surrounding social order, dazzling storytelling skills, beautifully fluid prose, and adventurous experimentation with form.

Born in Salamanca into a cultured and harmonious family, Martín Gaite received an excellent education. Her early schooling began with private tutors. She attended an academic high school instead of a finishing school, a rare choice among women in her social sphere. A superior student, she earned a *licenciatura* (roughly equivalent to the M.A. degree) from the University of Salamanca in 1948. In 1949 Martín Gaite moved to Madrid to pursue a doctorate in philology, but she fell in with a group of writers and began publishing fiction at the same time. Her academic career was sidetracked when her fiction began winning prizes.

Martín Gaite and the friends who once distracted her from her studies—Ignacio Aldecoa (1925–1969), Medardo Fraile (1925–), Alfonso Sastre (1926–), Jesús Fernández Santos (1926–1988), and her future husband (and later ex-husband) Rafael Sánchez Ferlosio (1927–)—are presently classified by scholars as the landmark "generation of mid-century" of contemporary Spanish literature. Martín Gaite is the only member of that elite group who has continued to write important fiction over the years. As of 1996, she had published seven novels, two novellas, two volumes of short stories, three novels for young readers, and a book of poetry, while also creating a stage play, screenplays, and translations from English and Italian. Having finished the Ph.D. in 1972, Martín Gaite also published eight volumes of literary analysis and social history.

Martín Gaite's literary career began with a novella entitled *El balneario* (1954; The Spa), which won the Premio Gijón, an elite award from critics. It introduced techniques that would not become well known for another two decades, including a fantastic episode and an exploration of the main character's unconscious through a dream. In 1957 Martín Gaite burst into the national consciousness when she won Spain's then most publicized literary prize, the Premio Nadal, for her novel *Entre visillos* (1958; Behind the Curtains, 1990). *Entre visillos* was part of the mainstream of social realism in Spain in the 1950s, offering a sweeping documentary of provincial society in the postwar era. At the same time, this novel had the audacity to depict the everyday lives of young women. They are also the subjects of her novella *Las ataduras* (1960; Bonds) and of many of her short stories, most of which were written in the 1950s and 1960s and which appear in the two volumes headed by novellas.

Martín Gaite's second novel, *Ritmo lento* (1962; Slow Motion), moved beyond objective realism to a synchronic narrative collage, about a young man whose honesty and idealism render him unable to adapt to the surrounding society. Martín Gaite created a new genre with her next novel, *Retahílas* (1974; Extended Skeins), which she wrote following a hiatus devoted to scholarship. Her third novel is composed of a series of spontaneous, interlocking verbal missives exchanged between a young man in his twenties and his forty-something aunt. With the newfound freedom that followed the demise of Franco in 1975, Martín Gaite's fourth novel was an early entry to the action-adventure genre that swept Spain in the 1980s. *Fragmentos de interior* (1976; Glimpses inside a House) depicts the brittle superficiality of Madrid sophisticates and chronicles the emerging European youth culture.

Martín Gaite's fifth novel remains her most acclaimed: *El cuarto de atrás* (1978; The Back Room, 1983) was a critical sensation when it appeared, winning the 1978 Premio Nacional de Literatura and attracting interest on both sides of the Atlantic. This novel is a unique hybrid. At once a fantastic novel, telling the story of a mysterious night-long encounter between the narrator (who exactly resembles Martín Gaite) and a man in black, it also is a realistic memoir of growing up female in Franco's Spain, including long-suppressed political details. Personal memories retrieved from the author's mental "back room" found an echo in the collective history of her generation and especially among the half of the population that also recalled the socialization of women in postwar Spain.

Her sixth novel, *Nubosidad variable* (1992; Variable Cloud, 1995), details the changing lives and enduring friendship of two middle-age women: a mother who does not work outside the home and an unmarried psychiatrist. Her next novel for adult readers, *La reina de las nieves* (1994; The Snow Queen), rewrites the quest plot of Andersen's "The Snow Queen," set in Spain in the late 1970s. During the late 1990s, Martín Gaite published two more significant novels depicting women's quest for autonomy, *Lo raro es vivir* (1996; What Is Marvelous Is Life) and *Irse de casa* (1998; Leaving Home), which shows an attractive widow facing a new journey into the unknown: life as a senior citizen, coping with aging, seeking purpose with her children grown, with lives of their own, distance between them growing. The mature heroine (not yet "geriatric") is a unique protagonist.

Martín Gaite's books for young readers also are noteworthy. These include the short works *El castillo de las tres murallas* (1981; The Castle with Three Walls) and *El pastel del diablo* (1985; The Devil's Pastry) and the full-length novel *Caperucita en Manhattan* (1990; Little Red Riding Hood in Manhattan). In all her fiction, certain overarching themes are evident: the complexity of women's lives, the need for communication, and the dilemma of the nonconformist in a traditional society. In 1999, she published a drama, *La hermana pequeña* (Little Sister) contrasting two half sisters and their quest for freedom.

Martín Gaite's nonfiction works are thematically integrated with her fiction. Particularly relevant are her historical study of the first stirrings of Spanish feminism in *Usos amorosos del dieciocho en España* (1972; *Love Customs in Eighteenth-Century Spain*, 1991); her books of literary theory *La búsqueda de interlocutor* (1973; The Search for an Interlocutor and Other Searches), and *El cuento de nunca acabar* (1983; The Never-Ending Story); and her chronicle of popular culture titled *Usos amorosos de la postguerra española* (1987; Customs of Love in post–Civil War Spain), winner of the Premio Anagrama de Ensayo of the same year. The latter is an important study of postwar society and its impact on women's ascribed and achieved status. In 1994 she published a tribute to Ignacio Aldecoa that also reconstructs the development of Spain's generation of midcentury, titled *Esperando el porvenir* (Waiting for the Future). The theme of passing time unites the essays of *Agua pasada* (1993; Water under the Bridge). The enduring concerns of Martín Gaite's work are emphasized in an anthology of selections from her writing in all genres, titled *Hilo a la cometa* (1995; Tail of the Comet), with an introduction by Emma Martinelli.

For her literary achievements over the past 50 years, Martín Gaite was honored with important prizes, including the Premio Príncipe de Asturias de las Letras (1988), the Premio Castilla y León de las Artes (1992), and the Premio Nacional de las Letras (1994). She also has been and continues to be honored in other meaningful ways: through critical attention and the veneration of readers in her country and the world. *See also* Fairy Tales in Novels by Spanish Women; Short Fiction by Women Writers: 1900–1975

Work by

Agua pasada. Barcelona: Anagrama, 1993.
Las ataduras. Barcelona: Destino, 1960.
The Back Room. Trans. Helen R. Lane. San Francisco, CA: City Lights Books, 2000.
El balneario. 2nd ed. Madrid: Alianza, 1968.
Behind the Curtains. Trans. Frances M. López-Morillas. New York: Columbia UP, 1990.
La búsqueda de interlocutor y otras búsquedas. Madrid: Nostromo, 1973.
Caperucita en Manhattan. Madrid: Siruela, 1990.
El castillo de las tres murallas and *El pastel del diablo*. In *Dos relatos fantásticos*. Barcelona: Lumen, 1986.
El cuarto de atrás. Barcelona: Destino, 1978.
El cuento de nunca acabar. Barcelona: Anagrama, 1983.
Cuentos completos. Madrid: Alianza, 1978.
Desde la ventana: Enfoque femenino de la literatura española. Madrid: Espasa-Calpe, 1987.
Entre visillos. 5th ed. Barcelona: Destino, 1967.
Esperando el porvenir: Homenaje a Ignacio Aldecoa. Madrid: Siruela, 1994.
La hermana pequeña. Barcelona: Anagrama, 1999.
Hilo a la cometa. La visión, la memoria, los sueños. Madrid: Espasa Calpe, 1995.
Lo raro es vivir. Barcelona: Anagrama, 1996.
Love Customs in Eighteenth-Century Spain. Trans. Maria G. Tomsich. Berkeley: U of California P, 1991.
Nubosidad variable. Barcelona: Anagrama, 1992.
El proceso de Macanaz: Historia de un empapelamiento. Madrid: Moneda y Crédito, 1970.
La reina de las nieves. Barcelona: Anagrama, 1994.
Usos amorosos de la postguerra española. Barcelona: Anagrama, 1987.
Usos amorosos del dieciocho en España. Madrid: Siglo Veintiuno, 1972.
Variable Cloud. Trans. Margaret Jull Costa. London: Harville, 1995.

Work about

Brown, Joan L. *Secrets from the Back Room: The Fiction of Carmen Martín Gaite*. Jackson: U of Mississippi P, Romance Monographs, 1987.
Carbayo Abengózar, Mercedes. *Buscando un lugar entre mujeres: Buceo en la España de Carmen Martín Gaite*. Málaga: Universidad, 1998.
Chown, Linda. *Narrative Authority and Homeostasis in the Novels of Doris Lessing and Carmen Martín Gaite*. New York: Garland, 1990.
Collins, Marsha. "Inscribing the Space of Female Identity in Carmen Martín Gaite's *Entre visillos*." *Symposium* 51.2 (Summer 1997): 66–78.
Jaffe, Catherine. "Patterns of Fiction and Desire: Childhood Reading in Carmen Martín Gaite's *Retahílas*." *Modern Language Notes* 112.2 (1997): 182–200.
Martinell Gifre, Emma. *El mundo de los objetos en la*

obra de Carmen Martín Gaite. Cáceres: U of Extremadura, 1996.

Roger, Isabel M. "La visión amorosa en algunos relatos de Carmen Martín Gaite y Medardo Fraile." *Revista Canadiense de Estudios Hispánicos* 21.2 (1997): 396–406.

Servodidio, M., and M. Welles, eds. *From Fiction to Metafiction: Essays in Honor of Carmen Martín Gaite.* Lincoln, NE: Society of Spanish and Spanish American Studies, 1983.

Joan L. Brown

Martín Recuerda, José (1925–): *Salvajes*, *Arrecogías*, and Other Women in His Theater

Like Federico *García Lorca (1898–1936), José Martín Recuerda writes plays set in his native Andalusia, and like Lorca, he excels in creating female characters. Martín Recuerda's *Como las secas cañas del camino* (1965; Like the Dry Stalks along the Way), based on an actual event that took place in the coastal town of Torrenueva, portrays a schoolteacher who falls in love with a former student and is forced to abandon her position, a victim of the villagers' cruelty and hypocrisy. The dilapidated school that Julita the teacher and the children decorate with chains of gaily colored paper has been her entire world. Now middle-aged, Julita, unmarried and childless, lives only for her pupils, through whom she attempts to rediscover the joy and beauty of life. The boredom and frustrations of women in a small town are seen also in the cases of La Reverenda Sra. Doña Carmela, widowed sister of the priest, Doña María, the mayor's wife, and La Piadosa Sra. Doña Carmen, a single woman. These women eagerly dance with circus members, whom they really scorn as social inferiors, during the fair that forms the background for the action. Although victims themselves, these women turn on Julita. The play ends with the arrival of a new teacher, full of the same idealism that characterized Julita some 10 years earlier, and with the departure of Julita after the neighbors stone her school. Her youth and vitality gone, Julita is as withered as the dry reeds along the road to school, the road it frightened her to travel alone and in which she doubtlessly foresaw her destiny. There are suggestions in Julita of both García Lorca's Doña Rosita la Soltera and Tennessee Williams's (1911–1983) Blanche Dubois.

Las salvajes en Puente San Gil (1963; The Savages in Puente San Gil) depicts a company of actresses who arrive at a provincial Andalusian town to perform a variety show. They are denounced to the ecclesiastical authorities by the intransigently puritanical Damas de Santa Úrsula (Ladies of St. Ursula), attacked brutally by village youths, and taken advantage of by the Damas' husbands to satisfy their own aggressive, ill-repressed sexuality. The play is based on the playwright's own observations as director of a university theater group that toured Spain in the 1950s and 1960s.

The Damas de Santa Úrsula, who are reminiscent of Julita's friends in the previous play, accuse the actresses of public scandal and prostitution and succeed in having the show canceled by the authorities. Their motive is distrust of their own husbands, whom they correctly suspect would be the first to seek out the showgirls. Like the village women in the preceding play, the Damas are themselves victims. Yet it is they who most staunchly uphold the morality responsible for their own suffering and attack the showgirls, branding them as "savages." The play's climax is the attack on several actresses by a group of drunken youths. After gaining entrance to the barricaded theater through the roof, the youths rape the actresses, causing the death of one actress who falls into the orchestra pit when trying to escape. While the actresses in the theater are attacked, those who have gone out to dance are exploited by the Damas' husbands. As they return, they wind up by chance in front of the house of the archpriest, who stated earlier that he would not allow them to endanger the souls of his parishioners. Holding him responsible for the actions of his people, one of the women physically assaults him.

The defiant replies of the actresses, after being charged with conspiracy to murder the archpriest, make clear the play's message. The accused become accusers as they denounce a repressive and hypocritical society, charging that "buyers" of sexual favors are as guilty as "sellers," if not more so. The real savages, as La Magdalena told the archpriest, are the men of San Gil. Her words point up the play title's ambiguity. As the women are led off to jail, they sing defiantly, realizing that they have nothing left to lose.

The collective female protagonist seen in Las salvajes en Puente San Gil appears also in Las arrecogías del Beaterio de Santa María Egipciaca (1974; The Inmates of the Convent of St. Mary Egyptian, 1985). Set in the Granada of Fernando VII, it depicts the last days of Mariana Pineda and her sister prisoners or recogidas (arrecogías in the popular speech of Granada). Martín Recuerda postulates the existence of other political prisoners in the beaterio founded as a reformatory for immoral women and links their stories with hers. He makes these women no less important than Mariana herself: Carmela "La Empecinada," a follower of Juan Martín; Paula "La Militara," a woman denounced as a mason by a royalist lover; Concepción "La Caratuana," a scrubwoman who carried the rebel flag from her village in the Alpujarras; Eva "La Tejedora," whose lover has fled with other liberal conspirators to Gibraltar; and Chirriana "La de la cuesta," a prostitute from Cádiz who fought with the Liberals. Whereas García Lorca's Mariana is implicated in the liberal conspiracy solely because of her lover, Martín Recuerda's heroine is the active revolutionary that she was historically.

Mariana and the prisoners who accept and identify with her, despite the difference in social class, expect the arrival of Casimiro Brodett, Mariana's lover, to free them. However, when he arrives, it is as a dying prisoner after the liberal conspiracy is crushed. The play's climax is Mariana's confession that she has opened her bedroom to politicians and noblemen of Granada to obtain the false passports and prison plans that saved so many Constitutionalists. When she perceives that he is wounded by the truth, she asks how (individual) human love can be placed above the freedom of an entire people. Martín Recuerda thus makes Mariana's convictions even stronger than her lover's.

Mariana's death sentence for having commissioned the embroidering of a rebel flag is read after she refuses to save herself by giving the names of the conspirators. The defiance of the other arrecogías, who demand to die with her, resembles that of the showgirls in Las salvajes en Puente San Gil as they are carted off to jail.

Martín Recuerda's female characters subsequent to Julita in Como las secas cañas rebel with impassioned fury against the conditions that oppress them: salvajes, arrecogías, dancers, and prostitutes in El engañao (1981; The Man Who Was Deceived) who support, with their bodies, Juan de Dios's hospital for victims of Carlos V's wars, as well as La Trotski and her cohorts, middle-aged dancers who could be the actresses of Las salvajes en Puente San Gil some 20 years later.

Work by

El engañao. Caballos desbocados. Ed. Martha T. Halsey and Angel Cobo. Madrid: Cátedra, 1981.

The Inmates of the Convent of St. Mary Egyptian. Adapted and trans. Robert Lima. Drama-Contemporary: Spain. Ed. Marion Holt. New York: Performing Arts Journal, 1985.

Las salvajes en Puente San Gil. Las arrecogías del Beaterio de Santa María Egipciaca. Ed. Francisco Ruis Ramón. Madrid: Cátedra, 1977.

El teatrito de Don Ramón. Como las secas cañas del camino. Ed. Gerardo Velázquez Cueto. Barcelona: Plaza y Janés, 1984.

La Trotski. La Trotski se va a las Indias. Sevilla: Biblioteca de la Cultura Andaluza, 1990.

Work about

Halsey, Martha. "Las arrecogías del Beaterio de Santa María Egipciaca: A Contemporary Celebration of Mariana de Pineda and Her Sisters." Kentucky Romance Quarterly 26.3 (1979): 305–318.

Weingarten, Barry. "José Martín Recuerda's *La Trotski*: Post-Franco Spain as *Esperpento*." *Estreno* 19.2 (1993): 44–47.

Martha T. Halsey

Martín Santos, Luis
See *Tiempo de silencio* (1962): Its Portrayal of Women

Martín Vivaldi, Elena (1907–   )

Born in Granada, poet Elena Martín Vivaldi studied philosophy and letters at the university there and in the early postwar years became a librarian (1942), working in various cities of Andalusia before returning to Granada in 1948. During these same years, following traumatic experiences in love and war, she began writing poetry; although written from 1942 to 1944, her first collection, *Primeros poemas* (1977; First Poems) remained unpublished for more than three decades. Although a significant poet, Martín Vivaldi is scarcely known, and her poetry is neither widely distributed nor easily accessible.

She was born at the same time as Carmen *Conde and, like her, matured during the aegis of the Generation of 1927. Logically, Martín Vivaldi's work contains frequent echoes of these poets (including Rafael Alberti, Vicente Aleixandre, Federico *García Lorca, and others). Nevertheless, her first published collection, *Escalera de luna* (1945; Moon Ladder), coincides not with early works of Conde and others of their generation but with the so-called writers of postwar *tremendismo* (inappropriately applied to poetry, this label for the neonaturalist novel of social realism was used by some critics of the day to refer to poetry that expressed postwar protest and existentialist angst). Martín Vivaldi's only point of coincidence with these younger poets appears in religious questioning. Critic José Ortega sees influences of Garcilaso, with Martín Vivaldi's elegiac tone and themes of impossible love in the *courtly love tradition being the most evident points of coincidence. Despite *garcilasismo* (a post–Civil War revival of the brilliant Renaissance poet Garcilaso de la Vega by pro-regime poets), Martín Vivaldi has little in common with this coetaneous group: She eschews their pastoral themes and use of traditional metrics, although she does occasionally cultivate the sonnet. Among other influences by earlier poets or affinities for Martín Vivaldi, critics have mentioned traces of Juan Ramón *Jiménez and, inevitably, of compatriot Granadan García Lorca. Asís also sees influences of Pedro Salinas and Jorge Guillén in her verse.

Like many women poets, working largely alone and away from contact with literary circles, Martín Vivaldi writes very personal, intimate, and confidential poetry. Hers is poetry in the confessional vein, stressing sentiment and psychic states—individual rather than collective—and thus quite unrelated to postwar social poetry, except for her use of plain, clear, simple language of great lucidity and precision, plus her preference for objective descriptions of concrete reality. While occasionally deliberately prosaic, as are the social poets, unlike them Martín Vivaldi avoids the colloquial register. And rather than focusing on the generic, the masses, the problematic, and unjust, as did the social poets, Martín Vivaldi prefers themes of love, love lost, or love in the past, as well as poems of pain, suffering, nostalgia, and oblivion. Her most significant theme, unrequited love, springs from autobiographical substrata, with frequent allusions to a tragic love affair when the love of her life ended their relationship. Unrequited love and resultant enduring loneliness constitute the major themes of *Primeros poemas* and another collection written at the same time (1942–1943), *El alma desvelada* (1953; Soul with Insomnia). Asís notes how here, baring her soul, the poetic persona appears as a metaphorical lemon tree, killed by the "hard freeze of life." Metaphors of solitude combine with references to darkness, death, and night, while faded flowers evoke remembered youth. Rejection and solitude are the poet's destiny, with life blurring into grayness. Nevertheless, it would be inaccurate to characterize Martín Vivaldi as sentimental; she strives to synthesize contemplation and passion with intellect.

Most of Martín Vivaldi's poetry was published in the 1970s; order of appearance in print has little connection with sequence of composition. *Diario incompleto de abril* (1971; Incomplete April Diary), subtitled "Homage to Bécquer," was written in 1947 during her residence in Seville, where *Bécquer had lived. Composed in free verse, the use of which Bécquer had pioneered in nineteenth-century Spain, the collection's compositions address April with dramatic monologues celebrating springtime. More rain than sunshine, however, makes for a somber and melancholy vision of nature's reawakening. Here as in other collections, the sea variously symbolizes life, death, and solitude.

Cumplida soledad (1953–1976) (1976; Fulfilled Solitude), *Arco en desenlace* (1963; Bow Unlaced [written 1953–1962]), and *Materia de esperanza* (1968; Matter of Hope [written 1958–1966]) are testimonials to the painful process of grieving and long, slow healing, as intense love and intense loss fade into acceptance of loneliness, the impossibility of another love, and the acceptance of solitude. While *Cumplida soledad* stresses suffering and solitude, it also contains poems of the night (symbolizing the inevitability of death), which critics have praised highly. *Durante este tiempo. 1965–1972* (1972; During This Time) is dedicated to the Generation of 1927 and considered one of Martín Vivaldi's best achievements. It figures among the most varied thematically and is perhaps her most accomplished technically. Three subdivisions correspond to three major preoccupations: "Día a día" (Day by Day) is composed of meditations on quotidian existence; "Paisajes" (Landscapes) abounds in both land and seascapes, rainy nocturnal reflections of internal "landscapes"; and "Las ventanas iluminadas" (Lighted Windows) opens on an urban environment, populous yet lonely. Unlike earlier collections, *Durante este tiempo* fixes its gaze on things beyond the poet, on experiences lived rather than imagined, for objective situations and other subjectivities, mourning the loss of friends (including an elegy on the death of poet Celia *Viñas). Time's passing becomes a significant theme, accompanying the poet's voicing of her sense of final, lasting, total solitude.

Martín Vivaldi's subsequent collections include *Nocturnos* (1981; Nocturnes [written 1974–1981]); *Y era su nombre mar* (1981; And His Name Was Sea [also 1974–1981]); *Los árboles presento* (1977; I Present the Trees), an anthology; and *Tiempo a la orilla* (1985; Time at the Water's Edge), which brings together 10 books published between 1942 and 1984, plus unpublished works and others that previously appeared only in periodicals. *Tiempo a la orilla* is not only the closest thing to a "complete works" edition that exists of Martín Vivaldi's poetry to date, but it includes an introduction by E. Molina Campos providing the best source for information on the poet's life and works.

Neither feminist nor activist, Martín Vivaldi does not present herself as victim, nor does she heap recriminations upon the man who some might see as ruining her life (although from her suffering and personal tragedy she has fashioned a major poetic opus). Her voice is profoundly feminine, and her writing is similarly gendered. Intelligence, sensitivity, spiritual qualities, and artistic achievement combine in an exceptional lyric accomplishment.

Work by

El alma desvelada. Madrid: Insula, 1953.
Los árboles presento. Prologue Antonio Gallego Morell. Granada: Universidad, 1977. Anthology.
Arco en desenlace. Granada: "Veleta al sur," 1963.
Cumplida soledad. Granada: "Veleta al sur," 1958.
Cumplida soledad (1953–1976). Granada: Silene, 1976. Anthology.
Diario incompleto de abril. Homenaje a Gustavo Adolfo Bécquer (1947). Ed. A. Caffarena. Málaga: Guadalhorce, 1971.

Durante este tiempo. 1965–1972. Barcelona: El Bardo, 1972.
Escalera de luna. Granada: "Vientos del Sur," 1945.
Materia de esperanza. Granada: "Albaicin," 1968.
Nocturnos. Granada: Don Quijote, 1981.
Primeros poemas (1942–1944). Intro. Fidel Villan Ribot. Málaga: Guadalhorce, 1977.
Tiempo a la orilla. Obra reunida 1942–1984. Study by Enrique Molina Campos. 2 vols. Granada: Silene, 1985.
Las ventanas iluminadas. Sel. Rafael Juárez and Luis García Moreno. Prol. and interview Luis García Moreno. Madrid: Hiperion, 1997.
Y era su nombre mar. Málaga: Cuadernos Jarazmin, 1981.

Work about

Asís, María Dolores de. "El sentimiento de la soledad en la poesía de Elena Martín Vivaldi." *Antípodas* 2 (December 1989): 129–140.
Gallego Morell, Antonio. "Prólogo" to *Los árboles presento.* Granada: Universidad, 1988.
Gutiérrez, José. *Manual de nostalgias.* Granada: Silene, 1982.
Molina Campos, E. "Introducción a la poesía de Elena Martín Vivaldi." *Tiempo a la orilla.* Granada: Silene, 1985.

Janet Pérez

Masoliver, Liberata (1911–)

Born in Barcelona, Liberata Masoliver cultivates the novel, romance, and children's fiction, writing primarily in Spanish but also in Catalan. Although details concerning her life are sparse, her writings express attitudes typical of the conventional, traditional, religious bourgeoisie of Catalonia in the years between the two world wars. From the late 1950s through the early 1970s, Masoliver published more than a dozen novels (and at least 17 titles), most treating realistically the Spanish Civil War and its aftermath, religious themes, or the life of the Catalan upper class in the postwar period. More in the romance vein are several tales of adventure in the jungles of equatorial Africa.

Masoliver repeatedly examines certain themes usually classed as feminist, that is, rape and adultery, but does not write from a feminist perspective: Her viewpoint is conservative, conformist, and supportive of the patriarchal establishment. Similarly, she treats several other potentially controversial topics—infidelity, impotence, sterility, divorce, rape, venereal disease, homosexuality, and surrogate paternity—but presents none as serious social problems. Instead, they function as catalysts, prompting characters to face ethical dilemmas and make moral decisions. Conflicts between religious faith or duty and the human heart or desires of the flesh provide the narrative conflict in several works, together with the "conversion" or repentance of the erring wife and/or mother who returns to her husband or family, having realized the evils of carnal love. Although a more searching analysis or less conventional resolution of many such problems in gender relations would likely have run afoul of the censors, Masoliver appears to have had no difficulty. Romantic illusion fades when confronted by reality in her fiction, and materialistic values collapse when juxtaposed to spiritual principles.

Chronicling contemporary upper-class Barcelona, *Los Galiano* (1957; The Galiano Family) presents young urban singles living a carefree existence devoted to literary pastimes, music, fashions, amusements, and fads of the day. *Selva negra, selva verde* (1959; Black Jungle, Green Jungle) features as protagonist an Italian adventurer and admirer of Mussolini (acceptable to Spain's fascist dictatorship) in a somewhat unlikely tale of life among a cannibal tribe. *Barcelona en llamas* (1961; Barcelona in Flames), a historical novel of the Civil War, traces the imprisonment of a Franco sympathizer by Loyalist Republican militia and her subsequent release, thanks to the intervention of a Republican friend, followed by sentimental involvement with a mysterious figure later discovered to be a priest in disguise. *La bruixa* (1961; The Witch), written for children and perhaps Masoliver's only work in Catalan, is a modern fairy tale in verse, re-creating the fantastic adventures of two children kidnapped by a witch whose broom crashes in their garden. *La mujer del colonial* (1962; The Colonist's Wife) returns to the equatorial jungle romance, this time with a female protagonist. Left behind to manage the ranch in the absence of her impotent husband, the wife indulges in a short-lived, tempestuous affair. As in the following novel, *Maestro albañil* (1963; Master Bricklayer), frustrated maternity is a major theme, and in both problems center upon children born of adulterous relationships. The colonist's wife repents and renounces her child to return to her husband, while the bricklayer's long-suffering spouse adopts the baby fathered by her husband during a short-lived affair with a scandalous adventuress. The theme reappears in *Pecan los buenos* (1964; When the Good Sin), with slight modification: A model wife—much as in *García Lorca's *Yerma*—discovers that her inability to conceive is her husband's fault, as premarital venereal disease rendered him sterile. Obsession with motherhood drives her to an affair with her husband's partner, but she quickly repents and returns to her marriage.

Masoliver sets several novels on the Costa Brava, in wealthy resorts favored by Barcelona's elite: this is the scene of *Maestro albañil*, of her next novel *Nieve y alquitrán* (1965; Snow and Tar), and of *Casino veraniego* (1968; Vacation Casino). *Nieve y alquitrán*, obvious opposites, suggest other aspects of a May–December relationship between two lonely outcasts, an adolescent girl and an aging recluse, starved for companionship and communication: He hangs himself when she falls in love with someone her own age. *Un camino llega a la cumbre* (1966; One Path Leads to the Summit) also approaches the question of suicide (viewed by Spain's faithful Catholics as an unpardonable, mortal sin). A devout girl, the victim of rape, contemplates suicide upon discovering that she is pregnant but sublimates her tragedy as implied by the title reference to spiritual ascent. Religious themes also dominate *La retirada* (1967; The Retreat), an ostensible documentary of the Civil War's final 18 months as experienced by two soldiers in the defeated Republican army, one a disillusioned leftist, the other a covert Franco sympathizer whose religious faith eventually leads to his companion's conversion, without completely displacing the chronicle of the retreat.

Casino veraniego, somewhat in the vein of the *novela rosa* (sentimental romance), provides the trivial chronicle of a wealthy young woman's selection between various suitors, against the backdrop of a Mediterranean summer resort, while *Hombre de paz* (1969; Man of Peace) revisits the Civil War, portraying the moral dilemma of a doctor who has courageously tended the sick and wounded of both sides but must kill to save his sister's life. His pangs of conscience and confession just prior to his postwar marriage preface his death in an auto accident. *Dios con nosotros* (1970; God with Us) is an exemplary novel re-creating the life of Christ, while *Estés donde estés* (1972; Wherever You May Be) portrays the life of the nineteenth-century founder of a missionary order. Contrasting with Masoliver's moralistic fiction is *Los mini-amores de Angelines* (1972; Angela's Mini-Loves) with its own didactic outcome: The selfish, sensual, flirtatious protagonist indulges in a series of affairs but meets her death, together with her latest paramour, at the hands of a jealous former lover.

Masoliver's obvious shortcomings include an abundance of stereotypes and predictable plots; counterbalancing narrative strengths are generally well-handled dialogue, realistic descriptions, and sustained narrative interest. She enjoyed considerable popular success during nearly a quarter century, leaving a work whose enduring literary merit is scant but that serves as a testimonial to Spain's traditional patriarchal values during those years. For gender scholars and feminists, it can be marked "Exhibit A," exemplifying the barriers to women's progress, education, liberation, and self-realization.

Work by

Barcelona en llamas. Barcelona: Barna, 1961.
La bruixa. Barcelona: Jaimes, 1961.

Un camino llega a la cumbre. Barcelona: Peñíscola, 1966.
Casino veraniego. Barcelona: Peñíscola, 1968.
Dios con nosotros. Barcelona: Jaimes-Libros, 1970.
Efún. Barcelona: Garbo, 1955.
Los Galiano. Barcelona: Janes, 1957.
Hombre de paz. Barcelona: Jaimes-Libros, 1969.
Maestro albañil. Barcelona: Peñíscola, 1963.
La mujer del colonial. Barcelona: Barna, 1962.
Nieve y alquitrán. Barcelona: Peñíscola, 1965.
Pecan los buenos. Barcelona: Peñíscola, 1964.
La retirada. Barcelona: Peñíscola, 1967.
Selva negra, selva verde. Barcelona: Barna, 1959.
Telón. Barcelona: Jaimes-Libros, 1969.

Janet Pérez

Maturana y Velázquez de Gutiérrez, Vicenta (1793–1859)

Her father, Vicente Maturana, was a knight of Calatrava, a *mariscal de campo* (field marshal), and general director of artillery. When Vicenta Maturana y Velázquez was four, the family moved to Madrid, where she received a careful education, learning French and drawing. She composed poetry at age nine, but due to parental displeasure, she began to write and study in secret. In 1807, the family moved to Seville, where her love of dancing earned her the name "Terpsicoris del Betis" (Dance Muse of the Betis [River]). Her parents died suddenly: the father at the Battle of Bailén, and her mother six months afterward. Between 1816 and 1820 she served as a *camarista* (maid of honor) of Queen María Josefa Amalia, who dearly loved the orphan girl and shared a mutual love of literature with her. This friendship gave rise to a palace intrigue in which Maturana was accused of plagiarizing the Queen's poems. To dispel this rumor Maturana published a short book of poetry, *Ensayos poéticos* (Poetic Essays) in 1818.

In 1820 Maturana left the palace to marry Colonel Joaquín María Gutiérrez. While married, she published anonymously her novel *Teodoro o el huérfano agradecido* (n.d.; Teodoro or the Grateful Orphan), as well as *Poesías* (n.d.; Poems), and a second novel, *Sofía y Enrique* (n.d.; Sophia and Henry). When the First Carlist War broke out, her husband took Don Carlos's side, and upon his death in 1838, Maturana exiled herself to France. There she published "Himno a la luna" (Hymn to the Moon), a prose poem in four cantos, striking for the originality of its composition. In 1841 she published an additional book of poetry in Paris. In the prologue to her poems she again defends herself from those who had accused her of plagiarism.

Maturana's poetry is characterized by a variety of themes and meters: *romances* (ballads), *liras*, *décimas*, tercets, sonnets, free verse. Her poems, reminiscent of neoclassic poet Meléndez Valdés's (1754–1817) verse, sing of nature in all its manifestations, her own emotions, and her deep existential concerns.

Work by

Ensayos poéticos. Madrid: Verges, 1828.
"Himno a la luna." Bayon: Dunhart-Fauvet, 1838.
Poesías. Paris: Lecointe et Lasserre, 1841.
Poesías. Madrid: Santiago Aguado, 1859.
Sofía y Enrique. Madrid: Vda. de Villalpando, 1829.

Work about

Serrano y Sanz, Manuel. *Apuntes para una biblioteca de escritoras españolas desde el 1401 al 1833.* 2 vols. Madrid: Rivadeneyra, 1903. Rpt. Madrid: Atlas, 1975.

María A. Salgado

Matute, Ana María (1926–)

She is recognized as one of Spain's most important and prolific writers of the Franco era. A precocious talent, Ana María Matute began writing as a child during the Civil War and had published her first short story, "El chico de al lado" (The Boy Next Door), by age 18 and her first novel, Nadal Prize finalist *Los Abel* (1948; The Abel Family), by age 22. For the next quarter century Matute steadily produced works for both adults (eight novels and numerous collections of short stories, novelettes, essays, and memoirs) and juveniles, many of which have been translated into several languages. Matute's fiction has garnered a number of prestigious literary awards, among them the Planeta Prize for *Pequeño teatro* (1954; Little Theater), the Critics' Prize and the National Literary Prize for *Los hijos muertos* (1958; The Dead Children), and the Nadal Prize for *Primera memoria* (1960; First Memoirs), and has received extensive attention from Spanish and non-Spanish critics.

Matute was born on July 16, 1926, in Barcelona, the second of five children of an upper-middle-class family. The author's formative years, marked by frequent moves between Barcelona and Madrid due to her Catalan industrialist father's work, and summers in Mansilla de la Sierra, in the Rioja region where her Castilian mother's family maintained an estate, were to strongly influence her fictional world. Barcelona and rural Old Castile are the most frequent settings for Matute's fiction. However, despite a happy family life, these moves produced in Matute a feeling of always being the outsider. This is reflected throughout her work in the constant repetition of the themes of alienation, solitude, inability to communicate, and despair that are linked to her primarily juvenile protagonists. Moreover, her contact with the backward, often primitive living conditions of the peasantry of Mansilla fomented in the author a marked sense of social injustice that permeates much of her fiction.

The most significant event of Matute's childhood, however, was the Civil War, the outbreak of which surprised the family in Barcelona. There Matute witnessed the brutal inter- and intrafactional battles that were to physically and emotionally scar the country. Her view of the civil strife, dominated by violence, degradation, and ultimately uselessness, impelled her to obsessively search for the causes of the conflict through her writing; this became the principal structural and thematic element of the majority of her work. This search is initiated in *Los Abel* by means of a diary format that reveals the decadence and internal strife of a family of Castilian rural gentry. The rivalry of the two eldest brothers, which introduces the Cain/Abel myth that is a constant of her narrative, and the relationship of the family to the land and to the rural peasantry foreshadows more direct symbolical representations in later novels (*Los hijos muertos*, *Fiesta al noroeste* [1959; Celebration in the Northwest, 1997], and the trilogy) of the social and economic injustice and personal/collective violence that comprise the roots of the Civil War.

While Matute's condemnatory thematic at times eluded the cutting hand of Francoist censors, thanks to her highly subjective, lyrical style and her use of an often misleading novelistic construction that diverts attention away from the subversive main narrative, this was not the case with the first novel she wrote, *Pequeño teatro*, nor her third novel, *En esta tierra* (1955; In This Land). Both were published only after substantial changes and in part due to the author's financial exigencies while laboring for seven years on the monumental *Los hijos muertos*. The latter, Matute's most lauded novel, characteristically focuses on the lives of three generations of orphaned youth during the decades framing the Civil War, combining personal conflicts with the political, economic, and moral crisis of the country. The distinct worlds of youth and adult, of peasants, proletariat, and the leisure class, as well as themes of authenticity, disillusion, guilt, and reconciliation are all key elements of the novel. Particularly significant in this work is the recurrent Matutian symbol of the wolf that explains the violence of the disinherited as forced by necessity.

The causes of violence and cruelty, especially among children, that are a consistent focus of Matute, come to the forefront in the first novel of the trilogy *Los mercaderes* (The Moneychangers). *Primera memoria* is a memoir narrated by the mature Matia, whose younger self is the protagonist, describing her difficult passage into adulthood that entailed the loss of her childhood/innocence/paradise.

Set on an island (Mallorca) during the initial months of the Civil War, and primarily using children as protagonists to represent the adult-engendered civil strife, the conflicts within families and between rival bands and social classes are provoked by individual as well as collective fear, jealousy, hate, and cowardice.

The preferred themes of Matute, continued in the remaining books of the trilogy, are also present in *La torre vigía* (1971; The Watchtower). While superficially quite different from prior fiction due to the medieval setting and a greater indulgence of fantasy, this subverted bildungsroman replete with biblical imagery in fact repeats numerous Matutian motifs such as the Cain-Abel conflict, materialism versus idealism, the illusory triumphs of warfare, the destructive nature of collective and personal vengeance, and the cyclical nature of human situations and types.

A full quarter-century after *La torre vigía* (which Pérez characterized as a "chivalric social novel"), Matute published the oft-announced and oft-delayed *Olvidado rey Gudú* (1996; Forgotten King Gudú), set in the tenth century in a mythic land at the edge of Europe—aspects of setting shared with the previous novel. *Olvidado rey Gudú*, however, is some four times longer and became a runaway bestseller, something of a cult classic with an almost limitless appeal. Chronicling the rise and fall of a medieval dynasty, it combines numerous chivalric and *fairy-tale figures and motifs with others already noted in *La torre vigía*, denouncing the feudal nobility's cruelty, rapaciousness, greed, and exploitation of the people—and especially of the young, of women, and of the defenseless. An antiwar novel that exposes knighthood and warlords as immoral and corrupt, it contains Matute's best-developed woman character, a rare empowered female, the orphan child become Queen Ardid. Also a novel of the fleeting nature of happiness and the doomed search for love, it anticipates Matute's latest novel to date, *Aranmanoth* (2000), also set in the Middle Ages amid chivalric trappings. But fantasy has displaced much of reality—the protagonist is only half human, the son of a water sprite—and magic abounds, all part of the backdrop for a tragic romance recalling *Tristan and Isolde*, replete with additional biblical symbology. All these things and more, *Aranmanoth* is above all a world extolling dreams and humanity's pursuit thereof. Since 1996, Matute has been a member of the Royal Spanish Academy, only the third woman in history to be so honored.

Matute's short fiction and juvenile literature have also been very successful. In the latter, motivated by the birth of her son Juan Pablo in 1954, Matute employs many themes recurrent in her adult literature such as social injustice (*Paulina, el mundo y las estrellas* [1960; Paulina, the World and the Stars]), allusions to the Civil War (*Carnavalito* [1962; Little Carnival]), and the termination of childhood (*El polizón del Ulises* [1965; The Cabin Boy of the Ulysses]). The notable presence of lyricism and fantasy in her juvenile literature is also apparent in her short fiction. Here, a wider range of characteristic Matutian themes are combined with varied stylistic techniques that provide additional insight into Matute's narrative. The collections of short stories, notable among them *Los niños tontos* (1956; The Stupid Children), *Historias de la Artámila* (1961; Stories of Artamila), and *Algunos muchachos* (1968; Some Boys), stand on their own as artistic creations and, at the same time, reinforce the evidence of the ultimate coherency of Matute's fictional world. *See also* Fairy Tales in Novels by Spanish Women; Short Fiction by Women Writers: 1900–1975

Work by

Los Abel. Barcelona: Destino, 1948.
Aranmanoth. Madrid: Espasa, 2000.
Celebration in the Northwest. Trans. and intro. Phoebe Ann Porter. Lincoln: U of Nebraska P, 1997.
The Heliotrope Wall and Other Stories. New York: Columbia UP, 1989.

The Lost Children. New York: Macmillan, 1965.
Olvidado rey Gudú. Madrid: Espasa-Calpe, 1996.
The School of the Sun. London: Quartet, 1991.
Soldiers Cry by Night. Pittsburgh: Latin American Literary Review P, 1994.
La torre vigía. Barcelona: Lumen, 1971.

Work about

Díaz, Janet. *Ana María Matute.* New York: Twayne, 1971.
El Saffar, Ruth. "En busca de Edén: Consideraciones sobre la obra de Ana María Matute." *Revista Iberoamericana* 116–117 (1981): 223–231.
Glenn, Kathleen M. "Apocalyptic Vision in Ana María Matute's *La torre vigía*." *Letras Femeninas* 16 (1990): 21–28.
Jones, Margaret E.W. *The Literary World of Ana María Matute.* Lexington: U of Kentucky P, 1970.
Kubayanda, José. "*La torre vigía* de Ana María Matute: Aproximación a una narrativa alegórica." *Revista de Estudios Hispánicos* 3 (1982): 333–345.
McGiboney, Donna. "The Sight/Site of the Father: Learning to Be Silent in Ana María Matute's *Primera memoria*." *Romance Languages Annual* 9 (1997): 613–618.
Nichols, Geraldine. "Creced y multiplicad: Niños y números en *Algunos muchachos* de Ana María Matute." *Compás de Letras* 4 (1994): 215–226.
Pérez, Janet. "Apocalipsis y milenio, cuentos de hadas y caballerías en las últimas obras de Ana María Matute." *Monographic Review/Revista Monográfica* 14 (1998, pub. 1999): 39–58.
———. "The Fictional World of Ana María Matute: Solitude, Injustice and Dreams." *Women Writers of Contemporary Spain: Exiles in the Homeland.* Ed. Joan L. Brown. Newark: U of Delaware P, 1991. 93–115.
Roy, Joaquín, Marie Lise Gazarian, Margaret E.W. Jones, and Janet Pérez. *The Literary World of Ana María Matute.* Coral Gables: Iberian Studies Institute, U of Miami, 1993.
Sotelo Vásquez, Marisa. "*Primera memoria* de Ana María Matute: La vida es una infancia repetida." *Salina: Revista de Lletres* 13 (1999): 171–178.
Soufas, C. Christopher. "Narrative Form as Feminist Ideology: Feminist Consciousness/Criticism in Laforet's *Nada*, Matute's *Primera memoria* and Moix's *Julia*." *Discurso: Revista de Estudios Iberoamericanos* (Asunción, Paraguay) 11.1 (1993): 153–161.
Vásquez, María. "Hablando con Ana María Matute." *Suplemento Literario de la Nación* (Buenos Aires), October 27, 1996: 3.

Kathleen Thompson-Casado

Maura, Julia (1906–1971)

Best known as a dramatist, Julia Maura, granddaughter of the famed conservative leader Antonio Maura and cousin of Constancia de la *Mora (1906–1950), also wrote newspaper articles, prose fiction, and essays. She was born in Madrid but spent much of her youth in her family's home in the Sierra de Guadarrama. Like most aristocratic young women of her time, Maura received a traditional education. She traveled a great deal, returned to live in Madrid in 1922, and married Andrés Covarrubias Castillo in 1931. It appears that the conflict between caring for her five children and her desire to write was a source of concern for her, although she always put her family first. Following the Spanish Civil War, Maura's plays enjoyed great popularity, and she became the most successful female playwright in Spain. After her original triumphs, however, critics began to write negative reviews of her works, sometimes without even having seen the productions. At one point Maura was involved in a scandal in which she was accused of plagiarizing Oscar Wilde in three newspaper articles in order to elicit the usual negative criticism. Her plan was to reveal subsequently that the famous Wilde was the true author of the pieces. She continued writing for most of the remainder of her life, with her final published play, *Jaque a la juventud* (Checkmate to Youth), appearing in 1965. Nine of her plays, the last written in 1966, remain unpublished.

Women's issues underlie the themes of most of Maura's works. In general her protagonists are females who fall victim to jealousy, false rumors, and the patriarchal system. Women of strong character and great integrity, they suffer unjustly at the hands of gossip mongers, domineering husbands, and the patriarchal system. In spite of their admirable personal characteristics, her female protagonists, like Maura herself, hold the traditional view of women's obligations, accepting marriage as the only role for women and putting family ahead of personal concerns. Her male characters usually personify the male stereotype as the overbearing husband, philandering and selfish. The exception is an occasional minor character who speaks up to express support for a female character.

The first play that Maura published, titled *La mentira del silencio* (1944; The Lie of Silence), deals with a woman who admits to an illicit affair with a man who has been killed by her husband. After much anguish, she concludes that tarnishing her reputation is a small price to pay for covering up her husband's theft of company funds, which had been discovered by the murdered man. As in many of Maura's plays, the innocent woman suffers in order to protect her family. In *La riada* (1956; The Torrent) the protagonist is a village woman wrongly accused of being unfaithful to her husband, a man who kills one of his employees whom he suspects of having an affair with his wife. At the end of the play the woman returns to her home, vowing to remain inside, impenetrable to the destructive force of village gossip.

In contrast to her earlier works, Maura's last published play, *Jaque a la juventud* (1965), takes place in an urban rather than rural setting and focuses on how the other characters react to the pregnancy of an upper-class family's unmarried daughter. Since the expected baby's father is a married man, the dilemma is resolved by her marriage to a cousin in order to give the child a legitimate birth. Although Maura implies that the new generation of young people have other alternatives, the young woman finally acquiesces to the established order.

Most of Maura's other writings concern the conflict she and her contemporaries faced between finding their own identities and staying within the bounds of the traditional social order. Although she did not openly rebel against these restrictions, she chose them as the focal point of her works and was one of the most noteworthy of the Spanish women writers of the first half of the twentieth century who helped pave the way for later female authors to deal openly with the problems inherent in the paternalistic society in which they lived.

Work by

Artículos de fe. Madrid: A. Vassallo, 1959.
Como la tierra y el mar. Madrid: Aguilar, 1945.
Estos son mis artículos. Madrid: Aguilar, 1953.
La eterna doña Juana. Madrid: Alfil, 1954.
Eva y la vida. Madrid: Aguilar, Ediciones Cristol, 1950.
Jaque a la juventud. Madrid: Alfil, 1965.
La mentira del silencio. Madrid: Biblioteca Teatral, 1944.
La riada. Madrid: Alfil, 1956.

Work about

Levine, Linda Gould, Ellen Engelson Marson, and Gloria Feiman Waldman, eds. *Spanish Women Writers: A Bio-Bibliographical Source Book*. Westport, CT: Greenwood P, 1993. 321–329.
O'Connor, Patricia W. *Dramaturgas españolas de hoy*. Madrid: Fundamentos, 1988.
———. "Lark in a Hostile Garden." *Estudios sobre escritoras hispánicas en honor de Georgina Sabat-Rivers*. Ed. Lou Charnon-Deutsch. Madrid: Castalia, 1992. 233–245.
———. "Women Dramatists in Contemporary Spain and the Male-Dominated Canon." *Signs* 15.2 (1990): 376–390.
Valdivieso, L. Teresa. "Ambiguedad epistemológica en un drama de Julia Maura." *Letras Femeninas* (1974–1994): 49–56.

Jean S. Chittenden

Mayoral, Marina (1942–   )

Born in Mondoñedo, Galicia, this professor of Spanish literature at the Universidad Complutense in Madrid has achieved a solid reputation as a literary scholar for her works on two Galician writers, Rosalía de *Castro (1837–1885) and Emilia *Pardo Bazán (1852–1921). She has published two major studies of Castro's poetry, *La poesía de Rosalía de Castro* (1974; Rosalía de Castro's Poetry) and *Rosalía de Castro y sus sombras* (1976; Rosalía de Castro and Her Shadows), and has edited two of her books, *Follas Novas* and *En las orillas del Sar*, as well as Castro's *Obras completas* in 1993. Mayoral's interest in Pardo

Bazán is evidenced in the annotated edition of four of her major works, *Los Pazos de Ulloa*, *Insolación*, *Dulce dueño*, and *La Quimera*. Mayoral's numerous essays and articles include studies on literary theory, authors such as Pérez Galdós (1843–1920), *Bécquer (1836–1870), *Azorín (1873–1967), León Felipe, Miguel Hernández, Castro, Pardo Bazán, and romantic writers, especially women.

As a creative writer, Mayoral has published seven novels in Spanish: *Cándida, otra vez* (1979; Candida Again), *Plantar un árbol* (1980; Planting a Tree), *Al otro lado* (1980; On the Other Side), *La única libertad* (1982; The Only Freedom), *Contra muerte y amor* (1985; Against Death and Love), *Recóndita armonía* (1994; Hidden Harmony), and *Tristes armas* (1994; Sad Weapons); and three in Galician: *Unha arbore, un adeus* (1988) (Galician version of *Plantar un árbol*); *O reloxio da torre* (1988), translated into Spanish as *El reloj de la torre* (1991; The Clock Tower); and *Chamábase Luis* (1989), with Spanish and Catalan translations, *Se llamaba Luis* (1995; His Name Was Luis) and *Es deia Lluís* (1995). Her shorter fictional works have appeared in newspapers, journals, anthologies, and in three collections: *Morir en sus brazos* (1989; To Die in His Arms); *Querida amiga* (1995; Dear Friend); and *Recuerda, cuerpo* (1998; Remember, Body).

Mayoral concentrates on the development of her characters in the environment of Galicia, reflecting critically the region's patriarchal, feudal past. Even when Mayoral enlarges her vision and sets action in Madrid, the characters are Galician. Her technique is that of an ironic observation and rendering of reality with regard to the relationship of the opposite sexes, sexual identity, homosexuality, incest, love, and friendship, in a parodical treatment of nineteenth-century romantic and realistic novels. Her characters are frequently eccentrics who subvert traditional sex roles—that is, a girl who loves boxing, men seduced by women, or a female scion in complete and ruthless control of her family estate.

An excellent storyteller, Mayoral's main themes are death and love, dealt with in a self-conscious and relativistic mode. Her metafictional narrations reject one single perspective, offering instead a myriad of voices through which subjectivity is problematized. Some of Mayoral's works contain on the surface elements of the detective novel; but a close reading reveals the ironic treatment of the popular subgenre through humor, parodical intertextual references, and the introduction of a supernatural reality. In the end, the mystery is the human psyche.

Mayoral has created a mythical Brétema, a metamorphosis of a Galician city, in which greedy aristocratic families, such as the Monterroso de Cela, have kept common people in bondage. This seacoast setting and many of the same characters reappear in *La sombra del ángel* (1999; Shadow of the Angel), one of whose narrators is the novelist Lucila Monterroso, a possible mask of the author. Mayoral's interest is not in social issues or politics but in psychology, that universal human longing for identity and fulfillment.

Mayoral is married to the painter Jordi Teixidor. *See also* Galician Woman Writers: A Brief History; Short Fiction by Women Writers: 1975–1998, Post-Franco

Work by

Cándida, otra vez. Ed. intro., and notes G. Gullón. Madrid: Castalia, 1992.
Contra muerte y amor. 2nd ed. Madrid: Cátedra, 1985.
Dar la vida y el alma. Madrid: Santillana; Alfaguara, 1996.
Morir en sus brazos. Alicante: Aguaclara, 1989.
Recóndita armonía. Madrid: Alfaguara, 1994.
Recuerda, cuerpo. Madrid: Alfaguara, 1998.
La sombra del ángel. Madrid: Alfaguara, 1999.

Work about

Alborg, Concha. "Marina Mayoral's Narrative: Old Families and New Faces from Galicia." *Women Writers of Contemporary Spain: Exiles in the Homeland*. Ed. Joan L. Brown. Newark: U of Delaware P, 1991. 179–197.
Bellver, Catherine G. "Entrevista con Marina May-

oral." *Letras Peninsulares* 6.2–3 (1993–1994): 383–389.

Camino Noia, María. "Claves de la narrativa de Marina Mayoral." *Letras Femeninas* 19.1–2 (Spring–Fall 1993): 33–44.

Gullón, Germán. "La (cambiante) representación de la mujer en la narrativa española contemporánea: *Chamábase Luis*, de Marina Mayoral." *Discurso femenino actual*. Ed. Adelaida López de Martínez. Puerto Rico: U of Puerto Rico, 1995. 33–51.

Johnson, Roberta. "Marina Mayoral's *Cándida, otra vez*: Invitation to a Retroactive Reading of *Sonata de otoño*." *Ramón del Valle-Inclan: Questions of Gender*. Ed. Carol Maier. Lewisburg, PA: Bucknell UP, 1994.

Juana Amelia Hernández

Medianera
See Celestina, La. Comedia o tragicomedia de Calisto y Melibea; Tercera.

Medina Sidonia, Duchess of
See Alvarez de Toledo, (Luisa) Isabel, Duchess of Medina Sidonia (1930–)

Medio, Dolores (1911–1996)

Short story writer and novelist Dolores Medio belongs to the group of significant women authors emerging in Spain after World War II. She wrote her major works in the 1940s and 1950s prior to the surge of feminism worldwide and certainly prior to the advent of strong feminist impulses in Spain, which began after the death of Franco in 1975. Medio wrote some nine works that could be classified as novels and at least eight collections of short stories. In addition, she composed poetry and published guidebooks, biographies of historical figures, and children's fiction. In both her life and her works Medio espoused feminist causes.

While she experimented in all genres, Medio's first success came in 1945 when her short story "Nina" won the prestigious Concha Espina Prize. It was then that she moved from the life of a provincial teacher to the Spanish capital of Madrid. Medio's first literary success graphically relates the oppression of the young victim, Nina, who is forced into prostitution. This acclaim was followed in 1953 with her family epic, *Nosotros los Rivero* (We, the Rivero Family), which in 1952 took the Nadal Prize, the most important award then given annually to Spanish novelists. With a highly sympathetic portrayal of the female protagonist, Lena Rivero, whose life experiences parallel Medio's own, *Nosotros los Rivero* follows the Spanish literary tradition of realism, chronicling not only the Rivero family but also the entire post–World War I epoch in Spain. This turbulent time of revolution, betrayal, and disillusionment is dramatized through the thinly veiled description of Medio's own family in Asturias, a region in northwestern Spain. As a young woman, Medio herself had believed in the ideals of the Second Republic but was shocked at the behavior of some revolutionaries. Behind her home in Oviedo was one of the places of execution for dissenters, and the family could hear the Nationalist (or Francoist) firing squads. This sense of intense immediacy pulsates through *Nosotros los Rivero* and renders it a compelling novel, despite occasional sentimental lapses. Medio's use of autobiographical material and the focus on female characters dominate not only *Nosotros los Rivero* but all her work.

In 1967 with the publication of *Andrés*, Medio expanded her treatment of the oppressed by focusing on the plight of children, often presented in shocking, disturbingly realistic tales. This collection won the prestigious Premio Sésamo literary award. Thereafter, Medio never achieved the same degree of success. She continued to write but spent her later years composing largely sentimental accounts of her native region, revising earlier work, or supervising her foundation, established to encourage and reward young authors from throughout the world, writing in the Spanish language. At the height of her success, Medio saw her works presented on television in Spain, and some, such as *Funcionario público* (Public Servant), originally published in Spain in 1956, were translated into Russian, German, and Rumanian. In 1963, *Funcionario público* was made into a text for English speakers studying Spanish. During this time of acclaim, Medio lived a somewhat flamboyant life in Madrid, occasionally sporting a men's dress shirt and tie and puffing away on her ever-present cigarette while talking animatedly about the state of art and politics in contemporary Spain. In 1990, she returned permanently to Oviedo, where she died on her eighty-fifth birthday, December 16, 1996. Ironically, the next day Medio was to have been honored by her natal city with publication of a long-suppressed novel, *Celda común* (Shared Cell), which may ultimately become her most important contribution to feminist literature.

Celda común (written 1963) documents her experiences while in prison for being present at a women's demonstration in 1962, offering a panoply of characters drawn from the people Medio encountered during her one-month incarceration, exacted because she could not pay the fine authorities imposed on her. Rebels and outcasts, these women become a metaphor not only for the plight of women but also for the problems of freedom and repression in Spanish society under Franco.

Equally ironic as the posthumous publication of *Celda común* and its potential impact on Spanish letters is the importance of Medio's novel *Bibiana* (1963), the first novel in the unfinished trilogy *Los que vamos a pie* (We, Pedestrians). Based on the well-meaning but completely inept and ineffectual figure of a middle-class Spanish housewife named Bibiana, in many ways this novel is even more significant than *Nosotros los Rivero*, with its highly romanticized heroine, Lena Rivero. Bibiana, in contrast, is human. She has wants and desires that, given the confines of Spanish society at that time, she is completely incapable of expressing—much less ever realizing. In this sense, Bibiana is painfully modern, stripped of all epic grandeur, too weak to be considered even tragic, yet treated with gentle humor by Medio.

In depicting Bibiana as an essentially trapped individual, Medio remains true to her literary roots and also to the great Asturian writers Leopoldo Alas (1852–1901) and Ramón *Pérez de Ayala (1880–1962), who, despite their protestations to the contrary, often wrote in the naturalistic vein, with an emphasis on contemporary social reality within a deterministic framework. Women, because their lives have so often been prescribed by society, become an appropriate vehicle to project Medio's naturalistic tendencies. At the same time, women in Medio's fiction become a symbol of all humanity; and while she often sees them as trapped, her sentiments, her exhortations, clearly urge them to change their lot. What further distinguishes Medio's fiction is her enormous sympathy for her characters—an outgrowth of her lifelong concern for the oppressed. Her early training in psychology and work as a teacher, dealing with students and parents of all classes, also enrich her work. Medio documents this important part of her life in the fictionalized account *Diario de una maestra* (1961; A Teacher's Diary), which she considered her best work, although she acknowledged that *Nosotros los Rivero* had been her best-received novel.

While fitting squarely in Spanish literary tradition with her reliance on realistic portrayal of character and linear development of plot, as in *Nosotros los Rivero*, Medio also participated in important stylistic innovations in Spanish fiction. In *El pez sigue flotando* (1959; The Fish Continues Afloat), Medio uses the technique of the perspective of multiple characters to give a sense that all of society is trapped in the same way as her individual characters. Here, she uses a wide lens and recalls the sense of simultaneous action employed by Camilo José *Cela (1916–2002). In this way and others, Medio also followed the vogue in Spain in the 1960s and

1970s of the *novela objetivista* (objective novel), a phenomenalist approach stressing the visual, the auditory, the surface structures. Medio also fits squarely within contemporary fiction in her treatment of the recurring theme of alienation, which she often sees as the result of gender and class differences and clashes. Solitude and noncommunication, or lack of communication, feed into this thematic concern as well.

In both her life and her fiction, Medio accomplished something that few women have achieved—even today: She often managed to immortalize female characters, such as Lena in *Nosotros los Rivero*, or Irene in *Diario de una maestra*, who live an independent single existence. While there were men in the lives of both Medio and her characters, she managed to explode the myth of the "old maid" in Spain by showing women living the single life in a positive light. She was the first woman writer of her generation who lived a full and active life without ever having to marry—or divorce—a man to achieve it. Just before her death, in a series of telephone interviews, Medio declared herself *una luchadora* (a fighter) who continues to struggle for feminism. *See also* Feminism in Spain: 1900–2000

Work by

Atrapados en la ratonera: Memorias de una novelista. Madrid: Yalce, 1980.

Celda común. Oviedo: Nobel, 1996.

Cinco cartas de Alemania. Madrid: Huerga y Fierro, 1995.

Funcionario público. Ed. and trans. Beatrice P. Patt and Martin Nozrick. New York: Oxford UP, 1963.

Nosotros los Rivero. Barcelona: Destino, 1970.

Work about

Díaz, Janet. "Three New Works of Dolores Medio." *Romance Notes* 9.2 (Fall 1969): 244–250.

Galerstein, Carolyn. "Dolores Medio: Women in Wartime." *Letras Femeninas.* 12.1–2 (Spring–Autumn 1986): 45–51.

Jones, Margaret E.W. *Dolores Medio.* Boston: Twayne, 1974.

———. "Dolores Medio: Chronicler of the Contemporary Spaniard's Interaction with Society." *Women Writers of Contemporary Spain: Exiles in the Homeland.* Ed. Joan L. Brown. Newark: U of Delaware P, 1991. 59–71.

Ordóñez, Elizabeth J. "Diario de una maestra: Female Heroism and the Context of War." *Letras Femeninas.* 12.1–2 (Spring–Autumn 1986): 52–59.

Pérez, Janet. "Portraits of the femme seule by Laforet, Matute, Soriano, Martín Gaite, Quiroga and Medio." *Feminine Concerns in Contemporary Spanish Fiction by Women.* Ed. Roberto Manteiga, Carolyn Galerstein, and Kathleen McNerney. Potomac, MD: Scripta Humanistica, 1988. 54–77.

———. "Silencios, alusiones, infantilismo: Dolores Medio y la retórica precavida de los cincuenta." *Letras Femeninas* 14.1–2 (1988): 32–40.

Ruiz Arias, Carmen. *Dolores Medio.* Oviedo: Caja de Ahorros, 1990.

Smoot, Jeanne J. "Freedom and Feminism against a Naturalistic World Order: The Life and Works of Dolores Medio." *Estudios en honor de Janet Pérez: El sujeto femenino en escritoras hispánicas.* Potomac, MD: Scripta Humanistica, 1998. 257–269.

———. "Realismo social en la obra de Dolores Medio." *Novelistas femeninas de la postguerra española.* Ed. Janet Pérez. Madrid: José Porrúa, 1983. 95–102.

Jeanne J. Smoot

Medrano, Luisa (Lucía) de (1484?–1527?)

A member of the Medrano Bravo family of the province of Soria, Luisa Medrano's fame rests on a public oration she delivered at the University of Salamanca in 1508 that was acknowledged by the rector of the institution, Pedro Torres, in 1517. In Book 25 of his *Cosas memorables de España*, Marineo Sículo describes her as a "woman of rare and admirable eloquence." In a letter to her he equates her with the classical figure of Hortensia for her eloquence.

According to Oettel, Medrano may have filled the chair of Latin rhetoric vacated by philologist Antonio de Nebrija during the academic year 1508–1509. Others speculate that she did not teach but gave the single oration witnessed and attested to by Marineo Sículo.

Work about

Oettel, Therese. "Una catedrática en el siglo de Isabel la Católica: Luisa (Lucía) de Medrano." *Boletín de la Real Academia de la Historia* 107 (1935): 289–360.

Siculus, Lucius Marineus. *Epistolarum Familiarum*. Valladolid, 1514.

———. *Obra de las Cosas memorables de España*. Alcalá de Henares, 1533.

Elizabeth T. Howe

Méndez, Concha (1898–1986)

Born in Madrid but forced into exile at the outset of the Spanish Civil War, Concha Méndez settled in 1943 in Mexico for the rest of her life. Of a rebellious nature from an early age, in 1928 she left her family in search of adventure and freedom, traveling first to England and then to Argentina. Known among contemporaries for her love of sports, loquacity, and free-spiritedness, her friends included many primary figures of the Generation of 1927, such as Luis Buñuel, Federico *García Lorca (1898–1936), Rafael Alberti (1902–), Luis Cernuda (1902–1963), and José Moreno Villa (1887–1955). Together with her husband, poet Manuel Altolaguirre (1905–1959), whom she had married in 1932, she founded the literary magazines *Héroe* and *Caballo verde para la poesía* in Madrid and *1616* in London. They also published important poetry of the period in their collections "La Tentativa Poética" and "Héroe." They continued their publishing efforts in Cuba with the collections "Verónica" and "El caballo griego."

Although her first books of poetry have often been dismissed as imitative tributes to Alberti, much of her imagery, the tonality of her verses, and the posture assumed by their speaker reveal a distinctly female presence. A joyous desire for liberation and self-assertiveness runs through Méndez's early poems. She celebrates her release from spatial confinement and revels in physical mobility and incorporates the visual quality, fragmented structure, and many motifs favored by *ultraísmo* (ultraism, an important early-twentieth-century literary movement). The sea, travel, freedom, and love prevail as her themes; and brevity, simplicity, and unpretentiousness establish themselves as the characteristic disposition of her poetry. With *Vida a vida* (1932; Life to Life) and especially *Niño y sombras* (1936; Little Boy and Shadows), inspired by the death of her first child, her poetry becomes more introspective. The loss of her son, exile, and divorce imbued her poetry with somber tones and a preoccupation with solitude and sadness. Pain and consolation, darkness and light, intermingle in poems that lose their impulse for experimentation. In her late poetry, memories, dreams, and the past replace the strong preference for life and adventure that defined her early writing.

Méndez also wrote a play containing motifs, settings, and structures stemming from vanguard currents, two short works of children's theater, and three versions of a play written in verse. Near the end of her life, she dictated her memoirs to her granddaughter.

Work by

El ángel cartero y El personaje presentido. Madrid: Galo Sáez, 1931.

Antología poética. Sel. María Dolores Arana. Mexico: Joaquín Mortiz, 1976.

Canciones de mar y tierra. Buenos Aires: Talleres Gráficos Argentinos, 1930.

Entre el soñar y el vivir. Mexico: Universidad Autónoma Nacional de Mexico, 1981.

Lluvias enlazadas. Havana: La Verónica, 1939.

Niño y sombras. Madrid: Héroe, 1936.

Poemas (1926–1986). Sel. James Valender. Madrid: Poesía Hiperión, 1995.

Vida a vida y Vida o río. Intro. Emilio Miró. Madrid: Caballo Griego para la Poesía, 1979.

Work about

Aub, Max. "Concha Méndez Cuesta." *Conversaciones con Buñuel*. Madrid: Aguilar, 1985. 241–251.

Bellver, Catherine G. "Exile and the Female Experience in the Poetry of Concha Méndez." *Anales de la Literatura Española Contemporánea* 18 (1993): 27–42.

———. "Mothers, Daughters and the Female Tradition in the Poetry of Concha Méndez." *Revista Hispánica Moderna* 51.2 (December 1998): 317–326.

———. "*El personaje presentido*: A Surrealist Play by Concha Méndez." *Estreno* 12.2 (1991): 292–303.

———. "Voyages, Flights and Other Patterns of Passage in *Canciones de mar y tierra* by Concha Méndez." *Pacific Coast Philology* 30 (1995): 103–116.

Miró, Emilio. "La contribución teatral de Concha Méndez." *El teatro en España. Entre la tradición y la vanguardia.* Ed. Dru Dougherty and María Francisca Vilches de Frutos. Madrid: C.S.I.C., Fundación García Lorca, Tabapress, 1922. 439–451.

Ulacia Altolaguirre, Paloma. *Concha Méndez: Memorias habladas, memorias armadas.* Madrid: Mondadori, 1990.

Valender, James. "Concha Méndez escribe a Federico y otros amigos." *Revista de Occidente* 211 (December 1998): 129–149.

Wilcox, John C. "Ernestina de Champourcin and Concha Méndez: Their Rescission from the Generation of 27." *Siglo XX/20th Century* 12.1–2 (1994): 291–317.

Catherine G. Bellver

Mendoza y de la Cerda, Ana
See Eboli, Princess of, Doña Ana de Mendoza y de la Cerda (1540–1592)

Meneses, Leonor María de (early 1620s–1664)

A member of a well-educated family from the highest Portuguese nobility (during the time when Spain ruled Portugal [1580–1640]), but to date little else is known of this recently rediscovered author of a courtly novella. Married twice, Leonor María de Meneses probably lived in Madrid, Lisbon, and possibly Paris; she wrote *El desdeñado más firme* (1655; Steadfast in Rejection) under the pseudonym "Laura Mauricia." It is a tale of love, jealousy, duels, death, and mistaken identities built around five suitors for two lovely cousins (each named Lisis) and a father/uncle attempting to arrange marriages for his two charges. Within this conventional mix of ingredients, Whitenack finds that Meneses departs significantly and purposefully from various conventions of the genre, particularly in her portrayal of the *mujer esquiva* (the woman averse to marriage and love, so popular in Golden Age theater), her treatment of jealousy, her multidimensional characters, and her defense of a woman's right to marry whom she wants rather than being forced to submit to the desires of others.

Work by

El desdeñado más firme. Primera parte. Ed. Judith A. Whitenack and Gwyn E. Campbell. Potomac, MD: Scripta Humanistica, 1994.

Work about

Whitenack, Judith A. "A Lost Seventeenth-Century Voice: Leonor de Meneses and *El desdeñado más firme.*" *Journal of Hispanic Philology* 17.1 (Fall 1992): 19–42.

Maureen Ihrie

Midwife
See Comadrona

Mieza, Carmen Farrés de (1931–1976)

Born a few years before the Spanish Civil War, Carmen Farrés de Mieza published two novels inspired by her own life experiences. Her father fled Spain, taking exile in Mexico, but Mieza remained in Spain until she had completed her education to be a teacher. Then she traveled to Mexico to join her father and returned to Spain in 1954. In 1976, she died in her home, but accounts of the incident are conflicting. Her first novel, *La imposible canción* (1962; The Impossible Song), portrays the lives of five Catalonian exiles living in Mexico City but longing to return to the homeland, a hope they sense can never be fulfilled. Their dreams to return to a free Spain once bolstered the diverse political convictions that they had upheld. Unfortunately, after more than 10 years in exile, they have fallen into a weakened, apathetic state; they routinely attend functions they dislike but gradually stray from the partisan activism that had held great significance for them. They feel unsettled, like ghosts wandering through a strange land because of their lingering homesickness for Spain. One of them, the communist Carrasco, does try to forget Spain and goes off to make a new life away from the others. In their struggle to hold on to their past and traditions, the men try to form close ties with their children. However, their children's inevitable assimilation with the Mexican culture only causes them more pain. The children feel that Spain no longer is their homeland; although they have experienced the trauma of expatriation, they need to go forward. Only one of the younger generation, Daniel Artigas, understands his father's suffering and the void that the separation from Spain has created. Daniel is the only child who wants to go back to seek his identity.

Una mañana cualquiera (1965; Any Morning), which won the Premio Urriza in the city of Lérida, also chronicles Spaniards exiled in Mexico. The novel deals with the complex relationship between a daughter, Angela, and her exiled father who has remarried. María, his uncultivated Mexican wife, seems to have married him by devious means and makes life difficult for Angela. The father, Pedro, a doctor, has made a life for himself in a small town; nonetheless he experiences the harsh desolation of exile, but his daughter does not share his sentiments. She remembers what had been taken from her as a child and does not want to look back. Pedro sees that the outlook for his daughter is promising and feels as alienated from Angela as he is from Spain. The novel intertwines the longings and uneasiness of the exiles with Angela's growing disaffection, with the presence of María, and with Angela's new friendships in Mexico. The forces of the novel compound the depiction of misery in exile as the complexities of Pedro's marriage to María widen the gap between father and daughter. Angela feels her father's world consists of shattered illusions and stagnation. Pedro sees the present as a tangible reflection of the past that he constantly remolds like fresh clay. At the end, no longer able to tolerate the situation created by María and her father, Angela finds the strength to walk away in search of a new space where she can make a future for herself and the man she has fallen in love with. While *Una mañana cualquiera* reflects a bitter moment of Spain's history, it is also a woman's coming-of-age story. After her return to Spain, Mieza established a publishing firm, Ediciones Marte. She also published several short stories, one of which won the 1960 story contest in El Correo Catalán of Barcelona; a travel book, *Barcelona, Tarragona, Lérida* (1966), part of the series Rutas de España (Routes of Spain); and *La mujer del español* (1977; The Spaniard's Wife), a collection of interviews of prominent women.

Work by

La imposible canción. Barcelona: Plaza y Janés, 1962.
Una mañana cualquiera. Madrid: Círculo de Amigos de la Historia, 1976.
La mujer del español. Barcelona: Marte, 1977.

Work about

Galerstein, Carolyn. "The Second Generation in Exile." *Papers on Language and Literature* 21.1 (1985): 220–228.
———. "Spanish Women Novelists and Younger-Generation Writers: Outsiders or Insiders?" *Latin America and the Literature of Exile*. Ed. Hans-Bernhard Moeller. Heidelberg: C. Winter, 1983. 137–148.

Glenn Morocco

Millán Astray, Pilar (1879–1949)

A conservative writer who enjoyed the favor of the bourgeoisie public during the 1930s, Pilar Millán Astray's plays always feature a strong, independent, hardworking woman as the main character. As participant in the debate about women's place in society that started after World War I, she defended a more active role for women, including their right to work. She publicly condemned the battering of women by her own relatives and exposed what is known nowadays as sexual harassment. At the same time, she defended the indissolubility and sacredness of marriage. Although she upheld the moral superiority of the Catholic Church, she attacked corruption within the clergy and the Church hierarchy's lack of concern for the proletariat. In similar fashion, although she was a defender of "true" aristocracy, she attacked the idle members of this class, asking them to conduct their businesses in a manner that could benefit society as a whole. Her thoughts provide a fascinating example of the evolution of conservative thinking in the pre–Civil War Spain.

Millán Astray moved to Madrid when her father was named director of the regional prison. She married Javier Pérez de Linares but was then widowed at a young age and so embarked on a literary career that made her one of the most popular playwrights of the 1920s and 1930s. For the 1932–1933 season she was the impresario of the Muñoz Seca theater in Madrid. She spent the Civil War years in Loyalist prisons of Alicante and Murcia, where she contracted illnesses that left her infirm the rest of her life. Her brother, General Millán Astray, was cofounder of the Foreign Legion in Spain with Francisco Franco.

El juramento de la Primorosa. Sainete en tres actos, en prosa (1924; Primorosa's Vow. Comic Sketch in Three Acts, in Prose) is a play that defends the need for literacy among the poor, the right of women to work, and the *honor of working-class women. Primorosa, a hairdresser in a working-class neighborhood of Madrid, is a matriarch in charge of preserving the honor of her daughter and her assistants. Rather than accusing the play of a reactionary message, it is more accurate to place it on the puritan side of feminism. Primorosa is a synecdoche of genuine Spain, the independent but conservative working-class woman who represents, according to Millán, the traditional and true values of Spain. *Juramento* made Millán one of the most popular *sainete* authors of the day.

La mercería de la dalia roja. Comedia asainetada en tres actos (1932; Red Dahlia Notions Store. Sainete-Style Play in Three Acts) takes place in Madrid during the profound changes brought by the Second Republic (1931–1936). It is a moral drama (not the comedy announced in the title) that tells the story of Alicia, marchioness of San Clodio. Abandoned by her husband after he squandered the family fortune, Alicia uses her last 75,000 pesetas to buy a notions store in a working-class neighborhood of Madrid. There, she lives a decent life and dedicates herself to helping poor families, teaching young women good manners, and instructing them how to read and write. She falls in love with Rafael, an Andalusian doctor, but cannot wed him because she is still married. Her friends recommend a divorce, an idea introduced by the Republic, but she refuses to abandon her Catholic beliefs. By the play's end her husband is again in Madrid and ready to oblige her to live with him. Nonetheless, Alicia refuses to go with Rafael and instead denounces Republican immorality and its attempt to introduce non-Christian doctrines in Spain. The play contains allusions against Catalonia, depicted as accomplice to the amoral forces at work in Spain. Madrid's working-class neighborhoods, Galicia, and Andalusia are portrayed as the true Spain.

Her most famous play is *La tonta del bote* (1925; The Silly Boat Girl), which tells the story of Susana, a Cinderella- or Eliza Doolittle–like character who gains fame and wealth when discovered by Felipe, who transforms her into the most famous Spanish dancer of her time.

After the war Millán Astray published *Cautivas. 32 meses en las prisiones rojas* (1940; [Women] Prisoners. 32 Months in Red Prisons), a book of fascist and religious poems that express her feelings while in prison. The texts are conventional and lack literary value, but some of the illustrations by other prisoners merit attention.

Work by

Al rugir el león. Comedia. Madrid: R. Velasco, 1923.
Cautivas. 32 meses en las prisiones rojas. Madrid: Saturnino Calleja, 1940.
El juramento de la Primorosa. Sainete en tres actos, en prosa. Madrid: Sociedad de Autores Españoles, 1924.
La mercería de la dalia roja. Comedia asainetada en tres actos. Madrid: Sociedad de Autores Españoles, 1932.
Pancho Robles. Comedia en tres actos. Madrid: Sociedad de Autores Españoles, 1926.
La tonta del bote. Sainete en tres actos, prosa. Barcelona: Cisne, 1936.

Work about

Nieva de la Paz, Pilar. "Tradición y vanguardia en las autoras teatrales de preguerra: Pilar Millán Astray y Halma Angélico." *El teatro en España entre la tradición y la vanguardia. 1918–1939.* Ed. Dru Dougherty and María Francisca Vilches de Frutos. Madrid: Tabapress, 1992. 429–438.
Rodríguez Sánchez, María de los Angeles. "Una escritora teatral, autora de comedias populares: Pilar Millán Astray y Terreros (1879–1949)." *Pedro Muñoz Seca y el teatro de humor contemporáneo.* Ed. and intro. Marieta Cantos Casenave and Alberto Romero Ferrer. Pref. Andrés Amorós. Cádiz: Universidad de Cádiz, Fundación Pedro Muñoz Seca, 1998. 237–243.

Salvador A. Oropesa

Misogyny in Medieval and Early Modern Spain

In Spain, as in the rest of Europe, society's ideas about women hearken back to classical, philosophical, scientific, literary, and religious texts. (For an overview of such writings, see Blamires, McLeod, Rogers.) Greek classical literature, so admired by Renaissance humanists, also reflected a society that scorned women and excluded them from all social, political, and cultural life. Classical writings like those of Hesiod (c. 750 B.C.) brand women the deceitful plague of man and source of evil. Roman society, in which women did attain more rights and control, nonetheless produced literature that denigrated marriage and generally found women to be fickle, frivolous, and duplicitous. Ovid (43 B.C.–A.D. 19), whose love poetry and recipes for seduction (*Art of Love*) were sources for much medieval literature, also exposes male duplicity, yet he denigrates women, characterizing them as licentious, greedy, and hypocritical, eager to outmaneuver vigilant parents and easy for a suitor to fool. Juvenal's (early second century A.D.) invectives depict women as domineering, lustful, deceitful, insufferable if they have studied, and fond of covering themselves with vile *cosmetics. Plutarch presents male and female virtue as equal in *The Virtues of Women*; but he also clearly considers woman subject to male control; his more egalitarian attitude, however, is uncommon. These writings and many, many others handed down through the centuries form a relatively consistent picture of woman as carnal, sinful, weak, and flawed, clearly in need of being controlled.

One key reason why medieval writers continued these primarily negative portrayals is the strong, enduring influence Aristotle's work had throughout Europe. Among other things, he defends the subjugation of women in Greek society (*Politics*) via his concept of the natural hierarchy of the world—just as the soul should govern the body, so should the intellect rule the emotions, and so should the male control the female. The "scientific" explanation Aristotle developed to distinguish woman from man defines her as an imperfect or defective male, as passive, fleshly "matter" lacking (and desirous of) rational "form," the essential characteristic of males. Although she does possess a soul, it is not the same degree or quality of soul that men have. Thereby, as putatively weaker vessel, or animal, woman needs the superior soul, intellect, and active quality of man to mold and guide her. This theoretical biology of inferiority, and its pathological implications, provided major underpinnings for perpetuating negative attitudes toward women in medieval Europe. Grounded in the idea that human bodies were composed of varying proportions of four "humors" (blood, choler, black bile, and yellow bile) that derive their properties from the basic four elements of creation (air, fire, earth, and water), and that determine human gender and personality traits, women were classified as phlegmatic, cold, and wet. This biological condition rendered them incapable of much intellect or reason, for those talents needed a hot, dry environment. The male gender was defined to be choleric, hot, and dry; men's biological makeup fostered reason and intellect, guaranteeing their superiority. In late-sixteenth-century Spain, Juan Huarte de San Juan further codified, extended, and repopularized the theory of four humors in his *Examen de ingenios* (1575; Examination of Men's Wits), which enjoyed enormous popularity throughout Europe.

A second essential underpinning of misogyny in Spain, as in Europe, is found in religious writings and Church doctrine. Beginning with the Bible, the single most significant account is the Old Testament story of the Fall, because of the devastating interpretations subsequently made of Eve's role as temptress in corrupting Adam and provoking God's ire and punishment of the human race. Proverbs and Ecclesiastes similarly emphasize woman's wiles and seductive powers, giving the impression that virtuous women are a rarity. Certainly there are stories of good women (Sara, Moses's mother, Deborah, Esther), but these are not the stories most frequently selected to illustrate women's nature in later writings. The advent of Christianity introduced a further radical change in biblical attitudes by endorsing celibacy and virginity as the preferable, most virtuous states of being. Paul's New Testament writings additionally offer harsh words for women; he condemns sex and advises that women be fully subject to male control: Women should not speak, particularly outside the home; they should not teach; they should obey their husbands (not tempting them like Eve), just as their husbands obey God; and they should veil themselves in church (*cubiertas*) to avoid corrupting men.

Clearly, Aristotelian notions of natural hierarchy and the biological inferiority of women complement Paul's attitudes, and Christian Church Fathers did build on these ideas, exalting virginity as the preferred state and condemning as sinful whatever provoked deviation from chastity. The married state was therefore inferior; procreation was the only justification for sex, and consequently woman's sexual attractiveness and her beauty were judged sinful and corrupting features. Tertullian called woman "the devil's gateway" and "first deserter of the divine law." He argued for her confinement (*encierro*), insisting that for a true virgin, public exposure is, for her, tantamount to rape. St. Augustine described a woman's embrace as "vile, detestable, shameful, and dreadful," and St. John Chrysostom deemed a woman's beauty "the greatest snare." Centuries later, medieval ideology insisted on granting responsibility for the first sin to Eve, generalizing from there about the wiles women used to accomplish their ends. The topic of *women's deceits—the idea of the innate trickiness of women, manifested through deceptive appearances (cosmetics, jewelry, long hair, clothes), words (lies or clever tongues), or deeds—became a staple of Spain's medieval literature (as seen in the *Corbacho, *Disciplina clericalis, Libro del *conde Lucanor, El, *Libro de buen amor, the *Celestina, and also in popular proverbs and anecdotes) and indeed throughout the Golden Age (Cervantes's novella *El casamiento engañoso*, writings by *Quevedo, countless plays of the day). Goldberg, however, notes the need to carefully study humorous stories because the primary target of sexual humor is not invariably the woman but often the foolish cuckold or otherwise incompetent male.

Yet another aspect of Christianity came to exercise a crucial, paradoxical role in defining society's attitudes about women. The cult of the Virgin Mary (*Marianism) first appeared as a grassroots movement during the early centuries of Christianity. By the eleventh century, the phenomenon was sweeping across Europe. On the one hand, Mary's positive role did to some extent improve attitudes toward women and provided a female deity that women might feel closer to and that both women and men could address for comfort and strength. On the other hand, as Warner and others eloquently maintain, the Church's constant pairing of Mary versus Eve as good versus evil role models for women held devastating implications for women. The concept of virgin birth espoused by the Church essentially negates a woman's role in reproduction and is rooted in deeply contemptuous views of woman's role in parturition. Mary's virginity could not be more perfect. As Virgin Mother, co-redeemer of humanity and corrector of Eve's error, descriptions of Mary and her experience—born without sin, conceiving immaculately, painlessly giving birth, and (still intact) ascending bodily to heaven, impervious to mortal decay—emphasize mortal woman's proximity to Eve—carnal temptress and principal agent of the Fall, subject to painful deliveries and normal body functions—and her distance from the churchly ideal of Mary. This very distinction is drawn by *Alfonso X el Sabio in his introduction to the *Cantigas a Santa Maria*, where he dedicates the work to his "true" (heavenly) beloved Mary, rejecting the "false" (earthly) maidens who had deceived him. Warner concludes that for a woman to approach perfection in the Catholic Church she must reject her beauty, her feminine body, and the biological functions that make her a woman.

These various themes from Greco-Roman literature, Aristotelian doctrine of natural hierarchies and biology, biblical teachings, writings of the early Christian Church Fathers, and the cult of the Virgin Mary mingle in various ways to encourage a discourse of misogyny. One striking manifestation in which misogyny figures is the complex *courtly love phenomenon, which flowered from the eleventh through the fifteenth centuries and endures in various ways to this day. In the world of courtly love, a man's goal is physical conquest, and he alternately worships his lady (when hopeful) as a goddess, obeying her every whim and command, and vilifies her at length (when spurned). Bloch points out several essential parallels between courtly love and antifeminism: (1) In each system, woman is perceived as "other," as sensual, as ornament, as body and appetite; (2) in each, virginity is key; (3) each stance pursues a "theology of renunciation"; (4) each tries to reconcile woman as redeemer with woman as source of suffering and evil, bringing us back to the Ave Maria/Eve paradox of the Church.

The notion that woman is biologically inferior to man surfaces throughout medieval society. In law and definitions of conduct, Alfonso X's groundbreaking legal code *Las siete partidas* (1256–1265; Seven Divisions) uses the idea of woman as "inferior vessel" consistently to legislate restriction of her rights by male guardians. Women are not differentiated by distinctions of nobility, class, or occupation; woman is simply "a virgin over 12, and all others." In *Doce trabajos de Hércules* (1417; The Twelve Labors of Hercules) the Marqués de Villena divides society into 12 principal estates: princes, prelates, knights, religious men, citizens, merchants, laborers, servants, teachers, students, solitary ones, and women. If the topic of women was subdivided into more categories, as in moral literature, the divisions were made more or less according to the state of a woman's womb: single women, married women, widows, and nuns. Distinctions of class held little, if any, relevance when the topic of women and their roles was debated.

In science, medieval (mis)understandings of love also encouraged misogynist attitudes and writings, an aspect that Solomon has studied with reference to two Spanish authors of misogynist tracts. Love was considered a physical affliction, a disease. Medicine at that time made no distinction between physical and psychological ailments; thus the extreme emotions that love and sexual desire provoke were considered physical pathology and harmful to the body. Medieval theorists also believed that erotic stories, descriptions, and literature could literally *feed* the disease; thus, certain writers (like physician Jaume Roig [?–1478] and Martín de Cordoba [1398?–1468], author of the *Corbacho*) composed derogatory, misogynist tracts as medicine—an antidote to protect men from the physical illness that woman's beauty caused.

The activity of the Reconquest (717–1492) in the Middle Ages did attenuate somewhat the negative position and attitudes toward women at times in certain parts of Spain. Sponsler has demonstrated how women from northern Christian Spain came to exercise a goodly measure of authority managing home and family finances while husbands and male relatives fought in the campaign. Women in the southern Arab-dominated portion of the peninsula lived enclosed in harems and were regarded as chattel, without legal recourse.

In the fifteenth century the question of a woman's nature and worth generally revolved around whether she was good (*Grisel y Mirabella*, *Libro de las virtuosas y claras mujeres*, *Cárcel de amor*, by Diego de *San Pedro, *Tratado en defensa de las virtuosas mujeres*) or evil (*Corbacho*, *Repetición de amores*). In the following century (Castillejo's *Diálogo de mujeres* being a notable exception) the focus was generally on whether she should receive some sort of education (*Vives, Luis de *León). Erasmus and other humanist authors provided a positive, moderating influence, arguing that women needed some instruction in order to educate children effectively, and additionally, the Renaissance ideal of man as perfectable and worthy included also his need for a worthy partner to share with him. Nonetheless, the sixteenth and seventeenth centuries witnessed a clear increase in misogynist attitudes toward women in Spain. El Saffar connects it to the increasing demands of conforming to one religion and one culture, combined with Inquisition activities, and the technological changes, wars, and New World exploration that separated males from attachments to home and family. She sees a clear connection between these conditions and the dramatic upsurge in female visionaries and also the distinctly masochistic behavior that many female mystics practiced, having internalized the idea that women must reject or rise above their bodies in order to attain a purer existence (see Isabel de *Jesús for a striking example). Vigil has studied the writings of sixteenth- and seventeenth-century moralists, using them to identify strategies that women devised to resist their condition as virtual domestic prisoners, on one hand subject to a rigid *honor code and on the other hand offered the courtly love stereotype of woman as conduct model as in the tremendously popular theater of late-sixteenth- and seventeenth-century Spain (Lope de *Vega's *El caballero de Olmedo*, for example). Interestingly, McKendrick maintains that the dramatic character of the *mujer esquiva*, the woman not interested in marriage or men, was invented by Lope for the purpose of bringing the ongoing social debate over women and their role into the public arena. Uncovering such indications of concern over women, their proper role, and detecting patterns of deviation from/ resistance to such definitions of gender roles, is ongoing. *See also* Eiximenis, Francesc (1330?–1409): His Views on Women; Sáenz-Alonso, Mercedes (1917–): *Don Juan y el donjuanismo*

Work about

Blamires, Alcuin, ed. *Woman Defamed and Woman Defended. An Anthology of Medieval Texts.* Oxford: Clarendon P, 1992.

Bloch, R. Howard. *Medieval Misogyny and the Invention of Western Romantic Love.* Chicago: U of Chicago P, 1991.

Boxer, C.R. *Mary and Misogyny. Women in Iberian Expansion Overseas 1415–1815. Some Facts, Fancies and Personalities* [sic]. Worcester and London: Trinity P, 1975.

Castro Lingl, Vera. "Juan de Flores and Lustful

Women: The *Crónica incompleta de los Reyes Católicos*." *La Corónica* 24.1 (1995): 74–89.

El Saffar, Ruth Anthony. *Rapture Encaged: The Suppression of the Feminine in Western Culture*. London: Routledge, 1994.

Goldberg, Harriet. "Sexual Humor in Misogynist Medieval Exempla." *Women in Hispanic Literature: Icons and Fallen Idols*. Ed. Beth Miller. Berkeley and Los Angeles: U of California P, 1983. 67–83.

McKendrick, Melveena. "Women against Wedlock: The Reluctant Brides of Golden Age Drama." *Women in Hispanic Literature: Icons and Fallen Idols*. Ed. Beth Miller. Berkeley and Los Angeles: U of California P, 1983. 115–146.

McLeod, Glenda. *Virtue and Venom. Catalogs of Women from Antiquity to the Renaissance*. Ann Arbor: U of Michigan P, 1991.

Misogyny, Misandry, and Misanthropy. Ed. and intro. R. Howard Bloch and Frances Ferguson. Berkeley: U of California P, 1989.

Ornstein, Jacob. "La misoginia y el profeminismo en la literatura castellana." *Revista de Filología Española* 3 (1941): 219–232.

Rogers, Katharine M. *The Troublesome Helpmate. A History of Misogyny in Literature*. Seattle: U of Washington P, 1966.

Solomon, Michael. *The Literature of Misogyny in Medieval Spain. The Arcipreste de Talavera and the Spill*. Cambridge: Cambridge UP, 1997.

Sponsler, Lucy. *Women in the Medieval Spanish Epic and Lyric Traditions*. Lexington: U of Kentucky P, 1975.

Vigil, Mariló. *La vida de las mujeres en los siglos XVI y XVII*. 2nd ed. Madrid: Siglo Veintiuno, 1994.

Warner, Marina. *Alone of All Her Sex. The Myth and the Cult of the Virgin Mary*. New York: Random House, 1983.

Maureen Ihrie

Moix, Ana María (1947–)

Born in Barcelona, Ana María Moix has written poetry, fiction (for adults and children), and essays, she has contributed extensively to journals and newspapers, and she has done translations. She began her literary career with two volumes of poetry that merited her inclusion as the only woman in José María Castellet's *Nueve novísimos* (1970), an important anthology of poets who represent a break from the "social poetry" tradition of the 1950s and 1960s, a greater international dimension, the influence of popular culture, an iconoclastic view of life through irony and parody, and a penchant for literary experimentation. These characteristics are apparent in her various collections of poetry, into which experimental forms also weave themes of loneliness, alienation, and an obsession with the past and memory.

Her first novel, *Julia* (1970), is the poignant story of a young woman who reviews her past during a long night after an unsuccessful attempt at suicide. The pressures of middle-class Catalonian society are partially responsible for her alienation: hypocritical, pretentious, conservative, their mores, represented by her dysfunctional family, leave her no room for personal growth. The feminist treatment of certain themes includes the stifling expectations of conformity for a girl growing up in bourgeois Catalonia; Julia's thwarted desire to bond with other women; a range of acceptable and unacceptable female role models (a cold, hypocritical mother, a matriarchal grandmother, and a fascinating independent career woman to whom Julia is attracted). The awful revelation of her rape at age six by a family friend explains her obsession with the past.

The 10 stories in *Ese chico pelirrojo a quien veo cada día* (1971; That Red-headed Boy I See Every Day) present characters who range from unusual to supernatural, most of whom are unhappy, disaffected, or maladjusted in some way. Perplexity, alienation, or even madness suggest the outcome for people subjected to a stifling, conformist society and the patriarchal expectations that underlie its values. However, the addition of fantasy and the supernatural and a humorous, sardonic tone undermine the serious criticism, introducing the note of ambiguity that will later become Moix's trademark.

The novel *Walter, ¿Por qué te fuiste?* (1973; Walter, Why Did You Leave?) adds more sophisticated techniques to themes from previous works. Continuing to depict the conflict between the individual and society, Moix widens *Julia*'s cast of characters to include a family of cousins growing up in the same restrictive bourgeois atmosphere. Physical and psychological spaces bring back memories of the past: The dreams and idealism of the young cousins contrast sharply with their present unhappiness and failures as adults. Rigid demands for conformism affect both sexes, but the girls can foresee a bleak future within the system. Contrast appears in the character of Lea, a free spirit whose bisexuality and individualism symbolize a new type of independent female unconcerned with conventions of society. Multiple narrative strands, intertextuality, metafiction, and the heavy influence of popular culture (e.g., the cinema and popular music) make this a particularly complex novel of high quality.

Twelve years passed before another book of adult fiction appeared. During the intervening time, however, Moix wrote children's literature, translated books, and published several works of nonfiction. She made a significant contribution to the feminist journal *Vindicación feminista as coordinator of the cultural sections, reviewing books, theater, movies, and the like, and writing "Nena no t'enfilis (Diario de una hija de familia)," a regular column in the form of a diary that combines humor and wit with social satire in her depiction of life in a bourgeois family. Her description of the adversarial relationships and of the difference between expectations and reality is amusing and witty, but beneath the humor is critical, bitter social satire that reveals the tensions inherent in the patriarchal structure of twentieth-century Spain.

Las virtudes peligrosas (1985; *Dangerous Virtues*, 1997) won the Premio Ciudad de Barcelona; the five short stories in this collection are masterful variations on the theme of solitude, lack of fulfillment, and alienation, but the frame and references have become abstract and ambiguous. In several stories, parody, irony, and humor undermine the gravity of the situation. The intriguing title story describes a mysterious bond between two women who never speak to each other but whose enduring and powerful relationship is indecipherable to the husband of one of them. Unable to fathom this mystery with logic and reason, he eventually goes mad and commits suicide. Obvious feminist issues include, on one hand, an understated indictment of the patriarchy, which wishes to control women and sees them as objects (particularly translated through the metaphor of the gaze), and, on the other, the subversive answer through women's bonding, an alternative mode of communication by means of speaking with the body. "The Dead" re-creates the mental processes of a woman at her own anniversary party. Skillful details reveal her minimal place in the life of her family, where she is considered only in terms of her relationship to others, particularly to her selfish poet-husband. The interior narrative poignantly lays bare her resultant alcoholism and depression. The other stories are equally fascinating: "Erase una vez" (Once Upon a Time) subverts all notions of the traditional fairy-tale (*Fairy Tales) genre by bringing stock characters (Snow White, Sleeping Beauty) and conventional phrases ("Once Upon A Time," "Happily Ever After") to life and describing their unhappy, ineffectual rebellion against their subjugation to the power of the written word. "El problema" describes the dilemma of a Problem whose aspirations to a brilliant career as an abstract, insoluble problem eventually shatter when he becomes a sexual problem for a bickering couple; "El inocente" (The Innocent One) uses an interior perspective to chronicle the progressive drunkenness and loss of control of an arrogant young man. Experiment in form and theme characterizes this collection. Linear development dissolves into a static inner landscape where ambiguity and enigma temper the sharp conflict between desire and reality. The absence of resolution or fulfillment and the occasional sardonic note support a postmodern perspective.

Vals negro (1994; Black Waltz) introduces fictional biography into the list of Moix's accomplishments. Multiple individuals and narrative perspectives provide a moving, human portrait of Elizabeth, empress of the Austro-Hungarian Empire, emphasizing the strain and unhappiness caused by the demands of royal behavior.

Moix's writings reveal a literary and human sensitivity that embraces both feminist and universal concerns. She couches highly original themes in narrative devices that are postmodern in outlook and expressed with the lyrical subtlety of a poet. *See also* Short Fiction by Women Writers: 1975–1998, Post-Franco

Work by

A imagen y semejanza. Barcelona: Lumen, 1983.
Dangerous Virtues. Trans. and afterword Margaret E.W. Jones. Lincoln: U of Nebraska P, 1997.
Ese chico pelirrojo a quien veo cada día. Barcelona: Lumen, 1971.
Julia. Barcelona: Seix Barral, 1970.
Vals negro. Barcelona: Lumen, 1994.
Las virtudes peligrosas. Barcelona: Plaza y Janés, 1985.
Walter, ¿Por qué te fuiste? Barcelona: Barral, 1973.

Work about

Brooksbank Jones, Amy. "The Incubus and I: Unbalancing Acts in Moix's *Julia*." *Bulletin of Hispanic Studies* 72 (1995): 73–85.
Bush, Andrew. "Ana María Moix's Silent Calling." *Women Writers of Contemporary Spain: Exiles in the Homeland*. Ed. Joan L. Brown. Newark: U of Delaware P, 1991. 136–158.
Jones, Margaret E.W. "Ana María Moix: Literary Structures and the Enigmatic Nature of Reality." *Journal of Spanish Studies: Twentieth Century* 4 (1976): 105–116.
Levine, Linda Gould. "Ana María Moix." *Spanish Women Writers: A Bio-Bibliographical Source Book*. Ed. Linda Gould Levine, Ellen Engleson Marson, and Gloria Feiman Waldman. Westport, CT: Greenwood P, 1993. 337–349.
———. "Behind the 'Enemy Lines': Strategies for Interpreting *Las virtudes peligrosas* of Ana María Moix." *Nuevos y novísimos: Algunas perspectivas críticas sobre la narrativa española de los sesenta*. Ed. Richard Landeira and Luis González-del-Valle. Boulder, CO: Society of Spanish and Spanish-American Studies, 1987. 97–111.

Schumm, Sandra J. "Progressive Schizophrenia in Ana María Moix's *Julia*." *Revista canadiense de estudios hispánicos* 19 (1994): 149–171.
Stewart, Melissa. "(De)Constructing the Text and Self in Ana María Moix's *Walter, ¿Por qué te fuiste?*" *Hispanófila* 124 (September 1998): 23–33.
Valis, Noël M. "Reality and Language in Ana María Moix's *Walter, ¿Por qué te fuiste?*" *Ojáncano* 4 (1990): 48–58.

Margaret E.W. Jones

Mojigata, La (1804)

The fourth of five comedies written by Leandro Fernández de *Moratín (1760–1828), *La mojigata* (The Pious Deceiver) criticizes the abuse of parental authority with regard to the education of daughters. The title derives from *mojigato*, a word of Arabic origin that means concealed or feigned. In this drama of the Spanish Enlightenment, *la mojigata* refers to a woman who feigns piety in order to indulge in questionable behavior on the sly, even as she appears to meet the obligations of a dutiful, moral daughter.

Moratín's play contrasts the educational methods employed by two brothers in preparing their daughters for adulthood. Don Luis, the kind, calm man of reason, has raised his child Doña Inés in an open atmosphere in which she enjoys love, respect, and freedom. His brother Don Martín, an excitable and overbearing man, has raised his daughter Doña Clara in a strict, oppressive environment with no consideration for her wishes or dreams. Don Martín selfishly destines Clara for the convent so that he can collect her inheritance. To no avail Don Luis warns him that Clara is actually a hypocrite, *una mojigata* who pretends religious devotion to blind her father to her secret indulgences—flirting with men and reading scandalous romances. When the dim-witted wastrel Don Claudio comes to town to court Inés, the sensible maiden ignores the boor, while her cousin Clara sets her cap for him. Moratín vindicates Don Luis's system of education at the end of *La mojigata*. The legator shifts the coveted inheritance from Clara to Inés, leaving

Clara and Claudio, now promised in marriage, as well as Don Martín, without the wealth they desire. The virtuous Doña Inés then offers to share the inheritance with her cousin Clara. Her father concurs with her generous decision but determines that Inés will control the money and the household and, by example, will educate Clara and Claudio in moderate, moral conduct.

Well versed in classical literature, Moratín found inspiration for *La mojigata* in Terence's *The Brothers* (160 B.C.). Other possible influences include Molière's *L'Ecole des maris* (1661), which Moratín later adapted for the Spanish stage as *La escuela de los maridos* (1812; School for Husbands), Tirso de *Molina's *Marta la piadosa* (1615; Compassionate Marta), and *Calderón's *Guárdate del agua mansa* (1649; Beware of Still Waters). Yet matters of literary influence aside, *La mojigata* bears witness to Moratín's belief in the power of theater to reform the public. This didactic comedy fulfills the neoclassical precept that literature should entertain and instruct in the way in which it punishes vice, rewards virtue, and maintains domestic harmony. Don Martín has overstepped the judicious use of paternal authority by treating his daughter in a venal, exploitative fashion, as a means to a profitable end. Doña Clara repays him in kind with immoral conduct that reveals little respect for her father or her own reputation. The fact that Doña Inés has the upper hand and Don Luis the final words at the conclusion of *La mojigata* makes clear that Moratín advocates a more liberal, humanistic approach to educating young women. Through the behavior of the exemplary father-daughter combination, the playwright shows that the foundation for good domestic pedagogy should be mutual love and respect manifested in frank, considerate discussions in which there is a fruitful exchange of ideas and opinions. As always in the orderly universe of Moratín's theater, moral, rational people triumph over immoral, irrational individuals.

The views toward parental authority and the education of women that are expressed in *La mojigata* identify Moratín as a spokesperson for the reform policies of Spain's Bourbon monarchy. The *ilustrado* (enlightened) elite associated women and the domestic sphere of activity with the moral improvement of society and the creation of a happy and industrious middle class. Thus, at the end of *La mojigata* Moratín charges Doña Inés, as embodiment of the female ideal of the Spanish Enlightenment, with the complementary tasks of domestic management and moral instruction of the wayward Doña Clara and Don Claudio. *See also* Feminism in Spain: 1700–1800; *Sí de las niñas, El* (1806)

Work

Obras de Nicolás y Leandro Fernández de Moratín. BAE 2. Madrid: Rivadeneyra, 1857.

Work about

Fernández Cabezón, Rosalía. *Como leer a Leandro Fernández de Moratín.* Madrid: Júcar, 1990.

Marsha S. Collins

Molina, María de (1259–1321)

Tres veces reina (three times queen) of Castile and León, niece of Fernando III the Saint, María Alfonso de Meneses was born in Tierra de Campos and received a rigorous education under the tutelage of María Fernández Coronel. She married Sancho IV the Brave, son of King *Alfonso X the Wise, in 1281, but the liaison was not sanctioned by the Church because of their blood ties. Nevertheless, María remained at her husband's side throughout his unsettled reign, and when Sancho died in 1295 she declared herself regent of Castile for her son Fernando IV. She had to face tremendous opposition from rival factions of nobles and pretenders to the throne (a period in her life eloquently dramatized in Tirso de *Molina's [1582?–1648] masterpiece *La prudencia en la mujer*), but with the support of the people and the local councils she retained the monarchy for her son until his majority in 1301. Throughout his reign, she remained active in politics, breaking up a plot by Aragón to dismember Castile (1303) and working for a renewal of the Crusades to Jerusalem. When Fernando IV died in 1312, María again became regent for her grandson Alfonso XI, governing at first with her daughter-in-law and two male relatives and then alone after 1319. Threatened again by nobles and rivals to the throne (in particular Don Juan Manuel [1282–1348], author of *Conde Lucanor), María had to resort once more to popular support; and shortly before her death in 1321 she convinced the Council of Valladolid to assume guardianship of her grandson.

This extraordinary woman, *tres veces reina*, stands out as one of the truly popular Spanish leaders in the Middle Ages, protecting the monarchy and the people from the tyranny of nobles, rival pretenders to the crown, and the Church.

Work about

Gaibrois de Ballesteros, Mercedes. *María de Molina: Tres veces reina.* Madrid: Espasa-Calpe, 1967.

Hors Bresmes, E., ed. *Tirso de Molina: "La prudencia en la mujer."* Zaragoza: Ebro, 1958.

David H. Darst

Molina, Tirso de, Pseudonym of Gabriel Téllez (1582–1648): Women in His Theater

Tirso de Molina is universally acknowledged as the best creator of female protagonists in the Spanish Golden Age. From queens (*La prudencia en la mujer* [Prudence in Women]) to nuns (*Santa Juana*) to amazons (*Antona García*) to countless girls in love, "Tirso" gives his women characters a strength of will that drives them to accomplish the deeds they respectively set for themselves. Tirso was especially adept at presenting women who resort to male disguises (*disfraces varoniles*) to achieve their desired goals. Since these women in a *disfraz varonil* are all protagonists of social comedies, their goal is to win the man whom they love or who has betrayed them in some way. In effect, Tirso wrote at least 24 plays (one-third of his extant production) in which the main female personage assumes a masculine garb in order to pursue the man she adores, and in virtually every case, she wins him. In such pieces as *El melancólico* (The Melancholy Man), *Don Gil de las calzas verdes* (Sir Gil of the Green Breeches), *La villana de Vallecas* (The Village Girl of Vallecas), and *El amor médico* (Love as Physician), the protagonist assumes another "nature" by taking upon herself an artistic disguise so as to bewilder, deceive, and overcome her adversaries. Her success is due to the fact that the diverse personages willingly accept the appearance she creates for reality, and many times reject reality for the appearance, which seems to be more natural and logical than its counterpart. The woman's success thus lies in her ability to split consciousness and functions in her opponents' minds so that they readily accept her created universe. In the abovementioned plays, for example, an essential conflict arises first within the woman's mind between her will and her reason, since she views her desires thwarted by circumstances. However, the woman seizes upon her strength of will (usually expressed in terms of *las industrias del ingenio* [the inventions of wit]) to force the outward reality to adjust itself to her desired outcome, which occurs in every case when she wins her man in the closing scene.

Essential to the woman's success is her ability to control events, and this control appears to be an aspect of her character that Tirso instituted incrementally as his dramatic career advanced. In *El melancólico*, *Esto sí que es negociar* (Now That's Negotiating), and *El vergonzoso en palacio* (The Dishonorable Man in the Palace), Tirso presents actions in which the diverse characters appear to be blindly pushed along to completion by a benevolent and far-seeing nature. Some, as Leonisa in the first two plays, have no control over events; others, such as Magdalena in *El vergonzoso en palacio*, believe that they are forging their own destinies, only to understand at the finale that they have accomplished through industry what natural processes would have achieved if the obstructive efforts of the men in the plays—true blocking characters—had not impeded the normal course of events. In later plays, such as *Don Gil de las calzas verdes*, *La villana de Vallecas*, and *El amor médico*, the respective heroines immediately seize control of events and manipulate the other participants in what becomes a "play within a play" wherein they exploit the inadequacies of the male antagonist to their own advantage.

Tirso's creativity of woman protagonists also undergoes a development in terms of his portrayal of character development, namely, the ability to characterize the woman's cognizance of her own motivations and the reasons that cause her to act in the decisive way she does. Leonisa and Magdalena never attempt to understand what forces cause them to respond so adamantly to their circumstances, whereas later protagonists are cognizant of their desires, although they may have been blind to certain interior motivations that also played a part in their intentions. In very late plays such as *El amor médico* and *La mujer por fuerza* (Women by Necessity), self-awareness becomes almost total, and the women become virtual models of the feminine will at work. This maturation in Tirso's aesthetic awareness thus translates into the characters of the comedia as a growth toward self-knowledge of one's inner motivations as well as self-control of one's will and reason; and these in turn translate into the woman's ability to control events in the objective world and the actions of the men who populate it to such a degree that the outcome in these comedies always matches the woman's expectations. See also *Burlador de Sevilla, El* (1627–1629): Its Women Characters

Work by

Obras dramáticas completas. Ed. Blanca de los Ríos. 3 vols. Madrid: Aguilar, 1946–1958.

Work about

Abraham, James. "The Other Speaks: Tirso de Molina's *Amazonas en las Indias*." *El arte nuevo de estudiar comedias: Literary Theory and Spanish Golden Age Drama*. Ed. and intro. Barbara Simerka. Cranbury, NJ: Bucknell UP—Associated UP, 1996. 143–161.

Allatson, Paul. "Confounding Convention: 'Women' in Three Golden Age Plays." *Bulletin of the Comediantes* 48.2 (Winter 1996): 212–213, 261–273.

Darst, David H. *The Comic Art of Tirso de Molina*. Chapel Hill, NC: Estudios de Hispanófila, 1974.

Ganelin, Charles. "Designing Women: Tirso's *La mujer por fuerza* on Stage." *Hispanic Essays in Honor of Frank P. Casa*. Ed. and intro. Robert A. Lauer and Henry W. Sullivan. New York: Peter Lang, 1997. 135–145.

———. "Who Was That Masked Woman? Female Identity in Tirso de Molina's *La mujer por fuerza*." *Indiana Journal of Hispanic Literatures* 6–7 (Spring–Fall 1995): 103–121.

Stoll, Anita K. "Achilles: Gender Ambiguity and Destiny in Golden Age Drama." *A Star-Crossed Golden Age: Myth and the Spanish Comedia*. Ed. and intro. Frederick A. de Armas. Lewisburg, PA: Bucknell UP; London, England: Associated UP, 1998. 112–125.

Vila, Juan Diego. "La educación del galán: Magdalena y la pedagogía genérica en *El vergonzoso en palacio* de Tirso de Molina: Homenaje a Marc Vitse." *El escritor y la escena, V: Estudios sobre teatro español y novohispano de los Siglos de Oro*. Ciudad Juárez, Mexico: Universidad Autónoma de Ciudad Juárez, 1997. 199–210.

David H. Darst

Montemayor, Jorge de (c. 1520–1561)

He spent his life in the service of queens, which may explain his exaltation of what are usually perceived as female values. As a musician of the Portuguese Infanta Doña María, Jorge de Montemayor moved with her to Castile upon her marriage to Philip II. After her death he entered the service of the Infanta de Castilla Doña Juana, mother of the Portuguese king Sebastián, and spent two years in Portugal. He returned to Castile in 1554 and became engaged to a woman at court who jilted him after he left for England as part of Philip II's entourage. Later he traveled in Flanders; he died in the Italian Piedmont in a duel over a woman.

Montemayor's poetical works include *Exposición moral sobre el psalmo ochenta y seis* (1548; Ethical Exegesis of Psalm 86) and a two-volume edition of his profane and devout verse *Las obras de George de Montemayor, repartidas en dos libros y dirigidas a los muy altos y muy poderosos señores don Iuà y doña Iuana, principes de Portogal* (1554; The Works of George de Montemayor, in Two Books and Dedicated to the Very High and Very Mighty Don Juan and Doña Juana, Prince and Princess of Portugal). He also translated Ausiàs March's (c. 1397–1459) poetry. Montemayor's profane verse, published separately after 1562 as the *Cancionero*, develops Petrarchan ideas and forms; most poems like his four eclogues are dedicated to high-ranking court ladies. Doña María de Aragón, his muse, may have been a sister to Fernando de Herrera's (1534–1597) muse, Leonor de Milá, the countess of Gelves. Montemayor also wrote songs to shepherdesses and *villancicos* (carols) developing popular love themes as well as burlesques such as a dialogue among a lady's clothes. He directed sonnets to Marfida and to Vandalina. The theme of the lover's uncomplaining suffering with a division between soul and body and the insistence that he expects no reward dominates the poems.

In his devout poetry Montemayor celebrates the Virgin as site of Christ's incarnation. In "Sicut Laetantium Omnium Habitatio Est In Te" he declares the Virgin stronger than most women: "el ser de mujer te puso/ pero no la condición" (you were given woman's being, but not her nature). He imagines the Virgin playing cards with the devil and producing the three trumps of the Trinity in "Ensalada del juego de la primavera" (Medley of the Springtime Game). Here he follows tradition in perceiving Eve as leading Adam into sin but does not heap opprobrium on her, nor does he do so in the first "Auto." In "La Pasión de Cristo" (Christ's Passion) Montemayor compares the apostle Peter, who denied Christ, to a *flaca mujer* (feeble woman) whose only weapon is her tongue. In the same poem he frequently addresses the Virgin; he describes Eve as a "lost innocent" and recounts Herod's wife's dream that Christ should not be killed. He evokes the pathos of Mary embracing Christ, *su esposa y nuestra luz* (his wife and our light) on the road to Calvary; blood runs from her heart as well as from that of Christ, *hijo y padre* (son and father) of the Virgin.

"Glosas sobre las Coplas de Manrique" (Glosses on Couplets by Manrique) contains Montemayor's warning to worldly women against vanity; he does not condemn them more than men. In his first "Auto" Montemayor presents Christ dressing himself in the suit of nature in the womb of sinless Mary. The surprising union of the sacred and the comic can be seen in Montemayor's introduction of a comic interlude between Bobo (Fool) and Viejo (Old Man) about the parentage of Bobo, product of an ass and a burro. The comic characters ridicule David and Solomon for allowing their wisdom to be bamboozled by women. In "Cántica Sexta" Montemayor asks Christ's help to overcome Original Sin (*en pecados me concibió mi madre* [my mother conceived me in sin]), which makes the body rule the spirit. Judging from the whole of Montemayor's poetry, the reader must conclude that he seldom criticizes women. In his last exchange "A don Juan Hurtado de Mendoza" he blames only himself for allowing the body to triumph over the spirit. The sonnet closing the book develops the orthodox ideal of the Christian soldier whose faith and good works win heaven.

Montemayor's pastoral novel *Los siete libros de la *Diana* (The Seven Books of the Diana), written around 1556 and existing in various undated editions by 1559, underwent 26 editions in the sixteenth century and 14 in the seventeenth century. It was placed on the Portuguese *Index* from 1581 to 1624 but never on the Spanish *Index*, which, however, did prohibit his devout works in 1559. Father Bartolomé de Ponce (1600–?), who transformed Montemayor's work into religious pastoral in *Clara Diana a lo divino* (1599; Illustrious Diana in the Religious Way), perceived Montemayor's death as divine punishment for his celebration of profane love.

In the *Diana* Montemayor most closely reflected his own experience in love in the shepherd Sereno. Despite the Renaissance practice of arranged marriages and the insistence on the obedience of children, Sireno and Sylvano blame Diana, their chosen lady, for her capitulation to a forced marriage to Delio. The errors and accidents of love as well as the purifying suffering love brings are developed in their story and in that of Selvagia, Ismenia, Alanio, and Montano. Although they shun bodily contact, the lovers' goal is consummation of their love in marriage rather than the maintenance of *courtly love relationships. Avalle-Arce describes the novel as a combination of Petrarchism with León Hebreo (1460–1521?) and Castiglione (1478–1529). Moya Jiménez observes that women are not merely objects but loving subjects in the *Diana*, and they need not maintain secrecy since their relationships are not adulterous. Creel believes that Montemayor, like Luther, regarded physical attraction leading to marriage as not inherently sinful. Nevertheless, as Pérez points out, any physical manifestations of carnal love among the unmarried characters are perceived as *apetito baxo y deshonesto* (base and indecent appetite): Montemayor follows Hebreo in perceiving physical consummation as the end of love's pain. Thus, the continuance of the amorous tensions upon which the plot hinges necessitates their remaining unconsummated. Wardropper explains that the pastoral presupposes a safe environment where the characters, motivated by eroticism, control their carnal instincts. Neither age nor wealth nor even sex proves a barrier in erotic attraction.

Book II contains a debate between Selvagia, who argues that the lover can recover from an unhappy love affair to love again, and Sylvano, who argues eternal constancy. As critic Siles Artés points out, Montemayor does not endorse all his characters say and frequently shows their actions belying their words as in Sylvano's case. Male idealism is contrasted with female pragmatism in this debate. Book II also contains Felismena's rescue of three nymphs who are being attacked by three hairy wild men. The nymphs prefer death to rape. In their beauty and lifelong chastity they symbolize the essence of femininity or, according to critic Renato Poggioli's interpretation, Goethe's "eternal feminine." The savages symbolize lust and represent man in his primitive state of physical supremacy and aggression. Civilization requires the union of male strength and valor with female beauty and chastity: Felismena, an androgynous warrior/shepherdess in Cull's interpretation, kills the wild men. Since the episode takes place before Sireno, Silvano, and Selvagia, it serves as a warning to them of what Vigier calls "la déraison inhérente à l'amour" (love's inherent lack of reason).

In Book IV, the heart of the novel, the lovers reach Felicia's temple with its fountain and commemorative chapels. Men are honored for valor and force in Mars's patio, which houses statues of famous Greek, Roman, and Spanish warriors including the Cid (1043–1099) and Bernardo del Carpio. Women are honored for chastity in the Sala de Castidad, the Sala de Diana, and the cemetery of nymphs and chaste women. Lucretia, Medea, and Doña María Coronel are among the honored. The nymphs reward Felismena by arraying her in rich robes and jewels that in Márquez Villanueva's interpretation symbolize various aspects of her loyalty, purity, hopefulness, humility, firmness, chastity, valor, and pride. Orpheus sings a paean to the queens and noblewomen of Spain and Portugal, and the characters discuss the nature of love. In allegorical interpretations of this tale Orpheus in his attempted rescue of

Eurydice from the underworld was perceived as a type of Christ, who rescued the human soul from sin. The shepherdess Diana is not allowed to enter Felicia's palace because of her unfaithfulness to Sireno and perhaps because she is a married woman. Mújica points out that Diana links the pastoral to the real world in which parental injunctions hold sway. Montemayor may have intended the reader to see a parallel between Diana and Eurydice: Human love improves the soul, and its cultivation may bring happiness, but divine grace is ultimately necessary for the redemption of erring souls.

In the Valladolid edition of the *Diana* of 1561 the Moorish tale of Abindarráez (*Abencerraje) was intercalated in Book IV as a story told by Felismena. Although Montemayor himself may not have wished this inclusion, the tale does balance Felismena's heroism with that of male characters famous for virtue and valor (Rodrigo de Narváez) and for valor, beauty, and courtesy (Abindarráez), according to Glenn's reading. The importance of honoring one's word provides a counterexample to such characters as Don Felis, Ysmenia, and Diana, who fail to keep theirs.

In Book V, Sireno, Selvagia, and Sylvano drink Felicia's magic potion, which makes them forget their unhappy love; the potion is usually perceived as a symbol for the healing effect of time (see Solé-Leris). In Book VII, Felismena comes to the rescue of her faithless lover, Don Felis, who is being attacked by three men on horseback. Symbolically Felismena helps Don Felis gain control of the three aspects of the mind (will, imagination, and reason) as in Plato's allegory of the mind and the passions in Damiani's interpretation. Felismena administers Felicia's magic potion to Don Felis, and his love for her is restored. The weddings of Felismena and Felis, of Belisa and Arsileo, and of Selvagia and Silvano take place in Felicia's palace.

Subirats argues that Felicia is based on María of Hungary, who held official festivities to honor her father Charles V and his entourage including Montemayor on a visit to Binche in 1549. De Oliveira e Silva's elucidation of the names of Felismena (from *feliz* [happy] and Philomena and *mente* [mind]), Felicia (*feliz*), and Felis (*feliz* and felino [feline]) shows how they underscore the theme of the pursuit of happiness through love. Damiani has demonstrated the importance of music in the novel, especially as a refined talent that enhances human worth. He associates the three nymphs Felismena saved as the three Graces (Castitas, Pulchritudo, and Amor) and with the theological virtues of Hope, Faith, and Charity. He relates Felismena to the active life pictured in Montemayor's *Diálogo espiritual* (Spiritual Dialogue) as well as to the Virgin Mary who represents virtue, justice, and consolation in Montemayor's couplets to the Virgin. The latent homosexuality of several relationships between female characters (Selvagia/Ismenia, Felismena [Valerio]/Celia, and Armia/Duarda) is dismissed by Wardropper and Solé-Leris as illustration of the Neoplatonic doctrine that love arises from the perception of beauty, regardless of sex. Pérez points out that *lesbianism arises from narcissism in Freudian theory and that only women are permitted physical expression of affection in the *Diana*. Both he and Cull believe Montemayor was deliberately titillating the reader with such descriptions. Mújica points out that sexual ambivalence in the *Diana* has serious consequences, leading even to death.

Like Creel, Damiani and Rhodes emphasize the consistency of Montemayor's philosophy of love throughout his religious and profane works. Damiani also points to the social and moral values exemplified in the novel in contradistinction to Darst who dismisses the novel as empty romance appealing primarily to an uneducated female audience. Darst follows Menéndez y Pelayo and other early critics who denigrated the pastoral as an artificial, effeminate genre. Damiani follows Wardropper, who in 1951 argued that the feminine values exemplified in the novel constitute its strength by giving voice to psychological differences between the sexes suppressed in most other Renaissance fiction. Within the protected world of the pastoral Nature acts as nurturing mother who erases class distinctions and the strife of men in society. Shepherds and shepherdesses are on equal footing in the expression of love and in occupation. In fact, female characters dominate the dialogue. Rhodes attributes the condemnation of the pastoral precisely to its cultivation of feminine values: emotional interdependence, the importance of inner worth over power and wealth, peaceful rather than military occupations, and the emphasis on communal relationships over individuation. She points out that women's freedom to choose their own partners and to move freely within the world ceases with marriage so that women's lives are still ultimately controlled by men's decisions. The popularity of the pastoral novel resulted from the changing role of the courtier (from warrior to aristocrat aesthete), the impetus of humanism that endorsed contemplative ideals and the influence of religious reform. *See also* Marianism in Spain

Work by

El cancionero del poeta George de Montemayor. Ed. Angel González Palencia. Madrid: Sociedad de Bibliófilos Españoles 9, 1932.

Los siete libros de la Diana. Ed. Francisco López Estrada. 3rd ed. Madrid: Espasa-Calpe, 1962.

Work about

Avalle-Arce, Juan Bautista. *La novela pastoril española*. Madrid: Revista de Occidente, 1959.

Creel, Bryant L. "Aesthetics of Change in a Renaissance Pastoral: New Ideals of Moral Culture in Montemayor's *Diana*." *Hispanófila* 33 (1990): 1–27.

Cull, John T. "Androgyny in the Spanish Pastoral Novels." *Hispanic Review* 57 (1989): 317–334.

Damiani, Bruno M. *La Diana of Montemayor as Social and Religious Teaching*. Lexington: UP of Kentucky, 1983.

———. " 'Et in Arcadia ego': Death in *La Diana* of Jorge de Montemayor." *Revista Canadiense de Estudios Hispánicos* 8 (1983): 1–19.

———. "Journey to Felicia: *La Diana* as Pilgrimage: A Study in Symbolism." *Bibliothèque d'Humanisme et Renaissance: Travaux et Documents* 45 (1983): 59–76.

———. "Music in *La Diana* of Jorge de Montemayor." *Hispanic Review* 52 (1984): 435–457.

———. "The Mythological Framework of *La Diana*." *Spanische Literatur—Literatur Europas: Wido Hempel zum 65 Geburtstag*. Ed Frank Baasner. Tübingen: Niemeyer, 1996. 115–150.

———. "Sermoneo y ejercicio de las virtudes cristianas en (*La Diana*) de Jorge de Montemayor." *Revista de Literatura* 46 (1984): 5–18.

———. "Social and Historical Realities of Montemayor's *Diana*." *Crítica Hispánica* 4 (1982): 111–125.

Darst, David H. "Techniques of Evasion in Montemayor's *Diana*." *Symposium* 43 (1989): 184–193.

de Oliveira e Silva, J. "Recurrent Onomastic Textures in the *Diana* of Jorge de Montemayor and the *Arcadia* of Sir Philip Sidney." *Studies in Philology* 79 (1982): 30–40.

Gillette, María. "Foolish Fancies? Maybe Not: Symptoms of Melancholy in *La Diana*." *Romance Notes* 39.1 (Fall 1998): 95–101.

Glenn, Richard F. "The Moral Implications of *El Abencerraje*." *Modern Language Notes* 80 (1965): 202–212.

Manero Sorolla, María Pilar. "La configuración imagínistica de la dama en la lírica española del Renacimiento: La tradición petrarquista." *Boletín de la Biblioteca de Menéndez y Pelayo* 68 (1992): 5–71.

Márquez Villanueva, Francisco. "Los joyeles de Felismena." *Revue de Litterature Comparée* 52 (April–December 1978): 267–278.

Moya Jiménez, Virgilio. "El amor cortés en *Los siete libros de la Diana*." *Letras de Deusto* 19 (1989): 177–182.

Mújica, Bárbara. *Iberian Pastoral Characters*. Vol. 30. Washington, DC: Scripta Humanistica, 1986.

Pérez, José C. "El amor en la *Diana* de Montemayor." *Explicación de textos literarios* 19 (1990–1991): 60–66.

Rhodes, Elizabeth. "Skirting the Men: Gender Roles in Sixteenth-Century Pastoral Books." *Journal of Hispanic Philology* 11.2 (Winter 1987): 131–149.

———. *The Unrecognized Precursors of Montemayor's Diana*. Columbia: U of Missouri P, 1992.

Siles Artés, José. *El arte de la novela pastoril*. Valencia: Albatrós, 1972.

Solé-Leris, Amadeu. *The Spanish Pastoral Novel*. Boston: Twayne, 1980.

Subirats, Jean. "La 'Diana' de Montemayor, roman à clef?" *Etudes Ibérique Latino-Americaines*. IVe Congrès des Hispanistes francais. Paris: Presses Universitaires, France, 1968. 105–118.

Vigier, Francoise. "La folie amoureuse dans le roman pastoral espagnol (2e moitié du XVIe siècle)." *Visages de la folie (1500–1650) (domaine hispano-italien)*. Ed. Augustín Redondo and André Rochon. Paris: Publications de la Sorbonne: Série "Etudes" 16, 1981. 117–129.

Wardropper, Bruce W. "The *Diana* of Montemayor: Revaluation and Interpretation." *Studies in Philology* 48 (1951): 126–144.

Judy B. McInnis

Montero, Rosa (1951–)

A lively curiosity about people and a desire to understand them and their world characterize the writing of Rosa Montero. A prolific journalist and novelist, she has worked for Spain's leading newspaper *El País* since 1976. To date three volumes of her interviews have appeared: *España para ti para siempre* (1976; Spain for You Forever), *Cinco años de País* (1982; Five Years of "Country" [referring both to Spain and to the newspaper]), and *Entrevistas* (1996; Interviews). Skilled at drawing out her subjects and gifted with a sharp eye for their weaknesses, Montero is confrontational when it serves her purpose. She does not hesitate to expose literal and figurative warts nor to reveal her own reactions to, for instance, the charm of Harrison Ford, the aggressiveness of Manuel Fraga, the stubbornness of Margaret Thatcher, or the monstrosity of Yasir Arafat, whom she describes as the most frightening public figure she has ever interviewed. Comparably personal are the columns collected in *La vida desnuda: Una mirada apasionada sobre nuestro mundo* (1994; Naked Life: A Passionate Look at Our World), which touch on a wide range of topics, including sexual harassment, mistreatment of the elderly, child abuse, racism, cruelty to animals, and political corruption. Heavy sarcasm, ridicule, exaggeration, and the use of familiar language are frequent strategies. Montero sees herself as a champion of the weak, and her open advocacy of liberal and feminist causes has won her fans as well as foes. Her recent *Historias de mujeres* (1995; Stories of Women), expanded versions of biographies she published in *El País*'s weekend supplement, consists of portraits of women who for one reason or another fascinated her, whether because of their lifelong battle against chaos and disorder (Agatha Christie), their implacability (Simone de *Beauvoir), their intensity (George Sand), or their destructiveness (Laura Riding). All, argues Montero, were abnormal in the sense that they departed from the norm.

Montero's powers of observation, psychological perception, linguistic skills, and talent for telling a good story have made her a bestselling novelist. As the title of her first novel suggests, *Crónica del desamor* (1979; *Absent Love: A Chronicle*, 1991) is an account of Montero's generation, and it foregrounds issues of special interest to women: sexual stereotyping, female sexuality, and male-female relationships. Ideological rather than artistic concerns predominate. In *La función Delta* (1981; *The Delta Function*, 1991), Montero again explores the tension between emotional needs and the demands of a career and engages in a sustained reflection on love and death. Chapters from the protagonist's memoirs of the year 1980 alternate with entries from her hospital journal in 2010, when she comes to realize that she is dying. The counterpoint of past and present, youth and age, and two concepts of love (as passion and as companionship) is paralleled by the contrast between Lucía's version of events and that of Ricardo, who reads and criticizes her memoirs. These metafictional comments and an awareness of the unreliability of representations of the self and of the past enrich the book.

Montero has described her third novel, *Te trataré como a una reina* (1983; I'll Treat You Like a Queen), as a bolero, a grotesque melodrama. The action revolves around a seedy nightclub and a group of characters who are desperately lonely. The images of romantic love projected by sentimental literature, popular songs, and films weigh heavily upon the women, whose lives do not measure up to the myths they pursue. As Javier Escudero has pointed out, biting humor, excremental imagery, emphasis upon physical decay, and a bleak vision of the human condition link Montero to baroque moralist and satirist Francisco *Quevedo (1580–1645). The issue of who has power and who does not is central in *Amado amo* (1988; Beloved Boss). It is a devastating portrait of a weak, egotistical man, ironically named César. The world of business in which he moves is divided into winners and losers, and so he does not think twice about betraying a woman friend in order to save his own neck.

Montero's next three novels reflect the interest in fantasy that is characteristic of much recent Spanish fiction. *Temblor* (1990; Trembling), a blend of romance, Gothic novel, dystopia, and allegory, is set in a distant future. The female hero, Agua Fría (Cold Water), embarks on a journey of initiation and quest for knowledge, but unlike her male counterparts in the traditional monomyth, she rejects reintegration into society and at the novel's end sets out in search of a place where she and her unborn child can "dream new dreams." Inversion and subversion are important strategies of this novel, and the description of the fantasy world portrayed therein allows the author to comment obliquely upon political systems, social conventions, and sexual roles in contemporary society. The children's book *El nido de los sueños* (1991; The Nest of Dreams) is an outgrowth of *Temblor* and, like its predecessor, is a fantasy and adventure story. Young Gabi emerges victorious from a series of trials without the assistance of male protectors and proves herself to be strong, brave, and resourceful. The child's invention of her own world and naming of its features parallels Montero's creation of a literary world by means of the written word. The author's favorite themes—love or its absence, loneliness, aging, death, the precariousness of memory, the lack of communication and understanding between the sexes—reappear in *Bella y oscura* (1993; Beautiful and Dark), whose action occurs in an excentric space populated by social outcasts. Sordid reality is offset by the magic and poetry of tales told by the Lilliputian Airelai, and the corruption of the adults is countered by the innocence of the children, who are victims of their elders' violence. Life, insists Montero, is a blend of beauty and darkness. The novel features a series of well-drawn female characters, an emphasis upon "women's wisdom," and revisionist mythmaking.

In 1997, Montero published a lengthy "historical" novel, *La hija del canibal* (The Cannibal's Daughter), based in part on documented historical background and the "true adventures" of anarchist opponents of the Franco regime. This factual portion of Montero's bestseller is subordinated to the first-person narrative of Lucía, whose husband disappears in Madrid's Barajas Airport. Helping her to search for him—a search that also leads to self-encounter and lengthy auto/biographical reconstructions—are two extraordinary characters, one an octogenarian anarchist and onetime trigger-man with Durruti. Thus Montero combines history and mystery, humor and irony, with an exploration of aging, marriage, and the enigma of being human. *Amantes y enemigos* (1998; Lovers and Enemies) is a collection of short stories published in varied outlets over some 15 years, united by their common focus on male-female relationships, their combination of melancholy and humor, and their lucid portraits of passion and despair.

Work by

Absent Love: A Chronicle. Trans. Cristina de la Torre and Diana Glad. Lincoln: U of Nebraska P, 1991.
Amado amo. Madrid: Debate, 1988.
Amantes y enemigos. Madrid: Alfaguara, 1998.
Bella y oscura. Barcelona: Seix Barral, 1993.
The Delta Function. Trans. Kari Easton and Yolanda Molina Gavilán. Lincoln: U of Nebraska P, 1991.
Entrevistas. Madrid: El País/Aguilar, 1996.
La hija del canibal. Madrid: Espasa-Calpe, 1997.
Historias de mujeres. Madrid: Alfaguara, 1995.
El nido de los sueños. Madrid: Siruela, 1991.

Temblor. Barcelona: Seix Barral, 1990.
Te trataré como a una reina. Barcelona: Seix Barral, 1983.
La vida desnuda: Una mirada apasionada sobre nuestro mundo. Madrid: El País/Aguilar, 1994.

Work about

Amell, Alma. *Rosa Montero's Odyssey*. Lanham: UP of America, 1994.
Brown, Joan L. "Rosa Montero: From Journalist to Novelist." *Women Writers of Contemporary Spain: Exiles in the Homeland*. Ed. Joan L. Brown. Newark: U of Delaware P, 1991. 240–257.
Davies, Catherine. *Contemporary Feminist Fiction in Spain: The Work of Montserrat Roig and Rosa Montero*. Oxford: Berg, 1994.
Escudero, Javier. "*Te trataré como a una reina*: La visión excremental de Rosa Montero." *Letras Peninsulares* 8 (1995): 113–132.
Gascón Vera, Elena. "From Struggle to Commitment: The Essays of Rosa Montero." *Spanish Women Writers and the Essay: Gender, Politics, and the Self*. Ed and intro. Kathleen Glenn and Mercedes Mazquiarán de Rodríguez. Columbia: U of Missouri P, 1998. 250–263.
———. "Rosa Montero ante la escritura femenina." *Anales de la Literatura Española Contemporánea* 12 (1987): 59–77.
Glenn, Kathleen M. "Victimized by Misreading: Rosa Montero's *Te trataré como a una reina*." *Anales de la Literatura Española Contemporánea* 12 (1987): 191–202.
Harges, Mary C. "Role-Reversal in Speculative Fiction: An Alternate Vision of the Future in *Temblor*." *Hispanófila* 123 (May 1998): 31–36.
Miguel Martínez, Emilio de. *La primera narrativa de Rosa Montero*. Salamanca: U de Salamanca, 1983.
Zatlin, Phyllis. "The Novels of Rosa Montero as Experimental Fiction." *Monographic Review/Revista Monográfica* 8 (1992): 114–124.

Kathleen M. Glenn

Montoro, Antón de

See Isabel I, Queen of Castile: The Vision of the Queen in *Converso* Poetry (c. 1474–c. 1480)

Montseny Mañé, Federica (1905–1994)

Catalan anarchist Federica Montseny, whose political, journalistic, and literary career spanned more than 50 years, contributed to numerous anarchist journals and newspapers, wrote libertarian novels, and remained a powerful force within the Spanish anarchist movement until her death in 1994. Born in Madrid to Catalan anarchist leaders Joan Montseny and Teresa Mañé, Montseny never attended formal school but rather was educated according to the teachings of María Montessori and Ferrari i Guardia by her mother. In 1912 the family returned to their homeland, Catalonia, where, after various farming enterprises in the outlying areas of the city, they established their residence in Barcelona. At 17, she joined the clandestine anarchist labor union CNT (National Confederation of Workers); contributed to numerous anarchist publications such as *Solidaridad Obrera*, *Tierra y Libertad*, and *Nueva Senda*, among others; and published her first novel under the name "Blanca Montsan" in the series "La Novela Roja."

In 1923, Montseny urged her parents to relaunch the anarchist journal of cultural criticism *La Revista Blanca*, which they had previously published between 1898 and 1905. Likewise, the Montseny family established the publishing firm *Ediciones de La Revista Blanca*, specializing in promoting libertarian ideals throughout the 1920s and 1930s. Federica Montseny participated as an editor of the serials "La Novela Ideal" and "La Novela Libre," writing many of the novels herself. The "Novela Ideal" had a weekly edition of 50,000 issues and the "Novela Libre," a monthly publication of 64 pages, 20,000 issues. Montseny proudly recalls in her autobiography *Mis primeros cuarenta años* (1987; My First 40 Years) that "La Novela Ideal," in Franco's view, poisoned three generations of Spaniards. As an anarchist intellectual, Montseny supported women's emancipation throughout her writing career. In her many novels, short stories, and articles for the anarchist press she analyzed the origins of the deplorable status of women in Spanish society and presented theories that challenged her readers' beliefs regarding women's capabilities.

Montseny was 25 years old when the Second Republic was proclaimed. By then married to fellow anarchist Germinal Esgleas, mother of a child, still dedicated to her family's publishing business, and active in trade union affairs, Montseny was the epitome of modern womanhood. As a propagandist for the CNT she traveled throughout Spain during the first half of the 1930s, lecturing about labor union's policies while promoting the local labor associations. Montseny's talent for public speaking, complemented by her political credentials and her astute defense of the FAI (Federación Anarquista Ibérica, the leftist faction of the CNT) in internal disputes, promoted her public career so that within a short time she was a prominent member of the labor union's National Committee.

In November 1936, Montseny was appointed minister of health and public assistance by Largo Caballero. During her six-month tenure as health minister, Montseny initiated a series of measures and implemented numerous programs that were ahead of their time. She downsized the ministry's bureaucracy in favor of efficiency and made it her policy to incorporate women into leadership positions. She additionally established the basis for what was to become the Republican refugee program throughout the war, she allocated funding to construct rest homes for battle-worn troops, and established a national home program to evacuate orphaned and displaced children from besieged cities such as Madrid. Taking advantage of the Republic's legal reforms, Montseny likewise secularized charity (formerly the domain of the Catholic Church) by creating programs to distribute federal aid to those in need. A series of reforms that Montseny implemented directly affected women's health policy. This progressive view favored sexual education, family planning, and the legal termination of pregnancy, among other programs sympathetic to women's needs.

Another innovation was the *liberatorios de prostitución*, halfway houses for women trying to break free of prostitution. Along with feminist advocate Dr. Amparo Poch, Montseny launched a nationwide campaign to prevent the spread of venereal diseases through education and vaccination campaigns among civilians and troops.

The events of May 1937 precipitated the fall of the Largo Caballero government and signaled the rise of the Soviet-supported Spanish Communist Party. Refusing to join the cabinet of the new prime minister Dr. Juan Negrín, all anarchist ministers, including Montseny, resigned their posts. Montseny continued to hold a variety of political offices in the CNT and the FAI throughout the remaining war effort: president of the UGT Union General de Trabajadores (General Workers Union)–CNT committee, secretary of propaganda of the National Committee of the CNT, and member of the Peninsular Committee of the FAI. During this last year of the war, Montseny remained in Barcelona with her family. Pregnant with her second child, she limited her activities and speaking engagements.

At the end of the war, Montseny, like hundreds of thousands of Spaniards who had defended the Republic, fled over the Pyrenees into France. The holder of a diplomatic passport, she was able to enter France with most of her family. However, her husband, father, and half sister María were interned in refugee camps until they were later reunited with Montseny in Paris. Until the German occupation, Montseny was busy rebuilding the CNT labor union in exile. In 1942 she was imprisoned at Perigueux and later in Limoges as she awaited extradition to Spain. Pregnant at the time with her third child, her extradition was denied, and she was confined to house arrest until the end of the war. During the long exile that was to be the destiny of many Spaniards following the end of the Spanish Civil War, Montseny continued to participate in the Spanish anarchist movement after the 1944 liberation of France. She collaborated with the anarchist newspaper *CNT/L'Espoir*, published in Toulouse, and traveled throughout Europe on lecture tours denouncing the Franco regime while simultaneously supporting the continued existence of the Spanish anarchist trade union CNT in exile.

Unlike the majority of the exiled activists who had returned to Spain upon reestablishment of democracy, Montseny chose instead to continue her residence in Toulouse. During the brief periods Montseny spent in Spain, especially Catalonia, she sought to recover that "other" Spanish history that, for obvious reasons, had been banished from collective memory. Toward the end of her life she was perceived more as a catalyzing symbol, comparable to Dolores *Ibarruri, rather than as a political leader capable of uniting the diverse political forces of the anarchist movement.

Work by

Cien días en la vida de una mujer. Barcelona: Galba, 1977.
El éxodo: Pasión y muerte de los españoles en el exilio. Barcelona: Galba, 1977.
Federica Montseny en Andalucía, verano de 1932. Seville: Las Siete Entidades, 1994.
La Indomable. Ed. Mª Alicia Langa Laorga. Madrid: Castalia. 1991.
Mis primeros cuarenta anos. Barcelona: Plaza y Janés, 1987.
Mujeres en la cárcel. Toulouse: Universo, 1948.
¿Qué es el anarquismo? Barcelona: La Gaya Ciencia, 1976.
Seis años de mi vida (1939–1945). Barcelona: Galba, 1978.

Work about

Alcalde, Carmen. *Federica Montseny: Palabra en rojo y negro*. Barcelona: Argos Vergara, 1983.
———. *La mujer en la guerra civil española*. Madrid: Cambio 16, 1976.
Greene, Patricia V. "Federica Montseny: Chronicler of an Anarcho-Feminist Genealogy." *Letras Peninsulares* 10.2 (Fall 1997): 333–354.
Mangini, Shirley. *Memories of Resistance*. New Haven, CT: Yale UP, 1995.

Patricia V. Greene

Moratín, Leandro Fernández de (1760–1828): His Portrayal of Women

This famous man of letters of the Spanish Enlightenment followed in the footsteps of his father, noted poet and dramatist Nicolás Fernández de Moratín (1737–1780), to become the premier playwright of the Enlightenment. Although he experienced great success during his lifetime, Moratín also encountered numerous frustrations in staging his plays and endured several skirmishes with the Inquisition. His theater is synonymous with neoclassicism and the values and ideals of *ilustrado* (enlightened) reform. Like other members of the ruling minority of eighteenth-century Spain, Moratín led a privileged life. He enjoyed the friendship of powerful political figures, such as the count of Cabarrús, Jovellanos, and Manuel Godoy, and met accomplished artists, including Goya and Goldoni. He traveled extensively in Europe, to France, England, and Italy. Named Secretary for the Interpretation of Languages in 1797, he later served as Royal Librarian to José Bonaparte. As is the case of many Bonaparte supporters, he died in exile in France.

Moratín wrote varied works, if few in number, including poetry, the prose satire *La derrota de los pedantes* (1789; The Defeat of Pedants), an edition with critical commentary of the seventeenth-century pamphlet *Auto de fe celebrado en la ciudad de Logroño en los días 7 y 8 de noviembre del año de 1610* (1812; Act of Faith [i.e., execution by the Inquisition] Celebrated in the City of Logroño on November 7 and 8 in the Year 1610), published under the pseudonym of Ginés de Posadilla, and a history of Spanish theater, *Orígenes del teatro español* (1831; Origins of Spanish Theater). He also translated *Hamlet* (1798) and adapted Molière's *L'Ecole des maris* (1661) and *Le Médecin malgré lui* (1666), rendered, respectively, as *La escuela de los maridos* (1812; School for Husbands) and *El médico a palos* (1814; The Doctor in

Spite of Himself). Moratín's enduring reputation, however, rests almost exclusively on his five original plays. These dramatic works are all comedies that to different degrees engage with women's issues, especially regarding parental authority and the education of women.

Moratín's first play, *El viejo y la niña* (1790; The Old Man and the Girl), pits the young heroine Doña Isabel against her elderly, unscrupulous husband Don Roque, who tricked her into marriage. Recent criticism of this *comédie larmoyante* (tearjerker) in verse has focused on its ambiguous conclusion, in which Isabel rejects an illicit amorous liaison with her former young suitor and escapes her husband's control by entering the convent. Some critics regard the heroine's choice to withdraw from society as the ultimate act of submission to the highest and most just male authority, God. Others interpret her decision as an assertion of independence that frees her from an abusive male's authority.

In *La comedia nueva* or *El café* (1792; The New Comedy or the Cafe), the author employs a play-within-a-play motif to satirize incompetent playwrights and their foolish dramas, which dominated the eighteenth-century Spanish stage. Moratín also lampoons the presumptuous bluestocking Doña Agustina for unnatural behavior, while he implicitly approves the more traditionally feminine Doña Mariquita, who cultivates domestic skills and yearns only for marriage and children.

Moratín reworked a *zarzuela* (vaudevillesque operetta) he had composed earlier to create the comedy in verse *El barón* (1803; The Baron). When an overly ambitious widow tries to impose an unequal marriage to a baron, actually an imposter, on her commoner daughter Isabel, the young heroine's beloved and her uncle intervene to set things right. Love triumphs over hypocrisy and overweening pride in the end, as the widow sees the error of her ways and the wisdom of the young people's match.

La *mojigata (1804; The Pious Deceiver) juxtaposes two methods of raising daughters. The play rewards the sincere, virtuous Doña Inés, the product of a more liberal education provided by a kind, tolerant father, and penalizes *la mojigata*, the pious hypocrite Doña Clara, the result of a strict education imposed by a selfish, authoritarian father.

Moratín's best drama is *El *sí de las niñas* (1806), the literary masterpiece of the Spanish Enlightenment. The play synthesizes the themes of his previous comedies, supporting improved education for women, frank communication between parents and daughters, and a woman's right to participate in the selection of her husband without parental coercion. Although Moratín follows closely the precepts of neoclassicism in his final original dramatic work, *El sí de las niñas* sparkles with wit and humor, much of it generated by the narrow-minded Doña Irene, one of the innovative character parts for older women that the playwright introduced to the Spanish theater.

Moratín promoted the neoclassical ideal that the theater should entertain and instruct. He observed the Aristotelian unities of time, place, and action and strove for verisimilitude in plot and dialogue. According to this master playwright, drama should depict people as they are, focusing on domestic life, national habits, and common vices to provide a representation at once pleasing and didactic. He directed his plays to the new middle class, the backbone of the Bourbon monarchy's reform program. Noted *ilustrados* such as Jovellanos almost invariably identified virtue, utility, and happiness as the tripartite, comprehensive goal of their reform efforts. This ideological position explains Moratín's predilection for comedy, a genre that lends itself to struggles between virtue and vice and in which virtue always wins, which leads to a happy conclusion.

The fact that Moratín's plays focus on women's issues mirrors the reform agenda of the *Ilustración* (Enlightenment) as well. The ruling elite targeted the domestic sphere of activity as the basis for the creation of a moral, industrious middle class. As wives and mothers, women were valuable to society for their roles as the principal educators of Spain's youth and as promoters of civility and citizenship, which guaranteed social stability and commitment. The *ilustrado* (enlightened) minority argued that females should be treated with dignity and respect, that women's ideas and opinions should be taken seriously, and that women should be educated for their social function as purveyors of the values of the Spanish Enlightenment. These beliefs enliven and inform Moratín's theater, and in this context, the master of neoclassical Spanish drama emerges as a consistent advocate for women's rights. *See also* Feminism in Spain: 1700–1800

Work by

La comedia nueva. El sí de las niñas. Ed. John Dowling and René Andioc. Madrid: Castalia, 1978.

Teatro completo. Leandro Fernández de Moratín. Ed. Manuel Fernández Nieto. 2 vols. Madrid: Nacional, 1977.

Work about

Andioc, René. "Sobre Goya y Moratín hijo." *Hispanic Review* 50 (1982): 119–132.

———. *Teatro y sociedad en el Madrid del siglo XVIII.* 2nd ed. Madrid: Castalia, 1987.

Dowling, John. *Leandro Fernández de Moratín.* New York: Twayne, 1971.

———. "Moratín's Creation of the Comic Role for the Older Actress." *Theatre Survey* 24 (1983): 55–63.

Kish, Kathleen. "A School for Wives: Women in Eighteenth-Century Spanish Theater." *Women in Hispanic Literature: Icons and Fallen Idols.* Ed. Beth Miller. Berkeley and Los Angeles: U of California P, 1983. 184–200.

Lázaro Carreter, Fernando. *Moratín en su teatro.* Oviedo: Universidad de Oviedo, 1961.

Llanos M., Bernardita. "Integración de la mujer al proyecto de la Ilustración en España." *Ideologies and Literature* 4 (1989): 199–223.

Maravall, José Antonio. "The Idea and Function of Education in Enlightenment Thought." *The Institutionalization of Literature in Spain.* Trans. Terry Cochran. Ed. Wlad Godzich and Nicholas Spadaccini. Minneapolis: Prisma Institute, 1987. 39–99.

Martín Gaite, Carmen. *Usos amorosos del dieciocho en España.* Madrid: Siglo Veintiuno de España. 1972.

Sherman, Alvin F., Jr. "Women's Feet: Moratín's Metaphor of Freedom and Progress." *Ojancano* 11 (April 1996): 51–65.

Marsha S. Collins

Mora y Maura, Constancia de la (1906–1950)

Born in Madrid to Germán de la Mora, chief executive officer of one of Madrid's most important electric companies, and Constancia Maura, the eldest daughter of Conservative politician and many times over Prime Minister Antonio Maura, Constancia de la Mora y Maura states in her autobiography that she was aware quite early in her life of belonging to Spain's privileged class of the rich, even before she could verbalize such awareness. The eldest of five children, she was brought up by an Irish nanny until her formal education began at the Handmaids of the Sacred Heart school. De la Mora criticized the instruction provided by the nuns as severely limited, finding herself upon completion of her course of study with a narrowly focused and parochial education. Too young to attend finishing school or make her societal debut, at age 14 she convinced her parents to send her to Great Britain, where she attended St. Mary's Convent School in Cambridge.

Upon her return to Spain in 1923, de la Mora prepared for her debut into society. This period of her life was filled with the never-ending social and religious obligations suitable for a young girl of her social stature. In 1926 while vacationing at the exclusive French seaside resort of St. Jean-de-Luz she met Manuel Bolín of Málaga, whom she wed a year later. Troubles in the relationship appeared almost immediately following the ceremony. De la Mora bitterly recalled in her autobiography that on her wedding night she realized before morning that she would never love this man. During this brief marriage the couple lived in the southern provincial city of Málaga. In 1928 de la Mora gave birth to her only child, a girl, named Constancia Maria de Lourdes Bolín de la Mora. Unable to earn their livelihood in Málaga, de la Mora returned to Madrid with her husband and child and set out to find a job in order to help support her family. Through Zenobia Camprubí, a businesswoman in her own right, and wife of poet and Nobel Prize winner Juan Ramón *Jiménez, de la Mora secured her first job, working as a Spanish tutor to American journalists. In the fall, de la Mora continued to work at Arte Popular, a folk-art shop owned by Camprubí and Inés Muñuz. In 1931, de la Mora sought a legal separation from Bolín.

As an independent single parent, de la Mora became keenly aware of the importance of public policy and its impact on the individual. Her newfound political awareness was closely bound to the difficulties she encountered as a working mother. De la Mora's alternative lifestyle met with great disapproval by her family and friends, many of whom deserted her. She aligned herself with the Republic, taking a job with the PNT (the National Tourist Board), which supervised the writing and distribution of tourist information about Spain. De la Mora hoped to help dispel the myths about Spain by producing well-written, accurate, and useful information for national and international tourists.

In 1931 de la Mora met Air Force Major Ignacio Hidalgo de Cisneros. As their relationship intensified, de la Mora decided to divorce her husband and marry Cisneros. On March 2, 1932, divorce became legal in Spain, and she wed Cisneros in a civil ceremony on January 16, 1933, in Alcalá de Henares. The next few years, de la Mora lived in Rome and Berlin, where Cisneros had been assigned the post of military attaché. These experiences enabled de la Mora to witness firsthand National Sindicalism in the Third Reich and fascism in Mussolini's Italy. In 1935, de la Mora returned to Spain and resumed employment in Madrid, this time as a partner in the art shop.

On July 17, 1936, General Francisco Franco and his troops staged a military revolt against the legally elected government of the Republic. De la Mora clearly sympathized with the democratic forces under siege and quickly volunteered her services in defense of the Republic. Aided by her closest friends, she took charge of an abandoned orphanage, caring for displaced children. During this period she joined the Spanish Communist Party and became an active member in the National Committee of Antifascist Women, the central governing organ of AMA, the Agrupación de Mujeres Antifascistas (National Organization of Anti-Fascist Women). Evacuated to Alicante in fall 1936, de la Mora established a convalescent home there for wounded aviators, relinquishing her leadership of the children she had brought from Madrid. In December, accepting the offer made by the Soviet government to care for Spanish Republican children until the end of the conflict, de la Mora sent her only daughter, Luli, to the USSR while she herself moved with the Republican forces to Valencia. De la Mora's remarkable command of foreign languages led friends to suggest that she could better help the antifascist war effort abroad by joining the Foreign Press Bureau (FPB). In 1937 she became the only woman to join the staff of censors of the FPB. That year she also attended the International Anti-Fascist Writers Conference held in Valencia. In 1938, now a government official, she left Valencia to take up residence in Barcelona as chief of the Foreign Press Bureau, becoming the only woman to hold this position in Spanish history. In May, she accompanied Foreign Minister Julio Alvarez del Vayo as translator and spokesperson for the Republican government to the League of Nations Assembly.

Following the disastrous Ebro campaign, Republican forces abandoned Barcelona. In

January 1939, with the help of her staff, she completely dismantled her office, destroyed all incriminating documents, and left for the northern town of Figueras. In February 1939, she crossed the Pyrenees on foot into France, set up a makeshift press agency in Toulouse, and found herself functioning as an impromptu spokesperson for the government of the Spanish Republic, now in exile. On February 10, 1939, she sailed for the United States, intending to request military and humanitarian aid for the Spanish cause. Her mission was cut short by General Franco's victory.

At the urging of journalist Jay Allen, de la Mora wrote her autobiography *In Place of Splendor* during those few months she spent in the United States. It has been translated into French, German, Italian, Spanish, and Russian, among other languages. In 1940, de la Mora relocated with her husband to Cuernavaca, Mexico, shortly thereafter becoming a Mexican citizen. In 1946 she was reunited with her daughter Luli. In Mexico, she continued her Communist Party affiliation, becoming a close associate of Diego Rivera and other members of the Democratic Revolutionary Party (PRD). She also continued her efforts to support Spanish refugees, working with the Joint Anti-Fascist Refugee Committee from 1940 to 1945.

At age 43, on January 25, 1950, en route to the Guayaquil airport in Guatemala, she was killed in an automobile accident.

Work by

In Place of Splendor: Autobiography of a Spanish Woman. New York: Harcourt, Brace, 1939.

Work about

Bolloten, Burnett. *The Spanish Civil War.* Chapel Hill: U of North Carolina P, 1991.
Broué, Pierre, and Emile Teminé. *The Revolution and the Civil War in Spain.* Trans. Tony White. Cambridge: MIT P, 1970.
Greene, Patricia V. "Constancia de la Mora's *In Place of Splendor* and the Persistence of Memory." *Journal for Interdisciplinary Literary Studies* 5.1 (1993): 75–84.

Guttman, Allan. *The Wound in the Heart: America and the Spanish Civil War.* New York: Free P of Glencoe, 1962.
Mangini, Shirley. *Memories of Resistance. Women's Voices from the Spanish Civil War.* New Haven, CT: Yale UP, 1995.
Seghers, Anna. *Anna Seghers, Constancia de la Mora Tell the Story of the Joint Anti-Fascist Refugee Committee.* New York: National Office, 1944.
Ugarte, Michael. "Women and Exile: The Civil War Autobiographies of Constancia de la Maura and María Teresa León." *Letras Peninsulares* 11.1 (Spring 1998): 207–222.

Patricia V. Greene

Moreto, Agustín de (1618–1669): Women in His *Entremeses*

Women are the most important characters of the *entremeses* (brief comic interludes) of Spain's Golden Age, and their presence runs the gamut of all female types, all within some canons of conformity with the society that surrounds them. They are prostitutes of better or worse fortune; they are married or single; most of them are of the lower classes; they are rustics or courtesans with their own hierarchy and their own laws, completely apart from the hierarchy and laws of the society of the time. Even so, all have something in common: They have keen intelligence, they are always ready to deceive, and they want more than they have. Usually the action of the *entremés* moves around their greed for possessions; most of them will achieve their objectives, but others will lose. When a woman character perpetrates the act of deceit, the audience never doubts that the one deceived will be a man. Javier Huerta points out that because of the difficulty in classifying and defining the traits of the female character, one might consider her a leitmotiv of the genre and the initiator of most of the plots. This point is clear in the *entremeses* of Agustín Moreto y Cabaña, for women are his strongest figures, the best developed, and the most perfected from every point of view.

Until now, studies of the characters of the

entremés have relegated to a secondary level the roles played by women, thus suggesting that their action in the plot is not an important one. In fact, the opposite is true. An examination of the work of Moreto is sufficient to reveal the importance of the woman in these short works. We begin by making a division of social type between outcasts (prostitutes and thieves) and those who live within socially acceptable boundaries. The reason for this division has nothing to do with morality but with theme, which varies according to the plot of the *entremés*. Even though the plot always involves trickery in the end, the motives and forms of carrying it out are usually different. Women in these works are decisive, assertive, and astute, since they live in a society in which it is difficult for them to survive simply because they are women.

Within the first category, that of social outcasts, Moreto presents three different types of women in three *entremeses*: *Entremés del aguador* (1661; Interlude of the Waterboy), *Doña Esquina* (1668; Miss [Street]Corner), and *Entremés de los gatillos* (1661; Interlude of the Kittens/Thieves). In *Del aguador*, the protagonist is named Doña Estafa, who, as her name indicates, is a fraud, a swindler: She is duplicity personified in the figure of woman. This woman has only one goal at this stage of her life: to improve her social position and to be called "your ladyship." The only way that she can realize her dream of grandeur is through marriage to a man of superior class, of position, and especially, of wealth, something that interests her as much as being called "your ladyship." The disdain she shows toward men will work to her disadvantage and will become the trick of the *entremés*, bitter in its resolution for the defeat it inflicts upon a woman who wants to improve her lot in life through questionable artifices. It is the men who in the end laugh at the desolate situation in which the woman finds herself.

The second work, *Doña Esquina*, is the only *entremés* in which women bear the exclusive burden of the plot. All principal characters are women except for Osorio and the porter, neither of whom carries much weight. This is one of Moreto's best *entremeses* and one of the most complete and polished. This *entremés* also plays with language through frequent use of double meanings. The only character in this play who has a proper name is the protagonist. Her name, Esquina, besides being her name is also the common noun "corner," which connotes ambivalence because it refers both to her profession (streetwalker) and to geometric and mental sharpness. The rest of the characters (excepting Osorio) have no name, nor do they need one for the actions they present. The neighbors fawn upon Esquina because she treats them well and continually gives them gifts, but they turn into vipers when an occasion arises that allows them to take away Esquina's man. If Esquina seems ingenuous when she fully trusts her neighbors to protect her, she disproves this idea by her skillful and witty manipulation of the neighbors' evil gossip, turning it to her advantage. Thanks to them, she is able to present herself as the victim and not as the offender that she is. Esquina is a resourceful, independent woman, a woman sure of herself and not in need of male protection.

The male presence on stage gives a visual representation of Esquina's work and her modus vivendi, the source of her income and, of course, her pleasure. Esquina knows who she is, what her position is, and more than anything else, how to profit from it. She does not offend by words, nor does she accuse her neighbors of treachery. By her actions she places them in situations that sooner or later force them to return her favors. She manages to resolve the misunderstanding with her lover in the blink of an eye. Of course, her motive in so doing is her own profit since she not only keeps the lunch that Osorio brought but also keeps Osorio, who represents for Esquina the hen that lays the golden eggs.

In the third work, the *Entremés de los ga-*

tillos, the female protagonist has no proper name, but stage directions indicate that "Manuela (the actress) comes out dressed as Marquillos." From the time she comes on stage it is clear that she is mistaken for a boy and henceforth participates in the only *entremés* by Moreto dedicated to the underground life and thievery. The word *gato* means both cat and petty thief, and in this *entremés* the petty thieves are known by the diminutive *gatillos* (kittens) in recognition of their youth. There is also a stage indication that this young protagonist, dressed in a tight buttoned-up gown, was a simpleton, for such garb was the traditional costume of these characters in the theater. She is identified as a simple boy by all the characters on stage and by the audience, which suits her dirty tricks very well. The trickery of the *entremés* is double in this case: Not only is the protagonist not a fool, but the male character was played by Manuela Escamilla, an actress well recognized by the public. The rascal she plays is the typical swindler who looks like a simpleton but who obtains all she/he wants. She observes her surroundings with great care, analyzes what she sees, formulates her plan of attack, and carries it out. Part of her success depends on her astute refusal to trust her luck, no matter how good it may be. She maintains her adopted role as a village fool because this disguise allows her to survive life on the street.

This character and that of Doña Esquina are comparable in behavior; both observe, make sure of the situation, and then carry out their plan, without forgetting for a moment who they are. In this way they differ from Doña Estafa, who, once her plan is ready, does not make sure of its practicability and consequently finds herself caught and tricked by those that she wanted to deceive. Nevertheless, these three women cannot be discarded as imaginary or impossible. They are fully developed as characters with defects and virtues typical of any woman in any era.

The second group of women is usually poor but finds socially acceptable methods for getting what is needed to escape the hole they are in. Servant women belong to this group who, although they have a job and some economic means, want to live in better circumstances. Two of Moreto's *entremeses* showcase the intelligence of such women: *La Mariquita* (1659) and *La Perendeca* (1639). *La Mariquita* presents Mariquita's plan to escape poverty by marrying Lorenzo, the doctor's simple-minded nephew. Lorenzo represents the dream candidate of any woman seeking to improve her socioeconomic status. He is simple-minded, so she can manage him, and he is so rich she can also forgive or ignore said defect if the situation so demands. The trickery of this *entremés* consists in convincing the youth that he is married when he is not and in persuading him that the winner in this marriage is he, not Mariquita. With the help of two friends she carries out the deceit, securing a home, husband, and much-improved economic situation. Like Esquina, Manuela, or Estafa, Mariquita is determined to succeed. And, like the first two, she has planned well and knows how to accomplish her plan. The message in this type of *entremés* is that marriage is a matter of economics and not of love.

In *La Perendeca*, the protagonist is pursued by several men, but like Esquina, she is an independent spirit. Perendeca, which means "streetgirl," has her work and wants to maintain it because of the freedom it gives her. Accepting a suitor's courtship would mean a total loss of freedom and acceptance of the subservient "wife" role. Like Esquina, Moreto plays with her name by changing a nominalized adjective into a proper noun. In this way, while he opens Perendeca's moral character to question, she is not another Esquina, for Perendeca is not a prostitute. This is an *entremés a palos* "with sticks or thrashings," a classification given to the old *entremeses* that concluded with blows, in contrast to the newer ones that ended with music or dances. Figuratively speaking, Perendeca controls the action behind the scenes, for she directs, plans, and observes without entering directly into the action until the end of the play, when she participates and the trickery is revealed. If men love her, it is not her fault; their relentless pursuit creates the action of the play. To avoid the displeasure of her master, who has given orders about whom she may see, Perendeca creates situations in which her suitors literally become objects: the blacksmith's shop, a forge, and finally some benches and a table for her master. When the last ruse is revealed, the old men, her master and a friend who is visiting him, begin to fight with sticks against Perendeca and her suitors, who must flee. The passage of time, from 1639 to 1668, shows a mellowing in Moreto's treatment of women in his *entremeses* as women characters move from stereotypical images to beings full of life and intelligence. They are their own persons, not reflections of their fathers or husbands. They think, decide, and choose what suits them. And on most occasions, they do not show the coldness or calculation of other authors' characters at that time.

Work by

Buendía, Felicidad. *Antología del entremés. (Desde Lope de Rueda hasta Antonio de Zamora) Siglos XVI y XVII*. Madrid: Aguilar, 1965. Contains *Doña Esquina, El aguador*.

———. *Los gatillos*. Ed. Celsa Carmen García Valdés. *Antología del entremés barroco*. Barcelona: Plaza y Janés, 1985.

Work about

Castañeda, James A. *Agustín Moreto*. New York: Twayne, 1974.

Finn, Thomas P. "Manipulating Identity across the Pyrenees." *French Review* 73.1 (1999): 60–70.

Huerta Calvo, Javier. *Teatro breve de los siglos XVI y XVII. Entremeses, loas, bailes, jácaras y mojigangas*. Madrid: Taurus, 1985.

Kennedy, Ruth L. *The Dramatic Art of Moreto*. Smith College Studies in Modern Languages Vol. 13, No. 1. Northampton, MA: n.p., 1932.

McKendrick, Melveena. *Theatre in Spain 1490–1700*. Cambridge: Cambridge UP, 1989.

Parker, J.H. "Some Aspects of Moreto's *Teatro Menor*." *Philological Quarterly* 51.1 (1972): 205–217.

Ruth Sánchez Imizcoz

Morris, Rocq
See Ballesteros, Mercedes (1913–)

Mujeres libres (1936–1938)

Mujeres libres (Free Women) was the publication of a women's anarchist association, Federación Nacional de Mujeres Libres, founded in April 1936. Thirteen issues of *Mujeres libres* were published. In addition, some uncomplicated brochures targeted readers with no education. The association founders were Lucía Sánchez Saornil, Mercedes Camposada, and Amparo Poch y Gascón. The objective of *Mujeres libres* was, essentially, the emancipation of the working woman—and of the working class—and her development as a member of the libertarian movement. *Mujeres libres* proclaimed a worker's feminism in opposition to bourgeois feminism. Its view of women's emancipation existed always in the context of proletarian freedom. Since women suffer three kinds of slavery—slavery from ignorance, slavery as workers, and slavery as women—*Mujeres libres* sought to transform the female population into a conscious, responsible force, through social and cultural education and via political praxis. Cultural education for women included elementary classes, movies, lectures, and commented readings. The political position of *Mujeres libres* was clearly very radical: The association argued that equality between sexes could only be achieved through the Social Revolution. *See also* Feminism in Spain: 1900–2000; Women's Situation in Spain: 1931–1975: The Second Spanish Republic, the Spanish Civil War and Its Aftermath

Work

Mujeres libres. Madrid and Barcelona: n.p., 1936–1938.

Work about

Nash, Mary, ed. *"Mujeres libres": España 1936–1939*. Barcelona: Tusquets, 1976.

Perinat, Adolfo, and María Isabel Marrades. *Mujer*,

prensa y sociedad en España, 1800–1939. Madrid: Centro de investigaciones sociológicas, 1980.

Carmen de Urioste

Mujer moderna y sus derechos, La (1927)

Novelist and journalist Carmen de *Burgos authored this 319-page defense of feminism six years after acceding to her first openly political position as president of two closely related feminist organizations, the Cruzada de Mujeres Españolas (Spanish Women's Crusade) and the Liga Internacional de Mujeres Ibéricas e Iberoamericanas (International League of Iberian and Hispanic-American Women).

In this text, de Burgos recounts that in 1921, the first year of her presidency, women of the Liga and the Cruzada were responsible for the first act of Spanish suffragists. They brought their demand for *suffrage to the public's attention by distributing copies of their feminist manifesto to members of the Cortes, approaching them on a Madrid street. This document, signed by thousands of women of all social classes, called for each woman's right to be *electora y elegible* (voter and eligible for public office). The deputies offered the suffragists their support in 1921; nevertheless, only minor revisions were made in the electoral law, and the Civil Code was not changed. In *La mujer moderna*, de Burgos expresses her impatience with such Spanish governmental inaction and with Spanish women's lack of support for suffrage. She laments the profound divisions that exist in the feminist camp, despite the indivisible nature of women's cause. A particular concern is the tendency among women's organizations to focus on *feminismo sensato*, sensible feminism, which only seeks protection for women and thereby excludes suffrage from their social programs.

In earlier years, de Burgos too had been ambivalent toward female suffrage, but in *La mujer moderna* she asserts that limiting feminist goals to seeking civil equality for women, while ignoring their political rights, is simply a new deceptive way to maintain women in inaction. De Burgos asserts that women will never obtain the reforms they seek without full political equality. This determination leads de Burgos to analyze and dispute the antifeminist ideology that informed the Spanish polemic on women's roles. She begins with a consideration of the origins of feminism in the cultural changes brought about by World War I and proposes a (re)definition of the word *feminism* stripping it of the negative connotations that make it seem either *ridícula y risible* (ridiculous and laughable) or *terrible, capaz de disolver la sociedad* (horrific, capable of destroying society). Perhaps alluding to the successful American union between suffragists and abolitionists, de Burgos describes that movement as one that works to achieve a justice that does not enslave half of humanity, to the detriment of the whole.

De Burgos continues her vindication of the women's cause by methodically attacking the major arguments used to restrict women to subordinate roles in Spanish culture. Citing evidence from experts in order to refute others whose theories contributed to the repression of women, she addresses doctrines of alleged female cerebral inferiority, moral difference, and innate suitability to the domestic role. The dedication of three chapters to the latter topic reveals de Burgos's continuing preoccupation, first shown in her 1903 survey on divorce, with legal regulation of personal relationships and women's private lives. De Burgos concludes that her work successfully refutes and eliminates the argument of mental and moral inferiority.

Quotations de Burgos employs to lend credence to her arguments reveal her acquaintance with nineteenth- and twentieth-century thought in philosophy (Bebel, Simmel) and biological theory (Lamarck, Marañón), as well as her familiarity with news about foreign events relating to women (Los Angeles divorce procedures, the Fatty Arbuckle case). At times, she appears to have a partial or inaccurate grasp of information, which may indicate that it was supplied to her by other sources. Her insistence on equal opportunities for women is problematized by her frequent citations of Spanish scientist Gregorio Marañón (1887–1960), whose essays on sexuality reinforced the theory of women's complementary, maternity-based social role.

In *La mujer moderna*, de Burgos is optimistic about the potential for improvement in the lives of women. She notes, however, that the inaction of conservative governments in Spain has preserved a Civil Code based on the *Partidas* of *Alfonso X (1221–1284), thereby maintaining women in antiquated roles. De Burgos suggests that Spain look to the United States and other republics for models of modernity based on social change. She urges her readers to seize this propitious moment, with the electoral census revealing that women were slightly more numerous than men, to choose modernity and insist that equality for women be written into law. Treading the line between radical reform and loyalty to the Constitution of 1876, however, de Burgos alleges that nothing in the document specifically prohibits women from exercising the right to vote. She insists, rather, that it is time for women to assume that the constitutional definition of Spanish nationality includes women as well as men.

By highlighting the *labor unánime, sin fronteras* (unanimous work, without [national] borders) of international organizations like the Liga, de Burgos exhorts Spanish women's organizations to abandon notions of national feminism limited by assumptions of complementary gender roles and to join the transcontinental effort for full gender equality. She contends that the march of civilization collaborates with feminism, while insisting on the urgency of converting controversy into legislative change before the opportunity is lost. *See also*: Feminism in Spain: 1900–2000; Women's Situation in Spain: 1786–1931: The Awakening of Female Consciousness

Work

La mujer moderna y sus derechos. Valencia: Sempere, n.d. [1927].

Work about

Fagoaga de Bartolomé, Concha. *La voz y el voto de las mujeres, 1877–1931*. Barcelona: Icaria, 1985.

Nash, Mary. "Experiencia y aprendizaje: La formación histórica de los feminismos en España." *Historia Social* 20 (1994): 151–172.

Scanlon, Geraldine. *La polémica feminista en la España contemporánea: 1868–1974*. Madrid: Akal, 1986.

Lynn Thompson Scott

Mulder, Elisabeth (1904–1987)

Her background and education set her apart from other women writers of her lifetime, especially those of the period following the Spanish Civil War. Elisabeth Mulder was born to an affluent Barcelona family; her Dutch father was half Spanish, and her Puerto Rican mother's ancestors were from Catalonia and Italy. An only child, she did not receive a traditional education but was taught by private tutors and learned English at the same time as Spanish, and four other languages as well. This allowed her in later life to translate the works of Pushkin (1799–1837), Baudelaire (1821–1867), and Pearl S. Buck (1892–1973), among others. She also took charge of the English literature section of the Madrid literary review *Insula* in the 1950s. Mulder commenced her literary career quite young as a poet and stopped publishing poetry in 1934 when she began to devote her creative efforts to the prose writing for which she is best known. Her first novel, *Una sombra entre los dos* (1934; A Shadow between the Two), is considered to have a feminist thesis because it depicts the choice that Patricia, a doctor, makes between her profession and her marriage to a conventional man who forbids her to practice medicine.

At the outbreak of the Spanish Civil War, Mulder decided to remain in Barcelona in the same house she had occupied with her husband, Ezequiel Dauner Foix, until he died in 1931. She would later share the same house with her son and his family until her death. The period of the 1940s and the 1950s was extremely productive in Mulder's literary output, and she was well received by conservative literary critics. At this time she concentrated her efforts on novels, novellas, short stories, and children's stories. Although she spent most of her time translating in the years immediately after the Civil War, she published *Preludio a la muerte* (1941; Prelude to Death) in which she analyzes friendship and love. It is the story of two women studying in Switzerland who become friends, then rivals. The disillusioned protagonist's suicide at the end created problems with the censor. The novel was made into a movie in 1950 but without the original ending.

In one of her then most famous works, *El hombre que acabó en las islas* (1944; The Man Who Ended Up in the Islands), Mulder utilized techniques similar to *tremendismo* (the first post–Civil War literary movement, characterized by neonaturalist images and expressionist methods) as well as Gothic and romantic aspects. This four-part novel, set in Spain, Sweden, and the Caribbean, relates the maturation process of a young man whose skepticism ultimately brings him to renounce civilization to live on a tropical island. *Las hogueras de otoño* (1945; The Bonfires of Fall) relates the anguish of a mature married couple who face a turning point when a third party comes between them. *Alba Grey* (1947), often classified as escapist literature, was recently reprinted in Spain and described as the Mulder novel that represents her best and most characteristic traits: lyricism, refined settings described with stylized traits, keen irony, and profound psychological analysis of her characters. Mulder's idiosyncratic characters typify the spoiled, decadent, melancholy, perhaps even frivolous generation of upper classes who inhabited Europe during the period between wars. The plot is constructed around a trip to Egypt via Italy as the protagonist (Alba Grey) deliberates the attraction she feels for two men who represent distinct aspects of love. Alba herself symbolizes the union of two cultures as she is the child of distinguished European lineage and a great American fortune.

El vendedor de vidas (1953; The Vendor of Lives) has been called the most *Baroja-like of Mulder's novels, an attribute the author herself admitted. It takes place in a lower-class section of Barcelona destroyed by the Civil War where life is a struggle and where initiation to the adult world takes place for young Julio Regás, one of the characters. In addition, this work presents an element of fantastic literature; while predicting the future, another character, an astrologer, sees a death in the beginning of the novel only to discover later that it would be his own.

Eran cuatro (1954; There Were Four), a short novel, deals with a mother whose four sons died in the Spanish Civil War. One of them was on the side of the Republic, while the others fought with Franco's victorious Nacionalistas. Hoping to overcome her loss, the mother undertakes a journey to visit the important places and people of her sons' lives. Her search results in failure, and she lapses into madness before dying. This work is attributed to the fiction of the 1950s that examined the consequences of the Civil War in a nonpartisan way.

Luna de máscaras (1958; Moon of Masks), often considered one of Mulder's best-written pieces, was the last novel published in her lifetime. Built on a perspectivist technique, the parts of the narrative belong to the different points of view of the novel's characters. Following a car accident, Mulder reconstructs a love triangle in segments, focusing each one on the thoughts of a single individual involved in the story. The action is set in affluent Mediterranean vacation resorts and art colonies.

Mulder also wrote several books of children's stories such as *Los cuentos del viejo reloj* (1941; Stories of the Old Watch) and *Las noches del gato verde* (1963; Nights of the Green Cat). An earlier book about a cat, *La* historia de Java (1935; The Story of Java), has also been called children's literature, but the author clearly expressed her intentions of writing it as a parable about the spirit's absolute freedom from love's domination. In the 1960s and 1970s Mulder translated a collection of books on painting and engaged in an intense schedule of lectures for organizations and universities in Spain and abroad. In the next decade, after recovering from a serious illness, she continued to write, but almost all that work remains unpublished. However, two stories that have been published indicate that Mulder had begun to develop a more contemporary writing style.

From 1940 on, Mulder was an active participant in Barcelona's cultural life, serving in an administrative capacity in such organizations as the Instituto de Estudios Norteamericanos, the Ateneo Barcelonés, and the Academia del Faro de San Cristóbal. Mulder is not typical of the women who wrote in postwar years and has been quite forgotten by readers and academics. New editions of some of Mulder's works released in Spain in the 1990s consider the author and her artistic principles misunderstood, often misinterpreted. Thus it seems her work is due for a fair reappraisal. *See also* Short Fiction by Women Writers: 1900–1975

Work by

Alba Grey. Ed. María del Mar Mañas. Madrid: Castalia, 1992.

Work about

Redondo Goicoechea, Alicia, ed., intro. and notes. *Relatos de novelistas españolas 1939–1969*. Madrid: Castalia/Instituto de la Mujer, 1993.

Glenn Morocco